GOETHE
ITALIAN JOURNEY

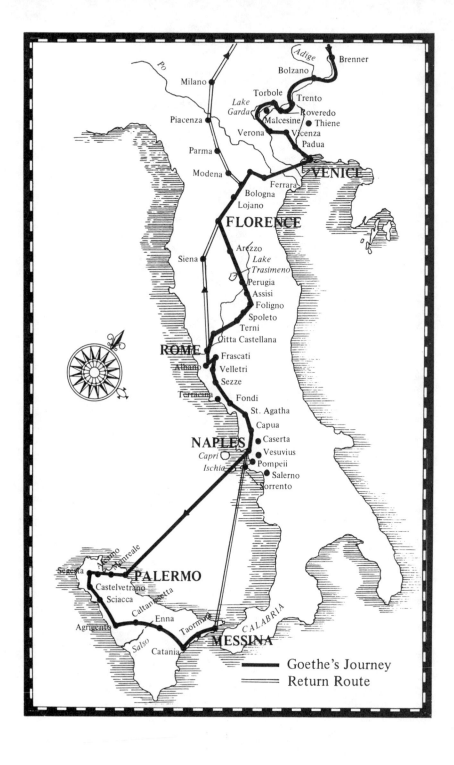

Goethe's Journey
Return Route

GOETHE

Selected Poems
Faust I & II
Essays on Art and Literature
From My Life: Poetry and Truth (Parts One to Three)
From My Life: Campaign in France 1792 • Siege of Mainz (Part Four)
Italian Journey
Early Verse Dramas and Prose Plays
Verse Plays and Epic
Wilhelm Meister's Apprenticeship
Conversations of German Refugees & Wilhelm Meister's
Journeyman Year or The Renunciants
The Sorrows of Young Werther • Elective Affinities • Novella
Scientific Studies

Collected Works in 12 Volumes

Goethe's Collected Works, Volume 6

Johann Wolfgang von
GOETHE

Italian Journey

Translated by Robert R. Heitner
Introduction and Notes by Thomas P. Saine

Edited by Thomas P. Saine and Jeffrey L. Sammons

Princeton University Press
Princeton, New Jersey

Published by Princeton University Press, 41 William Street,
Princeton, New Jersey 08540
In the United Kingdom by Princeton University Press, Chichester, West Sussex
Copyright © 1989 by Suhrkamp Publishers New York, Inc.

This is Volume 6 in the Collected Works of Johann Wolfgang von Goethe;
the hardback is published by Suhrkamp Publishers and distributed by
Princeton University Press; the paperback is published by
Princeton University Press by agreement with Suhrkamp Publishers

Library of Congress Cataloging-in-Publication Data

Goethe, Johann Wolfgang von, 1749–1832.
[Italienische Reise. English]
Italian journey / Johann Wolfgang von Goethe ; translated by
Robert R. Heitner ; introduction and notes by Thomas P. Saine ;
edited by Thomas P. Saine and Jeffrey L. Sammons.
p. cm.—(Princeton paperbacks)
Originally published: New York : Suhrkamp, 1989 (Goethe's
collected works ; v. 6
Includes index.
ISBN 0-691-03799-X
1. Goethe, Johann Wolfgang von, 1749–1832—Journeys—Italy.
2. Italy—Description and travel—Early works to 1800. 3. Authors,
German—18th century—Journeys—Italy. I. Heitner, Robert R.
II. Saine, Thomas P. III. Sammons, Jeffrey L. IV. Title.
V. Series: Goethe, Johann Wolfgang von, 1749–1832. Works. English.
1994 ; v. 6.
PT2026.A1C94 1994 vol. 6
[PT2027.I7]
831'.6—dc20
[838'.603]
[B] 94–3216

First Princeton Paperback printing, 1994

Princeton University Press books are printed on acid-free paper and meet
the guidelines for permanence and durability of the Committee on
Production Guidelines for Book Longevity of the Council on Library Resources

Printed in the United States of America

1 3 5 7 9 10 8 6 4 2

CONTENTS

viii   Contents

GOETHE
ITALIAN JOURNEY

Introduction*

Goethe grew up with a father whose most important formative experience—at least to hear Goethe tell it—had been an extended trip to
Italy after the completion of his legal studies. That Johann Caspar
Goethe had been to Italy was something rather unusual for a young
bourgeois gentleman in the first half of the eighteenth century. Young
aristocrats might include Italy on their cavalier's tour, that rite of passage which put the final touch to their social polish, their manners, and
their culture, if they planned a really extensive trip. Otherwise they
headed for Paris. From the early Renaissance on young artists too went
to Italy to receive instruction from the acknowledged masters and to
experience Europe's largest store of inspiring artworks. In the mid-
eighteenth century it was unusual for German Protestants, apart from
artists and archaeologists, to travel in Catholic Italy. There was absolutely no pressing reason for Johann Caspar Goethe to visit Italy
around 1740.

Yet Goethe's father, already demonstrating at an early age the stout
independence that marked him throughout his life, had been to Italy
and had made the most of it. His house was filled with mementos of
the journey: pictures, books, small artworks. He had learned to speak
and write Italian well and had composed an extensive account of his
journey in Italian. He held up Italy as an ideal and imposed it on his
children in the form of language lessons, stories about his Italian journey, and the aspiration for his son to follow in his footsteps and visit
the country himself at an early age. He was prepared at practically any
time to send young Wolfgang Goethe off to the south for his final polishing.

Yet Wolfgang did not gratify Johann Caspar by traveling to Italy

---

*See also the general introduction to Goethe's autobiographical works in
Volume 4.

during his father's lifetime. On two occasions before his departure for
Weimar in the fall of 1775 he either had the opportunity or even intended
to do so—but on both occasions he held back, or was held back by
the feeling that it was not yet time. In June of 1775, on his first trip to
Switzerland, he climbed up the St. Gotthard pass and looked down on
Italy. His companion urged him forward, but he refused to go on and
returned to Zurich and Frankfurt. In the fall of the same year, when
he had long waited in vain for the carriage that was to take him from
Frankfurt to Weimar, he resolved—at his father's urging—to forget
about Weimar and head for Italy instead. He started on his way and
got as far as Heidelberg before a dispatch rider sent from Frankfurt
caught up with him to convey apologies for the delay and a renewed,
even more urgent invitation to proceed to Weimar.

It was to be almost another eleven years before Goethe finally realized
the dream of Italy. Those years were devoted to hard work in government administration as perhaps the closest friend and one of the chief
advisers and functionaries of Duke Carl August, seeking to influence
the ruler and help modernize the Weimar and Eisenach territories. For
all the dedication and good will Goethe brought to the task of government, he was bound to feel considerable frustration over the difficulty
of transforming rulers by persuading them, or mankind by governing
it in an enlightened manner. In those eleven years he came more and
more to feel that by using himself up in Carl August's service he was
depriving himself both as an artist and as a human being. His cultural
accounts were in deficit and he had had no time or opportunity to grow.
He had not yet discovered his true calling as a man of letters and still
suffered under the illusion that he had considerable untapped ability in
the visual arts. His emotional life had become onesided and unfulfill-
ing—one may even say stunted—by his long-term Platonic relationship
with Charlotte von Stein, with whom he discussed his soul daily without
enjoying any sensual gratification whatsoever.

Goethe's departure for Italy in 1786 had every appearance of a flight
from unsatisfying Weimar reality to an almost mythical promised land.
Italy was appealing because of its climate: it was the South, where
nature was free to be itself instead of constantly being under pressure
and constraints as in the North. Here were the treasures of Renaissance
painting and sculpture and the cultural and architectural legacy of Rome.
In the northern European mind Italy had come to be invested with the
attributes of "Arcadia" as well. Strange as it may seem to us today,
in the eighteenth century Italy came to function as the repository of
the Greek ideal, an attitude sanctioned and nurtured by Winckelmann's
enthusiasm for the remains of Greek antiquity he had encountered in
Rome and points south. Travel to Greece was extraordinarily difficult,
however, as all of Europe east of Venice was ruled by the Turks, who

were continually at war with the Mediterranean Christian countries. Only privileged and hardy citizens of nations that had good relations with the Porte—primarily England and France—could ever hope to become familiar with the extensive remains of the Greek and Hellenistic civilization that had flourished in the eastern Mediterranean until Roman imperial times. Anyone else who ventured into the Mediterranean had to keep an eye out for pirates and raiders—dramatically illustrated by Goethe himself when, on his return trip from Sicily to Naples, he opted to travel on a neutral French ship. Northern Europeans in general—like Winckelmann and Goethe—had to settle for what they could find of Greece in Rome, southern Italy, and the once-flourishing Greek colony of Sicily. Idealizing what they found there, even though it was often only Roman copies of late Greek works that they encountered, they made serious blunders in their historical treatment of Greek art—epitomized by their enthusiasm for the Laocoon group, a late Hellenistic work. One will seek in vain in Goethe's *Italian Journey* for any similarly fervid appreciation of Roman visual art, yet his (and other Germans') appreciation of Greek art was still stamped by Rome.

Goethe had been vacationing in Carlsbad since late July 1786 in the company of Charlotte von Stein, Carl August, Johann Gottfried Herder and his wife, and other less intimate acquaintances. Charlotte left the Bohemian spa on August 14. After staying long enough to celebrate Goethe's thirty-seventh birthday on August 28, Carl August also left. Having asked the duke only in very general and vague terms for an "indefinite leave," Goethe stole away from Carlsbad at three in the morning on September 3 without telling anyone where he was going. Only the servant he left behind knew what his master had in mind. He hurried through Bavaria and Austria, over the Brenner Pass into the Tyrol, through Bolzano and Trent, Verona, Vicenza, and Padua before stopping to catch his breath at Venice. He wrote home for the first time from Verona, sending letters by way of his servant in Weimar without giving the recipients any hint of his whereabouts. It was not until he had arrived in Rome that he revealed his destination and his plans. Herder understood his need to get away from home in this fashion and for an extended period of time. Charlotte was less satisfied with her soulmate. Faced with a *fait accompli,* Carl August did not demand that Goethe return home soon. If he had had to say what he intended to do before he left, Goethe would probably never have gone. As it turned out, however, he was to enjoy almost two years in Paradise, coming to terms with himself and refreshing himself for the rest of his life. It was not nostalgia alone which later led Goethe to claim more than once that he had never again really been happy since leaving Rome, and his citation of Ovid at the conclusion of the *Italian Journey* reinforces that lament.

In Rome Goethe concealed himself under the incognito of "Filippo Miller, painter." Only the artist Wilhelm Tischbein knew at first who he really was. In the long run it was not possible to preserve his incognito at all times, and Goethe gradually became acquainted with a circle of fairly sophisticated people who could accept him on his own terms, the principal ones being Councilor Reiffenstein, Angelica Kauffmann, Karl Philipp Moritz, and Heinrich Meyer. The only reason for the incognito one can deduce from the *Italian Journey* itself is that Goethe wanted to avoid being identified and pestered everywhere as the author of *The Sorrows of Young Werther,* as which—due to the fact that he had published nothing significant since 1774 to erase or modify that first impression of himself—he was still notorious. Equally obvious, however, is the fact that as a high Weimar official who had recently been ennobled (1782) he would have been under considerable pressure to lead a very different life in Italy, had his identity become generally known. He would have had to frequent aristocratic circles and he probably could not have totally escaped becoming involved in diplomacy and affairs of state, since this was a period of *rapprochement* between post-Friderician Prussia—with whose policy Carl August increasingly became aligned—and Rome. (In fact, Goethe had not stolen away from Germany as cleanly as he thought: the Austrian intelligence service kept an eye on him while he was en route to Rome, suspecting diplomatic intentions on his part.) As it was, Goethe was charged on several occasions with representing his master's interests in Rome, he received communications through Prussian diplomatic channels and presumably was fairly well informed about affairs, and during the last months of his stay he was involved in the planning for Dowager Duchess Anna Amalia's trip to Italy in the fall of 1788.

What Goethe sought by remaining incognito was above all the opportunity to mingle and live with his own kind—artists—and to be his own man for an extended period of time. One could say that he was intentionally descending below his attained social class, renouncing his privileges whenever and as long as it pleased him to do so, and returning to his origins as an artist. In the pressure-free atmosphere he created for himself in this way he was free to grow in whatever direction he could. The pages of the *Italian Journey* are dominated by three major themes: the observation of nature and his efforts to formulate a law for the metamorphosis of plants, the progress of his writings for the eight-volume edition of his collected works he had contracted to put out with the Berlin publisher Georg Joachim Göschen, and above all his encounter with Renaissance art and the cultural monuments of antiquity. In the course of 1788, after the arrival in Rome of the Frankfurt-born musician and composer Philipp Christoph Kayser, music and work on his operettas also played a considerable role in his life. He summed up the effect of his Italian experience by claiming that in Rome he had learned to see for the first time. The encounter with the South, together with the freedom to pursue his inclinations to the point of fulfillment or to the point of certainty that fulfillment was impossible for him, led Goethe to proclaim that he had experienced a rebirth and even to feel that he had not really lived before arriving in Rome.

Goethe had sketched and dabbled in the visual arts all his life. Until near the end of his stay in Italy he struggled with his artistic talents and sought to develop them to the fullest. When he set out he still believed he possessed as much talent for the visual arts as for letters, only that this talent had never been developed the way his writing had. By the end of the second sojourn in Rome he finally admitted to himself and others that he had been mistaken and he had discovered that his true calling was to be a writer and a scientist. He renounced his ambitions in the visual arts and returned to Weimar full of ideas for literary and scientific projects that were enough to occupy him for years. He retained a lively interest in art and art history and even succeeded in getting the art historian Heinrich Meyer to settle in Weimar soon after his own return home, but he knew now once and for all that he was only an art lover and connoisseur, not a creative talent. Though of course a source of great disappointment to him, Goethe's realization that he was not destined to paint with oil on canvases was a salutary one—perhaps the greatest benefit of the Italian experience both for himself and for the history of German literature. However, the Italian experience had something of a negative effect on his life after returning to Weimar: the personal development Goethe had undergone and the insights he considered himself to have gained in Italy began once and for all to set him apart from other German intellectuals. Once back in Germany he began to feel himself more and more isolated. The productive friendship with Friedrich Schiller from 1794 to 1805 was a boon to him, but proved to be only an episode in the process of his estrangement from much of Weimar society and German intellectual life.

From the outset of his trip Goethe intended to write and talk about the Italian journey when he got back to Weimar. He kept a detailed diary of the trip from Carlsbad to Rome, which he sent back to Charlotte von Stein in installments with the suggestion that she should transcribe it in a large format, leaving out everything that was directed to her personally and might not be fit for others to hear or read. He hoped upon his return first to fill in the details and explicate his experiences for her at greater length—after all, the diary was mainly for *her*—and then to share it with others in one form or another as well. During the two stays in Rome he did not keep an extensive diary, but he wrote numerous quite detailed letters—above all to Charlotte, the Herders, and Duke Carl August. During the trip to Naples and Sicily in early

1787 he again kept a detailed diary and wrote letters as well. Upon his return to Weimar in the summer of 1788 he asked to have back the diary for Charlotte and the letters he had written to her and his other friends, with the intention of using them to write about his Italian journey. (Of all these materials, only the diary for Charlotte and the letters from the first stay in Rome still survive—Goethe later destroyed most of the diaries and letters which formed the basis for the Naples-Sicily part of the *Italian Journey* and the treatment of his second stay in Rome.) Yet he did not finally write about the journey itself until much later, and when Herder asked to borrow the travel diary in preparation for his own journey to Italy Goethe refused to let it out of his hands on the grounds that it lacked substance. He published a dozen or so articles and essays on various topics in Wieland's *German Mercury* in 1788 and 1789, a little illustrated book on the Roman Carnival, and a paper on Count Cagliostro, but he did not write about the journey itself and his Italian experiences until he was already rather far along with the project of writing his autobiography.

Towards the end of 1813, after he had completed the first three parts of *Poetry and Truth,* Goethe began working on the diary of the Italian journey. By the summer of 1814 he was able to announce to his publisher, Friedrich Cotta, that printing could begin in the fall. Yet other projects interfered and it was not until the summer of 1816 that the manuscript of the first part of the *Italian Journey* could go to the printer. The first volume, ending with the departure for Naples in February 1787, appeared in November 1816. The second volume, ending with the return from Naples to Rome at the beginning of June 1787, followed fairly soon afterward in October of 1817. These two volumes combine travel narrative with letters to friends at home. They are similar in character and form and are based on the voluminous raw materials in Goethe's possession—the diaries and the letters he had written to his friends. At their first publication both went under the general title "From My Life," like *Poetry and Truth.* When they were republished in the final authorized edition of Goethe's collected works (the "Ausgabe letzter Hand") they received the simple new title, "Italian Journey," parts I and II. This sets them off from the last part of the work dealing with Goethe's second stay in Rome from June 1787 to April 1788.

The last part of what we today call the *Italian Journey,* but to which Goethe gave a different title—"Second Sojourn in Rome"—and apparently did not regard as part of the "Italian Journey" as such, has a completely different character. Some would also feel that it is inferior to the first two parts. Goethe did not complete it until 1829 in conjunction with work on the "Ausgabe letzter Hand." Its form and content were in part dictated by the disposition of the works in the "Ausgabe letzter Hand" and it was first published in that edition. Working without the benefit of an extensive diary for this part of his stay in Italy, Goethe apparently felt that the letters he had in his possession were not enough by themselves to provide the richness of experience and texture that characterize the first two parts of the work. He therefore resorted to a new format, seeking to compensate for the lack of diary material by introducing a month-by-month narrative "Report" following the correspondence for each month. He also resorted to including materials from other sources, for example letters by Wilhelm Tischbein, essays by Heinrich Meyer, and an extract from Karl Philipp Moritz's essay *On the Creative Imitation of Beauty*. Finally, he included in the account of the second stay in Rome some materials for which there was no longer any logical place elsewhere in the "Ausgabe letzter Hand" (most of the essays from the *German Mercury* had already been published in a previous volume). The most prominent instances of this are the essay on St. Philip Neri, which he only completed in 1829 while working on the volume, and the *Roman Carnival*. The *Second Sojourn in Rome* thus became an archive of Goethe's experience and of the products of that experience rather than the straightforward and, on the whole, probably more satisfying account of the experiences and thoughts of the Italian sojourner produced in the first two parts of the work published in 1816 and 1817. There is often a certain amount of repetition between what is presented in the correspondence and what is narrated in the "Reports," and, whereas the first two parts of the work generally manage to give the impression of recapturing the immediate experience of 1786–1787 with a minimum of intrusion by the author who is editing his experiences from the viewpoint of 1816–1817, the *Second Sojourn in Rome* contains numerous lapses in perspective and later editorial comments. Writing more than forty years afterwards, the later Goethe often intrudes visibly on his former self.

A Note on the Translation and the Commentary

Readers and reviewers may well ask why it was necessary to provide a new translation of the *Italian Journey* when there is already a magnificent work by W.H. Auden and Elizabeth Mayer that goes under the title of Goethe's *Italian Journey (1786–1788)*. Originally published by Pantheon Books in 1962 and issued in an attractive new paperback edition by the North Point Press in 1982, the Auden/Mayer translation might seem to make a new translation of such a substantial work a rather dubious undertaking. In fact, work on this volume of the Suhrkamp edition was long postponed while we sought to clarify the situation with regard to the Auden/Mayer version. It certainly would have saved a considerable amount of labor if we had become convinced that it was advisable simply to reprint Auden/Mayer with emendations and annotation. We wish to thank Edward Mendelson, Auden's literary executor, for his interest in the Suhrkamp project and his willingness to allow us to revise Auden/Mayer, as well as Pantheon Books for granting us permission in the end to do with the Auden/Mayer text as we saw fit. Certainly it would have been conceivable to publish a version of the *Italian Journey* legitimately labeled as "based on Auden/Mayer" while seeking the fidelity to Goethe's text that is the goal of the Suhrkamp edition.

In the end, however, we decided that we had to bring out a new translation after all. Close analysis of the Auden/Mayer text by Jeffrey Sammons revealed literally hundreds of instances in which Auden/Mayer departs from Goethe's text in one way or another. The instances range from simple mistakes to the omission of words and phrases to the deletion of sentences and paragraphs to the deletion and transposition of entire entries. One would have had to choose between the alternatives of correcting and supplementing Auden/Mayer without explicitly noting each individual instance, correcting Auden/Mayer in the notes, or correcting Auden/Mayer in the text in italics or square brackets. Obviously such a production would no longer have been an authentic Auden/Mayer text. One might be able to defend treating some-one else's translation in such a way, but not the translation by W. H. Auden and Elizabeth Mayer. That would have been similar to trying to publish a "correct" version of Goethe's own German translation of Benvenuto Cellini's autobiography. Both the Suhrkamp Goethe Edition and Auden/Mayer are best served by Robert R. Heitner's new trans-lation.

In our annotation of the *Italian Journey* we have kept to the same principles observed in *Poetry and Truth, Campaign in France 1792,* and *Siege of Mainz.* Because of the large number of artists and artworks mentioned, discussed, and described in Goethe's text, a certain level of annotation is, if possible, even more necessary here than in volumes four and five. Every historical person mentioned in the text (excepting only those who can reasonably be considered to be well known to the educated reader) has been identified, where possible, at least by full name, birth and death dates, and primary occupation or position. The artworks mentioned or discussed by Goethe have been identified, where possible, with some indication whether or not the work is still commonly ascribed today to the artist to whom Goethe and his contemporaries ascribed it, and the present location of the work if it is no longer in the place where Goethe saw it. Goethe's *Italian Journey* is an important work for art historians and historians of art history, because it provides a detailed picture not only of what Goethe thought about art and art history, but also of what his contemporaries considered to be either common knowledge or striking new insights in their day. For a hundred years and more scholars have studied *Poetry and Truth* and the *Italian Journey,* putting together the names, facts, and dates necessary to elu-cidate the works. It is practically impossible to do significant new re-search in this area and we must frankly admit the near-total lack of originality in our annotation. We have relied heavily on Herbert von Einem's extensive commentary in volume 11 of the *Hamburger Aus-gabe,* which represents the apex reached so far in this cumulatory scholarly enterprise. Further, we have made use, to a lesser extent, of the commentary and biographical index in volumes 14 and 16 of the *Berliner Ausgabe,* and, less frequently, of the notes in the Auden/Mayer translation. There are probably inevitable mistakes, and there are per-sons and works which, after all these years, scholars still have not been able to identify. The inclusion of an index in this volume, prepared by Dagmar Garcia, makes it possible as a rule to offer the pertinent in-formation the first time a person or work is mentioned without having to refer the reader later to a previous page or note.

T. P. S.

PART ONE

I, too in Arcadia

From Carlsbad to the Brenner

I stole out of Carlsbad at three in the morning, for otherwise I would never have gotten away. Since my friends had been kind enough to celebrate my birthday on the twenty-eighth of August, no doubt they had earned a right to keep me there, but I could delay no longer.[1] All alone, with no more luggage than a portmanteau and a satchel, I leapt into a mail coach and reached Zwoda at seven-thirty on a fine, still, misty morning. The higher clouds were like strips of wool, the lower ones heavy. I took this for a good sign that I might hope, after such a bad summer, to enjoy a good autumn. At twelve I was in Eger, in hot sunshine; and now I remembered that this town was on the same latitude as my native city. I was happy to eat my midday meal on the fiftieth parallel again, under clear skies.

In Bavaria one immediately comes upon the Waldsassen monastery—the choice possession of clerical gentlemen, who were clever sooner than other people.[2] It lies in a basin more like a dish than a kettle, in a lovely, grassy hollow surrounded by gentle, fertile hills. Other properties owned by the monastery are spread far and wide in the area. The soil is decomposed shale. The quartz present in this species of rock neither decomposes nor weathers away, and it makes the ground friable and thoroughly fertile. The land rises as far as Tirschenreuth. The streams, heading for the Eger and the Elbe, flow toward me. To the south of Tirschenreuth the land slopes downward, and the streams run into the Danube. The smallest stream, once I have determined its direction of flow and the system it belongs to, quickly gives me a grasp of any region. Thus, even in areas one cannot survey, one forms a mental picture of the correlated hills and valleys. At the town mentioned there begins an excellent highway of granitic sand: it is the most perfect one imaginable, for the decomposed granite, which consists of gravel and clay, provides both a firm basis and a fine cohesive material, so that the road is as smooth as a threshing floor. But in consequence the region it runs through only looks worse: it too is of granitic sand, flat and marshy. Therefore the fine road is all the more desirable. Since the land also slopes downhill, one travels at an incredible speed that is quite a contrast to the snail's pace in Bohemia. The enclosed sheet lists the various stations along the way. Suffice it to say, the next morning I was in Regensburg and thus had covered these twenty-four and a half miles[3] in thirty-nine hours. At daybreak I found myself between Schwandorf and Regenstauf, where I noticed an improvement in the farmland. It was no longer detritus from the hills but mixed alluvial soil. In primeval times, all the valleys which at present empty their waters into the Regen river were affected by the ebb and flow from the Danube valley, and thus arose those natural polders which support agriculture. This observation holds true in the vicinity of all rivers large and small, and with this guideline the spectator can readily explain any cultivable soil.

Regensburg is beautifully situated. The region naturally attracted a town, and the clerical gentlemen carefully considered their own advantage too. All the fields around the town belong to them, and in the town there is one church and one institute standing next to the other. The Danube reminds me of my old Main. The river and bridge look better at Frankfurt, but here Stadtamhof, which lies opposite, has a nice appearance. I went straight to the Jesuit college, where the students were putting on their annual theatrical spectacle, and I saw the end of the opera and the start of the tragedy. They performed no worse than any other inexperienced amateurs and were beautifully, indeed almost too gorgeously costumed. This public show convinced me anew of the Jesuits' astuteness. They scorned nothing that could be in some way effective, and they knew how to treat it with loving attention. This is not shrewdness in any abstract sense, for their delight in the thing, their empathetic and personal pleasure, which results from making use of life, is obvious. This great religious society not only has members who are organ builders, carvers, and gilders, but certainly also some with the inclination and ability to attend to the theater. Just as they distinguish their churches with a pleasing magnificence, so these judicious men make use of worldly sensuality with their decorous theater.

Today I am writing at the forty-ninth parallel, which shows great promise. The morning was cool, and here too people are complaining about the cold, damp summer; but the day turned out to be splendid and mild. The balmy air that comes with a great river is something quite unique. The fruit is not remarkable. I have eaten some good pears, but I long for grapes and figs.

I am fascinated by the activities and ways of the Jesuits. Their churches, towers, and buildings have a grandeur and completeness that fill everyone with secret awe. The decorations made of gold, silver, metal, and polished stones are massed together in such splendor and abundance that beggars of all classes must be dazzled by them. Here and there, as a sop and magnet to the common people, something taste-less is included. This is the genius of Catholic public worship in general; but I have never seen it applied with as much intelligence, skill, and consistency as by the Jesuits. Everything is designed, not, as with other religious orders, to preserve an old, worn-out form of worship, but to revive it with pomp and splendor to suit the spirit of the times.

A strange type of rock is processed here which looks like a kind of new red sandstone but must be considered older, primary, indeed por-phyritic. It has a greenish admixture of quartz, is porous, and shows large spots of a sort of breccia. One bit was temptingly instructive and appetizing but could not be separated from the stone; and I have sworn not to load myself down with rocks on this trip.

Munich, September 6.

On September fifth at twelve-thirty PM I left Regensburg. Near Abach and extending almost as far as Saal is a beautiful area in which the Danube surges against limestone rocks. This limestone is dense like that near Osteroda in the Harz, but porous nevertheless. At six o'clock in the morning I was in Munich and spent twelve hours seeing the sights, but shall comment on just a few of them. In the picture gallery I felt like a stranger; I must first accustom my eyes to paintings again. The collection is excellent. I was greatly delighted with the Rubens sketches from the Luxembourg gallery.[4]

Also here is that elegant toy, a model of Trajan's column.[5] Gilded figures against a background of lapis lazuli. It is certainly a fine piece of work and pleasant to look at.

In the hall of classical sculpture[6] I could soon tell that my eyes were not trained to appreciate such objects and so did not want to stay and waste time. Many pieces did not appeal to me at all, though I could not have said why. A Drusus attracted my attention, two statues of Antoninus pleased me, as did a few other things. On the whole they were not placed to advantage, despite being meant as decoration; and the room, or rather the vaulted basement, would have profited from being kept neater and cleaner. In the natural history section I found beautiful specimens from the Tyrol which were already familiar to me in small samples which, indeed, I own.

A woman selling figs approached me, and, being my first ones, they tasted delicious. But in general the fruit is not especially good, con-sidering that this is the forty-eighth parallel. People here complain bit-terly about the cold and dampness. A fog scarcely distinguishable from

rain greeted me this morning outside of Munich. All day the wind blew
in very coldly from the Tyrolean mountains. When I looked in that
direction from up in a tower I found the mountains shrouded and the
whole sky overcast. Now the setting sun is still shining on the old tower
that faces my window. Excuse me for paying so much attention to wind
and weather: the traveler by land depends on both almost as much as
the seafarer, and it would be a pity if my autumn abroad should prove
to be as little favored as the summer at home.

Now I am going straight to Innsbruck. How much I am neglecting
on all sides in order to carry out my *one* intention, which I have waited
almost too long to do!

Mittenwald, September 7, evening.

It seems that my guardian angel is saying Amen to my Credo, and
I thank him for having brought me here on such a fine day. The last
postilion, shouting happily, said that it was the finest one of the whole
summer. I am silently nurturing my wishful belief that the good weather
will continue, but my friends must forgive me for talking again about
air and clouds.

When I rode away from Munich at five o'clock the sky had cleared.
Huge cloud masses clung motionless to the Tyrolean mountains. Nor
did the strips in the lower regions move. The road goes along the heights,
below which one sees the Isar flowing past drifts of piled-up gravel.
Here one can understand the effects of currents in the primeval sea.
In many a granite boulder I found siblings and relatives of the pieces
in my collection, which were a gift from Knebel.[7]

The mists from the river and the meadows persisted for a while, but
at last they too were dissipated. Between the gravel hills I have mentioned, which must be imagined as several hours' journey long and
wide, was the finest, most fertile soil, as in the Regen river valley. Now
the way leads back to the Isar, where one sees a profile of the slope
of the gravel hills, a good hundred and fifty feet high. I arrived in Wolf-
rathshausen and reached the forty-eighth parallel. The sun burned
fiercely. No one expects the good weather to continue, there is wailing
about the evils of the current year and lamenting that our great God is
not tending to His business.

Now a new world opened up to me. I was approaching the mountains,
which rose up before me gradually.

Benediktbeuern is choicely located, and the first sight of it surprises.
In a fertile plain there is a long, broad white building with a broad,
high, rocky ridge behind it. Now the road ascends to Lake Kochel;
then higher up into the mountains to Lake Walchen. Here I greeted

the first snow-capped peaks, and when I expressed my amazement at
already being so close to snowy mountains, I heard that it had thundered
and lightninged yesterday in the region and snowed in the mountains.
In these phenomena hope was seen for better weather, and the first
snow was presumed to mean a change in the atmosphere. The rocky
cliffs surrounding me are all limestone of the oldest type, which does
not yet contain fossils. Enormous uninterrupted ranges of these limestone mountains reach from Dalmatia to the St. Gotthard and beyond.
Hacquet[8] has toured a great section of this chain. It rests on a fundament
rich in quartz and clay.

I got to Lake Walchen at four-thirty. About an hour's journey from
the place I met with a pretty adventure: a harp player was walking
ahead of me with his daughter, a girl of eleven years, and he asked me
to take the child into my carriage. He went on with the instrument, I
put the girl on the seat beside me, and she carefully placed a large new
case at her feet. A polite, accomplished little creature, already quite
well traveled. She and her mother had made a pilgrimage on foot to
Maria Einsiedeln,[9] and the two had been about to start on a longer
journey to Santiago de Compostella when the mother departed this life
without fulfilling her vow. The girl said that nothing was too much
when it was a question of honoring the Mother of God. She herself had
seen a whole house burnt down to the ground after a great conflagration,
yet over the door, behind a glass, was a picture of the Virgin, quite
undamaged, which was obviously a miracle. She had made all her trips
on foot, had just played for the elector in Munich, and as a matter of
fact had performed before twenty-one princely personages. She entertained me very well. Lovely big brown eyes, a stubborn forehead which
sometimes puckered a little. She was pleasant and natural when she
spoke, and especially when she laughed loudly, like a child. On the
other hand, when she was silent she seemed to want to intimate something and curled her upper lip disagreeably. I discussed many things
with her, she was at home everywhere, and very observant of things.
Thus she asked me once what kind of a tree that was? It was a fine
big maple, the first I had seen on the whole trip. Naturally she had
noticed it at once, and when several others appeared one by one, was
glad that she too could identify this tree. She said she was going to the
fair at Bolzano, where I was also presumably heading. If we met there
I was to buy her a present, which I promised to do. There she would
also wear the new bonnet she had had made for herself in Munich from
her earnings. She wanted to give me a look at it in advance. So she
opened her case, and I was required to share her joy in the richly embroidered and much-beribboned head adornment.

We also took mutual pleasure in another happy prospect. Namely,
she assured me the weather would be good. They had a barometer with

them, that is to say, the harp. When the treble rose in pitch, that meant good weather, and it had done so today. I gladly accepted the omen, and we parted in the best of humor, hoping for an early reunion.

On the Brenner, September 8, evening.

Here I was practically compelled to stop for a rest, in a quiet place that was everything I could have wished for. The day was of a kind that can be enjoyed in retrospect for years. At six o'clock I left Mittenwald, a brisk wind cleared the sky completely. The cold was of a degree permissible only in February. Now, however, the gleam of the rising sun over the dark foregrounds covered with fir trees, the gray limestone rocks between them, and in the background the highest snowy peaks—those were exquisite, constantly changing pictures.

At Scharnitz one enters the Tyrol. The border is closed off by a rampart which seals the valley and adjoins the hills. It looks good; on one side the rock is fortified, on the other it rises up vertically. After Seefeld the road gets more and more interesting, and whereas from Benediktbeuern on it ascended from height to height and all the waters flowed into the Isar basin, now we look over a ridge into the Inn valley, and Inzingen lies before us. The sun was high and hot, I had to lighten my clothing, which I often change because of the day's changeable atmosphere.

At Zirl one rides down into the Inn valley. The locality is indescribably beautiful, and the sunny vapor made it look quite magnificent. The postilion hurried more than I wanted him to; he had not yet been to mass, and wished to hear it all the more devoutly in Innsbruck, today being the Virgin's Nativity. Now we kept on rattling down the Inn, past St. Martin's Wall, an enormous, steeply descending limestone face. It would have been at best a foolhardy undertaking, but I was confident that even without angels fluttering about I could reach the place where Emperor Maximilian[10] is said to have lost his way while climbing.

Innsbruck is splendidly situated in a broad, fertile valley among high cliffs and mountains. At first I wanted to stay there, but I had no rest. For a short time I was amused by the innkeeper's son, my Söller[11] in the flesh. Thus I meet my characters one by one. Everything is decorated in celebration of the Nativity of the Virgin. Crowds of people, looking healthy and prosperous, made the pilgrimage to Wilten, a shrine a quarter of an hour's walk from town in the direction of the mountains. At two o'clock, when my rolling carriage parted the cheerful, colorful throng, everybody was happily on the move.

Above Innsbruck the landscape grows more and more beautiful, no words can describe it. On very smooth roads one goes up a gorge that sends its water to the Inn, a gorge that offers the eye innumerable changes of scenery. While the road comes close to very sheer cliffs, indeed is cut into them, on the opposite side the land slopes gently and can support the finest agriculture. Villages, houses, cottages, huts, all painted white, stand among fields and hedges on the high, broad, sloping surface. Soon everything changes: the land is usable only for meadow, until that too disappears in a steep declivity.

I have gained much to support my view of the creation of the world, but nothing altogether new and unexpected. I have also mused a great deal about the model I have talked about for such a long time, by means of which I would like to make intelligible some ideas revolving in my mind that I cannot readily demonstrate in nature.

Now it grew darker and darker, details merged, the masses became larger and more imposing, but at last, when everything was just moving before me like a mysterious, murky picture, I suddenly saw the high, snowy peaks again, illumined by the moon. Now I wait for the morning to brighten this rocky gorge that hems me in, here on the boundary between south and north.

I shall add some remarks about the atmospheric conditions, which are favoring me, perhaps in gratitude for the many reflections I devote to them. In level country good and bad weather is received fully developed, but in the mountains one is present at its origin. This has happened to me so often on trips, walks, and out hunting, when I have spent days and nights in mountain forests, among rocky cliffs; and so a fanciful thought arose in me, which I do not pretend was anything else but which I cannot rid myself of, as indeed fanciful thoughts are the hardest to get rid of. I see it everywhere, as if it were a fact, and so I shall express it, since in any case I often find myself testing the patience of my friends.

Whether we contemplate the mountains from nearby or afar, now seeing their peaks agleam in the sunshine, now shrouded in fog, encircled by rushing clouds, whipped by pelting rain, or covered with snow, we ascribe it all to the atmosphere, since our eyes plainly see and grasp its movements and changes. On the other hand, the mountains stand there before our external senses, motionless, in their customary form. We consider them to be dead because they are rigid; we think them inactive because they are in repose. For some time, however, I have not been able to desist from ascribing the changes seen in the atmosphere in great part to an inner, quiet, secret action of the mountains. Namely, I believe that the mass of the earth generally, and, as a result, also especially its projecting foundations, do not exercise any constant, unchanging power of attraction, but that this power of attraction expresses itself in a certain pulsation, so that it is alternately increased and diminished through inner, necessary, perhaps also outer, incidental causes. All other attempts to demonstrate this oscillation may be too limited and crude, but the atmosphere is delicate and vast enough to instruct us about those quiet operations. If that power of attraction is diminished in the least, this action is indicated to us by the decreased heaviness, the diminished elasticity of the air. The atmosphere can no longer bear the moisture allocated to it chemically and mechanically, clouds descend, rains pour down, and streams of rain water flow toward the flat land. However, if the mountains increase their gravity, then the elasticity of the air is immediately restored, and two important phenomena occur. Once the mountains have assembled enormous cloud masses around themselves, they hold these firmly and rigidly overhead like second peaks, until, moved by the inner struggle of electrical energies, they descend as storm, fog, and rain; then the elastic air, which is now again capable of absorbing, vaporizing, and processing more water, affects the residue. I quite distinctly saw such a cloud being consumed; it was hanging around the steepest peak, the setting sun shone on it. Slowly, slowly its ends detached themselves, some tufts were drawn away and wafted upwards; they disappeared, as did gradually the whole mass, and it was quite literally unspun before my eyes by an invisible hand, like a distaff.

If my friends have smiled about this ambulant weather observer and his bizarre theories, some other reflections of mine will perhaps make them laugh. For I must confess, since my journey was in the nature of a flight from all the inclement weather I experienced on the fifty-first parallel, that I had hoped to enter a true Goshen on the forty-eighth. But I was deceiving myself, as I should have known earlier; for it is not the latitude alone that makes climate and atmosphere, but also the mountain ranges, especially those that cut across the regions from east to west. Great changes are always occurring in these, and the lands lying to the north suffer the most from them. Thus the weather this summer in the whole north seems to have been determined by the great Alpine chain on which I am writing this. During the last months it has rained constantly here, and southwest and southeast winds have driven the rain straight northwards. In Italy the weather is said to have been beautiful, indeed *too* dry.

Now a few words about the plant realm, which is not independent, but is conditioned in the most varied way by climate, altitude, and moisture. In this sphere too I have found no special change, but nevertheless some gain. Apples and pears are common already in the valley outside of Innsbruck, but peaches and grapes are imported from Italy, or rather the southern Tyrol. Around Innsbruck much Indian corn and buckwheat are grown, which they call "Blende."[12] On the way up to the Brenner I saw the first larch trees, at Schönberg the first stone pine. Would the girl harpist, I wonder, also have asked questions here?

With respect to plants I still feel very much a novice. As far as Munich I believed I was really seeing only the usual ones. To be sure, my hasty night-and-day trip was not conducive to any very fine observations. Now, although I have my Linnaeus[13] with me and have impressed its terminology on my mind, where shall I find the time and leisure for analysis, which in any case, if I know myself rightly, can never become my strong point? Therefore I direct my eye at general characteristics, and when I saw my first gentian at Lake Walchen, it struck me that heretofore also I had always found new plants first by the water.

What attracted my attention still more was the influence that the high altitude seemed to have on the plants. Not only did I find new plants there but also alteration in the growth of the old ones; if in the lower region the branches and stems were thicker and stronger, the buds closer to each other and the leaves broad, then higher in the mountains the branches and stems were more delicate, the buds separated by greater intervals from node to node, and the leaves shaped more lanceolately. I noticed this both in a willow and a gentian and became convinced that it was not, as one might think, a question of different species of these plants. Also at Lake Walchen I noticed longer and slimmer rushes than in the lowland.

The limestone Alps, which I had been traversing up to now, have a gray color and beautiful, curious, irregular forms, although the rock is divided into seams and strata. But because arched layers also occur, and the rock in general is unevenly weathered, the faces and peaks look strange. This species of rock reaches far up the Brenner. In the vicinity of the upper lake I found a change in it. Attached to a dark-green and dark-gray micaceous slate, heavily mixed with quartz, was a dense white limestone that was micaceous at the separation line and outcropped in large but infinitely fissured masses. On top of it I found micaceous slate again, which seemed more fragile to me than the first type. Farther up a special kind of gneiss manifests itself, or rather a type of granite which is being transformed into gneiss, as in the Ellbogen area. Up here, opposite the house, the rock is micaceous slate. The waters coming out of the mountain carry along this rock and gray limestone.

The granite mountain mass, on which everything is based, cannot be far distant. The map shows that we are on the side of the actual great Brenner, out of which the waters pour all around.

I have perceived the following with regard to the appearance of the people. This nation is honest and straightforward. Their figures show little variation, brown, wide-open eyes, and, among the women, finely drawn black eyebrows; among the men, however, thick blond eyebrows. The latter wear green hats that give them a cheerful look amongst these gray rocks. They trim the hats with ribbons or broad sashes of fringed

taffeta that are pinned together quite neatly. Each man also has a flower
or a feather on his hat. On the other hand the women disfigure themselves with very wide caps of tufted white cotton that look like shapeless
masculine nightcaps. These give them a very odd look, whereas when
in foreign parts they will wear the green men's hats, which become
them very nicely.

I have had occasion to see how the common people value peacock
feathers, and how any colorful feather at all is honored. Anyone planning
to travel through these mountains should pack some along with him.
Such a feather offered at the right place would serve as the most welcome gratuity.

While separating, gathering, fastening, and arranging these pages in
such a manner that they may not only soon provide my friends with a
cursory review of my adventures to this point but also relieve my mind
of what I have experienced and thought, I am on the other hand viewing
with a shudder some packets about which, without further ado, I must
confess: they are indeed my companions! Will they not exert a great
influence on the coming days?

I had taken all my works along with me to Carlsbad, intending finally
to compile the edition to be published by Göschen.[14] For a long time
I had possessed beautiful copies of the unprinted writings, prepared
by the skillful hand of Secretary Vogel.[15] That worthy man had also
come along this time to lend me his dexterous assistance. Consequently,
with Herder's most faithful cooperation I was enabled to send off the
first four volumes to the publisher, and was going to do the same with
the last four. In part these consisted of works only in outline, nay, of
fragments, for my bad habit of beginning many things, losing interest,
and then letting them lie had gradually worsened with the years, because
of other occupations and distractions.

Since I had all these things with me I was glad to heed the request
of that discerning circle of friends in Carlsbad and read everything aloud
to them that was as yet unknown, whereupon they complained bitterly
because I had not completed those works and thus entertained them
longer.

My birthday celebration consisted chiefly in my receiving several
poems written in the name of works I had begun but neglected, in which
each of them complained in its own way about my procedure. Especially
noteworthy among them was a poem in the name of the "birds," in
which a deputation of these cheerful creatures, having been sent to
"True Friend,"[16] implored him finally to establish and equip the realm
promised to them. No less understanding and graceful were the statements about my other fragments, so that suddenly all of them came to
life for me again, and I gladly told my friends about my projects and
complete plans. This gave rise to urgent demands and wishes and made

it easy for Herder to persuade me to take these papers along with me again, and above all to devote some well-deserved attention to *Iphigenia*. The play in its present form is more a sketch than a finished work; it is written in poetic prose that sometimes goes astray into iambic meter and indeed also resembles other meters.[17] This of course detracts a great deal from the effect, unless one is a very good reader and can mask the defects by means of certain techniques. He put this to me very earnestly, believing, since I had concealed my larger travel plans from him as from everyone else, that it was merely a question of another tramp through the mountains. Because he was always scornful of mineralogy and geology he said that I should, instead of hitting barren rocks, apply my tools to this work. I obeyed these many well-meant importunities; however, until now it has not been possible to turn my attention in that direction. Now I am separating *Iphigenia* from the packet and taking it along as my companion into the beautiful warm country. The day is so long, my reflections are undisturbed, and the splendid sights in the world around me by no means inhibit the poetic sense. Rather, along with movement and open air, they evoke it all the more quickly.

From the Brenner to Verona

Trent, September 11, 1786, morning.

After having been awake and in constant movement for fully fifty hours, I arrived here yesterday evening at eight o'clock, soon retired, and now am again able to continue my narrative. In the late afternoon of the ninth, when I had concluded the first section of my journal, I still tried to sketch the hostel, the posthouse on the Brenner, and its environs, but I did not succeed. I could not grasp its character and went back inside half peevishly. The innkeeper asked me if I did not want to leave, inasmuch as there would be moonlight and the road was in the best condition; and did I know that he needed the horses to-morrow morning for bringing in the hay and would like them home again by that time? So his advice was self-serving, but I accepted it anyway because it coincided with my inner desire. The sun reappeared, the air was tolerable, I packed up, and drove away at seven o'clock. The atmosphere kept the clouds in check and the evening was beautiful.

The postilion fell asleep and the horses trotted downhill very fast, off and away on the familiar road; when they came to a level spot they went a great deal more slowly. The driver woke up and urged them on, and thus, between high rocks, I very swiftly got down the rushing Adige river. The moon rose and illumined enormous objects. Several mills across the foaming stream, among very old fir trees, were perfect Everdingens.[18]

When I arrived in Sterzing at nine o'clock, it was made clear to me that I was not to linger there. In Mittenwald at twelve o'clock sharp I found everyone fast asleep, except the postilion, and so it went until Brixen, where again I was practically abducted, so that I arrived in Kollmann at dawn. The postilions drove at breakneck speed, but, sorry as I was to travel through these splendid regions at night and so dread-fully fast, as though flying, I rejoiced inwardly that a favorable wind was blowing in back of me, driving me to my longed-for goal. At daybreak I caught sight of the first vine-clad hills. A woman selling pears and peaches approached me, and then it was off to Teutschen, where I arrived at seven o'clock and was at once sent further. Now in the full sunshine, after having traveled northwards[19] again for a while, I finally beheld the valley in which Bolzano lies. Girt by steep mountains which are cultivated up to a considerable height, it is open toward the south, but blocked to the north by the Tyrolean mountains. A mild, gentle air filled the region. Here the Adige turns south again. The hills at the foot of the mountains are planted with grapevines. The stocks are drawn over long, low arbors, from the tops of which the blue grapes hang down very prettily and ripen from the warmth of the ground. Even on the valley floor, where usually only meadows are found, grapes are grown in arbors, in such close-standing rows that the Indian corn between them develops higher and higher stalks. I have often seen them as much as ten feet high. The fibrous male blossom has not yet been cut off, as will happen when the fertilization period has been over for a while.

I arrived at Bolzano in cheerful sunshine. Seeing so many merchant-faces gathered in one spot pleased me. Their expression very clearly bespeaks a purposeful, comfortable existence. On the square were sitting female fruit vendors with flat, round baskets over four feet in diameter, in which peaches lay side by side, so as not to press each other. The pears likewise. Here I was reminded of what I had seen written on the window of the inn in Regensburg:

> Comme les pêches et les melons
> Sont pour la bouche d'un baron,
> Ainsi les verges et les bâtons
> Sont pour les fous, dit Salomon.[20]

It is obvious that this was written by a northern baron, and of course in these parts he would alter his views.

The Bolzano fair occasions active marketing of silk; woolen cloths are also brought here, and whatever leather the mountainous regions can produce. But many merchants come chiefly to collect debts, take orders, and extend new credit. I was very much minded to describe all the products assembled in one place, but the desire, the restlessness, which drives me onward leaves me no peace, and I at once hurry away again. But I am consoled by the thought that in our statistical era all this is no doubt already printed, and one can learn about it from books at one's convenience. At present I am only concerned with sense impressions, which no book, no picture, can give. The fact is that I am taking an interest in the world again, am trying my powers of observation, and testing the extent of my knowledge and scientific training. Is my eye clear, pure, and bright, how much can I grasp in passing, can the creases be eradicated that have formed and fixed themselves in my heart? These last few days, during which I have had to be my own servant and always be watchful and alert, have already given quite a new elasticity to my spirit; I have to worry about exchange rates, change money, pay, make notes, and write, instead of, as usual, just thinking, wanting, meditating, ordering, and giving dictation.

From Bolzano to Trent the road goes along for nine miles through an increasingly fertile valley. Everything that tries so hard to grow in the higher mountains certainly has more life and strength here, the sun is hot, and I believe in a God again.

A poor woman shouted at me please to take her child into my carriage because the hot ground was burning its feet. I did this charitable deed in honor of the great heavenly light. The child was dressed up and adorned in a strange fashion, but I could not get a word out of it in any language.

The Adige now flows more gently and leaves broad deposits of gravel in many places. On the land near the river everything is planted and intertwined so closely up the hillsides that it seems one thing will surely strangle the other—vineyards, maize, mulberry trees, apples, pears, quinces, and nuts. Dwarf elder cascades gaily over the walls. Ivy grows up the rocks on strong trunks and spreads widely; lizards slip through the gaps and all the people walking to and fro remind one of the most charming artistic images. The tied-up braids of the women, the men's bare chests and light jackets, the fine oxen they drive home from the market, the laden little donkeys, all of it constitutes a living, moving Heinrich Roos.[21] And now when evening comes and, in the mild air, only a few clouds rest against the mountains, standing rather than drifting in the sky, and right after sunset the shrill chirping of the cicadas makes itself heard, then I feel at home at last, and not as though I were in hiding or exile. I pretend that I was born and raised here, and have now returned from a trip to Greenland, catching whales. I even welcome the dust of the fatherland that sometimes whirls around my carriage, not having experienced it for so long a time. The chiming of the cicadas, like big and little bells, is delightful, penetrating but not unpleasant. It creates a merry sound when mischievous boys whistle in competition with a field of such singers; I fancy that they really intensify each other. The evening too is perfectly mild, like the day.

If someone living in the south, who was a native of the south, were to hear my raptures over this, he would consider me very childish. Alas, what I am describing here has long been known to me, as long as I have suffered beneath an evil sky, and now I am happy to feel, just as an exception to the rule, a joy which should be ours as a perpetual natural necessity.

Trent, September 10, evening.[22]

I have walked around in the town, which is very old but has well-constructed new houses in some streets. In the church there hangs a picture of the assembled council listening to a sermon of the Jesuit general.[23] I wonder what he has made them believe! The red marble pilasters on the facade mark the church from the very outside as belonging to these fathers; a heavy curtain covers the doorway to keep out the dust. I lifted it up and entered a small anterior church; the church itself is closed off by an iron grating, but in such a way that one can see everything. All was quiet and deserted, for services are no longer held in it. The front door stood open only because all churches are supposed to be open at vesper time.

While I stood there and reflected on the design, which I found similar to the other churches of these fathers, an old man entered and immediately doffed his little black cap. His shabby old black coat indicated that he was an impoverished cleric; he knelt down before the grating and, after a short prayer, stood up again. Turning around, he said softly to himself: "Now that they have driven out the Jesuits, they should also have paid them what the church cost. I certainly know what it cost, and the seminary, many thousands." Meanwhile he had gone out and the curtain had fallen behind him, which I lifted, keeping silent. He had stopped on the upper step and was saying: "The emperor did not do it, the pope did it."[24] With his face turned to the street and unaware of my presence, he continued: "First the Spaniards, then we, then the French. Abel's blood cries out against his brother Cain!" And thus he went down the steps and up the street, still talking to himself. Probably he is someone the Jesuits supported who lost his reason over the tremendous fall of the order. Now he comes daily to look in this empty receptacle for its former inhabitants and after a short prayer curses their enemies.

A young man whom I asked about the curiosities of the town showed me a house called the Devil's House, which the otherwise all too eager Destroyer is said to have built in a single night with quickly procured stones. The good man failed to notice its really curious feature, namely, that this is the only house in good taste that I saw in Trent, certainly erected by a good Italian at an earlier time.

I traveled off at five in the evening; the same spectacle as yesterday evening, and the cicadas, which begin to shrill right at sunset. For at least a mile one rides between walls, over which grapevines can be seen; other walls are not high enough to prevent passersby from picking the grapes, and stones, thorns, and so forth have been used in an attempt to make them higher. Many proprietors spray the first rows with lime, which makes the grapes unpalatable but does not injure the wine at all because fermentation eliminates everything again.

September 11, evening.

Here I am now in Roveredo, which is the language border; north of it there is still alternation between German and Italian. Now for the first time I had a typical Italian postilion, the innkeeper speaks no German, and I must try out my linguistic skills. How happy I am that from now on the beloved language will be alive, the language of everyday use.

Torbole, September 12, after dinner.

How I wish my friends were here for a moment to enjoy the view I have before me!

I could have been in Verona this evening, but there was one more magnificent work of nature off to my side, a choice spectacle I did not want to miss, Lake Garda; and I was splendidly rewarded for making the detour. After five I rode away from Roveredo and up a side valley that pours its waters into the Adige. Having ascended it, one sees an enormous rocky barrier rising in the background, which must be crossed in order to get down to the lake. Here the most beautiful limestone rocks came into view, good for artistic studies. When one comes down there is a little town at the northern end of the lake, a small harbor or, rather, landing place, called Torbole. Fig trees in great numbers had already accompanied me on the way up, and as I descended into the rocky amphitheater I found my first olive trees, full of olives. Here for the first time I came upon what Countess Lanthieri[25] had promised me I would: little white figs as ordinary fruit.

A door leads down to the courtyard from the room I am sitting in; I have moved my table in front of it and sketched the view with a few strokes. Almost the whole length of the lake can be surveyed, only at the end, to the left, does it elude our eyes. The shore, framed on both sides by hills and mountains, gleams with innumerable little settlements.

After midnight the wind blows from north to south, so whoever wants to go down the lake must travel at this time; for already a few hours before sunrise the air current turns and goes northward. Now in the afternoon it is blowing toward me, cooling the hot sun quite delightfully. At the same time my Volkmann[26] informs me that the lake was formerly called Benacus and quotes a verse from Virgil mentioning it:

Fluctibus et fremitu resonans Benace marino.[27]

This is the first Latin verse whose content has come to life before me, and which is as true at this moment, when the wind is growing ever stronger and the lake is casting higher waves against the landing place, as many centuries ago. Many things have changed, but the wind still churns the lake, and the sight is still ennobled by a line of Virgil.

Written at the latitude of forty-five degrees and fifty minutes.

In the cool of the evening I went for a walk, and now I truly find myself in a new land, in a completely foreign environment. The people lead a careless life of ease: firstly, the doors have no locks, but the innkeeper assured me that I need not worry even if my bags contained nothing but diamonds; secondly, the windows are fitted with transparent oiled paper instead of glass panes; thirdly, a most necessary amenity is lacking, so that one comes rather close to a state of nature here. When I inquired of the porter about a certain facility, he pointed down to the courtyard, saying, "Qui abasso può servirsi!" I asked, "Dove?"— "Da per tutto, dove vuol!"[28] he answered amicably. Indeed I see the greatest negligence, but plenty of life and activity. The neighbor women carry on a lively conversation, a hubbub, all day long, and yet at the same time they are all doing something, working at something. I have not yet seen an idle woman.

The innkeeper announced to me with Italian pomposity that he considered himself fortunate to be able to serve me the choicest trout. They are caught near Torbole, where the brook comes down from the mountains and the fish are seeking a way up it. The emperor's share of this catch amounts to ten thousand gulden. They are not actual trout but big fish sometimes weighing fifty pounds, with bodies all speckled, up to the head; the taste is between trout and salmon, tender and excellent.

However, my real delight is in the fruit, in figs, also pears, which must surely be choice in a place where even lemons grow.

September 13, evening.

This morning at three o'clock I set out from Torbole in a boat with two oarsmen. At first the wind was favorable, and they could use the sails. The morning was splendid—cloudy, to be sure, but tranquil with dawn. We went past Limone, whose mountainside gardens, arranged in terraces and planted with lemon trees, have a rich and well-kept appearance. The whole garden consists of rows of square white pillars, placed at certain intervals, which ascend the mountain in steps. Strong poles are laid over these pillars so that the trees planted in between may be covered in winter. Contemplation and inspection of these pleasant objects was favored by our slow journey, and so we were just past Malcesine when the wind shifted completely, taking its usual day-time direction and blowing toward the north. Rowing was of little help against this superior force, and so we had to land in the harbor of Malcesine. It is the first Venetian town on the east side of the lake. When traveling by water one cannot say, I shall be here or there today. I want to use this stop to the best advantage, and especially for drawing the castle situated at the water's edge, a beautiful object. I made a sketch of it today as we were passing.

September 14.

The headwind that drove me into the harbor of Malcesine yesterday also caused me to have a dangerous adventure, which I got through with good humor and, in retrospect, find amusing. As planned, I went in the early morning to the old castle, which, having no gates or guards or keepers, is accessible to everyone. In its courtyard I sat down opposite the old tower built on and into the rocks; I thought I had found a very convenient little spot for drawing: next to a locked door at the top of three or four steps, and in the doorjamb an ornate little stone seat of the kind that can also still be seen in old buildings in our country.

I had not sat there long when various people entered the courtyard, looked at me, and walked back and forth. The crowd grew larger and finally stood still, surrounding me. I could plainly see that my sketching had created a stir, but I did not let this disturb me and calmly continued. At last a man not of the best appearance pushed close and asked what I was doing there. I answered that I was drawing the old tower as a souvenir of Malcesine. Thereupon he said that this was not allowed and I should stop it. Since he spoke in the vulgar Venetian dialect and in fact I scarcely understood him, I answered that I did not understand. At this, with true Italian composure, he seized my sheet, tore it up, but let it lie on the cardboard. Hereupon I detected a note of dissatisfaction among the people standing around, and one elderly woman in particular said that this was not right, the *podestà*[29] should be called, for he knew how to judge such matters. I stood on my steps, my back against the door, and surveyed the constantly growing audience. The inquisitive, unswerving looks, the good-natured expression on most of the faces, and whatever else may characterize a mass of foreign folk, made the most comical impression on me. I imagined I had the chorus of birds in front of me that I, as True Friend, had often made fools of on the stage at Ettersburg.[30] This put me into the most cheerful mood, so that when the *podestà* arrived with his clerk I greeted him without reticence and modestly answered his question as to why I was drawing their fortress by saying that I did not recognize this pile of masonry as a fortress. I pointed out to him and the people the decay of these towers and walls, the lack of gates, and, in short, the indefensibility of the whole thing, and I assured him that I had nothing else in mind except to see and draw a ruin.

His answer was, if it was a ruin, then what did I find remarkable about it? I answered, trying to gain time and favor, in great detail that they well knew how many travelers came to Italy only for the sake of its ruins, that Rome, the capital of the world, laid waste by the barbarians, was full of ruins which have been drawn many hundreds of times, and that not everything from antiquity was as well preserved as the amphitheater in Verona, which I also hoped to see soon.

The *podestà,* who was standing in front of me, but on a lower level, was a tall, somewhat gaunt man of about thirty years. The blunt features of his stupid face were in complete harmony with the slow and dreary way he brought forth his questions. The clerk, smaller and nimbler, also seemed a little confused by such an unusual new case. I said more things of the same kind, they seemed willing to hear me and, turning to some kindly female faces, I thought I perceived agreement and approval.

However, when I mentioned the amphitheater at Verona, which is known locally by the name "Arena," the clerk, who had meanwhile collected his thoughts, said that might be true, for that was a world-famous Roman building. But the only remarkable thing about the towers here was that they marked the boundary between the Venetian realm and the Austrian empire, and therefore ought not to be spied on. I explained at length that I did not agree, that not only Greek and Roman antiquities deserved attention, but also those of the Middle Ages. Of course these people should not be blamed for not being able to discover as much picturesque beauty as I could in this building they had known from childhood on. Fortunately, the morning sun was shedding the most beautiful light on the towers, rocks, and walls, and I began to describe this picture to them enthusiastically. However, because my listeners had their backs to these lauded objects and did not want to stop facing me altogether, they abruptly turned their heads around like those birds called wrynecks to see with their eyes what I was praising to their ears. Indeed the *podestà* himself turned to the picture being described, though with a little more dignity. The scene looked so ridiculous to me that my good spirits rose higher, and I spared them no details, least of all the ivy, which had already had centuries of time to adorn the rock and masonry very richly.

The clerk answered that this was all very well, but Emperor Joseph was a restless ruler who surely still had evil designs on the Republic of Venice, and I might well be his subject, delegated to spy out the borders.

"Far from belonging to the emperor," I exclaimed, "I can boast as well as you to be the citizen of a republic. To be sure, it cannot be compared in might and size to the illustrious Venetian state, but it also rules itself and is second to no city in Germany in commercial activity, wealth, and the wisdom of its officials. That is to say, I am a citizen of Frankfurt-on-Main, a city whose name and reputation must have reached your ears."

"From Frankfurt-on-Main!" shouted a pretty young woman. "There, Mr. *Podestà,* you can see right away what kind of a person this foreigner is, and I consider him a good man. Send for Gregorio, who was in service there for a long time, and he will be able to decide best in this affair."

Already there were more numerous benevolent faces around me, the first disagreeable one had disappeared, and when Gregorio arrived, the case turned completely in my favor. He was a man perhaps in his fifties, a brown Italian face of the familiar type. He spoke and behaved like someone to whom a foreign thing is not foreign, told me at once that he had been in domestic service to the Bolongaros[31] and would like to hear something from me about this family and the town he remembered with pleasure. Fortunately he had been there during my younger years, and I had the dual advantage of being able to tell him exactly the state of things at his time and what had changed since then. I told him about all the Italian families, none of which were strangers to me; he was very pleased to hear many details, for example that Mr. Allesina had celebrated his golden wedding anniversary in 1774, that a medal had been struck for the occasion which I owned myself; he remembered quite well that this business magnate's wife had been born a Brentano.[32] I also had to tell him about the children and grandchildren of these families, how they had grown, been provided for, had married, and produced grandchildren.

While I gave him the most exact information concerning almost everything he asked about, cheerfulness and seriousness alternated on the man's features. He was happy and touched, the people grew increasingly cheerful and could not get enough of hearing our conversation, a part of which, of course, he first had to translate into their dialect.

Finally he said, "Mr. *Podestà,* I am convinced that this is an honest, accomplished man, well brought up, who is traveling in order to educate himself. Let us send him on his way in a friendly manner, so that he will speak well of us to his countrymen and encourage them to visit Malcesine, whose lovely location certainly merits the admiration of foreigners." I reinforced these friendly words with praise of the region, the locality, and the inhabitants, not forgetting to praise the justice officers as wise and prudent men.

All this was declared good, and I received permission to inspect the town and its environs with Master Gregorio as I pleased. Now the innkeeper with whom I was staying joined us, already looking forward to the foreign visitors who would be flocking also to him when the good qualities of Malcesine were properly brought to light. He looked at my articles of clothing with lively curiosity, but particularly envied me those little pistols that can be stuck into one's pockets so conveniently. He said those people were lucky who were permitted to carry such fine arms, which were forbidden here under the severest penalties. I interrupted my friendly importuner several times in order to express gratitude to my deliverer. "Do not thank me," answered the worthy man, "you owe me nothing. If the *podestà* understood his trade and the clerk were not the most self-seeking of men, you would not have gotten away like that. The former was more embarrassed than you were and the latter would not have received a farthing for your arrest, the reports, or the transference to Verona. He thought this over quickly and you were already freed before our conversation was at an end."

Toward evening the good man took me out into his vineyard, which was very well located lower down the lake. His fifteen-year-old son accompanied us and had to climb the trees to pick me the best fruit, while his father selected the ripest grapes.

Between these two unworldly, kindly people, and quite alone in the infinite solitude of this corner of the world, I felt very keenly, reflecting on the day's adventures, what a strange creature man is: what he could enjoy with security and comfort in good company, he often makes uncomfortable and dangerous for himself, simply out of a whim to assimilate the world and its contents in his own special way.

Toward midnight my innkeeper, carrying the little basket of fruit that Gregorio had presented to me, accompanied me to my barque, and so, with a favorable wind, I left the shore which had threatened to become Laestrygonian for me.[33]

Now, concerning my lake trip! It ended happily after the magnificence of the watery expanse and the adjacent Brescian shore had refreshed me to the very heart. There, where the west side of the mountains ceases to be steep and the landscape slopes more gently towards the lake, lie Gargnano, Bogliaco, Cecina, Toscolano, Maderno, Verdom, Salo in a row stretching out for approximately an hour and a half's journey, all of them rather elongated also. Words cannot express the charm of this thickly populated region. At ten o'clock in the morning I landed at Bardolino, loaded my bags onto one mule and myself onto another. Now the way led over a ridge which divides the valley of the Adige from the lake basin. The primeval waters seem to have worked against each other here in vast currents from both sides and to have raised this colossal dam of pebbles. Fertile soil was washed over it in calmer epochs; but the farmer is nevertheless constantly plagued by deposits that keep coming to the surface. Every possible attempt is made to get rid of them, they are piled up in rows and layers, and by that means very thick quasi-walls are formed along the road. At this altitude, on account of insufficient moisture, the mulberry trees look sad. There are no springs at all. Occasionally one finds pools of collected rainwater, at which the mules, and their drivers too, for that matter, quench their thirst. Below, at the river's edge, bucket wheels are set up to water at will the plantations situated at the lower levels.

But there are no words to describe the magnificence of the new region which one now surveys while descending. It is a garden that extends for miles both in length and breadth, lying there quite flat and extremely well kept at the foot of high mountains and jagged rocks. And so on the 10th of September,[34] just before one o'clock, I arrived in Verona. Here I am first of all writing this, in order to conclude and stitch together the second installment of my journal. Then towards evening I hope to see the amphitheater in a happy frame of mind.

I report the following about the atmospheric conditions of the last few days. The night of the ninth to tenth was by turns bright and overcast; the moon always had a halo around it. In the morning not long before five o'clock the whole sky became covered with gray but not heavy clouds, which disappeared as daylight progressed. The lower I descended, the more beautiful the weather became. While in Bolzano the great mountain mass remained northerly, the air showed quite a different quality; namely, at the various hollows in the landscape, which were very pleasingly differentiated by a somewhat lighter or darker blue, one could see that the atmosphere was full of equally distributed vapors, which it could bear, and which therefore were neither precipitated as dew or rain, nor gathered into clouds. As I descended further I distinctly noticed that all the vapors rising from the Bolzano valley and all the cloud strips from the more southerly mountains were drifting toward the higher northerly regions, not concealing them but enveloping them in a kind of haze. In the farthest distance, over the mountains, I could detect a so-called "blister," an incomplete rainbow. To the south of Bolzano they have had the finest weather all summer, only a little "water" from time to time (they call gentle rain "acqua"), and then sunshine again right away. Yesterday too a few drops fell from time to time, while the sun kept shining. It has been a long time since they have had such a good year; everything is prospering; they have sent *us* the bad weather.

I shall mention the mountains and minerals only briefly, because Ferber's trip to Italy[35] and Hacquet's through the Alps give us enough information about this stretch of the road. A quarter hour away from the Brenner is a marble quarry, which I rode past in the twilight. It may, and must, lie atop micaceous slate, like the one on the other side. I found this slate near Kollmann when daylight came; farther down, porphyries manifested themselves. The rocks were so magnificent, and heaps of them along the highway so conveniently broken to pieces, that from them one could have immediately formed and packed up little collections like Voigt's.[36] I can also take along a piece of each sort without inconvenience, provided that I accustom my eyes and desires to smaller proportions. Not far below Kollmann I found a porphyry which splits into regular slabs, and a similar one between Branzoll and Neumarkt, in which the slabs further divide into prisms. Ferber considered these to be volcanic products, but that was fourteen years ago, when, in people's minds, the whole world was on fire.[37] Hacquet already ridicules that idea.

Concerning the humans, I can only say a little, and little of a pleasant nature. At daybreak, as I was riding down from the Brenner, I noticed a definite change in their appearance and was especially displeased by the brownish pallor of the women. Their expressions indicated poverty, the children looked just as pitiful, the men a little better, the basic features, however, quite regular and good. I believe the cause of their morbid condition is to be found in their copious use of Indian corn and buckwheat. The former, which they call yellow "Blende," and the latter, called black "Blende," are ground up, the flour cooked in water to a thick paste, and eaten like that. The Germans on the northern side pick the dough apart and fry it in butter. The Italian Tyrolean, on the other hand, eats it as it is, sometimes grating cheese on it, and no meat during the entire year. That must necessarily clog and stop up the first digestive passages, especially in women and children, and their cachetic color indicates such corruption. They also eat fruit and green beans, which they boil and mix with garlic and oil. I asked whether there were not also some rich peasants.—"Yes, indeed!"—"Do they not treat themselves well? Do they not eat better?"—"No, that is what they have always been used to."—"What do they do with their money? How else do they spend it?"—"Oh, as you know, they have their lords, who relieve them of it again."—That was the sum of a conversation with the daughter of my innkeeper in Bolzano.

I also heard from her that the winegrowers, who appear to be the most well-to-do, are the worst off, because they are in the clutches of the urban merchants, who advance them their living expenses in bad years, and then in good ones appropriate the wine for a pittance. But that is the same everywhere.

What confirms my opinion about nutrition is the fact that the women in the towns always look better. Pretty, plump, girlish faces, the body a little too short for its stoutness and the size of the heads, occasionally some quite friendly, obliging faces, however. We know the men because of the Tyrolean journeymen. At home they do not look as ruddy as the women, probably because the latter have more physical work, more activity, while the men are sedentary shopkeepers and tradesmen. At Lake Garda I found the people very brown, and without the slightest reddish glow on their cheeks, but not unhealthy either, instead quite fresh and comfortable-looking. This is probably caused by the intense sunshine to which they are exposed at the foot of their cliffs.

Verona to Venice

So the amphitheater is the first significant monument of ancient times that I have seen, and so well preserved! On entering it, but still more while walking around its rim, I felt strange because I was seeing something great and yet actually seeing nothing. Of course it should not be seen empty, but brimful of people, as has been arranged in recent times in honor of Joseph II and Pius VI.[38] The emperor, who surely was used to facing masses of humanity, is said to have been astonished by this. But only in the earliest times was the effect complete, when the populace was more of a populace than it is now. For in truth such an amphitheater is perfectly suited for impressing the populace with itself, for entertaining the populace with itself.

When anything worth looking at takes place on level ground and everyone gathers to see it, the individuals in back try in every possible way to raise themselves above the ones in front; people climb on benches, roll up barrels, drive up in carriages, pile up boards, occupy an adjacent hill, and quickly a crater is formed.

If the spectacle occurs on the same spot quite often, light scaffoldings are built for those who can pay, and the remaining masses help themselves as best they can. It is the business of the architect to satisfy this universal need. He prepares a crater like this by means of art, making it as simple as possible, so that the populace itself will be the decoration. Once having seen itself, it could only be amazed; for whereas it was otherwise accustomed only to see itself running about in confusion, to find itself as a milling crowd without order or particular discipline, now the many-headed, many-minded, fickle, errant beast sees itself united into a noble body, induced into oneness, bound and consolidated into a mass, as if it were one form, enlivened by one spirit. The simplicity of the oval is agreeably perceptible to every eye, and each head serves as a measure of the vastness of the whole. Seeing it empty now, I have no criterion, I do not know whether it is large or small.

The Veronese deserve praise for the way they have maintained this
structure. It is built of a reddish marble that is attacked by the elements,
for which reason the eroded steps are constantly being restored, in
rotation, and they all seem almost new. An inscription commemorates
one Hieronymus Maurigenus[39] and the incredible industry he expended
on this monument. Only one piece of the outer wall remains, and I
doubt that it was ever completely finished. The lower vaults, which
abut on the great square, called "il Brà," are rented out to craftsmen,
and it is surely a cheerful sight to see these cavities full of life again.

Verona, September 16.

The most beautiful but always closed gate is called "Porta stuppa"
or "del Palio."[40] As a gate, and considering the great distance at which
it is visible, it is not well conceived; for the merit of the structure can
only be recognized close up.

They offer various reasons for its being closed. Yet my conjecture
is this: the artist obviously intended this gate to effect a relocation of
the Corso, for it does not fit at all with the present street. The left side
has nothing but hovels, and the line at right angles to the middle of the
gate leads to a convent, which would certainly have had to be torn
down. No doubt this was perceived, also the rich and aristocratic probably did not wish to settle in this remote quarter. Perhaps the artist
died, and so the gate was closed, putting a sudden end to the matter.

Verona, September 16.

The portal of the theater building[41] looks quite respectable with its
six large Ionic columns. But over the door, in a painted niche supported
by two Corinthian columns, the life-size bust of Marchese Maffei in a
great wig seems by contrast insignificant. It has an honorable position,
but in order to maintain itself against the size and excellence of the
columns the bust should have been colossal. Now it stands meanly on
a little console, out of harmony with the whole.

The gallery encircling the forecourt is also insignificant, and its fluted
Doric dwarfs cut a pitiful figure next to the smooth Ionic giants. But
let us excuse that in view of the lovely display set up under the columned
porticos. Here a collection of antiquities has been installed that were
excavated mostly in and around Verona. Some are even said to have
been found in the amphitheater. There are Etrurian and Greek objects,
Roman ones down into the inferior period, and also modern things.
The bas-reliefs are fixed into the walls and provided with the numbers
given them by Maffei when he described them in his work *Verona il-*

lustrata. Altars, column fragments, and similar remains; a quite excellent white marble tripod on which genii busy themselves with attributes of the gods. Raphael imitated and transfigured such subjects in the spandrels of the Farnese palace.

The breeze wafting hither from the graves of the ancients comes laden with fragrance, as if over a mound of roses. The gravestones are heartfelt and touching and always depict life. There is a man who, with his wife beside him, looks out of a niche as though from a window. There stand a father and mother, their son between them, looking at each other with inexpressible naturalness. Here a pair join hands. Here a father, resting on his sofa, is apparently being entertained by his family. I was deeply touched by the absolute immediacy of these stones. They are of a later period of art, but simple, natural, and universally appealing. Here there is no man kneeling in his armor, awaiting a happy resurrection. The artist, with more or less skill, has just presented the simple daily life of people, thus continuing their existence and making it permanent. They do not fold their hands, do not gaze into heaven; on the contrary they are down on the earth, as they were and as they are. They stand together, take an interest in one another, love each other, and that, despite a certain lack of professional skill, is most charmingly expressed in these stones. A very richly decorated marble pillar also gave me some new ideas.

Laudable as this exhibit is, it is nevertheless obvious that the noble spirit of preservation which established it no longer lives on in it. The valuable tripod will soon be ruined because it stands free and is exposed toward the west to the atmosphere. This treasure could easily be preserved with a wooden sheath.

The unfinished palace of the Proveditore, if it had been completed, would have made a fine piece of architecture. Otherwise the *nobili* still do a great deal of building, but each one, unfortunately, builds on the site where his older dwelling stood, therefore often in narrow lanes. Thus the splendid facade of a seminary is now being put up in a little lane in the farthest suburb.

When I was walking with a casual companion past the great, somber gate of a remarkable building, he asked me amiably if I would not care to enter the courtyard for a moment. It was the Palace of Justice, and owing to the height of the building the courtyard looked exactly like a huge well. "Here," he said, "all the criminals and suspects are kept in custody." I looked around and saw that all the stories contained open corridors, provided with iron railings, that went past numerous doors. When the prisoner stepped out of his cell to be led to trial, he stood in the open air but was also exposed to general view; and because

there were probably several hearing rooms, the chains would clatter
first over this, then over that, corridor through all the stories. It was
a detestable sight, and I do not deny that the good humor with which
I had dispatched my birds would have had some difficulty maintaining
itself here.

I walked along the rim of the amphitheatrical crater at sunset, enjoying
a most beautiful view over the town and its environs. I was quite alone,
while down below crowds of people were walking on the broad paving
stones of the Brà. Men of all classes and women of the middle class
promenade. From this bird's-eye perspective the latter look just like
mummies in their black outer garments.

The *zendale* and *vesta,* which form the main wardrobe of this class,
are after all perfectly suitable dress for a people which, although not
very careful about cleanliness, still likes to appear in public constantly.
The *vesta* is a black taffeta skirt worn over other skirts. If the woman
has a clean white one under it, she deftly lifts the black skirt up on one
side. The latter is belted in such a way that it marks the waistline and
covers the ends of the bodice, which can be of any color. The *zendale*
is a large bonnet with long side pieces. The bonnet itself is made to
stand up high over the head by means of a wire frame, but the side
pieces are tied around the body like a sash, with the ends hanging down
behind.

Verona, September 16.

Today, after leaving the "Arena," I came upon a modern public
spectacle a few thousand paces away. Four noble Veronese were playing ball with four men from Vicenza. Ordinarily they did this among
themselves all year long at about two hours before nightfall; this time,
on account of the foreign opponents, an incredible throng of people
attended. There may well have been four or five thousand spectators.
I saw no women from any class.

Above, while speaking of the needs of the crowd in such a situation,
I have already described the type of natural, incidental amphitheater
that I saw here, with people positioned one over the other. Even from
a distance I heard lively clapping of hands; every significant stroke was
accompanied by this. The game proceeds as follows: Two gently sloping
wooden ramps are set up at an appropriate distance from each other.
The player who hits out the ball stands at the top of the ramp, his right
hand armed with a broad, spiked wooden ring. As another man on his
team throws him the ball, he runs down to meet it, and in this way
increases the power of the stroke with which he hits it. The opponents

try to hit it back, and this alternates until at last it remains lying on the court. While this is going on, the most beautiful poses are seen, which are worthy of being copied in marble. Since the players are all well-developed, robust young men in short, close-fitting white garments, the teams are distinguishable only by a colored emblem. The posture assumed by the hitter when he runs down the ramp and lifts his arm to strike the ball is especially beautiful; it is much like that of the *Borghese Warrior*.

It seemed odd to me that they perform this exercise next to an old city wall where the spectators do not have the slightest comfort. Why do they not do it in the amphitheater, which would be the very place for it!

Verona, September 17.

I shall just touch briefly on the pictures I have seen and add a few observations. I was making this remarkable journey not to deceive myself but to become acquainted with myself through objects, and so I tell myself quite honestly that I understand little of the art and craft of painters. My attention, my contemplation, can only be directed to the practical part, that is, to the subject and its general treatment.

San Giorgio[42] is a gallery of good paintings, all altarpieces, perhaps not of equal worth yet certainly noteworthy. But the unfortunate artists, what they had to paint! and for whom! A shower of manna, some thirty feet long and twenty high![43] the miracle of the five loaves as a companion piece![44] What was there to paint? Hungry people who pounce on the little kernels, countless others to whom bread is being presented. The artists tried desperately to lend significance to such paltry matters. And yet genius, stimulated by coercion, produced beautiful things. One artist, who had to depict St. Ursula with the eleven thousand virgins, handled the problem very intelligently.[45] The saint stands in the foreground as if she had victoriously taken possession of the land. She is very noble, virginal in an Amazon-like way, lacking in charm; her companions, on the other hand, are seen disembarking from the ship and advancing in procession in the distance, which makes everything diminutive. Titian's *Assumption of the Virgin*,[46] in the cathedral, is very blackened, but it is a laudable idea that the goddess-to-be is not looking heavenwards but down at her friends.

In the Gherardini gallery I found very beautiful works by Orbetto[47] and acquainted myself at once with this meritorious artist. At a distance one learns about only the greatest artists, and then often merely their names. However, when one comes nearer to this star-studded sky and even those of the second and third magnitude begin sparkling, each one also emerging as a part of the whole constellation, then the world grows wide and art becomes rich. Here I must praise the conception of one picture. Only two half-figures. Samson has just fallen asleep in Delilah's lap, and she is quietly reaching over him for the scissors, which lie on a table beside a lamp. The idea has been carried out very well. In the Canossa palace[48] my attention was drawn to a Danae.

The Bevilacqua palace[49] contains the choicest things. A so-called *Paradise* by Tintoretto,[50] which is actually the coronation of the Virgin as Queen of Heaven in the presence of all the patriarchs, prophets, apostles, saints, angels, etc., an opportunity for displaying the whole range of that most happy genius. Lightness of brushwork, spirit, variety of expression—to admire and enjoy all this one should own the picture personally and gaze at it for a lifetime. The work goes into infinite detail, even the last angels' heads that disappear into the glory still have character. The largest figures may be a foot in height, Mary and Christ, who is placing the crown on her, about four inches. The Eve is the most beautiful little woman in the picture, however, and, traditionally, still a little lustful.

A few portraits by Paul Veronese[51] have only increased my esteem for this artist. The collection of antiquities is magnificent, a recumbent son of Niobe is superb, the busts mostly very interesting regardless of the restored noses, an Augustus with the civil crown, a Caligula, and others.

It is my nature to be willing and happy to revere what is great and beautiful; and to develop this tendency with the help of such magnificent objects day after day, hour after hour, is the most blissful of all sensations.

In a land where people enjoy the day, but especially delight in the evening, nightfall is most significant. Then work ceases, then the promenader returns, the father wants to see his daughter back at home again, the day is at an end; but we Cimmerians scarcely know what day is. In our eternal fog and gloom it is immaterial to us whether it is day or night; for how much time do we really have to stroll and divert ourselves beneath an open sky? When night falls here the day, which consisted of evening and morning, is definitely past, twenty-four hours have been lived, a new account begins, the bells ring, the rosary is said, the maid enters one's room with a burning lamp and says: "Felicissima notte!" This cycle changes with every season, and the person who lives a lively life here cannot become confused because every joy of his existence is related not to the hour, but to the time of day. If a German clock were forced on this people they would become confused, for their clock is most intimately connected with their nature. One or one and a half hours before nightfall the nobility begins to drive out, it goes to the Brà, down the long, wide street leading to the Porta Nuova, out of the gate, away from town, and when the bell tolls night, everyone turns around. Some of them drive to the churches to pray the "Ave Maria della sera," some stop on the Brà, the cavaliers step up to the coaches, converse with the ladies, and that lasts a while; I have never waited to the end, the pedestrians stay until late in the night. Today just enough rain fell to settle the dust, it was really a lively, cheerful sight.

In order to adapt myself to an important point of local custom, I have invented a device to help me more easily assimilate their way of telling time. The following diagram can give an idea of it. The inner circle signifies our twenty-four hours, from midnight to midnight, divided into two times twelve, as we count and our clocks show. The middle circle indicates how the bells chime here in the present season, namely, also up to twelve twice in twenty-four hours, only in such a way that it strikes one when with us it would strike eight, and so on until fully twelve. In the morning at eight o'clock according to our clock hand, it strikes one again, and so on. Finally, the outermost circle shows how in daily life one counts to twenty-four. For example, at night I hear seven strike and know that midnight is at five, so I subtract this number from that and therefore have two o'clock past midnight. If in the daytime I hear seven strike and also know that noon is at five o'clock, I proceed in the same fashion and get two o'clock in the afternoon. However, if I want to tell the hours according to the local manner I must know that noon is seventeen o'clock, then add two more and say nineteen o'clock, The first time one hears and reflects on this, it seems extremely complicated and hard to put into practice; but quite soon one becomes accustomed to it and finds this an entertaining occupation. The people also delight in this endless back-and-forth reckoning, like children with difficulties that can easily be overcome. Besides, they always have their fingers in the air, figure everything in their heads, and like to work with numbers. Furthermore the matter is all the easier for the native because he really is not concerned about noon and midnight and, unlike the foreigner in his country, does not compare two clock hands with each other. They count the evening hours only as they strike, in the daytime they add the number to the varying noonday number, which is known to them. The rest is explained by the annotations attached to the figure.

Verona, September 17.

The populace here moves around in very lively confusion, and things look especially busy in the streets where shops and craftsmen's stalls are closely crowded together. The shop or workroom does not have a

Comparison chart

for the

Italian and German clocks, also the Italian clock hands for the
second half of September.

Noon

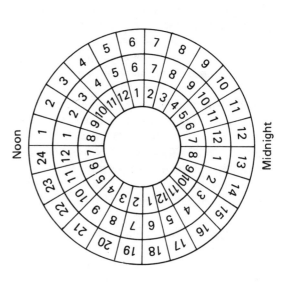

Midnight

The night increases a half hour with every half month.

Month	Day	Becomes night by our clock hand	Is midnight then at
August	1	8½	3½
	15	8	4
Sept.	1	7½	4½
	15	7	5
Oct.	1	6½	5½
	15	6	6
Nov.	1	5½	6½
	15	5	7

From then on the time stands still and is

		Night	Midnight
December } January }		5	7

The day increases a half hour with every half month.

Month	Day	Becomes night by our clock hand	Is midnight then at
Feb.	1	5½	6½
	15	6	6
March	1	6½	5½
	15	7	5
April	1	7½	4½
	15	8	4
May	1	8½	3½
	15	9	3

From then on the time stands still and is

		Night	Midnight
June } July }		9	3

door, as might be expected; no, the whole width of the house is open, one can peer all the way inside at everything that is happening. The tailors sew, the cobblers pull and pound, all of them halfway out into the street; indeed the workplaces make up a part of it. In the evening, when lights are burning, it all looks very much alive.

The squares are very full on market days, vast amounts of vegetables and fruit, garlic and onions to one's heart's content. Moreover they shout, joke, and sing all day long, and never stop swaggering and scuffling, exulting and laughing. The mild air, the low cost of food, makes their life easy. Everyone who possibly can be is outside beneath the open sky.

At night the singing and clamor begin in earnest. In all the streets one hears the little song about Marlborough,[52] then a dulcimer or a violin. They practice all the birdcalls on their pipes, the strangest tones ring out everywhere. The mild climate also gives the poor an exuberant joy in life, so that even this shadow populace seems deserving of respect.

The lack of cleanliness and comfort in the houses, which we find so striking, also stems from this: they are always outside, and are so carefree they think of nothing. The common people take life as it comes, the middle-class man also lives from one day to the next, the rich and aristocratic person secludes himself in his residence, which is also not as comfortable as it would be in the north. Their parties are held in public assembly rooms. Forecourts and colonnades are all befouled with ordure, for nature takes its course here. The populace is always edging forward. The rich man can be rich, build palaces, the *nobile* may rule, but when he installs a colonnade or a forecourt, the populace uses this for its needs, of which the most pressing one is to rid itself as quickly as possible of what it has consumed as copiously as possible. Anyone unwilling to tolerate this must not play the great lord, that is, he must not act as though a part of his residence belonged to the public, but simply close his doors; and that is all right too. The people absolutely refuse to give up their claim on public buildings, and this is what foreigners complain about all over Italy.

Today, while going through town on various streets, I observed the costume and manners especially of the middle class, which seems to be very numerous and busy. They all swing their arms when they walk. Persons of a higher class swing only one arm, because they wear a sword on certain occasions and are used to holding the left arm still.

Although the populace attends to its affairs and needs very light-heartedly, it nevertheless has a sharp eye for anything foreign. Thus in the first days I noticed everyone looking at my boots, which are too expensive an article of clothing here to be worn even in winter. Now that I am wearing shoes and stockings, no one looks at me anymore. But this morning, when they were all running around in confusion with flowers, vegetables, garlic, and so much other market produce, I found it remarkable that nobody failed to notice the cypress branch I held in my hand. A few green pine cones hung from it, and besides I was holding some blooming branches of caper. Everybody, child or adult, looked at my fingers and seemed to be having strange thoughts.[53]

I brought these branches from the Giusti garden, which is excellently situated and has enormous cypresses, all of which stand straight up in the air, like German broom. Probably the trimmed and tapered yews of northern horticulture are imitations of this magnificent natural product. A tree whose branches from bottom to top, the oldest as well as the youngest, all strive toward heaven, which lasts its good three hundred years, is surely worthy of veneration. Judging from the time when this garden was laid out, these trees have already reached that great age.

Vicenza, September 19.

The road here from Verona is very pleasant, one travels northeastwards past the mountains, with the foothills, which consist of sand, limestone, clay, and marl, always on the left; on these hills are situated towns, castles, houses. The straight, wide, well-maintained road goes through fertile fields; one looks into deep rows of trees on which grapevines are drawn up high and then descend as if they were airy branches. Here one can form an idea of what festoons are! The grapes are ripe and burden the tendrils, which hang down long and sway. The road is filled with people of every kind and trade, I was especially delighted by the wagons with low, dish-like wheels, which, drawn by four oxen, transport back and forth the great vats in which the grapes are brought from the gardens and pressed. When these were empty the drivers stood in them; it looked much like a Bacchic triumphal procession. The soil between the rows of vines is used for all kinds of grain, especially Indian corn and millet.

Toward Vicenza little hills rise up from the north and south, they are said to be volcanic, and end the plain. Vicenza lies at their feet and, as it were, in a bosom that they form.

Vicenza, September 19.

I arrived here a few hours ago, have already walked about the town and seen the Olympian theater and the buildings of Palladio.[54] A very pretty little book with engravings and an expert text has been published for the convenience of foreigners.[55] Only when these works are actually seen can one recognize their great merit; for they must fill the eye with their true size and concreteness and satisfy the spirit with the beautiful harmony of their dimensions, not only in abstract outlines but with all their projecting and receding parts seen in perspective. And so I say of Palladio: he was intrinsically and through and through a great man. The greatest difficulty confronting him, like all modern architects, was the proper use of the columnar orders in civil architecture; for to combine columns and walls is, after all, a contradiction. But how he has managed that! How he impresses with the presence of his works and makes us forget that he is only being persuasive. There is really something godlike about his designs, like the power of a great poet to take truth and lies and out of them frame a third entity, whose borrowed existence enchants us.

The Olympian theater is a theater of the ancients on a small scale and inexpressibly beautiful, but compared to ours it seems to me like a rich, aristocratic, handsome child compared to a clever man of the world, who is neither so aristocratic, rich, nor handsome, but knows better what he can achieve with the means at his disposal.

When, here on the spot, I contemplate the magnificent buildings erected by that man and see how they have been disfigured by people's narrow, base needs, how these designs were mostly beyond the abilities of the builders, how poorly these choice monuments to a lofty human spirit harmonize with the life of the rest of mankind, then it occurs to me that this after all is the way of the world. For one gets little thanks from people when one tries to exalt their inner urges, to give them a lofty concept of themselves, to make them feel the magnificence of a true, noble existence. But when one deceives the birds, tells them fairy tales, leads them along from day to day, debases them, then one is their man; and that is why the modern era delights in so many tasteless things. I do not say this to disparage these friends of mine, I am only saying that this is how they are, and one must not be surprised if everything is as it is.

It is impossible to describe how Palladio's basilica looks next to an old castle-like building bespeckled with dissimilar windows, which the great architect certainly imagined as being absent, tower and all, and in a curious way I have to steady myself; for here too, unfortunately, I find the very things I am fleeing side by side with those I am seeking.

September 20.

Yesterday was the opera, it lasted until after midnight and I longed to retire. *The Three Sultans* and *The Abduction from the Seraglio*[56] have furnished many scraps, out of which this play was patched together with little intelligence. The music was easy to listen to, but is probably by an amateur, without a single striking new thought. On the other hand the ballets were delightful. The leading couple danced an allemande that was as graceful as could be.

The theater is new, charming, beautiful, modestly sumptuous, everything uniform, as is appropriate for a provincial town; every box has a tapestry of the same color draped over it, the box of the *capitano grande* being distinguished only by a somewhat longer overhang.

The leading female singer, very much favored by the whole populace, receives tumultuous applause when she appears, and the birds grow wild with joy when she does something well, as she often does. She is an unaffected creature, pretty figure, lovely voice, a pleasant face, and a quite decorous manner. Her arms could be a little more graceful. However, I shall not be coming again; I feel that I shall never make a good bird.[57]

September 21.

Today I visited Doctor Turra;[58] for some five years he concentrated passionately on botany, assembled a herbarium of Italian flora, and, under the previous bishop, established a botanical garden. But that is all past. Natural history was displaced by medical practice, the herbarium is food for worms, the bishop is dead, and the botanical garden has been replanted, as is proper, with cabbages and garlic.

Doctor Turra is a really fine, good man. He told me his story with candor, purity of heart, and modesty, and in general spoke very precisely and pleasantly. But he was not inclined to open his cabinets, which probably were not in any presentable condition. Our conversation soon faltered and stopped.

September 21, evening.

I went to the old architect Scamozzi,[59] who edited the work on Palladio's buildings and is a worthy, dedicated artist. Pleased with my interest, he gave me some guidance. Among Palladio's buildings there is one I have always been especially partial to, it is said to have been his own residence;[60] but, close up, there is much more to it than is shown in the picture. I would like to have a drawing of it, illuminated with the colors given it by its age and material. But one must not imagine that the master erected a palace for himself. It is the most modest house in the world, having only two windows, which are separated by a broad space meant to contain a third window. A painting of it including the neighboring houses, to show how it is inserted between them, would also be pleasant to look at. Canaletto[61] should have painted that.

Today I visited the palatial house called the Rotonda,[62] which is located on a pleasant height about a half hour from the town. It is a square building which encloses a round salon lighted from above. One climbs up broad steps on all four sides and each time arrives at a vestibule formed of six Corinthian columns. Perhaps there has never been more extravagant architecture. The space occupied by the steps and vestibules is much greater than that of the house itself; for each individual side would make a suitable view of a temple. Inside it can be called habitable, but not comfortable. The salon is very beautifully proportioned, the other rooms also; but they would hardly meet the needs of an aristocratic family for a summer sojourn. On the other hand one can see it from all sides in the whole area, rising up most magnificently. There is great variety in the way its central mass together with the projecting columns moves before the spectator's eye as he walks around it. The owner has completely achieved his goal, which was to leave behind a large entailed estate and at the same time a tangible memorial to his wealth. And just as the building can be seen in its splendor from all points in the area, so too the view away from it is most pleasant. One sees the Bachiglione flowing, carrying ships down from Verona to the Brenta. At the same time one surveys the extensive possessions that Marchese Capra wanted to preserve intact within his family. The inscriptions on the four gable sides, which together make a whole, surely deserve to be recorded:

> *Marcus Capra Gabrielis filius*
> *qui aedes has*
> *arctissimo primogeniturae gradui subjecit*
> *una cum omnibus*
> *censibus agris vallibus et collibus*
> *citra viam magnam*
> *memoriae perpetuae mandans haec*
> *dum sustinet ac abstinet.*[63]

The conclusion in particular is rather strange: a man who had so much wealth and willpower at his disposal still feels that he must endure and abstain. That can be learned with less expense.

                                                        September 22.

This evening I was at an assembly held by the Academy of Olympians.[64] A mere pastime, but a good one, it provides the people with a little intellectual spice and liveliness. A great hall next to Palladio's theater, well lighted, the *Capitano* and some nobility present, indeed altogether an audience of cultivated persons, many clerics, in all about five hundred.

The question proposed by the president for today's session was whether invention or imitation has been of greater benefit to the fine arts. To be sure, the notion was a happy one, for if the alternatives contained in the question are separated they can be discussed from this side and that for a hundred years. The academic gentlemen took full advantage of this opportunity and said various things in prose and verse, many of them good.

Moreover, the audience is very lively. The listeners shouted "bravo," clapped, and laughed. If only we could stand before our nation and personally entertain it! We offer our best efforts in black and white; each reader sits owl-like in a corner and picks at it as best he can.

As can be imagined, Palladio was cited here again at every possible juncture, whether the subject was invention or imitation. At the conclusion, where a most humorous tone is always required, someone had the happy notion of saying that since everyone else had preempted Palladio, he would praise Franceschini, the great silk manufacturer. He then proceeded to show what benefits had accrued to this man, and through him to the city of Vicenza, by the imitation of Lyonnaise and Florentine materials, from which it would follow that imitation is far superior to invention. And he said this in such a humorous way that it caused universal laughter. In general the proponents of imitation won greater approval, for they said nothing but what the multitude thinks and is capable of thinking. At one point the audience, with loud hand-clapping, gave its hearty approval to a very crude sophism, whereas it had not reacted to many good, indeed excellent statements in favor of invention. I am very glad also to have experienced this, and then it is most refreshing to see that Palladio, after so long a time, is still revered by his fellow citizens as a lodestar and paragon.

September 22.

This morning I was in Thiene, which lies northward toward the mountains, where a new building[65] is being erected according to an old design, surely a commendable idea. Thus it is that everything from the good period is honored here, and people are wise enough to build something new on the basis of an inherited plan. The palace is quite admirably situated in a great plain, with the limestone Alps in the background and no mountains in between. The visitor is greeted by waters flowing toward him on both sides of the perfectly straight highway that leads to the building, and these irrigate the broad rice fields through which he rides.

Although as yet I have seen only two Italian cities and spoken with few people, I already know my Italians well. Like courtiers, they con-

sider themselves the foremost people in the world, and they can imagine
this smugly and with impunity because of certain undeniable advantages
they have. The Italians seem to me a very good nation; I need only
look at the children and common folk, as I now see and can see them,
since I am always among them and mix with them. And what faces
and figures they have!

I must especially praise the Vicentians, because they grant me the
privileges of being in a large city and do not stare at me, no matter
what I do; however, when I address them they are pleasant and com-
municative, and the women delight me particularly. I do not mean to
criticize the Veronese women, they have good facial structure and
strong profiles; but mostly they are pale, and the *zendale* makes this
worse, because one expects to see something charming under that
beautiful headgear. Here, however, I find quite pretty creatures, especially a brunette type, which particularly interests me. There is also
a blonde type, which is not as much to my taste.

Padua, September 26, evening.

I rode over here today in four hours in a little single-seat chaise called
a *sediola,* packed with all my belongings. Usually the trip is made comfortably in three and a half hours; however, since I wanted to enjoy
this delightful day under the open sky, I was glad that the *vetturino*[66]
was laggard in his duty. The route is straight southeastwards through
the most fertile plain, between hedges and trees, without any other
view, until finally on the right the beautiful mountains stretching from
the east to the south are seen. The opulence of the plants and fruits
hanging over walls and hedges and down from the trees is indescribable.
Pumpkins weigh down the roofs, and the oddest cucumbers hang from
laths and trellises.

I could survey the splendid location of the city very clearly from the
observatory. To the north the Tyrolean mountains, snow-covered, half
hidden by clouds, and joined in the northwest by the Vicentian mountains; finally, to the west and closer in, the mountains of Este, whose
shapes and hollows can be seen distinctly. To the southwest a green
sea of vegetation without a trace of elevation, tree on tree, bush on
bush, plantation on plantation, innumerable white houses, villas, and
churches peeping out of the greenery. On the horizon I saw the tower
of St. Mark's in Venice and other lesser towers quite distinctly.

Padua, September 27.

At last I have acquired the works of Palladio, to be sure not the
original edition with woodcuts,[67] which I saw in Vicenza, but an exact

copy, indeed a facsimile with copperplates put out by an excellent man, Smith,[68] the former English consul in Venice. It must be granted to the English that they have known for a long time how to appreciate what is good and have a grandiose manner of displaying it.

In connection with this purchase I entered a bookstore, which in Italy has quite a characteristic appearance. All the books stand around unbound, and good company is found there all day long. Those secular clergymen, nobles, and artists who are to any degree connected with literature walk to and fro here. A person may request a book, look something up, read, and converse, as he pleases. Thus I found some half-dozen men standing together, all of whom looked around at me when I inquired about Palladio's works. While the owner of the store was searching for the book, they praised it and gave me information about the original and the copy, for they were very well acquainted with the work itself and the merits of its author. Since they took me for an architect, they praised me for proceeding to this master's studies in preference to all others. They said that he provided more material for practical use and application than Vitruvius[69] himself did, for he had thoroughly studied the ancients and antiquity and tried to adapt it to our requirements. I conversed for a long time with these friendly men, learned some more things about the city's noteworthy sights, and took my leave.

Since whole churches have been built for the saints, surely a place can be found in them for monuments to men of reason. The bust of Cardinal Bembo[70] stands between Ionic columns, a handsome face, drawn back into itself by force, if I may put it thus, and a mighty beard; the inscription reads:

> *Petri Bembi Card. imaginem Hier. Guerinus Ismeni*
> *f. in publico ponendam curavit ut cujus ingenii*
> *monumenta aeterna sint ejus corporis quoque*
> *memoria ne a posteritate desideretur.*[71]

The university building alarmed me by all its solemnity. I was glad I did not have to study there. An academic situation as crowded as that is inconceivable, even to someone who, as a student at German universities, has experienced discomfort on lecture hall benches. The anatomical theater especially is a model of how students can be squeezed together. The listeners are layered above one another in a high, sharply tapering funnel. They look almost straight down at the narrow space where the table stands, on which no light falls, so that the teacher must demonstrate by lamplight. In contrast, the botanical garden is pleasant and bright.[72] Many plants can stay outdoors even in the winter, if they are set next to the walls or not far from them. In October the whole place is covered over, and then it is heated for a few months. It is agreeable and instructive to wander amidst vegetation that is foreign to us. We eventually think no more at all about plants we are accustomed to, like other long familiar objects; and what is observation without thought? Here in this newly encountered diversity that idea of mine keeps gaining strength, namely, that perhaps all plant forms can be derived from one plant. Only in this way would it be possible truly to determine genera and species, which, it seems to me, has heretofore been done very arbitrarily. My botanical philosophy remains stuck on this point, and I do not yet see how to proceed. The depth and breadth of the problem seem equally great to me.

The large square, called the Prato della Valle, is a very wide space, and in June the main market is held there. The wooden booths in the middle of it do not look very attractive, but the inhabitants assure me that a *fiera*[73] of stone, like the one in Verona, will soon be seen here. Indeed some basis for this hope is to be found in the surroundings of the square, which provide a very beautiful and significant sight.

An enormous oval is set around with statues representing all the famous men who have taught and studied here. Every native and foreigner is permitted to erect a statue of a specified size to any countryman or relative, as soon as there is proof of that person's merit and of his academic sojourn in Padua.

The oval is surrounded by a moat. On the four bridges crossing it stand popes and doges of colossal size; the rest are smaller and were placed by guilds, private persons, and foreigners. The king of Sweden[74] had Gustavus Adolphus[75] put up here because it is said that he once heard a lecture in Padua. Archduke Leopold[76] revived the memory of Petrarch and Galileo. The statues are made in a worthy modern style, few are excessively manneristic, some very natural, all of them in the costume of their rank and time. The inscriptions are also laudable. None of them are tasteless or trivial.

This would have been a happy idea at any university, and is particularly so at this one, because it is very comforting to see a completely vanished past evoked again. This can become quite a handsome square if the wooden *fiera* is replaced by one of stone, as is said to be the plan.

In the meetinghouse of a brotherhood dedicated to St. Anthony are some rather old pictures which bring the old German masters to mind, alongside them also some by Titian. The latter already show the great step forward that was not taken by anyone north of the Alps. Directly after that I saw some of the newest pictures. When these artists could no longer attain high seriousness, they very successfully turned to humorousness. The beheading of John by Piazzetta[77] is a very worthy picture of this kind, if one accepts the master's manner. John kneels, holding out his folded hands, his right knee against a stone. A hireling soldier, who holds him bound from the back, bends around his side and looks into his face, as if amazed by the composure with which this man submits himself. Up above stands another soldier, who is to execute the stroke, but he does not have the sword and only makes the gesture with his hands, as though practicing in advance. A third man, below, draws the sword out of its sheath. The concept is felicitous, though not great, the composition striking and very effective.

In the church of the Anchorites I saw pictures by Mantegna,[78] one of the older painters, who astonishes me. What a sharp, sure immediacy is displayed in these pictures! It was from this altogether genuine quality of immediacy—by no means specious, with no false effects that speak only to the imagination, but a robust, pure, bright, detailed, scrupulous, circumscribed immediacy, which at the same time had something stern, diligent, laborious about it—that the subsequent artists proceeded, as I noticed in Titian's pictures. And now the liveliness of their genius, the energy of their nature, illuminated by the spirit of these predecessors and invigorated by their strength, could climb higher and ever higher, rise from the earth and bring forth heavenly but true forms. It was thus that art developed after the barbarous times.

The audience room of the city hall,[79] rightly named "Salone," with the augmentative suffix, is a self-contained structure so enormous that it cannot be imagined or even, shortly afterwards, clearly remembered. Three hundred feet long, one hundred feet wide, and one hundred feet high beneath the vaulted roof that covers its whole length. These people are so accustomed to living in the open air that the builders found a marketplace to roof over for them. And there is no question that the huge arched-over space produces a peculiar sensation. It is an enclosed infinity, more analogous to man than the starry sky is. The latter draws us out of ourselves, the former very gently presses us back into ourselves.

For this reason I also like to linger in the church of St. Justine. It is four hundred eighty-five feet long, correspondingly high and wide, a vast but simple building. This evening I sat down in a corner and did some quiet meditating. I felt quite alone, for if any person in the world was thinking of me at that moment, he would certainly never have looked for me there.

Now it is time to pack up again, for tomorrow morning my way goes by water on the Brenta. It rained today, now it has cleared up again, and I trust that my first view of the lagoons and the sovereign city wed to the sea will be in beautiful daylight. And from her bosom I shall send greetings to my friends.

Venice

So it was written on my page in the Book of Fate that in 1786, on the twenty-eighth of September, at five o'clock in the evening by our reckoning, I should for the first time lay eyes on Venice, sailing out of the Brenta into the lagoons, and soon thereafter enter and visit this wonderful island city, this beaver republic. And so, God be thanked, Venice too is no longer a mere word to me, a hollow name which has often made me uneasy, me, the mortal enemy of verbal sounds.

When the first gondola approached the ship (this is done so that passengers who are in a hurry may be taken to Venice more swiftly), I remembered an early childhood toy I had not thought about for perhaps twenty years. My father owned a pretty model gondola that he had brought back; he prized it highly, and I felt very honored when I was actually allowed to play with it. The first prows of shiny iron plate, the black gondola cabins, all of that greeted me like an old acquaintance, and I reveled in a pleasant, long-forgotten childhood impression.

I am well lodged in the "Queen of England," not far from St. Mark's square, and that is the best feature of the inn; my windows open on a narrow canal between tall houses, directly below me a single-arched bridge, and opposite me a busy, narrow lane. Thus I live and thus I shall remain for a while until my packet for Germany is ready and until I have seen my fill of the sights of this city. I have often sighed longingly for solitude, and now I can really enjoy it; for nowhere does an individual feel more alone than in a bustling crowd, through which he presses, unknown to all. Perhaps there is only one person in Venice that knows me, and we shall not soon meet.

Venice, September 28, 1786.

Just a few words about my trip from Padua: The voyage on the Brenta, on a public ship in mannerly company (for the Italians are on their guard with each other) is seemly and pleasant. The banks are adorned with gardens and summer houses, little settlements come down to the water, and for a while the busy highway runs alongside it. Since one descends the river by means of locks, there is often a little delay, which one can use for looking around on shore and enjoying the fruit that is abundantly offered. Then one embarks again and moves through a colorful world of fertility and life.

In addition to so many alternating images and forms there was another apparition which, even though coming from Germany, was really quite appropriate here, that is to say, two pilgrims, the first I have seen close up. They have the right to be transported free of charge on this public conveyance; but because the rest of the company shuns their vicinity they do not sit in the covered space, but in the stern with the helmsman. Being a rare phenomenon nowadays, they were stared at and received little respect because formerly much riffraff wandered about under this guise. When I heard they were Germans and knew no other language I joined them and learned that they came from the Paderborn territory. Both were men over fifty, of swarthy but good-natured physiognomy. They had first of all visited the grave of the three sainted kings at Cologne, then had traveled through Germany, and now were on their way together to Rome. Then they intended to return to upper Italy, whereupon one of them would walk back to Westphalia while the other would first pay his respects to St. James at Compostela.

Their clothing was the customary kind but they had tucked it up and so looked better than the "pilgrims" in long taffeta robes we usually see at our balls. The great collar, the round hat, the staff, and the shell serving as the humblest drinking vessel, everything had its significance, its immediate usefulness; the metal case contained their passports. But the most remarkable things were their little morocco wallets holding various small instruments that were probably suitable for filling whatever simple need might arise. They had taken these out, having discovered something on their clothes that needed patching.

The helmsman, much pleased to have found an interpreter, had me ask them several questions; from this I learned something about their views, but more about their journey. They complained bitterly about their coreligionists, including monks and secular priests. Piety, they said, must be a very rare thing, because theirs was not credited anywhere, and in Catholic lands they were treated almost entirely like vagrants, even though they displayed their prescribed clerical itinerary and their episcopal passports. On the other hand, they related with feeling how well the Protestants had received them. They spoke of one particular country parson in Swabia and especially of his wife, who had been able to persuade her somewhat reluctant husband to let her provide them with abundant refreshment, which they had been in great need of. Indeed on their departure she had given them a thaler, which had stood them in good stead when they reentered Catholic territory. Hereupon one of them said with all the solemnity of which he was capable. "We also include this woman in our daily prayer and ask God to open her eyes as He opened her heart to us, and to accept her, even though late, into the bosom of the only true Church. And so we certainly hope to meet her some day in Paradise."

Seated on the little stairs leading to the deck, I explained as much as was necessary and useful of all this to the helmsman and a few other persons who had come out of the cabin to crowd into this narrow space. Some meager refreshments were extended to the pilgrims; for the Italian does not like to give. Hereupon they drew out little consecrated slips of paper showing a picture of the three sainted kings along with Latin prayers in their honor. The good men asked me to give these to the little group with an explanation of their great value. I was quite successful in this, for when the two men seemed very much at a loss, Venice being so big, as to how they would find the monastery designated to receive pilgrims, the emotionally stirred helmsman promised that on landing he would at once give a lad a three-penny piece to conduct them to that distant location. To be sure, he added confidentially, they would find little comfort there; the institution, although laid out on a grand scale for the reception of I do not know how many pilgrims, had at present rather deteriorated, and its revenue was being turned to other uses.

Entertained thus, we had come down the beautiful Brenta, passing many a magnificent garden, many a magnificent palace, viewing with a hasty glance the wealthy, busy towns along the shore. As we now sailed into the lagoons, our ship was immediately surrounded by a swarm of gondolas. A Lombard quite familiar with Venice bade me keep him company so as to get into town more speedily and escape the misery of the Dogana.[80] With a moderate gratuity he was able to fend off some people who tried to detain us, and so in the bright sunset we floated quickly to our goal.

The 29th, Michaelmas, evening.

So much has already been told and printed about Venice that instead of a detailed description I shall just give my personal impressions. What again claims my attention above all else is the populace, a great mass, a necessary, instinctive existence.

This race did not flee frivolously to these islands, it was not caprice that prompted subsequent settlers to unite with them; necessity taught them to seek their security in this most disadvantageous location, which later became so advantageous for them and made them wise when the whole northern world still lay captive in darkness; their increase, their riches, were a necessary result. Now their dwellings crowded together ever more closely, sand and swamp were replaced with rocks, the houses sought the air, like trees that stand close to each other, and had to gain in height what they lacked in width. Niggardly with every span of ground and compressed into narrow spaces from the very outset, they allowed the lanes no more breadth than was required for separating two opposite rows of houses and preserving scanty passageways for the citizen. Furthermore water served as their streets, squares, and promenades. The Venetian had to become a new species of creature, just as Venice can only be compared with itself. The great serpentine canal is second to no other street in the world, and nothing can really match the expanse before St. Mark's square: I mean the great watery surface which on this side is embraced in a crescent shape by the main part of Venice. To the left across the water one sees the island of San Giorgio Maggiore, somewhat more to the right the Giudecca and its canal, still farther to the right the Dogana and the entrance to the Grand Canal, where immediately several huge marble temples gleam at us. There, with a few strokes, are the chief objects that catch our eye when we step out from between the two columns of St. Mark's square. All the views and prospects have been engraved so often that anyone who likes prints can easily get a vivid idea of them.

After dinner, I first hastened to obtain a general impression and, without a companion, noting only the points of the compass, plunged into the labyrinth of the city, which, although thoroughly cut up by larger and smaller canals, is connected again by larger and smaller bridges. One cannot imagine the narrowness and density of the whole without having seen it. Usually the width of the lanes can be nearly or completely measured by stretching out one's arms; in the narrowest, a person walking with arms akimbo will hit against the walls with his elbows. There are indeed wider lanes, even an occasional little square, but everything can be called relatively narrow.

I easily found the Grand Canal and the Rialto, the principal bridge; it consists of a single arch of white marble. The view down from it is grand, the canal thickly dotted with boats that bring in all the necessities from the mainland and dock and unload chiefly here, in between them a swarm of gondolas. Especially today, it being Michaelmas, the view was lively and very beautiful; but in order to describe it to some degree I must give a few more details.

The two main sections of Venice, which are divided by the Grand Canal, are connected by a single bridge, the Rialto, but rowboats provide additional communication at specific crossing points. It looked very good today when well-dressed but black-veiled women, in large groups,

had themselves rowed over to reach the church of the fêted archangel.
I left the bridge and approached one of those crossing points to get a
close look at the disembarking women. I found some very lovely faces
and figures among them.

Having grown tired, I got into a gondola and left the narrow lanes.
To enjoy the spectacle on the opposite side properly, I rode through
the northern part of the Grand Canal, around the island of Santa Clara
in the lagoons, into the canal of the Giudecca, up toward St. Mark's
square, and was now suddenly a co-sovereign of the Adriatic sea, like
every Venetian when he reclines in his gondola. At this point I thought
respectfully of my good father, whose greatest pleasure was to tell about
these things. Will I not do the same? Everything around me is estimable,
a great, venerable accomplishment of collective human strength, a
magnificent monument, not of a ruler, but of a people. And even if
their lagoons are gradually filling up, evil vapors hover over the swamp,
their trade is weakened, their power diminished, yet the whole structure
and substance of this republic will not for a moment seem less honorable
to the observer. It is succumbing to time, like everything that has a
visible existence.

                                                        September 30.

Toward evening, again without a guide, I lost my way in the remotest
quarters of the city. The bridges here are all fitted with steps, so that
gondolas and probably also larger boats can pass comfortably under
the arch. I tried to find my way in and out of this labyrinth without
asking anyone, again only directing myself by the points of the compass.
Finally one does disentangle oneself, but it is an incredible maze, and
my method, which is to acquaint myself with it directly through my
senses, is the best. Also, up to the last inhabited tip of land I have
noted the residents' behavior, manners, customs, and nature; these are
differently constituted in every quarter. Dear Lord! what a poor, good-
natured beast man is!

A great many small houses stand right in the canals, but here and
there are found beautifully paved embankments on which people can
stroll back and forth very pleasantly between water, churches, and palaces. The long embankment on the north side is bustling and pleasant;
the islands are visible from there, especially Murano, which is Venice
in miniature. The lagoons in between are busy with gondolas.

                                                   September 30, evening.

Today I again increased my knowledge of Venice by procuring a map
of the city. After having studied it for a while, I climbed the tower of

St. Mark's, where a unique spectacle meets the eye. It was noon and
the sunshine was bright, so that I could clearly recognize places near
and far without a telescope. Floodtide covered the lagoons, and when
I turned my gaze to the so-called Lido (it is a narrow strip of land
closing off the lagoons), I saw the sea, with some sails on it, for the
first time. In the lagoons themselves lie galleys and frigates that were
supposed to join up with Cavaliere Emo,[81] who is waging war against
the Algerians, but that are idled by unfavorable winds. The Paduan
and Vicenzian mountains and the Tyrolean range conclude the picture
most admirably between west and north.

October 1.

I went out to view various aspects of the city, and since it was Sunday
I was struck by the great uncleanliness of the streets, which started
me reflecting. There is indeed a type of policing of this material, for
the people shove the refuse into the corners, and I see large boats plying
back and forth which stop at many places and load the refuse—these
are people from the surrounding islands who need fertilizer. But these
arrangements lack both regularity and strictness; and since this city
was completely planned for cleanliness, just as much as any city in
Holland, its uncleanliness is the more inexcusable.

All the streets are paved with flagstones. Even in the remotest quarters, wherever necessary, at least bricks are laid in them, set lengthwise
and upright, a little raised in the middle, with depressions at the side
to catch the water and conduct it into covered drains. Some other architectural devices in the well-considered original design also testify
to the fact that its excellent builders intended to make Venice the
cleanest city, just as it is the most extraordinary one. As I strolled
along, I could not resist drafting a set of regulations for this purpose,
preparing the way, in my thoughts, for a sanitary supervisor who would
take his task seriously. Thus one is always ready and eager to sweep
before someone else's door.

October 2.

First of all I hurried into the Carità;[82] in Palladio's works I had read
that he had proposed to build a monastery here which would depict
how rich and hospitable ancients lived at home. I was greatly delighted
with his plan, which was admirably designed both as a whole and in
its individual parts, and I expected to find a marvel. But alas, scarcely
a tenth part has been built, though even this is worthy of his genius,
having a perfection of arrangement and an exactness of execution that

are beyond anything known to me. Years should be spent in contemplating such a work. I think that I have never seen anything more sublime or more perfect, and I believe I am not mistaken. Let us imagine this excellent artist, born with an inner sense of the grand and gracious, who first, with incredible effort, attains to the cultural level of the ancients, so that he may reestablish them by himself. This man is given the opportunity to carry out a favorite idea, to erect a monastery, designated as a dwelling for many monks and a shelter for many strangers, in the form of an ancient private residence.

The church was already standing; one steps out of it into an atrium with Corinthian columns, which is charming and dispels any air of priestliness. On one side is the sacristy, on the other a chapter room, next to this the most beautiful spiral staircase in the world, with a broad, open newel and stone steps that are fixed into the wall and layered in such a way that each supports the other; I could not get enough of climbing up and down it. How well it turned out can be deduced from the fact that Palladio himself declares it well done. From the forecourt one steps out into the great inner court. Unfortunately, only the left wing of the building that was supposed to surround it has been erected: three orders of columns placed one above the other, large rooms on the ground floor, on the second a colonnade along the cells, the upper story a wall with windows. But this description must be supplemented by a look at the plans. Now a word about the construction.

Only the bases and capitals of the columns and the keystones of the arches are of hewn stone, everything else is not exactly of brick, but terra-cotta. Such bricks are quite new to me. The frieze and cornice are also made of them, likewise the members of the arches, everything partially fired, and in the final analysis the building is held together only with a bit of lime. It stands there as though all of one piece. If the whole edifice had been completed, and it could be seen cleanly rubbed down and colored, it would surely be a glorious sight.

However, the plan was too grand, as is the case with so many buildings in recent times. The artist had not only assumed that the existing monastery would be razed, but also that the adjacent houses would be bought; and then funds and interest may have dwindled away. Dear Destiny, why have you favored and immortalized so many stupid follies instead of allowing this great work to be completed?

October 3.

Il Redentore church,[83] a great, beautiful work by Palladio, its facade more praiseworthy than that of San Giorgio. Many copperplate engravings have been made of them, but these works have to be actually seen before my statement can be appreciated. Just a few words here.

Palladio was thoroughly imbued with antiquity and reacted to the petty narrowness of his own times like a great man, not surrendering but determined to remodel everything in accord with his noble ideas, as far as possible. He was, as I gather from a hint in his book, dissatisfied because Christian churches continued to be built in the old basilica form; therefore he tried to make his sacred buildings approximate the form of ancient temples. This resulted in certain inappropriate features which I think were successfully avoided in Il Redentore but are all too evident in San Giorgio. Volkmann mentions this, but does not hit the nail on the head.

The interior of Il Redentore is also exquisite, everything by Palladio, even the design of the altars. Unfortunately the niches, which were meant to hold statues, can only boast flat, cut-out, painted board figures.

October 3.

The *Patres Capucini* had richly decorated a side altar in honor of St. Francis; the only stone objects left visible were the Corinthian capitals; everything else seemed to be covered with a magnificent but tasteful embroidery in the arabesque style, as nicely as one could wish to see. I was particularly taken with the broad, gold-embroidered tendrils and foliage; but when I went nearer, I discovered a very pretty fraud. Everything I had imagined to be gold was actually straw, pressed flat, glued to paper in beautiful designs, and the background painted in vivid colors. This amusing thing, of totally worthless materials and probably made right in the monastery, was so varied and tasteful that it would have cost several thousand thalers if genuine. We could certainly imitate it if the occasion arose.

On an embankment overlooking the water I had already noticed more than once a plebeian fellow who told stories in the Venetian dialect to larger or smaller numbers of listeners. Unfortunately I cannot understand a word of it, but no one laughs, indeed the audience, which is mostly drawn from the lowest class, rarely smiles. Nor is there anything striking or ridiculous in the storyteller's manner, rather, something very sober, while the admirable variety and precision of his gestures indicates conscious artistry.

October 3.

Map in hand, I tried to find my way through the strangest labyrinth to the church of the Mendicanti. The conservatory there is at present considered the best one. The young women were performing an oratorio behind the choir screen, the church was full of listeners, the music very

lovely, and the voices magnificent. An alto sang King Saul, the main
personage of the poem. I had never before experienced such a voice;
some passages in the music were infinitely beautiful, the text perfectly
singable, such Italianate Latin that I found some passages laughable;
but music has great latitude here.

It would have been a choice pleasure, if the wretched choir director
had not beaten time on the screen with a roll of music, as unconcernedly
as if he had been instructing schoolboys. The girls had often rehearsed
the piece, so that his slapping was quite unnecessary and spoiled the
whole impression, just as if someone had tried to explain a beautiful
statue by pasting scarlet patches on its joints. The alien sound destroys
all the harmony. This man is a musician, and he does not hear that?
More likely, he wants to make us aware of his presence by means of
an impropriety, when he would be better off letting us surmise his worth
from the perfection of the performance. I know the French are capable
of that, I would not have believed it of the Italians, and the audience
seems accustomed to the noise. This would not be the first time it has
been deluded into thinking that something is contributing to enjoyment
when it is actually ruining enjoyment.

October 3.

Yesterday evening, opera at St. Moses (for theaters are named after
the nearest church); not very good! The libretto, the music, the singers—
everything lacked that certain inner energy which is the only thing that
can lend excitement to such a presentation. No one part of it could be
called poor, but only the two women made an effort both to act well
and project themselves agreeably. That is at least something. The two
have beautiful figures and good voices, and are charming, sprightly,
appealing little persons. As for the men, however, not a trace of inner
strength or any desire to create an illusion for the audience, and no
particularly fine voices.

The ballet was very poorly conceived and was generally hissed at;
however, there was enthusiastic applause for several excellent male
and female acrobats, the latter of whom felt an obligation to acquaint
the spectators with every detail of their physical charms.

October 3.

But today I saw a different sort of comedy, which pleased me more.
I heard a legal case being tried in public in the ducal palace; it was an
important one and, luckily for me, undertaken during the council recess.
One of the lawyers was everything any exaggerated *buffo* should be.

Portly figure, short but agile, a monstrously aquiline profile, a voice of brass, and a vehemence implying that what he said was meant from the bottom of his heart. I call this a comedy, because no doubt everything is settled before these public presentations take place; the judges already know the verdict, and the litigants know what to expect. However, this method pleases me a great deal more than the way we crouch in small rooms and lawyers' offices. And now I shall try to describe the circumstances and how agreeably, unpretentiously, and naturally everything proceeds.

In a spacious hall of the palace the judges sat at one side in a semi-circle. Opposite them the lawyers for both parties, on a rostrum capable of holding several persons side by side, and on a bench directly in front of them, the plaintiff and defendant in person. The plaintiff's lawyer had stepped down from the rostrum, for today's session was not scheduled to include any controversy. All the documents, pro and contra, although already printed, were to be read aloud.

A haggard clerk in a wretched black robe, a thick pad of paper in his hand, readied himself to perform the duty of reader. Moreover the hall was crowded with spectators and listeners. The legal question itself, as well as the persons it concerned, could not but seem significant to the Venetians.

Entailments are distinctly favored in this nation; once a possession is stamped with this character, it keeps it forever. Even if by some twist or circumstance it was sold several hundred years ago, and has passed through many hands, finally, when the case comes up, the descendants of the original family have the last word, and the estates must be handed over.

This time the lawsuit was extremely important, for the complaint was against the doge himself, or rather, against his wife,[84] who accordingly, veiled by her *zendale,* was sitting there in person on the little bench, only a short distance away from the plaintiff. A lady of a certain age, noble figure, comely face, on which a serious, nay, if you will, somewhat irritated expression was to be seen. The Venetians were very proud of the fact that their sovereign lady had to appear before them and the court in her own palace.

The clerk began to read, and only now did I grasp the significance of a little man sitting on a low stool behind a small table in view of the judges, not far from the lawyers' rostrum, and especially of the hourglass he had laid down in front of him. Namely, as long as the clerk reads, the sand does not run; but the lawyer, when he wants to comment, is generally allowed only a certain time period. The clerk reads, the hourglass is recumbent, the little man has his hand on it. When the lawyer opens his mouth, the hourglass is immediately set upright, but is lowered again the moment he is silent. The great skill here resides in interrupting

the flow of reading, in making fleeting comments, in arousing and demanding attention. Now the little Saturn gets into the most embarrassing
difficulties. He is required to change the horizontal and vertical positions
of the hourglass every moment, he sees himself in the situation of the
evil spirits in the puppet play, who, when the mischievous harlequin
quickly alternates his "berlique! berloque!"[85] do not know whether
they should come or go.

Anyone who has heard lawyers collating documents in their chan-
ceries can imagine this reading aloud—rapid, monotonous, but still
enunciated with sufficient clarity. A skillful lawyer knows how to interrupt the tedium with jokes, and the audience shows its delight in
them with most immoderate laughter. I must mention one joke, the
most memorable among those I understood. The clerk was just reciting
a document in which one of these owners deemed unlawful was dis-
posing of the estates in question. The lawyer bade him read more slowly,
and when he distinctly pronounced the word, "I give, I bequeath!" the
orator vehemently attacked him, shouting, "*What* do you intend to
give? bequeath *what?* You poor hungry devil! You know that nothing
in this world belongs to you. But," he continued, seeming to reflect
on the matter, "that illustrious owner was in the very same situation,
what he meant to give, to bequeath, belonged to him as little as to
you." There was a tremendous burst of laughter, but the hourglass
immediately resumed its horizontal position. The reader hummed on,
making an angry face at the lawyer; but those jests were all prearranged.

October 4.

Yesterday I saw a comedy at the San Luca theater which greatly
delighted me; it was an extemporized play with masks, performed with
much temperament, energy, and bravura. To be sure, they are not all
on a par; the Pantalone[86] very good, one of the women, strong and well
built, no extraordinary actress, speaks excellently, and knows how to
conduct herself. A nonsensical subject matter, similar to what is treated
in Germany under the title *The Partition*.[87] It was three hours of incredibly varied entertainment. But here again the folk is the basis on
which everything rests, the spectators join in the action, and the crowd
merges with the stage to make a single whole. All day long on the
square and at the shore, in the gondolas and the palace, buyers and
sellers, the beggar, the boatman, the neighbor woman, the lawyer and
his opponent, they are all lively and bustling and interested, speak and
assert, cry wares and shout, sing and play, curse and make noise. And
in the evening they go to the theater to see and hear their daily life
artfully structured, more neatly shaped, interwoven with fairy tales,

removed from reality by masks, brought closer by manners. They take a childish delight in this, cry out again, clap, and yell. From morning to night, indeed from midnight to midnight, everything is always just the same.

I doubt that I have ever seen more natural acting than that done by these maskers, which can only be attained by rather long practice and with an especially fortunate natural disposition.

As I write this, they are making a tremendous racket on the canal below my window, and it is past midnight. They are always involved with each other, whether for good or evil.

October 4.

I have now heard public speakers: three fellows on the square and the stone embankment at the shore, each telling tales in his own fashion; then two lawyers, two preachers, the actors, among whom I must especially praise the Pantalone; all these have something in common, not only because they belong to one and the same nation, which, always living in public, is always engaged in passionate speaking, but also because they imitate each other. In addition, there is a definite language of gestures, with which they accompany the expression of their intentions, sentiments, and feelings.

Today, on the festival of St. Francis, I was in his church alle Vigne.[88] The Capuchin's loud voice was accompanied, as though with an antiphon, by the shouting of the vendors in front of the church. I stood at the church door between them both, and it was certainly a strange thing to hear.

October 5.

This morning I was at the Arsenal,[89] which is always very interesting to me since as yet I am ignorant of maritime affairs and have been attending a lower school in the subject here. For truly the place reminds me of an old family which is still active although the best season of blossoms and fruit is past. Since I also investigate what the workmen are doing, I have seen many remarkable things and climbed up on the finished framework of a ship with forty-eight guns.

A similar one burned down to the waterline six months ago at the Riva de' Schiavoni, its powder magazine was not very full, and when it exploded no great damage was done. The neighboring houses lost their windowpanes.

I have watched the finest oak, from Istria, being processed, meanwhile reflecting quietly about the growth of this worthy tree. I cannot state strongly enough how my hard-won knowledge of natural things, which, after all, man needs as materials and uses for his benefit, constantly helps me to understand the procedures of artists and artisans. Thus, for example, my knowledge of mountains and the minerals taken from them has been of great advantage to me in art.

October 5.

To sum up the *Bucentaur*[90] in two words, I shall call it a state galley. The older one, of which we still have pictures, deserves this appellation even more than the present one, whose splendor blinds us to its origin.

I keep returning to my old theme: Give the artist a genuine subject, and he can accomplish something genuine. In this case the assignment was to build a galley worthy of taking the leaders of the republic, on the most festive day, to the sacrament of Venice's traditional mastery of the sea; and this task has been superbly executed. One cannot say that the ship is overladen with decoration, because it is *all* decoration, all gilded carving, otherwise useless, a true monstrance for displaying the nation's leaders to it in great magnificence. For well we know: just as the people like to decorate their hats, so they also want to see their superiors splendidly adorned. This ornate ship is a real bit of stage property, which tells us what the Venetians were and considered themselves to be.

October 5, night.

I have just come from the tragedy,[91] still laughing, and I must set this amusing experience down on paper right away. The play was not bad, the author had gathered together all the tragic heroes, and the actors had good roles. Most of the situations were familiar, some were new and quite felicitous. Two fathers who hate each other, sons and daughters from the divided families passionately in love with one another, one pair even secretly married. The action was wild and cruel, and in the end the only way left to make the young people happy was for the two fathers to stab each other to death, whereupon the curtain fell amid lively applause. Then, however, the clapping grew louder, they shouted "Fuora," and kept it up until the two leading couples consented to creep out from behind the curtain, make their bows, and leave on the other side.

The audience was still not satisfied, it continued clapping and shouted "I morti." That went on until the two dead men also came out and bowed, whereupon several voices shouted, "Bravi i morti!" They were held captive a long time by the clapping, until finally they too were allowed to go off. This nonsense seems much funnier to an eye- and earwitness who, like me, has his ears full of the "Bravo! Bravi!" which the Italians always have on their lips, and then suddenly hears even the dead summoned with this verbal tribute.

"Good night!" we Northerners can say, at whatever hour after dark we may be parting; but there is only one time when the Italian says "Felicissima notte!" and that is when a lamp is brought into the room as day is passing into night; and then it means something quite different. Thus the idiomatic expressions of one language cannot be translated into another; for, from the basest to the most sublime, every word relates to the nation's peculiarities, whether of character, sentiments, or conditions.

October 6.

Yesterday's tragedy taught me some things. First, I heard how the Italians manage their eleven-syllable iambics when declaiming them; second, I saw how cleverly Gozzi combined the masked figures with the tragic ones. That is the right sort of drama for these people, for they want to be moved in a crude way and do not take a heartfelt, affectionate interest in an unfortunate person. They are only pleased when the hero speaks well, for they put a high value on speaking; but then they want to laugh or see something silly.

They can only react to a drama as though it were reality. When the tyrant handed his son the sword and ordered the youth to kill his own wife, who stood opposite him, the people began loudly showing their displeasure at this unreasonable command, and very nearly interrupted the play. They insisted that the old man take back his sword, which of course would have invalidated the subsequent situations in the play. Finally the harried son took courage, stepped into the proscenium, and humbly asked them to have just a moment's patience and the affair would end exactly as they wished. But from an artistic standpoint, it was an absurd and unnatural situation under the circumstances, and I praised the people for their feelings.

Now I can understand better why there are such long speeches and back-and-forth discussions in Greek tragedy. The Athenians were still fonder of hearing speeches than the Italians, and were even sounder judges of them; they had learned a great deal from lounging around all day in the law courts.

October 6.

In Palladio's finished works, especially the churches, I have found many objectionable features side by side with the choicest ones. When

I meditated about how much justice or injustice I was doing to this extraordinary man, I felt as if he were standing beside me and saying: "That and that I did unwillingly, but did it nevertheless, because under the existing circumstances it was the only way in which I could come very close to my most sublime idea."

After much thought on the subject, it seems to me that when he contemplated the height and width of an already existing church or an older house, for which he was supposed to erect facades, he would just reflect, "How can you give the greatest form to these spaces? In the details, as necessity dictates, you will have to displace or botch something, here or there something unsuitable will result, but never mind, the thing as a whole will have a sublime style and you will be satisfied with your work."

And so the magnificent vision he cherished in his soul was applied even where it was not quite suitable, where he was forced to compress and stunt it in its details.

The wing in the Carità, on the contrary, must necessarily be of very great value to us because there the artist had a free hand and was allowed to carry out his intentions unconditionally. If the monastery had been completed, it would probably be the most perfect work of architecture in the whole modern world.

How he thought and worked becomes increasingly clear to me as I read on in his book and observe how he deals with the ancients. For although he uses very few words, they are all weighty. The fourth volume, which describes the ancient temples, is the right introduction for anyone who wishes to view the ancient remains with understanding.

October 6.

Yesterday evening I saw Crébillon's[92] *Electra* at the San Crisostomo theater, that is, in translation. I cannot tell you how tasteless the play seemed to me and how frightfully boring it was.

Generally speaking, the actors were good and were able to please the audience in individual passages. Orestes alone had three separate narrative speeches, poetically formed, in a single scene. Electra, a pretty little woman of medium height and girth, and of almost French vivaciousness, of good decorum, spoke the verses beautifully; only, as unfortunately the role demanded, she acted mad from beginning to end. Meanwhile I have again learned something. The Italian iambic verse with its invariable eleven syllables lends itself poorly to declamation, because the last syllable is quite short and rises in pitch, against the will of the declaimer.

October 6.

This morning I was at high mass in the church of St. Justina, which the doge must attend annually on this day because of a long-ago victory over the Turks.[93] The gilded barques land at the little square, bringing the sovereign and a portion of the nobility; strangely garbed boatmen busy themselves with the red-painted oars, on the shore stand the monks and clerics, crowding, surging, and waiting, with lighted candles stuck onto poles and portable silver candlesticks; then carpeted bridges are laid from the vessels onto the land. First the long violet garments of the *savii*[94] display themselves on the pavement, then the long red ones of the senators; finally the old man, adorned with his golden Phrygian cap, emerges in a golden robe, the longest of all, and an ermine cloak, and three servants take charge of his train—all of this, as it takes place on a little square facing the portal of a church before whose door the Turkish flags are held, suddenly made me think I was seeing an old, but very well-designed and colored, woven tapestry. To me, the refugee from the north, this ceremony was a great delight. In our country, where all festivities have short coats, and the greatest one imaginable is celebrated with shouldered muskets, something like this might not be in place. But here these dragging garments and peaceful processions are appropriate.

The doge is a very handsome, well-built man, who, in spite of being ill, for dignity's sake holds himself erect under his heavy robe. Aside from that, he looks like the grandpapa of the whole nation and is very gracious and genial. His clothing becomes him very well, the little skullcap under his head covering does not offend, because it is fine and transparent and rests on the whitest, cleanest hair in the world.

Some fifty *nobili* in long, dark, trailing garments were with him, mostly handsome men, not one deformed figure, several of them tall, with large heads that looked well in the blond, curly wigs; jutting features, flesh that is soft and white without looking bloated and repulsive, calm, self-confident, at ease in life, and overall a certain cheerfulness.

When everyone had taken his proper place in the church, the monks came in at the main door and left again by the one at the right side, after having, by pairs, received holy water and bowed to the high altar, the doge, and the nobles.

October 6.

For this evening I had commissioned the much-discussed song of the boatmen, the ones who sing Tasso and Ariosto to their own melodies. This must actually be ordered, it does not normally occur, rather it is one of the half-faded legends of olden times. In moonlight I got into a gondola, one singer was in the prow, the other at the stern; they began their song, alternating it verse for verse. The melody, which we know from Rousseau,[95] is a cross between chorale and recitative, always keeping the same cadence without having any rhythm; the modulation is also unvaried, except that, in accord with the content of the verse, both tone and measure are changed with a kind of declamation; but the spirit, the life, of it can be grasped, as follows.

I shall not inquire into the origin of the melody, suffice it to say that it is exactly right for an idle person who chants in different tonalities and imposes this kind of singing on poems he knows by heart.

With a penetrating voice—the common people prize strength above everything else—he sits on a barque at the shore of an island or canal and lets his song resound as far as he can. It spreads out over the quiet surface of the water. In the distance another man hears it; he knows the melody, understands the words, and answers with the next verse. The first man responds to this, and thus one is constantly the echo of the other. The song goes on for several nights, without their growing weary of this entertainment. The farther they are apart, the more charming the song can become; then if the listener stands between them both he is at the right place.

In order to let me hear this, they went ashore on the Giudecca and took up separate positions along the canal. I walked back and forth between them, always retreating from the one who was supposed to begin singing and approaching the one who had stopped. Thus the sense of the song was first revealed to me. Coming as a voice out of the distance it counds very strange, like a lament without grief; there is something incredibly moving about it, even bringing tears. I ascribed this to my mood, but my old servant said, "È singolare, come quel canto intenerisce, e molto più, quando è più ben cantato."[96] He wished that I might hear the women of the Lido, especially those of Malamocco and Pelestrina, who also sang Tasso to the same and similar melodies. He said further: "It is their custom, when their husbands are off in the sea, fishing, to sit down at the shore and let those songs ring out in the evening with penetrating voices, until from afar they hear the voices of their men and thus converse with them." Is that not very lovely? And yet it is quite likely that an auditor standing nearby would find little pleasure in listening to these voices compete with the waves of the sea. However, the idea of the song becomes human and true, and the melody, which was formerly a dead letter for us to rack our brains about, comes to life. It is a song sent out into the distance by a lonely individual, in the hope that someone else in the same mood will hear and answer.

October 8.

I visited the Pisani Moretta palace in order to see an exquisite painting by Paul Veronese: the women of Darius's family are kneeling before Alexander and Hephaestion, the mother kneeling in front takes the latter to be the king, he denies it and points to the right one.[97] According to legend, the artist was well received in this palace and worthily entertained there for some time; in return he secretly painted the picture as a gift, rolled it up, and shoved it under the bed. Truly, it deserves to have had a special origin, for it gives one an idea of this master's whole worth. His great artistry in producing the most exquisite harmony, not by spreading a universal tone over the whole piece, but by skillfully distributing light and shadow, and equally wisely alternating the local colors, is very visible here, since we see the picture in a perfect state of preservation, as fresh as if done yesterday. For to be sure, when a picture of this kind has decayed, our enjoyment of it is immediately marred, without our knowing the reason.

If anyone wanted to remonstrate with the artist about the costuming, let him just tell himself that the painting is supposed to depict a story of the sixteenth century, and that will settle the whole matter. The gradation from the mother to the wife and daughters is very true and felicitous; the youngest princess, kneeling at the very end, is a pretty little mouse, with a pleasing, headstrong, defiant little face; she does not seem at all ready to accept her situation.

Addendum to October 8.

My old gift for seeing the world with the eyes of any painter whose pictures have recently made an impression on me has led me onto a peculiar thought. Obviously the eye is formed by the objects it beholds from childhood on, and so the Venetian painter must see everything more clearly and brightly than other people. We who live on ground that is either dirty and muddy or dusty, that is colorless and dims reflections, and who perhaps even live in narrow rooms, cannot independently develop such a cheerful eye.

As I rode through the lagoons in the midday sunlight and watched the gondoliers on the rims of their gondolas, gently rocking, colorfully dressed, rowing, and sharply delineated in the blue air above the bright-green surface of the water, what I was seeing was the best, freshest picture of the Venetian school. The sunshine dazzlingly accentuated the local colors, and even the shadowed portions were so luminous that they, relatively speaking, could have served as highlights. The same was true of the sea-green water. Everything was painted bright on bright, and the foaming waves with flashes of light on them put the necessary dot on the i.

Titian and Paolo Veronese had this clarity to the highest degree, and wherever it is not found in their works, the picture has decayed or been painted over.

The dome and vaulted ceilings of St. Mark's church, along with its side areas, abound in pictures, colorful figures against a golden ground are everywhere, mosaic work is everywhere. Some things are very good, others inferior, according to which master prepared the designs.

It was brought home to me that everything really depends on the original conception, which must have the right proportions and true spirit; for with square bits of glass both the bad and the good can be reproduced, and here not even in the neatest way. The art which gave the ancients their floors and the Christians their vaulted church ceilings is now wasted on boxes and bracelets. These times are worse than one thinks.

October 8.

In the Farsetti palace[98] there is a valuable collection of plaster casts of the best ancient sculptures. I shall pass over the ones I already know from Mannheim[99] and elsewhere, and mention only the newer acquaintances. A Cleopatra in colossal repose, with the asp wound around her arm as she slumbers into death,[100] also Niobe, the mother shielding her youngest daughter from Apollo's arrows with her cloak, then some gladiators, a genius resting in his wings, philosophers both seated and standing.

These are works that can give the world enjoyment and culture for thousands of years, without the merits of the artists ever being fully comprehended.

The many significant busts carry me back into those splendid ancient times. But unfortunately I feel how far behind I am in this field of knowledge; yet I shall go forward, for at least I know my way now. The way to it, and to all art and life, has been opened for me by Palladio. This may sound a little odd, but surely not as paradoxical as Jakob Böhme's[101] being enlightened about the universe after having receiving an influx of Jovian radiance from the sight of a pewter bowl! Included in this collection is a piece of the entablature of the temple of Antoninus and Faustina[102] in Rome. The conspicuous presence of this magnificent architectural creation reminded me of the Pantheon capital in Mannheim. How very different these are from our Gothic decoration with its cowering saints stacked up over one another on little consoles, little painted towers, and crockets; thank God, I am rid of these now forever!

I want to mention a few more works of sculpture I have seen in the last few days, actually only in passing by, but with astonishment and edification nevertheless: two huge white marble lions before the gate of the Arsenal, one sitting upright, supported on its front paws, the other one reclining—splendid contrasts, lively and diverse.[103] They are so large that they dwarf everything around them, and we ourselves would be nullified, were it not that sublime objects exalt us. They are said to be from the best Greek period and to have been brought here from Piraeus in the republic's days of glory.

Likewise of possible Athenian origin are a couple of bas-reliefs embedded in the wall of the temple of St. Justina, who was victorious over the Turks; but unfortunately they are somewhat obscured by the pews. The sacristan pointed them out to me, because legend has it that Titian used them as models for the superbly beautiful angels in his picture portraying the murder of St. Peter the Martyr.[104] They are genii toiling along under a burden of divine attributes, but truly of an unimaginable beauty.

Next, with quite a strange feeling, I viewed the colossal nude statue of Marcus Agrippa in the courtyard of a palace; a dolphin twisting up against his side indicated that he was a naval hero. Amazing how such a heroic representation can make a mere man resemble the gods!

I took a close look at the horses on St. Mark's church.[105] From below it is easy to see that they are spotted, and in part have a beautiful yellow metallic sheen, in part are tarnished to a copper green. Nearby one sees and discovers that they were once completely overlaid with gold; and one sees that they are covered over and over with weals, because the barbarians did not want to file off the gold, but to cut it off. However, even that is all right, since at least the form remained.

A magnificent team of horses! I would like to hear a real expert on horses discuss them. What amazes me is that up close they look heavy, while from below in the square they seem as light as stags.

October 8.

This morning I went to the Lido with my guardian angel, to the tongue of land that closes off the lagoons and separates them from the sea. We got out of the boat and crossed over the tongue. I heard a mighty sound, it was the sea, and I soon saw it beating high against the shore as the tide went out; it was noon, the time of ebb. So now I have also seen the sea with my own eyes, and have followed after it on the beautiful smooth floor that is left behind when it recedes. I wish the children[106] could have been here, on account of the shells; childish myself, I picked up a supply of them, which, however, I devote to a curious use, namely to dry out some of the secretion of the cuttlefish, which flows away so copiously here.

On the Lido, not far from the sea, is where English people are buried, along with the Jews, for both are prohibited from resting in hallowed ground. I found the grave of the noble Consul Smith and his first wives; I owe my copy of Palladio to him, and I thanked him for it, standing at his unconsecrated grave.

And the grave is not only unconsecrated, but half covered with rubble. The Lido must be considered a mere dune; the sand is conveyed here, the wind drives it back and forth, it is piled up and pushed against everything. In a short time the monument, although quite elevated, will hardly be visible.

The sea is really a grand sight! I want to arrange for a ride in a fishing boat; the gondolas do not venture out there.

October 8.

At the seaside I have also found various plants whose similar character has led me to a better understanding of their nature. All of them are both plump and rigid, juicy and tough, and evidently it is the ancient salt of the sandy soil, and even more so the salty air, that give them these qualities; they are brimming with juices like water plants, they are firm and tough like mountain plants; in cases where the ends of the leaves have a tendency to become prickly, like thistles, these prickles are extremely pointed and strong. I found a cluster of such leaves, which seemed to me like our harmless coltsfoot, but armed here with sharp weapons, and the leaf was like leather, also the seedpods and stems, everything plump and fat. I am taking along seeds and some leaves preserved in brine *(Eryngium maritimum)*.

The fish market and the endless number of marine products give me much pleasure; I often go over there and inspect those unlucky creatures that have been snatched out of their home in the sea.

October 9.

A delightful day from morning to night! I went to Pelestrina, opposite Chiozza, where the republic is having great structures called *murazzi* raised up against the sea. They are made of hewn stones, and it is really the long tongue of land called the Lido, which divides the lagoons from the sea, that they are supposed to shield from this wild element.

The lagoons are an ancient work of nature. First, ebb and flood and earth acting in opposition to each other, then the gradual subsidence of the primeval waters, were responsible for the existence, at the upper end of the Adriatic sea, of a considerable stretch of swamp which is covered by the flood tide and partly relinquished by the ebb tide. Human ingenuity took over the highest spots, and so Venice is situated on a hundred islands grouped together and is surrounded by hundreds more. In conjunction with this, deep channels were dug into the swamp at incredible cost of money and labor, so that warships could get to the chief locations even at ebb tide. What human intelligence and hard work planned and executed in olden times must now be preserved by intelligence and hard work. The Lido, a long strip of earth, separates the lagoons from the sea, which can enter only at two points, namely at the fort and near Chiozza, at the opposite end. The flood tide normally comes in twice a day, and the ebb tide carries the water out twice, always by the same path in the same directions. The flood tide covers the inner marshy spots and leaves the more elevated ones, if not dry, at least visible.

It would be quite another matter if the sea were to seek new paths, attack the tongue of land, and surge in and out at will. Aside from the fact that the little settlements on the Lido, Pelestrina, San Pietro, and others, would be submerged, those communication channels would also be filled up; and while the water was making havoc of everything, the Lido would be transformed into islands, and the islands now lying behind it into tongues of land. To prevent this, the Lido has to be secured as well as possible, so that the element cannot arbitrarily attack and destroy what humans have already taken possession of and given form and alignment to, for a certain purpose.

In extraordinary cases, when the sea rises excessively, it is especially good that it can enter only at two places, while the rest remains closed; for it cannot penetrate with its full force and in a few hours must submit to the law of ebb tide and moderate its fury.

In other respects Venice has nothing to fear. The slow subsidence of the sea gives her millenia of time, and certainly they try to keep in possession of their city by cleverly improving the canals.

If only they kept their city cleaner, which is as necessary as it is easy, and really of great consequence for the centuries to come! Now it is true there is a heavy penalty for pouring anything into the canals or throwing rubbish into them. However, nothing prevents a hard rain from stirring up all the rubbish shoved into corners and dragging it into the canals, indeed what is worse, conducting it into the drains, which are designed only to carry off water, and clogging them so badly that the main squares are in danger of standing under water. I have even seen a few drains stopped up and full of water on the smaller St. Mark's square, although they are as cleverly installed there as on the large one.

A rainy day causes an intolerable mess; everybody curses and grumbles; while going up and down the bridges people soil their coats and the *tabarri*[107] they trail around in throughout the year; and since they all go about in shoes and stockings, these get spattered, and then they scold, for they have not been stained with ordinary, but with caustic filth. Once the weather is fine again, nobody thinks about cleanliness. How truly it is said: the public always complains about being badly served and does not know how to go about being served better. Here, if the sovereign so willed, everything could be done immediately.

October 9.

This evening I climbed up St. Mark's tower; having seen the lagoons in their flood-tide splendor from up there, I also wanted to see them in their ebb-tide lowliness, and these two images must be combined if one wishes to get an accurate idea. It looks strange to see land appearing all around where earlier there was an expanse of water. The islands are no longer islands, only spots of higher elevation in a large gray-greenish marsh, which is intersected by beautiful canals. The swampy part can come into view only gradually because it is profusely over-grown with aquatic plants that thrive in spite of being constantly agitated by ebb and flood, which give the vegetation no rest.

I shall turn once more to the sea in my narrative: Today I saw there the activities of sea snails, limpets, and common crabs, which thoroughly pleased me. What an exquisite, splendid thing a living creature is! How adapted to its condition, how genuine, how existent! How much profit I derive from my little bit of nature study, and how happy I am to continue it! But it can be described, and so I shall not tantalize my friends with mere exclamations.

The masonry raised against the sea consists first of several steep steps, then comes a gently upward-sloping surface, then another step, and a second gently upward-sloping surface, then a steep wall with an overhanging ledge above. Up these steps and surfaces the flooding sea now rises, until, in extraordinary cases, it finally crashes against the wall and its projection.

The sea is followed by its denizens, little edible snails, limpets, and whatever else is capable of movement, especially the common crabs. However, hardly have these animals taken possession of the smooth wall when the sea recedes again, yielding and swelling, just as it came. At first the swarm is at a loss, and keeps hoping that the salty flood will return; but it does not, the sun scorches and dries them out, and now their retreat begins. At this juncture the crabs seek their prey. There is nothing odder and more comical than the gestures of these creatures, which consist of a round body with two long scissors; for their spidery feet are not perceptible. They stalk along as though on stilt-like arms, and as soon as a limpet, hidden under its shield, starts to move away they rush up to stick their scissors into the narrow space between the shell and the masonry, upset the little roof, and dine on the meat. The limpet proceeds on its way slowly, but immediately adheres fast to the stone when it notices the approach of its enemy. The latter now makes strange gestures around the little roof, very dainty and monkey-like; but it lacks the strength to overcome the powerful muscle of the soft little animal. It abandons this prey, hurries off to another one that is wandering along, and the first one cautiously continues on its course. I did not see a single crab attain its goal, although I watched for hours as the swarm retreated, creeping down the two surfaces and the steps located between.

October 10.

Now I can say that I have also seen a comedy! Today at the San Luca theater they gave *Le Baruffe Chiozzotte,* which might possibly be translated as "The Noisy Brawls of Chiozza." The characters are all seamen living in Chiozza, with their wives, sisters, and daughters. The usual clamor of these people in joy or anger, their quarrels, vehemence, good nature, banality, wit, humor, and informal manners are well imitated. The play is an old one of Goldoni's,[108] and since I had been in this area only yesterday, and the voices and behavior of the sea and harbor people were still reverberating in my ears and reflecting in my eyes, I was most delighted with it. Although many an individual reference escaped me, I could get the gist of things quite well. The plot of the play is as follows: The women of Chiozza are sitting on the wharf in front of their houses, spinning, knitting, sewing, making pillow lace, as usual; a young man walks past and greets one of the women in a friendlier way than the others; immediately the teasing begins, does not stay within bounds, gets more intense and becomes mockery, rises to reproaches, one rude remark outdoes the other; then one vehement neighbor woman blurts out the truth, and now there is general, unrestrained scolding, reviling, and shouting, there are some downright insults, and finally the officers of the law must interfere.

The second act takes place in the courtroom; the clerk of the court, in place of the absent *podestà*—who as a *nobile* would not be permitted to appear on stage—the clerk, then, has the women summoned individually. This becomes a dubious matter, because he himself is in love with the female lead and, being very happy to talk to her alone, makes a declaration of love instead of interrogating her. Another woman, who is in love with the clerk, dashes in jealously, as does the excited lover of the first woman; the rest follow, new reproaches multiply, and now there is pandemonium in the courtroom, as earlier in the harbor.

In the third act the jest reaches a climax, and the whole affair ends with a hasty, makeshift denouement. The most felicitous idea, however, was to introduce a character who presents himself as follows:

An old seaman, whose limbs—but especially his organs of speech—have become halting because of the hard life he has led from youth on, comes on stage as a foil to the active, chattering, clamorous populace. He always starts out by moving his lips, and helps this along with hands and arms, until finally he is able to utter his thoughts. However, because he only succeeds in producing short sentences, he has taken on a laconic earnestness, so that everything he says sounds proverbial or sententious, and this nicely offsets the rest of the wildly emotional action.

But I have never experienced anything like the pleasure the people expressed at seeing themselves and their families represented so naturally. Uninterrupted laughter and jubilation from beginning to end. But I must also acknowledge that the actors performed excellently. According to the nature of the character portrayed, each of them had assumed one of the various voices that are typically heard among the folk. The main actress was charming, much better than she was recently in a passionate role and heroic garb. The women in general, but this one in particular, imitated the voices, gestures, and ways of the people most winningly. The author merits great praise for having created a most pleasant entertainment out of nothing. That can only be done, however, in direct contact with one's own vivacious people. It was certainly written by an expert hand.

Of the Sacchi troupe[109] that Gozzi wrote for, and which, by the way, is disbanded, I have seen the Smeraldina, a stout little figure full of life, versatility, and good humor. With her I saw the Brighella, a lean, well-built actor especially good at gestures and facial expressions. The masked characters, who in Germany seem almost like mummies, since they have neither life nor significance for us, are very much at home here as creatures of this landscape. The ages, characters, and conditions singled out for attention have been typified with strange clothing; and people who themselves run about in masks for the greatest part of the year find it quite natural to have black faces appear on stage as well.

October 11.

And since in the final analysis solitude is really not possible amid such a great mass of humanity, I have taken up with an old Frenchman who knows no Italian and feels himself betrayed and deceived because, in spite of all his letters of recommendation, he does not rightly know where he stands with people. A man of rank, very well mannered, but he cannot lower his reserve; he may be in his late fifties, and he has a seven-year-old son at home, news of whom he awaits anxiously. I have shown him some kindnesses; he is traveling through Italy comfortably but swiftly, in order to have seen it at last. He likes to learn as much as he can along the way, and I give him information about many things. When I spoke to him about Venice he asked me how long I had been here. Hearing that it had only been for a fortnight and was my first visit, he replied: "Il paraît que vous n'avez pas perdu votre temps."[110] That is the first testimony to my good conduct that I can point to. He has been here for a week now and leaves tomorrow. I was much amused to see a truly genuine Versailles courtier abroad. So that sort is traveling now too! And I am amazed to see that a person can travel without becoming aware of his surroundings, and yet in his way he is a very cultured, worthy, respectable man.

October 12.

Yesterday a new play was presented at San Luca, *L'Inglicismo in Italia*. Since many English people live in Italy it is natural for their manners to be noticed, and I hoped to learn here how the Italians view these rich and very welcome guests; but it amounted to nothing at all. A few successful clown scenes, as always, but the rest too heavy and seriously meant, and then actually not a trace of English feeling, just the customary Italian moral commonplaces, moreover only directed at the most commonplace matters.

Nor was it well received, and was on the verge of being hissed off; the actors did not feel in their element, they were not on the square in Chiozza. Since this is the last play I shall see here, it would seem that my enthusiasm for that national play was meant to be increased still more by the comparison.

After I have, in conclusion, gone through my journal and inserted little remarks from my notebook, the documents shall be referred to a higher court, namely, sent to my friends for their judgment. I have already found much in these pages that I could state more explicitly, amplify, and improve; but let them stand as a monument to first impressions, which we continue to delight in and treasure, even if they are not always true. If only I could send my friends a breath of this easier kind of life! Indeed the Italians have only a dim notion of the ultramontane, and to me too the other side of the Alps now seems dark; but friendly figures keep beckoning from the mist. Only the climate would tempt me to give preference to these regions over those; for birth and custom are strong ties. I would not care to live here or any other place where I would be idle; but at the moment I am very much occupied with new experiences. The architecture rises up out of its grave like an ancient ghost and bids me study its principles like the rules of a dead language, not so that I can practice it or enjoy it as something living, but only that I may, with a quiet spirit, honor the venerable, forever departed existence of past ages. Since Palladio relates everything to Vitruvius, I have procured the Galiani edition[111] for myself; but this folio volume weighs down my luggage as heavily as the study of it does my brain. Palladio, through his words and works, his manner of thought and action, has already brought Vitruvius closer to me and interpreted him better than the Italian translation can do. Vitruvius is not very easy to read; the book in itself is obscurely written and requires judicious study. Nevertheless I am glancing through it, and am left with many a valuable impression. Or better: I read it like a breviary, more out of piety than for instruction. Night is already falling earlier, which gives me more time for reading and writing.

God be thanked, how dear to me again is everything I have esteemed since childhood! How happy I am that I dare again to approach the ancient writers! For now I may say it, may confess my morbid foolishness. For some years I could not look at any Latin author or contemplate anything that revived in me the image of Italy. If it chanced to happen, I would suffer the most dreadful pain. Herder often taunted me with having learned all my Latin from Spinoza, for he had noticed that this was the only Latin book that I read; but he did not know how wary I had to be of the ancients and that it was only out of fear of them that I fled into those abstruse generalities. Finally I was made very unhappy by Wieland's translation of the *Satires;*[112] I had scarcely read two before I grew confused.

If I had not made the resolution I am now carrying out I would simply have perished, so ripe had the desire become in my heart to see these sights with my own eyes. Historical knowledge was of no benefit to me, for while the things stood there only a hand's breadth away, I was separated from them by an impenetrable wall. Even now I really do not feel that I am seeing the objects for the first time, but as if I were seeing them again. I have only been in Venice a short while, but I have adequately assimilated the local way of life and know that I am taking away a very clear and true, if incomplete, impression.

Venice, October 14, 2 hours after sundown.

Written in my last moments of being here: for I am going at once by courier ship to Ferrara. I am glad to leave Venice, for if I wanted to stay here with pleasure and profit, other steps would have to be taken, which are not in my plan. Also, everyone is leaving the city for his gardens and estates on the mainland. Meanwhile I have packed up well and shall carry the rich, strange, unique picture away with me.

Ferrara to Rome

October 16, morning, on the ship.

My traveling companions, men and women, quite tolerable and natural people, are all still asleep in the cabin. But I have spent both nights on deck, wrapped in my cloak. It only grew cool toward morning. Now I have actually entered the forty-fifth degree of latitude and I repeat my old song: the inhabitants of this country could keep everything else if only, like Dido, I could lay thongs around enough of this climate to surround our dwellings at home. Really, it is a different world. It was a very pleasant trip in splendid weather, the sights and views simple but charming. The Po, a friendly river, flows through great plains here, and only its bush- and forest-covered banks are visible, no distant places. Here, as along the Adige, I saw some absurd dikes, as childish and detrimental as those along the Saale.

Ferrara, the 16th, night.

Having arrived here this morning at seven by the German clock, I am preparing to leave again tomorrow. In this large and beautiful, levelly situated, but depopulated town I am for the first time overcome by a sort of aversion. These same streets were once enlivened by a brilliant court, Ariosto lived here discontentedly, Tasso unhappily, and are we to believe ourselves edified by visiting this place?[113] Ariosto's tomb contains a great deal of marble, poorly distributed. For Tasso's prison they show a woodshed or coalshed, where he was certainly not kept. Moreover there is hardly anyone in the house who knows what the visitor wants. Finally, for a gratuity, they do remember. It puts me in mind of Doctor Luther's inkspot,[114] which the castellan freshens up from time to time. Most travelers seem to have a touch of the journeyman about them and like to look around for such marks.[115] I had become quite disgruntled and took little interest in a fine academic institute that had been founded and enriched by a cardinal born in Ferrara, but some old monuments in the courtyard restored my spirits.

Then I was cheered by a painter's clever idea: John the Baptist before Herod and Herodias.[116] The prophet in his customary desert costume points vehemently at the lady. She looks quite calmly at the sovereign sitting beside her, and the sovereign looks quietly and shrewdly at the enthusiast. In front of the king stands a white dog of medium size, while a little Bolognese dog peeps out from under Herodias's skirt, and both of them bark at the prophet. In my opinion, that is a most happy thought.

Cento, the 17th, evening.

I am writing from Guercino's[117] native town, in a better mood than yesterday. But the situation is also quite different. A friendly, attractive little town of approximately five thousand inhabitants, productive, clean, in a vast cultivated plain. As is my custom, I immediately climbed up the tower. A sea of pointed poplar trees, among which I saw little farmsteads close at hand, each surrounded by its own field. Excellent soil, a mild climate. It was an autumn evening, but of a kind we can seldom enjoy even in our summertime. The sky, overcast all day, brightened, the clouds scudded north and southwards to the mountains, and I am in hopes of a beautiful day tomorrow.

Here for the first time I saw the Apennines, which I am coming closer to. The winter here lasts only through December and January, April is rainy, otherwise the weather is good, in relationship to the season. Never a prolonged rain; yet this September was warmer and better than their August. I nodded a friendly greeting to the Apennines in the south, for I am tiring of level country. Tomorrow I shall be writing over there at their foot.

Guercino loved his native town, and the Italians in general nurture local patriotism in a very high-minded way. This beautiful sentiment has given rise to many fine institutions, and indeed also the throng of local saints. Here, for example, an academy of painting was founded under that master's auspices. He left behind several pictures which still delight the townspeople and are certainly worthy of doing so.

Guercino is a sacred name, and is on the lips of children as well as adults.

I very much liked the picture showing the risen Christ when He appears to His mother.[118] Kneeling before Him, she looks up at Him with ineffable tenderness. Her left hand touches His body just below the wretched wound, which is a blot on the whole picture. He has placed His left hand around her neck and bends His body back slightly, so as to look at her more easily. This gives the figure a quality that is, if not forced, in any case odd, in spite of which it remains extremely pleasant. The quietly sad expression with which He looks at her is unique, as if the memory of their mutual sufferings, not immediately healed by the resurrection, were hovering before His noble soul.

Strange[119] has engraved this picture; I wish my friends could at least see that copy.

Next to win my affection was a Madonna. The Child demands her breast, she modestly hesitates to bare her bosom. Natural, noble, charming, and beautiful.

Furthermore a Mary, the Child standing in front of her and facing the spectators; she guides His arm, so that He may, with raised fingers, bestow the blessing. A very felicitous and often repeated idea, in the spirit of Catholic mythology.

Guercino is a profoundly good, wholesomely manly painter, without crudeness. Rather, his things have a delicate moral grace, a calm freedom and grandeur, and at the same time something unique, so that his works are unmistakable, once the eye has become accustomed to them. The lightness, purity, and perfection of his brushwork are astonishing. For the drapery he uses especially beautiful, subdued brownish-red pigments. These harmonize very well with the blue he also likes to apply.

The subjects of the remaining pictures are more or less unfortunate. The good artist did his utmost, but still his inventiveness and brushwork, his spirit and hand, were expended in vain. But I am surely very glad that I have also seen this beautiful group of paintings, even though there is little pleasure or instruction in racing past them so quickly.

                                        Bologna, October 18, night.

This morning, before daybreak, I rode away from Cento and arrived here in fairly good time. A nimble and well-informed hired servant, upon hearing that I did not plan to stay long, hurried me through all the streets and so many palaces and churches that I could hardly check them all off in my Volkmann; and who knows whether in the future these marks will help me remember all these places? Now, however, I shall mention a few high spots, where I felt a true satisfaction.

First, then, Raphael's *Cecilia!*[120] It is what I already knew it would be, but now I have seen it with my own eyes; he always *did,* what other artists only *wished* to do, and now all I would like to say is that it is by *him.* Five saints next to each other, none of whom concerns us, but of such consummate existence that we hope the picture may last forever, even though we ourselves must accept disintegration.

However, if we want to know him truly, appreciate him correctly, and also not honor him as a god who came into being, like Melchizedek, without father or mother, we must look at his precursors, his masters. These men based themselves on the solid ground of truth, laid the broad foundations diligently, indeed meticulously, and, in competition with each other, built up the pyramid step by step, until at last, benefiting from all these new techniques and inspired by his heavenly genius, he put the topmost stone in place, over and beside which no other can stand.

It especially awakens my historical interest to look at the works of older masters. Francesco Francia is a very respectable artist, Pietro of Perugia[121] such a worthy man that I was tempted to call him an honest German fellow. If only it had been Albrecht Dürer's good luck to have gone down farther into Italy! In Munich I saw a few works by him that were of incredible grandeur. The poor man, how he miscalculated in Venice, making an agreement with the priests that cost him weeks and months![122] How, on his trip to the Netherlands, he bartered magnificent artworks, with which he had hoped to make his fortune, for parrots and, to save gratuities, made a portrait of the servants who brought him a plate of fruit! I find such a poor fool of an artist infinitely touching, because basically this is also my fate, except that I am somewhat better able to take care of myself.

Toward evening I finally escaped from this venerable, scholarly old town, from the crowds of people who can amble back and forth, gape, buy, and carry on their affairs, protected from sun and weather by the arcades that are seen lining almost all the streets. I climbed up the tower[123] and enjoyed the open air. The view is splendid! In the north I saw the Paduan mountains, then the Swiss, Tyrolean, and Friulian Alps, in short, the whole northern chain, now covered by mist. Toward the west a limitless horizon, broken only by the towers of Modena. Toward the east a similar plain, up to the Adriatic sea, which can be glimpsed at sunrise. Toward the south the foothills of the Apennines, cultivated up to their summits and covered with growth, studded with churches, palaces, garden houses, like the Vicenzian hills. The sky was perfectly clear, without a wisp of cloud, only a sort of haze on the horizon. The warder asserted that this mist had been there in the distance for the last six years. Before that he had always been able, with the aid of his spyglass, to clearly make out the mountains of Vicenza with their houses and chapels, but now only rarely, even on the brightest days. And this mist clings mainly to the northern chain and makes our dear fatherland seem like a truly Cimmerian realm. The man also pointed out to me that the healthful location and air of the city were evident from the fact that its roofs looked like new, with none of the tiles attacked by damp and moss. It must be admitted that the roofs are all in fine condition, but the excellence of the tiles themselves may also be a contributing factor, at any rate in ancient times splendid tiles were manufactured in these regions.

The leaning tower[124] is an ugly sight, and yet in all likelihood it was built like this intentionally. I explain this foolishness to myself as follows: During the period of civil unrest every large building became a fortress, over which every powerful family raised a tower. Gradually this became a matter of pride and pleasure, everybody wanted to show off with a tower, and when straight towers became all too commonplace, a leaning one was built. And indeed the architect and the owner achieved their goal, for we look past the many straight, slim towers and seek out the crooked one. The bricks are laid in horizontal rows. Good, quick-setting cement and iron braces can be used to make some very absurd things!

Bologna, October 19, evening.

I have used this day to the best of my ability, looking, and looking again, but art is like life; the farther we advance into it, the broader it grows. New constellations that I cannot assess and that confuse me keep emerging in this sky, namely, the Caraccis, Guido, Domenichino, who arose during a later, happier artistic era.[125] Really to enjoy them, however, one needs knowledge and judgment, which I lack and can gain only gradually. The absurdity of their subjects is a great hindrance to pure contemplation and direct understanding of the pictures, which I would like to love and revere, but instead they drive me to distraction.

It is the same as when the children of God married the daughters of men, with the result that various monsters were born.[126] While you are attracted by Guido's beatific intent, by his brush, which should have painted only the most perfect things that can be gazed upon, at the same time you want to avert your eyes from the disgustingly stupid subjects, for which there are no words bad enough, and thus it is throughout. We cannot get away from the dissecting room, the gallows, the abattoir, and the sufferings of the hero; there is never any action, never any immediate interest, always some fantastic expectation from outside. Either sinners or ecstatics, criminals or fools, while the painter tries to save the situation by dragging in some naked fellow or a pretty female onlooker, or perhaps by treating his religious heroes as though they were lay figures to be draped with cloaks arranged in lovely folds. Nothing is there to suggest humanity! Ten subjects, not one of which should have been painted, and one that the artist was not permitted to treat in the right way.

Guido's large picture in the church of the Mendicanti[127] meets every painterly requirement, but nothing could be more nonsensical than the commission the artist was expected to carry out. It is a votive picture. I believe the whole senate praised it and also conceived the idea. The two angels, who would be worthy of consoling Psyche in her misfortune, here must—

St. Proclus, a beautiful figure; but the others, the bishops and priests! At the bottom are some cherubs playing with attributes. The painter, who had a knife at his throat, tried his best, he exerted himself to the utmost, just to show that it was not he who was the barbarian. Two nude figures by Guido: a John in the wilderness, a Sebastian.[128] How exquisitely they are painted! And what do they say? One has his mouth wide open, and the other writhes.

If I look at history in this bad humor I am tempted to say: faith gave renewed prominence to the arts, but superstition took them over and destroyed them again.

After dinner I was in a somewhat milder and less arrogant mood than this morning, and I noted down the following on my writing pad: In the Tanari palace there is a famous painting by Guido which depicts Mary nursing,[129] larger than lifesize, the head as if painted by a god; her expression as she looks down on the child at her breast is indescribable. To me it seems quiet, profound endurance, as if this were not a child of joy and love but a supposititious divine changeling that she only allows to nibble at her because the situation must simply be accepted, and in her deep humility she does not have the slightest idea why she was selected. The remaining space is filled with an enormous drapery, which is much praised by connoisseurs: I really did not know what to make of it. Besides, the colors have darkened; and the room and the day were not the brightest.

In spite of my current confusion I already feel that practice, acquaintance, and inclination are coming to my aid. Thus a *Circumcision* by Guercino[130] strongly appealed to me, because I already know and love the man. I excused the intolerable subject and took pleasure in the execution.—Painted with all imaginable skill, everything in it estimable and as perfect as if made of enamel.

And so I share the fate of Bileam, the confused prophet, who blessed when he intended to curse, and this would be the case still oftener if I were to stay here longer.

If, then, I come again upon a work of Raphael's, or at any rate one ascribed to him with some probability, I am at once completely healed and happy. Thus I have found a *St. Agatha*,[131] a precious, although not very well preserved picture. The artist has given her a wholesome, secure virginity, but without coldness and crudity. I have observed the figure well and in spirit will read my *Iphigenia* aloud to her, not letting my heroine say anything that this saint would not utter.

Now that I have once again mentioned the dear burden that I am
carrying with me on my wanderings, I cannot conceal that in addition
to having to work my way through great artistic and natural sights a
remarkable series of poetic figures is moving through my mind and
disturbing me. On my way here from Cento I wanted to continue my
work on *Iphigenia,* but what happened? The spirit moved me to think
of the plot of "Iphigenia of Delphi," and I had to develop it. Let me
sketch it here as briefly as possible:

Electra, certain in her hope that Orestes will bring the image of the
Tauric Diana to Delphi, appears in the temple of Apollo and dedicates
the cruel axe, which has wrought such havoc in the family of Pelops,
as her final sacrifice to propitiate the god. Unfortunately one of the
Greeks approaches her and tells how he accompanied Orestes and Pylades to Tauris, saw the two friends led to their deaths, and luckily
escaped. The passionate Electra is beside herself and does not know
whether to direct her fury at men or the gods.

Meanwhile Iphigenia, Orestes, and Pylades have likewise arrived in
Delphi. Iphigenia's saintly calm contrasts quite remarkably with Electra's earthly passion when the two figures meet without recognizing
each other. The fugitive Greek sees Iphigenia, recognizes her as the
priestess who sacrificed the friends, and reveals this to Electra. The
latter is on the point of murdering Iphigenia with the axe she has
snatched away again from the altar, when a fortunate turn of events
averts this last terrible evil from the sisters. If this scene works out
well, then it will very likely be as great and touching as anything ever
seen on the stage. But where shall my hands find the time, even though
the spirit were willing?[132]

Now, while fretting because too many good and desirable things are
claiming my attention, I must remind my friends of a seemingly quite
significant dream I had just a year ago. Namely, I dreamt I was in a
rather large boat that was landing at a fertile, opulently overgrown island
where I knew that the finest pheasants were available. And so I immediately bargained with the islanders for this fowl, of which they
promptly brought me many, already killed. They were pheasants, to
be sure, but since dreams alter everything, their long tails were studded
with colored eyes, like the tails of peacocks or rare birds of paradise.
The birds were now laid down in the boat like sheaves of wheat, and
piled up so neatly, with heads to the inside and long, varicolored tail
feathers hanging outside, that they made the most splendid stack
imaginable, and indeed such an ample one that little space was left
before or behind it for the helmsman and the oarsmen. In this fashion
we plowed the quiet waters, and I was already going over the names
of the friends with whom I would share these colorful treasures. Finally
arriving at a large harbor, I got lost among high-masted ships and clam-

bered from the deck of one to the other, seeking a secure landing place for my smaller craft.

We delight in such phantoms, which, since they arise out of ourselves, must surely have some analogy with the rest of our life and fortunes.

Now I have also visited the famous scholarly establishment called the Institute or "the Studies." The big building and especially its inner court look quite impressive in a solemn way, although the architecture is not of the best. The stairs and corridors are ornamented with stucco and frescos; everything is decorous and worthy, and I was duly amazed by the manifold beautiful and remarkable objects that have been collected here; nevertheless, Germans are accustomed to a freer method of study, and so the place made me feel uncomfortable.

An earlier observation came back to mind here, about how difficult it is, as time passes and alters everything, for human beings to sacrifice the original appearance of a thing even after its intended purpose has changed. Christian churches still adhere to the basilica form, although the temple form might be better suited to the ritual. Scholarly institutions still have a monastic appearance because it was in those pious precincts that studies found their first peaceful accommodation. The courtrooms in Italy are as spacious and lofty as a community's means permit; it is like being in those marketplaces where trials used to be held under the open sky. And do we not continue to build our largest theaters, with all their appurtenances, under a roof like those of the original kermess stalls, which were made of boards and not expected to last more than a short time? Because of the immense crowds of knowledge seekers at the time of the Reformation, students were forced to live in townspeople's houses, and yet how long it has taken us to open up our orphanages and provide those poor children with the same very necessary worldly education![133]

133

Bologna, the 20th, evening.

I have spent this whole bright, beautiful day in the open air. As soon as I come near to mountains I am attracted to their minerals again. I see myself as Antaeus, who always feels newly strengthened, the more forcefully he is brought into contact with his mother, the earth.

I rode on horseback to Paderno, where the so-called Bolognese heavy spar is found. Little cakes are made from it which, when calcined and then exposed to the light, will afterwards glow in the dark. Here they are called simply *fosfori*.

After passing some sandy clay hills on the way there, I soon found whole masses of selenite showing on the surface. A watery fissure descends near a brick kiln, with many smaller ones emptying into it. At first I supposed this was a soggy hill eroded by the rain, but on closer inspection I could detect the following about its nature: the solid rock composing this part of the range is a very thinly laminated shale alternating with gypsum. The shale is so intimately mixed with pyrites that it undergoes a complete change when in contact with air and moisture. It becomes distended, the strata disappear, a kind of clay is formed, conchoidal, crumbled, with gleaming surfaces like coal. The transition, or transformation, can only be convincingly demonstrated in large pieces; after cracking open several of them I clearly perceived both forms. At the same time it can be seen that the conchoidal planes are covered with white dots and sometimes have yellow parts; so the whole surface is gradually decaying, and in general the hill looks like weathered pyrites. Also, some of the strata are harder, green and red. I frequently found pyrites encrusted on the rocks too.

Then I ascended the crumbling, disintegrating mountains through ravines washed out by the last downpours, and to my delight found large amounts of the heavy spar I was seeking, mostly in imperfect ovoid form, showing on the surface at several spots where the mountains were in the process of falling to bits, some of it quite loose, some still tightly gripped by the shale in which it was situated. One glance sufficed to convince me that these were not detritus. Whether they originated simultaneously with the stratum of shale, or only when the latter swelled up and decomposed, merits closer investigation. The pieces I found, whether larger or smaller, come close to having an imperfectly ovoid shape, while the smallest are actually passing over into an indistinctly crystalline form. The heaviest piece I found weighs eight and a half ounces. In the same shale I also found loose, perfect gypsum crystals. When experts see the pieces I am taking along they will know how to define them more accurately. And so here I am, burdened with rocks again! I have packed up an eighth hundredweight of this heavy spar.

October 20, at night.

How much more there would be to say if I wanted to tell everything that went through my mind on this beautiful day! But my longing is stronger than my thoughts. I feel myself drawn irresistibly onwards, and I have to force myself to concentrate on what is at hand. And it seems that Heaven has heard my prayers. A *vetturino* has announced his intention of going straight to Rome, and so the day after tomorrow I shall set out in that direction without stopping along the way. Then today and tomorrow I must see to my affairs, attend to various matters, and dispose of them.

Lojano in the Apennines, October 21, evening.

Whether I drove myself out of Bologna today, or was chased out, I cannot say. In any case I impulsively grasped an opportunity to leave earlier. Now here I am in a miserable inn together with a papal officer who is going to his native town. When I seated myself next to him in the two-wheeled carriage I commented politely, just to make conversation, that I, being a German who was accustomed to associate with soldiers, found it very agreeable to be traveling now in the company of a papal officer.—"Do not take offence," he replied, "but I am not surprised you like the military, since I hear that in Germany everyone is a soldier. As for me, however, although our service is very easy and I have a perfectly comfortable life in Bologna, where I am garrisoned, still I wish I were rid of this jacket and were managing my father's little farm. But I am the younger son and so I have to put up with it."

The 22nd, evening.

Giredo, another little village high in the Apennines, where I feel quite happy because I am coming closer to my desires. Today we were joined by a lady and gentleman on horseback, an Englishman with his so-called sister. They have fine horses, but are traveling without servants, and it seems that the gentleman serves as both valet and groom. They have found something to complain about everywhere, it is like reading some pages out of Archenholz.[134]

I find the Apennines a remarkable part of the world. Upon the great plain of the Po basin there follows a mountain range that rises from the depths, between two seas, to end the continent on the south. If it were not so steep, so high above sea level, and so strangely tortuous, it would have been affected more and longer in primeval times by the ebb and flood, which would have washed over it and formed larger expanses of flat land. Then it would be one of the most beautiful regions in this most splendid latitude, somewhat higher than the other land. In actual fact, however, it is a curious web of mountain ridges facing each other; often it is not possible to find the point toward which the water is trying to drain. If the valleys were filled in more and the flat surfaces smoother and better watered, the region could be compared to Bohemia, except that these mountains have an entirely different character. Still, one must not imagine a high wasteland, but a countryside mostly cultivated, even though mountainous. Chestnuts develop beautifully here, and the wheat is excellent, the crop already a pretty green. Evergreen oaks with small leaves stand by the roadside, but the churches and chapels are surrounded by slim cypresses.

Yesterday evening the weather was gloomy, today it is bright and beautiful again.

The 25th, evening. Perugia.

For two evenings I have not written anything. The inns were so bad that there was nowhere to lay down a sheet of paper. Things are also beginning to get a bit tangled for me, because ever since my departure from Venice my travel distaff has not been spinning off as well and smoothly as before.

On the morning of the twenty-third, at ten o'clock German time, we came out of the Apennines and saw Florence lying in a wide valley, which is cultivated to an unbelievable degree and dotted with innumerable villas and houses.

I went through the city, the cathedral, the baptistery very hastily. Another new and unfamiliar world has opened up before me here, but I do not intend to linger in it. The Boboli garden has a choice location. I hurried out of it as fast as I went in.

The city shows the municipal wealth that built it; obviously it enjoyed a series of good governments. In Tuscany generally, one is immediately struck by the fine, grandiose appearance of public works such as roads and bridges. Everything here is both sturdy and well kept, the intention is to combine use and advantage with attractiveness, a spirit of precision is noticeable everywhere. In contrast, the papal state seems to survive only because the earth refuses to swallow it.

When I recently described what the Apennines *could* be, that is what Tuscany actually *is*. Owing to the much lower elevation, the primeval sea could perform its duty properly and heaped up a deep clay soil. It is bright yellow and easily tilled. They plow deeply, but still in the primitive way: their plow has no wheels and the plowshare is immovable. So the peasant has to shove it along, bent over behind his oxen, as he digs up the earth. Plowing is done as much as five times, and fertilizer is strewn by hand, very lightly. Finally they sow the wheat, then pile up narrow ridges with deep furrows between them, everything aimed at draining away rainwater. Now the crop grows up on the ridges, and they walk up and down in the furrows to weed. It would be an understandable procedure where there is danger of wetness; but I cannot see why they do it on the finest flat land. I carried out this inspection in the vicinity of Arezzo, where a magnificent plain unfolds. No field could be neater than this one, nowhere even a clod of earth, everything is as finely ground as if it were sifted. Wheat thrives very well here, apparently finding all the conditions appropriate to its nature. The second year they raise beans for the horses, which are not fed oats here.

Lupines are also sown and have already grown up splendid and green; they will bear fruit in March. The flax has come up already too; it survives the winter, and the frost only makes the fiber more durable.

The olive trees are curious plants; they closely resemble willows, losing their heartwood in the same way, and the bark splits. But in spite of that they have a fairly solid appearance. One can see that the wood grows slowly and has an incredibly delicate organic structure. The leaf is willow-like, but with fewer leaves to the branch. The hills around Florence are planted all over with olive trees and grapevines, the ground between them is used for grain. Near Arezzo and beyond it the fields are left freer. It seems to me that not enough is done to combat ivy, which is injurious to olive and other trees and could so easily be destroyed. One sees no meadows at all. They say that Indian corn exhausts the soil, and that other crops have suffered since its introduction. I can well believe that, in view of the meager fertilizer.

This evening I took leave of my captain with assurances and promises that I would visit him in Bologna on my return trip. Now a few things that particularly characterize him: Since I was often quiet and reflective, he once said, "Che pensa! non deve mai pensar l'uomo, pensando s'invecchia." Translated, that means: "Why do you think so much! A man must never think, thinking ages him." And after some conversation: "Non deve fermarsi l'uomo in una sola cosa, perchè allora divien matto; bisogna aver mille cose, una confusione nella testa." Translated: "A man must not concentrate on just a single thing, because that will drive him mad, he must have a thousand things, a confusion, in his head."

Of course the good man could not know that I was quiet and reflective for the very reason that my head *was* whirling with a confusion of old and new things. The cultural level of an Italian like him will be seen still more clearly from the following: Noticing of course that I was a Protestant, he eventually got up the courage to say I should please permit him certain questions, for he had heard so many curious things about us Protestants and finally wanted some reliable information on this subject. "May you really," he asked, "have an intimate relationship with a pretty girl without actually being married to her?—Do your priests allow you to do that?" I answered: "Our priests are clever men, who take no notice of such trifling matters. Of course, if we asked their permission, they would not give it."—"So you do not need to ask?" he exclaimed, "Oh, you lucky fellows! And since you do not confess to them, they do not find out about it." Hereupon he began a tirade against his priests and praised our blessed freedom.—"However, with respect to confession," he continued, "what is the situation there? We are told that all the people, even if they are not Christians, still must confess. But because they are too hardened to do it properly, they will confess to an old tree, which of course is very absurd and impious, but nevertheless it shows that they recognize the necessity of confession." Hereupon I explained our notions of confession to him, and how we went about it. That sounded very convenient to him, but he said it was approximately the same as confessing to an old tree. After some hesitation he besought me very earnestly for honest information on another point; that is to say, he had heard from the lips of one of his priests, who was a truthful man, that we were permitted to marry our sisters, which was certainly a great impropriety. When I denied this charge and tried to give him some sympathetic understanding of our doctrine, he did not pay any particular heed, for it seemed too ordinary to him, and he turned to another question:—"We are assured," he said, "that Frederick the Great, who has won so many victories even over the true believers and become famous throughout the world, that he, whom everyone considers a heretic, is actually a Catholic and has a papal dispensation to keep this a secret. For he does not go into any of your churches, as is well known; instead, he worships in a subterranean chapel, broken-hearted that he may not publicly confess the sacred religion. For if he did so, his Prussians, who are a bestial people and raging heretics, would kill him on the spot, which would not help the cause. Therefore the Holy Father has given him this dispensation, in return for which he quietly spreads and favors the only true religion as much as possible." I let all of that pass and merely answered: since it was a great secret, naturally no one could prove it. Our further conversation was in much the same vein, and I could not help feeling amazed at the clever clergy, who try to dismiss and distort everything that might penetrate and confound the dark realm of their traditional teachings.

I left Perugia on a splendid morning and felt the bliss of being alone again. The location of the town is beautiful, the view of the lake most delightful. I have impressed these pictures deeply on myself. First the road went down, then through a pleasant valley enclosed on both sides by distant hills. Finally I saw Assisi lying before me.

I knew from Palladio and Volkmann that a perfectly preserved, beautiful temple of Minerva, built in Augustan times, was still standing there. At Madonna del Angelo I left my *vetturino,* who continued on his way to Foligno, while I climbed up to Assisi in a strong wind; for I longed to wander on foot through what seemed to me a very isolated world. To my left were the enormous substructures over which, piled on top of each other in Babylonian fashion, are the churches where St. Francis rests;[135] but I turned away from them with repugnance, thinking to myself that the minds I found there would bear the same stamp as that of my captain. Then I asked a handsome lad about the Maria della

Minerva, and he led me up to the town, which is built on a mountainside. Finally we arrived in the actual old part of the town, and behold, there before my eyes stood the first complete monument from ancient times that I have seen. A modest temple, as befitted such a small town, and yet so perfect, so beautifully conceived, that it would stand out anywhere. Now, first of all, concerning its position! I have great respect for such matters after having read in Vitruvius and Palladio how towns should be built and temples and public buildings placed. In this regard too the ancients understood the grandeur of naturalness. The temple stands at the beautiful halfway point of the mountain, just where two hills meet, on the square which is still just called "the Square." The latter itself slopes upwards a little, and four streets come together on it, forming a very compressed St. Andrew's cross, two coming up from below, two down from above. The houses built opposite the temple were probably not standing in ancient times because they now block the view. If we could imagine them gone, we would look southwards into the most opulent region, and Minerva's temple would be visible from all sides. The layout of the streets may be ancient, for it is determined by the form and slope of the mountain. The temple does not stand in the middle of the square but is aligned in such a way that it is visible in very beautiful perspective to anyone coming up from Rome. Someone ought to draw not only the building but also its felicitous position.

In looking at the facade I became fascinated with the brilliant logic of the artist's procedure here too. The order is Corinthian, the space between the columns somewhat more than two column diameters. The tori and the plinths under them seem to stand on pedestals, but that is an illusion; for the socle is cut through five times, and each time five steps go up between the columns, and then one arrives at the surface on which the columns really stand, and from which one enters the temple. The bold decision to cut through the socle was appropriate here, for since the temple is situated on the mountainside, the steps leading up to it would have had to be placed too far in front and would have narrowed the square. It cannot be determined how many more steps were situated underneath; with few exceptions they are buried and paved over. Reluctantly I tore myself away from this sight and resolved to bring the building to the attention of all architects, so that we may obtain an exact plan of it. For in this instance I was struck again by how poorly things are transmitted. Palladio, in whom I had complete confidence, of course includes a picture of this temple, but he cannot have seen it himself, for he actually puts pedestals on the flat surface. This makes the columns disproportionately high, so that the result is an ugly Palmyric monstrosity,[136] whereas in reality one enjoys a serene, lovely sight that satisfies both eye and intellect. Contemplation of this

work awakens feelings in me that I cannot put into words, but they
will bear lasting fruit.

It was the most beautiful evening, and I was walking downhill on
the Roman road, wonderfully calm in spirit, when behind me I heard
rough, vehement voices raised in a quarrel. I supposed it might be the
sbirri[137] whom I had noticed earlier in the town. I coolly went on my
way, but kept listening to them in back of me. Then I soon realized
that their discussion was about *me*. Four such men, of unpleasant appearance, two of them armed with muskets, walked past me, muttered
something, returned after a few steps, and surrounded me. They asked
who I was and what I was doing here. I said I was a foreigner passing
through Assisi on foot, while my *vetturino* was driving on to Foligno.
They could not conceive of anyone's paying for a carriage and then
walking. They asked whether I had been in the Gran Convento.[138] I
said no, and assured them that this building had long been familiar to
me. But since I was an architect, this time I had inspected only the
Maria della Minerva, which, as they knew, was a model building. They
did not deny that but were much offended that I had not paid my respects to the saint, and aired their suspicion that my trade might be
the smuggling of contraband. I pointed out to them how absurd it was
to imagine that a man walking alone down the road, with empty pockets
and no knapsack, could be a smuggler. I offered to accompany them
back to town to see the *podestà* and show him my papers, whereupon
he would acknowledge me to be a respectable foreigner. They muttered
at this, saying it would not be necessary; and finally, while I maintained
a decidedly serious demeanor, they retreated towards the town again.
I watched them go. There in the foreground I saw those coarse fellows
walking, while behind them the lovely Minerva gazed at me again in a
very friendly and consoling manner. Then I looked to my left at the
mournful cathedral of St. Francis and was about to continue on my
way when one of the unarmed men detached himself from the group
and came up to me quite amicably. Greeting me, he said at once: "My
dear foreign sir, you should at least give *me* a gratuity, for I assure
you that I took you for an honest man right away and declared this
loudly to my companions. But they are hotheads who immediately get
angry, and they are ignorant of the world. You will also have noticed
that it was I who first applauded and accepted your words." I praised
him for this and asked him to safeguard respectable foreigners who
came to Assisi in pursuit of religion and art, especially architects, for
they would bring fame to the town by measuring and drawing the Minerva temple, which had not as yet been properly drawn and engraved.
I said he should be of service to them, for then they would certainly
show their gratitude—and with that I pressed several silver coins into
his hand, more than he expected. Very much delighted, he asked me

to be sure to return, and especially not to miss the saint's festival, where I would most certainly enjoy myself and be edified. In fact, if a handsome man like me should be interested in meeting a handsome woman, as was only right and proper, he could assure me that on his recommendation the most beautiful and respectable woman in all of Assisi would gladly receive me. Then he departed, swearing that he would mention me in his devotions at the saint's grave this very evening, and would pray for my subsequent journey. Thus we parted, and I was much relieved to be alone again with nature and myself. The road to Foligno afforded one of the most charming and beautiful walks I have ever taken. Four full hours along a mountainside, with a richly cultivated valley on my right.

One rides tolerably well with the *vetturini;* but the best part is that one can follow them easily on foot. I have had myself dragged along by them all the way here from Ferrara. This Italy, which enjoys nature's richest favor, has lagged very badly behind other countries with respect to mechanics and technology, which after all are the basis of a more modern and comfortable way of life. The carriage of the *vetturini,* which is still called *sedia,* or seat, is surely descended from the old sedan chairs in which women, or older and more aristocratic persons, had themselves drawn by mules. Two wheels were set underneath to replace the rear mule, which was then harnessed in front next to the tongue, and no further improvements were undertaken. The passenger is still rocked along as he was centuries ago, and they are like this in their dwellings and everything else.

If anyone wants to see the earliest poetic idea[139] still existing in reality, namely, that people lived mostly under the open sky and withdrew into their caves only when necessary, let him enter the buildings here, especially those out in the countryside, which are altogether cave-like in spirit and taste. The Italians are so incredibly insouciant because they do not want reflection to age them! With outrageous frivolity they neglect to prepare for winter and its longer nights, and consequently suffer like dogs for a good part of the year. Here I am in Foligno, in a truly Homeric domestic situation, where everyone assembles around a fire burning on the earthen floor of a great hall and, amidst shouting and clamor, dines at a long table, as in paintings of the marriage at Cana. Under the circumstances I would not have thought of inkwells, but somebody has had one brought in, and so I seize the opportunity to write this. But the page reveals how cold and uncomfortable my writing table is.

Now I surely feel how rash it was to come to this country unprepared and unaccompanied. Because of the various currencies, the *vetturini,* the prices, and the inferior inns there is no way for someone like me, traveling alone for the first time and looking hopefully for uninterrupted pleasure, to avoid feeling very unhappy day in, day out. But my one desire has been to see this land, cost what it may, and although they are dragging me to Rome on Ixion's wheel, I shall not complain.

Terni, October 27, evening.

Here I sit in another "cave," one that was damaged in an earthquake a year ago. The little town lies in a delectable region, which I happily surveyed while making the circuit of the walls. It starts off with a lovely plain between mountains, which all still consist of limestone. Terni is located at the foot of the range on this side, like Bologna on the other side.

The papal soldier having left me, I now have a priest as my traveling companion. He seems much more content with his situation than the former, and is very willing to instruct me, whom of course he recognizes as a heretic, when I ask him about the rituals and other matters of that kind. Truly, I am achieving my goal by constantly associating with different persons; and what a vivid picture of the whole country can be gained from just hearing the people converse among themselves! In the most remarkable way they are all adversaries, they feel the strangest fanatical loyalty to their province and town, are all very intolerant of one another, the classes are eternally at war, and all of this to the accompaniment of invariably lively, spontaneous emotion. All day long they perform a comedy for me and make fools of themselves; and yet at the same time they take the situation in and immediately notice when a foreigner is bewildered by their general behavior.

I climbed up to Spoleto and was on the aqueduct, which also serves as a bridge between two mountains. The ten arches of brickwork have stood there so calmly during the centuries, and water still gushes forth everywhere in Spoleto. This, now, is the third ancient structure I have seen, all of them with the same grandeur of design. A second Nature, one that serves civic goals, that is what their architecture is, and thus arose the amphitheater, the temple, and the aqueduct. Only now do I feel how right I was to loathe all capricious edifices, like the Winterkasten[140] on the Weissenstein for example, a nothing built for nothing, a huge decorative confection, and it is the same with a thousand other things. They all stand there stillborn, for whatever has no inner validity has no life, and can neither be nor become great.

How much pleasure and understanding I have derived from the last eight weeks! But they have also cost me considerable effort. I make sure to keep my eyes open all the time and let the sights impress themselves on me deeply. Even if it were possible, I would definitely not care to make judgments.

San Crocefisso,[141] a bizarre chapel next to the road, is in my opinion not the remains of any temple that stood on this spot. On the contrary, some columns, pillars, and pieces of entablature were found and patched together, not stupidly, but crazily. It beggars description, but surely there is an engraving of it somewhere.

And so it is disconcerting to us who are striving to acquire a concept of antiquity that we meet with nothing but ruins, on the basis of which we must try, with poor success, to reconstruct something we do not yet understand.

The situation is quite different with what is called classical soil. If, instead of losing oneself in fantasy here, one accepts the region as reality, just as it lies there, then it is still the definitive scene of action, which calls for the greatest deeds; and therefore up till now I have always made use of my interest in geology and topography to suppress my imagination and sentiment, and to preserve a free, clear view of the locality for myself. Then, in a remarkable fashion, history vividly links itself up with this, and I do not know what comes over me, but I feel the greatest longing to read Tacitus in Rome.

Nor must I entirely neglect the weather. When I was coming up the Apennines from Bologna the clouds were still moving northwards; later, they changed direction and moved toward Lake Trasimeno. Here they hung, then probably moved southwards. The great plain of the Po, which during the summer sent all its clouds to the Tyrolean mountains, now sends some of them to the Apennines, which may explain the rainy weather.

They are beginning to pick olives. It is done by hand here, in other places the trees are beaten with sticks. If winter comes prematurely, the remaining fruit continues to hang nearly until spring. Today I saw some of the largest, oldest trees on very stony ground.

The Muses' favor, like that of the demons, is not always bestowed on us at the proper time. Today I was inspired to work on a subject that is totally unsuited to the circumstances. Here I am, approaching the very heart of Catholicism, surrounded by Catholics, confined in a *sedia* with a priest, and also trying, with the purest of intentions, to observe and comprehend true nature and noble art, and what flashes through my mind very vividly is that all traces of original Christianity have been expunged. Indeed, when I visualized it in its pure form, as we see it in the Acts of the Apostles, I could not help shuddering at the deformed, nay, bizarre heathenism that now weighs upon those agreeable beginnings. Then I thought again of the Wandering Jew, who had witnessed all those curious, complicated developments and had experienced conditions so strange that when Christ Himself returned to inspect the fruits of His teachings, He was put in danger of being sacrificed a second time. That legend entitled *"Venio iterum crucifigi"*[142] was to provide me with the material for this catastrophe.

Such are the dreams I indulge in. For I am so impatient to be on my way that I sleep with my clothes on, and nothing pleases me more than to be waked before dawn, to sit down quickly in the carriage, and to ride into the morning in a state between sleeping and waking, letting my imagination create whatever images it wishes.

Città Castellana, October 28.

I shall not omit the last evening. It is not yet eight o'clock but everyone has already retired; so, to sum things up, I can recall the recent past and anticipate the near future. It was a very bright and splendid day today, the morning very chilly, the day clear and warm, the evening a little windy, but very beautiful.

We left Terni very early in the morning; we came up to Narni before daybreak, and so I did not see the bridge. Valleys and gorges, places near and far, exquisite regions—all of limestone, and not even a trace of any other rock.

Otricoli is situated on one of the gravel hills deposited by the ancient currents, and consists of lava brought from the other side of the river.

As soon as the bridge is crossed, one is in volcanic terrain, composed either of true lavas or of earlier rock that has been altered through roasting and smelting. One ascends a mountain that would seem to be of gray lava. This contains many white crystals formed like artillery shells. The highway leading from the summit to Città Castellana is of the same stone, worn nicely smooth by vehicles; the town is built on volcanic tufa, in which I thought I glimpsed ash, pumice, and pieces of lava. The view from the castle is very beautiful; Mount Soracte stands alone very picturesquely, probably a limestone mountain of the Apennine chain. The volcanic stretches are much lower than the Apennines, and have only been carved into mountains and cliffs by the waters rushing through them, resulting in the formation of some magnificently picturesque objects, overhanging crags, and other incidental topographical features.

So tomorrow evening I shall be in Rome. I can still hardly believe it, and if this wish is fulfilled, what shall I ever wish for afterwards? Nothing more that I can think of, except to land safely at home in my pheasant boat, and to find my friends healthy, happy, and kindly disposed to me.

Rome

At last I can open my mouth and send greetings to my friends with a light heart.[143] May they forgive my secrecy and my, as it were, underground journey here! I scarcely dared admit to myself where I was going, even during the trip I was still fearful, and not until I passed under the Porta del Populo was I certain that Rome was mine.

And now let me also say that I think of you again and again, indeed constantly, here in proximity to these sights that I never imagined I would have to see alone. Only when I saw that every one of you was chained body and soul in the north, and that all your interest in these regions had faded away, did I resolve to start out on this long, solitary journey in search of the focal point toward which I was drawn by an irresistible desire. Indeed, for the last few years this was becoming a kind of illness, which could only be cured by the sight and presence of Rome. I can confess it now: finally I could no longer bear to look at a Latin book or the picture of an Italian scene. My longing to see this land was more than ripe. Only now that it is satisfied have my friends and fatherland truly become dear to me again. Now I look forward to my return, indeed all the more so because I feel very certain that I shall not be bringing all these treasures back just for my own possession and private use, but so that they may serve both me and others as guidance and encouragement for an entire lifetime.

Rome, November 1, 1786.

Yes, I have finally arrived in this city, the capital of the world! I wish I had been in the fortunate position of seeing it fifteen years ago with good companions and some really intelligent man as guide. But since I was destined to visit it alone and see it through my own eyes, it is well that this joy was granted to me so late.

I have flown, so to speak, over the Tyrolean mountains, have seen Verona, Vicenza, Padua, and Venice well, Ferrara, Cento, Bologna superficially, and Florence scarcely at all. My desire to reach Rome was so great and increased so much with every passing moment that I could no longer stay anywhere, and stopped in Florence for only three hours. Now I am here and calm—calmed, it would seem, for the rest of my life. For it may well be said that a new life begins when something previously known inside and out, but still only in parts, is beheld in its entirety. Now I see all my childhood dreams come to life; I see now in reality the first engravings that I remember (my father had hung the prospects of Rome in a corridor); and everything long familiar to me in paintings and drawings, copperplates and woodcuts, in plaster and cork, now stands together before me. Wherever I go I find something in this new world I am acquainted with; it is all as I imagined, and yet new. And the same can be said of my observations, my thoughts. I have had no entirely new thought, have found nothing entirely unfamiliar, but the old thoughts have become so precise, so alive, so coherent that they can pass for new.

When Pygmalion's Elisa,[144] whom he had formed completely in accordance with his wishes and given as much truth and life as an artist can, finally came up to him and said: "It is I!" how different the living woman was from the sculpted stone!

It is also morally very beneficial to me to live among these entirely sensual people, who have been the subject of so much talk and writing, whom every foreigner judges by the standards he brings along from home. I excuse everyone who criticizes and chides them; they are too unlike us, and a foreigner finds it tiresome and expensive to deal with them.

Rome, November 3.

Among the chief reasons I imagined I had for hurrying to Rome was the All Saints' festival, the first of November. For I thought, if so much honor is accorded to an individual saint, what will it be like for all of them together? But how I deceived myself! The Roman church had not elected to have any conspicuous universal festival, and every order could celebrate the memory of its special patron quietly; for the name day and the day of honor assigned to him are really when each one shines in his glory.

Yesterday, however, on All Souls' day, I had better success. The memory of these is celebrated by the pope[145] in his private chapel in the Quirinal palace. Everyone is permitted to attend. I hurried to Monte Cavallo with Tischbein.[146] The square before the palace has a very particular, individual quality, and is as irregular as it is grandiose and charming. Now I caught sight of the two colossi![147] Neither eye nor mind is adequate to grasp them. We hurried with the crowd through the splendidly spacious courtyard and up a more than spacious staircase. In the anteroom opposite the chapel, with a view of the series of rooms, one feels strange to be under the same roof with the vicar of Christ.

The service had begun, pope and cardinals were already in the church. The holy father, a very handsome, dignified figure of a man, cardinals of various ages and countenances.

I was seized by a strange desire to see the supreme head of the church open his golden lips and enrapture us by rapturously describing the ineffable bliss of the souls in heaven. But when I saw that he was just moving back and forth before the altar, turning now to this side, now to that, gesturing and murmuring like an ordinary priest, then the Protestant original sin raised its head, and I was by no means pleased to see the familiar, usual mass celebrated here. Christ even as a boy, after all, had orally interpreted the Scriptures, and as a youth surely did not teach and persuade in silence; for He spoke gladly, wisely, and well, as we know from the Gospels. What would He say, I wondered, if He should enter and find His earthly counterpart mumbling and swaying back and forth? The words, *"Venio iterum crucifigi!"* came into my mind, and I plucked my companion's sleeve, so that we might get out into the openness of the painted and vaulted halls.

Here we found a crowd of persons intently contemplating the exquisite paintings, for this festival of All Souls is simultaneously the festival of all the artists in Rome. Like the chapel, the whole palace with all its rooms is accessible to everyone, and on this day is open free of charge for many hours; one does not need to give any gratuity and is not pestered by the castellan.

The wall paintings occupied my attention, and I met and learned to love and appreciate some additional excellent artists hardly known to me even by name, like the cheerful Carlo Maratti,[148] for example.

But the masterpieces of artists whose style I had already impressed upon my mind were especially welcome. I looked at Guercino's *St. Petronilla*[149] with admiration; it was formerly in St. Peter's, where now a mosaic copy has been installed to replace the original. The saint's corpse is being lifted out of the grave, and the same person, revived, is being received in the celestial heights by a divine youth. Whatever may be said against this double action, it is an inestimable picture.

I was still more amazed by a picture of Titian's.[150] It outshines all the others I have seen. Whether my faculties have already become sharper, or whether it really is the most superb one, I cannot tell. A huge chasuble, stiff with embroidery, indeed with figures of embossed gold, envelops a stately episcopal figure. His left hand on the massive crozier, he gazes upwards in rapture; in his right hand he holds a book out of which he seems just to have received a divine inspiration. Behind him is a lovely virgin, holding a palm branch and looking into the open book with sweet interest. However, a grave old man at his right, quite near to the book, seems to pay no attention to it; holding keys in his hand, he may well be confident about making his own interpretations. Opposite this group is a well-built nude youth, bound, and wounded by arrows, looking straight ahead with modest submissiveness. In the space between, holding a cross and a lily, are two monks who turn devoutly toward the heavenly beings, for the semicircular masonry that surrounds them all is open on top. There in the highest glory the mother turns to look down sympathetically. The lively, active Child on her lap with a cheerful gesture extends a wreath, indeed seems to be throwing it down. Angels, ready with more wreaths, hover on both sides. But over all these and above the threefold nimbus the heavenly Dove holds sway as both central point and keystone.

We tell ourselves: some underlying sacred old tradition must be the explanation for having brought these diverse, ill-assorted personages together in such an artistic and significant way. We do not inquire why and how, we accept it and admire the inestimable artistry.

A fresco by Guido[151] in his chapel is less incomprehensible but still mysterious. The most naively lovely, pious virgin sits quietly and demurely sewing, while two angels wait at her side for any sign that they should serve her. The dear picture tells us that youthful innocence and diligence are guarded and honored by the heavenly angels. No legend is needed here, no interpretation.

But now a cheerful adventure to temper this artistic seriousness: I could plainly see that several German artists, coming up to Tischbein because they were acquainted with him, looked at me and then walked back and forth. After having left me for a few moments, Tischbein returned and said: "I have a good joke for you! Everyone has heard the rumor about your being in Rome, and the artists have not failed to notice the only unknown foreigner present here today. But one of them has claimed for a long time that he associated with you, in fact was your friend, something we found difficult to believe. When we challenged this man to take a look and resolve the doubt about you, he flatly asserted it was not you, and that the stranger's face and figure did not resemble yours in the least. So your incognito is safe for the moment, at any rate, and afterwards we shall have something to laugh about."

I now circulated with less reserve among the group of artists, and inquired about the painters of various pictures whose artistic style was as yet unfamiliar to me. At last I found myself particularly attracted to a picture showing St. George, the dragon-slayer and liberator of virgins. No one could name the painter for me. Then a small, modest, previously silent man stepped forward and informed me that it was by Pordenone, the Venetian, one of his best pictures, which revealed all his merits.[152] Now I understood my preference very well: the picture had appealed to me because I was already quite well acquainted with the Venetian school and better able to appreciate the virtues of its masters.

The informative artist is Heinrich Meyer,[153] a Swiss, who has been studying here for several years along with a friend named Cölla.[154] He makes excellent copies in sepia of ancient busts and is very well versed in the history of art.

Rome, November 7.

I have been here seven days now, and a general concept of this city is gradually forming in my mind. We walk diligently here and there, I acquaint myself with the street plans of ancient and modern Rome, view the ruins, the buildings, visit this and that villa, and deal quite unhurriedly with the main objects of interest. I just keep my eyes open, look, and go, and come again, for only *in* Rome can one prepare oneself for Rome.

Let us admit, nevertheless, that it is hard, sad work to sort out the old Rome from the new, but one has to do it and hope for inestimable satisfaction at the end. We encounter traces of a magnificence and a destruction that are both beyond our comprehension. What the barbarians left standing, the builders of new Rome have ravaged.

When one looks at something that has existed for more than two thousand years and has been altered so diversely and thoroughly by the changing times, yet is still the same soil, the same hill, indeed often the same column and wall, and in the people still some vestiges of their ancient character, one becomes a participant in the great decisions of fate. And such conditions make it difficult from the outset for the observer to decipher how Rome follows on Rome, and not only the new on the old, but also the various epochs within the old and new Rome on one another. First I am just trying by myself to get the feel of the half-buried places, as only then can one make full use of the fine preliminary studies. For since the fifteenth century and up to the present day excellent artists and scholars have spent their whole lives working on these objects.

And the immensity of all this affects us very quietly as we hurry back and forth in Rome to get to the most outstanding sights. In other places one has to search for what is significant, here we are overwhelmed and surfeited with it. Go where we will, there is always a scene of some kind to look at, palaces and ruins, gardens and wilderness, vistas and confined areas, little houses, stables, triumphal arches and columns, often so close together that they could be drawn on one sheet of paper. A pen is useless here, one needs to write with a thousand slate pencils! And then in the evening I am tired out and exhausted from looking and marveling.

November 7, 1786.

Do forgive me, my friends, if you find me to be laconic from now on. The traveler gathers what he can along the way, every day brings something new, and he hastily thinks about it and evaluates it. Here, however, I have entered a great school indeed, where one day says so much that I dare say nothing about the day. Yes, a person would be well advised to linger here for years while preserving a Pythagorean silence.

On the same date.

I feel quite well. The weather is *brutto,* as the Romans say. There is a wind from the south, the sirocco, which brings varying amounts of rain every day; but I do not find such atmospheric conditions unpleasant, for the air remains warm, unlike rainy days in our country, even in the summer.

November 7.

I am steadily becoming better acquainted with Tischbein's talents, as well as with his plans and artistic goals, and am learning to esteem them more and more. He showed me his drawings and sketches, which include, and also promise, very many good things. His sojourn with Bodmer[155] turned his thoughts to the early times of the human race, when it found itself set on the earth and was faced with the task of becoming lord of the world.

As an ingenious introduction to the whole he has striven to present the great age of the world in a striking manner. Mountains covered with splendid forests, gorges dug out by streams of water, extinct volcanos emitting scarcely the faintest smoke. In the foreground, the mighty stump of an aged oak tree left in the ground, on whose half-exposed roots a stag tests the strength of his antlers, as well conceived as it is beautifully executed.

Then in a very remarkable drawing he has presented man both as a tamer of horses and also as superior in cunning, if not in strength, to all the animals of the earth, air, and water. The composition is extraordinarily beautiful, and it would make a very effective oil painting.[156] We must surely get a copy of that for Weimar. Then he is planning a group of old, wise, and time-tested men, in which he will take the opportunity to depict real persons. With the greatest enthusiasm, however, he is now sketching a battle in which two detachments of cavalry are attacking each other with equal ferocity at a place where they are separated by an enormous rocky gorge, over which a horse can jump only with the greatest effort. Defensive action is unthinkable here. Bold attack, wild resolve, success—or a plunge into the abyss. This picture will give him the opportunity to display in a very significant way his knowledge of horses and their anatomy and movements.

He would now like to see these pictures, and a series of subsequent and interpolated ones, linked together by some poems. The latter could serve to explain what was being depicted, and in exchange he would lend them substance and charm by means of specific figures.

It is a fine idea, but of course the execution of such a work would require us to be together for several years.

November 7.

Just now, at last, I have seen Raphael's loggias and the great paintings, *The School of Athens,* etc.,[157] and it is like studying Homer in a partly obliterated, damaged manuscript. The first impression is not altogether pleasant, and one's enjoyment is complete only after everything has been gradually inspected and properly studied. Best preserved are the painted ceilings of the loggias, which depict stories from the Bible, as fresh as if painted yesterday, to be sure very little of it by Raphael's own hand, but most excellently done from his drawings and under his supervision.

November 7.

In earlier years I sometimes had the odd notion that nothing could please me more than to be taken to Italy by some knowledgeable man, say, an Englishman well versed in art and history; and now in the meantime all that has turned out much better than I could ever have imagined. Tischbein has lived such a long time here as my affectionate friend, has lived here wishing to show me Rome; our relationship is old through letters, new with respect to physical presence; where could I have found a more valuable guide? My time here may be limited, but I shall enjoy and learn everything possible.

And, for all that, I see in advance that when I leave I shall wish I were just arriving.

November 8.

My curious and perhaps capricious semi-incognito[158] brings me un-expected advantages. Since everyone has pledged to pretend not to know who I am, and therefore no one may talk to me about myself, people have no alternative but to speak about themselves or the subjects that interest them. Consequently I get detailed information about what each of them is doing, or about whatever remarkable event occurs. Aulic Councilor Reiffenstein[159] put up with this whim; but since for a particular reason he could not abide the name I had assumed, he quickly dubbed me Baron, and now I am called the Baron vis-à-vis Rondanini.[160] That is designation enough, especially since the Italians only address people by their Christian name or their nickname. Suffice it to say, I have my way, and I avoid the constant inconvenience of having to give an account of myself and my works.

November 9.

Sometimes I stand still for perhaps a moment, and survey the highest peaks I already have behind me. With great pleasure I look back at Venice, that great entity sprung from the depths of the sea like Pallas from the head of Jupiter. Here in Rome, the Rotonda,[161] both inside and outside, has filled me with joyful respect for its magnitude. In St. Peter's, I have come to understand how art, as well as nature, can render all comparisons of size futile. And, in like manner, the *Apollo Belvedere* has taken me out beyond reality. For just as even the most exact drawing does not give a real concept of those buildings, so it is here with the marble original as opposed to the plaster casts, although earlier I have known some very fine ones.

November 10, 1786.

I am living here now with a feeling of clarity and calm that I have not had for a long time. My practice of seeing and taking all things just as they are, my constancy in keeping a clear eye, and my complete rejection of all pretensions are proving very useful again, and make me quietly very happy. Every day a new remarkable object, every day some new great, extraordinary pictures, and a totality that is past imagining, however long one might think and dream.

Today I was at the pyramid of Cestius,[162] and on the Palatine in the evening, up there on the ruins of the imperial palaces, which stand like rocky cliffs. I confess that I cannot describe any of this to you! Truly, there is nothing small here, although a few things may be objectionable and tasteless; but even they reflect the general grandeur.

Returning now to myself, as one so gladly does at every opportunity, I discover a feeling that infinitely delights me, and that I shall even venture to put into words. No one can take a serious look around this city, if he has eyes to see, without becoming solid, without forming a more vivid concept of solidity than he has ever had before.

His mind becomes certified as capable, it achieves seriousness without growing prosaic, and a steadiness combined with joy. I, at any rate, feel as if I had never appreciated the things of this world as properly as here. I look forward to the beneficial effect this will have on my whole life.

So let me gather up whatever comes, and it will put itself in order. I am not here to enjoy in my usual way; I want to apply my mind to the great objects, learn, and educate myself before I reach the age of forty.

November 11.

Today I visited the nymph Egeria,[163] then the racetrack of Caracalla,[164] the ruined sepulchers along the Via Appia, and the tomb of Metella,[165] which shows me for the first time what solid masonry is. These people built for eternity, their calculations took everything into account except the madness of the ravagers, before which everything had to bow. With all my heart, Charlotte,[166] I wished that you were here with me. The remains of the great aqueduct merit the highest respect. What a fine, great plan it was to give the people water by means of such an enormous installation! In the evening we arrived at the Coliseum when it was already twilight. When one looks at it, everything else seems small. It is so huge that one cannot keep the image of it in mind; it is remembered as smaller, and when one goes back there it seems larger again.

Frascati, November 15.

The company has gone to bed, but I am still writing, dipping into the shell full of India ink that has been used for drawing. We have had a few beautiful, rain-free days here, warm and friendly sunshine, almost like summer. The district is very pleasant, the town is situated on a hill, or rather, on a mountainside, and every step offers the sketcher the most magnificent subjects. The view is unlimited, one sees Rome lying there, and the sea beyond it, the mountains of Tivoli to the right side, and so on. In this cheerful region the country houses are truly designed for pleasure, and just as the ancient Romans formerly had their villas here, so for over a hundred years rich and haughty Romans have also established theirs on the most beautiful spots. We have already been walking around here for two days, and there is always something new and charming.

And yet it is a question whether the evenings are not passed even more pleasurably than the days. As soon as our stately hostess has set the three-branched brass lamp on the big round table and said "Felicissima notte!" we all gather in a circle and display the drawings and sketches made during the day. We discuss whether the subject should have been approached from a more favorable angle, whether its character has been captured, and anything else of a similar, elementary, general nature that can be demanded even of a preliminary design. Aulic Councilor Reiffenstein has the discernment and authority to be able to regulate and guide these meetings. However, this laudable society was actually founded by Philipp Hackert,[167] who could draw and finish the real views in a very tasteful fashion. Artists and amateurs, men and women, old and young were given no peace by him, he urged them individually to try out their own talents and abilities also, and he led with his good example. This manner of assembling and entertaining a group was faithfully continued by Aulic Councilor Reiffenstein after his friend's departure, and we think it is very commendable to rouse each person to active participation. The nature and peculiar qualities of the various society members emerge in a pleasant way. Tischbein, for example, as a historical painter, looks at the landscape quite differently from the landscape artist. He finds significant groups and other charming, meaningful subjects where someone else would perceive nothing. Thus he succeeds in catching many a naive human feature, be it in children, countryfolk, beggars, and other such natural creatures, or even in animals. He knows how to depict the latter very successfully with a few characteristic strokes, and in this way always supplies pleasant new material for our entertainment.

If conversation falters, then, as another legacy from Hackert, we read from Sulzer's *Theory;*[168] and even though from a higher point of view this work is not completely satisfactory, still one notices with pleasure its good influence on persons who are at a middle stage of cultural development.

Rome, November 17.

We are back! During the night there was a terrible rainstorm with thunder and lightning, now it is still raining and yet the air is warm.

However, I can describe the happiness of this day in just a few words. I saw Dominichino's fresco paintings in Andrea della Valle,[169] as well as Carracci's Farnese gallery.[170] Actually too much for months, let alone for one day.

November 18.

The weather is fine again, a bright, warm, friendly day.

In the Farnesina I saw the story of Psyche,[171] colored copies of which have brightened my rooms for such a long time. Then at St. Peter's in Montorio, Raphael's *Transfiguration*.[172] All old acquaintances, like friends I have made at a distance through correspondence, and who now are seen face to face. Living together is, after all, something very different; every true affinity and lack of affinity immediately become evident.

Everywhere there are also superb things which are not talked about so much, which are not so often distributed throughout the world in prints and copies. I am taking along some of these, drawn by good young artists.

November 18.

The fact that I have been on the best terms with Tischbein for such a long time by letter, and that I so often told him of my desire to come to Italy (hopeless as that seemed), at once made our meeting pleasant and productive. He had always kept me in mind and planned for me. He is perfectly familiar even with the types of stones used by the ancients and the moderns for building; he has studied them thoroughly, and here his artist's eye and artist's delight in physical objects stand him in good stead. Not long ago he sent a collection of specimens to Weimar especially selected for me, which will welcome me on my return. In the meantime a significant supplement to it has been found. A priest, who is now in France,[173] intended to complete a work on ancient minerals and through the good offices of the Propaganda[174] acquired some quite large pieces of marble from the island of Paros. These were cut up into specimens here, and twelve different pieces were set aside for me, ranging from the finest to the coarsest grain, from the greatest purity to varying admixtures of mica, the former usable for sculpture, the latter for architecture. It is quite obvious that in judging the arts it is very helpful to have exact knowledge of the material used in them.

There is plenty of opportunity here to amass a collection of such things. On the ruins of Nero's palace[175] we walked through freshly dug-up artichoke fields and could not refrain from filling our pockets with small slabs of granite, porphyry, and marble, which lie around here by the thousands and still act as an inexhaustible supply of witnesses to the ancient splendor of the walls they formerly covered.

Addendum to November 18.

Now, however, I must speak of a strangely problematical picture, which nevertheless bears comparison with those excellent paintings I have seen. Quite some years ago a Frenchman,[176] well known as an art lover and collector, was living here. He came into possession, no one knows from what source, of an ancient painting on limestone. He had Mengs[177] restore the picture and kept it in his collection as an esteemed work. Winckelmann speaks of it somewhere with enthusiasm.[178] It depicts Ganymede as he extends a wine bowl to Jupiter and receives a kiss in return. The Frenchman died and bequeathed the picture to his landlady as an ancient work. Mengs died and said on his deathbed that it was *not* an ancient work, he had painted it himself. And now everyone is arguing with everyone else. One side claims that Mengs just tossed it off as a joke, the other side says that Mengs could never have painted such a thing, indeed that it is almost too beautiful for Raphael. I saw it yesterday and must say that I too know nothing more beautiful than the figure of Ganymede, head and back. The rest is much restored. Meanwhile the picture is discredited, and no one wants to relieve the poor woman of her treasure.

November 20, 1786.

Since experience amply teaches us that drawings and engravings are desired for all sorts of poems, and since indeed the painter himself will dedicate even his best executed pictures to a passage from some poem, Tischbein's idea of having poet and artist work together, thus achieving unity from the outset, merits the highest approbation. Of course the difficulty would be greatly diminished if the poems were short and could be easily produced and taken in at a glance.

Tischbein also has some very pleasant idyllic ideas for this, and it is really remarkable that the subjects he wants treated in this fashion are of a kind that neither the art of poetry nor of painting, by itself, could adequately depict. He has told me about them on our walks, hoping to interest me in becoming involved in this. He has already designed the frontispiece to our joint work; if I was not afraid of entering into something new, I might well let him prevail on me.

Rome, November 22, 1786, on St. Cecilia's day.

I must jot down a few lines to preserve a vivid memory of this happy day and to give at least a factual description of what I enjoyed. It was the finest, calmest weather, a perfectly clear sky and warm sun. I went with Tischbein to St. Peter's square, where first we strolled up and down, then, when it got too warm for us, walked in the shadow of the great obelisk, which is just wide enough for two people, and ate the grapes we had bought nearby. Then we entered the Sistine chapel, which we also found to be bright and cheerful, the paintings well lighted. *The Last Judgment* and the manifold ceiling paintings by Michelangelo shared our admiration equally. I could do nothing but gaze and marvel. The manliness and inner certainty of this master, and his grandeur, are beyond all words. After we had looked at everything again and again, we left this holy place and walked towards St. Peter's church, which was most beautifully illuminated by the sunny skies, every part of it looking bright and clearly defined. We, who were only seeking enjoyment, took delight in its great size and splendor, and did not let ourselves be perplexed this time by overnice and oversophisticated questions of taste. We suppressed all keener judgment and simply took pleasure in something pleasurable.

Finally we climbed up to the roof of the church, where one finds what looks like a well-built town in miniature. Houses and storehouses, fountains, churches (to judge from their appearance), and a big temple, all of this high in the air, with beautiful paths in between. We climbed to the top of the dome and viewed the bright and cheerful Apennine region, Mount Soracte, the volcanic hills toward Tivoli, Frascati, Castel Gandolfo, the Campagna, and beyond that the sea. Directly at our feet lay the city of Rome in its whole length and breadth, with its palace-crowned hills, its domes, etc. Not a breeze was stirring, and inside the copper lantern it was as hot as in a greenhouse. After we had absorbed all of that, we climbed down and asked to have the doors opened that lead to the cornices of the dome, the drum, and the nave. One can walk around them to view these parts and the church itself from above. While we were standing on the cornice of the drum, the pope went past below us to say his afternoon prayers. So we missed nothing in St. Peter's. We climbed all the way down again, dined merrily and frugally at a nearby tavern, and continued on our way to the church of St. Cecilia.[179]

I would need many words to describe the ornamentation of this church, which was completely filled with people. There was not a stone of the architecture to be seen. The columns were covered with red velvet and wound about with golden braid, their capitals covered with embroidered velvet approximately imitating their form, and all the cornices and pillars were thus draped and concealed. All the wall spaces between were hung with vividly painted pieces, so that the whole church seemed veneered with mosaic; and over two hundred wax candles burned around and beside the high altar, in such a manner that one whole wall was lined with lights and the church fully illuminated. The side aisles and side altars were similarly decorated and lighted up. Opposite the high altar, under the organ, were two platforms, also draped in velvet, on one of which stood the singers, on the other the instrumentalists, continuously making music. The church was packed full.

I heard a lovely type of musical presentation here. Just as there are concertos for violins or other instruments, so they perform vocal concertos in which one voice, for example the soprano, dominates and sings solo, while the chorus breaks in from time to time and accompanies it, always with the full orchestra, of course. It makes a good effect.— The day had to end, and I must close also. In the evening we still managed to reach the opera house, where the *Litiganti*[180] was being given. But we had enjoyed so many good things already that we walked past without entering.

November 23.

But to save my beloved incognito from the fate of the ostrich, which believes itself hidden when it buries its head, I make certain compromises, while still asserting my old thesis. I was glad to meet the Prince of Liechtenstein,[181] the brother of my very dear Countess Harrach,[182] and dined with him several times. Then I soon became aware that my complaisance would take me a step farther, and so it happened. The prelude had been made by telling me about an abbé named Monti[183] and his tragedy entitled *Aristodemus,* which was soon going to be performed. The author, it was said, wanted to read his work aloud to me and hear my opinion of it. I let the matter drop without actually refusing, but in the end I encountered the poet and one of his friends in the prince's lodgings, and the play was read aloud.

The hero, as is well known, is a king of Sparta, who commits suicide on account of various qualms of conscience; and I was given to understand in a courteous way that the author of *Werther* would probably not be offended to see that several passages from his excellent book were used in this play. And so even within the walls of Sparta I could not escape the angry shade of that unhappy youth.

The play has a very simple, quiet action, both sentiments and language are in keeping with the subject, powerful and yet gentle. The work bespeaks a very fine talent.

In my own way, not the Italian one, to be sure, I proceeded to emphasize all of the play's good and laudable points, which pleased the author well enough, but with southern impatience he demanded something more. I was especially asked to predict how good an effect the play might be expected to have on the audience. I pleaded ignorance of local taste and ways of presentation, but was frank enough to add that I did not quite see how the pampered Romans, who were used to seeing a complete three-act comedy with an interlude consisting of a two-act opera, or a grand opera with very odd ballets as an intermezzo, could find pleasure in the noble, quiet action of an uninterrupted tragedy. Besides, the subject of suicide seemed to me quite foreign to the Italian mind. The killing of other people was something I heard about almost every day; but so far it had not come to my attention that anyone had taken his own dear life, or even considered such a possibility.

Hereupon I gladly listened to whatever objections were raised against my disbelief, and I yielded very willingly to those plausible arguments. I also asserted that nothing would please me more than to see the play performed, and that I, with a chorus of friends, would applaud it most sincerely and loudly. This declaration was most amicably received, and this time I had every reason to be happy about my complaisance—and of course Prince Liechtenstein is the soul of kindness and has arranged opportunities for me to go along with him and see quite a number of artistic treasures for which one needs the owner's special permission and therefore the influence of a high personage.

On the other hand my good humor failed when the Pretender's[184] daughter also expressed a desire to see the foreign marmot. I refused that request and very definitely submerged again.

And yet that is not quite the right behavior either, and I feel very strongly here what I have perceived earlier in life, namely that the well-intentioned person must be just as active and nimble in his dealings with other people as the selfish, small, or wicked person. It is one thing to see this; quite another to act accordingly.

November 24.

The only thing I can say about this nation is that it is made up of primitive people who, under all their splendid trappings of religion and the arts, are not a whit different from what they would be if they lived in caves or forests. What particularly strikes foreigners, and today again is the talk of the entire city—but only talk—is the homicides that take place so routinely. Just in the last three weeks four persons have been murdered in our district. Today a fine artist named Schwendimann, a Swiss,[185] a maker of medallions, Hedlinger's[186] last pupil, was attacked, exactly like Winckelmann.[187] He struggled with the murderer, who inflicted some twenty stab wounds on him; and when the police arrived, the scoundrel stabbed himself to death. That is not the usual style here. The murderer manages to reach a church, and that ends the matter.

And so, in order also to introduce shaded areas into my paintings, I ought to report something about crimes and calamities, earthquakes and floods; indeed, the current eruption of fire from Vesuvius has most of the foreign visitors here on the move, and it is difficult to keep from being swept along with the tide. This natural phenomenon really has something of the rattlesnake about it and irresistibly attracts people. At this moment all of Rome's art treasures go for naught; the foreigners in a body are interrupting the course of their contemplations and rushing off to Naples. I, however, shall stand fast, hoping that the mountain will still keep something in reserve for me.

December 1.

Moritz,[188] who has attracted our attention with his *Anton Reiser* and *Journey to England,* is here. He is a pure, excellent man, whom we enjoy very much.

December 1.

Many foreigners are seen here in Rome, not all of whom visit this capital of the world for the sake of higher art. On the contrary, they seek other kinds of entertainment, and the Romans are prepared with a variety of such. There are certain demiarts, which require dexterity and a delight in handicraft. These have been highly developed here, and foreign visitors are encouraged to take an interest in them also.

One of these is encaustic painting. With its preliminaries and preparations and then finally with the firing and whatever else is involved, this can keep anyone who has had any experience with watercolors busy doing mechanical things; and the artistic merit, which is often slight, can seem greater owing to the novelty of the undertaking. There are skilled artists who give instruction in this and, on the pretext of offering guidance, do most of the work themselves. Then, when the picture, gleaming because it has been intensified by encaustic, is seen at last in its golden frame, the fair pupil stands there in complete surprise at her unsuspected talent.

Another pleasant occupation is to make impressions from hollow-cut stones in a fine clay. This is also done with medallions, both sides being reproduced at once.

Lastly, then, there is the process of making the actual glass replicas, which requires more skill, attention, and diligence. Aulic Councillor

Reiffenstein has all the implements and arrangements necessary for these things in his house or at least very near at hand.

December 2.

By chance I have found Archenholz's *Italy* here. A scribble of that sort certainly shrivels up in the locality itself, just as if one had laid the little book on hot coals, so that it gradually became brown and black, and the leaves curled and went up in smoke. He has seen the things, to be sure; but he has far too little knowledge to support his pompous, contemptuous manner, and he blunders both in his praise and his censure.

Rome, December 2, 1786.

It is something quite new to me to have beautiful, warm, calm weather, only occasionally interrupted by a few rainy days, at the end of November. We spend the nice days in the open, the bad ones in our rooms, and there is always something to enjoy, learn, and do.

On November 28th we returned to the Sistine chapel and had the gallery opened, where one has a closer view of the ceiling. It is admittedly very narrow, and one squirms along past the iron bars with some difficulty and seeming danger, for which reason those prone to vertigo do not go up. But it is all repaid by the sight of this supreme masterpiece. And at the moment I am so captivated by Michelangelo that even nature, compared to him, has lost its charm for me, since I cannot see it with his great eyes, after all. If there were only some means of truly fixing such pictures in my mind! At least I am taking along as many engravings and drawings of his works as I can lay my hands on.

From there we went to Raphael's loggias, and I hardly dare admit it, but we could not look at them. Our eyes were so dilated and so spoiled for anything else by those huge forms and the superb perfection of all the parts that we did not care to view the clever, playful arabesques; and the Biblical stories, as beautiful as they are, did not bear comparison with those others. It must be a great joy to contrast these works more frequently, and to compare them at greater leisure and without prejudice; for indeed interest always starts out as one-sided.

From there we strolled, in sunshine that was almost too warm, to the Villa Pamfili,[189] where there are very beautiful gardens, and we stayed until evening. A large level meadow bordered with live oaks and tall pines was entirely planted with oxeye daisies, all with their little faces turned to the sun. Now my botanical speculations started in, and I continued to indulge in them the next day on a walk to Monte Mario, the Villa Melini,[190] and the Villa Madama.[191] It is most interesting to observe the workings of a vegetation that is never dormant and is uninterrupted by severe cold; there are no buds here, and only now do I begin to understand what a bud really is. The strawberry tree *(arbutus unedo)* is blooming again now while its last fruits are ripening, and the orange tree also displays blossoms along with ripe and half-ripe fruits (yet the latter trees, if they do not stand between buildings, are now covered). The cypress, the most stately tree of all when quite old and well grown, gives me a great deal to think about. Very soon I shall visit the botanical garden[192] and hope to learn many things there. Nothing can compare with the new life a reflective individual receives from contemplating a new country. Although I am still the same person, I think I am changed to the very marrow of my bones.

I close for this time and shall fill up my next pages with calamities, murders, earthquakes, and misfortunes, so that some shadows also get into my paintings.

December 3.

So far, the atmospheric conditions have changed mostly in six-day cycles. Two quite splendid days, one that is gloomy, two or three rainy days, and then fine ones again. I try to make the best use of each one in its own way.

But these magnificent objects still seem like new acquaintances to me. I have not lived with them, have not determined their characteristics. Some of them seize us by force, so that for a while we are indifferent, nay, unjust to the others. Thus, for example, the Pantheon, the *Apollo Belvedere,* some colossal heads, and recently the Sistine chapel have so captivated my mind and heart that I see almost nothing anymore but them. But how can we, as small as we are and used to what is small, place ourselves on the same level with something so noble, so huge, so refined? And even if I could put it into some sort of order, I am beset again on all sides by another huge mass of things that meet me at every step, and each demands the tribute of attention for itself. And how will I extricate myself? The only way is patiently to let it grow and have its effect, and diligently to take note of what others have done to assist us.

The new edition of Winckelmann's history of art, in Fea's translation,[193] is a very useful work, which I obtained right away. Here on the spot, in the good company of people who can interpret and instruct, I find it very helpful.

The Roman antiquities are also beginning to delight me. History, inscriptions, coins, which I formerly neglected, all are thronging up to me. What I experienced in natural history is happening to me again, for the whole history of the world is linked with this city, and I count the day when I entered Rome as my second natal day, a true rebirth.

December 5.

In the few weeks that I have been here I have already seen many foreign visitors come and go, and I am amazed at how lightly most of them take these noble sights. I thank God that from now on none of these birds of passage will be able to impress me at home in the north when he speaks to me about Rome; not one will stir my heart again. For I have seen it too, after all, and already know fairly well what to make of it.

December 8.

Now and then we have the most beautiful days. The occasional rains that fall make the grass and potherbs green. Evergreen trees also stand here and there, so that the fallen leaves of the others are scarcely missed. Orange trees, full of fruit, stand in the gardens, growing right out of the ground and uncovered.

I was going to give a detailed account of a very pleasant excursion we made to the sea, and about the catch of fish, but then in the evening poor Moritz broke his arm while riding back, when his horse slipped on the smooth Roman pavement. That spoiled all our pleasure and badly disturbed the peace of our little circle.

Rome, December 13.

How sincerely pleased I am that you all have taken my disappearance entirely as I wished. Now reconcile me also with every heart that might have been offended by it. I did not want to hurt anyone, and cannot say anything to vindicate myself now, either. God forbid that I should ever grieve a friend by telling my reasons for this decision.

Now I am gradually recuperating from my *salto mortale*,[194] and devote myself more to study than to pleasure. Rome is a world, and one needs years just to find one's place in it. How fortunate those travelers are who merely look and leave!

This morning I happened to get hold of the letters Winckelmann wrote from Italy.[195] With what emotion I began to read them! He came here thirty-one years ago, at the same season, a still poorer fool than I, and he took the same serious German approach to a thorough and certain knowledge of the art and antiquities. How worthily and well he worked his way through! And how much the memory of this man means to me in this place!

Except for objects in nature, which is true and consistent in all its parts, nothing really speaks as loudly as the trail left by a good, intelligent man, or as genuine art, which is just as logical as nature. One can truly feel that here in Rome, where willfulness has run so wild, where money and power have perpetuated so many absurdities.

I was especially pleased with a passage in Winckelmann's letter to Franke:[196] "One has to be somewhat phlegmatic about looking for all the things in Rome, or else one is taken for a Frenchman. Rome, I believe, is all the world's university, and I too have been tested and purified."

These words correspond exactly with my way of investigating things here, and certainly, before coming to Rome, no one has a notion of how he will be schooled here. He must be, so to speak, reborn, and will look back on his former ideas as though they were children's shoes. The most ordinary person becomes something here, at least he gets an idea of the extraordinary, even if it cannot become a part of his nature.

This letter will be my greeting to you for the new year, and I wish all of you much happiness at its beginning; before its end we shall see each other again, and that will be no small pleasure. The past year has been the most important one in my life; it does not matter whether I die now or last a while longer, in either case I am content. Now, in closing, a word to the little ones.

You can read or relate the following to the children: It does not seem like winter, the gardens are planted with evergreen trees, the sunshine is bright and warm, snow can be seen only on the most distant mountains to the north. The lemon trees, which are planted next to the garden walls, are gradually being covered over with reed matting, but the orange trees remain without cover. Many hundreds of the most beautiful fruits hang on such a tree, which is not trimmed and planted in a tub, as in Germany, but stands glad and free in the earth in a row with its brothers. There is no prettier sight imaginable. One can eat as many of the oranges as one likes for a small gratuity. They are very good already, but will be still better in March.

Recently we were at the seaside and had a net put down for fish. It brought up the most oddly shaped creatures, fish, crabs, and curious monstrosities, also the fish that gives an electric shock to anyone who touches it.

December 20.

And yet all that is more trouble and worry than enjoyment. The rebirth, which is remolding me from within, is still in progress. I certainly expected to learn something worthwhile here; but I did not imagine that I would have to go so far back in school and unlearn, indeed relearn, so much in a thoroughly different way. Now, however, I am truly convinced and have submitted totally; and the more of myself I must renounce, the happier it makes me. I am like an architect who wants to raise a tower but has laid a poor foundation for it; he perceives that just in time and gladly pulls down what he has already erected, tries to expand and ennoble his plan, to become surer of his base, and rejoices beforehand in the more reliable solidity of the future edifice. May God grant that when I return, the moral consequences of having lived in a wider world will also be manifest in me. Yes, along with my artistic sense my moral one is undergoing a great renovation.

Doctor Münter[197] is here, having returned from his trip to Sicily. He is an energetic, vehement man; I do not know what his goals are. In May he will go to Germany and have much to tell all of you. He has traveled in Italy for two years. He is unhappy with the Italians because they have not sufficiently honored the significant letters of recommendation he brought with him, and which were supposed to give him access to many an archive, many a private library. And so he has not fully accomplished what he desired.

He has collected beautiful coins and owns a manuscript, so he told me, that explains numismatics on the basis of well-defined distinguishing marks, like those of Linné. Herder will probably make further inquiries about it, and perhaps a copy will be permitted. Such a thing is possible to make, good, once it is made, and, after all, we must delve into this subject more seriously sooner or later.

December 25.

I am already beginning to see the best things for the second time, and find my first amazement giving way to a feeling of companionship with the object and to a purer sense of its worth. In order for the mind to absorb the highest concept of what these people have accomplished, it must first attain absolute freedom.

Marble is a remarkable material, which is why the *Apollo Belvedere* is so immensely pleasing. For the finest bloom of this living, youthfully free, eternally young being fades at once even in the best plaster cast.

Across from us in the Rondanini palace stands a Medusa mask[198] which expresses the anxious stare of death with ineffable precision in the nobly beautiful form of its larger than life-size face. I already possess a good cast of it, but the spell of the marble has been lost. The elegant semitransparency of the yellowish, nearly flesh-colored stone has disappeared. The plaster always looks chalky and dead in comparison.

And yet what a joy it is to enter a cast maker's workshop, where one sees the magnificent limbs of the statues issue individually from the molds and so obtains entirely new views of the figures. Things that are scattered all over Rome are seen here side by side, which is an invaluable aid to comparison. I was not able to resist purchasing a colossal head of Jupiter.[199] It stands opposite my bed, in a good light, so that I can immediately direct my devotions to it in the morning. For all its grandeur and dignity, however, it has provided us with a most amusing little story.

When our old landlady comes in to make the bed, her beloved cat usually slinks in after her. I was sitting in our big room and heard the woman going about her work in there. All at once, and with unaccustomed haste and vehemence, she opened the door and shouted that I should come in quickly to see a miracle. When I asked what it was, she replied that the cat was worshipping God the Father. She said that she had long since noticed that this animal had the intelligence of a Christian, but this was really a great miracle. I hurried to see this with my own eyes, and it truly was quite remarkable. The bust stands on a high base, and the body is cut off much below the chest, so that the head accordingly juts into the air. Now the cat had leapt on the table, had placed her paws on the god's chest, and, stretching her limbs to the utmost, had stuck her muzzle right into the sacred beard. This she was licking with the greatest daintiness, and was not disturbed in the least either by the landlady's exclamations or my interference. I allowed the good woman her amazement, but my own explanation for this curious feline worship was that the animal with its acute sense of smell probably detected the grease from the mold that had settled into the recesses of the beard and been preserved there.

December 29, 1786.

There is still much to tell in praise of Tischbein, how he developed himself, on his own, into something entirely original and German; then I must declare my gratitude to him because during his whole second sojourn in Rome he very kindly saw to my interests by having a series of copies of the best masters made for me, some in black chalk, others in sepia and watercolors. These will attain their true value once I am back in Germany and far removed from the originals, for then they will bring the best things back to mind.

In the course of his artistic career, since he at first intended to be a portrait painter, Tischbein came into contact with significant men, especially in Zurich, and that helped him to strengthen his feeling and broaden his understanding.

I was made doubly welcome for bringing the second part of *Scattered Leaves*[200] along with me here. Herder ought to have the reward of hearing in great detail about the impact this little book has even after repeated readings. Tischbein could not fathom how anyone could have written something like it without having been in Italy.

December 29.

Living in this artistic milieu is like being in a room full of mirrors, where there is no way to avoid seeing oneself and others reflected many times. I noticed that Tischbein was often closely observing me, and now it comes out that he plans to paint my portrait. His design is finished, he has already stretched the canvas. I am to be presented life-size as a traveler wrapped in a white cloak, sitting in the open air on a fallen obelisk and surveying the ruins of the Campagna, which are located far in the background.[201] That makes a beautiful picture, but one too large for our northern houses. No doubt I shall creep back into their shelter, but there will be no room for the portrait.

December 29.

Moreover, I do not waver, in spite of all the attempts that are made to draw me out of my obscurity, and the poets who read their works aloud to me or have them read, and the fact that I would merely have to express the wish if I wanted to play a role in affairs; and it rather amuses me, because I have now observed enough to know how things operate in Rome. For the many little social circles at the feet of the mistress of the world now and then betray a certain provincialism.

Yes, it is the same here as everywhere, and I am bored with whatever might be done with me and through me, even before it happens. One must join a party, help to defend their enthusiasms and cabals, praise artists and dilettantes, belittle competitors, and agree with everything said by the rich and great. On account of this whole litany one would like to run from the world, and I am expected to join in and chant it here, to no purpose whatever?

No, I shall only go in deeply enough to be sure of that, and then stay at home satisfied in this regard also, and disabuse myself and others of all desire for the great wide world. I want to see the enduring Rome, not the one that passes away every ten years. Even if I had the time,

I would want to make better use of it. From this vantage point, history especially is read differently from anywhere else in the world. In other places one reads from the outside in, here we imagine we are reading from the inside out, everything lies spread around us and also extends out from us. And that holds true not only of Roman history, but also of all world history. From here I can accompany the conquerors as far as the Weser and the Euphrates. Or, if I am content merely to gape, I can await the returning conquerors in the Sacred Street and partake of all this magnificence in comfort, having been supported meanwhile by gifts of grain and money.

January 2, 1787.

Say what one will in favor of written and oral communication, it is very rarely adequate, for it cannot transmit the actual character of any entity, not even in intellectual matters. But if one first has taken a careful look, then one is glad to read and hear, for that joins itself to the living impression; now one can think and judge.

You have all often scoffed and wanted to pull me back when, with special fondness, I observed stones, plants, and animals from certain definite points of view; now I am directing my attention to architects, sculptors, and painters, and shall learn to find my way here also.

January 6.

I have just been to see Moritz, whose arm is healed and was unbound today. He is getting along quite well. What I have seen and learned in the past forty days,[202] while serving this patient as nurse, confessor, and confidant, as finance minister and privy secretary, may subsequently be of advantage to us. During this time, the most wretched suffering always went hand in hand with the noblest pleasures.

Yesterday, for my edification, I set up the cast of a colossal head of Juno[203] in our salon; its original stands in the Villa Ludovisi. This was my first love in Rome, and now I own it. No words can give an idea of it. It is like a song of Homer's.

But surely I have earned the right to have such good company near me in the future, for now I can announce that *Iphigenia* is finished at last. That is to say, two fairly identical copies are lying before me on my table, one of which will soon be on its way to you. Be kind to it, for admittedly what you will find on this paper is not what I was supposed to write; but no doubt you will be able to divine what I was trying to do.

You have all complained several times about obscure passages in

my letters which indicate that in the midst of these most splendid sights
I was oppressed by a burden. My Grecian traveling companion had no
little part in this, for she kept urging me to work, when I should have
been looking at things.

I was reminded of that excellent friend of mine who had made arrangements for a long journey; indeed it could have been called a voyage
of exploration. After he had studied and economized for several years
in preparation for it, finally he took it into his head to elope with the
daughter of an eminent family, thinking that he could kill two birds
with one stone.

I resolved just as wantonly to take *Iphigenia* along to Carlsbad. I
shall briefly record at which places I especially passed my time with
her.

When I left the Brenner, I withdrew her from the largest packet and
put her in my pocket. At Lake Garda, while the powerful noonday
wind was driving the waves onto the shore, and where I was at least
as alone as my heroine was on the shore of Tauris, I drafted the first
lines of the new version, which I continued in Verona, Vicenza, Padua,
but most diligently of all in Venice. Then, however, the work came to
a standstill, and I was led to invent something new, namely, to write
"Iphigenia on Delphi."[204] Moreover I would have done so at once, if
I had not been hindered by distractions and a sense of duty towards
the older play.

But in Rome the work went on with due persistence. In the evening
before going to sleep I would prepare for the next morning's task, which
I would attack immediately upon awakening. My method was quite
simple: I would calmly transcribe the play and read it aloud in a regular
rhythm, line for line, period for period. What resulted from that is for
you to judge. The process was more one of learning than of doing.
Several additional comments are being sent along with the play.

January 6.

That I may speak once again on ecclesiastical subjects, I shall relate
that we roamed around on Christmas Eve and visited the churches
where services are held. One in particular is very well attended, where
the organ and the music in general are structured in such a way that
none of the typical sounds of pastoral music are missing, neither the
shepherds' shawms, nor the twittering of the birds, nor the bleating of
the sheep.

On Christmas day I saw the pope and the whole clergy in St. Peter's,
where he celebrated high mass partly in front of his throne, partly while
sitting on it. The spectacle is unique in its way, splendid and quite

dignified, but I am such a long-time Protestant Diogenist that I find
this magnificence more repellent than attractive. Like my pious pred-
ecessor I would wish to say to these ecclesiastical world conquerors:
"Do not hide the sun of higher art and pure humanity from me."

Today being Epiphany, I have seen and heard the mass celebrated
according to the Greek ritual. The ceremonies seemed to me more
stately, more austere, more thought-provoking, and yet of a more popular nature than the Latin ones.

But even there I felt again that I am too old for anything except truth.
Their ceremonies and operas, their processions and ballets, all of that
runs off me like water off an oilcloth cloak. On the other hand, a natural
phenomenon, like the sunset seen from the Villa Madama, or an artwork
like my much-honored Juno, make a deep and lasting impression on
me.

Now I am already shuddering to think of the theater season. Next
week seven theaters will be opened.[205] Anfossi[206] himself is here and
is giving *Alexander in India;* a *Cyrus* will be given too, and *The Conquest
of Troy* as a ballet. The children would enjoy that.

January 10.

So, then, this letter will be followed by my child of sorrows, for
Iphigenia deserves this sobriquet in more than one respect. While
reading it aloud to our artists I marked several lines, some of which I
have improved to the best of my ability; others I have let stand, hoping
that perhaps Herder will want to insert a few strokes of his pen. I have
grown quite dull working on it.

The real reason that I have preferred to work in prose for the last
several years is that our prosody is in an extremely uncertain condition.
Accordingly, my discerning, learned friends and colleagues have relied
on their feeling and taste to decide many questions, a procedure lacking
in all guiding principles.

I would never have ventured to transpose *Iphigenia* into iambs, if a
guiding star had not appeared to me in the form of Moritz's *Prosody*.[207]
My association with the author, especially during the time he was confined to bed, enlightened me still more, and I entreat my friends to give
it their favorable consideration.

It is a striking fact that we find only a few syllables in our language
that are definitely short or long. The rest are treated according to our
taste or caprice. Now Moritz has puzzled out a certain order of precedence among syllables, according to which a syllable with more significant meaning, juxtaposed to another of lesser meaning, becomes
long, while making the latter short. The former, however, will become

short again if it happens to be near a syllable of still greater intellectual weight. Here, then, at least we have a basis, and even if it is not definitive, surely for the time being it provides a guideline that one can cling to. I have frequently consulted this maxim and found it in agreement with my instincts.

Having spoken earlier about a reading, I must briefly describe how it went. These young men, being accustomed to my earlier vehement, vigorous works, had expected something in the *Berlichingen* style,[208] and could not immediately become reconciled to the calm pace; but the pure and noble passages did not fail to make their effect. Although Tischbein could hardly accept this almost total abandonment of vehement emotion, he created an appropriate image or symbol for it. He compared it to a sacrifice whose smoke, kept from rising by a gentle atmospheric pressure, travels along the ground, thus giving the flame more liberty to shoot upwards. He drew this very prettily and significantly. I am enclosing the page from his sketchbook.

And so this work, which I intended to put behind me quickly, has for a full three months claimed and delayed me, occupied and tormented me. This is not the first time I have neglected what was most important, and let us not worry and argue about it any further.

I am enclosing a prettily carved stone, a little lion with a gadfly buzzing at its nose. The ancients loved this subject and used it repeatedly. I want you all in future to seal your letters with this little trinket, so that by means of it a kind of artistic echo will resound from you over to me.

January 13, 1787.

How much I could have written every day, and how greatly I am held back by exertions and distractions from putting an intelligent word down on paper! Moreover, there are some cool days, when it is better to be anywhere than in our rooms, which have neither stoves nor fireplaces, so that they are only comfortable for sleeping in. Nevertheless I must not pass over a few happenings of the last week.

In the Giustiniani palace stands a Minerva[209] that I profoundly revere. Winckelmann scarcely mentions it, at least not in the right place, and I do not feel myself worthy enough to say anything about it. When we viewed the statue, taking a long time to do so, the custodian's wife told us that this used to be a sacred image, and the *Inglesi,* who followed this religion, still were accustomed to honor it by kissing one of its hands. And actually this hand was completely white, whereas the rest of the statue was brownish. She added that a lady of this religion had recently been there, had kneeled down, and worshipped the statue.

She, as a Christian, had not been able to look at such a curious action without laughing, and had run from the room so as not to explode. Since I could not tear myself away from the statue either, she asked me if I by any chance had a sweetheart who resembled this marble image, to make it attract me so strongly. The good woman knew only worship and love, and had no notion about the pure admiration of a magnificent work, or of one's fraternal respect for a human spirit. We were pleased about the English girl, and left, hoping to return; and I certainly shall go there soon again. If my friends want to be informed in greater detail, they should read what Winckelmann says about the *high* style of the Greeks. Unfortunately, he does not adduce this Minerva. If I am not mistaken, however, she belongs to that high, austere style just as it is merging into the beautiful style, the opening bud, and a Minerva besides, whose character is so very suitable for this transition!

Now about a spectacle of a different kind! On Epiphany, the festival of the salvation proclaimed to the heathen, we were in the Propaganda. There, in the presence of three cardinals and a large audience, the first item was a discourse on the subject: where did Mary receive the three Magi, in the stable or elsewhere? Then, after the reading of several Latin poems on the same subject, some thirty seminarians stepped up, one after the other, and read short poems, each in his native language: Malabaric,[210] Epirotic,[211] Turkish, Moldavian,[212] Elenic,[213] Persian, Colchian,[214] Hebrew, Arabic, Syrian, Coptic, Saracenic,[215] Armenian, Hibernian,[216] Madagascarian,[217] Icelandic, Bohemian, Egyptian, Greek, Isaurian,[218] Ethiopian, etc., and several whose names I could not catch. The little poems, mostly in the respective national meters, seemed to be recited in the respective national styles of declamation, for barbaric rhythms and sounds came forth. The Greek rang out like a star appearing at night. The audience laughed loudly at the foreign voices, and so this presentation too turned into a farce.

One more little story about how frivolously holy things are treated in holy Rome. The late Cardinal Albani[219] was in a festive assembly of the kind I have just described. One of the schoolboys, turning to the cardinals, began to say "Gnaja! gnaja!" ("Worship! worship!") in such a strange dialect that it sounded approximately like "Canaglia! canaglia!" Albani turned to his fellow cardinals and said, "That one obviously knows us!"

January 13.

How much Winckelmann left undone, and how much he left us to wish for! The reason he built so swiftly with the materials he had acquired was to get them under roof. Were he still living—and he could still be vigorous and healthy—he would be the first one to give us a revision of his work. How much more he would have observed and corrected, how much he would have used of what others, following his principles, have done, observed, newly excavated, and discovered. And then too, Cardinal Albani, for whose sake he wrote, and perhaps withheld, so much, would be dead.

January 15, 1787.

And so at last *Aristodemus* has been performed, and indeed very successfully, to the greatest applause. Since Abbé Monti has a family connection with the *Nepote*[220] and is highly esteemed by the upper classes, a good reception was to be expected from them—and indeed the loges did not spare their applause. The parterre was won over right from the start by the poet's beautiful diction and the actors' excellent recitation, and missed no opportunity to make its satisfaction evident. The German artists' bench distinguished itself particularly, since it is always a little boisterous; but this time that was quite appropriate.

The author had remained at home, full of worry about the success of his play, but gradually his apprehensiveness turned into the greatest joy, as favorable reports came in from act to act. Now the performance will surely be repeated, and everything is proceeding very well. Thus the most disparate things, provided that each has its own distinct merit, can please both the crowd and the connoisseurs.

But the performance was also very commendable, and the principal actor, who dominates the whole play, spoke and acted superbly; I thought I was seeing one of the ancient emperors on the stage. They had done very well at creating a splendid theatrical version of the costume that impresses us so much on the statues, and it was evident that the actor had studied the antiquities.

January 16.

Rome faces a great artistic loss. The King of Naples[221] is having the *Farnese Hercules*[222] brought to his capital. All the artists are grieving, but meanwhile this will be an opportunity for us to see something that was concealed from our predecessors.

The statue in question, that is to say, from the head to the knees, plus the feet below and the base on which they stand, were found on Farnese property; but the lower legs were missing. These were replaced by Guglielmo Porta,[223] and it has stood on them up to the present day. In the meantime the genuine ancient legs had been found on Borghese property, whereupon, of course, they were displayed in the Villa Borghese.

Now Prince Borghese[224] has brought himself to present these choice remains to the King of Naples. The Porta legs are being removed and replaced by the genuine ones, and although the former were previously found quite satisfactory, we now expect an entirely new perception and more harmonious enjoyment.

January 18.

Yesterday being the festival of St. Anthony the Abbot, we made a merry day for ourselves; it was the finest weather in the world, there had been frost during the night, but the day was warm and bright.

It can be observed that all religions which have expanded either their public worship or their theological speculations eventually have had to grant a certain participation in ecclesiastical favors even to animals. St. Anthony, the abbot or bishop, is the patron of four-footed creatures, his festival a saturnalian holiday for the usually burdened animals and for their keepers and drivers as well. All gentlefolk must stay at home on this day or go on foot. Invariably, dubious stories are told concerning aristocratic unbelievers who obliged their coachmen to drive on this day and were punished with very serious accidents.

The church is built on a square so vast that it could almost be called desolate, but on this day it is very busy and cheerful. Horses and mules, their manes and tails beautifully, indeed gorgeously interwoven with ribbons, are led before a little chapel somewhat removed from the church. There a priest armed with a large whisk sprinkles holy water unsparingly on the gaily decorated beasts, from the butts and tubs that stand before him. He does this roughly, sometimes even roguishly, to provoke them. Devout coachmen bring along larger or smaller candles, their masters send alms and presents, so that their useful, expensive animals may be kept safe from all accidents for the coming year. Donkeys and horned cattle, equally useful and valuable to their owners, likewise receive their allotted share of this blessing.

Afterwards we diverted ourselves with a long walk under such a happy sky, surrounded by the most interesting sights, to which we now paid slight attention, preferring to let joking and merriment reign completely.

January 19.

So the great king, whose fame carried throughout the world, whose deeds would even make him worthy of the Catholic Paradise, has also finally departed this life and is conversing with heroes of his ilk in the realm of the shades.[225] How willing one is to observe a moment of silence when such a man has been laid to rest.

Today we gave ourselves a good time: we viewed a part of the Capitol that I had neglected until now, then we crossed the Tiber and drank Spanish wine on a ship that just landed. It is claimed that Romulus and Remus were found in this area, and so, as though this were a doubled and tripled Pentecost festival, we could become intoxicated simultaneously with the sacred spirit of art, the mildest weather, antiquarian memories, and Spanish wine.

January 20.

Something that in the beginning provided pure enjoyment, when it was approached superficially, later becomes a troublesome burden on the mind, when one sees that without thorough knowledge there can be no true enjoyment.

I am fairly well trained in anatomy and, not without effort, have acquired a certain degree of knowledge about the human body. Here, as a result of endlessly contemplating statues, my attention is constantly drawn to it, but in a loftier manner. In our medical-surgical anatomy it is just a question of recognizing a part, and even a wretched muscle will serve. In Rome, however, parts mean nothing unless they go together to make a noble, beautiful form.

In the great San Spirito hospital[226] a very beautiful écorché figure has been set up for the use of artists. The beauty of it is amazing; it could really be looked upon as a flayed demigod, a Marsyas.

Thus, guided by the ancients, we are accustomed to study the skeleton complete with its musculature, not as just a mass of bones artificially strung together, and so it acquires life and movement.

If I now mention that in the evening we also study perspective, that is surely proof we are not idle. But, for all that, we always intend to do more than we actually accomplish.

January 22.

It can well be said of artistic sense and artistic life in Germany: one hears ringing, but no chiming. When I think now of the magnificent things in our vicinity and of the scant use I made of them, I could almost despair; and then I look forward again to my return home, when I can expect to understand those masterpieces I merely groped around on.

But even in Rome too little provision is made for someone who seriously wants to study his way into the total concept. He must piece it all together from innumerable, although extremely valuable ruins. Admittedly, few foreign visitors are truly serious about seeing and learning anything worthwhile. They follow their own whims, their own notions, and of course that fact is not lost on those who have to do with them. Every guide has particular ends in view, each one tries to recommend some tradesman or promote some artist, and why not? Does not the inexperienced visitor spurn the most superb things that are offered him?

It would have been a tremendous advantage to study, indeed a special museum would have come into being, if the government, which has to grant permission before any ancient relic can be exported, had firmly demanded that a plaster cast of the item always be furnished. But even if a pope had had such an idea, there would have been general opposition, for in a few years people would have been appalled at the value and importance of the things that had been exported, since permission to do so in individual cases can be obtained secretly and by various means.

January 22.

Even before the performance of *Aristodemus,* but especially then, the patriotism of our German artists awoke. They did not leave off praising my *Iphigenia,* individual passages were asked for again, and finally I found myself required to repeat the whole play for them. Then I discovered again that many a passage came more smoothly from my lips than it was written down on paper. Of course, poetry is not made for the eye.

Its good reputation now reached the ears of Reiffenstein and Angelica.[227] and I was bidden to perform my work again for them. I requested some delay, but at once explained the plot and action of the play in some detail. This presentation won greater approval from the persons mentioned than I thought it would, and even Mr. Zucchi, from whom I expected it least, was very openly and sensitively interested in it. However, this can be explained very well by the fact that the play approaches the form that has long been familiar in Greek, Italian, and French drama, and which still remains the most appealing one to a person who has not yet become accustomed to the English audacities.

Rome, January 25, 1787.

Now it is constantly getting harder for me to give an account of my

Roman sojourn; for just as the sea is found to be ever deeper, the farther one goes into it, so it is with me in my inspection of this city.

The present cannot be understood without the past, and comparison of the two requires more time and leisure. The very location of this capital of the world leads us back to the building of it. We soon see that it was not a large, competently led, nomadic tribe which settled here and wisely established the hub of a realm; no powerful prince chose this as the appropriate place for a colony to dwell. No, shepherds and riffraff were the first to take up their abode here, and a pair of robust youths laid the foundation for the palaces of the rulers of the world on a hill at whose foot they had once been deposited, between swamps and reeds, by the caprice of an obedient servant. Accordingly, the seven hills of Rome do not rise toward the land lying behind them, but toward the Tiber and the primeval bed of the Tiber, which became the Campus Martius. If further excursions are possible for me in the spring, I shall describe the unfortunate location more extensively. I already feel a cordial sympathy with the sorrows of the Alban women,[228] wailing and lamenting as they saw their town destroyed. They had to forsake a place selected by a clever leader, in order to live among the fogs of the Tiber and dwell on the miserable hill Coelius, from which they could look back at their lost paradise. As yet, I know little of the region, but I am convinced that no other town of the ancient world is situated as poorly as Rome. And when the Romans had at last used up all their land, they had to move outside with their country villas, back to the sites of the ruined towns, in order to live and enjoy life.

January 25.

The many people who live here quietly, each of them occupied in his own fashion, offer a subject for very peaceful meditations. At the house of a cleric who, though without great native talent, has devoted his whole life to art, we saw very interesting copies he has done in miniature of some excellent paintings. His choicest one was of Leonardo da Vinci's *Last Supper* in Milan. The moment seized is when Christ, sitting happily and amicably at table with the disciples, declares and says: "Verily I say unto you, that one of you shall betray me."

There is hope that a print will be made either from this copy or from others that are being worked on. It will be the greatest gift to the general public, if a faithful copy is published.

A few days ago I visited Pater Jacquier,[229] a Franciscan, at Trinità de' Monti. He is a Frenchman by birth, known for his mathematical writings, advanced in years, very pleasant and intelligent. He knew the best men of his time, and even spent a few months with Voltaire, who had great affection for him.

And so I have met still other good, solid men, who are here in vast numbers, but are kept apart by priestly mistrust. The book trade provides no connections, and new literary productions rarely bring any benefit.

And so it befits the solitary person to seek out the hermits. For after the performance of *Aristodemus,* which we had really been instrumental in furthering, I was led into temptation again. But it was only too obvious that the interest was not in me personally, but in strengthening a party, in using me as an instrument; and if I had been willing to step forward and declare myself, I could have played a brief phantom role. Now, however, since they see that I am not to be swayed, they let me alone, and I continue to walk my sure path.

Yes, my existence has taken on ballast, which gives it the proper weight; now I am no longer afraid of the ghosts that so often played with me. Be of good cheer, you will hold me above water and pull me back to you.

January 28, 1787.

Since they have become clear to me, I shall not fail to indicate two meditative thoughts, which permeate everything and to which I am bidden to return at every moment.

First, then, this city possesses enormous riches, but they are all in ruins, and in the case of every object I feel called upon to determine the era which produced it. Winckelmann urgently spurs us on to separate the epochs, to recognize the various national styles, which in the course of time were gradually developed and eventually spoiled. Every true art lover became convinced of this. We all acknowledge the justice and importance of the demand.

But how to obtain this insight! Little preliminary work has been done. While the concept has been correctly and magnificently put forward, the individual details are obscure and uncertain. It requires years of thoroughly training the eye, and one must learn before one can ask. It is useless to waver and hesitate, for attention is now actively being given to this important point, and everyone who takes the matter seriously can see that no judgment is possible in this field unless it can be developed historically.

The second thought is concerned exclusively with the art of the Greeks and aims at discovering how those incomparable artists went about developing their circle of godly figures—which is perfectly complete and lacking neither any main features nor the transitions and intermediate stages—out of the human form. My supposition is that they proceeded according to the same laws by which nature proceeds, and which I am tracking down. But something else is involved that I cannot put into words.

February 2, 1787.

Unless a person has walked through Rome in the light of the full moon he cannot imagine the beauty of it. All individual details are swallowed up in the great masses of light and shadow, and only the largest, most general images present themselves to the eye. For three days we have been thoroughly enjoying the brightest and most splendid nights. The Coliseum offers a particularly beautiful sight. It is closed at night, a hermit lives there in his tiny little church, and beggars nest in the dilapidated archways. They had laid a fire on the level floor, and a quiet breeze drove the smoke first toward the arena, so that the lower part of the ruins was covered and the huge walls above jutted out over it darkly. We stood at the grating and watched the phenomenon, while the moon stood high and clear in the sky. Gradually the smoke drifted through the walls, holes, and openings, looking like fog in the moonlight. It was an exquisite sight. This is how one must see the Pantheon, the Capitol, the forecourts of St. Peter's, and other great streets and squares illuminated. And so the sun and the moon, just like the human spirit, are quite differently employed here than in other places, here, where their gaze meets huge and yet refined masses.

February 13.

I must mention a stroke of luck, albeit a minor one. But all good fortune, large or small, is of a kind, and always welcome. The foundation for a new obelisk is being dug at Trinità de' Monti,[230] up there where the ground is composed of fill from the ruins of the gardens of Lucullus, which later became the property of the emperors. My wigmaker went by there this morning and in the rubble found a flat pottery shard with some figures, washed it, and showed it to us. I immediately appropriated it. Not quite as big as my hand, it seems to have come from the rim of a large bowl. Two griffons are standing at an altar table; they are most beautifully done and delight me very much. If they were on a carved stone, how gladly I would seal letters with it!

Many other items are being added to my collection, none of them pointless or empty, for that would be impossible here; they are all instructive and significant. But dearest to me is what I am taking along in my mind, an amount that is growing and can be constantly increased.

February 15.

Before my departure for Naples I could not avoid giving one last
additional reading of my *Iphigenia*. Madame Angelica and Aulic Councilor Reiffenstein were the auditors, and even Mr. Zucchi had insisted
on attending, because his wife wanted to. Meanwhile he kept working
on a large architectural drawing, something he knows how to do exceedingly well in a decorative style. He was in Dalmatia with Clérisseau,[231] had actually entered into partnership with him, and drew the
illustrations for the latter's edition of the buildings and ruins. While
doing this, he learned so much about perspective and effects that in
his old age he can still worthily amuse himself by using his skills on
paper.

The play made an incredibly deep impression on Angelica's tender
soul. She promised to create a drawing from it, which I should keep
as a souvenir. And now, just as I am preparing to leave Rome, I am
forming affectionate bonds with these kind people. It is at once a pleasant and a painful feeling to be certain that they do not like to see me
go.

February 16, 1787.

The safe arrival of *Iphigenia* was announced to me in a surprising
and pleasant manner. On my way to the opera I was brought a letter
written in a well-known hand, doubly welcome this time because it was
sealed with the little lion, as a token, for the time being, of the safe
arrival of the packet. I pushed my way into the opera house and in the
midst of this crowd of strangers tried to find a seat under the big chan-
delier. Here I felt myself brought so close to my friends that I would
have liked to jump up and embrace them. My cordial thanks for reporting the bare arrival, and may you accompany your next letter with
a kind word of approval!

Here follows the list of how I want the copies that I expect to receive
from Göschen divided among my friends. For while the public's opinion
of these things is a matter of complete indifference to me, I nevertheless
hope that they may give my friends some pleasure.

But a person tends to undertake too much. When I think of my last
four volumes as a whole, I almost grow dizzy; I must attack them individually, and then it will be all right.

Would I not have done better to stay with my first resolve, which
was to send these things out into the world in fragmentary form, after
which, with fresh courage and energy, I could have undertaken new
subjects, in which I had a fresher interest? Would I not do better to
write "Iphigenia on Delphi" than to struggle with the melancholy fancies

of *Tasso?* And yet I have also put too much of my own self into this
for me to leave it unfinished.

I have sat down by the fireplace in the vestibule, where the warmth
of what is, for once, a well-fueled fire gives me fresh courage to begin
a new page. For it is really very wonderful indeed that one can reach
so far into the distance with one's newest thoughts, indeed can remove
one's immediate surroundings, by means of words, to that distant point.

The weather is quite splendid, the days are growing markedly longer,
laurels and box trees are in bloom, also the almond trees. This morning
I was surprised by a remarkable sight: I saw from a distance high, pole-
like trees densely covered in the most beautiful violet. Closer investigation revealed that it was the tree known in our hothouses by the
name Jew tree, but called *cercis siliquastrum* by botanists. Its violet
papilionacious flowers are produced right on the trunk. The poles I saw
before me had been stripped of twigs last winter, and now the well-
formed, colorful flowers were bursting forth from the bark by the thousands. Oxeye daisies are emerging from the ground like hordes of ants;
crocuses and adonises appear more rarely, but look all the daintier and
more decorative.

What joys and revelations are no doubt in store for me in the more
southerly land, and what results these will bring me! It is the same with
natural things as with art: so much is written about them, and yet anyone
who sees them can arrive at new conclusions in regard to them.

When I think of Naples, indeed also of Sicily, what I hear and what
I see in pictures impresses me with the fact that these paradises of the
world are also where a volcanic hell violently opens up, and for thousands of years has startled and dismayed those who live there so en-
joyably.

But I am glad to banish all thought of those very significant scenes
from my mind, so that I may make proper use of this ancient capital
of the world once more before my departure.

For two weeks I have been on my feet from morning to night; what
I have not yet seen, I go to see. The very best things are being viewed
for the second and third time, and now some sort of order is emerging.
For as the principal objects assume their correct positions, sufficient
room is left between them for many lesser things. My affections are
being purified and determined, and only now can my spirit rise to meet
what is greater and most genuine with calm interest.

Yet I envy the artist, who, by imitating and reproducing, comes closer
in every way to those great intentions, and understands them better,
than the mere viewer and thinker. But in the last analysis everyone
must do what he is able to, and so I unfurl the sails of my spirit and
try to navigate these coasts.

The fireplace is really thoroughly warmed now, heaped up with the

finest coals, a rare event at our place because no one is likely to have
the time or desire to devote a few hours of attention to the fire; and
so I shall take advantage of this lovely atmosphere to rescue some
already half-obliterated remarks from my slate.

On February second we went to the Sistine chapel for a service held
to consecrate the candles. I immediately felt uncomfortable and soon
left again with my friends. For I thought: those are the very candles
that have darkened these magnificent paintings for three hundred years,
and that is the same incense which, with holy impudence, has not only
clouded this unique artistic sun, but from year to year has made it
dimmer, and will finally plunge it into darkness.

After that we sought the open air and at the end of a long walk reached
San Onofrio, in a corner of which Tasso lies buried. His bust stands
in the monastery library. The face is of wax, and I am willing to believe
that it is an actual death mask. Although not quite sharply defined, and
decayed in places, on the whole it still suggests, more than any other
of his portraits, a talented, sensitive, subtle, self-contained man.

So much for this time. Now I shall consult Part Two of honest Volkmann, which contains Rome, to extract from it what I have not yet
seen. Before I travel to Naples, the harvest must at least be reaped;
surely some good days will also come for binding it into sheaves.

February 17.

The weather is incredibly and inexpressibly fine, with a clear, bright
sky throughout February except for four rainy days, almost too warm
toward noon. Now we seek the open air, and whereas previously we
only cared to deal with gods and heroes, now the countryside is suddenly coming into its own again, and we frequent the environs, which
are enlivened by the most splendid daylight. Sometimes I recall how
artists in the north try to make something out of thatched roofs and
ruined castles, how they dawdle at brook and bush and crumbled rock
to capture a picturesque effect; and then I feel quite strange, especially
since those things still cling to me from long habit. But two weeks ago
I plucked up my courage and, equipped with a small sketch pad, began
walking out among the villas, uphill and down, where without much
reflection I have been sketching small, striking, truly southern and Roman objects and now am trying, with the help of some good luck, to
give them lights and shadows. It is quite peculiar that we can clearly
see and know what is good and better, but when we try to make use
of this, it withers in our hands, as it were, and we do not reach for
what is correct but for what we are accustomed to hold. Only through
regular practice would it be possible to make progress, but where am

I to find the time and concentration for that? Meanwhile, nevertheless, I feel myself considerably improved by my two weeks of passionate endeavor.

The artists like to instruct me, for I grasp things quickly. But what I have grasped is not immediately put into effect. To grasp something quickly is, moreover, what the mind is fitted for; but to do something worthwhile, for *that* one needs a lifetime of practice.

And yet the amateur, feeble though his efforts at emulation may be, should not let himself be deterred. The few lines I draw on my paper are often overhasty and seldom correct, but they make it easier for me to form each of my ideas of material things, for one can more readily proceed to a general concept if one observes individual objects more closely and precisely.

Only one must not compare oneself with the artists, but work along in one's own way; for nature has provided for its children, and the least of them has as much right to exist as the most excellent one: "A little man is also a man!"[232] And there we shall let the matter rest.

I have seen the sea twice, first the Adriatic, then the Mediterranean, but only, as it were, to pay a call. In Naples we shall become better acquainted. Everything is suddenly falling into place for me: why not sooner, why not more cheaply! How many thousand things, many of them entirely new and unfamiliar, I could tell you!

February 17, 1787.
In the evening, the carnival folly having died away.

I do not like to go away and leave Moritz alone. He is on the right path, but when he walks alone, he immediately looks for popular hiding places. I have encouraged him to write to Herder, the letter is enclosed here, and I hope for an answer containing something appropriate and helpful. He is an unusually good man, and he would have advanced much further if from time to time he had found persons capable of explaining his situation to him, and kind enough to do it. If Herder would permit him to write occasionally, that would be the most beneficial connection Moritz could make at present. He is engaged in a laudable antiquarian undertaking, which certainly merits support.[233] Friend Herder could scarcely find his efforts better expended anywhere, or plant his teachings in a more fertile soil.

The big portrait of me that Tischbein has undertaken is already sprouting from the canvas. The artist has had an accomplished sculptor make him a little clay model, which has been very elegantly draped with a cloak. He paints diligently from that, for of course he was to have progressed to a certain point before our departure for Naples, and it takes time just to cover such a large canvas with paint.

February 19.

The weather continues to be so fine that it is beyond words. This was a day I spent painfully among the fools. At nightfall I recuperated at the Villa Medici; the new moon is just past, and next to the slender crescent moon I could see the whole dark disk dimly with the naked eye, and quite distinctly through the telescope. Hovering over the ground all day is a vapor which is familiar to us only from the drawings and paintings of Claude Lorrain;[234] but in nature the phenomenon is rarely seen as beautifully as here. Now flowers that I do not yet know are appearing on the ground, and new blossoms on the trees; the almonds are blooming and are an airy new presence among the dark-green oaks; the sky is like a piece of light-blue taffeta shone on by the sun. To think how it will be in Naples! We find that almost everything is already green. My odd botanical notions are reinforced by all this, and I am on the way to discovering beautiful new conditions under which nature—that invisible immensity—develops the greatest variations from a simple entity.

Vesuvius is spewing out rocks and ash, and at night they see its summit glowing. May active nature give us a lava flow! Now I can scarcely wait for those great sights to be mine also.

February 20, Ash Wednesday.

Now the foolishness is at an end. The innumerable lights yesterday evening were another sad spectacle. To have seen the carnival in Rome completely rids one of the wish ever to see it again. It offers nothing whatever to write about, but an oral presentation of it might possibly be entertaining. While it was going on I had the unpleasant feeling that the people lacked inner joy and did not have enough money to indulge the slight inclination they may still feel. Persons of rank are economical and hold back, the middle class is without means, and the common folk are impotent. There was incredible noise in the last days, but little real gaiety. The sky, so infinitely clear and beautiful, looked down so nobly and innocently at these antics.

However, since I cannot keep from working at art here, to please the children I have drawn some carnival masks and characteristic Roman costumes, and then colored them. These may compensate our dear little ones for a chapter left out of the *Orbis pictus*.[235]

February 21, 1787.

I shall use the moments while I pause from packing to catch up with a few things. Tomorrow we are going to Naples. I look forward to that new place, which is said to be inexpressibly beautiful, and in that paradisiacal natural environment I hope to regain my freedom and desire to return to the study of art in solemn Rome.

Packing is easy for me, I am doing it with a lighter heart than half a year ago, when I was separating myself from everything that was so dear and valuable to me. Yes, it is already a half year, and not a moment of the four months I have spent in Rome has been wasted, which is indeed saying a great deal, but not too much.

I know that my *Iphigenia* has arrived; may I hear at the foot of Vesuvius that it got a good reception!

It is of the greatest importance for me to make this journey with Tischbein, who has as magnificent an insight into nature as into art; but, being true Germans, we cannot exist without plans and prospects for work. We are buying the finest drawing paper, although the great number, beauty, and brilliance of the sights will most probably set limits to our good intentions.

I have controlled myself in one respect, and of all my poetic works am taking along only *Tasso,* the one I have best hopes for. If I knew what all of you are saying about *Iphigenia,* it would guide me, for *Tasso* is a similar work, its subject matter almost even narrower than that of *Iphigenia,* and needing even more elaboration of detail. But I do not yet know what it can become, and I must discard everything I have already written, for it has been neglected too long. Neither the characters, nor the plot, nor the tone have the slightest relationship to my present views.

While clearing up I have come upon some of your dear letters, and in reading through them I see that you reproach me with having contradicted myself in mine. Of course I cannot see that, for what I write I always immediately send off. But I believe that it is very likely, since I am tossed about by tremendous forces, and so it is only natural that I do not always know where I stand.

They tell of a boatman who, being overtaken at night by a storm on the sea, tried to steer homewards. His small son, clinging to him in the darkness, asked: "Father, what is that odd little light over there, that I see first above us, then below us?" The father promised that he would explain it the following day, and it turned out that this had been the flame of the lighthouse, which seemed now below, now above to the eye of someone rocked up and down by the wild waves.

I too am steering to port on a tempestuous sea, and I just keep a close watch on the glow of the lighthouse; even if it seems to change its position, nevertheless I shall at last arrive safely on shore.

Somehow, leaving for a trip always brings every past departure spontaneously to mind, as well as the future final one. And at the same time, more forcefully now than usual, the thought is welling up in me that we encumber our lives with far too many things. For here we are, Tischbein and I, turning our backs not only on these many splendors, but even on our well-stocked private museum. Three Junos are standing there now in a row, for comparison with each other, and we are leaving them as if none was there at all.

PART TWO

Naples

Velletri, February 22, 1787.

We arrived here in good time.—The skies were already growing dark the day before yesterday, the fine days had brought us some dismal ones; yet there were a few signs in the air that the weather might consent to improve again, and this is what happened. The clouds gradually separated, here and there the blue sky appeared, and finally the sun lit up our path. We came through Albano after having stopped near Genzano at the entrance of a park whose owner, Prince Chigi,[1] keeps it—but does not keep it up—in a strange way and therefore does not want anyone to look around in it. A true wilderness has sprung up there: trees and bushes, weeds and vines, grow as they will, wither, fall over, rot. But that is all right and so much the better. The area before the entrance is beautiful beyond words. A high wall shuts off the valley, one can look in through a latticed gate, then the hill rises up, with the castle located on top. It would make the grandest picture, if undertaken by a real artist.

I must not go on describing now but merely say that when, from the heights, we caught sight of the mountains of Sezza, the Pontine marshes, the sea, and the islands, in that very moment a heavy squall was moving across the marshes toward the sea, and light and shadow, alternating quickly, enlivened that desolate area quite diversely. Several sunlit columns of smoke rising from scattered, scarcely visible huts introduced a very beautiful additional effect.

Velletri is very pleasantly situated on a volcanic hill that is connected to other hills only on the north and provides a most unobstructed view in three directions.

Now we looked at the collection of Cavaliere Borgia, who, being favored by his relationship with the cardinal and the Propaganda,[2] was able to assemble excellent antiquities and other remarkable things here: Egyptian idols formed of the hardest stone; little metal figures of earlier and later times; terra cotta bas-relief sculptures, excavated in the area, on the basis of which it is claimed that the ancient Volsci had a style of their own.

The museum possesses examples of various other rarities. I noted two Chinese paint-boxes, on the surfaces of one of which the whole breeding of silkworms is depicted, on the other the cultivation of rice, both subjects very naively treated and worked out in detail. The boxes and their wrappings are exceptionally beautiful and are certainly not inferior to the book in the library of the Propaganda that I have already praised.

Of course it is inexcusable that we had this treasure so close to Rome and did not visit it more frequently. But the inconvenience of any excursion in these regions and the powerful enchantment of Rome may serve as an excuse. When we walked toward the inn, several of the women sitting at their front doors called to us, asking if we did not want to buy antiquities also. But when we proved eager to do so, they produced oid kettles, fire tongs, and other simple household utensils, and nearly died laughing because they had duped us. We were irritated by this, but our guide set matters right again by assuring us that it was a traditional joke and all strangers were required to render the same tribute.

I am writing this in a very miserable inn and am neither comfortable enough nor strong enough to continue. Therefore a very friendly "Good night!"

Fondi, February 23, 1787.

We were already on our way at three o'clock in the morning. At dawn we found ourselves in the Pontine marshes, which are by no means as wretched in appearance as generally described in Rome. To be sure, one cannot, while just passing through, judge such a large and extensive undertaking as the proposed drainage of the marshes; but it does seem to me that the works ordered by the pope will attain the desired goals at least for the most part. Imagine a wide valley stretching from north to south with little declivity, but lower eastwards toward the mountains, and higher westwards toward the sea.

The old Via Appia has been restored in a straight line through the whole length of the valley, and the main canal has been dug along the right side of the road. The water flows down through it gently, and by this means the soil on the right side, toward the sea, has been drained and given over to agriculture. As far as the eye can see, it is cultivated or, except for some patches that are situated much too low, cultivable, if tenant farmers could be found.

However, the left side toward the mountains presents a more difficult problem. To be sure, transverse canals go under the highway into the main canal; but since the ground slopes toward the mountains, it cannot be freed of water by this means. It is said that a second canal will be cut alongside the mountains. Great stretches, especially in the direction of Terracina, have been planted with willows and poplars by windblown seeds.

One relay station consists merely of a long straw hut. Tischbein sketched it and for his reward enjoyed a pleasure that only he can fully appreciate. A white horse had gotten loose on the dried-out terrain and was making use of its freedom to dash back and forth on the brown soil like a streak of lightning. This was really a splendid sight, made particularly significant by Tischbein's delight in it.

To designate the central point of the area, the pope has had a large and beautiful building erected where the town of Meza formerly stood. The sight of it makes one more hopeful and confident about the whole undertaking. And so we kept moving onward, conversing animatedly, being mindful of the warning that one must not fall asleep on this road; and indeed, the blue vapor which was already hovering over the ground at a certain height at this time of year drew our attention to a dangerous layer of air. Therefore the rocky location of Terracina seemed all the more desirable and pleasing to us, and hardly had we enjoyed this view of the town when we caught sight of the sea directly in front of it. Shortly afterwards the other side of the populated mountain provided us with a display of new vegetation. Indian figs thrust their large, fleshy, leaflike bodies between low-growing, grayish-green myrtles, amidst yellow-green pomegranate trees and pale-green olive branches. Along the road we saw new, quite unfamiliar flowers and bushes. Narcissus and adonis were blooming on the meadows. For a time the sea is on the right, while the limestone rocks remain close by on the left. These are the continuation of the Apennines, coming across from Tivoli to join the sea, from which they are later separated by the Roman Campagna, then by the volcanoes of Frascati, Albano, and Velletri, and finally by the Pontine marshes. Monte Circello, the promontory opposite Terracina, where the Pontine marshes end, may likewise consist of a series of limestone rocks.

We left the sea and soon came onto the lovely plain of Fondi. This small area of fertile and cultivated soil, enclosed by moderately rugged mountains, must surely be a welcome sight to everyone. Most of the oranges are still hanging on the trees, the grain, all of it wheat, is up and green; there are olive trees in the fields, the little town is at the end. A palm tree stands out prominently, and we hailed it. So much for this evening. Excuse my hasty pen. To write at all, I must do it without thinking. There are too many sights, accommodations are too

poor, and yet my desire to commit a few things to paper is all too
strong. We arrived at nightfall, and now it is time to seek rest.

St. Agata, February 24, 1787.

My report of this lovely day must be written in a cold little room.
When we rode out of Fondi it had just become light, and we were
greeted at once on both sides of the road by the oranges hanging over
the wall. The trees are as full of fruit as can possibly be imagined. The
young foliage at the top is yellowish, but below and in the middle it is
of the juiciest green. Mignon was certainly right to long for this.[3]

Then we drove through well plowed and cultivated wheat fields,
planted with olive trees in appropriate places. The wind made them
sway and exposed the silvery underside of their leaves, while the
branches bent gently and gracefully. It was a gray morning, but a north
wind promised to drive away all the clouds completely.

Then the road led through a valley, between stony but well-cultivated
fields, with young wheat of the most beautiful green. At a few places
we saw spacious, round, paved areas surrounded by little low walls.
Here the grain is threshed at once, without being carted home in
sheaves. The valley grew narrower, the road went uphill, limestone
rocks stood nakedly on both sides. The storm blew more violently behind us. Hail fell, and melted very slowly.

We were surprised by some walls of reticulated work remaining from
ancient buildings. The high areas are rocky, yet are planted with olive
trees wherever there is the slightest amount of soil to support them.
Next we crossed a plain with olive trees, then went through a little
town. Here we found altars, ancient gravestones, and fragments of all
kinds built into the garden enclosures, then solidly constructed base-
ments of old villas, now filled up with soil and overgrown with little
forests of olive trees. Then we caught sight of Vesuvius, with a cloud
of smoke at its summit.

Mola di Gaëta greeted us with more of the most opulent orange trees.
We stayed for several hours. The bay in front of this small town affords
one of the most beautiful views, the sea washes in this far. If the eye
follows the right shoreline as far as the tip of the crescent, one sees
the fortress Gaëta on a cliff, at a moderate distance. The left tip of the
crescent is much farther away; first a series of mountains is visible,
then Vesuvius, and then the islands appear. Ischia lies almost opposite
the middle.

Here I found my first starfish and sea urchins washed up on the
shore. A lovely green leaf, like the finest vellum, but also some remarkable detritus: mostly the usual particles of limestone, but also ser-

pentine, jasper, quartz, breccia pebbles, granites, porphyries, types of
marble, glass of green or blue color. The last-named minerals were
hardly produced in this region; they are probably remnants of old
buildings, and so we see how the waves can play before our eyes with
the splendors of the ancient world. We lingered gladly and were amused
by the nature of the people, who behaved nearly like savages. The view
is still beautiful as one leaves Mola behind, even though the sea disappears. The last view of it is of a lovely inlet, which we sketched.
Next follows a good grainfield, fenced in with aloes. We glimpsed an
aqueduct which led from the mountains toward shapeless, tangled ruins.

Then the Garigliano river must be crossed. Next, the road wanders
off through rather fertile regions toward a mountain range. Nothing
exceptional. Finally the first hill of volcanic ash. Here begins a large,
magnificent area of mountains and valleys, towered over at the end by
snowy peaks. On the nearer heights an elongated, quite conspicuous
town. St. Agata is located in the valley, a very respectable inn, where
a lively fire was burning in a fireplace built as a small adjacent room.
For all that, our chamber is cold, no windowpanes, only shutters, and
I hasten to close this letter.

Naples, February 25, 1787.

Have finally also arrived here safely and with good omens. Only this
much about today's journey: we left St. Agata at sunrise, the wind
blew violently behind us, a northeaster that kept up all day. Not until
afternoon did it chase away the clouds; we suffered from cold.

Our road again went through and over volcanic hills, where I thought
I did not observe many more limestone rocks. At last we reached the
plain of Capua, soon after that Capua itself, where we ate our noonday
meal. In the afternoon a beautiful level field opened before us. The
highway cuts a broad swath through green wheatfields, the wheat is
like a carpet and easily a span high. Poplars are planted on the fields
in rows, their lower and middle branches stripped off, and grapevines
drawn up on them. Thus it goes all the way into Naples. A pure, splendidly loose soil, and well tilled. The grapevines of unusual strength and
height, their tendrils swaying like nets from poplar to poplar.

Vesuvius kept to our left, violently emitting smoke, and I was filled
with quiet delight at seeing this remarkable sight with my own eyes.
The sky grew clearer and clearer, and at last the sun shone quite hotly
into our cramped house-on-wheels. We approached Naples in an atmosphere of the purest brightness; and now we really found ourselves to
be in a different country. The buildings with their flat roofs indicate
that we are at a different point of the compass; presumably they are

not very cheerful inside. Everybody is out on the street and sitting in the sun, as long as it goes on shining. The Neapolitan believes himself in possession of Paradise, and has a very dismal conception of the countries to the north: "Sempre neve, case di legno, gran ignoranza, ma danari assai." That is how they picture our circumstances. For the benefit of all German tribes, this characterization translates as follows: "Perpetual snow, wooden houses, great ignorance; but plenty of money."

Naples itself appears to be happy, free, and lively, vast numbers of people running about in mingled confusion, the king is out hunting, the queen[4] is expecting a child, and so things could not be better.

Naples, Monday, February 26.

"Alla Locanda del Sgr. Moriconi al Largo del Castello." Letters from all four corners of the world could reach us now at this address, which sounds both cheerful and grand. In the vicinity of the big citadel located by the sea there is a large space which, although surrounded by houses on all four sides, is not called a square, but a wide place *(largo)*, probably ever since early times, when this was still an open field. On one side is located a large corner house, and we established ourselves in a spacious corner room, which affords an unobstructed and pleasing view over the always lively expanse. Outside, an iron balcony extends past several windows, and even around the corner. If the sharp wind were not so penetrating, we would not budge from there.

The room is gaily decorated, especially the ceiling, whose hundred sections of arabesques announce the nearness of Pompeii and Herculaneum. Now that is all very well, but there is no fireplace, no flue to be seen, even though February exercises its rights here too. I was longing for some warmth.

A tripod was brought to me which was elevated high enough above the floor so that I could hold my hands over it easily. A flat pan containing very gently glowing coals, with a smooth cover of ashes, was fastened on top of it. Here one must be economical, as we had already learned to be in Rome. With the lug of a key one carefully draws away the surface ashes from time to time, in order to expose some of the coals to the air. However, if one were to stir up the fire impatiently, then greater heat would be felt momentarily, but very soon one would use up the whole fire, whereupon, against payment of a certain sum, the pan would have to be refilled.

I was not entirely satisfied and would certainly have wished for more comfort. A reed mat served to ward off the chill of the stone floor; furs are not usually worn, so I decided to don a seaman's cowl we had taken along as a joke. It served me well, especially after I had tied it around my waist with a portmanteau cord, which gave me the very odd feeling that I was something halfway between a sailor and a Capuchin. Tischbein, returning from visits to friends, could not keep from laughing.

Naples, February 27, 1787.

Yesterday I rested all day, waiting for a small physical discomfort to pass, but today we feasted and spent the time in looking at the most magnificent sights. They can say, tell, and paint whatever they want, there is more here than all of that. The shores, bays, and gulfs of the sea, Vesuvius, the suburbs, the citadels, the pleasure grounds!—That evening we still went to the grotto of Posillipo,[5] just when the setting sun was shining in from the other side. I forgave all those who lose their minds over Naples, and I was moved by memories of my father, who had retained an indelible impression especially of the things I was seeing that day for the first time. And just as it is said that someone who has seen a ghost will never be happy again, so it might be said of my father, in reverse, that he could never become completely unhappy, because he returned to Naples again and again in his thoughts. Now, as is my fashion, I am very quiet and just open my eyes wide, very wide, when it all becomes too much for me.

Naples, February 28, 1787.

Today we visited Philipp Hackert, the famous landscape painter, who enjoys the special confidence and most particular favor of the king and queen. They have assigned him a wing of the Francavilla palace, which he has had furnished with artistic taste and lives in contentedly. He is a very resolute, intelligent man, who knows how to combine incessant hard work with enjoyment of life.

Then we walked to the sea and saw all sorts of fish and curiously shaped creatures pulled from the waves. The day was splendid, the tramontane wind bearable.

Naples, March 1.

Already in Rome, more sociability than I liked had been demanded of my stubbornly reclusive mentality. Granted, it seems strange for someone to go out into the world in order to stay alone. So I had not been able to resist the Prince of Waldeck,[6] who invited me in a very friendly fashion and through his rank and influence enabled me to participate in many good things. We had hardly arrived in Naples, where he had already been staying for a while, when he sent us an invitation to join him on an excursion to Pozzuoli and the adjacent region. I had intended to go to Vesuvius today, but Tischbein urges me to take this trip. Pleasant in itself, it promises a great deal of joy and profit because of the very beautiful weather and the company of such a perfect and well-educated prince. Also, back in Rome we had seen a beautiful lady who, along with her husband, was inseparable from the prince. She likewise is to be in the party, and we expect a very happy time.

I am also quite well known to this noble company from having entertained them on an earlier occasion. That is to say, when we first became acquainted the prince asked me what I was currently working on, and my *Iphigenia* was so present in my mind that during the evening I was able to narrate it in considerable detail. They entered into the spirit of it; but nevertheless I got the impression that something livelier, wilder, had been expected of me.

In the evening.

It would be difficult to give an account of this day. Who has not had the experience that the hurried reading of a book he could not put down has had very great influence on his whole life, and has had such a decisive effect that subsequent rereading and serious meditation could hardly contribute anything more to it? That happened to me once with *Sakuntala,*[7] and is it not the same for us with significant persons? A boat trip to Pozzuoli, easy drives on land, pleasant walks through the most amazing region in the world. The clearest sky above, the most unstable ground below. Ruins of what was unimaginable affluence, mutilated and depressing. Boiling waters, holes exhaling sulfur, slag heaps resistant to plant life, bare, loathsome areas, but then at last an always lush vegetation, taking hold wherever it can, rising over all the dead things, surrounding the lakes and brooks, even maintaining the most magnificent oak forest on the walls of an ancient crater.

And so we were propelled back and forth between the acts of nature and of nations. I wanted to think and felt myself incompetent to do so. Meanwhile the living man keeps on merrily living, and we did not fail to do so either. Cultured persons, not foreign to the world and its ways, but also, having been warned by solemn fate, prone to contemplation. Unrestricted views over land, sea, and sky, then called back into the proximity of a charming young lady, who is accustomed and inclined to receive homage.

Amidst all this tumult, however, I did not neglect to take note of many things. The map used on the spot and a hasty sketch by Tischbein will be the best aids to future editing; it is not possible for me to add even the slightest thing today.

On March 2

I ascended Vesuvius, although the weather was gloomy and the summit covered with clouds. I reached Resina by carriage, then by mule up the mountain between vineyards; next, on foot over the lava from the year '71, which had already grown a covering of fine but sturdy moss; then up alongside the lava. The hermit's hut stayed to my left on the heights. Then up the mountain of ashes, which is hard work. Two thirds of this summit was covered with clouds. At last we reached the ancient crater, which is now filled up, and found the new lavas from two months and fourteen days ago, also even a meager one five days old, already cooled. We climbed over them and up a newly created volcanic hill, which was smoking on all sides. The smoke was moving away from us, and I wanted to go toward the crater. We were approximately fifty paces into the smoke when it grew so thick that I could scarcely see my shoes. Holding up a handkerchief did not help. I also lost sight of the guide, and my steps were unsure on the little fragments of lava that had been cast up. I thought it best to turn back and save the desired sight for a sunny day with less smoke. Meanwhile I have also learned how difficult it is to breathe in such an atmosphere.

Except for that, the mountain was altogether quiet. Neither flames, nor roaring, nor showers of stones, as has always been the case since our arrival. Now that I have reconnoitered it, I can, so to speak, besiege it as soon as the weather consents to improve.

The lavas that I found were mostly composed of minerals I am familiar with. But I discovered a phenomenon that seemed very remarkable to me, and I want to investigate it more closely and get information from experts and collectors. It is a stalactitic coating on a volcanic chimney that was formerly domed over but is now open and projects from the old, filled-in crater. I believe that this solid, grayish, stalactitic mineral must have been formed through sublimation of the very most delicate volcanic exhalations, unassisted by moisture and without fusion. It occasions further thought.

Today, March the third, the sky is overcast and a sirocco is blowing; good weather for a mailing day.

By the way, I have already seen a good many very diverse people, fine horses, and strange fishes here.

Not one word about the splendors of the city's location, which have been described and praised so often. "Vedi Napoli e poi muori!" they say here. "See Naples and die!"

Naples, March 3.

That no Neapolitan wants to leave his city, and that its poets sing in mighty hyperbole of the blissfulness of this locality, should not be held against them, not even if there were a few more Vesuviuses in the vicinity. Here all thought of Rome is forgotten; compared to the openness of this location, the capital of the world in its Tiber valley seems like an old, poorly placed monastery.

The world of ships and the sea is also something entirely new to me. Yesterday the frigate to Palermo sailed away with a pure, strong tramontane wind. Surely this time it has not spent more than thirty-six hours on the way. With what a longing gaze I followed its billowing sails, as the ship passed between Capri and Capo Minerva and finally disappeared. To see a beloved person sail away like that would surely make one die of longing! Now the sirocco is blowing; if the wind gets stronger, the waves around the Molo will be quite brisk.

Today being Friday,[8] the nobility held its grand promenade, when each one displays his equipages, especially the horses. Nothing more graceful than these creatures here could possibly be seen; for the first time in my life my heart opens to them.

Naples, March 3.

I am sending several closely written pages here to give you a report on the initiation fee I paid here; also the envelope of your last letter, with a smoke-blackened corner as evidence that I took it along with me up Vesuvius. But I do not want all of you imagining, either while awake or in dreams, that I am surrounded by danger. Be assured that where I walk there is no more danger than on the highway to Belvedere.[9] It can surely be said in regard to this: the earth is everywhere the Lord's! I seek no adventures out of curiosity or eccentricity, but since I am usually perceptive and able to distinguish the special features of a thing quickly, I can do and dare more than someone else. Going to Sicily is not dangerous at all. A few days ago the frigate left for Palermo under a favorable northeast wind; it passed Capri on the right and certainly covered the distance in thirty-six hours. It does not seem as dangerous over there in reality as people choose to believe from a distance.

No earthquakes at all are being felt now in the lower part of Italy, but Rimini and nearby towns in the upper part were recently damaged. Earthquakes are capricious, and are discussed here just like the wind and the weather, or as fires are in Thuringia.

I am glad that you are now becoming reconciled to the new version of *Iphigenia;* but I would be still happier if you had felt the difference more keenly. I know what I have done to it and am entitled to talk about that, because there is still more I could do. If it is a pleasure to enjoy what is good, it is a greater one to perceive what is better, and in art only the best is good enough.

Naples, March 5.

We used the second Sunday in Lent to wander from church to church. Whereas in Rome everything is very solemn, here all is merry and gay. Also, it is only in Naples that one can understand the Neapolitan school of painting. Here one sees with amazement that a whole church front has been painted from bottom to top, Christ above the door, expelling the buyers and sellers from the temple, and the latter tumbling down the stairs on both sides, brightly and gracefully terrified. Inside another church the space over the entrance is richly decorated with a fresco painting that depicts the banishment of Heliodorus. Luca Giordano[10] surely had to hurry in order to fill such an expanse! Nor is the pulpit always a reading desk or teacher's chair, as it is elsewhere, but a gallery, on which I saw a Capuchin stride back and forth, reproaching the people for their sinfulness first from one end, then from the other. And how many more things I could tell!

But beyond telling or describing is the magnificence of the brightly moonlit night we enjoyed while strolling through the streets and over the squares, on the Chiaja,[11] that endless promenade, then back and forth along the seashore. A feeling of the infiniteness of space really comes over one. It is truly worth the effort to dream like that.

Naples, March 5, 1787.

I must briefly, and in a very general way, mention an excellent man with whom I have become acquainted in the last few days. He is Cavaliere Filangieri,[12] known for his book on legislation. He is one of those noble young men who work for the happiness of human beings and their honorable freedom. His deportment bespeaks the soldier, the cavalier, and the man of the world, yet this correctness is tempered by the fine moral feelings expressed in his whole personality and very charmingly evident in his words and ways. He is also sincerely committed to the king and his kingdom, even though he does not approve of everything that is happening; but he too is oppressed by fear of Joseph II.[13] The image of a despot, even though it may still be just hovering in the air, is terrible to noble-minded persons. He spoke to me quite candidly about what Naples has to fear from the emperor. He likes to converse about Montesquieu, Beccaria,[14] and also his own writings, all of which show the same best intentions and the same warm youthful desire to accomplish good. He may still be in his thirties.

He very soon acquainted me with an old author whose inscrutable profundity is a source of great inspiration and edification to these modern Italian devotees of law. His name is Giovanni Battista Vico, and they prefer him to Montesquieu. My cursory glance at a book[15] they told me was a holy relic gave me the impression that here were sibylline presentiments of a goodness and justice which would or should come some day, presentiments based on a serious contemplation of life and traditions. It is really fine for a nation to possess such a patriarch; some day Hamann[16] will become a similar codex for the Germans.

Naples, March 6, 1787.

Reluctantly, but out of loyal comradeship, Tischbein accompanied me up Vesuvius today. As a visual artist, he always deals only with the most beautiful human and animal forms, and indeed with his sense and taste he gives humanity even to what is unformed, such as rocks and landscapes. This fearsome, shapeless heap of things, which keeps consuming itself and declares war on every feeling for beauty, cannot fail to seem quite hideous to him.

We drove in two caleches because we did not trust ourselves to be our own guides and wind our way through the confusion of the city. The driver keeps shouting, "Make way, make way!" so that donkeys, men carrying wood or rubbish, caleches coming in the opposite direction, people bearing burdens or walking unencumbered, children, and old men will beware and get out of the way, while the sharp trot continues unchecked.

The road through the outermost suburbs and gardens proved to be an early indication of something Plutonic. Since it had not rained in a long time, the naturally evergreen leaves were covered with a thick, ash-gray dust, and all the roofs, girdle ledges, and whatever else offered any kind of surface were likewise coated with gray, and only the splendid blue sky and the powerful, radiant sun were proof that we were still among the living.

At the foot of the steep incline we were met by two guides, an older and a younger one, both sturdy men. The first dragged me up the mountain, the second one. Tischbein. I say dragged, for these guides gird themselves with a leather strap, which the traveler takes hold of and, since he is being pulled upwards, this makes it all the easier for him to climb up on his own feet with a staff.

Thus we reached the surface over which the cone rises, the wreckage of Monte Somma to the north.

Like a curative bath, a glance westward over the region removed all the pains of exertion and all fatigue, and then we made a circuit around the cone, which is always smoking and ejecting stones and ashes. As long as there was enough room so that we could stay at a proper distance, it was a grand, inspiring spectacle. First a violent thunder resounding out of the deepest abyss, then thousands of stones, larger and smaller ones, hurled into the air, veiled in clouds of ash. The greatest part fell back into the abyss. The other fragments, driven sideways, made a curious noise when falling onto the outer side of the cone: first the heavier ones thudded onto the side of the cone and bounced down it with a hollow sound. The lesser ones clattered after them, and finally the ash trickled down. This all took place with regular pauses, which we could easily measure by calmly counting.

Between Monte Somma and the cone, however, the space grew quite narrow, numerous stones were already falling around us, making it unpleasant to walk around. Tischbein was now still more annoyed with the mountain, since this monster was not satisfied with being ugly, it wanted to become dangerous as well.

However, there is something exciting about a present danger and it challenges the contrary spirit in man to defy it. So I reflected that it must be possible, in the interval between two eruptions, to reach the abyss and return from it in that same space of time. I consulted with the guides about this under an overhanging rock of Monte Somma, where, securely encamped, we were refreshing ourselves with the supplies we had brought along. The younger guide was willing to try the adventure with me, we padded the crowns of our hats with silk and linen cloths, we put ourselves in a ready position, staffs in hand, I grasping his belt.

While the little stones were still clattering around us, the ash still trickling, the robust youth was already pulling me over the glowing rubble. Here we stood at the enormous yawning abyss, whose smoke was being drawn away from us by a light breeze but at the same time veiled the interior of the pit, which was fuming all around from a thousand fissures. Rock walls, burst asunder, could be glimpsed here and there through a gap in the smoke. The view was neither instructive nor pleasant, but the very fact that we saw nothing made us wait to see something. Failing to count calmly, we stood on a sharp edge of the immense chasm. Suddenly the thunder resounded, the terrible charge flew past us, we instinctively ducked down, as if that would have saved us from the falling lumps. The smaller stones were clattering already, and without reflecting that we could now anticipate another pause, just happy to have survived the danger, we arrived at the foot of the cone along with the still trickling ash, our hats and shoulders all covered with it.

Tischbein received, scolded, and revived me in the friendliest way, and now I could direct my special attention to the older and newer lavas. The aged guide was able to give their dates precisely. The older ones were smooth and already covered with ash; the newer ones, especially those that had flowed slowly, were a strange sight; for as they creep along, temporarily dragging with them the solidified surface masses, the latter naturally come to an occasional standstill. Although still urged onward by the glowing streams, they stand fast, shoved on top of each other to become jaggedly stiffened in a curious manner, more strangely than piled-up ice floes in a similar situation. There were also some large blocks among this desolate molten substance which, when chipped, at the fresh break looked exactly like a type of the primeval stone.[17] The guides claimed that these were ancient lavas from the profoundest depths, which the mountain sometimes ejected.

On our way back to Naples I noticed some oddly built, windowless little one-story houses, their rooms lighted only by the street door. The occupants sit in front of them from early morning until night, when at last they retreat into these caves.

In the evening the city is tumultuous in a different way, and made me wish I could linger here for some time, so as to sketch the lively picture to the best of my ability. But I shall not be so fortunate.

Naples, Wednesday, March 7, 1787.

And so this week Tischbein conscientiously showed me a large portion of the art treasures of Naples and explained them. Being an excellent connoisseur and painter of animals, he had drawn my attention earlier to a bronze horse's head in the Colombrano palace.[18] Today we went there. This artistic fragment stands in the courtyard directly opposite the carriage entrance, in a niche above a fountain, and is astonishing; when the head was combined into a whole with the other limbs, what an effect it must have made! The entire horse was much larger than those of St. Mark's; and the head, viewed more closely and by itself here, manifests its strength and character all the more distinctly and admirably. The majestic frontal bone, the snorting nostrils, the alert ears, the rigid mane! A highly excited, vigorous creature.

We turned around to take note of a female statue[19] standing in a niche above the entrance gate. Winckelmann considered it to be the portrait of a dancer, for such performers demonstrate in living movement, in the most varied manner, the qualities preserved for us in rigid nymphs and goddesses by the masters of sculpture. It is very light and beautiful; the head was broken off but has been successfully set back on. In other respects it is undamaged, and would certainly merit a better place.

Naples, March 9.

Today I received your very dear letters dated the 16th of February. Please continue to write. I have carefully arranged for my mail to be forwarded and shall do so again if I travel onwards. It really seems strange to me when I read at this great distance that my friends do not meet together; and yet it is often the most natural thing in the world for people who live so close to one another not to assemble.

The weather has grown cloudy, it is in transition, spring is coming, and we shall have rainy days. The summit of Vesuvius has not been in sunshine since I was up there. During the last few nights it was sometimes seen to flame, but now it has stopped again; a fairly strong eruption is expected.

The recent gales have shown us a magnificent sea, where the waves could be studied in their condign manner and form. Nature is truly the only book that offers great substance on every page. On the other hand I do not enjoy the theater at all anymore. During Lent, religious operas are given here, the only difference from the secular ones being that no ballets are inserted between the acts; nevertheless they are as full of variety as possible. In the San Carlo theater they are performing *The Destruction of Jerusalem by Nebuchadnezzar*.[20] To me it is nothing but a big raree-show. It seems that I have lost my taste for such things.

Today we were up at Capo di Monte with the Prince of Waldeck. This is where the great collection of paintings, coins, etc., is located, not attractively displayed, but precious things. A great many notions about tradition are now confirmed and defined for me. The coins, gems, and vases which come up north singly, like the trimmed lemon trees, look quite different in the mass, here where these treasures are indigenous. For where works of art are rare, the rarity itself gives them value; here one learns to esteem only what is worthy.

They pay a lot of money for Etrurian vases now, and certainly there are some beautiful and excellent pieces to be found among them. There is not a traveler who would not like to own one. People spend money more freely than when at home, and I fear I shall eventually be seduced myself.

Naples, Friday, March 9, 1787.

The pleasant thing about traveling is that even the commonplace begins to look like an adventure because it is new and surprising. After

returning from Capo di Monte, I still paid an evening visit to the Filangieris, where I found, sitting next to the lady of the house[21] on the
sofa, a young woman[22] whose outward appearance did not seem in
keeping with the familiar behavior she indulged in so freely. In a light
frock of striped silk, her hair done up strangely, this dainty little figure
looked like a milliner who, while busy adorning others, pays small attention to her own appearance. (They are so accustomed to seeing their
work paid for that they cannot conceive of doing anything for themselves gratis.) My entrance did not distract her from her chattering,
and she told a great many droll stories about what had lately happened
to her or rather what she had caused with her impetuosity.

The lady of the house wanted to give me an opportunity to say a
word, so she spoke about the splendid location of Capo di Monte and
the treasures there. However, the sprightly little woman leapt to her
feet, and when standing looked even prettier than before. She said
goodbye, ran to the door, and said to me while passing by, "The Filangieris are dining with me soon. I hope to see you there also!" She
was gone before I could accept. Now I learned that she was the Princess
***, a close relative of the family. The Filangieris are not rich and live
respectably but modestly. I imagined the princess to be in the same
circumstances, since such lofty titles are not unusual in Naples. I noted
down the name, day, and hour, and did not doubt that I would arrive
at the proper time and the right place.

Naples, Sunday, March 11, 1787.

Since my stay in Naples will not be a long one, I am exploring the
more distant points first; the nearer ones will take care of themselves.
I drove to Pompeii with Tischbein, where to the left and right all those
magnificent views familiar to us from so many landscape drawings now
appeared in their combined splendor. Everyone is astonished by the
small, cramped size of Pompeii. Narrow streets, although straight and
provided with stone walkways on the side; little windowless houses,
the rooms that lead from the courtyards and galleries lit only through
their doors. Even public works, the bench at the gate, the temple, and
then also a nearby villa[23] are more like models and doll houses than
buildings. But these rooms, corridors, and galleries are most brightly
painted, a solid color on the wall surfaces, but in the middle a detailed
painting (now mostly chipped away), and light, tasteful arabesques on
the edges and ends, which then are further developed into dainty figures
of children and nymphs, while on another side wild and tame beasts
emerge from thick garlands of flowers. And so even in its present desolate condition, a town first covered by a rain of stones and ash, then

plundered by its excavators, still indicates that a whole nation had a delight in art and pictures which even the keenest modern art lover can neither understand, nor feel, nor desire.

Considering the distance of this town from Vesuvius, the volcanic mass that buried it can neither have been hurled here nor driven over by a blast of wind; rather, we must imagine that the stones and ash hovered in the air for a while like a cloud until they finally settled down over this unfortunate place.

To form a still clearer picture of this event, one might possibly think of a mountain village buried by snow. The spaces between the buildings, indeed the crushed buildings themselves, were filled up, but masonry may well have continued to protrude here and there when, in the course of time, the hill was used for vineyards and gardens. And so certainly many a proprietor, digging on his portion of land, gathered a significant early vintage. Several empty rooms were found, and in one of them was a heap of ashes that concealed various little household utensils and artworks.

We washed the strange, half-disagreeable impression of this mummified town out of our minds as we sat under an arbor by the seaside in a humble inn and consumed a frugal meal. We rejoiced in the blue sky and the bright, sparkling sea, hoping to meet here again and enjoy ourselves in this little spot when it would be covered with vine leaves.

On the outskirts of the city I was struck again by the little houses, which look like perfect imitations of those in Pompeii. We asked permission to enter one of them and found it very neatly furnished. Nicely woven cane chairs, a chest of drawers gilded all over, decorated with colorful flowers, and varnished—evidence that this region, after so many centuries and innumerable changes, still invests its inhabitants with similar manners and customs, inclinations and fancies.

Naples, Monday, March 12.

Today I stole through the city, observing things after my fashion, and noted down many points for future description, about which I can unfortunately say nothing at the moment. Everything points to the fact that a happy land which abundantly supplies the prime necessities of life also produces people with a happy disposition, who can placidly expect every day to be equally good and therefore lead a carefree life. Immediate gratification, temperate enjoyment, cheerful toleration of temporary afflictions!—A nice example of the latter:

The morning was cold and somewhat damp, it had not rained much. I came to a square, where the large flat paving stones appeared to be neatly swept. On this completely smooth, even surface, to my great astonishment, I saw a number of ragged boys squatting in a circle, their hands turned toward the ground as if they were warming themselves. At first I thought it was a prank, but when I saw that their expressions were as calm and serious as though they had satisfied some need, I did my best to solve the mystery, but without success. Therefore I had to ask what it was that induced these little monkeys to assume such a position and gather in this regular circle.

Hereupon I learned that a neighboring blacksmith had heated a wheel rim on this spot, which is done as follows: The iron hoop is laid on the ground, and as many oak chips are heaped on it in a circle as are considered necessary for softening it to the requisite degree. The ignited wood burns off, the rim is fitted to the wheel, and the ashes are carefully swept away. At once the little Indians make use of the heat that has been conducted to the paving and will not budge until they have absorbed the last trace of warmth. There are innumerable examples here of such frugality and alertness to use something that would otherwise be wasted. I find these people to be most eagerly and ingeniously industrious, not in order to become rich, but to live in a carefree manner.

                                                    In the evening.

Today I wanted to arrive at the designated time at the peculiar princess's house and not lose my way, so I hired a guide. He took me to the courtyard gate of a great palace, and since I did not credit her with having such a grand house, I spelled the name to him again most distinctly; but he assured me I was at the right place. Now I found a spacious courtyard, lonely and quiet, empty and clean, surrounded by the main building and its wings. The architecture was of the familiar cheerful Neapolitan type, the coloring also. Opposite me a large portal and a broad, gently rising staircase. On either side of this was an ascending line of footmen in expensive liveries, who bowed very low as I climbed past them. I felt like the sultan in Wieland's fairy tale[24] and took heart from his example. Next I was received by the higher-ranking servants, until finally the most distinguished one of all opened the door to a grand salon, where I was met by a space that I found to be just as cheerful, but also just as empty of people, as the rest. Walking up and down, I glanced into a side gallery and saw a table gorgeously set, as befitted its surroundings, for some forty persons. A priest entered; without asking me who I was or whence I came, he accepted my presence as sufficient acquaintanceship and spoke to me about the most general things.

A pair of double doors opened for the entrance of an elderly gentleman, and immediately closed again behind him. The clergyman went up to him, I too; we greeted him with a few polite words, which he answered with barking, stuttering sounds in a Hottentot dialect, not a syllable of which I could make out. When he took up a position at the fireplace, the clergyman stood back, and so did I. A stately Benedictine entered, accompanied by a younger comrade. He too greeted the host, and was barked at, whereupon he retreated and joined us at the window. Monks, especially the more elegantly dressed ones, have the greatest advantage in society; their clothing indicates humility and renunciation, but at the same time lends them a marked dignity. They can seem obsequious in their behavior without degrading themselves, and then, when they straighten up at the hips again, a certain complacency is actually becoming to them, whereas it would not be acceptable in any other profession. This man was like that. I inquired about Monte Cassino, he invited me there and promised me the best reception. Meanwhile the room had filled with people: officers, courtiers, secular prelates, indeed even a few Capuchins were present. I looked in vain for a dinner partner, but was eventually not to lack one. Again a pair of double doors opened and closed. An old lady had entered, probably still older than the gentleman, and the presence of the lady of the house now fully convinced me that I was in a strange palace and totally unacquainted with its occupants. The food was already being served, and I was keeping close to the clerical gentlemen, so that I could slip into the paradisal dining room with them, when suddenly Filangieri entered with his wife, making his excuses for being late. Shortly after that, the princess also burst into the room and, amidst curtseys, bows, and nodding of heads, sped up to me past everyone else. "It is very nice of you to have kept your word!" she cried. "Sit next to me at the table, you shall have the best morsels. Just wait! I first have to select the right place, then you must sit next to me." Thus summoned, I followed the various twists and turns she made, and finally we reached our seats, directly opposite the Benedictines, Filangieri at my other side.—"The food is very good," she said, "all Lenten fare, but choice, and I shall point out the best to you. But now I must tease the clerics. I cannot abide those fellows; they feed off our family every day in the week. What we have, we should consume with our friends ourselves!"—The soup was passed around, the Benedictine ate decorously.—"Please do not be bashful, reverend sir," she cried out. "Is it possible the spoon is too small? I shall have a larger one brought to you, you gentlemen are used to a healthy mouthful."—The monk responded that everything was so excellently appointed in her princely house that more important guests than he would be most perfectly satisfied here.

The monk took only one of the little pastries, and she called to him that he should surely take half a dozen! He of all people ought to know, she said, that wafer dough was easily digestible. The prudent man took another pastry, thanking her for her gracious attention, as though he had not heard the blasphemous jest. And so a coarser pastry also gave her an opportunity to vent her malice; for when the monk stuck his fork into one of them and put it on his plate, a second rolled after it.— "Do take a third, Sir Monk!" she exclaimed. "Apparently you want to lay a good foundation!"—"If such excellent materials are offered, the builder has easy work!" answered the monk.—And so it continued, without a pause, except when she was conscientiously assigning me the best morsels.

Meanwhile I was discussing the most serious matters with my neighbor. As a matter of fact, I have never heard Filangieri utter a trivial word. In this respect as in many others he resembles our friend Georg Schlosser,[25] except that as a Neapolitan and man of the world he has a gentler nature and is more at ease in society.

During this whole time the clerical gentlemen were granted no respite from the mischievousness of the lady beside me; it was particularly the Lenten fish dishes, disguised as meat, that furnished her with inexhaustible material for making impious and improper remarks, in which she laid special stress on the desires of the flesh and approved of enjoying them at least in form, even if the substance is forbidden.

I noted down still more jests of this kind, but I cannot bring myself to recount them. Such things may seem quite acceptable in actual life and when issuing from pretty lips, but in black and white I myself have misgivings about them. And then the odd part about such bold impudence is that it pleases at the time, because it astonishes, but when retold later it seems offensive and obnoxious to us.

Dessert was served, and I was afraid that the teasing would continue as before; unexpectedly, however, my dinner partner turned to me quite calmly and said: "The clerics shall be allowed to swallow down their Syracusan wine in peace. In any case, I have not succeeded in annoying a single one to death or even in spoiling his appetite. Now let us talk sensibly! What a conversation you have had again with Filangieri! That good man! He makes a lot of work for himself. I have often told him: 'If you make new laws, then we shall have to make a new effort to figure out how we can immediately evade them; we had already done that with the old ones.' Just see what a fine place Naples is: people have lived here happily and light-heartedly for so many years, and even if somebody is hanged now and then, everything else goes along splendidly." Hereupon she suggested that I go to Sorrento, where she has a large estate. Her steward would stuff me with the best fish and the choicest milkfed veal *(mungana)*. The mountain air would cure me of all philosophy, and then she would come herself. Not a trace would remain of all my wrinkles, which in any case I was allowing to spread prematurely, and together we would lead a very merry life there.

Naples, March 13, 1787.

Today I shall write a few more words, so that one letter will chase the other. I am feeling well, but I am seeing less than I should. The place inspires indolence and leisurely living, but meanwhile I am gradually rounding out my picture of the city.

On Sunday we were in Pompeii.—There has been much calamity in the world, but little that has brought posterity so much pleasure. I really do not know of anything more interesting. The houses are small and cramped, but all of them are painted most attractively inside. The city gate, with the graves directly next to it, is remarkable. The grave of a priestess, made like a semi-circular bench with a stone back, the inscription carved on it in big letters.[26] Out past its back the sea and the setting sun are visible. A magnificent place, worthy of the splendid idea.

We found good, lively Neapolitan company there. These people are completely natural and happy-go-lucky. We ate at Torre dell' Annunziata, at a table by the seaside. The day was extremely beautiful, the view of nearby Castell a Mare and Sorrento exquisite. Our companions felt so satisfied about residing here that some of them said it must be impossible to live without a view of the sea. As for me, I am satisfied to have its picture in my mind, and like to return to the hill country occasionally.

Fortunately there is a landscape painter[27] here who can very faithfully transfer the quality of this rich, open environment to his drawings. He has already made several for me.

I have now also closely studied the rocks produced by Vesuvius. I should really devote the rest of my life to observation, for I would discover much that might increase human knowledge. Please inform Herder that my botanical studies are progressing farther and farther; the principle is always the same, but a lifetime would be needed to follow it through. Perhaps I shall still be able to trace the main lines.

Now I am looking forward to the Portici museum.[28] While it is usually the first thing one sees, we shall see it last. I still do not know what my future plans are: everybody wants me back in Rome for Easter. I shall let matters take their course. Angelica has set about painting a picture based on my *Iphigenia;*[29] the conception is very felicitous, and she will carry it out excellently. The moment when Orestes comes to his senses again in the vicinity of his sister and his friend. She has combined what is spoken in succession by the three personages into a simultaneous group and transformed those words into gestures. From this it can be seen how delicate her feeling is, and how skillfully she appropriates what belongs in her province. And really it is the axis of the play.

Farewell, and love me! All the people here like me, even if they do not know what to do with me; however, Tischbein suits them better: in the evening he lets them watch while he paints a few life-size heads, and during this and because of it they act like New Zealanders seeing a warship. Here is the amusing story about that:

Namely, Tischbein has the great gift of being able to sketch the contours of gods and heroes, as large as life and larger. He draws in a few hatchings and skillfully applies shadows with a wide brush, so that the finished head looks round and sublime. The people present were astonished to see how easily he accomplished this and were heartily delighted by it. Now their fingers itched to paint like that; they grabbed the brushes and—painted beards on each other and stained each other's faces. Is there not an element of primitive humanity in this? And it was a cultured assemblage in the house of a man who himself draws and paints quite enthusiastically. No one who has not seen this race of people can form any conception of them.

Caserta, Wednesday, March 14.

A visit to Hackert in the very comfortable apartments assigned to him in the old palace. The new palace is huge indeed, on the order of the Escorial,[30] built in a rectangle with several courtyards; suitably royal. The location extraordinarily beautiful, on the most fertile plain in the world, and yet its park extends up to the mountains. An aqueduct diverts a whole river to water both palace and region, and the entire volume of water can be projected over artificially arranged rocks to form the most magnificent cascade. The park is lovely and very appropriate for an area that is one big garden.

The palace, although truly royal, did not seem sufficiently animated to me, and people of our sort cannot feel comfortable in such huge, empty spaces. The king may have similar sentiments, for a building has been provided in the mountains which is more suited to human proportions and lends itself to the pleasures of hunting and living.

Caserta, Thursday, March 15.

Hackert lives very comfortably in the old palace, with plenty of room for himself and his guests. While he is always busy drawing and painting, he remains sociable and knows how to attract people by making each one his pupil. He has won me over completely too, because he is tolerant of my weakness for insisting first of all on precision in drawing and then on sureness and clarity in the disposition of light and shadow. When he draws with ink, three kinds of it always stand ready, and while he works from back to front, using one of them after the other, a picture emerges without one's knowing where it comes from. If only it were as easy to do as it looks. He said to me with his usual resolute candor: "You have talent, but you cannot do anything. Stay with me for eighteen months and you will produce something that will please both you and other people."—Is that not a text on which an eternal sermon could be preached to all dilettantes? Its effect on me remains to be seen.

The special trust with which the queen honors him is shown not only by the fact that he gives practical instruction to the princesses, but also and especially by his often being summoned of an evening to converse instructively about art and other related subjects. In so doing, he depends on Sulzer's *Dictionary,* from which he chooses this or that article, according to his own preferences and convictions.

I could not but approve of that, and at the same time smile at myself. What a difference there is between someone who wants to develop himself from the inside out and one who wants to influence the world and instruct it in a way suitable for home use! I have always detested Sulzer's theory because of its false basic principle, yet now I saw that even this work contains far more than people need. The many bits of knowledge it imparts, the way of thinking that satisfied so worthy a man as Sulzer, are they not adequate for laymen?

We spent several pleasant and significant hours with the art restorer Andres,[31] who, having been summoned from Rome, also lives here in the old palace and diligently continues with his work, in which the king is interested. I must not begin to tell about his skill in restoring old pictures, because I should likewise have to enlarge on the difficult problems with which this unique artistic craft is concerned, and how they are happily solved.

Caserta, March 16, 1787.

Your dear letters of February 19th reached me today, and an answer shall go off immediately. How gladly I collect my thoughts, with my friends in mind!

Naples is a paradise, and everyone lives, as it were, in a state of intoxicated self-forgetfulness. It is the same with me. I hardly recognize myself. I feel like a completely different person. Yesterday I thought: "Either you used to be mad, or you are now."

I have now also made an excursion from here to the ruins of ancient Capua and everything connected with them.

Only in this region does one begin to understand what vegetation really is and why land is tilled. The flax is already on the point of blooming, and the wheat is one span and a half high. The land around Caserta is completely flat, with fields worked as evenly and cleanly as garden plots. Poplars, with grapevines twined around them, are planted everywhere, and in spite of this shade the soil bears the most perfect crops. Just think what will happen when spring actually arrives! Heretofore, with this beautiful sunshine, we have had very cold winds, caused by the snow in the mountains.

It must be decided in a fortnight whether I go to Sicily. Never yet have I vacillated so strangely about a decision. Today something happens that recommends the trip to me, tomorrow some circumstance advises against it. Two spirits are fighting over me.

Confidentially to my women friends only, so that my male friends may not hear it! I can see clearly that my *Iphigenia* has met with a strange reception: its original form was so familiar and everyone knew the expressions, having assimilated them through frequent hearing and reading. Now it all sounds different, and I can see that basically no one is thanking me for the endless trouble I have taken. A work of this kind is never really finished, but simply has to be called finished, once everything possible has been done, as far as time and circumstances permit.

But this is not going to deter me from undertaking the same operation with *Tasso*. I would actually prefer to throw it into the fire, but I shall stick to my resolution, and since there is no other choice, we shall make a curious work out of it. Consequently I am not at all displeased that the printing of my works is proceeding so slowly. And yet it is also good to be threatened at some distance by the typesetter. Strange, indeed, that I expect, even demand, some urging to perform the freest action.

Caserta, March 16, 1787.

While Rome is conducive to study, here one just wants to live. The world and one's self are forgotten, and for me it is a curious feeling to associate only with pleasure-seeking people. Sir William Hamilton,[32] who still resides here as the English ambassador, has now, after long years of fancying art and studying nature, found the culmination of all his joy in art and nature in a beautiful girl. He has her living with him, an Englishwoman about twenty years old.³³ She is very lovely and has a good figure. He has had a Grecian costume made for her that suits her to perfection, and she lets down her hair, takes a few shawls, and varies her postures, gestures, expressions, etc. until at last the onlooker really thinks he is dreaming. In her movements and surprising variety one sees perfected what so many thousands of artists would have liked to achieve. Standing, kneeling, sitting, lying, grave, sad, roguish, wanton, penitent, enticing, menacing, fearful, etc., one follows upon the other and from the other. She knows how to choose and change the folds of her veil to set off each expression, and makes herself a hundred different headdresses with the same cloths. The old knight holds up the light for the performance and has devoted himself heart and soul to this art object. He sees in her all the antiquities, all the beautiful profiles on Sicilian coins, even the *Apollo Belvedere* itself. This much is certain, it is unique entertainment! We have already enjoyed it on two evenings. Tomorrow morning Tischbein will paint her.

What I have heard and conjectured about the personages and conditions at court must first be weighed and sorted. Today the king is on a wolf hunt; he hopes to bag at least five.

Naples, addendum to March 17.

When I try to write words, pictures always stand before my eyes, of the fertile land, the open sea, the fragrant islands, the smoking mountain, and I lack the faculties for describing all that.

Only in this region does one come to understand how it could have occurred to human beings to till the fields, here, where the soil produces everything, and where three to five harvests can be expected every year. It is claimed that in the best years Indian corn has been planted three times.

I have seen much and thought still more: the world opens to me more and more, and everything I have known for a long time only now becomes mine. What an early knowing and late practicing creature the human being is!

However, it is a pity that I cannot communicate my observations from moment to moment; true, Tischbein is with me, but as an artist and man he is pulled in this direction and that by a thousand thoughts, and his time is taken up by a hundred persons. His situation is unique and odd, and he cannot freely share in someone else's existence because he feels so constricted in his own endeavors.

And yet the whole world is just a simple wheel, completely the same in its whole circumference, and only looks so curious to us because we ourselves are driven around with it.

What I always predicted, has happened: only in this country am I learning to understand a great many natural phenomena and to clear up many confused opinions. I am summing up from all sides and shall bring a great deal back with me, certainly also great love of my fatherland and joy in living with only a few friends.

My Sicilian trip is still being weighed in the scales of the gods; the pointer moves this way and that.

Who can the friend be who has been so mysteriously announced to me?[34] I hope I do not miss him because of my aimless island trip!

The frigate has returned from Palermo; a week from today it will leave from here again. I still do not know whether I shall sail along or return to Rome for Holy Week. I have never before been so undecided; a moment, a trivial thing, may determine the matter.

I am getting along better with people now; only they must be weighed with shopkeeper's weights, by no means in gold scales, as even friends unfortunately often do among themselves, out of hypochondriacal caprice and strange expectations.

The people here pay no attention to each other and scarcely notice that they are walking back and forth side by side. All day long they run to and fro in a paradise, without looking very much at anything, and if those neighboring jaws of hell begin to rage, they seek help from the blood of St. Januarius,[35] just as the rest of the world seeks help against death and the devil, or would like to, with—blood.

It is a remarkable and salutary experience to walk through the midst of such an immense and restlessly active crowd. What a chaotic stream of people, and yet each of them finds his individual way and goal. Only amid such a multitude and so much activity do I feel really quiet and solitary; the noisier the streets, the calmer I become.

Sometimes I am critical of Rousseau and his hypochondriacal affliction, and yet I am beginning to understand how so finely organized a mind could be put into disarray. If I did not feel in such great sympathy with natural things, and if I did not see that in this apparent confusion there are a hundred observations which can be compared and put in order, just as a surveyor tests many individual measurements by drawing a line through them, I would often think that I myself was mad.

Naples, March 18, 1787.

Now we could no longer delay seeing Herculaneum and the collection of excavated objects at Portici. That ancient town, located at the foot of Vesuvius, was completely covered with lava, made deeper by subsequent eruptions, so that the buildings now lie sixty feet below the surface. It was discovered by someone who was digging a well and struck inlaid marble floors. A great pity that the excavation was not systematically carried out by German miners: for certainly the haphazard later digging has wastefully destroyed many a noble relic of antiquity. Sixty steps lead down into a vault where by torchlight one can gaze in amazement at the theater, which once stood under the open sky, and hear about all the things that were found there and brought up to the surface.

We entered the museum well recommended and were well received. But even so, we were not permitted to sketch anything. Perhaps, as a result, we paid that much closer attention and transported ourselves the more eagerly into that vanished era when all these items stood around for the active use and enjoyment of their owners. Those little houses and rooms in Pompeii now seemed to me both more cramped and more spacious: more cramped, because I pictured them crowded with all these worthy objects, more spacious, because these same objects were not there merely out of necessity, but were so very ingeniously and charmingly decorated and enlivened by visual art that they delight and expand the mind more than the most spacious interior could.

For example, we saw a magnificently shaped bucket, with the most elegant upper rim; on closer inspection, this rim can be raised up from two sides, the combined semicircle is grasped as a handle and the vessel can be carried most comfortably. The lamps are decorated with as many masks and scrolls as they have wicks, so that each flame illuminates a genuinely artistic creation. Tall, slim bronze stands are designed to hold the lamps; by comparison, the hanging lamps trail various ingeniously conceived figures which more than meet the goal of causing pleasure and delight by swinging and dangling.

Hopeful of returning, we followed the guide from room to room, and, whenever the moment permitted, we snatched bits of pleasure and instruction, as well as we could manage.

Naples, Monday, March 19, 1787.

In the last few days a new acquaintanceship has grown closer. During these four weeks Tischbein has been my faithful and helpful companion in seeing natural and artistic sights, and we were together yesterday in Portici. But now it has become clear from our mutual deliberations that his artistic objectives, and the affairs he must attend to in town and at court, because he hopes for a future position in Naples, do not blend with my aims, wishes, and favorite pursuits. Therefore, always being solicitous of me, he has suggested, as a constant companion for me, a young man whom I have frequently seen since my first days here, and not without sympathy and liking. It is Kniep, who sojourned in Rome for a while but then proceeded to Naples, where the landscape painter is most truly in his element. I had already heard him praised in Rome as a skilled draftsman, but he did not receive equal praise for his diligence. I have come to know him quite well and would prefer to call the censured fault indecision, which can certainly be overcome if we are together for a while. A good beginning confirms me in this hope, and if it is left to me, we shall remain good comrades for a considerable time.

Naples, addendum to March 19.

All one has to do in order to see the most inimitable pictures is to stroll along the street and keep one's eyes open.

Yesterday at the Molo, one of the noisiest corners in the city, I saw a Pulcinella on a wooden platform, fighting with a little monkey, while on the balcony above them a rather pretty girl was offering her charms for sale. Next to the monkey platform a quack doctor was holding out his cure-all elixirs to the credulous crowd. Painted by Gerrit Dou,[36] it would have made a picture worthy of delighting both contemporaries and future generations.

Today was also the festival of St. Joseph; he is the patron saint of all *frittaruoli,* i.e., makers of baked goods, baked goods in the crudest sense. Since intense flames constantly shoot out from their black and boiling oil, all fiery torments are in their province; therefore on the previous evening they had handsomely decorated the house fronts with paintings: souls in Purgatory, Last Judgments glowed and flamed all around. In front of the doors, large pans stood on lightly constructed cooking stoves. One journeyman kneaded the dough, another formed it, making it into rings, and threw these into the boiling grease. At each pan stood a third man with a little spit; he fished the pastry rings out with it when they were done, and shoved them onto another little spit held by a fourth man, who offered them to the bystanders. The last were two young fellows with curly blond wigs, something that signifies "angel" here. A few more figures completed the group, served wine to the workers, drank some themselves, and shouted the praises of the wares. The angels too, and the cooks, all shouted. The people crowded up; because this evening all baked goods are being sold more cheaply, with a part of the receipts even given to the poor.

Endless stories of this kind could be told; and this is how it is every day, always something new and more bizarre, just the variety of clothing met with on the street, the throngs of people in the Via Toledo alone!

And when one lives with the people there is much other singular entertainment; they are so natural that I could become natural along with them. For example, we find the Pulcinella, the actual Neapolitan masquerade character, the Harlequin, from Bergamo, and Hanswurst, the native of the Tyrol. Pulcinella, now: a truly calm, composed serving man, somewhat indifferent, almost lazy, and yet humorous. And waiters and porters of that type are found everywhere. Today I was especially amused by our man, and it was merely a matter of sending him to fetch paper and pens. Partial misunderstanding, hesitation, good will, and roguishness created the most charming scene, one that could be produced with good success on any stage.

Naples, Tuesday, March 20, 1787.

Word of a new eruption, which is not visible in Naples because the lava is flowing down to Ottaviano, prompted me to visit Vesuvius a third time. I had hardly sprung from my two-wheeled, one-horse carriage at the foot of the mountain when those two guides who had accompanied our earlier ascent appeared. I did not wish to be without either of them, and took the one along out of habit and gratitude, the other because of my confidence in him, and both for my greater convenience.

When we arrived at the summit, the older man stayed back with the cloaks and victuals, the younger one followed me, and we courageously advanced upon an enormous volume of smoke that was issuing from the mountain below the conical crater. Then we strode along the mountainside, going slightly downwards, until at last, under a clear sky, we saw the lava gushing forth from the wild smoke cloud.

We can hear about something a thousand times, but only direct observation will show us its peculiar characteristics. The lava was narrow,
perhaps not more than ten feet wide, but the way it flowed down a
gently sloping, fairly even expanse was quite striking; for as it cools
on the sides and upper surface during its flow, a canal is formed. This
grows higher and higher, because the molten material underneath the
fiery stream also stiffens, while the dross floating on the surface is
thrown down equally to the right and left. By this means a dam is gradually raised, on which the glowing river flows along as calmly as a mill
stream. We walked beside the dam, which was raised to a considerable
height, the dross regularly rolling down its sides as far as our feet. We
could see the glowing stream from below through several holes in the
canal, and from above as it flowed on down.

On account of the very bright sunshine the glow appeared dimmed,
and only a moderate volume of smoke rose into the clear air. I wanted
to approach the point where the lava breaks out of the mountain. There,
so my guide asserted, an arched roof was supposed to form over it
immediately, and he had frequently stood on one. To see and experience
this as well, we climbed back up the mountain to reach that point from
the rear. Fortunately we found the place exposed by a brisk current
of air, although not completely, for the smoke was belching from a
thousand fissures all around it; and now we were actually standing on
the rigid cover, which looked like coiled dough; but it extended so far
in front that we could not see the lava gush out.

We attempted another few dozen steps, but the ground grew more
and more incandescent; an overpowering cloud of smoke whirled up
to darken the sun and choke us. The guide, who had gone ahead of
me, soon turned back, took hold of me, and we extricated ourselves
from these hellish fumes.

After refreshing our eyes with the view, and our palates and hearts
with the wine, we walked around to observe still other incidental features of this hellish peak that had been raised up in the midst of Paradise.
I again carefully inspected some pits that are volcanic chimneys which
do not emit smoke but constant violent puffs of glowing air. I saw that
they were thoroughly coated with a stalactitic material that covered
their interiors up to the top with forms like nipples and barrel corks.
Since the chimneys were of unequal size, some of these pendant vapor
products were fairly well within reach, so that we could easily obtain
them with our staffs and some hooklike contrivances. I had already
found examples of these, classified as genuine lava, at the lava merchant's, and I was glad to discover that it was volcanic soot deposited
by the hot vapors, revealing the volatilized mineral parts contained in
them.

On the way back I was revived by the most magnificent sunset and a heavenly evening; but I could feel how confusing such an enormous contrast is to the senses. The terrible to the beautiful, the beautiful to the terrible, one cancels out the other, and the result is a feeling of indifference. Surely the Neapolitan would be a different human being if he did not feel himself wedged between God and Satan.

Naples, March 22, 1787.

If I were not driven by my German mentality and a desire to learn and do, rather than to enjoy, I would linger somewhat longer in this school of light and merry living and try to profit from it more. It is quite pleasant to be here, but I wish it was possible to establish myself just a little. No praise can be too great for the city's location and its mild climate, but a foreigner also does not have much more than this to fall back on.

To be sure, anyone who takes the time, and is wealthy and adroit, can settle down very comfortably here. Thus Hamilton has created a lovely existence for himself and is enjoying it now in the autumn of his life. The rooms he has decorated in the English taste are charming, and the view from the corner room is perhaps unique. Below us the sea, Capri facing us, Posillipo to the right, the Villa Reale promenade nearer by, to the left an old Jesuit building, in the distance the coast from Sorrento to Capo Minerva. There may well be nothing in Europe to match this, at any rate not in the middle of a large, populous city.

Hamilton is a man of universal tastes, and after having wandered through all the realms of creation, he has come upon a beautiful woman, the masterpiece of the Great Artist.

And now, after all this pleasure and hundreds of others, the Sirens are luring me across the sea, and, if the wind is favorable, I shall leave at the same time as this letter, it to the north, and I to the south. The human mind balks at limits, and I, especially, have great need of the wide world. Now I must concentrate less on persevering than on quickly apprehending. If I have just grasped the fingertip of an object, I shall be able to seize its whole hand by dint of hearing and seeing.

Oddly enough, a friend[37] has lately called my attention to *Wilhelm Meister* and demanded a continuation of it. That would probably not be possible in these climes, but perhaps some of this atmosphere can be imparted to its last books. I hope that my existence may mature sufficiently for that, its stem grow longer, and its blossoms burst forth more abundantly and beautifully. Certainly it would be better for me not to come back at all, if I cannot come back reborn.

Naples, addendum to March 22.

Today we saw a picture by Correggio[38] which is for sale, to be sure
not perfectly preserved, but with its very delightfully distinctive charm
intact. It portrays a Virgin, just at the moment when the Child is hes-
itating between His mother's breast and some pears being offered Him
by a little angel. Thus, a "Weaning of Christ." I find the idea extremely
delicate, the composition lively, natural, and pleasant, and the execution
most charming. It immediately brings the *Vow of St. Catherine* to mind,
and seems to me unquestionably by the hand of Correggio.

Naples, Friday, March 23, 1787.

My friendship with Kniep has now developed and become established
in a very practical way. We were at Paestum together,[39] where he
sketched very busily, as he also did on the way there and back. This
resulted in the most magnificent drawings, and he himself is pleased
with this active, industrious life, which has awakened a talent in him
that he hardly credited himself with having. Here it is a question of
being resolute; and here is just where his precise and meticulous skill
is shown. He never fails to put a rectangular border around his drawing
paper, and sharpening and resharpening the best English pencils is almost as great a pleasure for him as the actual sketching; but that is
also why his outlines are all one could ask for.

We have now made the following agreement: From today onward
we shall live and travel together, his only duty being to sketch, as he
did during the last few days. All of his drawings will be my property;[40]
but so that he may have some further work out of this after our return,
he will finish a number of yet-to-be-chosen items for me, up to a certain
designated sum of money; in the meantime, considering his skill and
the significance of the views, and so forth, to be captured, the rest will
probably take care of itself. I am quite happy about this arrangement,
and now at last I can give a short account of our trip.

Sitting in a light, two-wheeled carriage and alternately taking the reins,
a good-natured, uncouth boy in back, we rolled through the magnificent
region, which Kniep greeted with an artist's eye. Presently we reached
the mountain gorge, through which one races over the smoothest road,
flying past the loveliest wooded and rocky sections. Then at last, in
the neighborhood of Alla Cava, Kniep could not refrain from fixing on
paper, cleanly and characteristically, the outlines, including the sides
and foot, of a splendid mountain directly in front of us that stood out
sharply against the sky. We were both delighted with this, regarding
it as the formal initiation of our alliance.

In the evening, a similar sketch was made from our windows in Salerno. It will spare me all description of this uniquely lovely and fertile region. Who would not have wanted to study here in those fine days when the university was flourishing?[41] Very early in the morning we drove on untracked, often marshy roads toward a pair of well-formed mountains, and passed through brooks and waters where we looked into the wild, bloodshot eyes of buffalos that resembled hippopotamuses.

The land grew increasingly flat and desolate, while the paucity of buildings indicated that farming was meager. Finally, uncertain whether we were riding through rocks or ruins, we could make out that several large, oblong masses we had already noticed from a distance were actually temples and monuments left over from a once very magnificent city.[42] Kniep, who on the way there had already sketched the two picturesque limestone mountains, quickly looked for a vantage point from which the character of this wholly unpicturesque area might be seized and depicted.

Meanwhile I had a local peasant guide me around the buildings; my first reaction was purely one of astonishment. I found myself in a totally alien world. For as the centuries move upward from the grimly serious to the pleasing, they move the human being along with them, indeed they breed him thus. Our eyes, and through them our whole inner being, are now so exclusively directed and definitely oriented to a slenderer type of architecture that these blunt, cone-shaped, dense columnar masses make us feel uncomfortable, even intimidated. But I soon pulled myself together, remembered my art history, bore in mind that the spirit of those times was in keeping with such architecture, pictured to myself the austere style of their sculpture, and in less than an hour I felt reconciled. Indeed I praised my tutelary genius for having let me see these very well-preserved remains with my own eyes, since no picture can give an adequate idea of them. For they seem more elegant in architectonic projections, cruder in perspective drawings, than they are. Only by walking around and through them can one really breathe life into them; and one feels it breathe out of them again, which is what the architect intended, indeed built into them. And I spent the whole day like this, while Kniep wasted no time in supplying us with the most precise sketches. How glad I was to have no worries in this regard and to acquire so many reliable aids for my memory. Unfortunately there were no facilities here for staying overnight, so we returned to Salerno and left for Naples early the next morning. Vesuvius seen from the back, in the most fertile countryside; poplars as colossal as pyramids along the highway in the foreground. We stopped for a bit and acquired this picture also.

Then we reached a high point; the broadest view opened up to us. Naples in its splendor, the row of houses stretching for miles along the flat shore of the bay, the promontories, the tongues of land, the walls of rock, then the islands, and behind them the sea—it was an enchanting view.

A hideous song, more like a shriek of pleasure and howl of joy, from the boy in back, who had now stood up, startled and annoyed me. He was the best-natured lad and had not heard a single cross word from us, but now I snapped at him angrily.

For a while he did not stir, but then he gently patted me on the shoulder, stretched out his right arm between us, and pointed his index finger, saying: "Signore, perdonate! questa è la mia patria!"—That means in translation: "Forgive me, sir! That is my fatherland!"—And so I was surprised a second time. Something like tears filled the eyes of this poor northerner!

Naples, March 25, 1787. Annunciation Day.

Although I felt that Kniep was eager to accompany me to Sicily, I could nevertheless tell that there was something he was loath to leave behind. With his candid nature, it did not long remain hidden from me that he had close and faithful ties to a sweetheart. It was quite charming to hear how they had become acquainted, and so far the girl's conduct recommended her; but now I was also to meet her, and see how pretty she was. Arrangements were made for this, and in such a way that I would at the same time be able to enjoy one of the most beautiful views over Naples. He led me to the flat roof of a house, from which I could survey especially the lower part of the city toward the Molo, the bay, and the coast of Sorrento. Everything farther to the right was shifted out of place in the oddest manner, something which can probably only be seen by standing at this spot. Naples is beautiful and magnificent everywhere.

As we were admiring the area, suddenly, although it was expected, a very pretty little head rose up from below. (For the entrance to a roof such as this is only an oblong opening in the stone floor, which can be covered with a trapdoor.) And now, when the little angel emerged completely, it occurred to me that older artists depicted the Annunciation in this way, with the angel coming up a stairs. However, this angel had in fact a beautiful figure, a pretty little face, and a good, natural demeanor. I was glad to see my new friend so happy, here beneath this magnificent sky, with a view over the most beautiful region in the world.

When she had gone again, he admitted to me that his reason for voluntarily enduring poverty heretofore had been both to enjoy her love and to learn to appreciate her frugality. Now he found his improved prospects and comfortable circumstances especially desirable because he would be able to make a better life for her as well.

Naples, addendum to March 25.

After this agreeable adventure I strolled by the sea and felt quietly happy. Then a good inspiration came to me concerning botanical matters. Please tell Herder that I shall soon have figured out the primeval plant. Only I fear that no one will be willing to recognize the rest of the plant kingdom in it. My much-discussed theory of cotyledons is so highly refined that it would be difficult to go any farther.

Naples, March 26, 1787.

Tomorrow this letter will go off to you from here. On Thursday the 29th I shall finally leave for Palermo with the corvette which, in my ignorance of maritime affairs, I raised to the rank of a frigate in my previous letter. My doubts about whether I should travel or stay made me uneasy during a part of my sojourn here. Now that I have decided, things are going better. This is a beneficial, in fact a necessary, trip for one of my disposition. Sicily points me toward Asia and Africa, and it is no trivial thing to stand in person on the remarkable spot that has been the focus of so much of the world's history.

I have treated Naples in my own fashion; I was by no means diligent, but I have seen much and formed a general idea of the country, its inhabitants, and their circumstances. Some things are still to be made up on my return, but only some, to be sure, for I must be back in Rome before June 29th. Even if I miss Holy Week, I shall at least celebrate St. Peter's Day there. My Sicilian journey must not divert me too far from my original intention.

The day before yesterday we had a violent storm with thunder, lightning, and torrents of rain. Now it has all cleared up again, and a splendid tramontane wind is blowing. If it remains constant, we shall have a very fast trip.

Yesterday my companion and I went to see our ship and inspect the little cabin we are to occupy. A sea journey is something I have never had any conception of; this little crossing and perhaps a circumnavigation of the coast will be an aid to my powers of imagination and expand my world. The captain is a young, lively man, the ship very graceful and trim, made in America, a good sailing vessel.

Everything is now starting to become green here, in Sicily I shall find it still more advanced. When you receive this letter, I shall be on the return trip and have Trinacria[43] behind me. That is the way of human beings: they constantly jump backwards and forwards in thought; I have not yet been there and am already back with all of you. But the confused state of this letter is not my fault; I am interrupted every moment, but would still like to finish writing this page.

A certain Marchese Berio[44] has just visited me, a young man who seems to know a great deal. Naturally he too wanted to meet the author of *Werther*. In general there is a great, urgent desire here for culture and knowledge. Only they are too lighthearted to go about it in the right way. If I just had more time, I would gladly devote that time to them. These four weeks—what were they compared to the tremendous life here! Now farewell! I shall probably learn how to *travel* on this trip, but whether I shall learn how to *live,* I do not know. The people who seem to understand it are so very different from me in type and nature that I could never aspire to this talent.

Farewell, and love me, just as I keep all of you affectionately in mind.

Naples, March 28, 1787.

These days are entirely taken up with packing and saying goodbye, with attending to things and paying bills, doing what has been neglected and making preparations. They are a total loss for me.

As I was taking leave of him, the Prince of Waldeck made me uneasy by suggesting nothing less than that on my return I should arrange to accompany him to Greece and Dalmatia.[45] Let him who goes out into the world and becomes involved with it beware lest he lose his bearings or actually his mind! I am not capable of writing another syllable.

Naples, March 29, 1787.

For several days the weather had turned uncertain, but today, on the designated date of departure, it is as beautiful as can be. The most favorable tramontane wind, a clear, sunny sky beneath which one wants to go out into the wide world. Now let me say one more sincere farewell to all my friends in Weimar and Gotha! May your love accompany me, for surely I shall always need it. Last night I dreamt that I was back at my work again. It does seem as though I could never unload my pheasant-ship anywhere except among you. But may it first be filled with a very stately cargo!

Sicily

Sea voyage, Thursday, March 29.

No brisk, beneficial northeaster was blowing now, as when the packet boat departed the previous time; instead, unfortunately, a mild southwester, the most unfavorable of all winds, was coming from the opposite side, and so we learned how dependent the seafarer is on the caprices of wind and weather. We spent an impatient morning alternating between the shore and the coffeehouse; at noon we finally embarked and enjoyed the most magnificent view in the finest weather. The corvette lay at anchor not far from the Molo. Clear sunshine, but a hazy atmosphere, so that the shaded rock walls of Sorrento had the loveliest blue color. Lively, sunny Naples gleamed with every hue. The ship did not move from the spot until sundown, and then only slowly, the contrary wind blew us over toward Posillipo and its extremity. The ship went calmly on its way all night. It was built in America, is fast-sailing, and equipped inside with pleasant little rooms and individual beds. The other passengers are lively but well behaved: opera singers and dancers, assigned to Palermo.

Friday, March 30.

At daybreak we found ourselves between Ischia and Capri, approximately a mile from the latter. The sun rose splendidly from behind the mountains of Capri and Capo Minerva. Kniep diligently drew the outlines of the coasts and island and various views of them; our slow progress was an aid to his efforts. We continued on our way with a weak, listless wind. Vesuvius disappeared from sight at about four o'clock, while Capo Minerva and Ischia were still visible. The sun sank into the sea, accompanied by clouds and a long streak of gleaming purple lights that extended for miles. Kniep also sketched this phenomenon. Now there was no more land to be seen, the horizon was a circle of water all around us, the night was bright, and the moon shone beautifully.

I had only had moments to enjoy these magnificent views when I was overcome by seasickness. I took myself off to my room, chose the horizontal position, refrained from eating or drinking anything but white bread and red wine, and felt quite comfortable. Being closed off from the outer world, I let the inner one prevail. Since the voyage promised to be a slow one, I immediately set myself a large task in order to have entertainment of a significant kind. Of all my papers, the only ones I had taken along over the sea were the first two acts of *Tasso,* written in poetic prose. These two acts, approximately the same as the present ones with respect to plan and action, but written ten years ago, had a soft, nebulous quality;[46] but this quickly evaporated when, in accord with my newer opinions, I concentrated on form and introduced meter.

Saturday, March 31.

The sun rose out of the sea, shining brightly. At seven o'clock we caught up with a French ship that had left two days before us. That is how much better we sailed, and still the end of our voyage was not in view. It was some consolation to see the island of Ustica but unfortunately, like Capri too, it was on our left as we passed, when it should have been on our right. Towards noon the wind was completely against us, and we did not move from the spot. The sea began to grow rougher, and almost everyone on board was sick.

I stayed in my accustomed position, rethinking the whole play from one end to the other, over and over again. The hours passed, and I would not have noticed the various times of day, had it not been for the roguish Kniep. The waves did not affect his appetite, and when from time to time he brought me bread and wine, he would at the same time maliciously praise the excellence of the noon meal and the cheerfulness and charm of the young captain, who regretted that I could not enjoy my portion with them. Kniep would also mischievously describe how individual members of the company made the transition from jesting and merriment to discomfort and illness; and he had a rich supply of these stories.

At four o'clock in the afternoon the captain turned the ship in a different direction. The big sails were hoisted again and our course was set directly on the island of Ustica, behind which, to our great joy, we saw the mountains of Sicily. The wind improved, we sailed more swiftly toward Sicily, and we caught sight of several more islands. The sunset was overcast, with the celestial orb hidden behind mists. All evening a quite favorable wind. Towards midnight the sea began to get very choppy.

Sunday, April 1.

At three o'clock in the morning a violent storm. In my sleep, and half dreaming, I worked on my dramatic plans, while in the meantime there was great activity on deck. The sails had to be lowered, and the ship was rolling on the high swells. Towards daybreak the storm abated, the atmosphere cleared. Now the island of Ustica lay completely to the left. A large turtle swimming in the distance was pointed out to us, a living dot easily discerned through our spyglasses. Towards noon we could very clearly distinguish the coast of Sicily with its headlands and inlets, but the wind was now much against us, and we tacked back and forth. Towards afternoon we were nearer the shore. We saw the entire western coast quite clearly from the Lilybaeic foothills to Capo Gallo, in fair weather and bright sunshine.

A school of dolphins accompanied the ship on both sides of the prow and kept darting out ahead of us. It was amusing to see how they would now swim alongside, covered by the transparent waves, now leap above the water, showing their fins and dorsal spikes and their sparkling gold and green sides.

Since we were being much affected by the wind, the captain headed straight for an inlet, right behind Capo Gallo. Kniep did not neglect this fine opportunity to draw the various views in considerable detail. At sunset the captain turned the ship back into the deep sea and sailed northeastwards, to reach the latitude of Palermo. I sometimes ventured on deck, but I never forgot my poetic goal, and I had brought the whole play more or less under control. Bright moonlight in a cloudy sky, the reflections on the sea infinitely beautiful. Painters, to gain an effect, often make us believe that the reflection of the celestial orbs in the water is broadest near the viewer, where it makes the strongest impression. Here, however, the reflection was seen to be broadest at the horizon, and to end like a pointed pyramid in glittering waves next to the ship. The captain changed his maneuvers a few more times during the night.

On Monday, April 2, at 8 o'clock in the morning we found ourselves opposite Palermo. This morning seemed a very delightful one to me. In these last days in the belly of the whale the plan for my drama had progressed nicely. I felt well, and now I could stand on deck and look attentively at the coasts of Sicily. Kniep went on busily sketching, and thanks to his skill and precision, several strips of paper became a very valuable souvenir of this delayed landing.

Palermo, Monday, April 2, 1787.

Finally, at three o'clock in the afternoon, with difficulty and strain, we arrived in the harbor, where a most delightful sight greeted us. Fully restored to health as I was, I felt the greatest pleasure. The city, situated at the foot of high mountains, is turned northwards; the sun shining over it in our direction, in accordance with the time of day. The bright shady sides of the buildings, illuminated by the reflection, gazed at us. Monte Pellegrino to the right, its pleasing contours in the most perfect light, to the left the lengthy shoreline with bays, tongues of land, and headlands. Another charming effect was that produced by the new green of graceful trees, the tops of which, lighted from behind, swayed back and forth in front of the dark buildings like great masses of vegetable glowworms. A transparent haze made all the shadows blue.

Instead of impatiently hurrying ashore, we stayed on the deck until we were driven off; where could we have hoped to find a similar vantage point and such an auspicious moment so soon again!

Through the curious gate[47] consisting of two huge pillars (it must remain open on top, so that St. Rosalia's towering cart[48] can pass through on her famous festival day) we were led into the city and immediately off to the left into a large inn.[49] The innkeeper, an easy-going old man long accustomed to seeing foreigners from all nations, showed us to a large room, from whose balcony we surveyed the sea and the wharf, St. Rosalia's mountain, and the shore. We also caught sight of our ship and could judge our first vantage point. Highly pleased with the location of our room, we almost failed to notice a raised alcove at the end of it that was hidden behind curtains, where the most spacious bed spread itself out. Resplendent with a silken canopy, it was altogether in keeping with the other stately, antiquated furnishings. Such a sumptuous room embarrassed us a little, and, as is customary, we desired to settle on the terms. The old man countered by saying this was unnecessary, he just wanted us to be happy in his inn. He said we should also use the anteroom, which was cool and airy, gay with several balconies, and directly adjacent to our room.

We diverted ourselves with the infinitely varied view and tried to sort out individual details of it for drawing and painting, since we could see a boundless harvest here for the artist.

The bright moonlight enticed us back to the waterfront again in the evening, and after our return it still kept us on the balcony for a long time. The lighting was unusual, the peace and charm great.

Palermo, Tuesday, April 3, 1787.

Our first aim was to get a closer look at the city, which is easy to survey but hard to become acquainted with—easy, because it is bisected from the sea to the foot of the mountains by a street miles in length, and this street is in turn bisected approximately in the middle by another one: whatever is located on these lines is easily found; however, the interior of the city is confusing for the stranger, and he needs a guide's assistance to make his way through this labyrinth.

Towards evening we watched the line of carriages in the familiar promenade of the more aristocratic persons, who were going out from the city onto the seafront in order to breathe some fresh air, to be entertained, and perhaps to pay court.

The full moon had risen two hours before nightfall and it made the evening indescribably beautiful. The fact that Palermo faces north puts the city and shore at a marvelous angle to the great celestial orbs, so that their reflection is never seen on the waves. Consequently, even today in the brightest sunshine we found the sea to be dark blue, somber, and seeming to press closer, not like at Naples, where from noon onwards it shines more and more brightly, merrily, and distantly.

Kniep had already let me go some places alone today to make my observations, so that he could draw a precise outline of Monte Pellegrino, the most beautiful headland in the world.

Palermo, April 3, 1787.

Here, in summary, a few more things, as a postscript and in confidence:

On Thursday, March 29th, we left Naples at sundown and did not land in the harbor of Palermo until four days later, at three o'clock. A little diary that I am enclosing reports our adventures in general. I have never begun a trip as calmly as this one and have never had a more peaceful time than on this voyage, which was much prolonged by the constant contrary wind. It did not even matter that during the first days I was confined to bed in a narrow little chamber by a severe attack of seasickness. Now my thoughts calmly turn to you; for if anything was ever decisive for me, it is this trip.

Whoever has not seen himself all surrounded by the sea can have no conception of the world and his relationship to the world. This grand, simple line has given me, as a sketcher of landscapes, entirely new ideas.

As the diary indicates, we had a variety of experiences on this short voyage and, as it were, lived a seafarer's life on a small scale. However, the safety and comfort of the packet boat cannot be praised enough.

The captain is a very fine and quite amiable man. The other passengers were a whole theatrical troupe, well mannered, unobjectionable, and agreeable. The artist I have with me is a good, loyal, lively person, who draws with the greatest accuracy; he sketched all the islands and coasts as they came into sight; when I bring all of this back, you will be very delighted with it. Moreover, in order to shorten the long hours of the crossing, he wrote down the mechanics of watercolor painting (*aquarelle*) for me. This has now attained a high degree of perfection in Italy, namely, how to use certain colors to produce certain tones that, without knowing the secret, one could not blend in a lifetime of trying. I had learned something about this in Rome, but never systematically. It was devised by artists in a land like Italy, or like this one. No words can describe the misty transparency that hovered around the coasts as we sailed up to Palermo on the most beautiful afternoon: the purity of the contours, the general softness, the distinctness of the tones, the harmony of sky, sea, and earth. To have seen it is to remember it for the rest of one's life. Now at last I understand the paintings of Claude Lorrain, and can hope that I shall be able, even someday in the north, to summon up mental images of this happy domain. If only everything trivial were as thoroughly expunged from my mind as the triviality of thatched roofs has been from my ideas about suitable subjects for drawing. Let us see what this queen of islands can do.

I lack words to express how she received us: with freshly leafed-out mulberry trees, evergreen oleanders, lemon hedges, etc. Wide beds of ranunculus and anemones stand in a public garden. The air is mild, warm, and fragrant, the wind soft. In addition, the full moon rose from behind a headland and shone on the sea—and this pleasure, after we had floated on the waves for four days and nights! Forgive me for scribbling this with a blunt pen out of an India ink shell that my companion uses for sketching outlines. But it comes over to you like a whisper, while I prepare a different memorial to those happy hours of mine for all of you who love me. I will not tell you what it is going to be, nor can I say when you will receive it.[50]

Palermo, Tuesday, April 3, 1787.

This sheet of paper, my beloved friends, should make you partakers, as far as possible, of the finest of pleasures: it should describe for you the incomparable bay shore, which encircles a great mass of water. Up from the east, where a rather flat headland extends far into the sea, up past many steep, well-shaped, wooded rocks to the fishermen's houses in the suburbs, then past the city itself, whose outer row of houses all face the harbor (as our inn does), up to the gate by which we entered.

Then it continues westward to the usual landing place, where the smaller ships tie up, and then as far as the real harbor on the Molo, the station for larger ships. There in the west, shielding all the vessels, rises Monte Pellegrino with its beautiful contours, after it has left a lovely, fertile valley (which extends to the sea on the other side) between itself and the actual mainland.

Kniep drew, I sketched outlines, both of us with great delight, and now that we have happily returned to our room neither of us feels energetic or courageous enough to rework and finish anything. Therefore our preliminary designs must be neglected until some future time, and this page is merely evidence of our inability to grasp these sights adequately, or rather the presumptuousness of our thinking we could capture and master them in so short a time.

Palermo, Wednesday, April 4, 1787.

In the afternoon we visited the pleasant, fertile valley that comes down past Palermo from the mountains to the south, with the Oreto river winding through it. Here too, if any picture is to be drawn, a painter's eye and a skilled hand are required, and yet Kniep quickly found a vantage point at the spot where the water flows down after being dammed up behind a half-ruined weir, in the shade of a delightful clump of trees, behind it several farm buildings and the open view up the valley.

The most beautiful spring weather and a burgeoning fertility spread a feeling of refreshing peace over the whole valley, but it was spoiled for me by the pedantry of our inept guide. He related in detail how Hannibal had once fought a battle here,[51] and told of the other great warlike deeds that had occurred in this place. I crossly rebuked him for so wretchedly evoking these departed spirits. I said it was bad enough that the crops had to be trampled down from time to time, if not always by elephants, then by horses and men; but at least my imagination should not be startled out of its peaceful reverie by these tales of tumult.

He was quite astonished that I should spurn classical memories in a place like this, and of course I was unable to make him understand how such mingling of past and present affected me.

It seemed still odder to our escort when I looked in all the shallows, many of which the river leaves quite dry, for little stones, and took along specimens of the various kinds. Again I was unable to explain to him that the quickest way to understand a mountainous region is to inspect the minerals swept down by the brooks, and that here too the

task was to use rubble in order to obtain an idea of those earthly antiquities, the eternally classical mountains.

And my booty from this river was actually quite rich, I assembled
almost forty pieces, which, it is true, could be listed under just a few
categories. Most of them were a mineral that in some cases looked like
jasper or hornstone, in others like shale. I found them in fragments
that were either rounded, or shapeless, or in rhomboidal form, of many
colors. Furthermore, many variations of the older limestone appeared,
as well as many breccias, with limestone as their bonding agent, but
the minerals combined in them were sometimes jasper, sometimes
limestone. There were also some fragments of shell limestone.

They feed the horses barley, chaff, and clover; in the spring they
give them green barley sprouts, in order to refresh them, *per rinfrescar,*
as they call it. Since they have no meadows, there is no hay. There is
some pasturage on the mountains, also on the fields, since a third of
them lie fallow. They keep just a few sheep of a breed from Barbary,
and in general more mules than horses, because the former tolerate the
calefactory fodder better than the latter.

The plain on which Palermo is located, as well as the area Ai Colli
outside of the city, also a part of the Bagaria, is on a base of shell
limestone, of which the city is built, and therefore great quarries are
found in these localities. At one place near Monte Pellegrino they are
over fifty feet deep. The lower strata are white in color. Many petrified
corals and crustaceans are found in them, principally large pilgrim shells.
The upper stratum is mixed with red clay and contains few shells, or
none at all. On the very top lies red clay, but not in a thick layer.

Monte Pellegrino rises up out of all this; it is of an older limestone
with many holes and cracks. More closely observed, the latter, for all
their irregularity, are seen to conform with the arrangement of the strata.
The stone is hard and it rings.

Palermo, Thursday, April 5, 1787.

We went through the city in detail. The architecture mostly resembles
that of Naples, but the public monuments—for example, the fountains—
are in still worse taste. There is no artistic spirit here to guide the work,
as there is in Rome; the structures receive their form and existence
merely from contingent circumstances. A fountain that is admired by
this whole island race would probably not exist if Sicily did not have
beautiful, colorful marble, and if a sculptor who was expert at animal

figures had not just then been in favor.[52] This fountain will be difficult to describe. On a medium-sized square stands a round architectural work, not quite one story high, base, wall, and rim of colored marble. A series of niches are carved into the wall, and out of these peer all sorts of white marble animal heads on outstretched necks: horses, lions, camels, elephants alternate with each other, and one would hardly expect to find a fountain behind this circular menagerie; however, openings have been left on four sides, through which marble steps lead up to the abundantly flowing water, so that it can be dipped out.

The situation is similar with respect to the churches, in which even the Jesuits' love of display has been outdone, not intentionally and out of principle, but by chance. Any craftsman who was at hand, any carver of figures or foliage, any gilder, lacquerer, or marbler was free to execute whatever he was capable of at certain spots, without taste or guidance.

Yet there is an evident ability to imitate natural things, as, for example, the rather good sculpting of those animal heads. Of course, this excites the admiration of the multitude, whose whole enjoyment of art consists in being able to see similarity between the imitation and the original.

Towards evening, I made a pleasant acquaintance when I stopped in at a small shopkeeper's in the long street to purchase various trifles. As I stood in front of his store to view the wares, a slight gust of wind arose and whirled along the street, immediately raising an immense cloud of dust and distributing it in all the shops and their windows. "By all the saints!" I exclaimed, "tell me why your city is so dirty! Can nothing be done about it? This street rivals the Roman Corso in length and beauty. There are stepping stones on both sides of it, which every shopkeeper or workroom proprietor is constantly sweeping clean; but everything is shoved into the middle of the street, which consequently just gets dirtier and dirtier; and every breath of wind sends back to you the rubbish you have consigned to the thoroughfare. In Naples donkeys are busy every day carrying the sweepings to the gardens and fields. Should not some similar arrangement come about or be instituted in your city?"

"Things with us are what they are," answered the man. "What we throw out of the house piles up and rots before our doors. Here you see layers of straw and reeds, of kitchen waste and all sorts of rubbish, the whole of which dries up and returns to us as dust. We combat it every day. But see, our nice, pretty, busy brooms finally get worn to a nub and just add to the rubbish in front of our houses."

And in his droll way he was quite right. They have pretty little brooms made of dwarf palms which, with slight alterations, could serve as fans. These wear down quickly, and thousands of their stubs lie in the street. To my repeated question whether no measures could be taken to remedy the situation he answered that popular opinion blamed the sanitation officials themselves; they were so influential that no one could compel them to use their monies as duty required. And besides, there was the curious circumstance that they feared, once the straw and manure were carted away, the bad condition of the underlying pavement would at last become clearly visible, which in turn would expose their dishonest administration of another public account. But all of that, he added with a comical expression, was only the interpretation given by malcontents. He himself agreed with those who claimed that the nobility retained this soft underlayer for its carriages, so that the traditional evening promenade could be accomplished comfortably on an elastic ground. And since the man was now in full swing, he joked about several other policing abuses, a consoling proof to me that human beings have enough humor left to make fun of what they cannot escape.

Palermo, April 6, 1787.

St. Rosalia, the patron saint of Palermo, has become so generally known, owing to the description of her festival given by Brydone,[53] that my friends will surely be pleased to read something about the place where she is especially honored.

Monte Pellegrino, a large rocky mass broader than it is high, is situated at the northwestern end of the Bay of Palermo. Its beautiful form cannot be described in words; an incomplete picture of it is found in the *Voyage pittoresque de la Sicile*.[54] It consists of a gray limestone from the earlier period. The rocks are quite bare, no tree or bush grows on them, while even the level sections are barely covered with a little grass and moss.

The saint's bones were discovered in a cavern of this mountain at the beginning of the last century and brought to Palermo. Their presence freed the city of the plague, and from that moment on Rosalia became the people's patron saint: they built chapels for her and held splendid festivities in her honor.

The pious diligently made pilgrimages up the mountain and, at great expense, a road was built that rests on pillars and arches like an aqueduct and rises zigzag between two cliffs.

The shrine itself is more in keeping with the humility of the saint who took refuge there than are the magnificent festivals which were instituted to honor her complete renunciation of the world. And it may be that all Christendom, which now for eighteen hundred years has based its possessions, its display, and its solemn revels on the poverty of its original founders and most zealous confessors, can point to no other holy place that is decorated and venerated in such a simple and sensitive manner.

After climbing up the mountain, one rounds the corner of a rock and stands just opposite a steep rocky wall, to which the church and convent are, so to speak, built fast.

The exterior of the church is neither inviting nor promising; the visitor opens the door without expectation, but is very greatly surprised upon entering. He finds himself under a vestibule that runs the width of the church and is open out toward the nave. It contains the usual receptacles for holy water and a few confessionals. The nave of the church is an open courtyard, bounded on the right side by crude rocks, on the left by a continuation of the vestibule. It is paved with flagstones laid so as to slope somewhat and allow the rainwater to run off; a little fountain stands approximately in the middle.

The cavern itself has been transformed into a choir, without sacrificing anything of its rugged natural form. Several steps lead upwards; immediately one faces the great lectern with the choir book, and there are choir stalls on both sides. All of it is illuminated by the daylight coming in from the courtyard or nave. In the middle, far back in the darkness of the cavern, stands the main altar.

As I have already said, nothing about the cavern has been changed; but since the rocks are always dripping water it was necessary to keep the place dry. This has been accomplished by means of lead gutters, which have been run along the edges of the rocks and combined in various ways. Since they are wide above, and down below taper to a point, and are also painted a dirty green color, it almost looks as if the cavern were overgrown inside with large varieties of cactus. The water is conducted partly to the side, partly to the back, into a transparent receptacle, from which believers draw it for use against all sorts of maladies.

While I was closely observing these sights, a priest stepped up to me and inquired whether by any chance I was a Genoese and wanted to have some masses read. I replied that I had come to Palermo with a Genoese, who would climb up tomorrow for the festival day. Since one of us always had to stay at home, I had come up today to look around. He replied that I should feel perfectly free, have a good look at everything, and perform my devotions. In particular, he pointed out an altar to me which stood to the left in the cavern, saying it was an especially sacred shrine; then he left me.

I saw lamps shimmering from under the altar through the openings of a large foliate grating made of chased brass, and I knelt down very close to look through these openings. Inside, another grating, of finely woven brass wire, was pulled across, so that the object behind it could only be distinguished as if through a veil.

By the gleam of some subdued lamps I caught sight of a beautiful woman.[55]

She lay as though in a kind of rapture, her eyes half closed, her head carelessly laid on her right hand, which was adorned with many rings. I could not get enough of looking at this image; it seemed to me to have quite special charms. Her gown is hammered out of gilded tin, which convincingly simulates a material richly woven out of gold. The head and hands, of white marble, may not be in what I would call high style, but are nevertheless worked so naturally and pleasantly that one would expect her to breathe and move.

A little angel stands next to her, appearing to fan her with a lily stalk.

In the meantime the priests had come into the cavern, had taken their seats, and were singing the vespers.

I sat down on a bench opposite the altar and listened to them for a while; then I went to the altar again, knelt down, and tried to see the beautiful image of the saint still more clearly. I yielded completely to the charming illusion of the figure and the place.

Now the priests' song died away in the cavern, the water trickled down and gathered in the container next to the altar, the overhanging rocks of the outer court, which is the actual nave of the church, enclosed the scene still more tightly. There was great stillness in this, so to speak, again deserted waste, and great cleanliness in a wild cavern; the Catholic divine service and its tinsel trappings, especially in the Sicilian version, here still close to its natural simplicity; the illusion produced by the figure of the beautiful sleeper, charming even to a practiced eye—suffice it to say, I could only with difficulty tear myself away from this place and did not get back to Palermo until late at night.

                                        Palermo, Saturday, April 7, 1787.

I spent some most enjoyable hours in the public garden adjacent to the waterfront. It is the most amazing place in the world. Although laid out regularly, it still seems fairy-like to us; though not planted long ago, it takes us back into antiquity. Green edgings enclose exotic plants, espaliered lemon trees adorned with a thousand red, carnation-like blossoms attract the eye. Trees entirely foreign and unknown to me, still without leaves, probably from warmer regions, spread their strange branches, a raised bench behind the level area affords a view of this curious tangle of vegetation, and finally one's gaze is drawn to large basins of water, in which gold and silver fish move about very prettily, now hiding under mossy reeds, now gathering in groups, lured by a bit of bread. All the plants have a green color we are not accustomed to, sometimes more yellowish, sometimes more bluish than at home. What lent the whole garden its most singular charm, however, was the thick haze uniformly diffused over everything, with such marked effect that objects just a few steps in back of one another were set off from each other by becoming more decidedly light blue, so that finally their true color was lost, or at least the eye saw them covered with a very blue tint.

The singular appearance given by this haze to more distant objects, such as ships and headlands, is quite worthy of notice by a painter's eye, since the distances can be accurately discerned, indeed measured; also, for this reason a stroll along the heights became very charming. I no longer saw nature, only pictures that a most artistic painter seemed to have gradated by applying a blue glaze to them.

But the impression of that marvelous garden stayed too deep within me; the blackish waves at the northern horizon, their surging up to the curves of the bay, even the particular smell of the misting sea—all of that recalled both to my senses and my mind the isle of the blissful Phaeacians.[56] I immediately rushed to buy a copy of Homer, read that canto to my great edification, and recited an impromptu translation of it to Kniep, who, with a good glass of wine, was comfortably resting up, as he well deserved to do, from a day of strenuous efforts.

Palermo, April 8, 1787. Easter Sunday.

Now, however, at daybreak, began the noisy rejoicing over the glad resurrection of the Lord. Petards, trains of gunpowder, firecrackers, squibs, and the like were set off by the boxful in front of the church doors, while the faithful crowded to the opened double portals. The sound of bells and of the organ, the choral song of the processions and that of the ecclesiastical choirs that came to meet them could really sound confusing to the ears of those not used to such tumultuous divine worship.

The early mass was hardly ended when two elegantly dressed footmen of the viceroy visited our inn for the dual purpose of extending his season's greetings to all the foreign visitors (and receiving a gratuity in exchange) and of inviting me to dine (for which reason my gift had to be increased somewhat).

After I had spent the morning visiting churches and observing the faces and figures of the people, I drove to the viceroy's palace, which is located at the upper end of the city. Having arrived somewhat too early, I found the upper rooms still empty, except for a lively little man who came up to me and whom I immediately recognized as a Maltese knight.[57]

When he heard that I was a German, he asked whether I could give him news of Erfurt, where he had spent some time very agreeably. I could satisfactorily answer his questions about the Dacheröden family[58]

and Coadjutor von Dalberg,[59] which pleased him very much, and then
he inquired about the rest of Thuringia. Hesitantly, but with interest,
he asked for news of Weimar. "How do things stand," he asked, "with
the man who at my time was young and full of life and caused both
rain and sunshine there? I have forgotten his name, but it is enough to
say he is the author of *Werther*."

After a little pause, as though I was reflecting, I answered: "The
person you are so kindly inquiring about is myself!"—Showing the
most visible signs of astonishment, he started back and cried: "Then
a great change must have taken place!"—"Oh, yes!" I replied, "between Weimar and Palermo I have undergone many a change."

At that moment the viceroy entered with his retinue and behaved
with tactful forthrightness, as befits such a ruler. However, he could
not help smiling about the Maltese knight, who continued to express
his amazement at seeing me here. I sat next to the viceroy at table,
where he talked about the purpose of my trip and asserted that he would
give orders to have me shown everything in Palermo and to have me
offered every assistance on my way through Sicily.

Palermo, Monday, April 9, 1787.

We were occupied all day today with the nonsense of Prince Palagonia,[60] and these follies too were quite different from what we had
imagined from reading and hearing about them. For however much he
loves the truth, the person who is to give an account of an absurdity
always is faced with a dilemma: because he wants to give an idea of
it, he makes something out of what is actually nothing, but wishes to
be considered something. And so I have to begin with still another
general reflection, namely that neither the most tasteless nor the most
excellent creations spring directly from *one* individual or *one* epoch;
rather, with a little perception one can establish a genealogical table
for the provenance of both.

That fountain in Palermo is one of the ancestors of the Palagonian
madness, except that the latter is on its own property here and can
display itself with the greatest freedom and latitude. I shall try to trace
the course of its development.

In this region, when a country seat is located more or less in the
middle of the whole property, and the manorial residence can only be
reached by driving through cultivated fields, kitchen gardens, and similar useful farm installations, the owners show themselves to be thriftier
than Northerners, who often turn a large stretch of good ground into a
park that beguiles the eye with bushes bearing no fruit. Instead, these
southerners raise two walls, between which one arrives at the manor

house without perceiving what goes on to the right or left. This road ordinarily begins with a large portal, indeed also with a vaulted hall, and ends in the courtyard. But to prevent the eye from being entirely disappointed between these walls, they are bent outwards on top and decorated with voluted ornaments and pedestals, on which here and there a vase may stand. The surfaces are whitewashed, divided into sections, and painted. The courtyard consists of a circle surrounded by one-story houses, where domestic servants and farm laborers live; the square manor house rises up over everything.

This is the traditional arrangement, and may be what existed here until the prince's father built his palace in tolerably good, although not the best, taste. However, while the present owner does not abandon those general fundamentals, he gives freest rein to his passionate appetite for misshapen, tasteless forms, and to credit him with even a spark of imagination would be paying him too much honor.

So we enter the large hall, which begins at the very edge of the property, and find an octagon that is very high in comparison to its width. Four huge giants with modern buttoned-up leggings support the cornice, on which, directly opposite the entrance, the Holy Trinity hovers.

The road to the palace is wider than usual, the wall transformed into a continuous high socle, on which excellent pedestals hold up bizarre groups, while several vases are set in the intervening spaces. The repulsiveness of these malformations, ineptly done by the most ordinary stonemasons, is increased by the fact that they are made of the loosest shell tufa; but a better material would only accentuate the worthlessness of the forms. I said "groups" above, and used an incorrect word, not applicable here; for these combinations are not the product of reflection or even mere caprice, they have simply been thrown together by chance. Each of the square pedestals is adorned by three of these, with their bases so arranged that together, in various positions, they fill up the square space. The most prominent one, whose base occupies most of the front part of the pedestal, usually consists of two figures; these are chiefly monsters in human and animal form. Two more pieces are needed to fill up the rear of the pedestal surface; the one of moderate size usually depicts a shepherd or shepherdess, a cavalier or a lady, a dancing ape or a dog. Now there is still a gap left on the pedestal: this is most often filled by a dwarf, a species which always plays a great role in stupid jests.

But to provide a complete description of the elements of Prince Palagonia's folly, we give the following list: *Humans:* beggars male and female, Spaniards male and female, Moors, Turks, hunchbacks, all kinds of deformed people, dwarfs, musicians, Pulcinellas, soldiers in ancient costumes, gods, goddesses, people in Old French costumes, soldiers with ammunition pouches and leggings, mythology with gro-

tesque additions, e.g., Achilles and Chiron with Pulcinella. *Animals:*
only parts of them, a horse with human hands, a horse's head on a
human body, disfigured apes, many dragons and serpents, all kinds of
paws on figures of every type, doublings, transposed heads. *Vases:* all
kinds of monsters and volutes which end below in rounded vase bottoms
and saucers.

Now imagine such figures produced in masses, created entirely without sense and understanding, and placed together without selection and
purpose; imagine this socle, these pedestals, and these monsters in an
endless row; then you can share the disagreeable feeling that must
overcome anyone who runs this insane gauntlet.

We approach the palace and are received into the arms of a semi-
circular forecourt; the main wall opposite us, with the gate going through
it, has fortresslike construction. We find an Egyptian figure embedded
in it, a fountain without water, a monument, vases lying around here
and there, statues intentionally laid on their noses. We enter the courtyard itself and find that the traditional circle of little buildings has been
shaped in scallops, for the sake of variety.

Most of the ground is covered with grass. On this, as if in a neglected
cemetery, stand oddly decorated marble vases from the father's time,
mixed haphazardly with dwarfs and other deformed creatures from the
new era, no place having been found for them as yet. We even come
upon an arbor crammed with old vases and other pieces of ornamental
stone.

But the height of such tasteless absurdity is shown in having the
cornices of the little houses hang at a decided slant to one side or the
other, so that our inner sense of the horizontal and perpendicular, which
is what really makes us humans and is fundamental to all harmonious
proportion, is bothered and confused. And these rows of roofs are also
bordered with hydras and little busts, with troops of monkeys making
music, and similar craziness: dragons, alternating with gods, an Atlas
carrying a wine barrel instead of the celestial globe.

But when one tries to escape from all this by entering the palace,
which was built by the father and has a relatively sensible outward
appearance, there, nearly in front of the door, one finds the laurel-
crowned head of a Roman emperor on the shoulders of a dwarf who
is sitting on a dolphin.

In the palace itself, whose exterior suggests a tolerable interior, the
prince's fever begins to rage again. The chair legs are sawn off un-
equally, so that no one can sit down, and the castellan warns the visitor
away from the chairs which could be sat on, because spikes are concealed under their velvet cushions. Standing in the corners are can-
delabras of Chinese porcelain, which on closer inspection prove to be
stuck together out of individual bowls, cups, saucers, and the like. There

is not a nook that does not have some capricious object looking out from it. Even the superb view across the headlands to the sea is spoiled by colored panes of glass, whose false tones either chill or inflame the landscape. I must also mention a small room which is paneled with old gilt frames cut up and juxtaposed. All the hundredfold carving patterns, all the various shades of older or newer, more or less dusty and damaged gilding, in close proximity to each other, cover all the walls and make the impression of being chopped-up rubbish.

Just describing the chapel would require several pages. Here we find an explanation for the whole insane idea, which could only have proliferated to this extent in a bigoted mind. I leave you to guess how many grotesque images of a misguided devotion have been placed here, but I shall not withhold the best one. Namely, a carved crucifix of considerable size, painted to look natural and covered with a mixture of varnish and gilt, is fastened flat against the ceiling. A hook is screwed into the navel of the crucified Christ, with a chain hanging from it that is attached to the head of a man kneeling in prayer. This figure, painted and varnished like all the other images in the church, hovers in the air, no doubt to symbolize the ceaseless devotion of the owner.

Moreover, the palace has not been completed inside: a salon, built by the father in a rich and varied manner, but not repulsively decorated, has remained unfinished, for the owner's boundless insanity cannot cope with all his follies.

Kniep, with his artistic sense, was driven to despair inside this madhouse, and for the first time I saw him become impatient; he forced me to leave as I was trying to represent and sketch in outline the individual elements of this false creation. Good-naturedly enough he finally drew one of the combinations, the only one that provided some kind of a picture. It shows a woman-horse sitting in an armchair and playing cards with a cavalier dressed in an old-fashioned way below, but adorned with a griffon head, crown, and a large wig. It is reminiscent of the Palagonia family's coat of arms, which remains very remarkable even when compared with all this foolishness: a satyr holds up a mirror to a woman with a horse's head.

Palermo, Tuesday, April 10, 1787.

Today we drove up to Monreale. A magnificent road, which an abbot put in at a time when that monastery was exceedingly wealthy: wide, with an easy ascent, trees here and there, but, in particular, large fountains fed by springs or pipes, profusely ornamented in almost Palagonian fashion but, for all that, giving refreshment to humans and animals.

The San Martino monastery, situated at the top, is a respectable es-

tablishment.[61] As can be seen with Prince Palagonia, one bachelor alone
has rarely produced anything sensible, whereas groups of them together
have created the very greatest works, as is shown by churches and
monasteries. But the religious societies probably only accomplished so
much because they could be more certain than any family patriarch of
a limitless progeny.

The monks let us see their collections. They preserve many beautiful
antiquities and natural specimens. We were especially struck by a medal
with the image of a young goddess, which was irresistibly charming.
The good brothers would gladly have given us an impression of it to
take along, but there was nothing at hand that would have been suitable
for making any sort of form.

After having showed us everything, not without making sad comparisons between their present and former circumstances, they conducted us into a pleasant little room with a balcony from which one
could enjoy a lovely view; places were set for us here, and we did not
lack for a very good noonday meal. After dessert was served, the abbot
came in, accompanied by his oldest monks, sat down with us, and stayed
at least half an hour, during which time we had to answer many questions. We parted most amicably. The younger monks escorted us once
more into the rooms which held the collections, and finally to our carriage.

We drove home with sentiments quite different from yesterday's.
Today we had to pity a great institution which is in decline just at the
time when, on the other side, a tasteless enterprise is putting forth new
growth.

The road to San Martino goes up the older limestone range. Workmen
crush these rocks and calcine lime out of them, which becomes very
white. For the calcining they use a long, sturdy type of grass, dried in
bundles. What is created now is calcareous earth. Red clay, which appears as the surface soil here, is found deposited up as far as the steepest
heights, the higher, the redder, little darkened by the vegetation. In the
distance I saw a pit almost like cinnabar.

The monastery stands in the midst of the limestone range, which
abounds in springs. The mountains round about are well cultivated.

Palermo, Wednesday, April 11, 1787.

Having now viewed two of the chief sights outside of the city, we
went to the palace, where an obliging footman showed us the rooms
and their contents. To our great dismay, the salon in which the antiquities are usually displayed was just then in the worst disorder, because

a new architectural decoration was being worked on. The statues were removed from their places, covered with cloths, and obstructed by scaffolding, so that in spite of all our guide's good will and some efforts on the part of the workmen, we could get only an incomplete idea of them. I was principally interested in the two bronze rams,[62] which were uplifting to my artistic sense, even when seen under these circumstances. They are shown in a recumbent position, with one hoof forward and their heads turned to opposite sides to make them a contrasting pair; powerful figures out of the mythological household, worthy of transporting Phrixus and Helle.[63] The wool not short and curly, but in long, descending waves, modeled with great realism and elegance, from the best Greek period. They are said to have stood in the harbor of Syracuse.

Next, the footman led us outside of the city into some catacombs,[64] which are laid out with architectural understanding and are by no means just quarries used as burial sites. Vaulted openings and, within them, coffins, several in a tier, have been carved in a vertically hewn wall of rather hardened tufa, everything out of the massive stone, without any auxiliary masonry. The upper coffins are smaller, and burial places for children are provided in the space above the pillars.

Palermo, Thursday, April 12, 1787.

Today we were shown Prince Torremuzza's[65] collection of medals. I was somewhat disinclined to go there. It is a subject about which I know too little, and a traveler who is merely curious is odious to true connoisseurs and art lovers. But since a beginning must be made somewhere, I submitted and derived much pleasure and benefit from doing so. How profitable it is to get even just a preliminary survey of how the ancient world was dotted with towns, the smallest of which bequeathed to us exquisite medals that demonstrate, if not a whole sequence of art history, at least a few epochs of it. An endless springtime of the blossoms and fruits of art, of a craft practiced lifelong on a higher plane, and a great deal more, smiles at us out of these drawers. The brilliance of the Sicilian cities, now dimmed, gleams freshly again from these molded metals.

Unfortunately we others, in our youth, possessed only the family medals, which mean nothing, and the imperial medals, which tiresomely repeat the same profile: pictures of rulers who can hardly be regarded as models of humanity. How sadly our youth was restricted to formless Palestine and form-confusing Rome! Sicily and New Greece give me hope again for a new life.

My indulging in general observations about these objects is proof that I have not yet learned to understand them very well; but that will gradually come, along with everything else.

Palermo, Thursday, April 12, 1787.

This evening another of my wishes was fulfilled, and in a peculiar way. I stood on the stepping stones in the big street, joking with the proprietor of that store; suddenly a tall, well-dressed footman approached me, briskly holding out a silver dish on which lay several copper pennies and a few silver coins. Since I did not know what this was about, I shrugged my shoulders and ducked my head, which is the customary way to indicate rejection, either because one does not understand, or does not like, the proposal or question. Just as quickly as he came, he left, and now I noticed that his comrades were engaged in the same activity across the street.

I asked the merchant what that signified, and he, with a cautious, almost furtive gesture, pointed to a tall, thin gentleman in court dress who was walking along decorously and coolly over the rubbish in the middle of the street. Curled and powdered, his hat under his arm, in silk clothing, a sword at his side, neat footwear with silver buckles: in this guise the venerable man walked along gravely and calmly; all eyes were turned to him.

"That is Prince Palagonia," said the shopkeeper, "who goes through the city from time to time begging money to ransom captive slaves in Barbary. To be sure, he never collects a great deal, but the subject does remain in mind, and persons who have held back in their lifetime often leave handsome sums for this purpose in their wills. The prince has headed this institution for many years and has done an infinite amount of good!"

"Instead of spending huge sums on those follies at his country seat," I cried, "he should have used them on this. Not a sovereign in the world could have accomplished more."

To this the merchant said: "But we are all like that! We gladly pay for our follies ourselves, but others are expected to provide the money for our virtues."

Palermo, Friday, April 13, 1787.

Count Borch[66] has done very diligent preliminary work for us in Sicily's mineral realm, and anyone who visits the island after him with the same interests will gladly express gratitude to him. I find it a pleasant duty to celebrate the memory of a forerunner. Am I not, after all, merely a precursor of others in the future, in life as on this journey!

However, it appears to me that the count was more active than knowledgeable: he proceeds with a certain self-satisfaction, which is not compatible with the modest, serious treatment that should be given to important subjects. Nevertheless, his quarto booklet devoted entirely to the Sicilian mineral kingdom has been of great benefit to me, and with this preparation I could make profitable visits to the lapidaries, who still ply their trade, although they had more work in former times, when the churches and altars were still in the process of being covered with marble and agates. I ordered specimens of soft and hard stones from them; for this is how they classify marble and agates, chiefly because the difference in price is based on this criterion. But besides these two they pride themselves highly on another material, which is a firing product of their lime-kilns. When the burning is over, a kind of molten glass is left in the kilns, ranging in color from the lightest to the darkest, indeed the blackest, blue. These clumps are cut into thin slabs like any other stone and are valued according to the intensity of their color and their degree of purity. They are successfully used instead of lapis lazuli to inlay altars, grave monuments, and other ecclesiastical ornaments.

The complete collection that I want is not ready and will only be sent to me in Naples. The agates are of the greatest beauty, especially those in which irregular spots of yellow or red jasper alternate with white—as though frozen—quartz to produce the loveliest effect.

An exact imitation of such agates, painted with enamels on the reverse side of thin glass panes, was the only sensible thing I managed to discover that day in the Palagonian nonsense. Such panels make a more attractive decoration than the genuine agate, for the latter has to be assembled from many little pieces, whereas the glass panels can be as large as the architect desires. This clever trick would be well worth imitating.

Palermo, April 13, 1787.

Italy without Sicily forms no image at all in the soul; only here is the key to everything.

The climate cannot be praised enough; it is the rainy season now, but with continual interruptions; today there is thunder and lightning, and everything is vigorously turning green. Some of the flax has already developed nodes, the rest is blooming. The fields of flax are so blue-green, lying down there in the valleys, that one takes them for little ponds. The charming sights are past counting! And my companion is

an excellent person, a genuine Good Hope,[67] just as I continue dutifully
playing True Friend. He has already made some quite beautiful outlines,
and the best is still to be done. What a prospect for me, to come home
safely some day with my treasures!

So far I have said nothing about the food and drink in this region,
and yet that is no small matter. The garden produce is splendid, especially the lettuce, which has the delicacy and taste of a milk; I understand why the ancients called it *lactuca*. The oil, the wine, all very
good, and could be still better if more care were taken in making them.
The best, most delicate fish. We have also had excellent beef since
being here, although usually it wins no praise.

Now, away from dining and to the window! onto the street! A criminal
was pardoned, which always happens in honor of the salutary Easter
week. A religious brotherhood led him under a mock gallows, he had
to say his prayers by the ladder and kiss it; then he was led away again.
He was a handsome fellow of the middle class, his hair dressed, a white
frock coat, a white hat, everything white. He carried his hat in his
hand, and if only someone had been permitted to pin colored ribbons
on him here and there, he could have gone to any fancy-dress ball as
a shepherd.

Palermo, April 13 and 14, 1787.

And so, shortly before our departure, I was still to be granted an
extraordinary adventure, which I shall at once relate to you in detail.

During our whole stay I had been hearing much talk at our public
table about Cagliostro and his origins and activities.[68] The Palermitans
were in agreement that a certain native of their city named Giuseppe
Balsamo had become notorious and then been banished on account of
numerous shabby tricks. But opinions were divided on whether he and
Count Cagliostro were one and the same person. Some, who had seen
Balsamo earlier, claimed to recognize him in that print[69] which is quite
well known in Germany and had also reached Palermo.

In the course of such conversations one of the guests referred to the
efforts made by a Palermitan legal scholar[70] to clarify this matter. He
had been commissioned by the French ministry to investigate the an-
tecedents of a man who had been so impudent as to introduce the most
ridiculous fabrications into a critically important trial,[71] in the face of
France and, one might well say, of the world.

It was told that this legal scholar had drawn up the family tree of
Giuseppe Balsamo and had sent off a memorandum, with certified enclosures, to France, where public use would probably be made of it.[72]

I expressed the wish to meet this legal scholar, about whom many other good things were related, and the narrator offered to make appointment for me and take me to him.

A few days later we went there and found him busy with his clients. When he had finished with them and we had taken breakfast together, he produced a manuscript containing Cagliostro's family tree, copies of the documents necessary to support it, and the first draft of a memorandum sent to France.

He laid the family tree before me and added the necessary explanations, of which I shall adduce as many here as are needed for easier understanding.

Giuseppe Balsamo's maternal great-grandfather was Matteo Martello. His great-grandmother's maiden name is unknown. Two daughters were born of this marriage, one named Maria, who married Giuseppe Bracconeri and became the grandmother of Giuseppe Balsamo. The other, named Vicenza, married Giuseppe Cagliostro, who was born in a little town called La Noara, eight miles from Messina. I note here that two bell-founders with this name are still living in Messina. This great-aunt afterwards became godmother to Giuseppe Balsamo; he received her husband's Christian name and eventually, when gone from home, also assumed his great-uncle's surname, Cagliostro.

The Bracconeri couple had three children: Felicità, Matteo, and Antonino.

Felicità married Pietro Balsamo, the son of a ribbon merchant in Palermo named Antonino Balsamo, who was presumably of Jewish extraction. Pietro Balsamo, the father of the notorious Giuseppe, went bankrupt and died in his forty-fifth year. His widow, who is presently still alive, bore him, besides the Giuseppe mentioned, a daughter, Giovanna Giuseppe-Maria, who married Giovanni Battista Capitummino. He produced three children by her, and died.

The memorandum, which the accommodating author read aloud to us and, at my request, entrusted to me for a few days, was based on baptismal certificates, marriage contracts, and other instruments that had been carefully assembled. It contained (as I see from an abstract of it that I made at the time) approximately the particulars that have now become known to us from the Roman trial records,[73] namely: that Giuseppe Balsamo was born in early June, 1743, in Palermo, that Vicenza Martello, married name Cagliostro, became his godparent, that in his youth he joined the Hospitalers, an order specializing in the care of the sick, that he soon showed great enthusiasm and aptitude for medicine, but was nevertheless dismissed because of his bad conduct, that subsequently he played the magician and dowser in Palermo.

He made good use of his great gift for imitating other people's handwriting (so the memorandum continues). He forged, or rather, he fabricated an old document, and in that way a controversy began over the ownership of some properties. He was investigated, thrown into jail, fled, and was under summons by public proclamation. He traveled through Calabria to Rome, where he married a tinsmith's daughter. From Rome he returned to Naples under the name Marchese Pellegrini. He risked going back to Palermo, was recognized, imprisoned, and only managed to get free again in a way that merits being related in detail.

One of the highest-ranking Sicilian princes, the owner of great estates, a man who held important posts at the Neapolitan court, had a son who combined a strong body and headstrong disposition with all the arrogance to which someone who is rich and great, but culturally undeveloped, thinks himself entitled.

Donna Lorenza was able to win him over, and he became the foundation on which the pretended Marchese Pellegrini based his security. The prince made a public show of being the patron of this newly arrived pair; and how furious he became when Giuseppe Balsamo was imprisoned again at the behest of the party injured by his trickery. He tried various means to free him, and since these were unsuccessful, he went to the prison governor's anteroom and threatened to maltreat the opposition party's lawyer physically if he did not immediately rescind Balsamo's arrest. When the opposing attorney refused, he took hold of him, struck him, threw him on the ground, kicked him, and could hardly be restrained from further misdeeds until the governor himself hurried out, having heard the noise, and called for peace.

The governor, a weak, dependent man, did not dare to punish the offender; the opposing party and its attorney were intimidated, and Balsamo was freed; but the dossier includes no official record of his release, neither who ordered it nor how it took place.

Soon afterwards he left Palermo and made various journeys, about which the author could only give incomplete information.

The memorandum ended with a shrewd argument proving that Cagliostro and Balsamo were one and the same person, a thesis that was harder to defend then than it is now, since we are completely informed about the whole story.

It would have been permissible for me to make a copy of the draft and inform my friends and readers earlier about many interesting details, but at the time I had to assume that public use would be made of it in France and that perhaps I would already find it in print on my return.

Meanwhile we have learned most—and more than that memorandum could contain—from a source out of which formerly only errors were wont to flow. Who would have believed that Rome could ever contribute as much to the enlightenment of the world, to the complete unmasking of an imposter, as was accomplished by the publication of that abstract from the trial records! This book could and should have been far more interesting; nevertheless it remains a fine document in the hands of any rational person who had to watch, chagrined, for years while the deceived, the half-deceived, and the deceivers honored this man and his tricks, felt superior to others because of their association with him, and from the heights of their credulous conceit looked down with pity, if not scorn, at healthy common sense.

Who did not prefer to keep silent during that time? And only now that the whole affair is finished and no longer subject to dispute can I bring myself to tell what I know, in order to complete the dossier.

When I found that so many persons in the family tree were indicated as still living, especially the mother and the sister, I told the author of the memorandum that I would like to see and meet the relatives of such an extraordinary man. He replied that this would be difficult to accomplish, since these poor but honest people lived in deep seclusion, were not used to seeing any foreigners, and the suspicious temperament of the nation would put all sorts of constructions on such a visit. But he would send me his clerk, who had access to the family and had procured for him the information and documents from which the family tree was drawn up.

The clerk appeared the following day and voiced some hesitation about the undertaking. "Up to now I have avoided coming face to face with these people again; for to obtain their marriage contracts, baptismal certificates, and other papers, so as to make legal copies of them, I had to resort to a peculiar stratagem. I took occasion to speak of a hereditary family subsidy somewhere that was unassigned, persuaded them that the young Capitummino was probably eligible for it, and that first of all a family tree must be drawn up, in order to determine the validity of the boy's claim. After that, of course, everything would depend on vigorously pursuing the matter, which I would undertake to do if, for my efforts, I was promised my fair portion of the sum received. The good people joyfully agreed to everything; I received the necessary papers, the copies were made, the family tree was drawn up, and since that time I have carefully kept my distance from them. Just a few weeks ago old mother Capitummino happened to see me, and the only excuse I could give was that such things proceed here in a dilatory way."

Thus spoke the clerk. But since I would not abandon my project, we agreed, after some reflection, that I should pose as an Englishman bringing the family some news of Cagliostro, who had gone to London directly after being released from the Bastille.

At the appointed hour, it was probably about three o'clock in the afternoon, we set out. The house was located in the turn of a lane named Il Cassaro, not far from the main street. We ascended a wretched staircase and came right into the kitchen. A woman of medium height, broad and robust, but not fat, was busy washing the cooking utensils. She was neatly dressed and pulled up one end of her apron when we entered, to conceal its dirty side from us. She looked at my guide happily and said: "Signor Giovanni, do you bring us good news? Have you accomplished something?"

He replied: "I still have had no luck with our affair; but here is a foreigner who has come to bring you greetings from your brother and tell you how he is getting along at present."

We had not completely decided on the greeting I was supposed to deliver, but at least the initial step had now been taken.—"You know my brother?" she asked.—"All Europe knows him," I replied, "and since no doubt you must have been worried about him up till now, I think you will be pleased to hear that he is safe and well."—"Go in," she said, "I shall follow at once." And I walked into the living room with the clerk.

It was so large and high that in our country it would have been considered a salon; but it also seemed to be the family's entire living space. A single window lighted the great walls, which once had been painted, and on which, all around, hung dark pictures of saints in golden frames. Two large, uncurtained beds stood against one wall, a little brown cabinet, in the form of a desk, against the other. Old chairs of woven rushes, whose backs had once been gilded, stood next to this, and the brick floor was deeply worn down in many places. But everything was clean and tidy, and we approached the family, which was gathered at the other end of the room by the only window.

While my guide explained the reason for our visit to old mother Balsamo, who was sitting in the corner, and repeated his words loudly several times on account of the old soul's deafness, I had time to observe the room and its other occupants. A girl of some sixteen years, well formed, but with features blurred by smallpox, stood at the window; next to her a young man whose unpleasant, pockmarked face also attracted my attention. In an armchair opposite the window sat, or rather, lay a very deformed sick person, who seemed to be afflicted with a kind of lethargy.

Once my guide had made himself clear, we were urged to sit down. The old woman asked me some questions, which I had to have interpreted before answering, since I was not familiar with the Sicilian dialect.

Meanwhile I observed the old woman with pleasure. She was of medium height, but well formed; her regular features, which had not been disfigured by age, were suffused with the peace that is usually enjoyed by people who have lost their hearing; the tone of her voice was soft and pleasant.

I answered her questions, and my replies, in turn, had to be interpreted for her.

The slow pace of our conversation gave me an opportunity to weigh my words. I told her that her son had been released in France and was now in England, where he had been well received. The joy she showed over this news was accompanied by sincerely pious sentiments, and since she now spoke somewhat more loudly and slowly, I could understand her better.

Meanwhile her daughter had entered and sat down next to my guide, who faithfully repeated to her what I had said. She had put on a clean apron and arranged her hair under a net. The more I looked at her and compared her with her mother, the more strikingly different their appearance seemed to me. A lively, wholesome sensuality shone out of the daughter's whole countenance; she was a woman perhaps forty years old. She looked around shrewdly with her bright blue eyes, but I could not detect any suspicion in her glances. In a sitting position her figure seemed taller than when she was standing; her posture was resolute, she bent her body forward as she sat and laid her hands on her knees. In general, her blunt, rather than sharp, features reminded me of the portrait of her brother known to us in the engraving. She asked me various things about my trip, about my plan to see Sicily, and was convinced that I would return to celebrate the festival of St. Rosalia with them.

Since the grandmother had again been addressing several questions to me, and I was busy answering her, the daughter conversed in an undertone with my companion, but in such a way that I could find an opening to ask what they were talking about. He answered that Signora Capitummino was telling him about the fourteen *oncie*[74] her brother still owed her; when he hurriedly left Palermo she had redeemed some items for him that he had pawned; but since that time she had neither heard from him nor received money or any support from him, although she had been told that he possessed great riches and lived on a princely scale. She asked whether, after my return, I would not undertake to remind him in a kindly way of his debt, and to arrange some support for her, indeed, whether I would not take along, or possibly deliver, a letter. I offered to do so. She asked me where I was staying, where she might send the letter to me. I declined to give my address, and volunteered to pick up the letter myself the next day, towards evening.

After this she told me about her precarious situation: she was a widow with three children, one of the girls was being educated in the convent, the other was present here; and her son had just gone for his lesson. Besides these three children she had her mother with her, whom she had to support, and out of Christian charity she had also taken in the unfortunate sick person, who increased her burden still more; all her hard work scarcely sufficed to provide the necessities for herself and her family. Of course she knew that God would not fail to reward her good works, but she nevertheless groaned under the burden she had already borne for such a long time.

The young people now joined in the conversation, and the talk grew livelier. While I was speaking to the others, I heard the old woman ask her daughter whether I too was devoted to their sacred religion. I noticed that the daughter cleverly tried to avoid answering. As far as I could understand, she indicated to her mother that the foreigner seemed to be well disposed to them, and that it was not proper immediately to question someone on this point.

When they heard that I intended soon to leave Palermo, they became more insistent and entreated me to come back again; they especially praised the paradisal days of the St. Rosalia festival, for there was nothing in the whole world as good as that to see and enjoy.

My companion, who had long been eager to leave, finally put an end to the conversation with his gestures, and I promised to return the next day towards evening and collect the letter. My companion was happy that everything had gone off so well, and we parted contentedly.

It can easily be imagined what an impression this poor, pious, well-meaning family made on me. My curiosity was satisfied, but their good, natural behavior had aroused my sympathy, which grew still stronger when I reflected on the matter.

However, I immediately began to worry about the next day. My sudden appearance, which had surprised them in the beginning, would naturally have set them thinking, once I had departed. From the family tree I knew that several other relatives were still living; and naturally they would call their friends together and have me repeat in their presence what they had been amazed to hear from me the day before. I had reached my goal, and the only thing left to do was to put a proper end to this adventure. Therefore the next day, right after dinner, I went alone to their home. They were astonished when I walked in. The letter was not yet finished, they said, and some of their relatives also wanted to meet me, but would not arrive until toward evening.

I replied that I had to leave the next morning, still had to pay some visits, and pack. Therefore I had preferred to come here earlier rather than not at all.

Meanwhile the son, whom I had not seen the day before, came in. He resembled his sister in face and figure. He brought the letter which they had wanted me to take along; as is customary in those parts, he had had it written outside by a notary public. The young man had a quiet, sad, and modest manner, inquired about his uncle, asked about the latter's wealth and expenditures, and also wondered sadly why he had so completely forgotten his family. "It would be our greatest happiness," he continued, "if he were to come here someday and agree to take care of us. But," he went on, "how did he come to tell you that he still has relatives in Palermo? We hear that he disowns us everywhere and poses as a man of noble birth." I answered this question, which had been prompted by my guide's incautiousness when we first entered, in a plausible manner, saying that although his uncle had reason to conceal his origins from the public, he made no secret of them to his friends and acquaintances.

The boy's sister, who had approached during this conversation, having gained courage from her brother's presence, probably also from the absence of yesterday's friend, likewise began to speak very pleasantly and vivaciously. They both implored me to remember them to their uncle if I wrote to him; and with equal warmth asked me to come back after I had made my trip through the kingdom and celebrate the St. Rosalia festival with them.

The mother joined in with her children. "Sir," she said, "although it is really not proper for me to receive strange men in my house, since I have a grown daughter, and there is every reason to be on one's guard against both danger and gossip, you will nevertheless always be welcome here when you return to this city."

"Oh, yes," echoed the children, "we shall guide the gentleman around at the festival, we shall show him everything, we shall take seats on the platform, where we can see the festivities best. How delighted he will be with the big cart and especially with the splendid illuminations!"

Meanwhile the grandmother had read and reread the letter. When she heard that I was about to take my leave, she stood up and handed me the folded paper. "Tell my son," she began, with a noble animation, indeed a kind of rapture, "tell my son how happy you made me with the news you brought me about him! Tell him that I clasp him to my heart thus"—here she stretched out her arms and pressed them back together again on her breast—"that I plead for him daily with God and our holy Virgin in my prayers, that I give my blessing to him and his wife, and that my only wish is to see him once more before my death with these eyes, which have shed so many tears over him."

The characteristic gracefulness of the Italian language facilitated the selection and noble arrangement of these words, and, moreover, they were accompanied with the lively gestures by means of which that nation customarily adds an unbelievable charm to its utterances.

I bade them farewell, not without emotion. They all offered me their hands, the children escorted me out, and as I descended the stairs they sprang out onto the balcony facing the street, by the kitchen window, called after me, waved, and, so that I should not forget, told me again to come back. When I turned the corner I saw them still standing on the balcony.

It goes without saying that my interest in this family made me very eager to be of use to them and help them in their poverty. Now I too had deceived them, and their hopes of sudden assistance were about to be disappointed a second time owing to the curiosity of a northern European.

My first intention was to give them, before I left, those fourteen *oncie* the fugitive owed them, and to disguise the fact it was a gift by making them believe that I expected to have him repay me this sum. But when I went back to my room to add up my accounts and go through my cash and papers, I could plainly see (this being a country where poor communications stretch distances out to infinity, as it were) that I would get into a predicament if I took it upon myself to remedy an impudent fellow's injustice with my heartfelt generosity.[75]

Toward evening I went once more to my shopkeeper and asked him how tomorrow's festival would turn out, when a great procession was to move through the city and the viceroy himself would accompany the holiest image on foot. For the slightest gust of wind would envelop both God and men in a very thick cloud of dust.

The jolly man replied that in Palermo people tended to rely on miracles. A mighty downpour had often fallen in such cases, so that the generally sloping street was washed at least partly clean and a path was cleared for the procession. The same hope was cherished for this occasion, and not without reason, for the sky was clouding over and promised rain during the night.

Palermo, Sunday, April 15, 1787.

And that is what happened! Last night a very heavy rain fell from the sky. In the morning I hurried into the street at once to witness the miracle. And truly it was quite remarkable. The stream of rainwater channeled between the stepping stones on both sides had driven the lightest rubbish down the sloping street, partly into the sea, partly into the sewers, insofar as they were not clogged up. The bulkier masses of straw were at least displaced, and as a result, curious meandering lines were marked on the pavement. Now hundreds of people came with shovels, brooms, and pitchforks to widen these clean spots and connect them by piling up the remaining rubbish on one side and then the other. The result was that when the procession began it actually beheld a cleared path winding through the quagmire, and not only the entire clergy with their long robes but also the nobility with their trim footwear, the viceroy at their head, could walk through unhindered and unsoiled. I thought I was seeing the children of Israel, for whom an angel's hand had prepared a dry path through bog and swamp, and with this parallel I ennobled for myself the intolerable sight of so many pious and decorous people praying and parading their way through a boulevard of damp rubbish heaps.

Just as before, the stepping stones enabled us to walk without getting dirty, but inside the city, where we intended to go this very day to see various things we had heretofore neglected, it was almost impossible to get through, although the business of sweeping and piling up was not unattended to here either.

This festivity gave us an incentive to visit the main church and inspect its noteworthy features, and also, since we were out and about anyway, to have a look at some other buildings. We were much pleased with a still well-preserved Moorish house[76]—not large, but with beautiful, wide and well-proportioned, harmonious rooms; not really habitable in a northern climate, but a most welcome abode in a southern one. Perhaps some experts in construction will make us a ground plan and vertical projection of it.

In a cheerless place we also saw various remnants of ancient marble statues, but we did not have the patience to puzzle them out.

Palermo, Monday, April 16, 1787.

Since it is now time for us to threaten ourselves with imminent expulsion from this paradise, today I hoped to find perfect refreshment once more in the public garden. I would read my daily portion of the *Odyssey,* and then, while walking to the valley at the foot of St. Rosalia's mountain, continue pondering the plan of *Nausicaa* and try to make a drama out of this subject matter. All of this happened, perhaps not with great success, but I did enjoy doing it. I wrote down the plot and could not keep from sketching and working out some parts that especially attracted me.

Palermo, Tuesday, April 17, 1787.

Truly, it is a misfortune to be pursued and tempted by many different spirits! This morning I went to the public garden with the firm, calm resolve to continue my poetic dreams, but before I realized it, another specter seized me, one that has been skulking behind me for the last few days. The many plants that otherwise I was used to seeing only in tubs and pots, indeed for most of the year behind glass windows, stand here, fresh and happy, under the open sky; and by fulfilling their intended purpose completely, they become clearer to us. Confronted with so many kinds of fresh, new forms, I was taken again by my old fanciful idea: might I not discover the primordial plant amid this multitude? Such a thing must exist, after all! How else would I recognize this or that form as being a plant, if they were not all constructed according to one model?

I took pains to investigate how the many diverse shapes differed from each other. And I invariably found them more similar than different. When I tried to apply my botanical terminology, I was able to, but there was no profit in that, it disquieted me without helping me to proceed. My good poetic intentions were upset, the garden of Alcinous[77] had disappeared, and a world garden had opened up. Why are we moderns so easily distracted, why are we so fascinated by challenges we can neither meet nor fulfill!

Alcamo, Wednesday, April 18, 1787.

Early in the morning we rode out of Palermo. Kniep and the *vetturino* had proved to be efficient at packing and loading. We moved slowly up the splendid road we had already become acquainted with on our visit to San Martino, and were again admiring one of the magnificent fountains along the way when we learned something about the frugal customs of this country. Namely, our groom had hung a little wine barrel around his waist on a strap, like our canteen women, and it seemed to have enough wine in it for several days. Therefore we were surprised when he rode up to one of the water pipes, opened the bung and let water run in. With true German astonishment we asked why he was doing that, and whether the little cask was not full of wine. He answered very calmly that he had left it a third empty, and because no one drank unmixed wine, it was better to mix it all at once, for then the fluids would be combined better; and indeed one could not be sure of finding water everywhere. Meanwhile the cask was filled, and we had to go along with this ancient Oriental marriage custom.[78]

Having arrived now on the heights behind Monreale, we saw areas of wondrous beauty, more of a historical than an agricultural kind. To the right we could look as far as the sea, which drew an absolutely straight horizontal line between the most wonderful headlands and past forested and unforested shores, and, because it was markedly calm, contrasted magnificently with the wild limestone rocks. Kniep did not omit to sketch several of these in small format.

Now we are in Alcamo, a quiet, tidy little town, whose well-equipped inn is to be praised as a fine establishment because it is conveniently located for visiting the temple of Segesta, which stands apart in a lonely spot.

Alcamo, Thursday, April 19, 1787.

Our pleasant quarters in this quiet little mountain town appeal to us, and we have decided to spend the whole day here. So let yesterday's events be discussed first of all. I have already denied that Prince Palagonia had originality; he had predecessors and found models. A fountain on the road to Monreale has two monsters standing by it, and several vases on its balustrades that look just as if the prince had commissioned them.

Behind Monreale, when one leaves the good road and enters the stony mountains, pieces of what I took for ironstone because of their weight and weathering obstruct the way up on the ridge. All the level areas are cultivated and bear crops, some better than others. The limestone was barren, also the weathered soil at such places. This red, clayey-limey soil is widely distributed, the ground hard, no sand underneath, but it bears excellent wheat. We found old, very thick, but stunted olive trees.

We refreshed ourselves with a light meal under the shelter of an airy structure built onto the front of an inferior inn. Dogs greedily devoured our cast-off sausage skins, a beggar boy drove them off and with good appetite ate the peels of the apples we were consuming, but he in turn was chased away by an old beggar. Professional jealousy is at home everywhere! In a ragged toga the old beggar ran back and forth as a porter or waiter. But I had already noticed before this that whenever an innkeeper is asked for something he does not have in his house at the moment, he has a beggar fetch it from a shopkeeper.

Usually, however, we are spared such distasteful service, since our *vetturino* is excellent—stable boy, cicerone, guard, shopper, cook, and everything.

The olive, the carob, and the ash are trees found even in the higher mountains. Also, they divide their agriculture into three-year cycles: beans, grain, and rest period, in connection with which they say: "Manure works more miracles than the saints." The grapevines are kept very low.

Alcamo is splendidly located on a height some distance from the bay; the grandeur of the region attracted us. High rocks with deep valleys, but breadth and variety. Behind Monreale one comes into a beautiful double valley, in the middle of which rises another rocky ridge. The fertile fields lie green and silent, while along the broad road wild bushes and massed shrubbery gleam with blossoms as though gone mad with blooming: the lentil bush, entirely covered with papilionaceous flowers, not a green leaf to be seen; the hawthorn, bunch after bunch of blooms; the aloes shooting upwards and hinting at blossoms; rich carpets of amaranthine-red clover; fly orchids, Alpine roses, hyacinths with closed calyxes, borage, garlic, asphodels.

The river flowing down from Segesta carries along not only limestone pebbles but many fragments of hornstone, very solid pieces, dark-blue, red, yellow, brown, in the most varied shades. I also found outcropping veins of hornstone or flint in limestone rocks, with selvages of lime. One finds whole hills of such detritus before reaching Alcamo.

Segesta, April 20, 1787.

The temple of Segesta[79] was never finished, and the space around it was never leveled off, the only smoothed-out area being that on which the columns were to be set; for even now, although there is no hill nearby from which rocks and soil could have washed down, the steps in many places are nine or ten feet below the surface. Also the rocks lie mostly in their natural positions, and no broken pieces are found among them.

All the columns are standing; two that had fallen have recently been set up again. It is hard to determine how much of a socle the columns were supposed to have, and this cannot be made clear without a drawing. Sometimes it looks as if a column were standing on the fourth step, in which case one must again go down a step to reach the interior of the temple; sometimes the uppermost step is cut through, then it looks as if the columns had bases; sometimes these gaps have been filled in again, and then we are back at the first case. May some architect determine this more precisely.

The long sides have twelve columns, not counting the corner ones, the front and rear sides have six including the corner columns. The bosses on which the stones were transported have not been chiseled away from the steps around the temple, a proof that the temple was not finished. But the best evidence of that is offered by the floor, which is indicated at various places by stone slabs extending inward from the sides, but the rough limestone rock still stands in the middle, higher than the level of the laid floor; therefore the paving can never have been completed. There is also no trace of a cella. Nor has the temple been covered with stucco, although that seems to have been the intention: the plinths above the capitals have projections to which, perhaps, the stucco was to be attached. The whole thing is constructed of a travertine-like limestone, now very much eaten away. The restoration of 1781 was of great benefit to the building. The seam that joins the parts is simple, but neat. I could not find the large individual stones mentioned by Riedesel.[80] Perhaps they were all used in the restoration of the columns.

The temple has an exceptional location: at the highest end of a long, wide valley, on an isolated hill, but nevertheless surrounded by cliffs,

it looks into the far distance, across much land but just a small corner
of the sea. The region is fertile, but quiet and sad; everything cultivated,
almost no dwellings anywhere. Innumerable butterflies swarmed over
blooming thistles. Wild fennel, last year's desiccated growth, stood eight
or nine feet high in such abundance and apparent order that it could
have been taken for part of a tree nursery. The wind soughed in the
columns as though in a woods, and birds of prey hovered screaming
over the entablature.

We had so much difficulty clambering around the insignificant ruins
of a theater that we lost our desire to visit the ruins of the town. Large
pieces of dense quartz lie at the foot of the temple, and the road to
Alcamo is strewn with endless fragments of the same material. Consequently a certain amount of silica gets into the soil and makes it looser.
In the fresh fennel I noticed the difference between the upper and lower
leaves, and yet it is always the same organ, developing from simplicity
into diversity. Weeding is done very diligently here; the men go through
the whole field as if they were flushing out game. Insects are also in
evidence. In Palermo I had only noticed worm-like creatures, lizards,
leeches, snails, no more beautifully colored than ours, in fact only gray.

Castel Vetrano, Saturday, April 21, 1787.

On the way from Alcamo to Castel Vetrano one goes over hills of
gravel alongside a limestone range. Between the steep, barren limestone
mountains are wide, hilly valleys, everything cultivated, but almost no
trees. The gravel hills full of large fragments, indicating ancient sea
currents; the soil well mixed, lighter than before, on account of the
sand in it. Salemi remained an hour's journey to our right, here we
went across gypsum rocks lying in front of the limestone, the soil more
and more excellently mixed. To the west the sea is visible in the distance. In the foreground the land completely hilly. We found budding
fig trees, but what excited our pleasure and admiration were the vast
masses of flowers that had established themselves on the very broad
road and were divided into a series of large, colorful, contiguous areas.
The loveliest wild convolvulus, hibiscus, mallows, and various kinds
of clover alternately predominated, with garlic and Galega bushes in
between. And we meandered through this colorful carpet on muleback,
following innumerable narrow, crisscross paths. In the midst of this
graze beautiful reddish-brown cattle, not large, very trimly built, the
shape of their horns especially graceful.

The ranges in the northeast all stand in rows; only one peak, Cu-
niglione, juts out from the middle. The gravel hills produce little water,

and heavy rains must be rare here, for one finds no gullies nor any washed-down debris.

During the night I met with a peculiar adventure. Very tired, we had thrown ourselves on our beds in an admittedly not very elegant inn. At midnight I awoke and saw the most delightful apparition above me: a star more beautiful, I thought, than any I had ever seen before. I was exhilarated by the lovely, propitious sight, but soon the gracious light disappeared and left me alone in the darkness. Only at daybreak did I perceive the cause of this miracle: it was a hole in the roof, and just at that moment one of the most beautiful stars in the sky had passed through my meridian. Nevertheless, we travelers confidently interpreted this natural event in our favor.

Sciacca, April 22, 1787.

The road here, mineralogically uninteresting, constantly goes over gravel hills. One arrives at the seashore, where occasionally limestone rocks tower up. All the level ground is extremely fertile, barley and oats standing most beautifully; saltwort has been planted; the fruit-bearing stems of the aloes have already grown higher than they were yesterday and the day before. The many kinds of clover did not abandon us. Finally we came to a little woods, bushy, with only individual taller trees; at last cork trees too!

Agrigento,[81] April 23. Evening.

A good day's journey here from Sciacca. Just before arriving at the above-named town we inspected the baths; a hot spring surges out of the rock with a very strong smell of sulfur; the water tastes very salty, but not foul. Is it not possible that the sulfurous vapor is created at the moment when the water emerges? Somewhat higher up is a fountain, cool, odorless. On the very top lies the monastery, where the steam baths are; heavy mist rises from them into the clear air.

Here the sea rolls in only limestone fragments, quartz and hornstone are cut off. I observed the small rivers: the Caltabellotta[82] and the Maccazzolo also carry only limestone fragments, the Platani carries yellow marble and flints, which never fail to accompany this nobler type of limestone. A few small pieces of lava caught my eye, but I do not imagine that there is anything volcanic in the area. Rather, I think they are remnants of millstones, or of pieces brought from a distance for some other use. Near Montalegro everything is gypsum: dense gypsum and mica, whole rocks of it in front of and amongst the limestone. The extraordinary lofty site of Caltabellotta!

Agrigento, Tuesday, April 24, 1787.

Surely never in our lives have we had such a magnificent springtime view as we had today at sunrise. New Agrigento is located on the lofty site of the ancient fortress, which has a perimeter large enough to accommodate inhabitants. From our windows we saw the long, broad, gentle slope of the old city, completely covered with gardens and vineyards, under whose greenery hardly a trace of the former large urban districts can be imagined. At the very end of this green and blossoming area the temple of Concordia can be seen to stand out, in the east the few remaining pieces of the temple of Juno. The rest of the ruins, those of the other religious buildings, are situated in a straight line with the aforementioned ones. The eye does not take note of them from above, but instead hastens farther south to the coastal area, which stretches out toward the sea as far as one can walk in half an hour. Today we had to forgo a descent into those splendidly green, blooming, promisingly productive expanses, and of being amid branches and vines; for our guide, a good little priest, asked us to devote this day to the town before all else.

First he had us inspect the quite well-made streets, then he led us up to higher points, where the greater width and distance made the view even more splendid; then, for artistic enjoyment, to the main church. This contains a well-preserved sarcophagus,[83] salvaged for use as an altar: Hippolytus with his hunting companions and horses is detained by Phaedra's nurse, who wants to give him a little tablet. The main intention here was to depict handsome youths, for which reason the old woman, quite small and dwarfish, is hewn out between them as an incidental feature that is not supposed to distract. I think I have never seen a more magnificent specimen of bas-relief, perfectly preserved besides. For the time being I shall take it as an example of the most charming period of Greek art.

We were transported back into earlier epochs by contemplating an exquisite vase of significant size,[84] perfectly preserved. Furthermore there seemed to be some architectural remains incorporated here and there in the new church.

Since there are no inns here, a friendly family took us in and assigned us a raised alcove in a large room. A green curtain separated us and our luggage from the family members, who used the big room for the manufacture of pasta, indeed pasta of the finest, whitest, and smallest type. The kind that commands the highest price is first given the shape of inch-long pegs, which are then twisted by skillful girlish fingers into a spiral form. We sat down next to the pretty children, had them explain the process to us, and heard that the pasta is made out of the best and heaviest wheat, called *grano forte*. Handwork plays a much greater role in this than machines and molds. And then they also prepared the choicest dish of pasta for us, but regretted that they did not have enough in stock for a dish of the very best sort, the manufacture of which was restricted to Agrigento, indeed to their own house. Apparently this could not be equaled for whiteness and tenderness.

All evening too, our guide managed to curb our impatient desire to go down the hill by leading us up again to splendid observation points where we could survey the locality and pick out all the notable things that we were to see close at hand the next day.

Agrigento, Wednesday, April 25, 1787.

At sunrise we did walk down, and at every step the surroundings grew more picturesque. Our little man, conscious of the fact that it was in our best interest, led us without stopping across the rich vegetation, past a thousand individual things, each of which offered a subject for idyllic pictures. The uneven ground contributes greatly to this, rolling in waves over hidden ruins, which could be covered all the more easily with fertile soil because the ancient buildings were composed of a light shell material. And so we arrived at the eastern end of the town, where the ruined temple of Juno[85] decays more every year, because the porous stone is being consumed by air and weather. Today we were to undertake only a cursory examination, but Kniep already selected the vantage points from which he wants to draw tomorrow.

Today the temple stands on a weathered rock. The city walls extended out from here, and directly eastward,[86] upon a limestone layer which stands at right angles to the flat shore left by the sea both before and after it had formed these rocks and washed against their foot. The walls were partly hewn out of the rocks, partly built with them; behind the walls rose the series of temples. No wonder, therefore, that the lower, ascending, and highest parts of Agrigento, together, made a significant sight from the sea.

The temple of Concordia[87] has withstood so many centuries; its slender architecture brings it quite close to our standards of beauty and grace; its relation to the temples of Paestum is that of a god's form to the shape of giants. I shall not complain about the tasteless way the laudable recent plan for preserving these monuments has been carried out—filling in the gaps with dazzling white plaster, so that, as a result, in a certain way this monument looks broken; but how easy it would have been to give the plaster the color of weathered stone! To be sure, seeing the easily crumbled limestone of the columns and walls, one marvels that it has lasted this long. But the builders, hoping for a posterity like themselves, had made provision for this: the columns still show traces of a delicate varnish, which was meant both to please the eye and insure permanence.

Then our second stop was at the ruins of the temple of Jupiter.[88] Like a gigantic bony skeleton, this lies stretched out inside of and underneath several small properties, is crossed by fences, and overgrown with plants of various sizes. Everything with form has disappeared from this rubbish heap except for a huge triglyph and a piece of semicolumn proportioned to it. I measured the former with outspread arms and could not span it. But the fluting of the columns can be judged by the fact that when I stood in one, as though it were a little niche, I filled it, with both shoulders touching the sides. Twenty-two men placed next to each other in a circle would approximately form the periphery of such a column. We left with the uncomfortable feeling that there was nothing here for an artist to draw.

The temple of Hercules,[89] on the other hand, still revealed traces of a previous symmetry. The two ranks of columns that bordered the temple on either side lay in the same direction, north to south, one rank up a hillside, the other down, as if they had all been felled at the same time. The hill may well have been created by the collapsed cella. The columns, probably held together by the entablature, fell suddenly, perhaps knocked down by the fury of a storm; and they still lie regularly, broken into their composite parts. Kniep, in his thoughts, was already sharpening his pencils in order to draw this remarkable phenomenon precisely.

The temple of Aesculapius,[90] shaded by the most beautiful carob tree and almost walled in by a small farm house, makes an agreeable picture.

Next we descended to the tomb of Theron[91] and delighted in the presence of a monument that we had so often seen pictured, especially since it served us as the foreground for a wonderful view. For we looked from west to east along the rocky layer on which not only the fragmentary town walls are visible, but also, through and over them, the remains of the temples. In Hackert's artistic hands this view has become a lovely picture; Kniep will also not fail to make a drawing of it.

Agrigento, Thursday, April 26, 1787.

When I awoke, Kniep was already prepared to start out on his drawing tour, and had a boy who was to show him the way and carry his portfolio. I enjoyed the most magnificent morning, seated by the window with my secret, silent, but not mute friend at my side. Out of pious respect I have heretofore not mentioned the name of the mentor to whom I look and listen from time to time; it is the excellent von Riedesel, whose little book I carry in my bosom like a breviary or talisman.

I have always been much disposed to mirror myself in natures that possess what I lack, and that is the case here: calm purpose, sureness of goal, clearly defined and suitable methods, preparation and knowledge, a deeply felt relationship with a superlative teacher, i.e., Winckelmann. I am without all of this, and all the other things that result from it. And yet I cannot blame myself for trying to take by stealth, by storm, by stratagem what has not been granted to me in the normal course of life. May that excellent man sense at this moment, amidst the tumult of the world, that his merits are being praised by a later traveler, solitary in this solitary place, which held so much charm for him also that he even wanted to spend his life here, forgotten by his family and forgetting them in turn.

Next I walked the same paths as yesterday with my little clerical guide, observing the sights from various directions and occasionally visiting my industrious friend.

My guide pointed out to me a beautiful custom of the old, mighty city. There are tombs, probably designed as resting places for brave and good men, in the rocks and masses of masonry that served as Agrigento's bulwark. Where could they be more beautifully interred, to their own glory and for everlasting emulation!

In the wide expanse between the walls and the sea one also finds the remains of a small temple,[92] which has been preserved as a Christian chapel. Here too, semicolumns are very beautifully combined with the smooth stones of the wall, and both, fitted into each other, are very pleasing to the eye. This, it would seem to me, is the very point that marks the consummate development of the Doric order.

We looked perfunctorily at some unpretentious ancient monuments, and then, with more interest, at the modern way of storing wheat underground in large, masonry-lined vaults. The good old guide told me quite a lot about civic and churchly conditions. I did not hear about anything that was undergoing even slight improvement. It was a conversation well suited to these steadily disintegrating ruins.

The layers of shell limestone all slope toward the sea. Seams of rock curiously hollowed out from beneath and behind, but with the upper and front sections partially preserved, so that they look like fringes hanging down. Hatred of the French, because they are at peace with the Berbers and are blamed for betraying the Christians to the infidels.

A gateway leading from the sea was carved into the rocks in antiquity. The still existent walls rest in stages on the rocks. Our cicerone was named Don Michele Vella, antiquary, living at the house of Maestro Gerio, in the vicinity of St. Maria.

They use the following method of planting broad beans: they make holes in the earth at appropriate intervals and put a handful of manure in them, wait for rain, and then plant the beans. They burn the bean straw, then wash their linen with the resulting ashes. They use no soap. The outer almond shells are also reduced to ashes, which are used in place of soda. First they wash the clothes in water and then in this kind of lye.

They rotate their crops from beans to wheat to *tumenia;* the fourth year is left for pasture. "Beans" here are to be understood as "broad beans." Their wheat is extremely good. *Tumenia,* whose name is supposedly derived from *bimenia* or *trimenia,* is a splendid gift of Ceres: it is a kind of summer grain that ripens in three months. They sow it from the first of January to June, and it is always ripe at the designated time. It does not need much rain, but does need great heat; at first it has a very delicate leaf, but it grows like wheat and eventually becomes very sturdy. Wheat is sown in October and November, and ripens in June. Barley sown in November is ripe on the first of June, faster on the coast, more slowly in the mountains.

The flax is already ripe. The acanthus has unfurled its superb leaves. *Salsola fruticosa* grows luxuriantly.

Sainfoin grows abundantly on uncultivated hills. In part it is leased out and taken to town in bundles. They pull up oats from amongst the wheat, and also sell these in bundles.

To facilitate watering, they make neat dividing lines, with little borders, in the soil where they intend to plant cabbages.

All the leaves were out on the fig trees, and the fruit had started to develop. It will be ripe on midsummer day, then the tree begins to bear again. The almond trees were very full; innumerable pods hung from a cropped carob tree. The grapes for eating are strung onto arbors supported on high columns. They plant melons in March, to ripen in June. These grow vigorously, without a trace of moisture, in the ruins of the temple of Jupiter.

Our *vetturino* ate raw artichokes and kohlrabi with great appetite; it must of course be admitted that they are much tenderer and juicier than in our country. When we walk through the fields, the peasants let us eat as many young beans, for example, as we like.

When I noticed some black, solid rocks that resembled lava, the antiquary told me they came from Etna, and that there were also some standing in the harbor, or rather, landing place.

There are not many indigenous birds, only quail. The migrant birds are: nightingales, larks, and swallows. *Rinnine,* small, black birds that come from the Levant, nest in Sicily and then go onward, or back. *Ridene,* waterfowl which come from Africa in December and January, alight on the river Akragas, and then go on to the mountains.

One more word about the vase in the cathedral. On it, a hero, presumably a recent arrival, stands in full armor before a seated old man, whose wreath and scepter indicate that he is a king. Behind him stands a woman, her head bowed, her left hand under her chin, a watchfully reflective posture. Opposite, behind the hero, an old man crowned with a wreath, talking with a spear carrier, who may be a member of the bodyguard. The old man seems to have introduced the hero and to be saying to the guard: "Just let him talk to the king, he is a worthy man."

The red is apparently the ground color of this vase, with the black being an overlay. Red seems to lie on black only in the woman's garment.

Agrigento, Friday, April 27, 1787.

If Kniep intends to carry out all his plans, he will have to draw incessantly, while I walk around with my little old guide. We strolled toward the sea, from which side, as the ancients assure us, Agrigento used to look very good. My glances were drawn to the expanse of waves, and my guide pointed out a long strip of clouds to the south, which seemed to lie on the horizon like a mountain ridge. This, he said, indicated the coast of Africa. Meanwhile another phenomenon struck me as curious: it was a narrow arc formed of light clouds, which, based with one foot on Sicily, curved up high into the blue, otherwise entirely clear sky, and seemed to rest with its other end on the sea. Quite beautifully colored by the setting sun and almost stationary, it was both a strange and agreeable sight for the eye. I was assured that this arc went in the exact direction of Malta and might well have let down its other foot on that island, a phenomenon that sometimes occurred. It would be quite extraordinary if the attractive force mutually exerted by the two islands were to manifest itself in the atmosphere in this manner.

This conversation made me question again whether I should abandon my plan of visiting Malta. But the difficulties and dangers we had thought about earlier remained the same, and we resolved to hire our *vetturino* to take us as far as Messina.

But at the same time we would act again in accordance with one of my obstinate notions. That is to say, heretofore I had seen few rich grain-bearing areas in Sicily, and our horizon had been limited everywhere by near and distant mountains, so that the island seemed to lack level spaces entirely, and we could not understand why Ceres was reputed to have so specially favored this realm. When I asked about this, the answer was that if I wanted to understand, I would have to bypass Syracuse and go cross-country, where I would encounter numerous wheatfields. We yielded to the temptation of giving up Syracuse, since we were not ignorant of the fact that little is left of this magnificent city but its glorious name. If necessary, we could easily reach it from Catania.

Caltanissetta, Saturday, April 28, 1787.

So today, at last, we can say that we have been shown in a graphic fashion how Sicily could receive the honorable title of being Italy's granary. The fertile ground began some distance after we had left Agrigento. There are no large areas, but the hill and mountain ridges meet gently and are, without exception, planted with wheat and barley, and present an unbroken mass of fertility to the eye. The soil that is suitable for these plants is so well utilized and husbanded that there is not a tree to be seen anywhere; indeed all the little villages and houses are located on the ridges of the hills, where an extensive series of limestone rocks makes the land unworkable in any case. The women live there all year, occupied with spinning and weaving, whereas the men, during the actual season of field work, spend only Saturday and Sunday with them, and stay down below on the other days, retiring to reed huts at night. And so our wish was fulfilled to the point of satiety, and we wished for the winged chariot of Triptolemos,[93] to escape from this monotony.

Now, in the hot sunshine, we rode through this desolate fertility and were happy to arrive at last in the well-located and well-built town of Caltanissetta, where, however, we looked in vain again for a tolerable inn. The mules may stand in splendidly vaulted stables, the stable boys sleep on the clover meant for the animals, but the stranger must begin his housekeeping from the beginning. If a room is perhaps made available to him, it first has to be cleaned. There are no chairs or benches, one sits on low trestles of sturdy wood; there are no tables either.

If those trestles are to be converted into feet for a bed, one must go to a carpenter and borrow as many boards as necessary, in exchange for a certain amount of rent. The large Russia leather bag that Hackert had lent us now came in very handy, and was temporarily filled with chaff.

Before anything else, however, arrangements had to be made for eating. Along the way, we had bought a hen, the *vetturino* had gone to get rice, salt, and spices; but because he had never been here before, for a long time it remained a mystery where we were actually going to cook, there being no facility for that in the inn itself. Finally an elderly citizen consented, for a small sum, to provide us with wood and a stove, as well as kitchen and table utensils. While the meal was cooking, he conducted us around the town and eventually to the marketplace, where, in age-old fashion, the most distinguished citizens sat around, conversed, and expected us to entertain them.

We had to tell about Frederick II, and their interest in this great king was so lively that we concealed the fact of his death, in order not to make ourselves odious to our hosts with such ill tidings.

Caltanissetta, Saturday, April 28, 1787.

Geological matters, as an addendum. Down from Agrigento along the shell limestone rocks a whitish earth appears, and is subsequently explained: we find the more ancient limestone again, with gypsum right next to it. Wide, level valleys, crops planted up as far as the peaks, often over them; the more ancient limestone mixed with weathered gypsum. Then a more porous, yellowish, easily crumbled new limestone appears: its color is clearly recognizable in the plowed fields, often merging into a darker shade, even violet. A little past the halfway point, the gypsum protrudes again. Sedum of a pretty violet color, almost rosy-red, frequently grows on it, as a beautiful yellow moss does on the limestone rocks.

That crumbly limestone often turns up again, most plentifully near Caltanissetta, where it lies in strata containing individual shells; then it looks reddish, almost like minium, with a hint of violet, as was mentioned earlier in connection with San Martino.

Only about halfway along did I find quartz fragments, in a valley that was closed on three sides but stood open to the east, and therefore toward the sea.

Standing out in the distance, to the left, were the high mountain near Camerata and another one, which was like a truncated cone. Not a tree to be seen for more than half the way. The grain had come up splendidly, although it was not as high as at Agrigento and the seashore; but it was as pure as is possible: no weeds in those vast wheat fields. First we saw nothing but fields that were turning green, then plowed ones, in damp places a bit of meadow. There are also poplars here. Just outside of Agrigento we found apples and pears, moreover some figs in the hills and near the few villages.

These thirty *miglia,*[94] along with all I could make out to the left and right, consist of older and newer limestone, with gypsum in between. The soil owes its fertility to the decomposition and mutual interaction of these three minerals. It may contain a little sand, for it crunches between the teeth. A supposition regarding the Achates river will be proved correct tomorrow.[95]

The valleys are beautifully formed, and although they are not completely level, I saw no marks left by heavy rains. There are just some scarcely noticeable brooks trickling down to the sea, for everything flows directly there at once. Not much red clover is to be seen, the low palms disappear, together with all the flowers and bushes of the southwestern side. Thistles are granted dominion over the road, but everything else belongs to Ceres. In general the area is much like the fertile hilly regions of Germany, for example that between Erfurt and Gotha, especially looking in the direction of the Gleichen.[96] A great many things had to concur to make Sicily one of the most fertile lands in the world.

Few horses were to be seen on the whole tour; they plow with oxen, and there is a ban against slaughtering cows and calves. We encountered many goats, donkeys, and mules. The horses are mostly dapple-grays with black fetlocks and manes; we saw the most sumptuous stalls with built-in bedsteads. The ground is manured for raising beans and lentils, the other crops grow after this summer one. As we rode by, bundles of barley, sprouting ears but still green, and of red clover were offered to us for sale.

On the mountain above Caltanissetta there was compact limestone with fossils: the large shells situated at the foot, the small ones at the top. In the pavement of the little town we found limestone with *Pectinidae*.[97]

Addendum to April 28, 1787.

Behind Caltanissetta the hills slope down abruptly into various valleys which pour their waters into the Salso river. The soil is reddish, very clayey, much of it lay uncultivated, the grain rather good in the cultivated parts, but not very far along compared to the previous regions.

Enna,[98] Sunday, April 29, 1787.

Today we noted still greater fertility and still greater desolation. Rainy weather had set in and made traveling conditions very unpleasant, since we had to go through several very swollen streams. At the Salso river, where we looked around in vain for a bridge, we were surprised by a curious arrangement. Strong men stood ready, and two by two they grasped our mules by the middle, complete with rider and baggage, and led them thus through a deep part of the river up to a big gravel bank; once the whole company was together here, the second arm of the river was crossed in the same fashion, with the men again holding the animals on the right path and upright against the current by pushing and shoving. There is some shrubbery at the water's edge, but this disappears again farther inland. The Salso river carries granite, an incipient gneiss, and both brecciated and monochromatic marble.

Now we saw before us the solitary ridge upon which Enna is situated and which gives the area a strange, somber character. As we rode up the long path ascending its side, we found that the mountain consisted of shell limestone; we collected some large, merely calcined shells. Enna only becomes visible after one arrives at the very top of the ridge, for it lies on the northern slope. The curious little town itself, with its tower, and the village of Calascibetta, some distance away to the left, face each other quite gravely. In the plain we saw beans in full bloom, but who could enjoy this view! The roads were horrendous, even more terrible because they had once been paved, and it kept on raining. Ancient Enna received us most ungraciously: a room with a stone floor and no window glass, just shutters, so that we either had to sit in the dark or put up again with the drizzling rain we had just escaped. We ate a few leftovers from our travel supplies, and spent a miserable night. We solemnly swore never again to make a mythological name the goal of our journey.

Monday, April 30, 1787.

A rugged, difficult mountain path goes down from Enna, and we had to lead the horses.[99] In front of us, the atmosphere was filled with very low-hanging clouds, whereupon a wonderful phenomenon appeared far above us. It was striped white and gray and seemed to be something physical; but how did something physical get into the sky? Our guide informed us that what was causing our astonishment was a side of Mt. Etna, which was showing through rents in the clouds: the stripes were formed by alternating ridges and snow; this was not even the highest peak.

Ancient Enna's steep rock now lay behind us, we passed through long, long, lonely valleys; they lay there untilled and uninhabited, given over to grazing cattle, which were a pretty brown, not large, with small horns, as neat, slender, and lively as little stags. These good creatures may have had enough pasture land, but it was being narrowed and gradually spoiled for them by enormous masses of thistles. These plants have the finest opportunity here for self-pollination and propagation of their species; they occupy an incredible area, large enough to serve as pasturage for several great landed estates. Since they are not perennials, surely it would be easy to eradicate them by mowing them down now, before they blossom.

While gravely pondering these plans for an agricultural war against the thistles, we were obliged to observe, to our shame, that they were not entirely useless after all. A pair of Sicilian nobles, who were traveling to Palermo because of a lawsuit, had come at the same time as we to an isolated inn, where we ate. With amazement we saw these two serious-looking men stand in front of a group of these thistles with sharp pocketknives and cut off the top part of the flourishing plants; then they cautiously grasped their prickly prize with their fingers, peeled the stem, and consumed the inside of it with pleasure. They spent a long time at that, while we refreshed ourselves with wine (unmixed this time!) and good bread. The *vetturino* prepared some stem pulp for us too, with the assurance that it was a healthful, cooling food; but it tasted no better to us than the raw kohlrabi at Segesta.

On the way, April 30.

Having arrived in the valley through which the San Paolo river winds, we found reddish-black soil and crumbly limestone; much fallow land, very wide fields, a beautiful valley, made very pleasant by the little river. The good, mixed, loamy soil is twenty feet deep in places, and mostly even. The aloes had sprouted vigorously. The grain looked beautiful, but occasionally flawed, and much retarded, compared to that on the southern side. Small houses here and there; no trees except directly below Enna. Much pastureland along the shores of the river, but reduced by the huge masses of thistles. Quartz minerals in the river deposits again, partly plain, partly like breccia.

Molimenti, a new village, very intelligently laid out amidst beautiful fields, on the little river San Paolo. Nearby was a really incomparable stand of wheat, to be harvested as early as the twentieth of May. There is still not a sign of volcanic activity to be seen in the whole region, even the river carries no such fragments. The soil, well mixed, heavy rather than light, has, on the whole, a coffee-brown color merging into violet. All the mountains to the left, which enclose the river, are of lime- and sandstone. I could not observe how these alternate; however, by decomposing they have created the great, evenly distributed fertility of the lower valley.

Tuesday, May 1, 1787.

Although nature designed this valley to be fertile throughout, it is not evenly cultivated, and we rode down it in some annoyance, because, after all the hardships we had endured, we found nothing at all there to serve our artistic goals. Kniep had drawn a rather significant distant scene, but since the middle and foreground were truly execrable, he, with tasteful playfulness, substituted a front part in the style of Poussin.[100] This was easily done, and made the page into quite a pretty little picture. I wonder how many illustrated travel books contain similar half-truths.

To soothe our disgruntled feelings, our groom promised us good lodgings for the evening, and did indeed lead us to an inn built only a few years ago. Located on this road at just the right distance from Catania, of course it was a welcome sight to the traveler, and for the first time in twelve days we could again take our ease to a certain extent in a tolerable establishment. But we were struck by an inscription penciled on the wall in a beautiful English hand: "Travelers, whoever you may be, beware of the inn of the Golden Lion in Catania; it is worse than if you had fallen into the clutches of the Cyclopes, the Sirens, and the Scyllas all at the same time." Although we thought that the well-meaning warner might have mythologically exaggerated the danger, we nevertheless firmly resolved to avoid the Golden Lion, which had been announced to us as such a ferocious animal. Therefore when the muleteer asked us where we wanted to stay in Catania, we answered: "Anywhere except in the Golden Lion!" Then he suggested that we make do with the inn where he stabled his animals; however, we would have to arrange for our own food there, as we had done heretofore. We were all satisfied: our sole wish was to elude the jaws of the lion.

Towards Paternò,[101] lava fragments are in evidence, brought down from the north by water. Above the roadway one finds limestone combined with various fragments, hornstone, lava, and chalk; then solidified volcanic ash, overlaid with lime tufa. The hills of mixed gravel continue almost as far as Catania, and up to and over them are lava streams from Etna. To the left is what seems to be a crater. (Directly below Molimenti the peasants were pulling flax.) Nature shows us its love of color here when it plays with the blue-black-gray lava: bright-yellow moss spreads over it, sedum of a beautiful red grows luxuriantly on it, as do some beautiful violet flowers. Careful cultivation is evident in the cactus plantings and the grapevines. Next, enormous lava flows press close to our path. Motta is a beautiful, significant rock. Beans grow here in very high bushes. The fields are varied, sometimes very gravelly, sometimes of a better mixture.

Our *vetturino,* who probably had not seen the springtime vegetation on the southeastern side for a long time, began to exclaim loudly about the beauty of the grain, and with smug patriotism asked us if there was anything like it in our country. Here everything is sacrificed to it, one sees little else, indeed no trees at all. We were charmed by a girl with a lovely, slim figure, a long-time acquaintance of our *vetturino,* who ran alongside his mule, chatting, and at the same time spinning her thread as gracefully as possible. Now yellow flowers began to predominate. Near Misterbianco, cactuses were already standing in the fences again; but fences made entirely of these curiously shaped plants become increasingly regular and beautiful in the vicinity of Catania.

Catania, Wednesday, May 2, 1787.

We were really very miserable in our inn. The food our muleteer could prepare was not very good. Still, a hen cooked in rice would have been acceptable if too much saffron had not made it both yellow and unpalatable. The extremely uncomfortable bed had almost forced us to get Hackert's Russia leather sack out again, for which reason we spoke with the friendly innkeeper early in the morning. He apologized for not being able to provide for us better: "But over there is a house where strangers are well looked after and have every reason to be satisfied."—He pointed to a large corner house, and the side of it facing us looked very promising. We immediately hurried over there and found an energetic man who said he was a hired servant. In the innkeeper's absence he showed us to a fine room next to a salon, at the same time assuring us that we would be served very cheaply. We did not fail to inquire in the customary way about what we would have to pay for our quarters, the host's table, wine, breakfast, and other matters that could be determined in advance. It was all reasonable, and we quickly brought over our few possessions in order to arrange them in the capacious, gilded chests of drawers. For the first time, Kniep had an opportunity to spread out his portfolio; he put his drawings in order, as I did my notes. Then, pleased with the beautiful rooms, we stepped out onto the balcony of the salon to enjoy the view. After contemplating and praising it sufficiently, we resumed our activities, and lo! there above our heads was a big golden lion. We looked at each other doubtfully, smiled, and then laughed. However, from now on we kept glancing around to see if one of those Homeric bogeys was peering out somewhere.

Nothing of the kind was to be seen, instead we found a pretty young woman in the salon. She was dandling a child perhaps two years old, but the next moment she was standing there being roughly scolded by the active assistant innkeeper: she should leave, he was saying, she had no business here!—"It is really cruel of you to chase me away," she said. "I cannot pacify the child at home when you are gone, and surely these gentlemen will allow me to calm the little one in your presence." Her husband did not leave it at that, but tried to send her away, the child screamed quite pitifully at the door, and at last we had to insist that the pretty little lady remain.

Having been warned by the Englishman, it was easy enough for us to see through this comedy, we acted the part of novices, of innocents, and he made a great show of being an affectionate father. The child was actually friendliest with him, probably the ostensible mother had pinched it when they were in the doorway.

And so she stayed there, looking very innocent, while the man went away to deliver our letter of recommendation to the family chaplain of Prince Biscari.[102] She continued playing with the child until he returned and announced that the abbé would come in person to give us detailed information.

Catania, Thursday, May 3, 1787.

The abbé, who had already greeted us yesterday evening, appeared early today and conducted us to the palace, which is built in one story on a high base, and, of course, we first looked at the museum, where marble and bronze images, vases, and all kinds of such antiquities stand side by side. Again we had an opportunity to broaden our knowledge; however, we were especially fascinated by the torso of a Jupiter,[103] a cast of which I already knew from Tischbein's studio, and which possesses greater merits than we were capable of judging. A member of the household gave us the most necessary historical information, and then we entered a large, high-ceilinged salon. The many chairs against the walls were evidence that sometimes large groups assembled here. We sat down in expectation of a favorable reception. At that moment a pair of women entered and walked up and down the length of the room. They spoke earnestly with each other. When they noticed us, the abbé stood up, I likewise, and we bowed. I asked who they were, and learned that the younger one was the princess,[104] the elder a Catanian noblewoman. We sat down again, and they walked back and forth as one would in a marketplace.

We were conducted to the prince, who, as had already been mentioned to me, was showing special confidence in us by displaying his coin collection. Apparently his father before him, and he too, had lost many an item when exhibiting the coins, and this had lessened his normal willingness to some extent. Here, to be sure, I could seem somewhat more knowledgeable, since I had educated myself by looking at the collection of Prince Torremuzza. Now I was learning again and helped myself along rather well on that durable Winckelmannic thread which leads us through the various artistic epochs. The prince, fully informed about these things, and seeing that we were not connoisseurs, but observant admirers, was quite willing to give instructive answers to all our questions.

After having devoted considerable, but still insufficient, time to examining the coins, we were about to take our leave; then, however, he brought us in to meet his mother, and that was also where the remaining smaller artworks were displayed.

We found a distinguished-looking woman[105] with a naturally noble air who received us with the words: "Do look around my room, gentlemen, you will find everything here just as my late husband[106] collected and arranged it. I owe this to my son's filial piety: he not only lets me inhabit his best rooms, but also will not permit the smallest thing that was acquired and set up by his father to be moved or taken away. Consequently I have the double advantage of living as I have been accustomed to for so many years and also, as formerly, of seeing and becoming acquainted with the fine foreign visitors who come from such distances to view our treasures."

Thereupon she herself opened the glass cabinet in which objects made of amber were kept. Sicilian amber differs from the northern type in that it ranges from transparent and opaque honey colors through all the shadings of a saturated yellow up to the most beautiful hyacinthine red. Urns, goblets, and other things were carved out of it, so that in some cases we imagined that the original chunks of material must have been impressively large. The lady took a special delight in these objects, as well as in the carved shells made in Trapani and in choice works out of ivory; she had many an entertaining story to tell about them.

The prince drew our attention to more important objects, and so several hours passed in a pleasant and instructive manner.

Meanwhile the princess had learned that we were Germans, and therefore inquired about Messrs. von Riedesel, Bartels, and Münter,[107] all of whom she knew and properly appreciated, having discerned their respective characters and behavior very well. We parted from her regretfully, and she did not seem to want us to leave. There is, after all, something solitary about this insular situation, and only the interest shown by persons passing through preserves and revives it.

Then the chaplain led us into the Benedictine monastery, to the cell of a brother who, while not very old, had a sad, withdrawn appearance that did not promise much cheerful conversation. He was nevertheless a talented man, the only one able to master this church's huge organ.[108] He silently granted our wishes, not so much hearing as surmising them: we went into the very spacious church, where, playing the splendid instrument, he filled the farthest corners with sound, both the lightest whispering breath and the most forceful, crashing tones.

Anyone who had not seen the man beforehand would have thought
a giant was exerting this power; but since we had already met him
personally, we only marveled that he had not been worn out long ago
by this struggle.

Catania, Friday, May 4, 1787.

Soon after we had dined, the abbé came with a carriage, since he
was supposed to show us the outlying parts of the town. A curious
dispute over precedence took place as were getting in. I had climbed
up first and was about to sit down on the left; but he, getting in after
me, emphatically demanded that I move over to the right. I asked him
to dispense with such ceremony. "Pardon me for making us sit this
way," he said, "for if I take my seat at your right, everyone will think
I am driving with you; but if I sit at your left, that is a sign you are
driving with me, that is, with me as the prince's representative to show
you the town." Obviously no objection could be raised to that, and we
did accordingly.

We drove up the streets where the lava which destroyed a large part
of this town in 1669 remains visible to the present day. The solidified
fiery stream was treated like any other rock; streets were even marked
out on it and partially built. I knocked down a piece of what was unquestionably molten material, keeping in mind the controversy over
the volcanic quality of basalts that had broken out in Germany before
my departure.[109] And I did the same at several spots, in order to obtain
a number of variations.

Yet the traveler would have to labor in vain for a long time if the
natives themselves, out of love for their region, and for the sake of
profit or science, were not avid collectors of the notable things in their
district. The lava dealer in Naples had already assisted me a great deal,
and here Cavaliere Gioeni[110] did so in a far higher sense. In his rich,
very tastefully displayed collection I found the lavas of Etna, the basalts
from its foot, and some minerals that, although altered, were more or
less recognizable; everything was very kindly shown to us. What I admired most were zeolites from the steep rocks standing in the sea below
Jaci.

When we asked the *cavaliere* about ways and means of climbing
Etna, he refused to hear a word about our venturing up to the summit,
especially at this time of year. "In general," he said, after asking our
pardon, "strangers arriving here take the matter much too lightly; we
who are neighbors of the mountain are quite satisfied if, after watching
for the right moment, we can reach the summit just a few times in our
life. Brydone, whose description first aroused interest in this fiery peak,

never went up there himself; Count Borch leaves the reader in doubt, but actually he too only got up to a certain height, and I could say the same of several others. At this time, the snow still extends too far down and presents insurmountable obstacles. If you take my advice, you will ride early tomorrow to the foot of Monte Rosso and climb to its top; from there you will enjoy the most magnificent view and at the same time see the old lava that erupted there in 1669 and unfortunately flowed to the town. The view is splendid and clear; you would be wise to let the rest just be told to you.''

Catania, Saturday, May 5, 1787.

In obedience to this good advice, we started out early and, always looking backwards as we rode on our mules, reached the region of lavas not yet subdued by time. Jagged clumps and slabs towered up before us, and the animals only found a haphazard path through them. We stopped on the first significant height. Kniep, with great precision, drew what lay before us farther up: the lava masses in the foreground, the double peaks of Monte Rosso to the left, and, directly above us, the forests of Nicolosi, out of which rose the snowcapped, barely smoking summit. We moved closer to the red mountain, and I climbed up: it is heaped up entirely out of red volcanic grit, ash, and rocks. Except for a violently raging morning wind that made every step unsure, I could have walked comfortably around the volcano's mouth. I had to take off my cloak to make even a little progress, but now my hat was in danger of being blown into the crater at any moment, and I after it. So I sat down to compose myself and survey the region; but this position did not help me either: the gale came straight from the east over the splendid land lying near and far below me, up to the sea. The coast, with its curves and inlets, stretched before my eyes from Messina to Syracuse, either altogether clear or just slightly covered by rocks at the shoreline. When I came down, quite dazed, Kniep had used his time well, sitting in a shelter: with delicate lines he had secured on paper what the wild gale had hardly let me see, much less capture.

Back again in the jaws of the Golden Lion, we found the hired servant, whom we had kept from accompanying us only with difficulty. He commended us for giving up the summit, but importuned us to take a sea excursion tomorrow to the rocks of Jaci;[111] that was the finest outing that could be made from Catania! We should take along food and drink, possibly also equipment for warming something. His wife would be glad to take over this task. Furthermore, he remembered the merry occasion when some Englishmen had even had a boatload of musicians accompany them, which was a pleasure beyond all imagining.

The rocks of Jaci strongly attracted me, I felt a great desire to hammer zeolites out of them as beautiful as the ones I had seen at Gioeni's. We could, after all, make it a short trip and decline to be accompanied by the wife. But the Englishman's warning spirit prevailed, we gave up the zeolites, and were not a little proud of our self-restraint.

Catania, Sunday, May 6, 1787.

Our clerical escort did not fail to appear. He guided us to see remains of old architecture, which of course require the viewer to have great talent for restoration. We were shown the remains of reservoirs, of a naumachia,[112] and other similar ruins, but the repeated destruction of the town by lava flows, earthquakes, and war has buried and lowered them to such an extent that only the most expert connoisseur of ancient architecture can derive any pleasure and instruction from them.

The abbé declined to procure us a second audience with the prince, but we parted with mutual warm expressions of gratitude and good will.

Taormina, Monday, May 7, 1787.

God be thanked that everything we saw today has already been sufficiently described, and may He be thanked still more because tomorrow Kniep intends to spend all day up above, drawing. After climbing to the top of the rock walls, which rise up steeply not far from the seashore, one finds two peaks connected by a semicircle. Art assisted whatever natural form this had, and made it into an amphitheatrical semicircle for spectators; walls joining with other outbuildings of brick supplied the necessary corridors and halls. The stage was built across the base of the graduated semicircle, forming a connection between the two rocks and perfecting a most enormous work of art and nature.[113]

Whoever sits down where the uppermost spectators once sat has to admit that no other theater audience has ever had such objects to behold. Fortifications rise up on fairly high rocks to the right, farther below lies the town, and although these structures date from more recent times, no doubt similar ones stood on the same spot in antiquity. Next, one looks past the entire long mountainous ridge of Etna, to the left is the seashore up to Catania, even to Syracuse; then the enormous, smoking volcano concludes the broad, wide-ranging picture, but not in a frightening manner, because the atmosphere has a softening effect that makes Etna look more distant and gentler than it is.

Turning from this view to the corridors installed behind the spectators, on the left one has all the rocky walls between which and the sea the road winds to Messina. Groups of rocks and rocky ridges in the sea itself, the coast of Calabria in the farthest distance; only if one looks closely can it be distinguished from some gently rising clouds.

We climbed down into the theater, lingered a while in its ruins (on which a skilled architect should try out his talent for restoration, at least on paper), then undertook to blaze a trail through the gardens to the town. But here we discovered what an impenetrable bulwark a fence of closely planted agaves can be: one looks through the crossed leaves and thinks there is a way of squeezing through, but the strong spikes that edge the leaves are a severe obstacle; if a person steps on one of those colossal leaves, hoping it will bear his weight, it collapses, and instead of getting across it into the open, he falls into the arms of a neighboring plant. Nevertheless we finally found our way out of this labyrinth, ate a light meal in town, but could not take leave of the area before sunset. It was infinitely beautiful to observe how this region, which is significant in all its parts, gradually receded into darkness.

Below Taormina, at the seaside, Tuesday, May 8, 1787.

Kniep, sent me by my good fortune, cannot be praised enough for ridding me of a burden I would find intolerable, and for restoring me to my own nature. He has gone up to draw in detail what we looked at superficially. He will have to resharpen his pencils several times, and I do not see how he will finish everything. I too might have seen all of that again! At first I wanted to go up with him, but then I felt tempted to stay here; I sought a narrow space, like a bird that wants to build its nest. In a wretched, neglected peasant garden I sat down on the branches of an orange tree and became lost in fanciful thoughts. It sounds rather odd for the traveler to be sitting on the branches of an orange tree, but there is nothing strange about it if one knows that an orange tree, left to itself, divides just above the root into twigs which in time become definite branches.

And so I sat, continuing to think out the plan of *Nausicaa,* a dramatic condensation of the *Odyssey.* I do not consider this impossible, but shall have to keep the basic difference between drama and epic clearly in mind.

Kniep has come down, happy and content because he has brought back two huge sheets, most neatly drawn. He will do finished versions of them both for me in everlasting memory of this splendid day.

Not to be forgotten is that we looked down from a small balcony at this beautiful shore, under the clearest sky, that we saw roses and heard nightingales. The latter, we are told, sing here for fully six months.

From Memory

Thanks to the presence and industry of a skilled artist, and to my own weaker, only sporadic efforts, I was sure that I would have permanent, well-chosen pictures of the most interesting regions and their individual parts—sketches, and also as many finished drawings as I wished. Therefore I was the more prone to yield to a gradually awakening urge: namely, to populate my present magnificent surroundings—the sea, the islands, the ports—with worthy poetic figures, and to create for myself, on and out of this locality, a composition with a spirit and tone unlike anything I had yet produced. The clear sky, the breeze from the sea, the haze which, as it were, dissolves the mountains, sky, and sea into a single element, all of this sustained my project; and while I strolled in that beautiful public garden,[114] between blooming oleander hedges, through arbors of fruit-laden orange and lemon trees, and lingered among other trees and bushes, which were unknown to me, I felt the foreign influence most pleasantly of all.

Convinced that this living environment was the best possible commentary I could have to the *Odyssey,* I had bought a copy and was reading it, in my fashion, with enormous interest. But quite soon I was moved to produce a work of my own, which, strange as it seemed at first, became ever dearer to me and eventually occupied me entirely. That is to say, I seized on the idea of treating the subject of Nausicaa as a tragedy.

It is not possible even for me to tell exactly what I would have made of it, but I soon decided on the plot. The main idea was to present Nausicaa as a lovely maiden with many suitors, who, feeling no affection for any of them, has refused them all. However, when a remarkable stranger stirs her heart, she emerges from her condition and, by prematurely declaring her affection, compromises herself, which makes the situation wholly tragic. This simple plot was to be made pleasing by a wealth of subordinate themes and particularly by the special sea-and-island tone of the actual finished work.

The first act began with the ball game. The unexpected acquaintance is made, and her scruples about not personally leading the stranger into the town become in themselves an early sign of her affection.

The second act set forth the family of Alcinous and the characters of the suitors, and ended with the entrance of Ulysses.

The third was devoted entirely to the significance of the adventurer, and I hoped to accomplish something artistic and pleasing in the dialogued narrative of his adventures, which make the most varied impressions on the various listeners. During the narration, passions rise, and Nausicaa's lively interest in the stranger is at last brought out into the open by means of effect and countereffect.

In the fourth act, Ulysses displays his bravery offstage, while the women remain behind and give way to affection, hope, and all the tender feelings. Hearing of the great advantages won by the stranger in the contests, Nausicaa controls herself even less and compromises herself irretrievably before her countrymen. Ulysses, who is half-guilty, half-innocent of having caused all of this, must at last announce his departure, and the poor girl has no choice but to seek death in the fifth act.

There was nothing in this composition that I could not have painted from life out of my own experiences. On a journey myself, in danger myself of arousing affections that, even without tragic endings, could still become quite painful, perilous, and injurious; in a position myself, so far from home, to entertain the company with vividly colored descriptions of remote objects, travel adventures, daily incidents, to be considered a demigod by the young, a braggart by more sedate persons, to receive many an undeserved favor, face many an unexpected obstacle; all of that made me so attached to this plan, to this project, that on account of it I dreamt away my sojourn in Palermo, indeed the greater part of my further Sicilian journey. For this reason I felt all the discomforts only slightly; I felt in a poetic mood on this supremely classical soil, and whatever I experienced, whatever I noted, whatever came my way, I could take hold of it all and preserve it in a pleasing receptacle.

In accordance with my praiseworthy or unpraiseworthy habit, I wrote down little or nothing of the play, but worked out the major part of it, to the last detail, in my mind. There it has languished, pushed into the background by subsequent distractions, until now, as I summon up just this superficial memory of it.

May 8. On the road to Messina.

There are high limestone rocks on the left. They grow more colorful and make beautiful bays; then follows a kind of stone that could be called shale or graywacke. Fragments of granite are already present in the brooks. The yellow apples of the genus *Solanum,* the red blossoms of oleander make the landscape gay. The river Nisi carries along mica-slate, as its tributary brooks do also.

Wednesday, May 9, 1787.

Battered by the east wind, we rode along between the billowing sea on the right and the cliffs we had looked down from the day before yesterday; today we were engaged in a constant battle with water. We

crossed innumerable brooks, a larger one of which, the Nisi, bears the
honorary title of river; but these waters, as well as the pebbles they
carry along, were more easily conquered than the sea, which raged
violently and at many places washed up over the road as far as the
rocks and splashed back on us travelers. It was a magnificent sight,
and the uniqueness of the event made its inconvenience bearable.

At the same time I was determined to make some mineralogical observations. When the huge limestone rocks crumble and fall down, their
soft parts are worn away by the action of the waves, but the mingled
harder pieces are left behind, and so the whole beach is covered with
colorful, quartzlike flints, several examples of which we packed in our
luggage.

Messina, Thursday, May 10, 1787.

And so we arrived in Messina. Not knowing any comfortable place
to stay, we submitted to spending the first night in the quarters of our
vetturino, and planned to look around for better accommodations the
next morning. This decision was responsible for giving us, as soon as
we entered, the most frightful concept of a destroyed city:[115] for a
quarter of an hour we rode past nothing but ruins before reaching the
inn, the only house in the entire district to have been rebuilt, with a
view from its upper-story windows only of a wasteland of jagged ruins.
There was no trace of man or beast beyond the precincts of this farm-
stead, at night there was a terrible stillness. The doors could neither
be locked nor bolted, there was as little accommodation for human
guests here as in any other such stable, and yet we slept peacefully on
a mattress that our obliging *vetturino* had talked the innkeeper into
giving up from his own bed.

Friday, May 11, 1787.

Today we parted with our honest guide, and rewarded him for his
faithful service with a large gratuity. We bade each other a friendly
farewell, but not before he had procured us another hired servant, who
was to lead us immediately to the best inn and show us all the sights
in Messina. The present innkeeper was so eager to get rid of us that
he helped us transport our cases and all the rest of our luggage very
quickly to pleasant lodgings nearer the inhabited parts of town, that is
to say, outside of the town itself. The situation is as follows: After the
dreadful calamity that struck Messina, in which twelve thousand inhabitants perished, there was no place for the remaining thirty thousand
to live. Most of the buildings had fallen down, the broken walls of the

rest did not provide a safe shelter. Therefore, on a big meadow to the north of Messina, a town was hastily erected out of boards. Anyone who has wandered around the Roman Hill in Frankfurt at fair time, or the market at Leipzig, can easily imagine this, for all the stores and workrooms are open to the street, and much of the activity is outside. Accordingly there are only a few large buildings, and they too are not particularly closed off from the public street, since their occupants spend much time under the open sky. They have lived under these conditions for three years now, and this living and working in booths, huts, and even tents has had a decided influence on the character of the inhabitants. The horror felt about that tremendous event and their fear of a similar one impel them to enjoy the delights of the moment with good-natured gaiety. Their anxiety about a new catastrophe was revived on April twenty-first, thus approximately twenty days ago, when a noticeable tremor shook the ground again. We were shown a small church where many people had been crowded together just at that moment and felt the shock. Some persons who had been there seemed not yet recovered from their fright.

Our guide for finding and observing these sights was a friendly consul, who voluntarily looked after us in many ways—something to acknowledge with gratitude especially in this wilderness of ruins. Moreover, when he heard that we wanted to leave soon, he put us in touch with a French merchant ship which was about to set sail for Naples. Doubly welcome, since its white flag would protect us from the pirates.

We had just mentioned to our kind guide that we would like to see one of the larger, though still only one-story, huts on the inside, so as to examine its furnishings and improvised housekeeping, when a friendly man joined us and identified himself as a teacher of French. At the end of our walk the consul told him of our wish to see one of these buildings, and requested him to take us to his home and introduce us to his family.

We entered the hut, whose sides and roof were made of boards. The impression was exactly like that of those fair booths where one can pay to see wild animals or other marvels: the timberwork was visible both on the walls and ceiling, a green curtain divided off the space in front, which was not boarded over but seemed to be beaten flat, like a threshing floor. There were some tables and chairs, but no other household items. The place was lighted from above by chance openings between the boards. We conversed for a while, and I was gazing at the green drapery and the inner framework visible above it, when suddenly on either side of the curtain several most charming girlish heads, with black eyes and black curls, peeped out inquisitively, but then, seeing that they had been noticed, disappeared like lightning. At the consul's request, but only after enough time had passed for getting dressed, the heads reappeared on dainty little well-adorned bodies; the girls looked extremely pretty, standing in front of the green hanging in their colorful dresses. From their questions it was obvious that they considered us fabulous creatures from another world, and our answers could not but confirm them in this charming error. The consul painted an amusing picture of our magical arrival; the conversation was very pleasant, parting was difficult. Only when the door had closed did it occur to us that we had not seen the inner rooms, and had forgotten the house's construction because of its female occupants.

Messina, Saturday, May 12, 1787.

The consul said, among other things, that it would be advisable, although not absolutely necessary, to pay our respects to the governor,[116] an eccentric old man who, according to his moods and prejudices, could do just as much harm as good. It would be to the consul's credit if he introduced significant foreign visitors, also a newcomer never knew whether he might need this man in one way or another. To please my friend I went along.

Entering the anteroom, we heard a quite appalling uproar from within, and a footman, making Pulcinella gestures, whispered into the consul's ear: "Evil day! perilous hour!" Nevertheless we went inside and found the aged governor with his back turned to us, sitting at a large table by the window. Great piles of old, yellowed correspondence lay before him, from which, with the greatest imperturbability, he cut off the pages that were not written on, thereby indicating his thrifty character. While engaged in this peaceful occupation, he scolded and cursed away fearfully at a respectable man who, to judge from his clothing, could have been connected with the Maltese Order, and this person was defending himself with great composure and precision, though given little opportunity to do so. Scolded and shouted at, he was calmly trying to allay the governor's apparent suspicion that he had entered and left the town several times without authorization; the man cited his passports and his well-known connections in Naples. All this was of no help, the governor cut up his old correspondence, carefully laid aside the blank paper, and continued raging.

Besides the two of us, some twelve other persons were standing in a wide circle as witnesses of this animal-baiting, probably envious of our position at the door, which was a good escape, should the angry man actually raise his crutch and start hitting with it. During this scene the consul's face had grown noticeably longer; but I was comforted by having the comical footman nearby, who was performing all sorts of antics behind me on the threshold to reassure me, whenever I turned around, that this was not to be taken too seriously.

And the ghastly affair was indeed settled in a perfectly mild fashion: the governor ended by saying that there was nothing to prevent him from jailing the embarrassed man and letting him languish in custody, but this time he would overlook the matter, he could stay the specified few days in Messina, but then he must go away and never return. Quite calmly, without changing his expression, the man took his leave, courteously saluted the assemblage, and us in particular, since he had to go between us to reach the door. When the governor wrathfully turned around to hurl one last invective after him, he caught sight of us, controlled himself immediately, beckoned to the consul, and we approached him.

A man of very great age, with a bowed head, looking out from deep-set black eyes under bushy gray eyebrows; quite a different man now from what he was before. He told me to sit next to him, and, continuing his work without interruption, inquired about various things. I gave him the requested information, and finally he added that I was invited to his table as long as I stayed here. The consul, who was as glad to go as I was, and even more so, because he knew better what danger we had escaped, flew down the steps; and I had lost all desire ever to come near this lion's den again.

Messina, Sunday, May 13, 1787.

Although we awoke to brightest sunshine, in a more pleasant room, we were still in unhappy Messina. A uniquely unpleasant sight is the so-called Palazzata, a sickle-shaped row of genuine palaces, which encloses and defines the seafront for about the distance of a quarter hour's walk. They were all five-story stone buildings; but although some of the facades are still intact up to the main cornice, others are broken down to the fourth, third, or second floors. As a result, this formerly sumptuous row now has a very repulsive gap-toothed appearance, and is also full of holes; for the blue sky looks through almost all the windows in the broken facades, behind which the actual inner apartments have all collapsed.

The cause of this curious phenomenon is that less wealthy neighbors of the rich people who had begun this splendid architectural project tried to emulate it externally; so they concealed their old houses, which were built of larger and smaller river pebbles stuck together with much lime, behind new facades of dressed stone. This intrinsically unsafe type of structure was broken up and crumbled by the immense shock, and naturally fell apart. So, for example, one of the many amazing rescues related in connection with this great calamity is the following: In the terrible moment, one occupant of these buildings had just stepped into a stone window recess when the house completely collapsed behind him; and so, up there in safety, he calmly awaited the moment of his liberation from this airy prison. That this inferior type of construction, resulting from a lack of nearby quarry stones, was responsible for the total ruination of the town is shown by the tenaciousness of solid buildings. The Jesuit college and church, built of sound ashlars, still stand undamaged, as sound as ever. Be that as it may, Messina's appearance is extremely disagreeable and is reminiscent of those primitive times when the Sicani and Siculi forsook this restless ground and built on the western coast of Sicily.

And after spending the morning thus, we went to eat a frugal meal in the inn. We were still sitting together quite happily when the consul's servant burst in breathlessly and announced that the governor was having the whole town searched for me; he had invited me to dine, and I had failed to appear. The consul was sending me the most urgent request to go there immediately, whether I had eaten or not, whether I had missed the hour on purpose or out of forgetfulness. Not until now did I feel how incredibly frivolous I had been to dismiss the Cyclops's invitation from my mind, glad to have escaped the first time. The servant would not let me delay, he expostulated most earnestly and convincingly, saying that the consul risked having that furious despot stand him and the whole nation on their heads.

While putting my hair and clothes in order, I plucked up my courage and followed my guide in a cheerful frame of mind, calling on my patron saint Odysseus to intercede for me with Pallas Athene.

When I arrived in the lion's den, the comical footman led me into a large dining room, where some forty persons were sitting in complete silence at an oval table. The place at the governor's right was unoccupied, and that is where the footman conducted me.

After greeting the master of the house and his guests with a bow, I sat down next to the former, using as excuse for my absence the vast extent of the town, also the mistakes I frequently made because I was unaccustomed to their way of counting the hours. He answered, with a fiery glance, that in foreign lands it was always incumbent on the traveler to become informed about local customs and abide by them. I replied that I always tried to do so, but had often found, in spite of my best intentions, that in the first few days, when a town is still new to us and the situation unfamiliar, one falls into certain errors. These of course would seem unpardonable, if people were unwilling to accept travel fatigue, distraction due to the objects of interest, and one's concern about tolerable lodgings, indeed even about continuing the journey, as grounds for excuse.

After that, he asked how long I planned to be here. I answered that I hoped for a rather long stay, so that, by punctiliously obeying his orders and directions, I could prove my gratitude for the favor he had shown me. Then, after a pause, he asked what I had seen in Messina. I briefly related my morning's activities, and added that I chiefly admired the cleanliness and order in this devastated town. And it really was admirable how all the streets had been cleared of ruins by means of throwing the rubble into the foundations of the collapsed buildings themselves, while the stones were set in rows against the houses; so the streets were unobstructed in the middle, open again to trade and traffic. In this connection I could flatter the dignitary with the truth when I assured him that all the citizens of Messina gratefully realized that they owed this benefit to his care.—"They realize it, do they?" he grumbled. "At first they screamed loudly enough about the harsh way in which they were forced to act to their own advantage." I spoke about wise governmental intentions, higher goals that could only be understood and appreciated later, and the like. He asked whether I had seen the Jesuit church, and I said no; whereupon he promised that he would have it shown to me, with all its appurtenances.

During this conversation, which was seldom interrupted by pauses, I saw the rest of the company putting bites of food into their mouths with as few motions as possible, and in the profoundest silence. And then, when the table was cleared and coffee served, they stood around at the walls like wax puppets. I went over to the household chaplain, who was supposed to show me the church, to thank him in advance for his trouble; he retreated sideways, humbly assuring me that he was only following His Excellency's orders. After that I talked to a young foreigner next to me, who, although he was a Frenchman, seemed rather ill at ease; for he too was as mute and rigid as the rest of the company, among which I saw several faces that had been uncomfortable spectators at yesterday's scene with the knight of Malta.

The governor left, and after a while the chaplain told me it was now time to go. I followed him; the other guests had very, very quietly dispersed. He led me to the portal of the Jesuit church,[117] which rises up ostentatiously and really imposingly, in the well-known style of these fathers. A doorkeeper was already approaching us with an invitation to enter, but the chaplain restrained me, saying that we first had to wait for the governor. The latter soon drove up, stopped on the square not far from the church, and beckoned, whereupon the three of us grouped ourselves close to the door of his coach. He ordered the doorkeeper not only to show me every part of the church but also to tell me in detail the history of the altars and other donated items; further, he should open the sacristies and point out to me all the noteworthy things contained in them. He said I was a man he wanted to honor, so that I should have every reason to speak well of Messina in my fatherland. "Do not fail," he said then, turning to me, with as much of a smile as his features could muster, "do not fail, as long as you are here, to come and dine at the right hour, you will always be well received." I hardly had time to return a proper answer to this before the coach moved off.

From this moment on, the chaplain grew more cheerful, and we entered the church. The castellan, as he might surely be termed in this enchanted palace, now bereft of divine services, was getting ready to fulfill the duty that had been so strictly enjoined on him, when the consul and Kniep burst into the empty sanctuary, embraced me, and showed extreme joy at seeing me again, for they had imagined me in custody. They had been in mortal terror until the nimble footman (probably well paid by the consul) related, with a hundred bits of nonsense, the happy outcome of the adventure. At this a cheering sense of relief had come over both of them, and when they heard about the governor's interest in the church, they immediately came to look for me here.

Meanwhile we stood before the high altar, listening as the precious old objects were explained. Columns of lapis lazuli, fluted, so to speak, by gilded bronze bars, pilasters and panels inlaid in the Florentine manner; magnificent Sicilian agates in profusion, bronze and gilding repeated over and over, tying everything together.

Now, however, a remarkable contrapuntal fugue ensued when, in interlocking fashion, Kniep and the consul expatiated on the awkward adventure, our docent, for his part, on the sumptuous, still well-kept treasures, all three full of their subject; and this gave me the double pleasure of feeling the significance of my fortunate escape and at the same time of seeing Sicilian minerals, which I had already taken some pains to study, used architecturally.

My exact knowledge of the individual elements composing this rich display helped me to the discovery that the so-called lapis-lazuli of those columns was really only limestone, admittedly of a more beautiful color than I had ever seen before, and splendidly joined. But even so, the columns remained worthy objects; for one must presuppose an enormous amount of that material, if pieces of such beautiful and identical color could be selected from it, and then the effort expended in cutting, grinding, and polishing is very significant. But was anything too difficult for these fathers?

In the meantime the consul had continued enlightening me about my menacing fate. Namely, the governor, dissatisfied with himself that I, at my first entrance, had been a witness of his violent behavior towards the quasi-Maltese knight, had resolved to honor me specially, and had made a plan to this effect; but my absence had upset the execution of it at the very beginning. Finally sitting down at table after a long wait, the despot had not been able to conceal his impatient displeasure, and the company had fearfully anticipated a scene either when I came or after the meal.

The sacristan, meanwhile, kept trying to get our attention, and opened the secret rooms, beautifully proportioned, appropriately, even splendidly, decorated, and many a movable religious implement still remained in them, formed and decorated in keeping with the whole. I saw nothing made of precious metals, nor any genuine older or newer artworks.

Our Italian-German fugue—for the priest and the sacristan were intoning in the former, Kniep and the consul in the latter—was drawing to a close, when we were joined by an officer I had seen at table. He was a member of the governor's retinue. This could have caused some renewed concern, especially since he offered to guide me to the harbor, where he would take me to points otherwise inaccessible to foreigners. My friends looked at each other, but I did not let this deter me from going off alone with him. After some casual conversation, I began to talk confidentially to him, confessing that I had definitely noticed several guests at table who, though silent, had made some friendly signs to let me know I was not alone among provincial people, but among friends, indeed brothers,[118] and therefore had nothing to worry about. I considered it my duty (I said) to thank him, and asked him to extend my thanks in like manner to the other friends. To this he answered that they had especially tried to reassure me, since, knowing their superior's temperament, they had not really feared for me. For an explosion like that against the Maltese knight was quite rare, and after such things the worthy old man would reproach himself, be on his guard for a long time, and then live for a while securely and light-heartedly performing his duty, until finally, surprised by some unexpected occurrence, he would lose control and become vehement again. My good friend added that nothing would please him and his comrades more than to become better acquainted with me; therefore I should be so kind as to identify myself more exactly, and tonight there would be a very good opportunity for that. I politely evaded this request by asking him to excuse a peculiar notion of mine, namely that on my travels I wished to be seen merely as a human being, and if I could inspire confidence and find sympathy on this basis, that would be my desire and pleasure; I was forbidden for various reasons to enter into any other relationships.

I did not intend to convince him, for after all I could not reveal my real reason to him. But it did seem quite remarkable to me that under this despotic rule right-minded men had so nicely and innocently banded together for their own protection and that of foreigners. I did not conceal from him that I was quite well aware of their connections with other German travelers; I enlarged on the praiseworthy goals that were to be attained, and astonished him more and more with my mixed confidentiality and stubbornness. He tried in every way to draw me out of my incognito, but did not succeed, partly because, having escaped one danger, I could not pointlessly expose myself to another, partly because I could see very clearly that the views held by these honest islanders were much too different from mine for them to derive any pleasure or consolation from associating more closely with me.

Instead, I spent a few more hours that evening with the solicitous and helpful consul, who enlightened me about the scene with the Maltese knight. This person, while not actually an adventurer, was a restless rover from town to town. The governor, from an illustrious family, honored for his seriousness and ability, and esteemed on account of his significant services, nevertheless had the reputation of being thoroughly self-willed, uncontrollably vehement, and rigidly inflexible. Being an old man and a despot, he was suspicious. And he was worried, rather than convinced, that he had enemies at court; therefore he hated such itinerant persons, all of whom he considered spies. This time the redcoat had crossed his path just when, after a rather long interval, he had needed to burst out angrily again, to relieve his liver.

Messina and at sea, Monday, May 13, 1787.

We both awoke with the same feeling, that is, vexed because impatience with our first desolate view of Messina had made us resolve to arrange our return passage on the French merchantman. Since my adventure with the governor had ended happily, since I was in contact with some worthy men to whom I only needed to identify myself more exactly, and because of a visit to my banker, who lived out in the country in a most pleasant area, I could hope for some very pleasant times if I stayed longer in Messina. Kniep was being well entertained by some pretty girls, and so his dearest wish was for the otherwise hated head wind to continue. Meanwhile we were in the disagreeable situation of having to keep everything packed and be ready to leave at any moment.

So, then, the call actually did come toward midday; we hurried on board, and among the crowd gathered on shore was also our good consul, to whom we said our grateful farewells. The yellow-clad footman pushed his way through to us, to collect his gratuities. He was rewarded and then commissioned to announce our departure to his master and excuse my absence from table.—''He who sails away is excused!'' he shouted; then, turning around with an odd sort of caper, he disappeared.

Inside the ship itself things looked different from aboard the Neapolitan corvette; but what held our attention as we gradually left the shore was the magnificent sight of the palace circle, the citadel, and the mountains rising up behind the town. Calabria on the other side. Then the open view into the strait running north and south, its expansive breadth provided with beautiful shores on both sides. As, moving along, we gazed at this in wonder, we were told to look to the left, where a considerable distance away there was some turbulence in the water, and to the right, but closer, where a rock projected from the shore; the former was Charybdis, the latter Scylla. People have seized upon these two curiosities, spaced so far apart in nature and moved so closely together in literature, to complain about the wild imagination of poets. They have not taken into consideration that when human fantasy wants to think of things as being significant, it always imagines them as larger than life, and thus provides the image with more character, gravity, and dignity. I have heard the complaint a thousand times that something known from a story is always disappointing in reality. The reason for this is ever the same: imagination and reality correspond to each other as do poetry and prose; the former will conceive of things as mighty and steep, the latter will always spread them out flat. Landscape painters of the sixteenth century, compared to ours, offer the most striking example. A drawing by Jodocus Momper[119] next to one of Kniep's outlines would make the whole contrast evident.

We entertained ourselves with these and similar conversations, since Kniep, who had already made preparations to sketch the coasts, found them insufficiently attractive even for him.

However, the unpleasant sensation of seasickness came over me again, and the condition was not, as on the trip out, made more bearable by comfortable privacy. Nevertheless the cabin was big enough to accommodate several persons, also there was no dearth of good mattresses. I assumed the horizontal position again, and Kniep most solicitously kept me nourished with red wine and good bread. In this situation our whole Sicilian journey failed to appear to me in any sort of pleasant light. We had really not seen anything except the completely useless efforts of the human race to maintain itself against nature's violence, time's spiteful tricks, and the rancor arising from its own hostile disagreements. The Carthaginians, Greeks, Romans, and so many later peoples built and destroyed. Selinunte lies there, methodically knocked down; two millenia did not suffice to demolish the temples of Agrigento, but a few hours, or perhaps just minutes, were enough to destroy Catania and Messina. These were the truly seasick reflections of someone rocked back and forth on the waves of life, and I did not allow them to gain mastery over me.

At sea, Tuesday, May 13, 1787.

My hope of getting to Naples more quickly this time, or of being freed of seasickness sooner, was not fulfilled. At Kniep's instigation,

I tried various times to go on deck, but was denied enjoyment of the sea's very diverse beauties; only a few occurrences made me forget my dizziness. The whole sky was overcast with a whitish cloudy vapor, through which the sun, although its image was not visible, illuminated the sea, turning it the most beautiful sky blue to be seen anywhere. A school of dolphins accompanied the ship, always keeping even with it, swimming and leaping. I imagine that from out of the depths and distance our floating building looked to them like a black spot, and they had taken it for some kind of prey and a welcome meal. At any rate the sailors did not treat them as escorts, but as enemies; one was struck by the harpoon, but not brought alongside.

The wind remained unfavorable, and our ship could only outmaneuver it by repeatedly changing course. Our impatience with the situation was increased when several experienced travelers asserted that neither the captain nor the helmsman understood his trade: the former might be a good merchant, the latter a good sailor, but they were not qualified to take responsibility for something as valuable as all these people and goods.

I begged these otherwise worthy persons to keep their apprehensions to themselves. The number of passengers was large and included women and children of various ages, for everyone had crowded aboard the French vessel, considering nothing except how the white flag would protect them against pirates. I pointed out that mistrust and worry would be extremely distressing to all, since heretofore they had felt very safe because of that colorless, unmarked bit of linen.

And truly, as a decisive talisman, this pointed white cloth fluttering between sky and sea is quite remarkable. By waving white handkerchiefs to exchange their last greetings, people who are leaving and those staying behind awaken in each other a unique sense of departing friendship and affection; and here, in this simple flag, the ship's origin is made sacred, just as if someone tied his handkerchief to a pole, in order to proclaim to the whole world that a friend was coming over the sea.

Being refreshed from time to time with bread and wine (to the annoyance of the captain, who demanded that I should eat what I had paid for), I managed to sit on deck and take part in some conversations. Kniep, instead of trying to make me envious by exulting over the excellent food, as he had done on the corvette, cheered me up this time by saying I was fortunate not to have any appetite.

Monday, May 14, 1787.

And so the afternoon passed without our sailing into the Bay of Naples as we had hoped. Instead, we were driven ever farther westward, and the ship, by coming close to the island of Capri, distanced itself more and more from Capo Minerva. Everyone was impatient and out of humor except for the two of us, who could be content because we looked at the world with painter's eyes; for at sunset we enjoyed the most superb view given us on the whole voyage. Capo Minerva and the mountains adjacent to it lay before our eyes, enhanced by the most glowing colors, while the rocks extending down toward the south had already taken on a bluish tone. The whole illumined coast stretched from the cape to Sorrento. We could see Vesuvius, over it a towering cloud of smoke, from which a long strip drew far eastwards, so that we could assume there had been a very strong eruption. Capri lay to the left, rising up steeply; we could distinguish the outlines of its rocky walls perfectly through the transparent bluish haze. Beneath a completely clear, cloudless sky sparkled the quiet, scarcely stirring sea, which eventually, in the total calm, lay before us like a limpid pond. We were enraptured by this sight, Kniep lamented that paints could never be mixed skillfully enough to reproduce this harmony, just as the finest English pencil would not enable the most practiced hand to trace these lines. I, however, was convinced that in the future I would be very glad to have any memento, even something far inferior to what this skilled artist could obtain for me, and so I encouraged him to exert his eye and hand one more time. He let himself be persuaded and produced a very exact drawing, which afterwards he colored, and left an example of how the impossible becomes possible to pictorial representation.[120] With equally eager eyes we followed the transition from evening to night. Capri now lay before us in complete darkness, and, to our amazement, the Vesuvian cloud ignited, as did the cloudy strip, more and more brightly the farther out it went, and finally we saw a considerable part of the atmosphere in the background of our picture illuminated, indeed, flashing with sheet lightning.

Because of these very welcome scenes we had failed to notice that we were threatened with a great misfortune; but the unrest among the passengers did not leave us long in doubt. More experienced than we were in what happens at sea, they bitterly reproached the ship's master and his helmsman: because of their incompetence not only had the channel been missed, but also the passengers entrusted to them were in danger of perishing, goods and all. We asked the reason for their alarm, since we did not understand why any calamity should be feared in this total calm. But it was this very calm which made those men despondent. "We are," they said, "already in the current that goes around the island and, because of the strange way in which the waves break, it moves slowly and irresistibly to the steep rocks, where we are not given a ledge even a foot wide, or any inlet, as an escape."

Alerted by these words, we now began to dread our fate; for although the night did not let us discern the increasing danger, we nevertheless noticed that the ship, swaying and jerking, was approaching the rocks, which stood more and more darkly before us, while a light evening glow was still spread over the sea. Not the slightest movement was to be felt in the air: everyone held up handkerchiefs and light ribbons outside, but there was no sign of the desired breeze. The crowd kept growing louder and wilder. The women knelt on the deck with their children, not praying, as might be expected, but wedged together because the space was too narrow for anyone to move. They scolded and raged at the captain more than the men, who, with presence of mind, were thinking about help and rescue. Everything that had been silently objected to on the whole voyage was now cast into the captain's teeth: poor, but high-priced, accommodations, inferior food, a manner that, if not unfriendly, was certainly uncommunicative. He had accounted to no one for his actions, indeed had maintained a stubborn silence about his maneuvers even on this last evening. Now they called him and his helmsman good-for-nothing shopkeepers with no knowledge of navigation, who out of mere self-interest had succeeded in making themselves owners of a ship, and now because of their incompetent bungling were destroying all the people entrusted to them. The captain said nothing and seemed still to be planning a rescue; but from youth on I have hated anarchy worse than death, and so it was impossible for me to keep silent any longer. I stepped forward and addressed them, with about as much composure as when I addressed the birds of Malcesine. I pointed out to them that their only hope for rescue was with those men whose ears and minds were being so confused at this very moment by noisy shouting that they could neither think nor hear each other speak. "As for you," I shouted, "come back to your senses, and then address your ardent prayers to the Mother of God. It depends on her alone whether she will intercede with her Son, so that He will do for you what He did for His apostles when, on the stormy Sea of Tiberias, the waves were already splashing into their ship. The Lord slept, but when the wretched, helpless men woke Him He immediately ordered the wind to cease, as He can now command the breeze to blow, provided it is His holy will."

These words had a very good effect. One of the women, with whom I had conversed earlier on moral and religious subjects, cried: "Ah! il Barlamé! benedetto il Barlamé!"[121] and since they were already kneeling anyway, they really did begin to pray their litanies, with more than the usual ardor and emotion. They could do this the more calmly because the seamen were trying another means of rescue, which at least was eye-catching: they let down the boat, which of course could hold only from six to eight men, and with a long rope fastened it to the ship, which the sailors then tried to pull after them by tugging mightily at the oars. For a moment we even believed they were moving it within the current, from which we hoped to see it soon safely released. But whether these efforts increased the counterforce of the current, or whatever it might have been, suddenly the boat and its crew, on the long rope, were hurled backwards in an arc against the ship, like the knot at the end of a whip when the driver cracks it. This hope too was abandoned!—Prayers alternated with laments, and the situation took a still more gruesome turn when the goatherds up on the rocks, whose fires we had seen for some time, raised the hollow cry that a ship was running aground down there! They kept shouting incomprehensible sounds at each other, in which some passengers familiar with the language thought they heard something about the men's anticipation of this and that booty they intended to fish out the next morning. Unfortunately, even the comforting doubt whether the ship was really getting so threateningly close to the rocks was dispelled all too soon by the crew's seizing thick poles, with which to hold the vessel off from the rocks, if it came to the worst, until finally these too would break and everything be lost. The ship swayed more and more violently, the breakers seemed to multiply, and this brought on my seasickness again, leaving me no choice but to go back down into the cabin. Half-dazed, I laid myself on my mattress, but with a certain feeling of pleasure which seemed traceable to the Sea of Tiberias; for the picture from Merian's illustrated Bible[122] hovered quite distinctly before my eyes. And so the strength of all physical-moral impressions never proves more effective than when a person is thrown back entirely on his own resources. I do not know how long I lay half-asleep, but I was awakened by a violent noise above me; I could distinctly hear that this was being made by big ropes as they were dragged back and forth on the deck; this gave me hope that the sails were being used. Shortly afterwards, Kniep leapt down and told me that we were saved, the gentlest breeze had risen; at the moment they were busy hoisting the sails, and he himself had not failed to lend a helping hand with this. He said we were already moving visibly farther away from the rocks, and although we were still not completely out of the current, there was nevertheless hope of soon overcoming it. Everything was quiet overhead; then several of the passengers came, announced the happy outcome, and lay down.

When I awoke early on the fourth day of our voyage, I felt fresh and well, just as I had at the same time on our trip out. Therefore even on a longer sea voyage I would probably have paid my tribute with an illness of just three days' duration.

From the deck I saw with pleasure that the island of Capri lay at some distance to the side, and that our ship was sailing in a direction that gave us hope of entering the bay, which then soon occurred. Now, after having survived a hard night, we had the pleasure of admiring, in an opposite light, the sights that had charmed us the evening before. Soon we left that perilous island behind us. While yesterday we had admired the right side of the bay from afar, now we we had the fortifications and the city directly in front of us, Posillipo to the left, and the tongues of land extending as far as Procida and Ischia. Everybody was on deck, in the front a Greek priest who was very prejudiced in favor of his Orient. When the local inhabitants, who greeted their magnificent fatherland rapturously, asked him how Naples compared with Constantinople, he answered very enthusiastically: "Anche questa è una cittá!"—"This too is a city!"—We arrived in port at the right time, with people buzzing around us; it was the busiest moment of the day. Hardly had our cases and other paraphernalia been unloaded and left standing on the shore when they were immediately seized by two porters; and hardly had we said that we would lodge with Moriconi when they ran off with their burden as though it were booty, so that we could not keep them in sight through the populous streets and across the busy square. Kniep had his portfolio under his arm, so we would at least have rescued the drawings, had those porters, less honest than the usual poor devils in Naples, robbed us of what the breakers had spared.

Naples

To Herder

Naples, May 17, 1787.

I am back here again, my dear friends, healthy and vigorous. My journey through Sicily was made quickly and easily, and when I return home you shall judge *how* I have seen. My old habit of always adhering and clinging to objects has given me an incredible ability to sightread, as it were, and I consider myself quite fortunate to have the great, beautiful, incomparable idea of Sicily so clearly, completely, and purely in my soul. Now there is nothing left in the south that I long to see, since I also came back from Paestum yesterday. The sea and the islands brought me enjoyment and affliction, and I return satisfied. Let me reserve the details for my homecoming. In any case, it is impossible to collect one's thoughts here in Naples. I shall describe this city to you better now than I did in my first letters. On the first of June I shall go on to Rome, unless prevented by a higher power, and I plan to leave there again at the beginning of July. I must see all of you again as soon as possible, and we shall have some good days together. I have taken on an immense load, and need some peace and quiet in order to assimilate it.

Herder, a thousand thanks to you for all your kind assistance with my writings; I kept trying to improve them so that they would also please you. I shall welcome any work of yours, wherever it may reach me; we are as close in our attitudes as is possible without being in absolute agreement, particularly in regard to the main points. While during this time you have drawn much from within yourself, I have acquired much, and I can hope for a good exchange.

To be sure, as you say, my thoughts are very much concentrated on the present, and the more I see of the world, the less I can hope that humanity will ever become a single wise, intelligent, happy mass. Perhaps among the millions of worlds there is one that can boast of such excellence, but ours is so constituted that I have as little hope for it as for Sicily.

On an enclosed sheet[123] I say something about the road to Salerno and about Paestum itself; it is the last and, I might almost say, the most splendid idea I shall now take along northwards in a complete form. Also, the middle temple,[124] in my opinion, is preferable to anything that can still be seen in Sicily.

With respect to Homer, it is as if scales had fallen from my eyes. The descriptions, the similes, etc., seem poetic and yet are inexpressibly natural, but drawn, to be sure, with a warmth and purity that startle one. Even the most bizarre fictional events have a naturalness that I never felt so strongly as in the vicinity of the things described. Let me briefly express my thoughts as follows: *they* depicted the substance, *we* usually the effect; *they* portrayed the terrible thing, *we* portray in a terrifying manner; *they* what is agreeable, *we* agreeably, and so on. This is the source of all the exaggeration, all the mannerism, all the false grace, all the bombast. For when one is creating effect and striving for effect, one thinks it can never be made strong enough. What I say may not be new, but I have new cause to feel it very intensely. Now that all these coasts and headlands, bays and inlets, islands and tongues of land, rocks and beaches, bushy hills, gentle pastures, fertile fields, ornate gardens, well-tended trees, hanging grapevines, cloudy peaks and always sunny plains, reefs and shoals, and the all-encompassing sea with its many changes and variations are present in my mind, only now has the *Odyssey* become a living word for me.

Furthermore I must confide to you that I am close to discovering the secret of plant generation and structure, and that it is the simplest thing imaginable. The finest observations can be made under this sky. I have quite clearly and unquestionably found the main feature, the location of the bud, and I already see everything else in a general way; just a few more points need to be better defined. The primordial plant is turning out to be the most marvelous creation in the world, and nature itself will envy me because of it. With this model and the key to it an infinite number of plants can be invented, which must be logical, that is, if they do not exist, they *could* exist, and are not mere artistic or poetic shadows and semblances, but have an inner truth and necessity. The same law will be applicable to every other living thing.

Naples, May 18, 1787.

Tischbein has returned to Rome[125] but meanwhile, as we can see, has arranged for us not to feel his absence. He seems to have recommended us so warmly to his whole group of friends here that they are all receptive, friendly, and helpful to us. This is what I need very much in my present situation, because not a day passes that I do not have to call on someone for a favor and assistance. I am just in the process of making a list summarizing the things I still would wish to see, since the brevity of my stay will remain the determining factor and indicate how much I can really still make up for.

Naples, May 22, 1787.

Today I met with a pleasant adventure, which certainly gave me something to ponder and is worth relating.

A lady[126] who had already shown me many kindnesses during my first stay asked me to come to her house in the evening at precisely five o'clock: an Englishman wanted to talk to me, because he had something to tell me about my *Werther*.

Six months ago I would surely have returned a negative reply to this, even if she had been twice as dear to me; but I accepted, proving to myself that my Sicilian journey had had a good influence on me, and I promised to come.

Unfortunately, however, the city is too large, and offers so much to see that I climbed the steps a quarter of an hour late. I was standing on the reed mat in front of the locked door, just about to ring, when the door opened and out stepped a handsome middle-aged man whom I immediately recognized as being the Englishman. He had barely looked at me before he said: "You are the author of *Werther*!" I admitted to this and excused myself for not having come earlier.

"I could not wait a moment longer," he said. "What I have to tell you is quite brief and can be said just as well here on the mat. I shall not repeat what you have heard from thousands of people, and the work has not affected me as strongly as it has others; but whenever I think of all that was involved in writing it, I am always amazed anew."

I was about to make some grateful reply, but he interrupted me, crying: "I cannot delay a moment longer, my wish has been fulfilled, for I have told you this personally; goodbye and good luck!" And so saying he went down the stairs. I stood for a while reflecting on this honorable text and finally rang the bell. The lady was pleased to hear about our meeting, and said many complimentary things about this unusual and eccentric man.

Naples, Friday, May 25, 1787.

I shall probably not see my frivolous little princess again; she really did go to Sorrento, having done me the honor, before her departure, of scolding me for preferring stony and desolate Sicily to her. Some friends informed me about this odd phenomenon. Born into a good but impecunious family, educated in the convent, she decided to marry a rich old prince, all the more easily persuaded to do so because nature had made her a good person, but one completely incapable of love. In these affluent but, because of the family situation, restrictive circumstances, she sought refuge in her wit; since she was hampered in her actions, she could at least give free rein to her tongue. I was assured that her actual mode of life was quite above reproach, but that she seemed determined to slap all convention in the face with her scandalous talking. It was jokingly said that no censor could ever approve her discourses, if they were written down, because every word she uttered was an offense against religion, the state, or morals.

The strangest and most amusing stories were told about her, and I shall repeat one of them here, although it is somewhat indelicate.

Shortly before the earthquake that struck Calabria,[127] she had gone to her husband's estates there. Near her palace was built a barrack, that is to say, a one-storied wooden house set directly on the ground, but with wallpaper and furniture, and suitably equipped. At the first sign of the quake, this is where she fled. She was sitting on the sofa, tatting, a small sewing table in front of her, opposite her an abbé, an old family chaplain. Suddenly the ground heaved, and on her side the building sank down, while the opposite side rose, lifting up both the abbé and the table. "Fie!" she cried, leaning her head against the sinking wall, "is that befitting such a venerable man? You act as if you wanted to ravish me. That is quite contrary to all morals and propriety."

Meanwhile the house had settled into place again, and she could not stop laughing about the foolish, lascivious figure supposedly cut by the good old man; and because of this joke she seemed not to be affected in the least by all the calamities, indeed the great losses, that had befallen her family and so many other people. Rare and fortunate is the character that can jest while the earth is preparing to swallow it.

Naples, Saturday, May 26, 1787.

Looking at the matter closely, one might approve of the fact that there are so many saints; for every believer can select his own and with complete trust turn straight to the one that really appeals to him. Today was my saint's day, and I celebrated it in his honor with cheerful piety, after his own manner and teachings.

Filippo Neri[128] is highly esteemed and at the same time remembered happily; it is edifying and pleasing to learn about him and his great piety, and at the same time to hear many stories about his good humor.

From his childhood years onward he felt the most fervent religious impulses, and in the course of his life he developed the greatest talents for religious enthusiasm: the gift of involuntary prayer, of profound unspoken worship, the gift of tears, of ecstasy, and at last even of rising from the ground and hovering over it, which is considered greatest of all.

With all these mysterious, singular spiritual qualities he combined the soundest common sense, the keenest appreciation, or rather depreciation, of worldly things, and the most active support of his fellowmen in their physical and spiritual needs. He strictly fulfilled all the duties incumbent on a devoutly religious man, with regard to festivals, church attendance, prayers, fasting, and the like. He similarly concerned himself with the cultural development of young people, with their musical and oratorical exercises, proposing not only spiritual but also intellectual topics, and in other ways starting lively conversations and disputations. What might well seem the most remarkable part is that he did and accomplished all of that on his own initiative and authority, and steadily pursued his path for years without belonging to any order or congregation, without even being ordained.

But it must strike us as more significant that this occurred precisely at Luther's time, that in the midst of Rome there was a capable, God-fearing, energetic, active man who likewise had the idea of combining religious, nay, sacred matters with worldly ones, of introducing the celestial into the secular, and, by so doing, himself prepared a reformation. For only here lies the key that shall open the papal prison and give the wide world its God again.

With such a significant man in its vicinity, in the precincts of Rome, and under its protection, the papal court did not rest until he was finally persuaded (and after all he was leading a clerical life, already resided in monasteries, taught and gave spiritual guidance there, indeed, was even about to found, perhaps not an order, but a free assembly) to be ordained and thus receive all the advantages he had heretofore lacked on his way through life.

Even if we are justly doubtful about his miraculous levitation, in spirit he was certainly raised high above this world; and therefore nothing repelled him as much as vanity, pretence, and arrogance, which he always vigorously combated as the greatest hindrances to a truly God-pleasing life. But he always did this in a good-humored fashion, as many a story tells us.

For example, he happened to be nearby when the pope was informed that a nun in the vicinity of Rome was attracting attention because of her many remarkable spiritual gifts. Neri was commissioned to investigate the validity of these tales. He immediately mounted his mule and, in spite of very bad weather and roads, soon arrived at the convent.

On being admitted, he conversed with the abbess, who was thoroughly convinced of these tokens of grace, and gave him all the details about them. The nun was summoned and entered, but his only greeting was to extend his muddy boot to her, indicating that she should pull it off. The pure, holy virgin started back in horror, and with angry words expressed her resentment of this impudence. Neri rose quite calmly, climbed back on his mule, and returned to the pope much sooner than expected; for Catholic confessors have very precise, significant precautionary measures prescribed to them for the testing of such spiritual gifts. While the church concedes that such spiritual favors are possible, it does not admit their authenticity without the most punctilious examination. Neri briefly communicated the result to the astonished pope: "She is no saint," he cried, "she performs no miracles! For she lacks the main attribute, humility."

This maxim can be regarded as the guiding principle of his whole life, for, to relate just one more story: When he had founded the Congregation of Padri dell' Oratorio, which quickly acquired great prestige and a good many people wanted to become members of it, a young Roman prince came asking admission and was granted the novitiate, along with the requisite clothing. However, when after some time he applied for actual entrance, he was told that first there were a few tests to be passed; and he declared himself ready for them. Then Neri produced a long foxtail and demanded that the prince have this attached to the back of his long frock and then walk quite gravely through all the streets of Rome. The young man, like the aforementioned nun, was horrified, and said that he had come forward to reap honor, not shame. Then Father Neri said that this could not be expected of their circle, where self-denial remained the supreme law. Whereupon the youth took his leave.

Neri had summed up his main doctrine in a short motto: *Spernere mundum, spernere te ipsum, spernere te sperni*.[129] And truly that said it all. No doubt a person who is subject to melancholy sometimes imagines himself able to fulfill the first two requirements; but in order to comply with the third, one would have to be on the way to becoming a saint.

Naples, May 27, 1787.

Yesterday, thanks to Count Fries,[130] who came from Rome, I received, at one and the same time, all of your dear letters from the end of last month, and I truly enjoyed myself reading and rereading them. Also included was the longingly awaited little box,[131] and I thank you a thousand times for everything.

But now it is high time that I flee from here; for in the midst of trying, at the eleventh hour, to fix Naples and its environs indelibly on my mind, to renew my impressions, and settle some affairs, I am swept away by the stream of daily events; and now some excellent people have attached themselves to me, both old and new acquaintances, whom I cannot simply send away. I found a charming lady[132] with whom I had spent the pleasantest days last summer in Carlsbad. How many hours we stole from the present with our very cheerful reminiscences! All our dear and cherished friends were discussed in turn, above all the cheerful good humor of our beloved prince. She had kept the poem[133] with which the girls of Engelhaus surprised him as he rode away on his horse. It recalled all the merry scenes, the witty teasing and mystifications, the clever attempts to take just revenge on one another. We promptly felt ourselves back on German soil, in the best German company, closed in by those rocky walls, kept together by that curious locality, but even more by esteem, friendship, and affection. But as soon as we stepped to the window, the Neapolitan stream rushed by so forcibly that we could not hold on to those peaceful memories.

Nor could I avoid becoming acquainted with the Duke and Duchess of Ursel.[134] Admirable persons of excellent breeding, with a pure understanding of nature and human beings, a decided love of art, kindness to people they meet. Lengthy and repeated conversation with them was most attractive.

Hamilton and his fair lady continued their friendliness to me. I dined at their residence, and later in the afternoon Miss Harte also demonstrated her musical and vocal talents.

At the urging of my friend Hackert, who is increasingly kind to me and would like to acquaint me with everything notable, Hamilton led us into the secret vault where he keeps his artworks and his rubbish. Confusion reigns there; the products of all epochs mixed up randomly: busts, torsos, vases, bronzes, various decorative objects out of Sicilian agate, even a miniature chapel, carvings, paintings, and whatever he had happened to buy up. In a long box on the ground, with a loosened top that I inquisitively shoved aside, lay two quite magnificent bronze candelabra. I made a sign to get Hackert's attention, and asked him in a whisper whether these were not similar to the ones in Portici. However, he made me a sign to keep silent; of course, they had probably found their way here obliquely from the Pompeian tombs. On account of these and similar fortunate acquisitions the baronet may well have let only his most intimate friends see these hidden treasures.

A box standing upright caught my eye, open in front, painted black inside, and surrounded by the most splendid golden frame. The space was large enough to hold a standing human figure, and we learned that indeed such was its purpose. This admirer of art and girls, not satisfied with seeing the lovely creature as a moving statue, also wanted to enjoy her as a colorful, inimitable painting. And so, inside this golden frame, dressed in many colors against the black ground, she had sometimes imitated the ancient paintings of Pompeii and even modern master-works. This period seemed to be over, and besides, the apparatus was hard to move around and properly illuminate: therefore we could not be favored with this spectacle.

This is the place to mention another favorite pursuit of Neapolitans in general. I mean the crèches (presepe), which are seen in all the churches at Christmas time, realistically depicting the adoration of the shepherds, angels, and kings, grouped together more or less completely, richly, and splendidly. In cheerful Naples these exhibits have also as-cended to the flat housetops, where a light framework, like a shed, is built and decorated with evergreen trees and bushes. The mother of God, the Child, and all the figures standing and hovering around are sumptuously decked out in a wardrobe on which the house spends great sums. However, what glorifies the whole display inimitably is the background, which includes Vesuvius and its surroundings.

It may even have occurred sometimes that living persons were min-gled with the dolls, and gradually it became one of the most significant entertainments in wealthy and aristocratic families also to present sec-ular pictures, drawn from history or literature, in their palaces for an evening's amusement.

If I may permit myself a remark which a well-treated guest should not venture to make, I must confess that our lovely entertainer really strikes me as an insipid creature, who no doubt has an attractive figure, but cannot make an impression on us with any soulful note in her voice, her way of speaking. Even her singing lacks appealing richness.

And that, in the final analysis, may also be the case with those rigid images. There are beautiful persons everywhere, but persons that feel deeply and also are gifted with pleasant speaking voices are much rarer; rarest of all are those who combine all this with a prepossessing figure.

I am eagerly looking forward to Herder's third part.[135] Save it for me until I can tell you where it should meet me. I am sure he has admirably worked out mankind's beautiful dream of being better off some day. I myself must say I also believe it is true that humane values will eventually triumph. My only fear is that at the same time the world will be one big hospital and everybody will be everybody else's humane nurse.

Naples, May 28, 1787.

My good and useful Volkmann occasionally forces me to disagree with him. He says, for example, that thirty to forty thousand idlers are to found in Naples, and who does not repeat this after him? Of course, very soon after I had acquired some knowledge of conditions in the south, I surmised that this might well be the Northern way of thinking, according to which anyone who does not toil scrupulously the entire day is considered an idler. Therefore I paid particular attention to the common people, whether in action or at rest, and could, to be sure, see many poorly clothed persons, but no unoccupied ones.

Therefore I asked some friends about the innumerable idlers, since, after all, I wanted to get to know them as well. But they could not show me any either, and so, because the investigation would be intimately connected with my viewing of the city, I went out hunting myself.

I began to acquaint myself with the various figures in this enormous maze, to judge and classify them by form, clothing, conduct, and occupation. I found this operation to be easier in Naples than elsewhere, because the individual is left more to his own devices here and shows even outwardly that he conforms with his station.

I began my inspection early in the morning, and all the people I saw standing around or resting here and there were ones whose calling required it at the moment.

The *porters,* who have their privileged posts at various places and wait for someone to make use of them; the *calash drivers,* with their boys and stablemen, who stand by their one-horse calashes on the big squares, look after their animals, and are at the service of anyone who wants them; *seamen,* who smoke their pipes on the Molo; *fishermen,* who lie in the sun, perhaps because an unfavorable wind is blowing and they cannot put out to sea. To be sure, I also saw some men walking aimlessly, but in most cases each of them carried with him a token of his activity. The only beggars I noticed were quite old, fully incapacitated and crippled persons. The more I looked around and the more closely I observed, the fewer true idlers of any age or sex I could find, either of the lower or the middle class, either in the morning or for the greatest part of the day.

I shall go into greater detail, so as to give more credibility and concreteness to what I am maintaining. The smallest children are occupied in a number of ways. A great army of them carry fish from Santa Lucia to sell in the city; others are often seen picking up the tiniest bits of wood in small baskets near the Arsenal, or wherever else carpenter work is being done and there are chips, also at the sea, which casts up twigs and small bits of wood. Children a few years old, who can scarcely do more than crawl along the ground in the company of older boys five to six years of age, engage in this little trade. Afterwards they carry their baskets farther into town and set up a market, so to speak, with their small portions of wood. The artisan, the humble citizen, buys it from them, burns it to coals on his tripod to warm himself, or uses it in his frugal kitchen.

Other children go around selling water from the sulfurous wells, which is copiously drunk, especially in the spring. Others try to make a little profit by purchasing fruit, spun honey, cake, and candy, then offering and selling them, like miniature merchants, to the rest of the children; at worst, just so they may have their own part of it free. It is really a pleasure to see how a boy like this, whose whole equipment consists of a board and a knife, carries around a watermelon or half a baked pumpkin, how a group of children gathers around him, and how he sets down his board and begins to cut the fruit into small pieces. The buyers watch very gravely to make sure they are getting enough for their small copper coin; and the little merchant negotiates the transaction just as carefully with his eager customers, lest he be cheated out of a little piece. I am convinced that during a longer stay I could collect many other examples of such childish businesses.

A very large number of people, some of them middle-aged, some of them boys, mostly very poorly dressed, are engaged in taking refuse out of the city on donkeys. The fields adjoining Naples are one big kitchen garden, and it is a delight to see what an enormous amount of produce is carted in every market day, and with what industry the people immediately bring back to the fields, in order to speed the cycle of growth, the superfluous parts thrown away by the cooks. Owing to the incredible consumption of vegetables, a large part of Neapolitan refuse actually consists of the stems and leaves of cauliflower, broccoli, artichokes, cabbage, lettuce, and garlic; and these are also particularly sought after. Two large baskets hang over the donkey's back, and both of these are not only filled, but, with special skill, piled high. No garden can exist without one of these donkeys. A farmhand, a boy, and sometimes the owner himself hurry to town as often as possible in a day, because it is a rich treasure trove for them at all hours. It can be imagined what a sharp eye these collectors have for the manure of horses and mules. They reluctantly leave the street when night falls, and the rich people, driving back from the opera after midnight, probably do not guess that a diligent man will be carefully looking before daybreak for the traces left by their horses. I am told that if a few such people join forces, buy themselves a donkey, and rent a small piece of vegetable-growing land from a major proprietor, they will soon be in a position, by dint of hard work—and thanks to this favorable climate, in which plant growth is never interrupted—to extend their business considerably.

I would be digressing too far, were I to speak here of the many different ways of selling that are a pleasant sight to see in Naples, as in every other large town; nevertheless I must mention the street vendors, because they deal especially with the lowest class of the populace. Some walk around with small barrels of ice water, glasses, and lemons, so that lemonade, a drink which not even the humblest person can do without, can be made everywhere immediately; others have salvers, on which bottles of various liquors and conical glasses stand in wooden rings, to keep them from falling; others carry around baskets with various baked goods, sweets, lemons, and other fruits; and it would seem that each of them wants to participate in and add to the great festival of eating and drinking that is celebrated in Naples every day.

Just as busy as this type of hawker is still another multitude of petty merchants who also walk around, and without much ado set out their paltry wares on a board, in a box top, or, in the squares, right on the open ground. It is not a question here of individual wares that are also found in larger stores, but of real secondhand goods. There is not a bit of iron, leather, woolen cloth, linen, felt, etc., that does not come back on the market as a secondhand ware, and that is not resold to one person or another. Many persons of the lower class also find work with merchants and artisans as errand boys and helpers.

It is true that one cannot go many steps without encountering some very poorly clothed or even ragged individual, but that does not mean he is an idler, a sluggard. Indeed, I am tempted to advance the paradox that in Naples, comparatively speaking, perhaps the greatest industriousness is to be found among the lowest classes. Of course we must not compare it with Northern industriousness, which has to provide not only for the day and hour, but on sunny days for bad and gloomy ones, and in summer for the winter. Nature compels the Northerner to make provisions and preparations, the housewife to pickle and cure, so as to supply the kitchen for the whole year, the husband to see to the stores of wood and grain, the fodder for the cattle, etc. Consequently the most beautiful days and hours are lost to enjoyment and devoted to work. For several months people are glad to stay out of the open air and secure themselves in their houses against storm, rain, snow, and cold. The seasons cannot be kept from following one another, and everyone has to become a householder, if he does not want to perish. For the question is by no means whether or not he *wants* to do without; he must not want to do without, he *cannot* want to do without, for he cannot do without; nature forces him to be busy, to work ahead. These natural influences, which have stayed the same for millenia, surely have determined the character of the northern nations, which are admirable in so many respects. On the other hand, Heaven has dealt very leniently with the southern peoples, and it is too severe of us to judge them from our viewpoint. What Mr. de Pauw dares to say in his *Recherches sur les Grecs*,[136] in connection with the Cynics, fits perfectly here. He believes that our notions about the miserable conditions of such people are not very correct; their principle of doing without everything is much favored by a climate that provides everything. In these regions, a poor and, to us, apparently miserable person is not only able to satisfy his most urgent and elementary needs, but can also enjoy the world in the finest way; and likewise, a so-called Neapolitan beggar might well scorn the position of viceroy in Norway, and decline the honor, should the Empress of Russia entrust him with the governing of Siberia.

Certainly a Cynic would not last long in our country, whereas in southern lands nature almost invites such behavior. There the ragged man is not yet naked; he who neither owns nor rents a house, spends the summer nights under overhanging eaves, in doorways of palaces and churches, in public halls, and in bad weather finds a place to sleep somewhere for a trifling sum, is not yet, on that account, a miserable outcast; a person is not yet poor because he has failed to provide for tomorrow. If we only consider what quantities of food are offered by the teeming sea, with whose products these people are required by law to nourish themselves several days a week; that all kinds of fruits and vegetables are available at every season; that the region in which Naples lies has earned itself the name *terra di lavoro* (not the land of labor, but of agriculture), and that the whole province has for centuries had the honorable title of "the happy country" *(campagna felice);* then it can surely be understood how easy life here can be.

Generally speaking, the paradox I ventured above would give rise to some reflections in anyone who was undertaking to write a detailed description of Naples, certainly a task requiring no small talent and many a year of observation. Perhaps, then, he would notice that on the whole the so-called *lazarone* is not a whit less active than all the other classes, but at the same time he would perceive that all of them, in their fashion, work not merely to *live,* but to *enjoy,* and that they even want to enjoy life while working. This explains a great deal: that the artisans, almost in every case, are far behind those of other lands; that no factories are built; that except for attorneys and physicians little erudition is to be found, considering the large mass of people, although individual worthy persons may strive for it; that no painter of the Neapolitan school has ever been painstaking and become great; that the clergy feel very comfortable in their idleness, and even the great nobles mostly prefer to enjoy their wealth by spending it on sensual delights, pomp, and amusements.

I am well aware of having spoken too generally, and that the character traits of each class can only be drawn clearly after closer acquaintance and observation; but I believe that on the whole one would arrive at the same results.

I return to the humble people in Naples. It is noticeable that, like happy children, when they are given some task, they will certainly perform it, but at the same time make play out of their work. Without exception this class of people has a very lively temperament and a candid, straightforward gaze. Their speech is said to be metaphorical, their wit very quick and caustic. Ancient Atella[137] was located not far from Naples, and just as their beloved Pulcinella still carries on those farces, so the very common class of people still keeps that humor alive today.

Pliny, in the fifth chapter of the third book of his *Natural History,* considers Campania worthy by itself of a detailed description. "So happy, charming, blessed are those regions," he says, "that nature obviously delighted in its work there. Witness this zestful air, the ever-salubrious mildness of this sky, such fertile fields, such sunny hills, such benign woodlands, such shady groves, such profitable forests, such lofty mountains, such spreading crops, such an abundance of grapevines and olive trees, sheep with such noble wool, bulls with such fat necks, so many lakes, such a wealth of watering rivers and springs, so many seas, so many ports! The earth itself, which everywhere opens its bosom to trade and, as though eager to assist man, stretches out its arms into the sea.

"I shall not mention the capabilities of the people, their customs, their strengths, and how many nations they have conquered by persuasion and by force.

"The Greeks, a people that used to praise itself excessively, pronounced the most honorable judgment on this land by calling a part of it 'Greater Greece'."

Naples, May 29, 1787.

A distinct gaiety is to be seen everywhere, and I share in it with the greatest pleasure. The multicolored flowers and fruits that embellish nature seem to invite humans to decorate themselves and all their implements with the brightest possible colors. Silk cloths and ribbons, flowers on the hats adorn everyone who can at all afford them. Chairs and chests of drawers in the humblest houses are decorated with colorful flowers on a gilt ground; even the one-horse calashes are painted bright red, the carvings gilded, the horses in front decked out with artificial flowers, bright-red tassels, and tinsel. Many have plumes on their heads, others even little flags that rotate with every movement they make while running. We usually call such indulgence in bright colors barbaric and tasteless, and in a certain way it can be and become that, but beneath a very clear blue sky nothing is really colorful, for nothing can outshine the brilliance of the sun and its reflection on the sea. The most vivid color is muted by that powerful light, and because every color—the various greens of the trees and plants, the yellow, brown, red soil—

strikes the eye with full force, even the colorful flowers and garments fit into the general harmony. The scarlet vests and skirts of the women of Nettuno, trimmed with broad strips of gold and silver, the other colorful national costumes, the painted ships, everything seems to strive for at least some degree of visibility against the brilliance of the sky and sea.

And as they live, so they bury their dead; no slow, black procession disturbs the harmony of their merry world.

I saw a child being carried to its grave. A large red velvet hanging, embroidered with broad strips of gold, covered a wide bier, on which stood a carved, heavily gilded and silvered coffin, wherein lay the corpse, dressed in white and completely covered with rose-colored ribbons. At the four corners of the coffin were four angels, each approximately two feet high, who held large bouquets of flowers over the recumbent child. Because they were attached underneath only with wires, they rocked with the movements of the bier and seemed to spread mildly invigorating flower perfumes. The angels swayed all the more since the procession was hurrying fast over the streets, and the priests and candle bearers at the head of it were nearly running.

There is no time of the year when one is not surrounded everywhere by items of food, and the Neapolitan not only enjoys eating but also wants the wares set out for sale to be beautifully presented.

In the Santa Lucia district the sea creatures are usually displayed in nice, clean baskets lined with green leaves, by individual species, crabs, oysters, sheatfish, small clams. The stores selling dried fruit and legumes are most diversely decorated. The Seville oranges and all kinds of lemons, with green foliage showing between, are very pleasing to the eye. But nothing is decorated more than the meat products, which the populace eyes with particular greediness, because doing without them periodically whets its appetite that much more.

The cuts of oxen, calves, and wethers are never hung out in the butcher's stalls without the fat, together with the side or leg, being heavily gilded. Various days in the year, especially the Christmas holidays, are famous as banqueting festivals; a universal Cockaigne, arranged for themselves by five hundred thousand people, is celebrated at those times. But then the Via Toledo and several neighboring streets and squares are also most appetizingly decorated. The greengroceries, where raisins, melons, and figs are displayed, make a most agreeable sight for the eye. Items of food hang across the street in garlands; great rosaries of gilded sausages tied with red ribbons; turkeys, all with a red flag stuck under their tails. It was stated that thirty thousand of them were sold, not counting those that people had fattened at home.

Besides this, a great many donkeys, laden with green vegetables, capons, and baby lambs, are driven through the city and over the marketplace; and the mounds of eggs seen here and there are so large that one would never have imagined that many being together. And it is not enough that all this is consumed: every year a police official rides through the city with a trumpeter and proclaims on all the squares and at all the street crossings how many thousand oxen, calves, lambs, pigs, etc., the Neapolitans have devoured. The people listen attentively, are overcome with joy at the large numbers, and everyone remembers his part in the feast with pleasure.

When it comes to foods made of flour and milk, which our German women cooks can prepare in so many ways, these people, who like to make short work of such things and do not have well-equipped kitchens, are doubly provided for. All types of macaroni (a soft dough of fine flour that is thoroughly kneaded, pressed into certain shapes, and cooked) is available everywhere for a trifling sum. Usually it is just boiled in water and served in bowls that are both greased and spiced with grated cheese. At the corners of almost every large street stand men with pans full of boiling oil who are busy, especially on fast days, immediately preparing fish and crullers to each customer's order. These individuals make an incredible number of sales, and many thousands of people carry away their noontime and evening meals from there on a little piece of paper.[138]

Naples, May 30, 1787.

Strolling through the city at night, I arrived at the Molo. There, with one glance, I saw the moon, its light on the edges of the clouds, its gently agitated reflection on the sea, brighter and livelier on the margin of the nearest wave. And then the stars in the sky, the lamps of the lighthouse, the fire of Vesuvius, its reflection on the water, and the many lights strewn over the ships. I would surely like to have seen this manifold problem solved by van der Neer.[139]

Naples, Thursday, May 31, 1787.

I was so determined to see the Corpus Christi festival[140] in Rome and, along with it, especially the tapestries made from Raphael's cartoons, that I by no means permitted all these magnificent natural phenomena to distract me, even though they are unequaled in the world, but instead persisted with my preparations for the trip. A passport was applied for, a *vetturino* had given me the rental deposit; for here, to protect the traveler, the custom is the opposite of ours in Germany. Kniep was busy moving into his new quarters, which are much better in regard to space and location than his former ones.

Earlier, when this change was under way, my friend had mentioned to me several times that, really, it was unpleasant and somewhat improper to move into a house without bringing along any furniture; even a bedstead would suffice to inspire some respect in the landlord and his wife. Today, while going through the endless trash from the enlargement of Castel Nuovo, I saw a pair of iron frames painted to resemble bronze, which I immediately bargained for and presented to my friend as the future basis for a quiet and solid place to sleep. One of the ever ready porters brought them and the necessary boards to the new quarters. This arrangement pleased Kniep so much that he proposed to leave me at once and move in here, and concerned himself with quickly procuring large drawing boards, paper, and everything else he needed. In accordance with our agreement, I turned over to him a portion of the outlines drawn in both Sicilies.

Naples, June 1, 1787.

The arrival of Marchese Lucchesini[141] has delayed my departure for a few more days; I was delighted to meet him. He seems to me one of those people who have a good moral stomach, so that they can always eat along with others at the great world table; whereas someone like me will gorge at times like a ruminating animal, and then cannot take another bite until he has finished chewing his cud and digesting it. I like *her* very much too, she is an honest German woman.

Now I am glad to leave Naples, indeed I must go. In these final days I have given in and been so complaisant as to see people; I have met mostly interesting persons, and do not regret the hours devoted to them, but another two more weeks and it would have led me farther and farther away from my goal. And then, one grows more and more indolent here. Since returning from Paestum I have seen little except the treasures of Portici, and some things are still left over for which I would not care to bestir myself. But, after all, the Portici museum is the alpha and omega of all collections of antiquities; there one really can see how far advanced the ancient world was in its joyful sense of art, even if it remained far behind us in strict technical proficiency.

Addendum to June 1, 1787.

The hired servant who delivered my completed passport told me, at the same time, that he was sorry I was leaving, because a considerable flow of lava had erupted from Vesuvius and was making its way to the sea. It was already almost down the steeper slopes of the mountain and in a few days could easily reach the shore. Now I found myself in the worst quandary. Today was spent in paying farewell visits that I owed to a great many kindly and helpful persons; I can already see how things will go for me tomorrow. Obviously it is impossible to avoid people completely along the way, but however much assistance and pleasure they give us, in the final analysis they turn us aside from our serious goals, while we do not advance them toward theirs. I am completely out of humor.

In the evening.

My farewell courtesy calls were actually quite pleasant and instructive. I was shown a number of things that had heretofore been postponed or neglected. Cavaliere Venuti[142] even let me see treasures that have not yet been made public. With great reverence I viewed his mutilated, but still invaluable Ulysses for a second time. In farewell, he took me into the porcelain factory, where I tried hard to impress the Hercules on my mind, and filled my eyes again with the Campanian vessels.

He was truly moved as he said a friendly goodbye, and at last confided to me where the shoe was really pinching him, namely, he wished very much that I could stay a while longer with him. My banker, at whose house I arrived just before mealtime, would not let me go. That would all have been well and good if the lava had not captured my imagination. When night came on, although I was busy taking care of various matters, paying bills, and packing, I still hurried off to the Molo.

Here I now saw all the fires and lights and their still more wavering reflections on the agitated sea; the full moon in its splendor next to the shower of sparks from the volcano, and then the lava, of which there has been none recently, on its solemn, glowing way. I ought to have driven out, but arrangements for that were too complicated, and I would not have arrived there until morning. Since I was enjoying the view, I did not want to spoil it for myself with impatience, and so I remained sitting on the Molo until my eyes began to fall shut in spite of the milling crowds who were pointing, telling stories, comparing, arguing about where the lava might flow, and generally being a nuisance.

Naples, Saturday, June 2, 1787.

And so I also spent this fine day with excellent persons, pleasantly and profitably, to be sure, but nevertheless not at all as I had intended, and with a heavy heart. I looked longingly at the smoke slowly moving down the mountain toward the sea, marking the path taken from hour to hour by the lava. The evening was not to be free either. I had promised to visit the Duchess of Giovane,[143] who lives in the palace, where I was obliged to climb up many steps and wander through many corridors, the uppermost of which was crammed with boxes, clothespresses, and all the disagreeable paraphernalia of a courtly wardrobe. In a large and high-ceilinged room without a particularly good view I found an attractive young lady who conversed in a very delicate and moral fashion. Having been born a German, she was not ignorant of the way our literature has developed in the direction of freer, wideranging humane values. Above all, she prized Herder's endeavors and anything like them, and Garve's[144] clear mind had also strongly appealed to her. She tried to keep abreast of the German authors, and it was obvious that her wish was to wield a pen skillfully and commendably herself. That was the drift of her remarks, which also disclosed her intention of influencing the daughters of the highest classes; such a conversation knows no limits. Twilight had already come, but no candles had been brought in. We walked up and down in the room, and she, approaching a side with shuttered windows, opened one of the shutters, and the sight was something one sees only once in a lifetime. If she meant to surprise me with it, she accomplished this totally. We stood at a window in the upper story, Vesuvius directly in front of us. The sun had set long ago, and so the flames from the descending lava glowed distinctly and were beginning to gild the attendant smoke. The mountain roared violently, above it was an enormous stationary cloud of smoke whose various masses, at every eruption, were illuminated in separate sections as though by lightning. Down from there, towards the sea, a strip of fire and glowing vapors; otherwise sea and earth, rock and vegetation distinct in the evening twilight, clear, peaceful, in an enchanted repose. To survey all this at one glance, and to see this most wonderful picture completed by the full moon, as it rose behind the mountain ridge, could hardly fail to cause astonishment.

From this vantage point my eye could take in everything at once, and although it could not scrutinize individual objects, it never lost the impression of the whole great scene. While our conversation was interrupted by this spectacle, it now took a more agreeable turn. Millenia would not suffice for expounding the text we now had before us. The more the night darkened, the greater clarity the area seemed to gain; the moon shone like a second sun; the columns of smoke were illuminated so that their strips and masses were individually distinct, indeed, with a weak spyglass it seemed possible to distinguish the glowing clumps of rock ejected onto the black cone. My hostess, as I shall call her because never has a more delicious evening meal been prepared for me, had candles placed at the opposite side of the room. The beautiful woman, standing in the moonlight, was the foreground of this incredible picture, and she seemed to me to become more and more beautiful. Indeed, what especially enhanced her loveliness was that in this southern paradise I was hearing a very pleasant German dialect. I forgot how late it was, until at last she pointed out to me that the hour was near when her galleries would be closed, in monastic fashion, and she had to send me away, although regretfully. And so I slowly departed from what was distant and what was near, blessing my fate because my grudging politeness during the day had been so well rewarded in the evening. Back beneath the open sky, I told myself that in no other way could I have enjoyed such a view and such a leave-taking from Naples; and had I gone close to this more abundant lava, I would only have seen a repetition of that previous, lesser flow. Instead of going home, I turned my steps toward the Molo, in order to see that great spectacle with a different foreground. But either fatigue after such a full day, or a feeling that the last beautiful picture must not be effaced, I do not know which, drew me back to my rooms at Moriconi's, where I found Kniep, who had come over from his new quarters to pay me an evening visit. Over a bottle of wine, we discussed our future relationship. I could promise him that as soon as I was able to show some of his work in Germany he would be recommended to Duke Ernst of Gotha,[145] an excellent man, and receive commissions from there. And so we parted in a happy, cordial manner, with the sure prospect of future mutually beneficial activity.

Naples, Trinity Sunday, June 3, 1787.

And so, half-dazed, I drove out through the vast life of this incomparable city, which I was probably destined never to see again. Yet I was pleased that I left neither sorrow nor pain in my wake. I thought about my honest Kniep and vowed to provide for him from afar to the best of my ability.

At the last police barrier in the suburbs I was bothered for a moment by a customs officer who looked into my face in a friendly way but quickly made off again. The customs men were not yet finished with my *vetturino* when out of the door of the coffee shack stepped Kniep, carrying on a tray the largest Chinese cup, full of black coffee. He slowly approached my carriage door, with an earnestness which, coming from the heart, suited him very well. I was astonished and touched, for this was an unparalleled token of appreciation. "You have," he said, "shown me so many kindnesses, and have had such an influence on my whole life, that I would like to offer you this symbol of my debt."

Since in any case I never know what to say on such occasions, I could only reply very laconically that he had already put *me* in his debt with his work, and that he would constantly be making our association closer by using and revising our common treasures.

We parted in a way unusual for persons who by chance have become partners for a short time. Perhaps we would derive more reward and benefit from life if we frankly told each other what our mutual expectations are. Once that is accomplished, both parties are content, and cordial feelings, which are the first and last of everything, ensue as a pure bonus.

On the road, June 4, 5, and 6.

Since I am traveling alone now, I have sufficient time to review my impressions of the last months; I am enjoying this very much. And yet quite often the fragmentary nature of my notations becomes evident, and although the journey, to the one who has made it, seems to pass by in a stream, appearing in his imagination as an unbroken succession, yet he feels that a real description of it is impossible. The narrator must set down everything separately: how can anything whole be formed from that in the mind of another person?

Consequently nothing could have been more comforting and pleasing to me than to find the assurances in your last letters that you are all busily occupied with Italy and Sicily, reading travel accounts and looking at prints; the good mark this gives my letters is my greatest consolation. Had you done or mentioned it sooner, I would have been even more zealous than I was. The fact that excellent men have preceded me, like Bartels, Münter, and architects of various nationalities, and that they certainly pursued external goals more painstakingly than I, who had my mind only on inner ones, has often comforted me when I was forced to consider all my efforts inadequate.

If, generally speaking, every human being is to be regarded simply as a supplement to all the others, and appears most useful and amiable when he behaves as such, then this must be particularly applicable to travelers and travel books. Personality, goals, time considerations, favorable and unfavorable contingencies, all these are different for each individual. Although I know his predecessors, I will also enjoy and make use of him, await his successor, and receive the latter amicably too, even if in the meantime I have been so fortunate as to visit the area myself.

PART THREE

THE SECOND SOJOURN IN ROME

Longa sit huic aetas dominaeque potentia terrae,
Sitque sub hac oriens occiduusque dies.[1]

June

Correspondence

I returned here safely the day before yesterday, and yesterday the solemn Corpus Christi festival immediately initiated me as a Roman again. I freely admit that it was painful for me to leave Naples; I was abandoning not only that magnificent region but also the mighty lava flow which was making its way from the summit to the sea. I should probably have looked at it close by and added its behavior to my store of experiences, since this is something I have read and been told so much about.

But today my longing to see that great natural wonder has already been stilled, and I have been led back into the sphere of higher meditations, not so much by the pious confusion of the festival (which, although generally imposing, still offends one's inner sense with occasional tasteless details) as by viewing the tapestries made from Raphael's cartoons.[2] The choicest ones, which almost certainly owe their origin to him, are displayed together, while others, probably designed by pupils, contemporaries, and artistic associates, join them not unworthily in covering the vast spaces.

Rome, June 16.

My dear friends, let me address another word to you. I am doing very well, I am regaining my old self more and more, and am learning to differentiate between what is akin and what is foreign to me. I am industrious, receptive to everything, and growing from the inside outwards. I have just spent some days in Tivoli,[3] where I saw one of the greatest natural spectacles. The waterfalls there, along with the ruins and the whole complex of the landscape, are among those sights that enrich us to the depths of our being when we have seen them.

I neglected to write on the last mailing day. In Tivoli I was very tired from walking around in the heat and drawing. I was out there with Mr. Hackert, who is incredibly expert at copying nature and immediately giving form to his drawings. I have learned much from him in these few days.

There is really nothing more I can say about it. Quite simply, it is one of the most remarkable things on earth. A very complicated declivity in the area produces the most splendid effects.

Mr. Hackert praised and criticized me and helped me to improve. Half in jest, half in earnest, he suggested that I spend eighteen months in Italy and practice according to good principles; after this time, he promised me, I would be pleased with my work. I can also plainly see what and how a person must study in order to overcome certain difficulties that would otherwise be a burden to crawl under for his entire life.

Another observation: Only now are the trees, the rocks, indeed Rome itself becoming dear to me; heretofore I have always just felt that they were foreign. On the other hand, I was pleased with unimportant objects that were similar to what I saw in my youth. Now I must begin to feel at home here also, and yet it will never be as close to me as those first things in my life. In this connection, I have had various thoughts concerning art and imitation.

During my absence, Tischbein discovered a painting by Daniele da Volterra[4] in the monastery at the Porta del Populo; the monks were willing to sell it for one thousand scudi, which Tischbein, as an artist, could not raise. Therefore he asked Meyer to offer a proposition to Madame Angelica, which she accepted; she paid out the aforementioned sum, took the picture to her house, and later, for a considerable amount of money, bought from Tischbein the half that was contractually his.[5] It was an excellent picture portraying the burial of Christ, with many figures. Meyer made a careful drawing of it that is still extant.

                                                         Rome, June 20.

Now I have again seen some exquisite works of art here, and my spirit is becoming purer and clearer. Nevertheless, I would need another year just in Rome, if I were to profit from my stay in my own fashion, and, as you know, that is the only way I can do anything. If I leave now, I shall only know that there is much I still do not understand, and there, for a while, the matter can rest.

The *Farnese Hercules* is gone, I still managed to see it with the genuine legs, which were restored to it after so long a time. Now it seems inconceivable that the first ones, by Porta, could have been considered good for so many years. It is now one of the most perfect works of ancient times. The king is going to have a museum built in Naples in which all the artworks he owns will be displayed together: the Herculaneum collection, the paintings from Pompeii, the paintings from Capo di Monte, the whole Farnese legacy. It is a grand and beautiful undertaking. Our countryman Hackert is the main impetus behind this work. Even the *Farnese Bull*[6] is supposed to migrate to Naples and be set up there on the Promenade. If they could take along the Carracci gallery from the palace, they would do that too.

Rome, June 27.

I was with Hackert in the Colonna gallery, where works by Poussin, Claude, and Salvator Rosa[7] hang side by side. He said many good and well-considered things to me about these pictures; he has copied some of them, and thoroughly studied the others. It pleased me that in general I had had the very same ideas on my first visits to the gallery. Everything he told me, instead of altering my concepts, merely expanded and defined them. If, then, one can immediately turn again to nature, and find and gather again what those men found and more or less imitated, that surely has to expand the mind and finally give it the highest intuitive concept of nature and art. I shall not rest until everything that is still merely words and tradition for me becomes a living concept. From my youth onwards this has been my desire and my torment; now that old age is approaching, I at least want to attain the attainable and do the doable, because for such a long time I have deservedly and undeservedly endured the fate of Sisyphus and Tantalus.

Continue to love and have faith in me! I get along tolerably well with people now and am pleasantly open with them; I feel good and am enjoying life.

Tischbein is a very worthy man, but I fear he will never be in a position to work happily and freely. I shall have more to tell you orally about this rather unusual man. My portrait is turning out well, it is an excellent likeness, and everyone is pleased with the concept. Angelica is also painting me, but it will not come to anything.[8] She is very upset because progress on the likeness eludes her. It may be a handsome fellow, but he does not resemble me in the least.

Rome, June 30.

The great festival of Saints Peter and Paul also finally arrived; yesterday, from the Castel, we saw the illumination of the dome and the fireworks. The illumination is an enormous fantasy, one cannot believe one's eyes. Since of late I only see objects, and not, as formerly, non-existent things accompanying them, it takes spectacles as grand as this to delight me. On my journey I have counted perhaps half a dozen, and this certainly qualifies as one of the best. To see the beautiful shapes of the colonnade, of the church, and especially of the dome, first in fiery outline, and then, when the hour is past, in a glowing mass, is unique and splendid. If we consider that during this moment the vast building serves merely as a framework, we shall readily understand that there can be nothing else in the world like this. The sky was clear and bright, the moon shone and dimmed the fire of the lamps to a pleasant radiance; eventually, however, when everything was set aglow by the second illumination, the moonlight was extinguished. The fireworks are beautiful because of the location, but are far from comparable to the illumination. This evening we shall see both again.

Now that is past too. The sky was beautiful and clear, and the moon was full, which made the illumination softer, and it was just like a fairy tale. To see the beautiful shapes of the church and the dome in, so to speak, a fiery vertical projection, is a grand and charming sight.

                                              Rome, end of June.

I have entered too great a school for me to leave it quickly again. My knowledge of art, my small talents must be thoroughly perfected here and ripen fully, otherwise I shall bring back only half a friend to you, and the longing, striving, creeping, and crawling will start all over again. I would never finish if I were to tell you how well everything has worked out for me here again this month, indeed how everything I could wish for has been presented me on a platter. I have fine quarters,[9] good service. Tischbein is going to Naples, and I shall occupy his studio, a large, cool salon. When you think of me, think of me as a happy person; I shall write often, and so we shall be and remain together.

I also have many new thoughts and ideas. Being left to myself, I am rediscovering my early youth in detail, and then in turn the supreme merit of the objects carries me up as high and far as my present inner life can reach. My eye is undergoing an incredible development, and my hand will not altogether lag behind. There is only one Rome in the world, and I am as happy as a fish in water here, and float on the surface in this quicksilver like a cannonball, which sinks in any other fluid. Nothing darkens the atmosphere of my thoughts except not being able to share my happiness with my dear friends. The sky is now splendidly bright, so that Rome is misty only in the morning and evening.

But on the mountains, Albano, Castello, Frascati, where I spent three days last week, the air is always bright and clear. That is a nature to study.

Comment

Since I now would like my report to reflect the conditions, impressions, and feelings of that time, I am beginning to extract passages of general interest from my own letters, which, certainly more than any later narrative, depict the special qualities of the moment; but in so doing I have also come across letters from friends that might serve this purpose even better. Consequently I have decided to insert these epistolary documents here and there, and begin at once by introducing some very lively accounts by Tischbein of his trip from Rome to Naples. They offer the advantage of immediately transporting the reader to those regions and directly into the situation of the persons. They especially illuminate the character of the artist, who had such a long, significant career, and even though he no doubt occasionally seemed rather odd, nevertheless deserves to be remembered gratefully for his efforts and accomplishments.

Tischbein to Goethe

Naples, July 10, 1787.

Our trip from Rome was very easy and pleasant. Hackert joined us in Albano; in Velletri we ate at Cardinal Borgia's table and looked at his museum, which I especially enjoyed because I observed many things that I had passed over the first time. At three o'clock in the afternoon we set out again through the Pontine marshes, which I liked much better now than in the winter, because the green trees and hedges give an agreeable variety to these great flat spaces. Shortly before twilight we found ourselves in the middle of the marshes, where one changes horses. However, while the postilions were applying all their eloquence to the task of extorting money from us, a spirited white stallion found an opportunity to break loose and run away. That made a spectacle which gave us much pleasure. It was a snow-white horse of magnificent proportions; he tore the reins with which he was tied, struck with his front hooves at the man who tried to stop him, kicked out behind, and whinnied so loudly that everyone stepped aside in fear. Then he jumped over the ditch and galloped across the field, still snorting and whinnying. His tail and mane fluttered high in the air, and there was such beauty of form in the freedom of his movements that everyone shouted: "O che bellezze! che bellezze!" Then he ran back and forth along another ditch, looking for a narrow place to jump over and get to the foals and mares, many hundreds of which were grazing on the other side. Finally he succeeded in jumping over, and now he ran among the mares, who were peacefully feeding. They were alarmed by his wildness and clamor, ran from him in a long row, fleeing across the flat field; but he kept after them, trying to cover one.

Finally he drove one mare to the side; but she then ran to another field and joined another numerous group of mares. The latter were also terrified and stampeded over to the first troop. Now the field was black with horses, with the white stallion leaping about among them, all of them wild and terrified. The herd ran back and forth across the field in long lines, the air rang and the earth thundered wherever the powerful weight of the horses flew across it. For a long time we watched with pleasure as the troop of so many hundreds galloped around on the field, now in a clump, now separately, sometimes running about singly and distractedly, sometimes racing across the ground in long lines.

Finally the darkness of oncoming night robbed us of this unique spectacle, and when the clearest moon rose from behind the mountains the light of our burning lanterns was extinguished. But after I had enjoyed its gentle gleam for a long time, I could not fight off sleep anymore, and for all my fear of unhealthy air I slept more than an hour, not waking until we arrived in Terracina, where we changed horses.

Here the postilions were very courteous, for Marchese Lucchesini had put them in awe of us. They gave us the best horses and drivers, because the road between the great cliffs and the sea is dangerous. Many accidents have occurred here, especially at night, when the horses shy easily. During the hitching up, and while the passports were being shown at the last Roman guardhouse, I went strolling between the high rocks and the sea, and beheld the greatest effect: the dark rock, brilliantly illuminated by the moon, cast a brightly sparkling column into the blue sea, and this glittered up as far as the waves that were tossing at the shore.

High up on the mountain peak, in shadowy blue, lie the fragments of Genseric's ruined castle;[10] they made me think of times past, I felt unhappy Conradin's longing to escape,[11] as well as Cicero's and Marius's,[12] all of whom had known fear in this locality.

It was beautiful to drive farther along the mountain in the moonlight, between the big boulders that have rolled down to the edge of the sea. The groups of olive trees, palms, and stone pines near Fondi were clearly illuminated; but we regretted not seeing the orange groves to advantage, for they only show their whole splendor when the sun shines on their gleaming golden fruit. Then we went over the mountain, where many olive and carob trees stand, and day had already dawned when we arrived at the ruins of the ancient town, where there are many remnants of grave monuments. The largest of these is said to have been erected for Cicero, on the very spot where he was murdered. It had already been daylight for several hours when we arrived at the delightful bay off Mola di Gaeta. The fishermen were already returning with their catch, which made the beach very lively. Some of them carried the fish and crustaceans away in baskets, others prepared the nets for a future haul. From there we drove to Garigliano, where Cavaliere Venuti is having excavations made. Here Hackert left us, for he was hurrying to Caserta, and we, abandoning the road, walked down to the sea, where a breakfast was made ready for us that could have served as our main meal. The excavated antiquities were put here for safekeeping, but they are sadly smashed to pieces. Among other beautiful things, we saw the leg of a statue that may not be much inferior to the *Apollo Belvedere*. It would be a stroke of luck if the rest of it could be found.

Being tired, we had lain down to sleep for a while, and when we woke up again we found ourselves in the company of a pleasant family that lives in this neighborhood and had come to give us a midday meal. To be sure, we probably owed this attentiveness to Mr. Hackert, but he had already left. So again a table stood prepared for us; but I could neither eat nor remain sitting, as good as the company was. Instead I went for a stroll along the sea, among the stones, of which there were some very odd ones, especially the many that have been perforated by marine insects, so that some of them resemble a sponge.

Here I encountered something quite pleasant: a goatherd drove his flock to the beach; the goats went into the water and cooled themselves off. Then the swineherd came also, and while the two herds were refreshing themselves in the waves, the two herdsmen sat down in the shade and made music, the swineherd on a flute, the goatherd on bagpipes. Eventually a full-grown naked boy rode up and went far out into the water, so far that his horse swam with him. It was indeed a fine sight when the well-built lad came so close to shore that one could see his whole form; and then he went right back into the deep sea, where nothing could be seen but the head of the swimming horse and the boy's head and shoulders.

At three o'clock in the afternoon we drove on, and when we were three miles beyond Capua—it was already an hour after nightfall—we broke the back wheel of our carriage. We were delayed several hours while it was being replaced with a different one. However, when this was done and we had covered another several miles, the axle broke. We were very much annoyed about this—so near to Naples and yet we could not speak to our friends. Finally we did arrive there several hours after midnight, and saw more people still on the streets than might have been seen at midday in another town.

I found all of our friends here sound and well, all of them happy to hear the same of you. I am staying at Mr. Hackert's place; the day before yesterday I was with Sir William Hamilton at his villa in Posillipo. Surely nothing more splendid can be seen on God's earth. After we had eaten, a dozen boys swam in the sea, which was a fine sight. How variously they grouped themselves and posed as they played! He pays them for it, in order to enjoy this pleasure every afternoon. I like Hamilton extremely well; I talked about many things with him, both in the house and when we were taking a boat ride on the sea. It made me extraordinarily happy to learn so much from him, and I am hoping for many more benefits from this man. Do write me the names of your other friends here, so that I can meet them and give them your greetings. You shall soon hear more from here. Give my greetings to all our friends, especially Angelica and Reiffenstein.

P.S. I find Naples a great deal warmer than Rome, with only this difference, that the air is more wholesome and there is always a bit of cool wind blowing, but the sun is much more intense; the first days were almost unbearable for me. I lived only on ice and snow water.

Later, undated.

I wish you had been in Naples yesterday: never in my life have I seen such a crowd of noisy people, who were only there to buy food-stuffs; nor will such a mass of food ever be seen again. The big Via Toledo was almost covered with all sorts of victuals. Only here does one get a concept of a race that dwells in a such a happy region, where the climate lets crops grow daily. Imagine, 500,000 people are engaged today in banqueting, and that in Neapolitan style! Yesterday and today I was at a table where feeding went on a rate that astonished me; a sinful superabundance was in evidence. Kniep was sitting there too and overate so greedily of all the delicious foods that I was afraid he would burst; but it did not affect him, and meanwhile he kept telling about his appetite on shipboard and in Sicily, while you paid your good money only to fast and practically starve, partly because of illness, in part deliberately.

Today everything that was sold yesterday has already been devoured, and it is said that tomorrow the street will be as full again as it was yesterday. The Via Toledo seems a theater for the display of super-abundance. The shops are all decorated with foodstuffs, which even hang over the street in garlands, and the little sausages are partly gilded and tied with red ribbons. The turkeys all have a red flag sticking in their rumps, thirty thousand of them were sold yesterday, not counting those fattened at home. It was startling to see the many donkeys laden with capons, likewise those weighed down with little Seville oranges, and the big heaps of this golden fruit that had been spilled onto the pavement. But probably most beautiful of all were the shops where fresh vegetables are sold and those that handle raisins, figs, and melons: everything laid out in such an attractive manner that it delights both eye and heart. Naples is a place where God sheds His blessings co-piously on all the senses.

Later, undated.

Here you have a drawing of the Turks who are being kept in captivity here. It was not the *Hercules*[13] that seized them, as was said at first, but a ship that was escorting the coral fishers. The Turks saw this Christian vessel and advanced on it to capture it, but they deceived themselves; for the Christians were stronger, and so they were overpowered and brought here as captives. There were thirty men on the Christian ship, twenty-four on the Turkish one; six Turks were killed in the fighting, one is wounded; not a single one of the Christians was killed, the Madonna protected them.

The ship's master made a fine catch; he found a great deal of money and goods, silk cloth and coffee, also some valuable jewelry belonging to a young Moorish woman.

It was remarkable to see the many thousands of people who went out there, in boat after boat, to look at the captives, especially the Moorish girl. Various admirers turned up who wanted to buy her and offered a lot of money, but the captain is not willing to let her go.

I went out there every day and once found Sir William and Miss Harte, who was very touched, and wept. When the Moorish girl saw that, she began to weep too; Miss Harte wanted to buy her, but the captain stubbornly refused to surrender her. Now they are no longer here; my drawing gives the further details.

Addendum

Papal Tapestries[14]

The great sacrifice I made by deciding to leave behind the lava flowing down from the mountaintop almost to the sea was richly rewarded by the goal I attained, that is, seeing the tapestries which, hung up on Corpus Christi day, were a very brilliant reminder to us of Raphael, his pupils, and his times.

The method of working tapestries with a high warp, called *hautelisse,* had already been raised to the peak of refinement in the Netherlands. I have not learned how the manufacture of tapestries was gradually developed and improved. In the twelfth century the individual figures may still have been embroidered or made in some other way and then joined together with specially worked connecting pieces. We still find such things above the choir stalls in old cathedrals, and this work has something in common with the colorful windows, whose pictures were also first put together out of quite small pieces of stained glass. In the tapestries, needle and thread substituted for solder and little tin bars. Art and technique always start out like this; we have seen valuable Chinese tapestries that were made in the same way.

Probably inspired by Oriental models, people in the commercially active and luxury-loving Netherlands had already developed this artistic technique to the highest point at the beginning of the sixteenth century. Works of this kind soon went back again to the Orient and were certainly also known in Rome, probably from imperfect examples and from drawings done in the Byzantine style. Leo X, with his great and, in many respects, free spirit, especially where art was concerned, probably wanted to see tapestries in his apartments that would portray with equal freedom and grandeur the same things he saw pictured on walls. At his request, Raphael created the cartoons: happily, with subjects that depicted Christ's relationship to His apostles and then the actions of these gifted men after the Master's ascension.

Not until Corpus Christi day did we become acquainted with the true purpose of the tapestries: here they transformed colonnades and open spaces into grand salons and galleries, meanwhile, to be sure, furnishing us with positive proof of this supremely gifted man's ability and giving us the most felicitous example of how art and craft, both at the highest point of perfection, can form an active partnership.

The Raphaelesque cartoons, hitherto kept in England, are still universally admired; some certainly can be attributed to the master alone, others may have been made from his drawings or his specifications, still others even only after his death. They all gave evidence of great, harmonious artistic intentions, and artists of all nations were congregating here in order to uplift their spirits and improve their capabilities.

This prompts us to consider the tendency of German artists, slight indications of which could already be detected at that time, to prefer and esteem particularly his early works.[15]

In any art, we feel a closer relationship with a richly talented, sensitive youth, whose mode is gentle, charming, and natural. Of course we dare not compare ourselves with him, but quietly compete with him and hope to match his accomplishments.

We do not turn to the fully developed man with the same confidence; for we sense the terrifying conditions imposed on even the most pronounced natural talent before it can rise to the highest possible success; and if we do not want to despair, we must go back and compare ourselves with someone who is still striving and becoming.

This is the reason why German artists bestowed their affection, respect, and trust on older, imperfect works. Next to them, they could feel that they too amounted to something, and might flatter themselves

with the hope of personally accomplishing something that had needed,
however, a succession of centuries to develop.

Let us return to Raphael's cartoons and state that all of them are
manly in concept; moral earnestness, awe-inspiring grandeur are dom-
inant everywhere, and, although occasionally mysterious, they nevertheless become altogether clear to those who are sufficiently informed
from Holy Scripture about the Savior's departure and the miraculous
gifts He bequeathed to His disciples.

First of all, let us look at the humiliation and punishment of Ananias,[16]
since we can do this quite well at any time by comparing the little
engraving (not unreasonably ascribed to Marcantonio)[17] from a detailed
drawing by Raphael with the reproduction of the cartoons by Dorigny.[18]

There are probably few compositions worthy of being placed next
to this one. Here is a grand concept, an action that is very important
because of its peculiar nature, and presented very clearly in spite of
its complete diversity.

The apostles waiting for each individual to offer up his possessions
to the common purse as a pious gift; on one side the faithful bringing
gifts, on the other the needy recipients, and in the middle the defrauder,
horribly punished; an arrangement whose symmetry proceeds from the
given facts and which is both concealed and enlivened by the demands
of the subject to be portrayed; just as the requisite symmetrical proportions of the human body only acquire vivid interest when in diverse
living motion.

While viewing this work of art would prompt no end of observations
we shall just emphasize one further important merit of this portrayal.
Two male persons who approach carrying bundled-up pieces of clothing
must necessarily belong to Ananias; but how are we to recognize from
this that some portion of the clothing has remained behind and been
withheld from the common property? Here, however, our attention is
drawn to a pretty young woman who, with a cheerful face, is counting
money from her right hand into her left; and we immediately recall the
noble saying: "Let not thy left hand know what thy right hand doeth,"
and do not doubt that this is meant to be Saphira, who is counting out
the money to be presented to the apostles, but is nevertheless with-
holding some, as her cheerfully cunning face seems to indicate. This
concept is astonishing and terrible, if one becomes absorbed in it. Before
us is the husband, already punished and twisted out of shape, writhing
on the floor in horrible convulsions; just a little in back of him, unaware
of what is happening, the wife, planning with self-confident craftiness
to take advantage of the godly men, without suspecting the fate that
is in store for her. In general, this picture stands before us as a perpetual
problem, which we admire more and more, the clearer and more possible its solution becomes for us. Comparison of the Marcantonio print,

from a drawing of the same size by Raphael, with Dorigny's larger one, after the cartoon, brings us again to profound meditations on the wisdom with which such a talent was able to alter and enhance the same composition in a second treatment. Let us gladly confess that for us such study has been one of the finest pleasures of a long life.

July

Correspondence

My present life is just like a youthful dream, we shall see whether I am destined to enjoy it or to discover that this too, like so much else, is merely futile. Tischbein is gone, his studio emptied, dusted, and washed clean, so that now I am glad to be in it. How necessary it is to have a pleasant home in this weather. The heat is intense. In the morning I get up at sunrise and go to the Acqua acetosa,[19] a chalybeate spring, about a half hour away from the gate at which I live; I drink the water, which tastes like a weak Schwalbach water but is nevertheless very effective in this climate. At about eight o'clock I am at home again and busily engaged in whatever my mood dictates. I am quite well. The heat gets rid of everything catarrhal and drives whatever is corrosive in the body out through the skin, and it is better for an evil to itch than for it to tear and pull. I continue to develop my taste and hand in drawing. I have begun to study architecture more seriously, everything is becoming amazingly easy for me (that is to say, the theory, for the practice requires a lifetime). The best part was: I had no conceit and no pretensions. I had no demands to make when I came here. And now I only insist that nothing remain just a name, a word for me. With my own eyes, I want to see and appreciate everything that is considered beautiful, great, and worthy of respect. Without copying, this is impossible. Now I must attempt the plaster busts. (Artists are suggesting the right method to me. I keep trying to do as well as I can.) At the beginning of the week, I could not refuse invitations to dine here and there. Now they want me to come to this place and that; I let it pass and remain quietly at home. My regular circle is made up of Moritz, some compatriots[20] living in the house, and a worthy Swiss. I also go to Angelica and Councilor Reiffenstein; I always have my reflective manner, and there is no one to whom I could open my heart. Lucchesini is here again; he sees everybody and, like everybody else, I see him. Unless I am much mistaken, he is a man who knows his profession. I shall write to you before long about several persons whom I hope soon to meet.

I am working on *Egmont*,[21] and I hope it will turn out well. At any rate, while writing it I have always felt symptoms that have proved trustworthy. It is quite strange that I was so often prevented from ending the play, and that now it is to be finished in Rome. The first act is in good order and fully developed, and there are whole scenes in the play that I do not need to touch.

I have had so much opportunity to think about all kinds of art that my *Wilhelm Meister* is really expanding.[22] But the older items shall be disposed of first. At my age, I must not delay if I still want to accomplish anything. As you can easily imagine, I have a hundred new things in mind, and it is not a question of thinking, but of *doing*. It is an accursed task to arrange things so that they finally stand one way and not another. I would like to talk quite a lot about art now, but without the artworks what is there to say? I hope to get past much that is insignificant, therefore grant me my time here, which I am spending so wonderfully and peculiarly, grant it to me by giving your loving approval.

I must close now, although I dislike sending one empty page. The heat of the day was great, and toward evening I fell asleep.

Rome, July 9.

From now on I shall write a few things throughout the week, so that neither the heat on a mailing day nor some other chance occurrence may prevent me from saying a sensible word to you. Yesterday I saw a great deal, not all of it for the first time. I was in perhaps twelve churches, where the most beautiful altarpieces are.

Then I went with Angelica to visit the Englishman Moore,[23] a landscape painter, whose pictures are mostly very well conceived. Among other works, he has painted a *Deluge* that is quite unique. Instead of showing an open sea, as others have done, which always just gives the impression of a wide, but not high, flood, he has depicted the ever-rising waters as they finally plunge even into a high, closed-off mountain valley. It can be seen from the shape of the rocks that the water is approaching their tops, and it makes a fearful effect that in back the valley is closed off crosswise, and all the cliffs are sheer. The painting is almost entirely gray on gray, the dirty, churned-up water is very intimately combined with the dripping rain, the water dashes up and trickles back from the rocks, as if those huge masses were also about to dissolve in the universal element; and the sun looks through the veil of water like a bleak moon, without shedding light, and yet it is not night. In the center foreground there is an isolated flat slab of rock on which some helpless humans have taken refuge just at the moment when the flood is swelling nearer and is about to cover them. The whole picture is incredibly well conceived. It is large, perhaps 7–8 feet wide and 5–6 feet high. I shall say nothing at all about the other pictures, a splendidly beautiful *Morning,* an exquisite *Night.*

For three full days there was a festival in Aracoeli for the beatification of two holy men from the order of St. Francis. The decoration of the church, the music, the illumination and fireworks at night attracted a great crowd of people. The nearby Capitol was illuminated also, and fireworks were set off on the Capitoline plaza. All of this together made a beautiful sight, although just an epilogue to St. Peter's. The Roman women, accompanied by their husbands or male friends, come out at night for this occasion in white dresses with a black girdle, and they are beautiful and well mannered. Now there is also much strolling and driving at night in the Corso, whereas in the daytime people do not leave the house. The heat is quite bearable, and a cool breeze has been blowing for the last few days. I keep to my cool salon and am quiet and happy.

I am industrious, and my *Egmont* is coming right along. It is strange that just now in Brussels they are playing the scene that I wrote down twelve years ago;[24] now much of it will be considered a pasquinade.

Rome, July 16.

It is already late at night, but does not seem so, for the street is full of people who walk up and down singing, playing zithers and violins, alternating with each other. The nights are cool and refreshing, the days not intolerably hot.

Yesterday I was with Angelica in the Villa Farnesina, where the legend of Psyche has been painted. How often and under how many circumstances I have looked at colored copies of these pictures in my rooms with all of you! I was really struck, since I know these pictures almost by heart because of those very copies. This salon or, rather, gallery has the most beautiful decoration that I have seen, even though much of it has now been damaged and restored.

Today there was animal baiting in the monument to Augustus.[25] This large, perfectly round building, which is empty inside and open above, has now been turned into a kind of arena or amphitheater for bull baiting. It can probably hold four to five thousand people. I did not find the spectacle itself very edifying.

On Tuesday, July 17, in the evening, I visited Albacini,[26] the restorer of ancient statues, to see a torso found among the Farnese possessions that are going to Naples. It is the torso of a seated Apollo,[27] and is of perhaps unequaled beauty; at least it ranks among the best things remaining from antiquity.

I dined at Count Fries's lodgings; Abbé Casti,[28] who is traveling with him, recited one of his novellas, "The Archbishop of Prague," which is a little indecent, but extraordinarily beautiful, and written in ottava rima. I already esteemed him as the author of my beloved *Rè Teodoro in Venezia.* Now he has written a *Rè Teodoro in Corsica,* of which I have read the first act, also an altogether charming work.

Count Fries is a great buyer, and among other things has purchased a Madonna by Andrea del Sarto[29] for 600 zechins. Just last March, Angelica offered 450 for it, and would have paid this whole sum at once if her closefisted husband had not raised some objection. Now they are both sorry. It is an incredibly beautiful picture, something that one can have no idea of without having seen it.

And so day in, day out, something new appears, side by side with the old and lasting, and gives great pleasure. My eye is being well trained, and with time I could become a connoisseur.

Tischbein complains in a letter about the terrible heat in Naples. It is bad enough here. Foreigners say that it was hotter here on Tuesday than they had ever felt it to be in Spain and Portugal.

Egmont has already progressed as far as the fourth act, and I hope it will please all of you. I expect to be finished in three weeks, and then I shall send it to Herder at once.

I am also busily drawing and coloring. One cannot leave the house or go for the shortest walk without encountering the worthiest objects. My imagination, my memory, are filling up with infinitely beautiful sights.

Rome, July 20.

In the last few days I have truly been able to identify two of my principal defects, which have pursued and tormented me my whole life. One is that I never cared to learn the technique of a craft that I wanted or was supposed to work at. That is the reason why I, with so much natural aptitude, have made and done so little. Either it was forcibly accomplished through strength of mind, with success or failure left to luck or chance, or, if I tried to do something well and thoughtfully, I would be timid and unable to finish. The other, closely related defect is that I never cared to spend as much time on a work or task as was required. Since I have the fortunate ability to think and deduce a great deal in a short time, I find a step-by-step execution boring and intolerable. I should think now would be the proper time and hour to correct this. I am in the land of arts, let us study the field thoroughly, so that we have peace and joy for the rest of our life and can go on to something else.

Rome is a splendid place for that. Not only are there objects of every kind here, but also people of every kind, who are serious-minded, who walk the right paths, in conversation with whom one can make progress quickly and comfortably. Thank Heavens, I am beginning to be able to learn and take from others.

And so I find myself healthier than ever in body and soul! May you see this in my productions and praise my absence. I am connected to you through what I produce and think, but otherwise, of course, I am very much alone and must adapt my conversation to the circumstances. However, that is easier here than anywhere else, because there is something interesting to discuss with everyone.

Mengs says somewhere,[30] concerning the *Apollo Belvedere,* that a statue combining equally great style with more realistic flesh would be the greatest thing imaginable. And in that torso of an Apollo or Bacchus, which I have already mentioned, his wish or prophecy seems to have been fulfilled. My eye is not sufficiently developed to be able to decide such a matter; but I myself am inclined to consider this fragment the most beautiful thing I have seen. Unfortunately, not only is it just a torso, but its epidermis has also been washed away in many places; it must have stood under a gutter.

On Sunday, July 22,

I ate at Angelica's; it is now already customary for me to be her Sunday guest. Beforehand, we drove to the Barberini palace to see the exquisite Leonardo da Vinci[31] and Raphael's beloved, painted by himself.[32] It is most pleasant to view paintings with Angelica, since her eye is very cultivated and her technical knowledge of art is so great. At the same time, she is very sensitive to everything beautiful, true, and tender, and is incredibly modest.

In the afternoon, I visited the Chevalier d'Agincourt,[33] a wealthy Frenchman, who is spending his time and money writing a history of art from its decline up to its revival. The collections he has formed are extremely interesting. We see how the human spirit continued to be active during that dark and gloomy era. If this work is ever finished, it will be a very remarkable one.

Now I am engaged on a project from which I am learning much; I have devised and drawn a landscape, and it is being colored, in my presence, by a skilled artist, Dies.[34] By this means my eye is becoming more and more accustomed to color and harmony. In general, I am making good progress, except that, as always, I am working at too much. My greatest joy is that my eye is being developed on the basis of reliable forms, and accustoms itself easily to shape and proportion. Meanwhile my old feeling for distribution of light and shadow within the whole is returning very strongly. Now everything depends on practice.

On Monday, July 23,

in the evening, I climbed Trajan's column[35] in order to enjoy the inestimable view. From up there, as the sun is setting, the Coliseum looks quite magnificent, the Capitol quite near, the Palatine is behind it, with the city adjoining. Not until late did I slowly walk back through the streets. The Monte Cavallo square with the obelisk is a remarkable sight.

Tuesday, July 24.

To the Villa Patrizzi, in order to see the sunset, to enjoy the fresh air, to fill my mind properly with the image of the great city, to expand and simplify the range of my vision with the long lines, and to enrich it with the many beautiful and diverse objects. This evening I saw the square containing the Antonine column:[36] the Chigi palace in the moonlight, and the column, black with age, against the brighter night sky, on a gleaming white pedestal. And what a countless number of other beautiful, individual objects one comes across on such a walk! But how much is involved in assimilating even only a small part of all this! A whole human life is needed for it, indeed the life of many persons, who learn from one another in stages.

Wednesday, July 25.

I went with Count Fries to see the Prince of Piombino's[37] gem collection.

Friday, the 27th.

Incidentally, all the artists, young and old, are helping me to shape and expand my small talent. I have made progress in perspective and architecture, also in landscape composition. There is still some difficulty with living creatures, that is an abyss, but with serious application it should be possible to advance in this too.

I do not know whether I mentioned the concert that I gave last week-end. I invited those persons to it who had provided me with many a pleasant time, and had the singers from the comic opera perform the best pieces from the latest intermezzos. Everyone was pleased and gratified.

Now my salon is beautifully cleaned up and straightened. It is very pleasant to live here in the extremely hot weather. We have had a dark, rainy day, a thunderstorm, and now a few bright, not very hot days.

On Sunday, July 29, 1787,

I was with Angelica in the Rondanini palace. You will all remember, from my first Roman letters, a Medusa that appealed to me so much even then, but now gives me the greatest joy. Just to conceive of there being something like that in the world, of its having been possible to make something like that, makes one twice as much of a person. How I would like to say something about it, if everything one can say about such a work were not an empty breeze. Art is there to be seen, not to be talked about, except perhaps in its presence. How ashamed I am of all the artistic babble that I formerly joined in with. If it is possible to obtain a good plaster cast of this Medusa I shall bring it along home, but it would have to be newly made. There are a few for sale that I do not like, since they spoil the concept more than they give and preserve it. The mouth especially is unutterably and inimitably great.

On Monday, the 30th,

I stayed at home all day and worked. *Egmont* is moving along toward the end, the fourth act is as good as finished. As soon as it is copied I shall send it with the postrider. What a joy it will be for me if I hear from you that this production, to some extent, has your approval! I feel really young again as I write this play; I hope it will also impress the reader as being fresh. This evening there was a little ball in the garden behind the house, to which we too were invited. Although this is not dancing weather, everyone was quite merry. The pretty Italian misses have their peculiar ways, some of which I might have put up with ten years ago, but this vein has now gone dry in me, and the little festivity was so uninteresting to me that I could hardly stay to the end. The moonlit nights are quite incredibly beautiful; the rising of the moon, before it has worked its way up through the mists, all yellow and warm, *come il sole d'Inghilterra,*[38] then for the rest of the night it is clear and friendly. A cool breeze, and everyone comes to life. Until nearly morning, there are still groups in the street, singing and playing, one hears various duets that are as beautiful as in an opera or concert, and even more beautiful.

On Tuesday, July 31,

several moonlight scenes were put on paper, then I made various other good artistic efforts. In the evening I went strolling with a countryman, and we argued about the relative superiority of Michelangelo and Raphael; I upheld the former, he the latter, and we ended up by joining in praise of Leonardo da Vinci. How happy I am that all these names are now ceasing to be mere names, and that I am gradually forming complete, living concepts of the value of these excellent men.

At night to the comic opera, a new intermezzo, *L'Impresario in angustie,*[39] is first-rate and will entertain us for many a night, no matter how hot it is in the theater. There is a very successful quintet in which the poet reads his play aloud and is applauded on one side by the impresario and the prima donna, while on the other the composer and the *seconda donna* criticize him, which finally leads to a general quarrel. The castrati disguised as women play their roles better and better, and please the audience more and more. For a small summer troupe that has just casually come together, it is quite adept. They act with great naturalness and good humor. The poor devils suffer pitifully from the heat.

Report

July

In order to give an appropriate introduction to what I now intend to present, I believe it is necessary to insert some passages here from the previous volume, which may have escaped notice there in the rush of events, and by means of them recommend this matter, which is of such great importance to me, to the friends of natural science.

Palermo, Tuesday, April 17, 1787.

Truly, it is a misfortune to be pursued and tempted by many different spirits! This morning I went to the public garden with the firm, calm resolve to continue my poetic dreams, but before I realized it, another specter seized me, one that has been skulking behind me for the last few days. The many plants that otherwise I was used to seeing only in tubs and pots, indeed for most of the year behind glass windows, stand here, fresh and happy, under the open sky; and by fulfilling their intended purpose completely, they become clearer to us. Confronted with so many kinds of fresh, new forms, I was taken again by my old fanciful idea: might I not discover the primordial plant amid this multitude? Such a thing must exist, after all! How else would I recognize this or that form as being a plant, if they were not all constructed according to one model?

I took pains to investigate how the many diverse shapes differed from each other. And I invariably found them more similiar than different. When I tried to apply my botanical terminology, I was able to, but there was no profit in that, it disquieted me without helping me to proceed. My good poetic intentions were upset, the garden of Alcinous had disappeared, and a world garden had opened up. Why are we moderns so easily distracted, why are we so fascinated by challenges we can neither meet nor fulfill!

Naples, May 17, 1787.

Furthermore I must confide to you that I am close to discovering the secret of plant generation and structure, and that it is the simplest thing imaginable. The finest observations can be made under this sky. I have quite clearly and unquestionably found the main feature, the location of the bud, and I already see everything else in a general way; just a few more points need to be better defined. The primordial plant is turning out to be the most marvelous creation in the world, and nature itself will envy me because of it. With this model and the key to it, an infinite number of additional plants can be invented, which must be logical, that is, if they do not exist, they *could* exist, and are not mere artistic or poetic shadows and semblances, but have an inner truth and necessity. The same law will be applicable to every other living thing.

But let this much be briefly stated here, to facilitate further understanding: Namely, it had become apparent to me that in the plant organ we ordinarily call the leaf a true Proteus is concealed, who can hide and reveal himself in all formations. From top to bottom, a plant is all leaf, united so inseparably with the future bud that one cannot be imagined without the other. To grasp, to endure such a concept, to detect it in nature, is a task that puts us into a sweet torment.

Intruding Meditations on Nature

Anyone who has personally experienced what it means to have a pregnant thought, whether it is original with him or transmitted and instilled by others, will bear witness to the passion with which it stirs the spirit and to the enthusiasm with which we anticipate in its entirety everything that will subsequently develop more and more, and the further discoveries to which that development will lead. When this is taken into consideration, I shall be pardoned for having been captivated and driven by a perception of this kind, as if by a passion, and for having been compelled to occupy myself with it, if not exclusively, nevertheless for the rest of my life.

But, as integral a part of me as this inclination had become, there was no possibility of any systematic study after my return to Rome; poetry, art, and antiquity, each of them demanded more or less my whole attention, and I doubt that I have ever spent more laborious, arduously busy days in my life. Perhaps it will seem absurdly naive to experts in the field when I relate how, day after day, in every single garden, on walks, on short excursions, I would appropriate plants that I noticed beside me. Especially when the seeds were beginning to ripen, it was important to me to observe how some of them emerged into daylight. So I turned my attention to the sprouting of *Cactus opuntia,* which grows misshapenly, and saw with pleasure that it unveiled itself in an innocently dicotyledonous manner in two tender little leaves, but then, with further growth, its future unlovely form developed.

I also had a remarkable experience with seedpods: I had brought home several pods of *Acanthus mollis,* and laid them down in a small open box; then one night I heard a rustling, and soon afterwards a sound as though of tiny bodies jumping around against the ceiling and walls. I could not immediately explain it to myself, but later discovered that my pods had burst open and scattered the seeds around. In a few days, the dryness of the room had ripened them to this state of elasticity.

Among the many seeds that I observed in this way, there are still several I must mention because they continued to grow either a shorter or longer time in old Rome, in memory of me. Stone-pine nuts opened quite remarkably, they raised themselves up as though enclosed in an egg, but soon cast off this hood, and the beginnings of their future destiny were already shown in a wreath of green needles.

Although the foregoing concerned reproduction by seeds, my attention had been equally drawn to reproduction by buds, and actually by Councilor Reiffenstein, who never went for a walk without tearing off branches here and there and asserting in an almost pedantic manner that each of these, if stuck into the earth, would immediately continue to grow. As decisive proof, he pointed to cuttings of that type in his garden which had taken root very well. And I certainly wish he had lived to see how significant such general attenpts at reproduction subsequently became for botanical gardening.

However, what struck me most was a carnation stalk that had grown up like a shrub. The phenomenal vitality and reproductive power of this plant are well known; bud crowds over bud on its branches, joint is funneled into joint. Here this was increased by age, and the buds were forced out of impenetrable confines into the highest possible development, so that the completed flower itself produced another four completed flowers from its bosom.

Seeing no available means of preserving this miraculous form, I undertook a precise drawing of it, and in this way arrived at ever deeper insights into the basic concept of metamorphosis. But the distractions caused by my many and various obligations only grew the more importunate, and my sojourn in Rome, the end of which I foresaw, became ever more painful and burdensome.

After I had for some time kept quietly to myself and far from all fashionable, distracting company, we committed a blunder that brought us to the attention of the whole quarter, as well as of society, which is on the lookout for new and strange events. The matter, however, was as follows: Angelica never went to the theater, for reasons we did not investigate. But, as passionate theatergoers, we could not praise the charm and skill of the singers and the effectiveness of our Cimarosa's music highly enough in her presence, and it was our dearest wish to have her share in these pleasures. So one thing led to another, and our young people—Bury in particular, who was on excellent terms with them—persuaded the singers and musicians to make a cheerful offer to play and sing on some occasion in our salon for us, their passionate admirers and enthusiastic applauders. This plan, frequently discussed, proposed, and delayed, finally became a happy reality, as the younger participants wished. Kranz,[40] the expert first violinist at the ducal court in Weimar, who was on leave for further training in Italy, arrived unexpectedly, and this brought about a speedy decision. With his talent tipping the scales in favor of the music enthusiasts, we saw ourselves in a position to invite Madame Angelica, her husband, Aulic Councilor Reiffenstein, Messrs. Jenkins and Volpato,[41] and everyone else to whom we owed a courtesy, to a proper festivity. Jews and tapestry hangers had decorated the salon, the proprietor of the nearby coffeehouse furnished the refreshments, and so, on the loveliest summer night, a brilliant concert was performed. Large crowds of people gathered under the windows and, as if they were in a theater, duly applauded the songs.

Indeed, the most striking thing was a big charabanc[42] occupied by an orchestra of music lovers, which had just then elected to make its pleasure rounds through the nocturnal city and had stopped under our windows. After lively applause for the efforts overhead, a lusty bass voice could be heard, accompanied by all the instruments, joining in on one of the most popular arias of the opera that we were performing piece by piece. We reciprocated with the heartiest applause, the populace clapped along, and all of them declared that while they had been present at many a nocturnal entertainment, they had never been at such a perfect, accidentally successful one.

Now, suddenly, our handsome but quiet apartment opposite the Rondanini palace attracted the attention of the Corso. It was said that a rich *mylordo* must have moved in there, but nobody could find and identify him among the well-known personalities. To be sure, it would have cost significant sums if we had had to pay money to give a festivity like the one we had staged here at moderate expense, because artists were performing as a favor to artists. Although we continued to live quietly, as before, from now on we could not dispel people's false assumption that we were wealthy and well born.

The arrival of Count Fries, however, was new cause for a livelier social life. With him was Abbé Casti, who delighted us very much by reading aloud from his then still unpublished gallant tales. His cheerful, spontaneous delivery seemed to bring those witty, uncommonly latitudinarian portrayals completely to life. We were only sorry that this well-meaning, wealthy art lover was not always served by the most reliable persons. His purchase of a falsely attributed carved gem gave rise to much talk and vexation. On the other hand, he could certainly be very content with his purchase of a beautiful statue depicting a Paris or, according to another interpretation, a Mithras. Its counterpart now stands in the Pio-Clementino museum; both were found together in a sandpit. But it was not only the negotiators in art transactions who lay in wait for him, he also had to experience many an adventure; and since he did not spare himself at all in the hot weather, he was inevitably attacked by various maladies, which made the last days of his stay miserable. But it was particularly painful for me since I had become greatly indebted to him for his kindness, as when, for instance, I was favored with an opportunity to examine the Prince of Piombino's superb gem collection with him.

Besides the art dealers to be found at Count Fries's lodgings, there were literary men of the sort who wander around in abbés' clothing. It was not pleasant to converse with them. Hardly would I begin to speak of the national poetry and try to get information on one point or another, when I would immediately and abruptly be asked which of the two poets, Ariosto or Tasso, I considered the greater. If I answered: God and nature should be thanked that two such outstanding men had been granted to one nation, that each of them, in accord with his time and circumstances, his condition and feelings, had given us the most splendid moments, had calmed and charmed us—no one would accept this rational statement. Then the preferred poet would be lauded to the skies, and the other one reduced to the depths by comparison. At first, I tried to speak in defense of the disparaged one and emphasize his merits; but this was to no avail, for sides had been taken, and nobody's mind was changed. Since the same thing happened to me again and again, and I did not want to argue captiously about matters I took so seriously, I avoided such conversations, especially when I noticed these people took no real interest in the subject, and were merely spouting clichés.

But it was much worse when Dante was being discussed. A young man of rank and intelligence, who was genuinely interested in that extraordinary poet, was not very receptive to my applause and approbation. He declared quite bluntly that no foreigner could hope to understand such an extraordinary spirit, whom the Italians themselves were unable to follow in every detail. After some talking back and forth, I finally became annoyed and said I would have to confess that I was inclined to agree with his statements, for I had never been able to grasp why anyone would want to bother with these poems. The *Inferno* struck me as quite horrible, the *Purgatorio* as ambiguous, and the *Paradiso* as boring. He was quite content with this, taking it as an argument in support of his assertion: this simply proved that I could not fathom the profundity and sublimity of these works. We parted the best of friends; he even promised to point out and explain to me some difficult passages which he had thought about for a long time and had finally interpreted to his own satisfaction.

Unfortunately, my conversations with artists and art lovers were no more edifying. However, I finally forgave in others the error I had to admit in myself. First it was Raphael, then Michelangelo whom I preferred, and in the end this only proved man to be such an obtuse creature that even if his spirit has opened to greatness he never acquires the ability to appreciate and recognize, in like manner, greatnesses of different kinds.

While we missed Tischbein's company and guidance, he made up for that as much as possible with his very lively letters. Besides witty accounts of some strange incidents, and some unconventional opinions, we learned from his drawings and sketches the details about a painting which was gaining him renown in Naples. In half-length figures it depicted Orestes at the sacrificial altar, just as Iphigenia recognizes him and the Furies, who have been pursuing him, flee. Iphigenia was the speaking likeness of Lady Hamilton,[43] then at the pinnacle of her beauty and prestige. One of the Furies was also ennobled by a resemblance to her, and in general she was used as a model for all heroines, muses, and demigoddesses.[44] An artist capable of doing that was very well received in the significant social circle of a Sir William Hamilton.

August

Correspondence

August 1, 1787.

Busy all day, but quiet because of the heat. The best part about this warm weather for me is my conviction that you must all be having a good summer in Germany too. It is the greatest delight to see hay being carted in here, since at this time it does not rain at all, and the fields can be cultivated at will—if only they cultivated them.

In the evening we bathed in the Tiber, in well-set-up, safe little bathhouses: then we strolled on Trinità de' Monti and enjoyed the fresh air and moonlight. Moonlit nights here are all one imagines or dreams them to be.

The fourth act of *Egmont* is finished, and in my next letter I hope to announce the completion of the play to you.

August 11.

I shall stay in Italy until next Easter. I cannot run away from my apprenticeship now. If I persevere, I shall certainly advance to the point where my work can give my friends some pleasure. You will continue to receive letters from me, then gradually my writings will come, and you will think of me as a living person who is absent, whereas you so often pitied me as a dead one who was present.

Egmont is finished and can be sent off at the end of this month. Then I shall painfully await your judgment of it.

Not a day passes that I do not grow in the knowledge and practice of art. Just as it is easy to fill a bottle by thrusting its open top under the water, so a person can easily be filled up here, if he is receptive and prepared; the artistic element rushes in from all sides.

I could predict from here that you would have a good summer. Our skies are always clear, and although the noontime heat is terrible, I can escape it fairly well in my cool salon. I shall spend September and October in the country, sketching from nature. Perhaps I shall go back to Naples in order to enjoy Hackert's instruction. Thanks to him, I progressed farther in our fortnight together in the country than I would have in years by myself. I am still not sending you anything, Charlotte, but am holding a dozen little sketches in reserve, so that I can send you something good all at once.

This week has passed in a quietly busy fashion. I have especially learned some things about perspective. Verschaffelt,[45] a son of the Mannheim director, has carefully studied this theory, and is teaching me his techniques. I have also drawn and colored several moonlight scenes, besides some other ideas that are almost too extravagant to warrant description.

Rome, August 11, 1787.

I have written the duchess[46] a long letter and advised her to postpone her trip to Italy for another year. If she leaves in October, she will arrive in this beautiful land just when the weather is changing, and that will spoil her pleasure. If she follows my advice in this and other matters, and has good luck, she can have a nice time. I am heartily pleased that she is going on this journey.

Both I and others are provided for, and we shall calmly await the future. No one can coin himself anew, or escape his destiny. From that same letter, Herder, you will see my plan and, I hope, approve of it. I shall not repeat anything here.

I shall write often and always be with all of you in spirit throughout the winter. Tasso will come after New Year's. Faust will be my courier, and announce my arrival on his cloak.[47] Then I shall have completed, and cleanly ended, an important epoch, and be able to begin again, and take action where it is necessary. I feel easier in my mind, and am almost not the same person I was a year ago.

My life is full to overflowing with everything that is particularly dear and valuable to me, and only during the last few months have I really enjoyed my stay here. For now things are unfolding, and art is becoming, as it were, a second Nature for me, born from the heads of the greatest humans, like Minerva from the head of Jupiter. Later on you shall be regaled with this for days, indeed for years.

I wish you a good September. At the end of August, when all of our birthdays coincide,[48] I shall often think of you. When the heat subsides, I am going out in the country to draw, in the meantime I do what I can indoors and must often stop for a while. One must be careful not to catch cold, especially in the evening.

Rome, August 18, 1787.

This week I had to moderate my Northern industriousness somewhat, the first days were entirely too hot. Therefore I have not done as much as I wanted to. Now, for two days, we have had the loveliest tramontane wind and very clear air. September and October will surely be two heavenly months.

Yesterday, before sunrise, I drove to Acqua acetosa; one could really lose one's mind over that landscape, because of its clarity, variety, transparent vapors, and heavenly coloration, especially at the distant points.

Moritz is now studying the ancient authors; he wants to humanize them and cleanse them of all bookish mustiness and pedantic dust, for the use of young people and of every thinking person.[49] He has a very felicitous, correct way of looking at these things, and I hope he will also take the time to be thorough. We go walking in the evening, and he tells me which part he has thought about during the day, and what he has read in the authors; so this gap is also being closed for me, which I would have to neglect because of my other occupations, and could fill in only belatedly and with difficulty. Meanwhile, I am looking at buildings, streets, the region, monuments, and when I return home in the evening, while we are chatting, I playfully draw a picture of whatever has particularly struck me. I am enclosing one of those sketches from yesterday evening. It gives a general idea of what one sees in coming up the Capitol from the back.

I went Sunday with our good friend Angelica to see Prince Aldobrandini's paintings, especially a superb Leonardo da Vinci.[50] She is not as happy as she deserves to be, in view of her truly great talent and daily increasing wealth. She is tired of painting pictures to sell, and yet her old husband delights in seeing such big money coming in for what is often little work. She would like to work for her own pleasure, with greater leisure, care, and study; and she could do this. They have no children, they cannot use up the interest on their investments, and every day, even without working very hard, she earns another sizable amount. But that is not how it is, and it never will be. She talks very candidly with me, I have told her my opinion, given her my advice, and encourage her whenever I am with her. Surely one may call it deprivation and misfortune when people who have enough cannot use it for their enjoyment! She has an incredible and, for a woman, truly prodigious talent. One must see and appreciate what she *does,* and not look for what she *omits.* How many artists' work would stand the test, if their omissions were taken into account!

And so, my dear friends, Rome and its character, art, and artists are constantly becoming better known to me, and I understand local conditions; living here and wandering to and fro are making them seem familiar and natural to me. Any mere visit gives one false notions. Here too, they would like to take me away from my quiet routine and draw me into the world; I guard against this as well as I can. I promise, delay, evade, promise again, and play the Italian among the Italians. The Secretary of State, Cardinal Buoncompagni,[51] has sent messengers to press me very hard, but I shall evade him until I go out into the country in the middle of September. I shrink from the ladies and gentlemen as though from the plague, I feel a pang even when I just see them out driving.

Rome, August 23, 1787.

Yesterday I received your dear letter No. 24, just as I was going to the Vatican, and I read it over and over both on the way there and in the Sistine chapel, whenever I paused in my looking and observing. I cannot tell you how much I wished that all of you had been with me, so that you would get an idea of what a single great human being can accomplish. Unless one has seen the Sistine chapel it is impossible to form an intuitive concept of what one person is capable of doing. We hear and read much about great and worthy people, but here we have it still completely alive above our heads and before our eyes. I held a great imaginary conversation with you, and I wish all of that were written on this sheet of paper. You want to know about *me!* How much I could say! For I really have been recreated and renewed and completed. I feel that all my powers are uniting and I hope still to accomplish something. During this time I have reflected seriously upon nature and architecture, have also attempted several things, and now can see where this will lead and how far it could be taken.

Now, at last, the alpha and omega of all things known to us, the human figure, has taken hold of me, and I of it, and I say, "Lord, I will not let Thee go, except Thou bless me, and even if I wrestle myself lame."[52] I had no success in drawing it, so I have decided on modeling, and that seems to show promise. At any rate, I have happened on an idea that makes things easier. To discuss it in detail would be too complicated, and it is better to do than to talk. Briefly, the main point is that my persistent study of nature and my careful procedure with comparative anatomy have now made me capable of seeing some things in general in nature and the ancient sculptures which artists have difficulty finding in the particular, and if they do eventually achieve this, they can only possess it for themselves and are unable to communicate it to others.

I have now retrieved all the physiognomical techniques that I had discarded because of my pique at the prophet,[53] and they come in very handy. I have begun a head of Hercules; if it is successful, we shall go on from there.

I am so remote from the world and all worldly affairs now that it seems strange to me when I read a newspaper. The form of this world is transitory. I prefer to occupy my mind exclusively with enduring conditions and thus, according to the teachings of ***,[54] truly procure eternal life for my spirit.

Yesterday I saw many drawings at Sir Richard Worthley's,[55] who has made a journey to Greece, Egypt, etc. I was chiefly interested in drawings of bas-reliefs in the frieze of the temple of Minerva in Athens, works by Phidias. Nothing more beautiful than these few simple figures can be imagined. Generally speaking, the many objects that were drawn had little charm; the surroundings were unattractive, the architecture was better.

Farewell for today. My bust is being made, and that has cost me three mornings this week.

August 28, 1787.

In the last few days many good things have come my way, and for my birthday today I received Herder's little book filled with worthy thoughts about God.[56] It consoled me to read something so pure and beautiful in this Babel, this source of so much deceit and error, and to think that this, after all, is now the time when such sentiments and feelings can and may be disseminated. I shall read this little book many more times in my solitude, take it to heart, and also make annotations to it that may lead to future discussions.

With respect to art, I have been gaining ground steadily in the last few days, and now can survey almost the whole task I still have to complete; and when it is completed, nothing will yet have been done. Perhaps it will give others an incentive to do better and more easily that to which their talent and aptitude direct them.

The French Academy[57] has exhibited its works, among them some very interesting things. Pindar,[58] who asks the gods for a happy demise, falls into the arms of a boy he loves very much, and dies. This picture has much merit. An architect has carried out a very pleasing idea, he has drawn present-day Rome from an angle which makes all of its parts look very good. Then on another sheet he has depicted ancient Rome, as if seen from the same perspective. It is known where the old monuments stood, and mostly what their form was, and the ruins of many are still standing. Now he has removed everything new, and has restored the old as it may have looked approximately in Diocletian's time, with as much taste as effort, and charmingly colored.

I do what I can, and take on as many of these concepts and talents as I can carry, and in this way shall manage to bring home what is most reliable.

Have I told you, Herder, that Trippel[59] is working on a bust of me? The Prince of Waldeck has commissioned him to make it, and the general impression is good. It is being worked in a very solid style. When the clay model is completed, he will make a plaster cast of it, and then immediately start on the marble, which he wants to finish from life; for what can be done in this material is unattainable in any other.

Angelica is now painting a picture that will turn out very well: the mother of the Gracchi showing off her children as her best treasures to a woman friend who was displaying her jewels. It is a natural and very successful composition.

How fine it is to sow, and reap a harvest! I have kept it completely secret here that today is my birthday, but I thought, when I got up: will nothing come from home for my celebration? And see, then your packet was brought to me, which delights me more than I can say. I sat right down to read it, and now that I am finished, I am writing at once to express my most cordial thanks to you.

Now I would really like to be with all of you, then a conversation would start in which we could enlarge on several points I have marked. Never mind, we shall have that too, and I thank you very much, Herder, for erecting a column from which we can now count our miles. I am walking with a firm tread in the fields of nature and art, and shall gladly come to meet you halfway from that direction.

Today, after receiving your letter, I carefully thought matters over once more, and must persist in this: my study of art, my activity as an author, all still require this time. I must advance in art to the point where everything becomes intuitive knowledge, where nothing remains tradition and name, and I shall make that happen in this half year; also, it can happen nowhere else but in Rome. I must at least finish my little works (for they seem very diminutive to me) with joy and composure.

Then everything will draw me back to the fatherland. And even if I were to lead an isolated, private life, I have so much to catch up on and combine that I can see no rest for ten years.

I am bringing back natural history specimens for you, Herder, that you do not expect. I believe I am coming very close to the How of structure. You will view these manifestations (not fulgurations)[60] of our God with delight, and then inform me who in ancient or modern times found and thought the same thing, and considered it from the same or a slightly different standpoint.

Report

August

At the beginning of the month I definitely made up my mind to remain in Rome also the coming winter. What finally decided me was my feeling and perception that I would be leaving this situation without having attained anything like maturity, and that nowhere else would I find such latitude and tranquillity for finishing my works. And now, once I had sent this announcement back home, a period of a new kind began.

The great heat gradually grew more intense and limited my all too energetic activities. It made me seek out places where I could spend my time profitably in pleasant quiet and coolness, and the Sistine chapel offered the best opportunity for this. It was just at this time that Michelangelo had again won the esteem of artists; in addition to his other great qualities, he was said to be unsurpassed even as a colorist, and it became fashionable to argue whether he or Raphael was the greater genius. The latter's *Transfiguration* was criticized very severely at times, and the *Dispute* was called his best work. This already heralded the predilection for works of the older school which arose later. But the quiet observer saw this only as an indication of inferior and unliberated talents, and could never take kindly to it.

It is hard enough to comprehend one great talent, let alone two at once. We make this easier for ourselves through partisanship, which is why the appreciation of artists and writers always fluctuates, and one or the other always exclusively dominates the day. Such disputes could not perplex me, since I did not enter into them, and occupied myself with direct contemplation of everything valuable and estimable. The artists quickly made their preference for the great Florentine known to the art lovers, and indeed, at this very time, Bury and Lips[61] had a commission from Count Fries to make watercolor copies in the Sistine chapel. We paid the custodian so well that he would let us in through the back door by the altar, and we did as we pleased inside. We also brought some food along, and I remember that once, when I was tired from the heat of the day, I indulged in a midday nap on the papal chair.

We made careful tracings of the lower heads and figures of the altarpiece, which we could reach with a ladder. First these were drawn with white chalk on framed pieces of black gauze, then with red chalk on large sheets of paper.

Inasmuch as people were turning to the older painters, Leonardo da Vinci became equally famous, and I went to see his highly esteemed picture, *Christ among the Pharisees,* in the Aldobrandini gallery with Angelica. It had become customary for her to drive by my place at noon on Sunday with her husband and Councilor Reiffenstein, and then, with as much composure as possible, we would proceed through the ovenlike heat to some collection, spend a few hours there, and then return to her house for a substantial meal. Each of these three persons was in his own way theoretically, practically, esthetically, and technically educated, and it was most instructive to talk with them in the presence of such significant artworks.

Sir Richard Worthley, who had returned from Greece, kindly let us see the drawings he had brought back. Among them, the reproductions of Phidias's works in the fronton of the Acropolis made a decided and indelible impression on me, an all the stronger one since Michelangelo's mighty figures had inspired me to devote more attention and study to the human body than heretofore.

But the exhibition of the French Academy at the end of the month created a great sensation in the lively art world. David's *Horatians*[62] had tipped the scales in favor of the French. It inspired Tischbein to begin his life-size *Hector Challenging Paris in the Presence of Helen.*[63] The fame of the French is now being upheld by Drouais, Gagneraux, Desmarais, Gauffier, and St. Ours, and Boquet[64] is making a good name for himself as a landscape painter in the style of Poussin.

Meanwhile Moritz had been applying himself to ancient mythology; he had come to Rome to write a travel book, and thus earn enough money for his journey, as he had done before. A publisher[65] had given him an advance, but during his stay in Rome he soon realized that he could not, with impunity, write a free and easy journal. As a result of our daily conversations and the contemplation of so many important artworks, he was stirred with the thought of writing a classical mythology from a purely human point of view, and to publish it later with illustrative drawings copied from carved stones. He worked diligently on it, and our group did not fail to exert some influence by discussing it with him.

I entered into an extremely pleasant, informative conversation, one directly coinciding with my wishes and goals, with the sculptor Trippel in his studio, as he was modeling my bust, which he was supposed to finish in marble for the Prince of Waldeck. Probably under no other conditions could I have come straight to a study of the human figure and had its proportions, both in ideal form and in divergent character, explained to me. This moment was made doubly interesting by the fact that Trippel had found out about a head of Apollo[66] which had previously lain unheeded in the Giustiniani palace collection. He considered it to be one of the noblest artworks, and nurtured the hope of buying it, which, however, was not fulfilled. The ancient sculpture has since become famous, and later went to Mr. de Pourtalès in Neuchâtel.

But I was like a man who had ventured out to sea and is compelled by wind and weather to steer now in this direction, now in that. Verschaffelt started a course in perspective, for which we gathered in the evening, and a numerous company listened to his teaching and immediately put it into practice. The best part was that we learned just enough, and not too much.

People would have liked to tear me away from this contemplatively active, busy tranquillity. Our unfortunate concert was much discussed in Rome, where gossiping about the events of the day is as customary as in small towns; attention had been drawn to me and my writings; I had read *Iphigenia* and other works aloud before gatherings of friends, and this too was a subject for discussion. Cardinal Buoncompagni demanded to see me, but I steadfastly remained in my familiar hermitage and could do so the more easily because Councilor Reiffenstein maintained firmly and obstinately that, since I had not let *him* present me, no one else could. This worked very much to my advantage, and I always made use of his prestige to preserve my self-imposed and unequivocal solitude.

September

Correspondence

September 1, 1787.

Today I can say *Egmont* has been finished; I still did some work recently on various parts of it. I am sending it via Zurich, because I want Kayser[67] to compose entr'actes for it and whatever other music is necessary. Then I wish you joy in reading it.

My artistic studies are proceeding nicely, my principle is universally applicable and explains everything to me. All the things that artists, with great effort, are forced to gather one by one now lie assembled before me openly and freely. I now see how much I do not know, and the way is open for me to know and comprehend everything.

Herder's ideas about God have been of great benefit to Moritz. They have certainly caused a turning point in his life, he has taken them to heart, and was prepared for them by his association with me. He burst into bright flames, like well-dried wood.

Rome, September 3.

Today it has been a year since my departure from Carlsbad. What a year! And what a singular turning point this day was for me, the duke's birthday and the day of my birth into a new life. At the moment, I can evaluate neither for myself nor others how I have used this year; I am hoping the time will come, the beautiful hour, when I can sum it all up with you.

My studies here are now only beginning, and I would not have seen Rome at all if I had left earlier. It cannot even be imagined what there is to see and learn here; away from Rome one can have no conception of it.

I have returned to the Egyptian relics. Recently I went several times to see the great obelisk which still lies broken up amidst rubbish and filth in a courtyard. It was the obelisk of Sesostris,[68] set up in Rome in honor of Augustus, and it stood as the gnomon to the great sundial that was formerly drawn on the surface of the Campus Martius. This, the oldest and most magnificent of many such monuments, now lies there in pieces, some sides of it defaced (probably by fire). And yet it still survives, and the undestroyed sides are still as fresh as though made yesterday, and worked most beautifully (after their fashion). I now am having molds made of one sphinx at the top, and of the faces of sphinxes, humans, and birds, for casting in plaster. I have to possess these invaluable things, especially since it is said that the pope wants to have it set up again, which would put the hieroglyphics out of reach. I want to do the same with the best Etrurian objects, etc. Now I am modeling in clay from these forms, in order to make it all really my own.

September 5.

I must write to you on a morning that is becoming a festive one for me. For today *Egmont* has really been completely finished. The title and list of characters are written, and I have filled in a few gaps that were left; now I am already anticipating the hour when you will receive and read it. Several drawings are also to be enclosed.

September 6.

I had intended to write you a great deal and say all sorts of things about your last letter, but now I have been interrupted, and tomorrow I am going to Frascati. The letter must be posted on Saturday, and I shall just say a few words now in farewell. Probably you also have the fine weather that we are enjoying under this more open sky. I keep having new thoughts, and since there are thousands of objects around me, they awaken me now to this idea, now to that. Everything is coming together at one point from many directions, so to speak, indeed I can now see clearly where I and my abilities are heading. I have had to get as old as this in order to have a tolerable understanding of my condition. So the Swabians are not the only ones who need forty years to grow wise.

I hear that Herder is not well, and this worries me; I hope to have better news soon.

I am still feeling good in body and soul, and can almost hope that the cure will be permanent. Everything seems easy for me to do, and sometimes a breeze from my youth wafts over to me. *Egmont* is going off with this letter, but will arrive later, because I am sending it by mail coach. I am quite curious and eager to hear what all of you will say about it.

Perhaps it would be good to start the printing soon. I would be delighted to have the play reach the public while it is still so fresh. Try to arrange that; I shall not delay with the remainder of the volume.

Herder's *God* is excellent company for me. Moritz is really elated with it, almost as if this work was all that was needed to put the keystone to his thoughts, which were always about to fall apart. His book[69] is becoming quite good. As for me, I feel encouraged to continue my study of natural things, in which, especially in botany, I have hit upon a ἓν καὶ πᾶν[70] that astonishes me. I myself cannot yet see how far its implications reach.

Every time I apply it, I become more convinced of the correctness of my principle for explaining artworks and elucidating all at once what artists and connoisseurs have been seeking and studying in vain ever since the restoration of art. It is really like Columbus's egg. Without revealing that I have this master key, I now discuss the parts with the artists in a relevant manner, and see how far they have come, what they have, and where there is a difficulty. I have opened the door, and am standing on the threshold, but unfortunately it is only from there that I shall be able to look around the temple before I leave again.

This much is certain: the ancient artists had as great a knowledge of nature as Homer, and just as sure a notion as he of what can be depicted, and how it must be depicted. Unfortunately, the number of first-class artworks is much too small. When one sees these, however, there is nothing more to wish for than to appreciate them properly, and then depart in peace. These sublime works of art are also the sublimest works of nature, created by men following true and natural laws. Everything arbitrary, everything imaginary crumbles away, there we have necessity, there we have God.

In a few days I shall see the works of a skilled architect who was himself in Palmyra,[71] and drew the objects there with great understanding and taste. I shall report on them at once, and then eagerly await your thoughts about these important ruins.

Rejoice with me that I am happy, indeed I can say with assurance that I have never been as happy as this: it is certainly not a small thing to be able to satisfy an inborn passion in the greatest peace and purity, and be entitled to promise oneself lasting profit from a continual pleasure. If I could only impart some of my pleasurable feelings to my dear friends!

I hope that the dark clouds in the political sky will dissipate.[72] Our modern wars make many people unhappy while they last, and no one happy when they are over.

September 12, 1787.

My dear friends, probably nothing can alter the fact that I am a person who lives on labor. In recent days I have again spent more time working that enjoying. Now the week is ending, and you shall have a letter.

It is a pity that the aloe in the Belvedere[73] has chosen this particular year to bloom, when I am absent. I was in Sicily too early, and here only one is blooming this year, not a large blossom, and so high up that one cannot reach it. To be sure, an Indian plant is not really at home even in these parts.

The Englishman's[74] descriptions give me little pleasure. The clergy has to tread very cautiously in England, but, on the other hand, it has the rest of the public on the run. The free Englishman must keep within strict limits in his moral writings.

I am not surprised by the tailed people,[75] judging from the description it is something very natural. Far stranger things meet our eyes daily, but we take no notice of them because they are not as closely related to us.

B.[76] is like many people who have no genuine religious feeling during their lives but grow pious, as it is called, in their old age, and that is quite all right, unless we are supposed to be edified by them.

For several days I was in Frascati with Councilor Reiffenstein, Angelica came on Sunday to call for us. It is a paradise.

Erwin and Elmira[77] is already half rewritten. I have tried to give the little play more life and interest, and have completely discarded the extremely insipid dialogue. It is a juvenile work, or rather, scribble. The charming songs, on which everything turns, of course all remain.

I am also pursuing the arts with all my might and main.

My bust has turned out very well; everyone is satisfied with it. Certainly it is fashioned in a beautiful and noble style, and I do not mind if this idea of my appearance lives on in the world. The carving in marble will now begin at once, and finally the marble will also be worked on from life. Transport is so cumbersome, otherwise I would send a copy of it at once; perhaps sometime by ship, for, after all, I shall eventually be packing up several cases.

Has Kranz not arrived yet with the box I gave him for the children?

Now, after two miserable failures, they again have quite a charming operetta at the theater in Valle. The cast acts with much enthusiasm, and everything harmonizes. Now I shall soon go out to the country. It has rained several times, the weather has cooled off, and the region is becoming green again.

The newspapers will tell you, or have already done so, about the great eruption of Etna.

September 15.

Now I have also read Trenck's[78] autobiography. It is quite interesting, and quite a few reflections can be made on it.

Tomorrow I shall meet a remarkable traveler,[79] and my next letter will tell you about that.

Moreover, be glad about my sojourn here! Rome is now quite familiar to me, and I hardly think there is anything left in it that would be beyond my powers. The art objects have gradually raised me up to their level. I am enjoying ever more purely, more knowledgeably, and good fortune will help me to go ever farther.

I have enclosed another sheet,[80] and would like to have it copied and shown to our friends. Another reason why my sojourn in Rome is so interesting is that this is a central point toward which so much is attracted. The drawings by Cassas are extraordinarily beautiful. In thought, I have stolen some things from him, and shall bring them along home to you.

I am always hard at work. Now I have drawn a little head from a plaster cast, in order to see whether my principle holds true. I find that it suits perfectly and facilitates the work amazingly. No one wanted to believe I had done it, and yet it is still really nothing. I see now how far one could progress with application.

Monday I am going to Frascati again. Nevertheless, I shall see to it that a letter is sent off a week from today. Then I shall probably go to Albano. I shall be drawing very diligently from nature. My sole desire now is to produce something and really pursue my inclination. I have suffered from this illness from youth onwards, and may God grant that I be relieved of it someday.

September 22.

Yesterday there was a procession in which they carried around the blood of St. Francis; while the monks were filing past I paid close attention to heads and faces.

I have acquired a collection of two hundred of the best imprints of ancient gems. They are the most beautiful ones of ancient make in existence, and were partly chosen also because of their pretty ideas. There is nothing more precious that one can take back from Rome, especially since the imprints are so extraordinarily beautiful and sharp.

How many good things I shall bring along with me when I return in my little ship, but, above all, a joyful heart that is more capable of savoring the happiness wished for me by your love and friendship! Only I must never again undertake anything that lies beyond the scope of my ability, where I just toil and accomplish nothing.

September 22.

I must hastily send you one more page, my dear friends, with this mail. Today has been a very noteworthy day for me. Letters from many friends, from the dowager duchess, news of the celebration held on my birthday,[81] and finally my writings.

It really gives me a strange feeling to have these four slender little volumes,[82] the products of half a lifetime, seek me out in Rome. I can truly say: there is not a letter of them that I did not live, feel, enjoy, suffer, or think, and now they all have that much stronger an appeal for me. My concern and hope is that the four subsequent volumes will not lag behind. I thank you for all that you have done for these pages, and I want to be able to bring you pleasure too. Do, with faithful hearts, look after the subsequent ones also!

You tease me about saying "provinces,"[83] and I admit that the expression is very inappropriate. But from that you can see how accustomed one becomes in Rome to think of everything in a grandiose way. It really seems I am becoming naturalized, for people accuse the Romans of only wanting to hear and speak of *cose grosse*.[84]

I am always hard at work and am now concentrating on the human figure. Oh, how long and wide art is, and how infinite the world becomes when one is trying to concentrate strictly on the finite.

On Tuesday the 25th I am going to Frascati, and there too I shall work hard. I am now beginning to succeed. If only I would truly succeed.

It has struck me that in a large city, in a wide circle, even the poorest, humblest person feels that he has his place, while in a small town the best, richest one does not, and cannot breathe freely.

Frascati, September 28, 1787.

I am very happy here, all day long and into the night I draw, paint, color, glue, and do arts and crafts quite *ex professo*.[85] My host, Councilor Reiffenstein, keeps me company, and we are lively and merry. In the evening we visit the villas by moonlight and draw their most striking motifs even in the dark. We have discovered several that I want to make finished drawings of sometime. Now I hope that the time will also come when my technique is perfected. But when one sees far, perfection lies only too far off.

Yesterday we drove to Albano and back, and on the way also shot many birds in flight. Here, in the midst of great profusion, one can profit from it, and really I am burning with a desire to assimilate everything; I feel that my taste is becoming more refined with every object my mind absorbs. If only, instead of all this talking, I could send you something good for once! Several trifles are going off to you with a fellow countryman.

I shall probably have the pleasure of seeing Kayser in Rome. So, then, music will join me too, and the circle of arts dancing around me will be complete, almost as if they wanted to keep me from attending to my friends. And yet I hardly dare broach the subject of how lonely I often feel, and how I am gripped by a longing to be with you. Basically, I just reel along from day to day, neither able nor willing to think further.

I spend quite profitable hours with Moritz and have begun to explain my plant system to him, and to write down in his presence how far we have progressed every time. This is the only way I have been able to put some of my thoughts on paper. But, in my new pupil, I can see how comprehensible even the most abstract points of this theory become when I expound it by the right method and find a prepared mind. He delights in it and keeps moving ahead with conclusions of his own. But, at all events, it is hard to write about, and impossible to comprehend merely by reading, even if it were all written ever so explicitly and vividly.

So I live happily, because I am about my Father's business. My greetings to all who wish me well in this, and help me directly or indirectly, and support and maintain me.

Report

September

This day, the third of September, was a doubly and triply noteworthy one for me to celebrate. It was the birthday of my prince, who has requited my loyal affection with such manifold benefits. It was the anniversary of my hegira from Carlsbad, and as yet I could not review what effect this wholly foreign situation, which I had experienced in such a significant way, had had on me, what it had brought to me, and bestowed on me; for I did not have time for much reflection.

The peculiar great advantage of Rome is that it must be considered a center of artistic activity. Cultured travelers stop by and gain great profit from their stay here, whether short or long; they travel on, actively accumulating knowledge, and when they return home enriched, they deem it an honor and a pleasure to display what they have learned, and to pay a debt of gratitude both to their distant and their local teachers.

A French architect named Cassas returned from his trip to the Orient. He had taken the measurements of the most important ancient monuments, especially of those not yet published, and had also drawn the areas as they should be viewed. He had likewise made pictorial representations of ancient buildings that are in a dilapidated and ruined condition, and he had outlined some of his very precise and tasteful drawings with pen and ink, using watercolors to present them vividly to the eye.

1. The Seraglio of Constantinople from the seaside, with a part of the city and the Sophia mosque. The residence of the sovereign is built on the most delightful extremity of Europe, in the most pleasing manner imaginable. Tall trees, always carefully preserved, stand behind each other in large, mostly tight groups, amidst them one does not see, as might be expected, great walls and palaces, but little houses, lattice

work, passageways, kiosks, outspread tapestries, mingled in such a modest, friendly, homelike way that it is a delight. Since the drawing is finished in color, it makes a very pleasant effect. A beautiful expanse of sea washes the coast that is built up in this way. Asia lies opposite, and one looks into the straits which lead to the Dardanelles. The drawing is some seven feet long and three to four feet high.

2. General view of the ruins of Palmyra, of the same size.

Beforehand, he showed us a ground plan of the city, as he had deduced it from the ruins.

A colonnade, approximately an Italian mile long, went through the city from its gate up to the temple of the sun, but not in a completely straight line, for it made a slight bend in the middle. The colonnade was composed of four ranks of columns, each column ten diameters high. No roof is seen on top; he believes that tapestries served the purpose. In the foreground of the large drawing, a part of the colonnade is shown still standing upright. A caravan, moving across just then, is a very felicitous touch. In the background stands the temple of the sun, and on the right extends a broad plain, over which some Janissaries are rushing at full gallop. The most curious phenomenon is this: the picture ends in a blue line, like a strip of sea. He explained to us that the desert horizon, which inevitably becomes blue in the distance, closes the range of vision in a way so much like the sea that it deceives one's eye in nature as it had first deceived us in the picture, although we knew that Palmyra is some distance away from the sea.

3. Grave monuments of Palmyra.

4. Restoration of the temple of the Sun at Baalbek, also a landscape with the ruins as they stand.

5. The great mosque at Jerusalem, built on the foundations of Solomon's temple.

6. Ruins of a small temple in Phoenicia.

7. Area at the foot of Mt. Lebanon, as charming as can be imagined. A little pine forest, a lake bordered by weeping willows, grave monuments under them, the mountains in the distance.

8. Turkish grave monuments. Each gravestone bears the headdress of the deceased, and since the Turks are differentiated by their headdress, the rank of the buried person is immediately obvious. Flowers are raised with great care on the graves of virgins.

9. Egyptian pyramid with the great sphinx head. Cassas says that it was carved out of a limestone rock, and, because of the latter's cracks and unevenness, the colossus had been coated with stucco and painted, as can still be seen in the folds of the headdress. One section of the face is approximately ten feet high. He had been able to stroll comfortably on the lower lip.

10. A pyramid, restored on the basis of several documents, sugges-

tions, and conjectures. Halls, with obelisks standing next to them, project on four sides; leading to the halls are passageways decorated with sphinxes of a type still found in Upper Egypt. This drawing is the most immense architectural concept I have ever seen in my life, and I do not believe it is possible to go any farther.

In the evening, after having viewed these beautiful things in an easy, leisurely manner, we went into the gardens on the Palatine, which have made the spaces between the ruins of the imperial palaces arable and charming. There, in an open assembly area where, under magnificent trees, the fragments of decorated capitals, smooth and fluted columns, broken bas-reliefs, and other things of the kind had been set around in a wide circle, in the way tables, chairs, and benches are normally arranged for cheerful gatherings in the open air—there we enjoyed the delightful weather to our heart's content. And when, with freshly washed and cultivated eyes, we surveyed a most varied view at sundown, we had to admit that this picture still could hold its own with all the others shown us today. If drawn and colored by Cassas in the same taste, it would enchant everyone. And so our eye is gradually attuned by artistic works to become increasingly receptive to the presence of nature, and increasingly open to the beauties it offers.

The next day, however, it struck us as very amusing that the grandeur and limitlessness we had seen yesterday at the artist's should be the very thing to induce us to go to a mean, shabby place. Those magnificent Egyptian monuments brought back to mind the mighty obelisk erected by Augustus on the Campus Martius, which had served as a gnomon, but now lay in pieces in a dirty corner, fenced around by a wooden partition, and waiting for the bold architect who might be competent to resurrect it. (NB. Now it has been erected again on the Monte Citorio square, and is serving again, as in Roman times, as a gnomon.) It is carved out of the most genuine Egyptian granite and covered all over with charming, naive figures, although in the notorious style. As we stood next to the apex, which under other circumstances was raised high in the air, it was remarkable to see on its tapered surfaces the most elegant images of sphinx after sphinx, at other times accessible to no human eye, only to sunbeams. Here we have a case where the religious function of art is not calculated on any effect that is to be made on human sight. We arranged to have these sacred images cast in plaster, so that we could see in convenient proximity what normally was raised toward the cloudy regions.

In the disagreeable place where we found ourselves with this most worthy work, we could not help viewing Rome as a potpourri, but of a unique kind, for even as such this enormous locality has the greatest merits. Chance created nothing here, it only destroyed: everything standing upright is magnificent, everything demolished deserves respect, the deformity of the ruins points to ancient regularity, which came to the fore again in the grand new forms of the churches and palaces.

Those quickly made plaster casts reminded me that the large Dehn collection of paste replicas,[86] imprints of which were for sale either in complete or partial sets, also included some Egyptian ones; and, since one thing leads to another, I selected the most outstanding items from this collection, and ordered them from the present owners. Such imprints are the greatest treasure, and a foundation that the art lover with limited resources can lay for himself for future great and diverse benefits.

The first four volumes of my works published by Göschen had arrived, and the presentation copy was immediately placed in the hands of Angelica, who said that it gave her renewed cause to praise her mother tongue.

However, I could not indulge in the thoughts that thronged into my mind when I looked back on my earlier activities. I did not know how far the road I had started on would lead me, I could not see to what extent my earlier endeavors would succeed, and to what extent the results of my yearning and wandering would recompense me for the effort expended.

But I had neither the time nor place to look backwards and think. My ideas about organic nature and how it is formed and reformed, with which I had been, so to speak, inoculated, permitted no standing still; and since one conclusion after the other was developing in my mind as I cogitated, I needed some sort of daily and hourly communication, for my own enlightenment. I attempted it with Moritz, and, as well as I could, expounded the metamorphosis of plants to him. He, a peculiar vessel that was always empty and in need of refilling, thirsted for things he could absorb and made an honest effort to participate, at least to the extent that I was encouraged to continue my discourses.

Here, however, a noteworthy book proved to be, perhaps not of direct assistance, but surely of significance as a stimulus: Herder's laconically titled work, in which he took pains to state in conversational form various opinions about God and godly things. This work took me back to the times when, at the side of this excellent friend, I was often moved to discuss these matters orally. But this volume, with its lofty atmosphere of pious meditation, contrasted strangely with the veneration expected of us for the festival of a special saint.

On the 21st of September there was a celebration in memory of St. Francis, and his blood was carried around the city in a lengthy procession of monks and true believers. I grew attentive as these many monks walked by, their clothing so simple that my eye was drawn to contemplate only their faces. It struck me that the hair and beard are really part of what is needed for forming a concept of a male individual. At first with attentiveness, then with astonishment, I inspected the line passing before me and was truly delighted to see that a face framed by hair and beard looked quite different from the beardless populace around me. And now I was convinced that such faces, if depicted in paintings, would certainly appeal very strongly to the viewer.

Aulic Councilor Reiffenstein, who had become expert at his task of guiding and entertaining foreign visitors, could of course see all too soon, in the course of his activities, that persons who come to Rome equipped with little more than a desire to see and be amused become painfully bored now and then, since, in a foreign land, they are usually totally without their customary means of filling idle hours. This practical observer of human nature also realized that mere sightseeing can be very tiring, and that it is necessary to entertain and calm one's friends with some sort of personal activity. Therefore he had selected two things toward which he usually directed their energies: encaustic painting and the manufacture of paste replicas. The first of these arts, which involves application of a wax soap to bond the colors, had only recently been reintroduced. Since the main concern of the art world is to keep artists busy in some fashion, a new method of doing old, familiar things always rekindles interest. It gives people a strong stimulus to attempt in a new way what they would not care to undertake in the old one.

The bold enterprise of actually copying Raphael's loggias for the Empress Catherine, so that this entire piece of architecture could be reproduced in St. Petersburg, was favored by this new technique, indeed, perhaps could not have been accomplished without it. The same panels, wall sections, socles, pilasters, capitals, and cornices were ordered to be made out of the strongest planks and blocks of a durable chestnut wood, and these were covered with linen, which, when primed, served as a secure base for the encaustic. This work, which had occupied Unterberger[87] for several years under Reiffenstein's direction, and was executed very scrupulously, had already been sent off when I arrived, and only the remains of the undertaking gave me some tangible idea of it.

But now, because of this project, encaustic painting became highly esteemed. Foreign visitors with some talent felt obliged to get practical knowledge of it; ready-made sets of paints were available at a low price; people cooked the soap themselves; in short, there was always something to do or putter with, whenever a free, idle moment presented itself. Also, mediocre artists were employed as teachers and assistants, and, indeed, several times I saw foreign visitors pack up their Roman encaustics and take them back home, deluded into very comfortably thinking that these were their own work.

The other occupation, that of manufacturing paste replicas, was more suitable for men. The best facilities for it were provided by a big old vaulted kitchen in Reiffenstein's district. Here we had more than enough room for this work. The refractory infusible mass was very finely pulverized and sifted, the dough kneaded out of it was pressed into a form, carefully dried, and then, surrounded with an iron ring, was placed on the fire; next, the molten mass of glass was pressed on it, and by this process a little artwork appeared that could not fail to delight anyone who had created it with his own hands.

Aulic Councilor Reiffenstein, who had found me willing and eager to be initiated into these activities, very soon noticed that a prolonged occupation of this kind did not appeal to me, that my actual inclination was to increase the powers of my hand and eyes by reproducing artistic and natural objects. So the intense heat was hardly over when he took me to Frascati, together with several artists, where we found accommodations and everything we needed in a well-appointed private house. After we had spent the whole day outdoors, we liked to gather in the evening around a large maple table. Georg Schütz from Frankfurt—adept, but not an outstanding talent, more given to a certain gentlemanly ease than to sustained artistic effort, for which reason the Romans also called him "il barone"—accompanied me on my walks and was useful to me in many ways. If one considers that for centuries the finest architecture flourished here, that the artistic ideas of first-rate minds took visible form and rose up on mighty substructures remaining from ancient times, then one can understand how charmed the eye and mind must be when, in every kind of light, one sees these multiple horizontal and thousands of vertical lines, interrupted and adorned, like a mute music, and how, not without pain, everything petty and narrow-minded in us is dislodged and driven out. Especially indescribable is the richness of the moonlight scenes, where individual enjoyable—perhaps they should be called intrusive—details recede, and there are only the great masses of light and shadow, which fill the eye with hugely graceful, symmetrically harmonious, colossal shapes. On the other hand, we did not lack for instructive, but also often playful, conversations in the evening.

Accordingly, we may not keep it secret that young artists who knew and noted our worthy Reiffenstein's peculiarities, usually called weaknesses, often talked about them privately in a mocking or joking manner. One evening, we were again discussing the *Apollo Belvedere,* which is an inexhaustible subject of conversation for artists, and someone remarked that the ears on its superb head were not especially well done. This quite naturally led the discussion around to the dignity and beauty of the organ in question, the difficulty of finding a beautiful example of it in nature, and of reproducing it equally well in art. Since Schütz was noted for his comely ears, I asked him to sit for me next to the lamp until I had carefully drawn the one that was especially well-shaped, which was unquestionably his right ear. In his rigid model's position, he happened to be sitting directly opposite Councilor Reiffenstein, from whom he was neither permitted nor able to avert his eyes. Now the former began to recite the precepts that he repeatedly extolled: namely, one must not immediately turn to the best, but first begin with the Carraccis, specifically those in the Farnese gallery, then proceed to Raphael, and at last draw the *Apollo Belvedere* often enough to know it by heart, and beyond that there would not be much else to hope or wish for.

Poor Schütz was seized by such an attack of silent laughter that he could hardly hold it in, and the longer I tried to keep him from moving, the worse his torment grew. Thus a teacher and benefactor can always expect mocking ingratitude if he has taken some individualistic, unreasonable stance.

We saw a splendid, although not unexpected, view from the windows of the villa of Prince Aldobrandini, who was out in the country just at that time. He kindly sent us an invitation, and entertained us festively at a bountiful table, in company with his clerical and secular retainers. As can be imagined, the mansion was designed in such a way that the magnificence of the hills and plain could be surveyed from it at a glance. Much is said about pleasant country seats; but the view from here convinces me that few houses could be more pleasantly situated than this one.

Here, however, I feel obliged to insert an observation whose serious significance warrants my commending it to your attention. It sheds light both over what has already been stated and what will follow; moreover, many an intelligent person who is developing culturally will be moved to self-examination by it.

Individuals whose minds are making lively progress are not satisfied with enjoying art, they demand knowledge. The latter stimulates them to personal activity, and, whatever success this may have, they come to the conclusion that nothing can be judged correctly except what one can produce oneself. But it is not easy for a person to see his way clearly in this matter, and that results in certain false endeavors, which become the more meticulous, the purer and sincerer his intention is. However, doubts and suspicions did begin to arise in me at this time, making me uneasy in the midst of these pleasant conditions; for soon I could not escape the feeling that the real wish and purpose of my stay would hardly be fulfilled.

But then, after an interval of several delightful days, we returned to Rome, where we were to be compensated for the loss of the open sky by a new, most charming opera in the bright, densely crowded theater auditorium. The German artists' bench, one of those at the front of the parterre, was, as usual, fully occupied, and this time too, so as to pay our obligations for present and past pleasures, we did not spare our applause and shouting. Indeed, by artfully crying "Zitti!"[88] at first rather softly, then more loudly, and finally in a commanding tone, we managed to silence the quite noisily chattering audience whenever the ritornello was played at the beginning of a favorite aria or some other enjoyable passage. For this reason, our friends up on stage showed us the courtesy of directing their most interesting presentations toward our side.

October

Correspondence

Frascati, October 2.

I must begin this little page at once if you are to receive it punctually. Actually I have much, and not much, to say. I continue to draw, and quietly think of my friends while doing so. Lately, great longing for home came over me again, perhaps because I feel the lack of what is dearest to me, even though things are going so well for me here.

I am in a really strange situation, but intend to pull myself together, use every day profitably, do what is to be done, and so work throughout this winter.

You will not believe how beneficial, but also how difficult it has been for me to live this whole year absolutely among strangers, especially since Tischbein—let this be kept in confidence—has not turned out as I hoped. He is a really good person, but not as pure, natural, and open as he seems in his letters. To avoid being unjust to him, I can only describe his character to you orally, and yet what does a description of that kind amount to? A person's life is his character. Now I have hope that Kayser will come, and he will be a great delight to me. May Heaven grant that nothing prevents this!

It is, and remains, my first concern to achieve a certain degree of skill in drawing, so that I can do something with ease, and not regress again, or be so long at a standstill, since unfortunately I have let the best time of my life slip by. But it is necessary to make excuses for oneself. To draw for the sake of drawing would be like talking for the sake of talking. If I have nothing to express, if nothing stimulates me, if I first have to search laboriously for worthy subjects, and even then can hardly find them, where will the urge to imitate come from? In these surroundings, one has to become an artist, because everything foists itself on one, one becomes fuller and fuller, and is compelled to make something. With my aptitude and knowledge of the way, I am convinced that I would progress very far here in a few years.

You have asked me, my dear friends, to write about myself, and can see how I am doing it. When we meet again, you shall hear quite a few things. I have had the opportunity to reflect a great deal about myself and others, about the world and history, and, in my fashion, I shall tell you many good things, even though they are not new. Eventually, everything will be contained and included in *Wilhelm*.

Thus far, Moritz has remained my favorite companion, although, in his case, I feared, and almost still do, that he will merely grow cleverer from his association with me, and neither more correct, nor better, nor happier, a worry that always restrains me from being completely open with him.

In general, I am quite content to live with several other people. I observe each individual's disposition and behavior. One wastes his time, the other does not; the latter will advance, the former, hardly. One gathers, one scatters. One is easily satisfied, the other, never. This one has talent, and does not use it, that one has none, and works hard, etc. I see all that, and myself in the middle of it; I am amused, and do not get out of humor, because I am not closely involved with these people, and am not responsible for them in any way. Only if each individual, my dear friends, while acting in his own way, nevertheless demands that we should become, be, and remain a whole—demanding it, first of all, of me—then I shall have no alternative but to leave or go mad.

Albano, October 5, 1787.

I intend to send this letter to Rome with tomorrow's mail, and shall say on this sheet only a thousandth part of what I have to say.

Yesterday, when I was about to drive away from Frascati, I received your letters, along with *Scattered Leaves* (I prefer "gathered"), the *Ideas,* and the four morocco volumes.[89] Now I have a rich supply for the whole *villegiatura.*[90]

I read "Persepolis"[91] last night. I am greatly delighted with it, but I cannot add anything to it, because that art and manner did not migrate here. Now I want to go to some library and see the books that were cited, and then thank all of you again. I beg you, continue, or continue because you must, illuminate everything with your light!

I have not yet touched the *Ideas* and the poems.[92] Let my writings go to press now, I shall continue to work faithfully. The four copper-plates for the last volumes are to be made here.

Our relationship with the men you mentioned was only a good-natured truce on both sides, as I well know; not much can come of it. The distance between us will continue to widen, and, if matters go well, it will quietly, informally, become a separation. The one man[93] is a fool whose head is stuffed with pretensions to simplicity. "My mother has geese" can be sung naively with more ease than "Honor be alone to God on high." Indeed, he is also a ___: "They are not confused by hay and straw, by hay and straw," etc., etc. Stay away from this tribe! The first ingratitude is better than the last. The second man[94] thinks he is coming from a foreign land to his own kind,[95] and comes to people who are looking for themselves, without wanting to admit it. He will find himself to be a stranger, and perhaps not know why. Unless I am much mistaken, the magnanimity of Alcibiades[96] is a sleight-of-hand trick of the Zurich prophet,[97] who is clever and skillful enough to exchange and mix up big and little balls with incredible dexterity, in order to make true and false appear and disappear, as his theological-poetical feelings dictate. May the Devil, who is a friend of lies, de-monology, premonitions, longings, etc., from the beginning, take or preserve him!

And I must get out a new sheet of paper, and ask you to read more with your spirit than your eyes, just as I am writing more with my soul than my hand.

Continue, dear brother Herder, to find, to combine, to compose poetry, to write, without worrying about other people. One must write as one lives, first for one's own sake; and then one also exists for kindred natures.

Plato would tolerate no ἀγεωμέτρητον[98] in his school; if I were able to found one, I would tolerate no one in it who had not chosen to study some aspect of nature seriously and exactly. Recently, I found the following nonsensical words in a tiresomely apostolic and Capuchin-like declamation by the Zurich prophet: "Everything that has life lives through something outside of itself."[99] Or it sounded approximately like that. Someone claiming to be a missionary to the heathen can write that, and his guardian angel does not pluck him by the sleeve as he revises? They have not grasped the first, most elementary truths of nature, and yet would be only too pleased to sit on the chairs around the throne, where other people belong, or where no one belongs. Leave it all at that, as I do also, although now, of course, it is easier for me!

I would prefer not to describe my life, because it would look far too merry. I am mainly engaged in drawing landscapes, and this sky and this earth make it a particularly inviting task. I have even found several idyllic scenes. How much more I shall still do! I see very well that a person like me only needs to be constantly surrounded by new objects, then he is safe.

Fare well and happily, and, should you have troubles, just remember that you are *together,* and what you mean to each other, whereas I, a voluntary exile, who intentionally goes astray, is purposely unwise, a

stranger everywhere, and everywhere at home, do not so much lead
my life as let it take its course, and, in any case, do not know where
it is heading.

Farewell, remember me to our Lady Duchess. In Frascati, Councilor
Reiffenstein and I planned her whole stay. If everything works out, it
will be a masterpiece. We are now in the midst of negotiations for a
villa that is, so to speak, in sequestration. Therefore it can be *rented,*
unlike other villas, which are either occupied, or would be vacated by
the great families only as a favor, which, in turn, would involve obligations and social relationships. I shall write just as soon as something
more definite can be said. There is also a beautiful detached house with
a garden ready for her in Rome. And so I want her to feel at home
everywhere, for otherwise she will not enjoy anything; time passes,
the money is spent, and one looks around as though for a bird that has
escaped from one's hand. If I can arrange everything for her so that
she will not dash her foot against a stone, I shall do it.[100]

Now I can write no more, even though there is still space. Farewell,
and excuse the hastiness of these lines.

Castel Gandolfo, October 8, actually the 12th,

for this week has gone by without my having a opportunity to write.
Therefore this little missive is hastily going to Rome, so that it will still
reach you.

We live here as one does in a spa, except that in the morning I go
off by myself to draw. Then for the rest of the day I must be part of
the company, which suits me quite well for this brief period. After all,
for once I am seeing people, and many of them at once, without sacrificing much time.

Angelica is also here, and is staying nearby; then, partly in this house,
and partly in the vicinity, there are some lively girls, some women,
and Mr. von Maron,[101] Mengs's brother-in-law, with his wife; it is a
merry group, and there is always something to laugh about. In the evening, we go to the comedy, where Pulcinella is the main personage,
and the next day we keep repeating the bons mots of the previous evening. *Tout comme chez nous*—except beneath a bright, exquisite sky.
Today a wind has come up and is keeping me at home. If anything
could coax me out of my shell, it would be these days, but I always
retire into it again, and my whole inclination is toward art. Every day,
I get a new perception, and it would seem that at least I shall learn
how to see.

Erwin and Elmira is as good as finished; it is just a question of a few
mornings when I am in a writing mood; everything has been thought
out.

Herder has called upon me to supply Forster[102] with some questions
and speculations for his voyage around the world. I do not know where
I shall find the time to concentrate on that, even though I would do it
with great pleasure. We shall see.

No doubt you are already having cold, dreary days, while we look
forward to another whole month of taking walks. I cannot tell you how
delighted I am with Herder's *Ideas*. Since I have no messiah to wait
for, this is my dearest gospel. Give my greetings to all, in my thoughts
I am always with you, and love me.

You did not get a letter on the last mail day, my dear friends, because
the activity in Castel Gandolfo finally became much too hectic, and
also I did want to draw.[103] It was like being at one of our spas, and,
since I was living in a house that was always full of visitors, I had to
be sociable. As a result, I saw more Italians than in the whole past
year, and this too was a gratifying experience.

I became interested in a Milanese girl[104] during her week's stay; she
stood out to great advantage against the Roman girls with her naturalness, common sense, and good manners. Angelica was, as she always
is, sensible, kind, pleasant, obliging. One cannot help being her friend,
and a great deal can be learned from her, especially how to work, for
it is incredible how much she accomplishes.

For the last few days, the weather has been cool, and I am quite
pleased to be back in Rome again.

Yesterday evening, when I went to bed, I really felt the pleasure of
being here. It was as if I were laying myself down on a very broad,
secure base.

I would like to speak with Herder about his *God*. There is one main
point to be noted, I believe: this little book, like others, is taken to be
food, when it is actually the *bowl*. The person with nothing to put in
it finds it empty. Let me continue to allegorize a little, and Herder will
be the one best able to explain my allegory. Men can move considerable
weights with a lever and rollers; they use winches, block and tackle,
and so forth to shift the pieces of the obelisk. The greater the weight,
or the finer the adjustment (as, for example, in a clock), the more complicated, the more intricate, the mechanism will be, but still possess
the greatest inner unity. That is how all hypotheses are, or, rather, all
principles.—Someone who does not have much to move reaches for
the lever, and spurns my block and tackle; and what does a stonemason
want with an endless screw? When L. tries with all his might to make
truth out of a fairy tale, when J. wears himself out idolizing the shallow
sentiment of a childish brain, when C.[105] would like to turn himself
from a simple messenger into an evangelist, it is obvious that they would
abhor anything that shines more light into the depths of nature. Would

the first one say with impunity: "Everything that lives, lives through something outside of itself"? would the second not be ashamed about the confusion of concepts, the mixing up of the words *knowledge* and *belief, tradition* and *experience?* would the third not have to move down a few benches, if they were not absolutely determined to place their chairs around the throne of the Lamb? if they did not carefully avoid setting foot on the firm ground of nature, where everyone is only what he is, where we all have the same rights?

By comparison, take a book like the third part of the *Ideas,* see first what it is, and then ask whether the author could have written it without having that concept of God! By no means; for the noble, great, profound qualities that this book has, it has precisely *in, from,* and *through* that concept of God and the world.

So if there is any defect, it is not in the ware, but in the buyers, not in the machine, but in those who operate it. I always tolerated it with a quiet smile when they did not take me seriously in metaphysical conversations; but, as an artist, such matters need not concern me. Rather, my concern should be not to divulge the principle by and through which I work. For my part, let everyone keep his lever! I myself have been using the endless screw for a long time, and do so now with even more joy and ease.

Castel Gandolfo, October 12, 1787.

To Herder

Just a quick word, and first my warmest thanks for the *Ideas!* They have come to me as the most captivating gospel, and all the most interesting studies of my life converge in them. Everything I have labored over for so long is now presented to me most completely. How much desire for everything good you have given me, and renewed in me, with this book! I am still only in the first half of it. Please have the passage from Camper[106] that you refer to on page 159 written out in full for me as soon as possible, so that I can see which rules of the Greek artistic ideal he has discovered. I can only remember how he demonstrated profiles on the basis of prints. In addition, write to me, and excerpt whatever else you consider useful to me, so that I may know what progress has been made lately with these speculations; for I am still like a newborn babe. Does Lavater's *Physiognomy*[107] contain anything intelligent about that? I shall gladly respond to your appeal in behalf of Forster, although I really do not see how it will be possible; for I cannot pose any individual questions, I have to explain and ex-

pound my hypotheses fully. You know how hard that will be for me
to do in black and white. Just write me the last date for completion,
and where it is to be sent. I am now sitting among the reeds, and am
so busy cutting whistles that I never manage to blow them. If I undertake
it, I shall have to resort to dictation; and I really look on it as a hint.
It seems I am supposed to put my house in order in all respects, and
settle my accounts.

The hardest part for me will be that I have to take absolutely everything out of my head. After all, I do not have a single page of my
collected notes with me, not a drawing, nothing, and the newest books
are entirely lacking here.

I shall probably stay two more weeks in Castello, and lead the life
of a spa guest. In the morning, I draw, then there are people, and more
people. I am glad that I see them in a group, individually it would be
a great annoyance. Angelica is here and helps to make everything tolerable.

The pope is said to have news that Amsterdam has been captured
by the Prussians.[108] The next newspapers will bring us certainty. That
would be the first expedition in which our century displayed itself in
all its greatness. I call that a *sodezza!*[109] Without a blow being struck,
just a few bombs, and no one wants to continue fighting for the cause!
Farewell, I am a child of peace, and want to be at peace with the whole
world forever, since I have at last made peace with myself.

Rome, October 27, 1787.

I am back in this magic circle, and immediately feel myself under its
spell again, contented, quietly working away, forgetful of everything
besides myself, and the figures of my friends visit me peacefully and
amicably. I have spent the first days writing letters, have cursorily
looked over the drawings I made out in the country, new work will
begin next week. The hopes that Angelica expresses for my landscape
drawings, if certain conditions are met, are too flattering for me to
repeat. At any rate I shall persevere, in order to come nearer to what
I shall probably never attain.

I am eagerly awaiting news about the arrival of *Egmont* and your
opinion of it. Surely I have already written that Kayser is coming here?
I expect him in several days, with the now completed score for our
Scapineries.[110] You can imagine what a festive occasion that will be!
We shall immediately start on a new opera,[111] and *Claudina* and *Erwin*
will be revised in his presence, with his advice.

I have now finished reading Herder's *Ideas* and enjoyed the book
tremendously. The conclusion is splendid, true, and uplifting, but, like

the book itself, will be of benefit to people only in the course of time and perhaps under an assumed name. The more a thoughtful person adopts this attitude of mind, the happier he will become. I have also found, living among strangers during the past year, that all really intelligent persons, to a greater or lesser extent, in a subtler or cruder way, come to and abide by the conclusion that the moment is everything, and that a rational person's advantage consists only in his conducting himself in such a manner that his life, insofar as it is under his control, will contain the largest possible number of rational, happy moments.

If I were to say what I thought about that book and its conclusion, I would have to write another book. Now I open it at random and reread passages, delighting in every page, for it is beautifully conceived and written throughout.

I find the section on the Greek period especially beautiful; that I miss some corporalities—if I may put it thus—in the part on the Roman period can perhaps be imagined without my saying it. This is only natural. At present, this state, as it was, reposes in my mind purely as a mass; for me it is like the fatherland, something exclusive. But you, my friends, would have to determine the worth of this individual existence in relationship to the whole enormous world, whereupon, of course, much would shrivel and perhaps go up in smoke.

So the Coliseum still remains imposing for me, even if I think about the time when it was built and the fact that the populace which filled up this enormous circle was no longer the old Roman populace.

A book on Roman painting and sculpture has also made its way to us. It is a German product, and, what is worse, by a German nobleman.[112] He seems to be an energetic but pretentious young man, who has taken pains to go around, take notes, to hear, to listen, to read. He has been able to give his work the appearance of comprehensiveness, and there is much in it that is good and true, but, simultaneously, much that is false and silly, imagined and parroted, also longueurs and blunders. Anyone who peruses it, even far from Rome, will soon see what a freakish cross between a compilation and an original work this voluminous opus has become.

The arrival of *Egmont* delights me and sets my mind at rest, and I am eager to have your opinion of it. Probably that is en route now. The morocco copy has arrived, and I have given it to Angelica. We shall handle Kayser's opera not as we have been advised to do, but more cleverly; your suggestion is very good, when Kayser comes, you shall hear more.

The review is in the old man's[113] usual style, too much and too little. My only concern now is to *do,* ever since I see that what has been *done,* even if it is not the most perfect work, can be *reviewed* for thousands of years, that is, something can be told about its existence.

Everyone is amazed that I came through the heat without paying a toll; but they do not know how I behaved, either. Our October was not the best, although we had some heavenly days.

Now a new epoch is beginning for me. My heart and mind have been so expanded by all I have seen and appreciated that I must limit myself now to some sort of work. A person's individuality is a curious thing. I have really become well acquainted with mine now, since, on the one hand, I have depended only on myself this year, and, on the other, I have had to associate with complete strangers.

Report

October

At the beginning of this month, in mild, consistently sunny, splendid weather, we enjoyed a true *villegiatura* in Castel Gandolfo, which saw us initiated and adopted into the midst of this incomparable region. Mr. Jenkins, the wealthy English art dealer, resided there in a very stately building, the former dwelling of the Jesuit general, where for a number of friends there was no lack of comfortable accommodations, nor of salons for cheerful sociability, nor of colonnades for pleasant strolling.

The best way to visualize an autumn holiday like this is to imagine it as a sojourn in a spa. Persons without the slightest connection to each other are momentarily placed by chance into the closest proximity. Breakfast and midday meal, excursions, serious and playful conversations quickly lead to acquaintance and intimacy. Soon, then, the most marked elective affinities emerge, and it would be a wonder if they did not, here where there is total idleness and not even any illness and cure to provide a kind of diversion. Aulic Councilor Reiffenstein had advised us, and quite correctly, to go out there early, so that we would have the time we needed for walks and other artistic wanderings into the mountains before the throng of people surged in and demanded our participation in group entertainments. We were the first arrivals, and without delay, as that experienced guide had directed us to do, we properly inspected the area, and found this most enjoyable and educational.

After some time had passed, I saw a very pretty Roman neighbor of ours, who lived not far from us in the Corso, arriving with her mother. Ever since I had been created a milord, they had both returned my greetings in a friendlier manner than before. Yet I had not addressed them, although I often passed by them closely enough when they sat outside their door in the evening; for I had remained completely true to my vow not to let myself be kept from my main goal by such relationships. But now we suddenly met like very old acquaintances, and that concert of mine provided enough subject matter for our initial conversation. There can hardly be anything more charming than a Roman girl of the type that freely and cheerfully engages in artless conversation, and, in the euphonious Roman tongue, rapidly but distinctly tells about her lively interest in pure reality, gracefully referring to her own participation in it; and this in the noble dialect which elevates even the middle class, and lends a certain dignity to the most natural, indeed commonplace things. To be sure, these qualities and peculiarities were known to me, but I had never before heard them in such an ingratiating sequence.

At the same time, they introduced me to a young Milanese, the sister of one of Mr. Jenkins's clerks, a young man who was in his employer's best graces because of his skill and honesty. The girls seemed to be very close friends.

These two beauties, for they really could be called beautiful, were definite, although not absolute, opposites: the Roman girl had dark-brown hair, the Milanese, light-brown; the former had a brown complexion, the latter was fair, with delicate skin; the latter with almost blue eyes, the former with brown; the Roman girl was rather serious, reserved, while the Milanese had an open, not only engaging, but also inquiring manner. I sat between the two young women at a type of gambling game, and had pooled my money with the Roman. In the course of the game, it happened that I also tried my luck in betting or otherwise with the Milanese girl. Suffice it to say, a kind of partnership arose also with her, while in my innocence I did not immediately notice that this divided interest was not meeting with approval. Finally, when the game was over, the mother, finding me alone, assured the esteemed foreigner in a polite way, to be sure, but with genuine matronly seriousness, that, since he had now shown such interest in her daughter, it was not proper to indulge in similar courtesies with another girl. It was considered etiquette at a *villegiatura* for persons who have to some extent become a couple to abide by that in company, and carry on an innocently pleasant exchange of courtesies. I excused myself as best I could, but with the demurrer that, as a foreigner, I might find it impossible to recognize such obligations, since in our part of the world it was traditional to be attentive and courteous to all the ladies in the company, to one as to the other, together or in turn, and that this would apply all the more here, since it was a question of two very close friends.

But alas! while I was trying to excuse myself in this way, I had the strangest feeling that I was already inclined toward the Milanese girl. This happened with the speed of light and much urgency, as is usually the case when an idle heart, smugly and calmly confident that it fears nothing, wants nothing, suddenly comes into contact with what is most desirable. However, at such a moment we fail to espy the danger threatening us beneath those charming features.

The next morning found the three of us alone, and then the scales tipped still more in favor of the Milanese. She had the great advantage over her friend that there was something in her remarks that denoted aspiration. She complained not about a neglected but an overtimid education: "We are not taught to write," she said, "for fear we would use our pens for love letters; we would not be allowed to read if we did not have to pore over the prayerbook; no one will consider instructing us in foreign languages, and I would give anything to know English. I get a feeling close to envy when I hear Mr. Jenkins often conversing in English with my brother, or Madame Angelica, Mr. Zucchi, and the Messrs. Volpato and Camuccini.[114] And those yard-long newspapers lying on the table in front of me, I can see that they have news in them from the whole world, but I do not know what they say."

"That is all the more unfortunate," I replied, "since English is so easy to learn, and you would certainly grasp and comprehend it in a short time. Let us try at once," I continued, picking up one of the voluminous English newspapers that lay around in profusion.

I quickly looked through it and found an article about a girl who had fallen into the water, but fortunately had been rescued and restored to her loved ones. There were circumstances about the case which made it complex and interesting, doubts remained about whether or not she had plunged into the water to seek death and which of her suitors, the favored or the scorned one, had bravely rescued her. I indicated the passage to her and asked her to look at it attentively. Then I began by translating the nouns for her and examined her on how well she had retained their meaning. Quite soon she was surveying the arrangement of the basic nouns and acquainting herself with the place they had taken in the sentence. Then I went over to the influencing, moving, determining words and pointed out, in a very humorous way, how these enlivened the whole thing. Then I catechized her until, finally, she read the entire passage aloud to me as if it were printed on the paper in Italian, which she could not manage to do without some movement of her dainty person. I doubt that I have ever seen such a combination of emotional and intellectual joy as she expressed while thanking me in the most charming way for this view into a new field. She could barely contain herself when she realized it was possible that her dearest wishes were near fulfillment, and saw them already achieved experimentally.

The company had grown more numerous, Angelica had arrived too; I had been placed to her right at a large table laid for a meal; my pupil stood on the opposite side, and, while the other people were exchanging pleasant remarks about their assigned places, she did not hesitate a moment to walk around the table and sit down next to me. The serious lady next to me seemed somewhat taken aback at this, and it did not require a clever woman's eye to perceive that something must have happened here, and that the friend who had previously, to the point of cool discourtesy, kept his distance from women had finally seen himself surprised, captured, and tamed.

Outwardly, I still stood reasonably firm; on the other hand, my inner agitation betrayed itself in the rather embarrassed way in which I divided my conversation between the two ladies. I tried to entertain the older, gentle, now taciturn lady in a stimulating manner. As for the other, who still seemed to be practicing the foreign language, and found herself in the situation of someone who is dazzled by the longed-for sunrise, and cannot immediately find his way in the surroundings, I attempted to calm her by showing a quietly friendly, somewhat aloof interest.

This agitated situation, however, was immediately subjected to a period of remarkable upheaval. Towards evening, as I was looking for the young women, I found the older ones in a pavilion which offered the most magnificent of views; my gaze wandered around it, but what passed before my eyes was something other than the picturesqueness of a landscape. The area had become suffused with a color tone that could be ascribed neither to the sunset nor the evening breezes alone. The glowing illumination of the high points, the cooling blue shadows over the depths, seemed more splendid than they ever could be in oils or watercolors; I could not get enough of looking at that, yet I felt that I would like to leave this place and do homage to the last gleam of the sun in a small, sympathetic group.

But, unfortunately, I had been unable to refuse the invitation of the mother and the other ladies to sit down with them, especially since they had made room for me at the window to get the best view. When I listened to their conversation, I perceived that they were talking about someone's trousseau, a perpetual and inexhaustible subject. Because the ladies had captured me for a later walk, I had to listen patiently while they wasted this lovely time reviewing necessaries of all kinds, and relating in minute detail the number and nature of the various presents, in part still a secret, such as basic family gifts, many contributions from male and female friends, and so forth.

Eventually the conversation came around to the merits of the bridegroom. They described him quite favorably, but were not willing to pass over his faults, in the confident hope that the charm, good sense, and amiability of the bride would suffice to moderate and improve them in the future married state.

Having finally grown restless, just as the sun was sinking into the distant sea, providing an inestimable view through the long shadows and muted, but still powerful, sidelights, I very meekly asked who the bride might be. In amazement, they asked me whether I did not know what everyone else did; and only now did they realize that I was not a fellow guest in that house, but a stranger.

Surely I need not describe how horrified I felt to hear that it was the pupil I had so recently grown fond of. The sun went down, and I managed to find some excuse for leaving the group that, without realizing it, had enlightened me in such a cruel way.

It is traditional and well known that if one yields to affections imprudently for a length of time, they turn into pain when the dream is finally over; but what perhaps makes this case interesting is the rare circumstance that here a pronounced mutual fondness was destroyed at the moment of its inception, and with it went anticipation of all the infinite happiness that such a feeling leads one to expect from future developments. I came home late, and early the next morning, with my portfolio under my arm, I took a rather long walk, having excused myself from coming to the table.

I was sufficiently old and experienced to regain my self-possession at once, painful as this was. "It would certainly be strange," I cried, "if a fate similar to Werther's had overtaken you in Rome and spoiled the conditions you have so far preserved and which are of such significance to you."

I quickly turned again to the natural landscape, which I had meanwhile neglected, and tried to reproduce it as faithfully as possible, but my real success was in seeing it better. The modicum of technique I possessed was scarcely adequate for the most unpretentious sketch, but the opulent corporality offered us by that area in the form of rocks and trees, inclines and declines, placid lakes, and lively brooks, was more perceptible to my eye than almost ever before, and I could not hate the pain that was able to sharpen my inner and outer senses to such a degree.

From now on, however, I must be brief. Throngs of visitors filled our house and the houses in the neighborhood, individuals could avoid each other without affectation, and carefully considered politeness, to which such an inclination disposes us, is well received in society everywhere. My behavior met with approval, and I experienced no unpleasantness, no discord, except once, with our host, Mr. Jenkins. That is to say, I had brought the most appetizing mushrooms back from a long walk through the woods and mountains, and turned them over to the cook, who was highly delighted to have a food that was rare, but very famous, in those parts, and he served them very tastily prepared. Everyone ate them with great relish, but when, only with the intention of honoring me, it was revealed that I had brought them back from the wilds, our English host became angry, although not openly, because a stranger had contributed food to the banquet without the knowledge of the master of the house, and not ordered and arranged by him. He felt it was improper to surprise someone at his own board, and serve foods he could not account for. It was left to Aulic Councilor Reiffenstein to tell me all of this diplomatically after the meal, to which I humbly replied (suffering inwardly from a different pain, one which could not be attributed to funguses) that I had assumed the cook would report it to his master, and assured him that if I should run across such edibles again on my walks I myself would present them to our host for his examination and approval. For, to be fair, his annoyance was due to the fact that this generally questionable food had come to his table without due inspection. To be sure, the cook had given me his assurances, and had recalled that similar mushrooms had been served to his master at this season, perhaps not often, but always with great approbation, because they were a special rarity.

This culinary adventure gave me cause to reflect in a quietly humorous way that I, who was myself tainted with a quite peculiar poison, had been suspected of poisoning, with equal imprudence, a whole social gathering.

It was easy to abide by my resolution, I tried at once to evade the English lessons by going away in the morning and never approaching the pupil I secretly loved, except when several other persons were there.

Quite soon, this situation was straightened out again in my busily occupied heart, and actually in a very agreeable way. For, as a fiancée and future wife, she was raised above trivial girlhood in my eyes, and since I felt the very same inclination toward her, but on a higher, disinterested plane, and, since in any case I no longer resembled a frivolous youth, I was quite soon able to treat her in a very friendly, relaxed manner. My service to her—if casual attentions deserve that name— was marked by a complete absence of importunity, and, when we met, almost by a kind of respect. But she, who also knew now that I was informed about her situation, could be perfectly satisfied with my conduct. The other people, however—and I conversed with them all—did not notice or suspect anything, and so the days and hours followed a calm, easy course.

There would be much to tell about the many different ways in which we were entertained. Suffice it to say, there was also a theater in this place, where the same Pulcinella we applauded so often in the carnival (who worked the rest of the time at his cobbler's trade, and also in other respects made the impression here of being a decent citizen of the lower middle class) knew how to entertain us very well with his pantomimic-mimic-laconic absurdities, and could put us in a very agreeable state of self-forgetfulness.

Meanwhile, letters from home had made it obvious to me that my long-planned, repeatedly delayed, and finally so rashly undertaken trip to Italy had stirred up some unrest and impatience in the friends I had left behind, indeed, even the wish to follow my example and taste the same happiness I had described so favorably in my cheerful, no doubt also informative, letters. Of course, it was customary in our Duchess Amalia's intelligent and art-loving circle always to view Italy as the New Jerusalem of truly cultured persons and, with a fervor such as only Mignon could express, always to set their hearts and minds on going there. The dam had finally broken, and gradually it became quite clear that, on the one hand Duchess Amalia and her associates, on the other hand Herder and the younger Dalberg,[115] were seriously proposing to cross the Alps. My advice to them was to let the winter pass, to go as far as Rome in the intermediate season, and then, by degrees, enjoy all the other good things offered by the surroundings of the old metropolis, etc., and by the southern part of Italy.

As honest and pertinent as my advice was, it nevertheless served my own interests as well. So far, I had been spending noteworthy days of my life in a most unfamiliar situation with quite unfamiliar people. I had really taken a fresh, new delight in the human condition, which, for the first time in a long time, I had been made aware of again in accidental but natural relationships. For a closed circle at home, a life amidst wholly familiar and kindred persons, eventually puts us in the strangest situation: it is one where reciprocal tolerance and sufferance, participation and abstention, produce a certain neutral feeling of resignation, so that sorrow and joy, annoyance and pleasure, cancel each other out in the normal routine. A neutral number, so to speak, is created, which completely nullifies the character of individual results, until at last, in our striving for comfort, we cannot yield freely either to joy or sorrow.

Overcome by these feelings and presentiments, I had definitely decided not to await my friends' arrival in Italy. For I was more convinced than ever, after having tried for a year to escape the Cimmerian ideas and attitudes of the North, and grown used to breathing and looking around more freely beneath a vault of heavenly blue, that my way of seeing things would not immediately be theirs. In the meantime, travelers coming from Germany had been continually very burdensome to me; they went to see things they were supposed to neglect, and could not recognize what they had long wished for, even when it was right in front of their eyes. I myself was still finding it difficult enough, by means of thinking and doing, to keep on the path I had decided was the right one.

Germans who were strangers could be avoided, but such closely connected, revered, beloved persons would have disturbed and hindered me, not only with their own mistakes and half-perceptions, but even by adopting my attitudes. The Northern traveler believes he is coming to Rome to supplement his own existence, to fill in the gaps; but then gradually he perceives, to his great discomfort, that he must completely change his way of thinking and begin again from the beginning.

As plainly as I saw this situation, I nevertheless wisely kept myself in uncertainty as to the day and hour, and continued without interruption using my time most conscientiously. Independent reflection, listening to others, looking at artistic efforts, my own practical attempts constantly alternated, or, rather, mutually interlocked.

I was especially encouraged in this by the interest of Heinrich Meyer of Zurich; my conversations with him, although somewhat infrequent, proved useful to me because, as a diligent and sternly self-critical artist, he knew how to make better use of his time than my circle of younger artists. For they frivolously believed it was possible to combine serious progress in concepts and technique with a merry, rollicking life.

November

Correspondence

Rome, November 3, 1787.

Kayser has arrived, and as a result I have not written all week. First he is tuning the piano, and, bit by bit, the opera will be played on it. His presence marks the beginning of another extraordinary epoch, and I see that it is best just to go one's way calmly, while the days bring both the best and the worst.

I am happy about your reception of my *Egmont;* and I trust that it will not lose from a second reading, for I know what I have written into it, and this cannot be read out of it all at once. The things you praise are what I was trying to accomplish; if you say that they are there, then I have attained my goal. It was an immensely difficult task, and I would never have completed it, if I had not had unlimited freedom to live and feel. Imagine what it means to take up a work written twelve years earlier, and finish it without rewriting it! The special circumstances of the time made the task both harder and easier for me. Now two more such stones lie in my path: *Faust* and *Tasso*. Since the merciful gods seem to have relieved me in future of the punishment of Sisyphus, I hope to roll these boulders up the mountain as well. Once I have brought them to the top, I shall begin something new, and try hard to deserve your applause, since you steadfastly give me your love, which I do not deserve.

Charlotte, I do not quite understand what you say about Clare, and I await your next letter. Evidently you feel some lack of nuance between the wench and the goddess. However, since I have made the relationship to Egmont her only one; since I attribute her love more to a belief in her beloved's perfection, her rapture more to an incredulous delight that *this* man is hers, than to sensuality; since I have her appear as a heroine; since she follows in her beloved's footsteps in the most heartfelt conviction that their love is eternal; and since she is finally glorified in his mind by means of a transfiguring dream, I do not know where I should place the intermediate nuance. Nevertheless, I admit that the shadings I have listed above may be too far apart and disconnected, or, rather, the connections too subtly indicated, owing to the pasteboard and lathwork required for a drama. Perhaps a second reading will help, perhaps your next letter will give me more details.

Angelica has drawn, and Lips engraved, a frontispiece for *Egmont*[116] that could not have been drawn and engraved elsewhere, at any rate not in Germany.

Rome, November 3.

Unfortunately, I now have to neglect the visual arts completely, for otherwise I shall not finish my drama projects, which also require special concentration and quiet reworking, if anything is to come of them. *Claudina*[117] is now in progress, and will be completely revised, with the old chaff of my existence winnowed out, so to speak.

Rome, November 10.

Kayser is here now, and, since music has been added to it, my life is threefold. He is an exceedingly good man, and fits in with us, we who really lead a life of nature as much as that is possible anywhere on earth. Tischbein is returning from Naples, and then quarters and everything else will have to be changed for the two of them; but, with our good natures, in a week all will be going smoothly again.

I have suggested to the dowager duchess that she should permit me to spend the sum of two hundred zechins for her in gradually buying various little artworks. Do lend your support to this suggestion, Charlotte, as you find it in my letter to her; I do not need the money immediately, and not all at one time. This is an important point, the whole significance of which you will grasp without much explanation; and you would realize the necessity of my advice and the usefulness of my offer even more if you knew the conditions here, which I can see so plainly. I shall give her great delight with trifles, and when she finds the things that I shall have had made, little by little, that will satisfy the desire for acquisitions that develops in every newcomer, whoever he may be, and which she could only suppress with painful resignation, or satisfy with expense and loss. I could fill many more pages on this subject.

Rome, November 10.

I am heartily pleased that my *Egmont* is meeting with approval. I have never completed a play with more freedom of spirit and more conscientiousness than this one. But, when one has already written other works, the reader is hard to satisfy; he always demands something like the earlier ones.

Rome, November 24.

In your last letter, Charlotte, you inquire about the color of the landscape in this area. I can answer that on sunny days, especially in the autumn, it is so *colorful* that in any picture it would look *mottled*. I am hoping to send you fairly soon some drawings made by a German who is now in Naples;[118] the watercolors by no means match the brilliance of nature, and yet none of you will believe it. The most beautiful feature is that, even at a slight distance, the vivid colors are muted by the tint of the air, and that the contrasts between cool and warm tones (as they are called) emerge so visibly. The clear blue shadows stand out very attractively from all the brightly lit green, yellowish, reddish, brownish parts, and combine with the bluish haze in the distance. There is a brilliance, and at the same time a harmony, a gradation, in the whole that cannot be imagined at all in the north. Where you are, everything is either hard or dull, mottled or monotonous. At least, I seldom remember having seen individual effects that gave me a foretaste of what I now see before me daily and hourly. Perhaps, now that my eye is better trained, I would also find more beauty in the North.

Moreover, I can surely say that I now pretty well recognize and see before me the true, direct routes to all the visual arts, but can also estimate the more clearly how far away they are. I am already too old to do more than dabble from now on; I also see how others fare, find many a person on the right path, but no one making great strides. It is the same as with happiness and wisdom, which merely hover before us as ideals, and at best we touch the hem of their garments.

Kayser's arrival, until we had put our domestic arrangements into some sort of order, had set me back to a certain extent, and my projects came to a standstill. Now things are proceeding again, and my operas are nearly finished. He is very worthy, sensible, honest, steady, and as solid and sure in his art as a man can be—one of those people in whose proximity one becomes healthier. In addition, he has a kind heart and a proper view of life and society, which make his otherwise stern character more flexible and lend a peculiar grace to his manners.

Report

November

Now, however, while I was quietly thinking about disassociating myself little by little, a new connection was close at hand with the arrival of a worthy friend from earlier years, Christoph Kayser, a born Frankfurter, who had come up at the same time as Klinger[119] and the rest of us. Gifted by nature with unique musical talent, he had already years ago, while composing the score for *Jest, Ruse, and Revenge,* begun to furnish suitable music for *Egmont.* I had written to him from Rome that the play had been sent off, but that I retained a copy. Instead of a lengthy correspondence, we found it advisable for him to come promptly in person; whereupon, without delay, he flew through Italy with the express mail coach. He arrived at our place very soon, and saw himself amicably received into the circle of artists which had established its headquarters in the Corso, opposite Rondanini.

At this juncture, however, instead of the concentration and collaboration that were so necessary, new distractions and disunity emerged.

First of all, several days passed while we procured a piano, and it was tried out, tuned, and put in order according to the wish and will of the strong-minded artist, who always found one more thing to demand and desire. However, the effort expended and time lost were very soon rewarded with performances given by a very skilled talent, one thoroughly suitable for its time, and capable of performing with ease the most difficult works of that era. And to make this clear at once to connoisseurs of musical history, I shall mention that at that time Schubart[120] was considered without a peer, and also that it was considered the test of a good pianist to execute variations, in which a simple theme, developed in the most intricate way, finally reappeared in its natural form, to let the listener catch his breath again.

He brought along the overture to *Egmont,* and this acted as a stimulus to my further endeavors, which were directed more than ever, both by necessity and inclination, toward the musical theater.

Erwin and Elmira, as well as *Claudina of Villa Bella,* were now also due to be sent to Germany; but, owing to my revision of *Egmont,* I had raised my standards so much that I could not bring myself to send them off in their first form. A good many of the lyrics they contained were dear and valuable to me; they bore witness to many perhaps foolishly, but happily, spent hours, and also to the grief and pain to which youth is exposed because of its reckless activity. On the other hand, the prose dialogue was too reminiscent of French operettas. The latter, to be sure, must be granted a kind mention, because they were the first to import a cheerful, singable essence onto our stage; but they no longer satisfied me, since as a naturalized Italian, I wanted to see the melodious airs at least combined with sung recitatives and declamatory passages.

Now both operas will be found revised in this manner; their musical settings pleased audiences here and there, and so they too, along with others, floated by on the dramatic stream of their time.

People usually revile Italian texts, and do so, indeed, in phrases that can be thoughtlessly repeated by one person after another. They may be merely light and cheerful, but they never make greater demands on the composer and the singer than both gladly submit to. I do not wish to go into too much detail about this matter, but I remember the text of *The Secret Marriage;*[121] the author is unknown, but whoever he was, he was one of the most skillful who have worked in this field. To proceed in this manner, to work for definite ends with like freedom, was my intention, but I myself could not say how close I came to my goal.

Unfortunately, I had already been involved for some time with friend Kayser in an undertaking that grew to seem ever more dubious and less practicable.

One must visualize that very naive era in German operatic history when a simple intermezzo like Pergolesi's *Serva Padrona*[122] was received with approval. Appearing at that time in German cities and towns were a German buffo named Berger[123] and his beautiful, stately, skillful wife, who, with simple costuming and meager musical accompaniment, gave rousing, comical salon performances, which of course always involved the deception and humiliation of an amorous old fop.

I had thought of adding a third, intermediate, and easily filled vocal role to these two, and so I had already written the operetta *Jest, Ruse, and Revenge* years ago and sent it to Kayser in Zurich; but this serious, conscientious man approached the work too earnestly, and treated it too fully. Actually, I myself had already made it too long for an intermezzo, and the subject matter, although it seemed slight, had generated so many songs that, even with economical, light musical accompaniment, the three persons would have gone on performing almost endlessly. Now Kayser had given the arias a thorough treatment in the old style, and quite successfully in places, it may be said, while the whole score was not without charm.

But how and where was it to be presented? Unfortunately, in line with earlier principles of moderation, it suffered from a paucity of voices; it contained nothing more ambitious than a trio, and at last we would have gladly brought the Doctor's theriaca boxes[124] to life in order to get a chorus. Consequently, all our efforts to confine ourselves to the simple and restricted went for naught when Mozart came on the scene. *The Abduction from the Seraglio*[125] struck everything down, and our so carefully wrought play has never been put on the stage.

The presence of our friend Kayser now heightened and broadened our love of music, which heretofore had been limited to what is offered in the theater. He carefully kept track of the ecclesiastical festivals, and so we felt obliged to go along with him and listen to the solemn concerts performed on such days. To be sure, we thought them quite secular because of the very complete orchestras, although singing still predominated. I remember having heard a bravura aria with choral accompaniment for the first time, on St. Cecilia's day; it had an extraordinary effect on me, as such things still do on audiences, when they occur in operas.

Besides this, Kayser had another virtue: namely, since he was much interested in older music and also devoted himself seriously to researching the history of the musical art, he visited libraries; thus, because of his steadfast diligence, he was especially well received and assisted at the Minerva.[126] At the same time, his study of books resulted in his calling our attention to the older illustrated works of the sixteenth century, and, for example, he made sure to remind us of the *Speculum romanae magnificentiae*[127] and the *Architectures* by Lomazzo,[128] as well as the later *Admiranda Romae,*[129] and other things of the kind. These collections of books and engravings, to which we others then also made pilgrimages, are of especially great value when one finds them in well-printed copies. They recall that earlier period when antiquity was viewed gravely and with awe, and its remains were depicted in a vigorous manner. So, for instance, we approached the Colossi as they still stood on their old spot in the Colonna garden; the semi-ruin of the Septizonium Severi[130] still indicated the approximate form of this vanished building; St. Peter's without its facade, the great central part without the dome, the old Vatican, in whose courtyard tournaments could still be held— all of this took us back to olden times, and simultaneously made us most clearly aware of the changes brought about by the following two centuries, and of the attempts, in spite of significant obstacles, to restore what had been destroyed and to recover lost ground.

Heinrich Meyer of Zurich, whom I have often had occasion to mention, lived reclusively and was very industrious, but still he was rarely absent where something of significance was to be seen, experienced, or learned; for the others also sought him out and wanted him, since in company he proved himself to be as modest as he was informative. He continued calmly along the sure path opened up by Winckelmann and Mengs, and, because of his ability to make sepia drawings of ancient busts in Seydelmann's[131] manner, no one had more opportunity than he to examine and become acquainted with the subtle gradations of earlier and later art.

When we now made arrangements for a torchlight visit to the museums both of the Vatican and the Capitol, which was desired by all the foreigners, whether artists, connoisseurs, or laymen, he joined the group. An enjoyable tour of this kind through the most magnificent artistic relics hovers, for the most part, before the mind's eye like a charming, gradually fading dream; but among my papers I find an essay[132] of his thanks to which it gains lasting significance, also with respect to its beneficial effects on knowledge and understanding.

"The custom of viewing the great Roman museums, e.g., the Pio-Clementino museum in the Vatican, the Capitoline, etc., by the light of wax torches still seems to have been fairly new in the eighties of the previous century, although I do not know when it actually began.

"Advantages of torch illumination: Every piece is observed individually, isolated from all the rest, and the viewer's attention remains directed to it exclusively. Then, in the powerfully effective torchlight, all the subtle nuances of the workmanship look much more distinct, there is an end to all troublesome reflections (especially annoying in highly polished statues), the shadows become more definite, the lighted parts emerge more brightly. But a chief advantage is unquestionably this, that poorly placed pieces thereby receive their due. Thus, for example, in the niche where it stood, the *Laocoon*[133] could only be seen properly by torchlight, because no direct light fell on it, just a reflection from the little round courtyard of the Belvedere, which was encircled by a columnar hall; the situation was the same with the *Apollo* and the so-called *Antinous* (Mercury).[134] Torch illumination was still more necessary for seeing both the *Nile*[135] and the *Meleager*[136] and appreciating their merits. To no other ancient statue is torch illumination as advantageous as the so-called *Phocion*,[137] because only then—not with the usual lighting, because it is badly positioned—can one perceive the parts of the body which appear in such marvelous subtlety through the simple garment. The superb fragment of a sitting Bacchus[138] also looks beautiful, as does the upper part of a Bacchus statue[139] with a handsome head, and the half-figure of a triton,[140] but, above all, that miracle of art, the famous *Torso*,[141] which can never be sufficiently praised.

"The monuments in the Capitoline museum are, to be sure, generally less important than those in the Museo Pio-Clementino, yet there are several of great significance, and it is advisable to see them by torchlight to become suitably acquainted with their merits. The so-called *Pyrrhus*,[142] superbly sculpted, stands on the staircase, and gets no light at all; in the gallery before the columns stands a lovely half-figure, considered to be a draped Venus,[143] which receives weak light from three sides. The nude *Venus*,[144] the most beautiful statue of this type in Rome, is not seen to advantage in daylight, since it is placed in a corner room, and the beautifully draped so-called *Juno*[145] stands against the wall between windows, where it just gets a little sidelight. The very famous *Head of Ariadne*[146] in the miscellany room can also not be seen in its entire splendor except by torchlight. And there are also several other pieces in this museum that are badly placed, so that torch illumination becomes absolutely necessary, if one is to see them properly and appreciate them as they deserve.

"However, like much of what is done for the sake of fashion, torch illumination turned into an abuse. It can only be profitable in the event one understands what it is useful for. It is necessary for seeing monuments which receive only dim light, as was reported above concerning several of them, since elevations and depressions, and the blending together of the parts, can then be more correctly discerned. But it will be particularly beneficial to works from the very best period of art (that is to say, if both the viewer and the person holding the torch know what is important); it will show the masses better and emphasize the subtlest nuances of the workmanship. On the other hand, works in the archaic style of art, whether of the mighty or even the sublime type, have not much to gain, provided that they stand in a bright light otherwise. For since the artists at that time were still not knowledgeable about light and shadow, how should they have taken light and shadow into consideration for their works? It is the same with works done later, when the artists began to grow more lax, and taste had already sunk so low that attention was no longer paid to light and shadow in sculptures, and the theory of masses was forgotten. What purpose would be served by torchlight on monuments of this kind?"

On such a festive occasion, it is in keeping with my reminiscences also to mention Mr. Hirt,[147] who had been useful and helpful to our group in more than one way. Born in 1759 in Fürstenberg territory, he felt an irresistible urge, after having completed his studies of the ancient writers, to betake himself to Rome. He had arrived there a few years earlier than I and had made a most earnest effort to become acquainted with ancient and modern works of art and architecture of every kind,

thereby equipping himself to be an informative guide for curious foreigners. With selfless interest, he also showed me this courtesy.

While his main study was architecture, this did not divert his attention
from the classical locales and the many other noteworthy things. His
theoretical views on art led to numerous lively discussions in conten-
tious and factious Rome. There especially, where art is always talked
about in every place, the diversity of opinions quite frequently results
in arguments which, in the vicinity of such magnificent objects, are
extremely stimulating and beneficial to the mind. Our friend Hirt believed that Greek and Roman architecture derived from the oldest, most
fundamental wooden construction, on which maxim he then based his
praise and criticism of the newer workmanship; and in so doing he
made adroit use of history and examples. Others declared, to the contrary, that tasteful fictions[148] occur in architecture as in every other
art, which the architect must never reject, since the cases presented
to him are so manifold that he has to seek help now in this way, now
in that, and is forced to depart from the strict rule.

With respect to beauty, he often found himself at odds with other
artists, since he based it on the element of character. Those who agreed
with him that character must of course be the foundation of every artwork were nevertheless convinced that the treatment should be left to
good taste and the sense of beauty, which should present each character
in both an appropriate and attractive manner.

However, although art consists in doing, and not in talking, people
will always talk more than do, and so it is easy to imagine that at the
time such conversations were endless, as they have remained into the
most recent times.

If the differing opinions of artists led to quite a variety of unpleas-
antnesses, and even to estrangements, it also, although rarely, happened
that humorous incidents took place on such occasions. The following
may serve as an example of that.

A group of artists had spent the afternoon in the Vatican, and, since
it was late, they avoided the long way home through the city by walking
out at the gate of the colonnade, along the vineyards, and down to the
Tiber. They argued on the way, arrived arguing at the riverbank, and
continued their lively discussion on the ride over. If they disembarked
at Ripetta, they would have to separate, and see the still remaining
arguments on both sides stifled at birth. Therefore they agreed to stay
together, and be rowed across and back again, allowing their dialectic
to take its further course on the swaying ferryboat. Once, however,
was not found sufficient; they were in full swing, and demanded that
the ferryman repeat the trip several times. The latter did not mind,
since every crossing and recrossing brought him one *bajacco* per person,

considerable earnings, which he could not have expected so late in the day. Consequently, he fulfilled their demands in total silence; but when his little son asked him in amazement: "Why do they want to do that?" he answered very calmly: "I do not know, but they are crazy."

At about this time, I received the following letter in a packet from home:[149]

"Sir, I am not surprised that you have bad readers; so many people prefer talking to feeling, but one must pity them, and congratulate one-self on not resembling them.—Yes, dear sir, I am indebted to you for having done the best deed of my life, which will engender many others, and for me your book is good. If I were fortunate enough to live in the same country as you, I would go to embrace you and tell you my secret, but, unfortunately, I live in one where nobody would credit my motive for taking such a step. Be content, sir, with having been able, at 300 leagues from your home, to lead the heart of a young man back to decency and virtue, an entire family will be relieved of worry, and my heart rejoices in a good deed. If I had the talents, the knowledge, or a rank that would enable me to influence the fate of men, I would tell you my name, but I am nothing, and I know what I would not want to be. I hope, sir, that you are young, that you enjoy writing, and that you are the husband of a Charlotte who has never seen Werther; in that case you are the happiest of men, for I believe that you love virtue."

December

Correspondence

Rome, December 1, 1787.

I can assure you of this much: I am more than certain of the most important points, and although there is no limit to the knowledge that could still be acquired, at least I have a sure, indeed a clear and communicable concept of this finite-infinite subject.

I am still planning the most remarkable things, and restrain my cognitive faculty, just so that my creative powers may make some headway. For there are magnificent things here, and as comprehensible as the palm of one's hand, once one has taken hold of them.

Rome, December 7, 1787.

I spent this week drawing, since I could make no progress with literary work; one must look and try to use all periods of time. Our domestic academy is still in progress, and we are endeavoring to waken old Anganthyr[150] from his sleep. In the evening we study perspective, and at the same time I am always seeking to learn how to draw some parts of the human body better and more confidently. But the basics are exceedingly difficult and must be practiced with great diligence.

Angelica is very dear and kind, she puts me in her debt in every way. We spend Sundays together, and I see her once a week in the evening. She works so much and so well that one cannot imagine how it is possible, and yet one would never think she was doing anything.

Rome, December 8.

You will not believe, Charlotte, how very delighted I am that my little ditty[151] pleased you, how glad I am to have struck a tone that

matches your mood. That is exactly what I wished for *Egmont,* of which
you say so little, and more about what you dislike than what you like.
Oh, we know quite well that we can hardly keep such a large composition in perfect tune; no one, after all, really understands the difficulty of art except the artist himself.

There is far more of the *positive,* that is to say, *teachable* and *trans-
mittable,* in art than is commonly believed; and there are a great many
mechanical techniques by means of which the most spiritual effects can
be produced (of course always with spirit). If one knows these little
techniques, then much that looks ever so marvelous is merely child's
play, and I believe that nowhere can more be learned about the high
and the low than in Rome.

Rome, December 15.

I am writing to you late at night, Charlotte, just to write you something. I have spent this week very pleasantly. Last week, I could make
no headway either with one work or the other, and since the weather
was so fine on Monday, and my knowledge of the sky led me to expect
some good days, I set out with Kayser and my other Fritz,[152] and from
Tuesday until this evening I walked through places I already knew,
and various parts I did not yet know.

Tuesday evening we reached Frascati, Wednesday we visited the
most beautiful villas, and particularly the exquisite *Antinous*[153] at Villa
Mondragone. Thursday we walked from Frascati up Monte Cavo, above
Rocca di Papa, of which you will get drawings someday, for verbal
descriptions are nothing; then down to Albano. On Friday, Kayser left
us, because he did not feel very well, and I went with Fritz II up to
Aricia and Genzano, along Lake Nemi, and back up to Albano. Today
we went up to Castel Gandolfo and Marino, and from there back to
Rome. The weather was unbelievably favorable, it was almost the best
weather of the whole year. Besides the evergreen trees, some oaks still
have their leaves, young chestnuts also have theirs, even though they
are yellow. There are color tones of the greatest beauty in the landscape,
and the magnificent great forms in nocturnal darkness! I felt great delight, which I communicate to you who are far away. I am very pleased
and well.

Rome, December 21.

It is a help, not a hindrance, to my literary powers that I am drawing,
and studying art; for one only has to write a little, but draw a great
deal. I just wish I could communicate to you, Charlotte, the concept
I now have of visual art; although still inadequate, it is pleasing because

it is true and points ever onward. If I was as though born anew when I arrived in Italy, now it is as if I were beginning to be educated anew.

What I have sent heretofore are only frivolous attempts. I am sending a roll along with Thurneisen,[154] on which the best things are not by me, and they will please you.

Rome, December 25.

This time, Christ has been born amidst thunder and lightning! Just at midnight we had a severe storm.

The splendor of the greatest artworks no longer dazzles me, I now go around in contemplation, with true, discerning perception. I cannot say how indebted I am for this to a quiet, solitary, diligent Swiss named Meyer. He was the first to make me aware of detail, of the properties of the individual forms, and to initiate me into the actual *making*. He is modest, and content with little. He really enjoys the artworks more than their aristocratic owners do, who do not understand them, and more than other artists, who are too anxiously driven by a desire to imitate what is unattainable. There is a heavenly clarity in his ideas, and an angelic goodness in his heart. Whenever he speaks to me I want to write down everything he says, so definite and correct are his words, so fixed on the one true course. His instruction gives me what no other person was able to, and his departure will be an irreparable loss to me. In proximity to him, after a period of time, I still hope to improve my drawing to a degree which I myself can hardly imagine. Everything I learned, tried, and thought in Germany stands in the same relationship to his teaching as the tree bark does to the stone of the fruit. I have no words to express the quiet, attentive bliss with which I now am beginning to view artworks; my mind is expanded enough to grasp them, and is training itself more and more to be really able to appreciate them.

Foreign visitors are here again, and sometimes I view a gallery with them. They remind me of the wasps in my room, which fly against the windows, mistaking the clear glass for air, then rebound again, and buzz on the walls.

I would not wish the silent, retiring mode of life even on an enemy. And to be considered *sick* and *obtuse,* as formerly, befits me less than ever. So think, my dear Herder, act, do what is best for me, and preserve my life for me, which otherwise will be ruined and of no use to anyone. Yes, I must say that I have been very spoiled this year in my dealings with other people. I stood alone for a while, quite cut off from everyone. Now an intimate circle has gathered around me again, all good men, all on the *right path,* which just shows that it is necessary to be well along on the right path in thought and actions in order to put up with me, to like me, and enjoy my company. For I am merciless and intolerant toward all those who dawdle or get lost along the way, and nevertheless want to be considered messengers and travelers. I frmtheap scorn and ridicule on them until they either change their lives or leave me. Of course I am speaking here only of good, sincere persons, for stupid and wrong-headed ones are winnowed out unceremoniously. Two people are already indebted to me for their altered mode of life and thought, nay, three,[155] and they will be grateful to me as long as they live. It is when my character can be influential that I feel the *health* of my nature and its *extension;* my feet hurt only in tight shoes, and I can see nothing when set before a wall.

Report

December

The month of December had begun with sunny, fairly stable weather, which inspired an idea that would provide a merry group of good companions with many pleasant days. We said, namely, "Let us imagine we had just arrived in Rome, and, as hurried foreign visitors, had to become informed quickly about the major sights. Let us begin a tour with this in mind, so that what we already know will become new again in our minds and senses."

We began to put the plan into effect at once, and, with some persistence, carried it out rather well. Unfortunately, very little is left of the many good things that were thought and said along the way. Letters, notes, drawings, and sketches from this time are almost entirely lacking; nevertheless, let something briefly be told about it.

Below Rome, not a far distance from the Tiber, is a medium-sized church called "The Three Little Fountains";[156] the latter were brought forth, so it is told, by the blood of St. Paul when he was beheaded, and they are still flowing to the present day.

The church is, in any case, situated in a low place, and so the piped springs gushing in its interior naturally increase the already existing misty dampness. The interior is sparsely decorated and almost forsaken, except for a rare divine service, and, though musty, it is tended and kept clean. What serves to embellish it very greatly, however, is the series of Christ and His apostles that is colorfully painted in life-size on the pillars of the nave, after drawings by Raphael. This extraordinary genius, who at other times, in the right place, presented these men identically dressed and in an assembled group, had depicted them here, where each individual appears separately, each with his own distinguishing mark—not as if he were in the retinue of the Lord but as if, left to his own devices after the latter's ascension, he now had to mold and endure his life in a way suitable to his character.

To instruct us about the merits of these pictures even when far away, however, we still had reproductions of the original drawings by the accurate hand of Marcantonio, which frequently gave us the opportunity and incentive to refresh our memory and write down our observations. We attach an excerpt from an essay that was included in the *German Mercury* in the year 1791.[157]

"The problem of representing in a fitting manner a transfigured Teacher with His twelve original and most distinguished disciples, who hung entirely on His words and life, and for the most part crowned their simple lives with a martyr's death, was solved by him with such naiveté, variety, sincerity, and profound artistic understanding that we can consider these drawings as one of the finest monuments of his beneficial existence.

"He used very sensitively all that has come down to us in writings or by tradition about their character, status, occupations, life, and death; and by that means he produced a series of figures that, without being alike, have an inner relationship to each other. We want to examine them individually, in order to draw our readers' attention to this interesting collection.

"*Peter.* He has placed him facing directly forward and given him a solid, stocky frame. In this, as in other figures, the extremities are slightly enlarged, so that the figure seems somewhat shorter. His neck is short, and his short hair is the curliest of all the thirteen figures. The main folds of his garment meet in the middle of the body, his face, like the rest of his form, is seen fully from the front. The figure is firmly compacted and stands there like a pillar that is capable of supporting a burden.

"*Paul* is also depicted standing, but turned to the side, like someone who is about to leave and is looking back once more; his cloak is pulled up and draped over the arm in which he holds the book; his feet are free, nothing hinders them from walking away; hair and beard are like flames, and his face glows with religious zeal.

"*John.* A noble youth with beautiful long hair, curled only at the ends. He seems calmly content to possess and display the outward symbols of religion, the book and the goblet. It is a very felicitous device that the eagle, while raising its wings, at the same time lifts up the garment, and, by this means, the beautifully arranged folds are laid most perfectly.

"*Matthew.* A well-to-do, placid man, satisfied with his life. His all too great calm and ease are balanced by a serious, almost timid look; his money pouch and the folds draped over his body make an indescribable impression of peaceful harmony.

"*Thomas* is one of the most beautiful figures, one of the most expressive in its extreme simplicity. He stands gathered into his cloak, which falls into almost symmetrical folds on both sides, but quite subtle variations make them completely dissimilar to each other. It would hardly be possible to create a quieter, calmer, more unassuming figure. The angle of the head, the gravity, the almost sad look, the delicacy of the mouth harmonize very beautifully with the calm of the whole figure. Only the hair is in motion, to indicate an emotional disposition under the gentle exterior,

"*James the Greater*. A gentle, muffled figure, a pilgrim walking past.

"*Philip*. If he is placed between the two previous figures, and the drapery of all three is compared, it will be conspicuous how rich, big, and broad the folds are on this figure, in contrast to the others. As rich and elegant as his raiment is, that is how securely he stands, how firmly he holds the cross, how sharply he looks at it, and the whole figure seems to indicate an inner grandeur, calm, and steadiness.

"*Andrew* does not just wear his cross, he embraces and caresses it. The simple folds of his cloak are very expertly arranged.

"*Thaddeus*. A youth who lifts up his long tunic, as monks customarily do when traveling, so that it will not impede his walking. This simple action creates very beautiful folds. In his hand, for a pilgrim's staff, he carries a halberd, the sign of his martyr's death.

"*Matthias*. A lively old man in a simple garment, which is given variety by means of some very expertly arranged folds, leans on a spear, his cloak hangs down behind him.

"*Simon*. The folds of the cloak, and of the other garment with which this figure, seen more from the back than from the side, is clothed, are among the most beautiful in the whole collection; and in general there is an indescribable harmony in the posture, the expression, the hair of the head.

"*Bartholomew* stands wrapped up carelessly and—with great art— artlessly in his cloak; his posture, his hair, the way he holds the knife might almost make one think that he is more prepared to flay someone else than to submit to this operation himself.

"*Christ,* last of all, will probably not satisfy anyone who might be expecting the miraculous figure of a God-man here. He steps forth simply and quietly to bless the people. It may justly be maintained that the garment pulled up in beautiful folds from below to reveal the knee and rest against the body cannot be kept that way for even a moment, but must immediately fall down. Probably Raphael assumes that the figure has raised and held the garment with the left hand, but has released it at the moment of lifting the arm in blessing, so that it must just be falling. This would be an example of the fine technique of indicating a recently completed action by the still existent condition of the folds."

But from this modest little church it is not far to the larger memorial dedicated to the great apostle; it is the church called St. Paul outside

the Walls,[158] a monument put together grandly and intricately from
magnificent ancient remains. This church makes a sublime impression
as one enters. The mightiest rows of columns support high, frescoed
walls which end above in the crossed timbers of the roof. While this
now may look somewhat barnlike to our pampered eye, surely the effect
of the whole on festival days, when the beams are hung with tapestries,
would be incredible. Many a wonderful remnant of highly decorated
colossal architecture is worthily preserved here, namely in the capitals
that were rescued by being taken from the ruins of the palace of Caracalla, which formerly stood nearby, but now has almost entirely disappeared.

Next, the racetrack still named for this emperor[159] gives us an idea
of what this immense expanse used to be, even though it is mostly in
ruins. If the sketcher were to position himself to the left of where the
charioteers emerged, then he would have on his right, up above the
crumbled spectator seats, the grave monument of Cecilia Metella, with
its modern surroundings. From the former seats the line goes off into
infinity, and, in the distance, significant villas and country houses can
be seen. When the eye returns from them, it can still follow the ruins
of the spina very well, and anyone who has architectural imagination
can visualize to some extent the high spirits of those days. In any case,
the ruins, as they now lie before us, would make a subject for a pleasant
picture, if it were undertaken by a talented and knowledgeable artist,
and of course it would have to be twice as long as high.

This time our eyes greeted the pyramid of Cestius[160] from outside,
and the actual appearance of the ruined baths of Antoninus or Caracalla,[161] of which Piranesi[162] has given us so many a rich imaginary
impression, could hardly satisfy even our artistically trained eye. But
in this connection we remembered Herman van Swanevelt,[163] who, using his burin delicately to express the purest of feelings for nature and
art, was able to revive these past glories, indeed, to remake them into
most attractive representatives of the living present.

On the square in front of St. Peter's in Montorio we greeted the
gushing waters of Acqua Paola,[164] which flow in five streams through
the portals and gates of a triumphal arch to fill a commensurately large
basin to the brim. By means of an aqueduct restored by Paul V, this
opulent stream makes a journey of twenty-five Italian miles from behind
Lake Bracciano, through a zigzag imposed by alternating heights, to
reach this spot. While spreading out in Trastevere, it provides for the
needs of various mills and factories.

Here, now, we friends of architecture praised the happy thought of
providing these waters with an openly visible triumphal entranceway.
The columns and arches, the cornices and attics, are reminiscent of
those magnificent gates through which, in earlier times, conquering
warriors used to enter; here the most peaceable nourisher enters with

equal power and strength and immediately receives thanks and admiration for the exertions of its long course. The inscriptions also tell us
that here the providence and beneficence of a pope from the Borghese
family hold, as it were, their eternal, uninterrupted, stately entry.

However, a recently arrived visitor from the North felt that it would
have been a better idea to pile up crude rocks here, in order to give
these floods of water a natural entry into the light of day. We replied
to him that this was not a natural stream, but an artificial one, and it
was perfectly justifiable to have decorated its place of arrival in similar
fashion.

But there was as little agreement about this as about the magnificent
picture of the Transfiguration, which we had an opportunity to admire
directly afterwards, in the adjacent monastery. Then there was much
discussion; but the quieter members of the group were annoyed to hear
a repetition of the old criticism that it has a double action. But that is
the way of the world, a worthless coin always stays in some kind of
circulation alongside a standard one, especially when one wants to
conclude a transaction quickly, and settle certain differences without
much reflection and hesitation. Nevertheless, it is odd that anyone
should ever have found fault with the grand unity of this conception.
In the Lord's absence, some disconsolate parents bring a demoniac
boy to the Holy One's disciples; the latter may already have attempted
to banish the spirit; someone has even opened a book to explore whether
a traditional formula might possibly be found effective against this evil;
but in vain. At this moment, the One who alone is mighty appears,
and, indeed, in transfigured form, acknowledged by His great predecessors; and, after this vision, some persons quickly point to Him as
the only source of cure. How, then, are those upper and lower parts
to be separated? The two are one: below, the suffering part, in need
of help; above, the effective, helpful part, both of them linked together.
To express the sense of this in another way: can the connection between
the conceptual and the real be severed?

The like-minded ones in the group were now reconfirmed in their
convictions. "Raphael," they said to each other, "particularly distinguished himself by the correctness of his thinking, and are we to suppose
that this divinely gifted man, who is positively recognizable by that
very quality, thought wrongly, acted wrongly, in the prime of his life?
No! He and nature are always right, and never more so than when we
least understand them."

A plan like the one we had agreed on, to obtain a cursory general
view of Rome in good, close-knit company, could not be carried out
in complete isolation, although that had been our intention. One person

or another would be missing, perhaps kept away accidentally, others again, if we were going their way, would join us to view this or that object of interest. Meanwhile the nucleus still held together, and we knew when to accept and when to exclude, when to lag behind and when to hurry ahead. Occasionally, to be sure, we were obliged to hear some very strange comments. There is a certain kind of empirical judgment which has been much in use for some time, thanks especially to English and French travelers; a spontaneous, impromptu judgment is expressed without consideration of the fact that every artist is conditioned in multiple ways, by his special talent, by his predecessors and teachers, by place and time, by patrons and clients. None of these are taken into account, although of course they are required for a true assessment, and therefore what results is an atrocious mixture of praise and criticism, affirmation and negation, by which all the true value of the objects in question is very definitely nullified.

Our trusty Volkmann, otherwise so alert and quite useful as a guide, seems to have relied completely on those foreign critics, for which reason his own appraisals make a very strange impression. Can anyone express himself, for example, more unfortunately than he does in regard to the church of Maria della Pace?

"Above the first chapel, Raphael painted several sibyls,[165] which are in bad condition. The drawing is correct, but the arrangement is weak, which presumably can be attributed to the inconvenient location. The second chapel is decorated with arabesques after drawings by Michelangelo;[166] these are highly esteemed, but are not simple enough. Three paintings are to be seen under the dome, the first, by Carlo Marati, depicts the visitation of Mary, and is coldly painted, but well composed; the second, the birth of Mary, by Cavaliere Vanni,[167] in the manner of Pietro da Cortona;[168] and the third, the death of Mary, by Giovanni Maria Morandi.[169] The composition is somewhat confused, and descends into crudeness. On the vault above the choir, Albani[170] pictures the assumption of Mary, with weak coloring. The paintings he did on the pillars under the dome turned out better. Bramante[171] designed the courtyard of the monastery attached to this church."

Inadequate, unreliable criticism of this kind thoroughly confuses the viewer who has chosen such a book for his guide. And then much is quite wrong, e.g., what is said here about the sibyls. Raphael was never hampered by the space that the architecture allotted to him, rather, it is part of the greatness and elegance of his genius that he knew how to fill and decorate any space most gracefully, as he obviously proved in the Farnese palace. Even such magnificent pictures as the *Mass of Bolsena*, the *Freeing of the Captive St. Peter*, and the *Parnassus*[172] could not be imagined as so superbly contrived without the curious limitation of space. Likewise, here too with the sibyls, what predominates, in the most ingenious manner, is the concealed symmetry, the most essential factor in composition. For, in art as in the natural organism, life manifests itself to perfection within the narrowest limits.

However that may be, let the manner of assimilating artworks be entirely left up to each individual. On this tour, I got the feeling, the concept, the perception of what might be called, in the highest sense, the presence of classical soil. By this, I mean the physical-intellectual conviction that greatness was, is, and will be here. It is in the nature of time and the wholly interactive moral and physical elements that what is greatest and most magnificent may pass. While making our very general inspection, we could not feel sad when passing the destroyed places, because we had reason to be happy that so much had been restored here, more splendidly and extravagantly than it had ever been before.

Certainly St. Peter's church is as grandly conceived as any of the ancient temples, indeed even more grandly and boldly, and we saw before us not only the destruction wreaked by two thousand years, but the new productions of a more advanced culture.

Everything indicated life and movement, even the shifting taste in art, now seeking the grandly simple, then returning to a multiplicity of smaller things; the history of art and mankind stood synchronically before our eyes.

It must not depress us if we cannot escape the conclusion that greatness is transitory; rather, when we see that the past was great, this must encourage us to accomplish something of significance ourselves, which, even if it falls into ruin, will hereafter stimulate our successors to noble activity, in which our ancestors were never deficient.

These very instructive and spiritually uplifting viewings were, I may not say disturbed and interrupted, nevertheless intermingled with a painful feeling that accompanied me wherever I went. For I had learned that the fiancé of that amiable Milanese girl had gone back on his word, I do not know under what pretext, and broken off his engagement to her. On the one hand, I congratulated myself on not having yielded to my affection, on having quickly drawn back from the dear child, which, under the code of that *villegiatura,* was not held against me in the least, as I ascertained after the most minute inquiry. On the other hand, I felt very bad to see my pleasant image of her, which had heretofore accompanied me so cheerfully and amicably, now clouded and marred; for I soon heard that the shock and horror of this event had caused her to fall ill with a violent, life-threatening fever. I sent for word about her daily, and, at first, twice a day, while I endured the torment of an imagination that tried to visualize the impossible, that is, to conceive of those cheerful features, which were meant only for the open, merry daylight, which were expressive of a simple, quietly progressing life, as stained now with tears and disfigured by illness—of such fresh youthfulness grown prematurely pale and fragile from inward and outward suffering.

In this mood, of course, I was very glad to be distracted by a sequence of the most significant sights, whose existence and imperishable value were enough to occupy both my eyes and imagination; but it was only natural that I looked at most of them with heartfelt sorrow.

While, after so many centuries, the old monuments had mostly decayed into misshapen masses, it was likewise sad, with respect to splendid, undamaged modern buildings, that so many families had declined in these latter days. Indeed, even those that were still in a fresh, lively condition seemed to be gnawed by a secret worm; for how should an earthly entity with no real physical strength maintain itself in our day only with moral and religious supports? And just as a cheerful frame of mind can revive even the ruins, and, like fresh, evergreen vegetation, endow tumbled walls and scattered stones with life again, so a sad frame of mind strips the finest adornment from living existence, and would like to foist it on us as a naked skeleton.

Nor could I resolve on a mountain trip our merry group still planned to make before the onset of winter, until, certain that she was improving, and having made careful arrangements to keep informed, I was to receive news of her recovery in the very places where, in those lovely autumn days, I had come to know her as someone both lively and charming.

The first letters from Weimar about *Egmont* already contained some objections to this and that; whereupon I observed, as I had before, that the comfortably situated friend of literature, unpoetical himself, usually takes exception at places where the poet has tried to solve, gloss over, or hide a problem. The comfortable reader wants everything to follow a natural course; but even the unnatural can be natural, although it does not seem so to the person who persists in his own views. A letter with this content had arrived, I took it and went to the Villa Borghese; there I was obliged to read that several scenes were considered too long. I thought it over but still could not have shortened them, since there were such important motifs to be developed. But what seemed most objectionable to my women friends was the laconic way in which Egmont bequeaths Clare to Ferdinand.

An excerpt from the answer I wrote at that time will best explain my sentiments and state of mind.

"How gladly I would fulfill your wish now and modify Egmont's bequest a little! On a splendid morning, I hurried straight to the Villa Borghese with your letter. For two hours I reflected on the action of the drama, its characters, and the situation, and could find nothing that I ought to shorten. How I would like to write you all my deliberations, my pros and contras! They would fill enough paper for a book and contain a dissertation about the economy of my play. On Sunday I went to see Angelica and submitted the question to her. She has studied the play and owns a copy of the manuscript. I wish you could have been present, Charlotte, to hear with what feminine delicacy she analyzed everything, and her main point was that all of you wanted the hero also to explain orally what is implicitly contained in the apparition. Angelica said: Since the apparition only represents what is happening in the mind of the sleeping hero, there are no words that could express more forcefully how much he loves and appreciates her than this dream does, which lifts the charming creature not merely up to him, but above him. Indeed, it pleases Angelica very much that this man, whose whole life has been, so to speak, a waking dream, who has more than appreciated life and love, or rather, has appreciated them only through gratification, that he at last, still in a waking dream, as it were, quietly tells us how deeply in his heart his beloved dwells, and what a preeminent and important place she occupies within it.—She added still more observations, to the effect that, in the scene with Ferdinand, Clare could only be mentioned in a subordinate way, so as not to take away interest from his farewell to his young friend, who at this moment was in any case not capable of hearing or realizing anything.''

Moritz as an Etymologist

Long ago a wise man[173] spoke these true words: "Let the person whose powers are inadequate for doing what is necessary and useful happily occupy himself with the unnecessary and useless." Perhaps many people will judge the following in this manner.

Our comrade Moritz, although surrounded now by the most sublime art and most beautiful nature, continued musing and meditating constantly about the inner nature of the human being, his attitudes, and their development; therefore he also, and primarily, occupied himself with the universal aspects of language.

At that time, in the wake of Herder's prize-winning essay "Concerning the Origin of Language,"[174] and in keeping with the general notions of the day, the prevailing idea was this: the human race did not spring from a single pair and come down from the high Orient to spread over the whole earth; instead, at a certain remarkably productive period on the globe, after nature had endeavored to create, in stages, the most varied types of animals, humankind had emerged here and there, more or less perfected, in many a favorable location. Language now was born with the human being, standing in the most intimate relationship to his organs and mental capacities. No natural guidance was needed for this, nor any transmittal. And in this sense there was a universal language, which each autochthonous tribe had tried to manifest. The kinship of all languages lay in the uniformity of the idea according to which the creative force had formed and physically constituted the human race. This was why, partly out of basic impulse, partly from external causes, the very limited number of vowels and consonants had been used to express feelings and ideas, aptly or inaptly. For it was natural, indeed necessary, that the most diverse autochthons had sometimes met together, sometimes moved away from each other, and subsequently this or that language had either deteriorated or improved. What was true of the basic words was also true of the derivatives which are able to express and more clearly designate the connections between individual concepts and ideas. This, then, as something inexplicable, which would never be decided with certainty, could be let stand, and not pursued further.

Among my papers, I find the following particulars about this matter:

"I am pleased to see Moritz turning away from his brooding idleness, ill humor, and self-doubt to a kind of activity, for then he becomes delightful. Then his fancies have a real foundation, and his reveries have some purpose and sense. He is now occupied with an idea which I have gone along with too, and which entertains us very much. It is hard to tell about, because it will immediately sound insane. Nevertheless, I shall try:

"He has invented an intellectual and emotional alphabet, and demonstrates with it that the letters are not arbitrary, but are rooted in human nature. All of them belong to certain areas of the inner sense, which they express when enunciated. The languages can be judged according to this alphabet, and then it is seen that all nations have tried to express themselves in conformity with the inner sense; but, by accident and caprice, they have been diverted from the right path. Accordingly, we search the languages for the words which have best hit the mark, sometimes it is one language, sometimes another; then we alter the words until they seem right to us, make up new ones, etc. Indeed, when we are really feeling playful, we invent names for people, investigate whether this or that person has the appropriate name, etc., etc.

"So many people are now engaged in playing with etymology, and here it is keeping us busy too in this cheerful way. As soon as we come together, we begin the game as though it were chess, and we try hundreds of combinations, so that anyone who happened to overhear us would surely think us mad. Also, I would prefer to have it confided only to our closest friends. Suffice it to say, it is the cleverest game in the world and an incredible exercise for one's linguistic talent."

Filippo Neri, the Humorous Saint[175]

Filippo Neri, born in Florence in 1515, appears to have been, from childhood on, an obedient, well-behaved boy with pronounced natural gifts. Fortunately, a portrait of him as such is preserved in Fidanza's *Teste scelte,*[176] Volume V, plate 31. No healthier, heartier, more straightforward boy could be imagined. As the scion of a noble family, he is taught everything then considered good and worth knowing, and finally, it is not reported at what age, he is sent to Rome. Here he develops into a perfect youth; his handsome face, his abundant locks, distinguish him; he is both friendly and reserved, grace and dignity accompany him everywhere.

Here, at the saddest time, a few years after the cruel sacking of the city,[177] he follows the procedure and example of many noble souls by devoting himself entirely to pious exercises, and his enthusiasm mounts with his fresh, youthful energy. Incessant visiting of churches, especially the seven main churches, ardent, insistent praying for aid, diligent confessing and taking of communion, imploring and striving for spiritual blessings.

Once, in such an enthusiastic moment, he throws himself down on the altar steps and breaks some ribs, which heal poorly, causing him lifelong palpitation of the heart and intensifying his feelings.

Young men gather around him to practice morality and piety, they prove to be indefatigable in caring for the poor and nursing the sick; and they seem to ignore their studies. In all likelihood, they use their subsidies from home for benevolent purposes, in short, they constantly give and help, keeping nothing for themselves. Indeed, he later expressly refuses all assistance for his flock, turning over to the needy the sums awarded them by charity, while they themselves live in poverty.

However, their pious actions were too heartfelt and vigorous for them not to want to discuss the most important topics in a sensitive, spiritual manner. The little group still did not have its own place, but looked for one now in this monastery, now in that, where suitable empty rooms

were likely to be found. After a short silent prayer, a text of Holy
Scripture was read, and one or the other would give a short talk, either
interpreting or applying it. To be sure, they also discussed it, exclusively
with reference to direct action; subtle and dialectical treatment was
absolutely forbidden. The rest of the day was regularly devoted to attentive care of the sick, service in hospitals, and assistance to the poor
and destitute.

Since this situation was not a restrictive one, and the men could
come and go as they pleased, the number of participants increased
amazingly, and the group's activities also became more serious and
extensive. Also, they often read aloud from the lives of the saints and
consulted passages from the church fathers and church history, after
which four of the participants had the right and duty to speak, each
for half an hour.

This pious but prosaic, indeed familiar-practical, treatment of the
highest spiritual concerns attracted increasing attention, not only among
individuals, but even among whole corporate bodies. The meetings were
transferred to the cloisters and rooms of this and that church, the throng
increased, especially the Dominican order showed a marked inclination
to be edified in this way, and many Dominicans joined the constantly
growing band, which, owing to the vigor and high-mindedness of its
leader, remained absolutely uniform, and kept advancing on the same
path, even though tried by all sorts of adversities.

In accordance with the high principles of their admirable superior
all speculation was banned, and every one of their regulated activities
was focussed on life; however, life is unimaginable without some
amusement, and our man was able to fulfill the innocent needs and
desires of his followers also in this regard. In early spring he led them
to San Onofrio, which was a very agreeable place to go in such weather
because it was located on a broad height. Here, where everything in
the young season should be young, a handsome boy stepped forward
after silent prayers and recited a sermon he had learned by heart; prayers
followed, and a choir of specially invited singers performed pleasingly
and movingly at the end. This was all the more significant since, at that
time, music was neither widespread nor highly developed, and here,
for perhaps the first time, a hymn was sung in the open air.

Continuing to function in this manner, the congregation increased,
growing not only in numbers but also in significance. The Florentines
all but compelled their countrymen to move into the monastery of San
Girolamo, a dependency of theirs; here the establishment continued to
expand and function in the same way, until finally the pope assigned
it, near the Piazza Navone, its own monastery, which had been rebuilt
from the ground up and could accommodate a considerable number of
the pious comrades. Nevertheless, there was no change in their earlier
policy of making the word of God, that is to say, noble religious sen-

timents, more understandable to ordinary intelligence and incorporating it into ordinary, everyday life. They assembled as before, prayed, heard a text, listened to discussions about it, prayed, and, at the end, were entertained with music; and what took place quite often then, indeed daily, still takes place now on Sundays. Certainly, any traveler who has acquired some knowledge of the holy founder will in future, when attending these simple services, be especially edified if he opens his heart and mind to what we have already related and what we shall tell next.

Here, now, is the place to remind ourselves that this whole establishment still bordered on the secular. Thus only a few of them had joined the actual priesthood, and there were only as many ordained clerics among them as were needed for hearing confessions and celebrating mass. And so Filippo Neri himself had reached the age of thirty-six without announcing himself for the priesthood, for he seems to have felt free in the status he had and much more independent than he would have felt if put into ecclesiatical bonds—highly respected, to be sure, as a member of the great hierarchy, but limited all the same.

But orders came from above not to leave it at that. His father confessor put it to him as a matter of conscience to take holy orders and enter the priesthood. And that, indeed, is what happened; now the church had prudently drawn into its circle a man who, heretofore of independent spirit, had aimed at creating a situation in which the sacred and the secular, the noble and the commonplace, would combine and harmonize with each other. But this change, the transition to the priesthood, seems not to have had the slightest effect on his outward conduct.

He simply practices renunciation even more strictly than before and, together with others, lives wretchedly in an inferior little monastery. So, during a great famine, loaves he has received as a gift are given by him to another man, who is still needier, and he continues to serve the unfortunate.

But priesthood has a remarkably intensifying effect on his inner self. The duty of celebrating mass puts him into a state of enthusiasm, of ecstasy, in which we entirely lose sight of the man who was previously so natural. He hardly knows where he is walking, he staggers on the way to the altar and in front of it. When he elevates the host he cannot bring his arms down again; it seems as if an invisible force is pulling him upwards. He trembles and shudders while pouring the wine. And when, after the completed transubstantiation, he is supposed to partake of these mysterious gifts, he acts in a bizarre, inexpressibly voracious manner. He bites passionately into the chalice, in the rapt belief he is drinking the blood of the body that, shortly before, he has devoured almost greedily. But once this frenzy is past, we find a man who may be vehement and odd, but is nevertheless very sensible and practical.

Such a youth, such a man, going about his work in such a lively and unusual way, could not but seem strange to people, and occasionally tiresome and offensive because of his very virtues. Probably this is something he has often experienced in the course of his earlier life; but after he has been consecrated as a priest, and is satisfied to live so meagerly and miserably, as a guest, so to speak, in a poverty-stricken monastery, adversaries come forward, and pursue him relentlessly with mockery and scorn.

But we shall look deeper and say that, although he was a most distinguished man, he tried to master the arrogance innate in every individual of this type, and to cloak the radiance of his being in renunciation, privation, benevolence, humility, and disgrace. What he persistently and exclusively aimed at, in endeavoring to educate himself, and then his followers, was the idea of appearing foolish to the world, and of becoming, by this means, the more truly immersed and trained in God and godly things. St. Bernard's maxim:

Spernere mundum,
Spernere neminem,
Spernere te ipsum,
Spernere se sperni.[178]

seems to have thoroughly permeated him, or rather, to have developed out of him anew.

Similar goals, similar circumstances, compel human beings to fortify themselves with the same maxims. It is certain that persons who are the most exalted, the most inwardly proud, conform to those principles only because they have resolved to sample in advance the unpleasantness of a world that always resists the good and great, to empty the bitter cup of experience to the dregs even before it is offered to them. Many of those little tales about how he tested his followers have come down to us; however, in limitless quantity and uninterrupted series they really try the patience of every worldly person who hears them, just as those who were supposed to obey these commandments could not help feeling them extremely painful and nearly intolerable. Consequently, not everyone survived this ordeal by fire.

But before we begin with these peculiar stories, which may be somewhat unwelcome to the reader, we prefer to turn once more to those great merits which his contemporaries conceded to him and praised highly. According to them, he received his knowledge and culture from nature rather than from instruction and upbringing; everything that others acquire with effort had just been poured into him, so to speak. Furthermore, he possessed the great talent of being able to discern personality, to appreciate the qualities and assess the abilities of people; at the same time, he had very astute insight into worldly affairs, to such a degree that he was believed to possess the spirit of prophecy. A decided power of attraction, which the Italians express with the beautiful word *attrativa,* was given him in great measure, and it extended not only to people, but to animals. As an example, the story is told that a friend's dog attached itself to him, followed him everywhere, and also refused to stay with its first owner, who wanted it back very badly and tried in various ways to recover it. However, it always went back to the attractive man and never left his side, but instead, after several years, ended its life in its chosen master's bedroom. This creature now serves to bring us back to those tests, an occasion for which was provided by the dog itself. As is well known, in the Middle Ages generally, and probably also in Rome, it was considered very degrading to lead or carry dogs. In view of this, the pious man customarily led that animal through the city on a chain, and his followers also had to carry it through the streets in their arms, and in this way expose themselves to the laughter and scorn of the crowd.

He also demanded that his followers and associates assume other undignified guises. A young Roman prince who thought he too should have the honor of being considered a member of the order was required to promenade through Rome with a foxtail attached behind, and, when he refused to do so, was denied acceptance into the order. He sent another through the city without his tunic, and yet another with torn sleeves. A nobleman took pity on the latter, and offered him a new pair of sleeves, which the youth declined, but afterwards, by the master's order, had to fetch gratefully, and wear. When the new church was being built, he compelled his followers to carry up materials, like day laborers, and hand them to the workmen.

In like manner, he knew how to unsettle and destroy any intellectual self-satisfaction a person might feel. If a young man's sermon was succeeding, and the speaker looked pleased with himself, he would interrupt him in mid-sentence, and continue the talk in his stead, and might even order less capable novices to come up without hesitation, and begin to speak. The latter, being so unexpectedly called on, then had the good fortune of proving to do better, without preparation, than ever before.

Let us put ourselves back into the second half of the sixteenth century, and into the devastated situation in which Rome, under various popes, resembled a stormy sea. Then it will be easier to grasp how this method could not fail to be effective and powerful. Through inclination and fear, devotion and obedience, it lent great strength to man's inmost wish to preserve himself in spite of all external conditions, to withstand everything that could occur, since it enabled him to renounce absolutely even what was reasonable and sensible, what was conventional and proper.

A remarkable, although already well-known story about a test bears repetition here because of its special charm. It was announced to the holy father that a miracle-working nun was gaining renown in a rural convent. Our man receives the assignment to investigate the particulars of an affair that was so important for the church. He mounts his mule to carry out these orders; but he returns sooner than the holy father had expected. Neri counters the amazement of his ecclesiastical commander with the following words: "Most holy Father, this woman performs no miracles, for she lacks the foremost Christian virtue, humility. I arrive at the convent, ill treated by the bad road and the weather. I summon her before me in your name, she appears, and, instead of a greeting, I extend my boot to her, indicating that she should pull it off. She starts back in horror. What do I take her for! she cries; she is the handmaid of the Lord, but not of just anyone who comes along and demands menial services of her. I rose calmly, got back on my mule, stand here again before you, and am convinced that you will find no need for any further tests." Smiling, the pope let it go at that, and probably she was forbidden to work any more miracles.

If he took the liberty of testing others in this way, he also had to submit to being tested himself by like-minded men who were following the same path of self-denial. A mendicant friar, but one already in the odor of sanctity, meets him in the most crowded street and offers him a drink from the bottle of wine that he providently carries with him. Without a moment's hesitation, Filippo Neri bends his head back and boldly puts the long-necked demijohn to his lips, while the populace laughs loudly and mocks because two pious men are drinking each other's health in this fashion.

Filippo Neri, who, in spite of his piety and devotion, may have been somewhat annoyed by this, thereupon said: "You have tested me, now it is my turn," and immediately set his square biretta on the bald-headed friar, who was now jeered at in the same way, but walked on quite calmly, saying, "Whoever takes it off my head can have it." Neri took it off him, and they parted.

To be sure, to dare such things and still exert the greatest moral influence was only possible for a man like Filippo Neri, whose deeds could very often be regarded as miraculous. As a confessor, he made himself formidable, and therefore worthy of the greatest confidence; he uncovered sins in his penitents that they had concealed, faults they had ignored. His ardent, ecstatic prayers seemed supernatural to those around him; they were astonished and put into a state wherein people think they are actually experiencing through their senses what has probably been pictured to them by their emotionally charged imagination. In addition to this, if something miraculous, nay, impossible, is told and retold, at last it completely usurps the place of the real, the commonplace. So it was that not only did people claim to have seen him elevated over the altar at various times during the mass, but also that witnesses were found who beheld him, when he was kneeling to pray for the life of a very dangerously ill person, raised so high above the floor that his head almost touched the ceiling of the room.

Given a situation so thoroughly devoted to feeling and imagination, it was only natural that the interference of loathsome demons also did not seem to be entirely absent.

The pious man once saw a repulsive creature, like an ugly monkey, hopping around among the dilapidated walls of the baths of Antoninus; but at his command it immediately disappeared among ruins and apertures. But more significant than this single event is the way he handled his followers when they ecstatically reported to him that they had been blessed with joyous visions of the Virgin Mary and other saints. Well knowing that such hallucinations usually give rise to religious conceit, the worst and most stubborn kind of all, he assured them that a hideous, diabolical darkness lay behind this heavenly brightness and beauty. To prove it, he ordered them, if a gracious maiden of this type returned, to spit right into her face; they obeyed, with successful results, for a devil's mask immediately emerged.

The great man may have commanded this consciously, or, as is more likely, out of deep instinct. Suffice it to say, he was sure that the image, which had been evoked by fanciful love and longing, would immediately be transformed into a monster by reacting to it boldly with hate and scorn.

However, he was entitled to use this very curious pedagogy because of his most extraordinary natural gifts, which appeared to hover between the extremely spiritual and the extremely physical: sensing the approach of a person as yet unseen, having a presentiment of distant events, reading the thoughts of someone standing in front of him, compelling others to accept his ideas.

These and similar gifts can be distributed among several persons, and many an individual can boast of having them at one time or other, but the uninterrupted presence of such abilities, the ready exercise of such astonishingly effective powers in every case, this is perhaps conceivable only in a century when concentrated, unfragmented powers of body and spirit could be displayed with amazing energy.

But let us consider this temperament—longing for and driven to independent, unrestricted spiritual action—when it must feel itself constrained again by the tight clasp of Roman-ecclesiastical bonds.

The missionary work of St. Francis Xavier[179] among the idolatrous heathen may well have caused a great sensation in Rome at that time. Stirred by this, Neri and some of his friends also felt themselves drawn to the so-called Indies and wanted to go there with papal consent. But the father confessor, probably acting under strict instructions from above, dissuaded them and made them reflect that there were Indies enough to be found in Rome itself for godly men whose aim was to help their neighbors and propagate religion, and that a worthy arena was open here for their activity. They were informed that a great calamity might soon be threatening the great city itself, since, for some time, the three fountains at the San Sebastiano gate had been flowing dark and bloody, which was to be viewed as an infallible omen.

So the worthy Neri and his associates, pacified by this, presumably continued their benevolent, miracle-working life inside Rome. This much is certain, that increasingly, from year to year, he won the confidence and esteem of great and small, old and young.

Let us now ponder the marvelous complexity of human nature, wherein the sharpest contrasts are adjusted, the material and the spiritual, the routine and the impossible, the repulsive and the charming, the restricted and the limitless—and we could continue with a long register of this kind. Let us consider such a conflict when it happens and is manifested in a superior person, how, because of the incomprehensible things that intrude, it confuses the mind, unfetters the imagination, goes beyond faith, and justifies superstition, thereby bringing the natural condition into direct contact with the most unnatural one, indeed unifying them. If we apply these observations to the extensively reported life of our man, then we can conceive of what an influence such an individual must have acquired through almost a whole century of ceaseless and unremitting activity on such a large stage in an enormous element. People's high opinion of him went so far that they not only derived profit, benefit, and a beatific feeling from his energetic actions when he was in good health, but found their confidence increased even by his illnesses, since they were moved to regard these as signs of his most intimate relationship with God and the most godly things. This makes us understand how, while still alive, he was advancing toward the dignity of sainthood, and his death merely reinforced what had been intended for him and granted to him by his contemporaries.

When, therefore, soon after his passing, which was accompanied by even more miracles than his life, the question was brought to Pope Clement VIII[180] whether it was permissible to start with the investigation, the so-called "process," that precedes a beatification, the pope answered: "I have always considered him a saint, and accordingly cannot object if the Church announces and presents him as such to believers in general."

Now, however, it might be considered worthy of attention that, in the long sequence of years granted him for his work, he experienced fifteen popes, having been born under Leo X[181] and ended his days under Clement VIII. Consequently, he presumed to maintain an independent posture even toward the pope, and while, as a limb of the Church, he certainly conformed to its general regulations, in individual matters he did not show submissiveness toward the supreme head of the Church, but even acted imperiously. This also explains why he absolutely refused the rank of cardinal, and, in his Chiesa Nuova, like a rebellious knight in an old castle, dared to behave rudely to the supreme lord protector.

All in all, the character of that relationship, which was still preserved in quite a curious form at the end of the sixteenth century from earlier, cruder times, cannot be presented more clearly to the eye, or more impressively to the mind, than by the petition issued to the new pope, Clement VIII, by Neri shortly before his death; and this received an equally curious response.

These provide us with an otherwise unobtainable glimpse into the relationship of a man nearly eighty years old, who was advancing to the rank of saint, with a sovereign head of the Roman Catholic church who reigned in a significant, capable, and very estimable manner for a considerable number of years.

Petition of Filippo Neri to Clement VIII

"Most holy Father! And, pray tell, who am I, that cardinals should come to visit me, and, in particular, yesterday evening the Cardinals of Florence and Cusano? And, because I needed a few flakes of manna,[182] the aforementioned Cardinal of Florence had two ounces of it fetched for me from San Spirito, since my Lord Cardinal had sent a great quantity to that hospital. Then he stayed two hours after nightfall, and said many good things about Your Holiness, far more than I thought proper; for, since you are the pope, you should be the soul of humility. Christ came at seven o'clock at night to embody Himself in me, and Your Holiness could come to our church sometime as well. Christ is man and God, and He visits me rather frequently. Your Holiness is just a human being, born of a holy and upright man, He, however, of God the Father. Your Holiness's mother is Signora Agnesina, a very God-fearing lady; but His is the Virgin of all virgins. How many more things I could say, if I were to vent my spleen fully! I command Your Holiness that you do my will with regard to a girl I want to send to Torre de' specchi.[183] She is the daughter of Claudio Neri, whose children Your Holiness has promised to protect; and let me remind you that it is nice for a pope to keep his word. Therefore leave the aforementioned affair to me and allow me to use your name if necessary; with all the more reason since I know the girl's wishes, and am certain that she is moved by divine inspiration. And with the greatest humility, which I owe you, I kiss your most holy feet."

The Pope's Resolution
Written in his Own Hand under the Petition

"The pope says that the first part of this writing contains something of the spirit of vanity, since he is supposed to learn from it that you are so often visited by cardinals; unless, perhaps, it is supposed to indicate to us that these gentlemen are religiously inclined, as we already know quite well. With regard to his not having come to see you, his answer is that Your Reverence does not deserve it, since you have refused to accept the cardinalate which has been so frequently offered to you. As far as the command is concerned, he is satisfied that you, with your customary imperiousness, give stiff rebukes to those good mothers who do not act according to your lights. Now, however, he commands you to take care of yourself, and not to hear confessions without his permission. But if our Lord comes to visit you, pray for us and for the most urgent needs of Christendom."

January

Correspondence

Rome, January 5, 1788.

Forgive me for writing so briefly today. I have begun this year with serious intent and diligence and can hardly spare a moment.

After an inactive period of several weeks, during which I was ill, I again have the finest revelations, as I may well call them. I am permitted to cast glances into the essence and relationships of things, and a vast mine of wealth opens up before me. These effects are produced in my spirit because I am always learning and, indeed, learning from others. When a person teaches himself, the generating and assimilating powers are one, and the steps forward must become smaller and slower.

I am now completely preoccupied with the study of the human body. Everything else pales beside it. It is something that has affected me strangely all my life, and again now. It is not something I can talk about; time will tell what I shall still accomplish.

The operas do not entertain me. Only what is profoundly and eternally true can delight me now.

Towards Easter, an epoch will reach its climax—I feel that. What will develop, I do not know.

Rome, January 10.

Erwin and Elmira comes with this letter, may this little play really please you, Charlotte! But an operetta, if it is a good one, can never be satisfactory when merely read; the music must be added, so that the whole idea the poet had in mind can be expressed. *Claudina* will follow soon. Both plays are more extensively revised than they appear to be, because it was only with Kayser that I finally made a proper study of the operetta form.

I continue diligently drawing the human body, for example evenings during the perspective lesson. I am preparing myself for my disengagement, so that I may submit to it without regrets, if the gods have ordained it for Easter. May all go well.

My interest in the human form now cancels out everything else. I am well aware of this, and used to turn away from it, as one turns away from the dazzling sun; moreover, any attempt to study it outside of Rome is in vain. Without the thread that one can only learn to spin here, it is impossible to find the way out of this labyrinth. Unfortunately, my thread will not be long enough, but at least it is helping me through the first passageways.

If I continue finishing my writings under the same constellations, then, in the course of this year, I shall have to fall in love with a princess to be able to write *Tasso* and succumb to the devil to write *Faust,* although I have little inclination to do either. For that has been the situation up to now. I was not even interested in my *Egmont* until the Holy Roman Kaiser picked a quarrel with the citizens of Brabant; and, to give my operas some degree of perfection, the Zurich Kayser came to Rome. So I must really be a "noble Roman," as Herder says, and I find it rather amusing to have become a final cause of actions and events which are not directed toward me at all. That is genuine good luck. So we shall patiently await the princess and the devil.

Rome, January 10.

Here is another little sample of German art and manner coming to you from Rome, *Erwin and Elmira.* It was finished sooner than *Claudina,* but I do not want it to be printed first.

You will soon see, Herder, that it is wholly designed to fit the requirements of the musical stage, which I did not have the opportunity to study before coming here: to employ all the personages in a certain succession, in a certain measure, so that each singer has enough rest intervals, etc. There are a hundred things to observe, to which the Italians sacrifice all the sense of the poem. I hope that I have succeeded in satisfying those musical-theatrical demands with a little play that is not completely nonsensical. Another consideration for me was that the two operettas be readable, and not disgrace their neighbor *Egmont.* No one reads an Italian libretto, except on the evening of the performance, and to print one in the same volume with a tragedy would be considered as impossible in these parts as anyone's being able to sing German.

With respect to *Erwin,* I must add that you will frequently find trochaic meter, especially in the second act; it is not an accident or habit, but taken from Italian examples. This meter lends itself especially well to music, and the composer can vary it to such a degree with different rhythms and beats that the listener never recognizes it. And in general the Italians like nothing but smooth, simple meters and rhymes.

Young Camper[184] is an enthusiast who knows a great deal and grasps quickly, but does not go deeply into things.

Congratulations on the fourth part of the *Ideas!*[185] The third part is a sacred book for us, which I keep locked away. Only now has Moritz been given an opportunity to read it, and he considers himself fortunate to live in this period of the education of the human race. He showed very good feeling for the book and was quite beside himself about the end of it.

If only someday I could entertain you on the Capitol in return for all your kindness! It is one of my dearest wishes.

My titanic ideas[186] were just chimeras haunting me on my way to a more serious epoch. I am now engrossed in the study of the human form, which is the non plus ultra of all human knowing and doing. The fact that I have diligently prepared myself by studying all of nature, especially osteology, helps me to progress rapidly. Only now do I see, only now enjoy, the most sublime relics of antiquity, that is, the statues. Indeed, I perceive that one could study for a whole lifetime and might still cry at the end: "Only now do I see, only now enjoy."

I am gathering up everything possible, so that around Easter I can conclude a certain epoch, the end of which is now in sight, and leave Rome without marked reluctance. I hope to be able to continue some studies in Germany, conveniently and thoroughly, although quite slowly. Here, the stream carries a person along as soon as he has boarded his little ship.

Report

January

Ah, Cupid, naughty, obstinate little fellow,
You asked to stay with me for just a few hours!
How many days and nights you've managed to linger,
And now are giving the orders and running the household.

Away from my broad couch I see myself driven,
And sit at night upon the earthen floor, tormented,
Your mischief stirs up flame on flame in the fireplace,
And burns my supply for the winter, while singeing me also.

You shift and shove my things, creating total disorder,
I look for them but feel confused, as though blinded,
You are so loud and awkward I fear my spirit
Will flee, so as to flee you, and cede you my dwelling.[187]

If the little poem quoted above is not taken literally, if my readers do not think here of the demon we usually call Amor, but imagine instead a group of active individuals who address and challenge a person's innermost being, pull him this way and that, and confuse him by dividing his interest, then, in a symbolical manner, they will be participating in the situation in which I found myself, and which has been sufficiently depicted in the excerpts from my letters and my previous narratives. It will be admitted that great effort was required of me to maintain myself against so many things, not to grow weary of active work, and not to become indolent about assimilating things.

Induction into the Arcadian Society[188]

As early as the end of the previous year, I was importuned with a proposal that I viewed as a result of that fatal concert by which we had rashly revealed our incognito. Yet there could have been other reasons why I was pressed from several sides to let myself be inducted into the "Arcadia" as a notable shepherd. I resisted for a long time but eventually had to give in to my friends, who seemed to attach a special importance to this.

It is known in a general way what is meant by this Arcadian Society; but probably no one will be averse to learning more about it.

Italian poetry seems to have deteriorated in various ways in the seventeenth century; for, towards the end of this period, cultured, well-intentioned men reproached it with having neglected substance, which was termed "inner beauty" at that time; it also certainly merited censure with respect to form, or external beauty. For, with barbaric expressions, intolerably harsh verses, defective figures and tropes, and especially with continual and unbridled hyperbole, metonymies, and metaphors, it had completely forfeited the qualities of charm and sweetness that are so much prized and enjoyed in the external form.

Nevertheless, as is usually the case, the writers who were mired in those wrong paths reviled what was genuine and excellent, so that their abuses might continue unchallenged. But then, at last, cultured and sensible people could no longer tolerate this, and, as a result, a number of circumspect and enterprising men met together in the year 1690 to discuss adopting another course.

But, to prevent their meetings from making a stir and inviting opposition, they went out into the open air, to bucolic garden surroundings, a good many of which are enclosed and marked off within the walls of Rome itself. This also gave them the benefit of getting close to nature and sensing the primeval spirit of poetry out in the fresh air. There they lay down on the grass at random spots or sat down on architectural ruins and blocks of stone, where even the cardinals who were present could be honored with nothing but a softer cushion. Here they talked with each other about their convictions, principles, and intentions; here they read poems in which they tried to revive the essence of higher antiquity and of the noble Tuscan school.[189] Then one of them cried out in rapture: "Here is our Arcadia!" This, as well as the idyllic quality of their arrangements, furnished the name of the society. They did not desire the protection of any great and influential man's patronage; they were not willing to acknowledge any master, any president. The Arcadian precincts were to be opened and closed by a custodian, who was to be assisted in the most necessary matters by a council of elected elders.

Here the name Crescimbeni[190] deserves honorable mention, for this man can surely be considered one of the founders; and, as the first custodian, he executed his office faithfully for many years, keeping watch over a better, purer taste and becoming increasingly successful at eliminating barbarisms.

His dialogues on *poesia volgare*—which should not be translated as "folk poetry," as might be expected, but as poetry befitting a nation because it is written by definite, genuine talents, and not spoiled by the fancies and oddities of individual eccentrics—his dialogues, in which he expounds the better doctrine, are obviously the fruit of Arcadian discussions, and very important as a parallel to our new esthetic endeavors. The poems of the Arcadia that he published also merit all our attention in this respect. For the present, we permit ourselves only the following observation.

Certainly the worthy shepherds had intended to get closer to nature by lying about on the green grass in the open air, and, under such circumstances, love and passion often attack the human heart by stealth. But this society consisted of clerical gentlemen and other dignified persons who were forbidden to become involved with the Amor of those Roman triumvirs, and therefore expressly eliminated him. However, since love is quite indispensable to the poet, they had no choice but to turn to spiritual, more or less Platonic, yearnings, and likewise to indulge in allegory. Consequently, their poems acquired a quite respectable, individual character, since, moreover, they could follow the example of their great predecessors, Dante and Petrarch, in this.

My arrival in Rome coincided with this society's one hundredth year of existence, and, in spite of various changes of location and sentiments, it had always maintained, even if not great prestige, at least its decorum in regard to external form. And foreign visitors who were in any way significant were seldom allowed to tarry in Rome without being lured into membership, especially since this was the only means by which the guardian of these poetic rusticities, whose income was modest, could eke out a living for himself.

But the actual ceremony proceeded as follows: In the anterooms of an elegant house, I was introduced to a distinguished clerical gentleman and informed that he was the one who was supposed to present me, acting, so to speak, as my sponsor or godfather. We entered a large, already rather crowded salon, and sat down in the very middle of the first row of chairs, opposite a lectern that had been set up. More and more auditors approached; the seat left empty at my right was taken by a stately older man, who I had to assume was a cardinal because of his clothing and the respect that was shown him.

The custodian made a general introductory speech from the lectern, then called on several persons, some of whom spoke in verse, others in prose. After this had gone on for a considerable time, the custodian began a speech whose content and form I shall pass over, since it corresponded entirely with the diploma I received and propose to append here. After this, I was formally declared one of their members, and was accepted and recognized amid much handclapping.

My so-called godfather and I had stood up meanwhile, and thanked them with many bows. He, however, made a well-composed, not excessively long, appropriate speech, whereupon general applause was heard again. After it died down, I had the opportunity to thank them individually, and take my leave. The diploma, which I received the next day, follows here in the original, and has not been translated, because in any other language it would lose its characteristic flavor. In the meantime, I sought to make the custodian very well satisfied with his new fellow shepherd.

C.U.C.

By Resolution of the Entire Society

Nivildo Amarinzio

Nivildo Amarinzio

Custode generale d'Arcadia

Custodian General of Arcadia

Travandosi per avventura a beare le sponde del Tebbro uno di quei
One of those geniuses of the first rank who flourish in Germany today,
Genj di prim' Ordine, ch'oggi fioriscono nella Germania qual' è l'Inclito
the famous and erudite Mr. von Goethe, privy councilor to his Serene
ed Erudito Signor DE GOETHE Consigliere attuale di Stato di Sua Altezza
Highness, the Duke of Saxe-Weimar, chancing to bless the shores of

Serenissima il Duca di Sassonia Weimar, ed avendo celato fra noi con
the Tiber with his presence, and with philosophical restraint concealing
filosofica moderazione la chiarezza della sua Nascità, de' suoi Min-
from us the illustriousness of his birth, his ministries, and his virtue,
isterj, e della virtù sua, non ha potuto ascondere la luce, che hanno
has not been able to hide the light diffused by his most learned pro-
sparso le sue dottissime produzioni tanto in Prosa ch' in Poesia per
ductions both in prose and verse, for which he has become celebrated
cui si è reso celebre a tutto il Mondo Letterario. Quindi essendosi com-
in the whole world of letters. Therefore this aforesaid Mr. von Goethe,
piaciuto il suddetto rinomato Signor DE GOETHE d'intervenire in una
having consented to attend one of our public Academy sessions, had
delle pubbliche nostre Accademie, appena Egli comparve, come un
hardly appeared, like an unknown celestial body in our forest, and in
nuovo astro di cielo straniero tra le nostre selve, ed in una delle nostre
one of our genial meetings, when the Arcadians, gathered together in
Geniali Adunanze, che gli Arcadi in gran numero convocati co' segni
great numbers, with signs of the most sincere joy and approval resolved
del più sincero giubilo ed applauso vollero distinguerlo come Autore
by voice vote to distinguish him, as the author of such celebrated works,
di tante celebrate opere, con annoverarlo a viva voce tra il più illustri
by numbering him among the very illustrious members of their pastoral
membri della loro Pastoral Società sotto il Nome di Megalio, e vollero
society under the name of Megalio, and have likewise resolved to assign
altresi assegnare al Medesimo il possesso delle Campagne Melpomenie
him possession of the Melpomenean fields sacred to the Tragic Muse,
sacre alla Tragica Musa dichiarandolo con ciò Pastore Arcade di Nu-
declaring him thereby one of the number of Arcadian shepherds. At
mero. Nel tempo stesso il Ceto Universale commise al Custode Gen-
the same time the whole Society commissioned its Custodian General
erale di registrare l'Atto pubblico e solenne di si applaudita anno-
to register the solemn public document of this so greatly applauded
verazione tra i fasti d'Arcadia, e di presentare al Chiarissimo Novello
initiation among the annals of Arcadia, and to present our new fellow
Compastore Megalio Melpomenio il presente Diploma in segno dell'
shepherd Megalio Melpomenio with the present diploma as a token of
altissima stima, che fa la nostra Pastorale Letteraria Repubblica de'
the highest esteem given in perpetual memory by our literary-pastoral
chiari e nobili ingegni a perpetua memoria. Dato dalla Capanna del
republic of illustrious and noble spirits. Given from the Cottage of the
Serbatojo dentro il Bosco Parrasio alla Neomenia di Possideone Olim-
Conservatory in the Parrasian forest at the neomenia of Poseidon,

piade DCXLI. Anno II. dalla Ristorazione d'Arcadia Olimpiade XXIV.
Olympiad DCXLI, Anno II, from the restoration of Arcadia Olympiad
Anno IV. Giorno lieto per General Chiamata.
XXIV, Anno IV. A joyous day by general acclaim.

Nivildo Amarinzio Custode Generale
Custodian General

The seal displays a wreath
half of laurel, half of
stone pine, in the middle a
panpipe, under it
"Gli Arcadi"

Corimbo
Melicronio
Florimonte
Egiréo

} *Sotto-Custodi*
Sub-custodians

The Roman Carnival[191]

In undertaking a description of the Roman carnival, we must fear the objection that such a festivity really cannot be described. Such a great living mass of sentient objects should move directly before one's eyes and be viewed and comprehended by each individual in his own way.

The objection becomes still graver when we ourselves have to admit that the Roman carnival makes neither a complete nor a pleasant impression on any foreign observer who is seeing it for the first time, and only can and wants to see; it neither particularly delights his eye nor satisfies his heart and mind.

The long, narrow street, in which innumerable people trundle back and forth, cannot be viewed in its entirety; even in the section of the tumult that the eye can encompass, hardly anything is distinguishable. The movement is monotonous, the noise deafening, the end of the period unsatisfactory. But these misgivings will soon disappear when we explain ourselves more clearly; and the main question will be whether the description itself vindicates us.

The Roman carnival is a festival that really is not given to the people, but one the people give themselves.

The state makes few arrangements for it, and goes to little expense. The circle of pleasures revolves by itself, and the police regulate it only with a lenient hand.

This is not a festival to dazzle the eyes of the spectators, like the many religious festivals of Rome. Here there are no fireworks to provide a unique, amazing view from Castel Sant' Angelo; here there is no illumination of St. Peter's and its dome, which attracts and pleases so many foreign visitors from every land; here there is no brilliant procession at whose approach the people are supposed to pray and marvel; rather, here a signal is given that everyone may be as foolish and absurd as he wishes, and that except for blows and stabbings almost everything is permitted.

The difference between high and low seems to be set aside for a moment; everyone draws closer to everyone else, everyone takes in good part whatever happens to him, and reciprocal impudence and license are balanced by a general good humor.

During these days the Roman rejoices still in our times that the birth of Christ, while delaying the festival of the Saturnalia and its privileges for a few weeks, could not abolish it.

We shall endeavor to make the joys and frenzy of these days come alive in the imagination of our readers. We also flatter ourselves that we can be of service to those persons who have actually once witnessed the Roman carnival and may now be pleased to have a lively reminder of those times; also to those who are still contemplating that trip and for whom these few pages will make it possible to survey and enjoy a rushed and quickly passing pleasure.

The Corso

The Roman carnival assembles in the Corso. This street delimits and defines the public festivities on these days. In any other place, it would be a different festival; and therefore, before all else, we must describe the Corso itself.

As is the case with several long streets in Italian cities, the name derives from horse racing, with which every carnival evening concludes in Rome, and which in other places ends other festivities, such as the festival of a patron saint or a parish fair.

The street goes in a straight line from the Piazza del Populo to the Venetian palace. It is some four and one-half thousand paces in length, and is lined by high, mostly magnificent buildings. Its width is not in proportion to its length and the height of the buildings. On both sides, raised pavements for pedestrians take away approximately six to eight feet. In the middle, at most places, a space of only twelve to fourteen paces is left for vehicles, and thus it is easy to see that at best only three of them can find room here to move next to each other.

The obelisk on the Piazza del Populo is the lower boundary of this street during the carnival; the Venetian palace is the upper one.

Promenade in the Corso

The Roman Corso is lively every Sunday and on all annual festival days. The wealthier and more aristocratic Romans go for a drive here one or two hours before nightfall in a very long procession; the carriages come down from the Venetian palace, keep to the left side and, if the weather is fair, drive past the obelisk, out at the gate, and onto the Flaminian Way, sometimes as far as Ponte Molle.

When, sooner or later, they turn around and come back, they keep to the other side; thus the two rows of vehicles move past each other in the best order.

The ambassadors have the right to drive up and down between the two rows. The Pretender, who was sojourning in Rome under the name "Duke of Albany,"[192] was likewise entitled to do this.

As soon as night is tolled, this order is interrupted; each driver turns where he pleases, looking for the nearest way out, often to the inconvenience of many other equipages, which are thereby hindered and delayed in the narrow space.

The evening promenade, which is brilliant in all large Italian cities, and imitated in every small one, even if only with a few coaches, attracts many pedestrians to the Corso; everbody comes to see or be seen.

As we shall soon see, the carnival is really just a continuation, or rather the culmination, of those customary Sunday and festival-day delights; it is nothing new, nothing unfamiliar, nothing unique, but, on the contrary, is just a natural adjunct to the Roman way of life.

Climate, Ecclesiastical Costumes

Nor will it strike us as strange when we now begin to see a multitude of masqueraders out in the open, since we are accustomed to seeing so many a curious scene in ordinary life all year long under this bright, sunny sky.

For every festival, the streets are transformed into great rooms and galleries, as it were, by stretching cloths above them, hanging out tapestries, and strewing flowers.

No corpse is carried to the grave unaccompanied by costumed brotherhoods; the many monks' habits accustom the eye to odd and unfamiliar figures; it seems to be carnival all year long, and the abbés in their black clothing seem to represent the nobler *tabarri* among the other ecclesiastical costumes.

The Early Period

From New Year's onward, the theaters are open again, and the carnival has begun. Here and there in the loges we see a beauty dressed as an officer, and with the greatest aplomb she will show off her epaulets to the populace. The promenade in the Corso includes more carriages; but what everyone is waiting for is the last week.

Preparations for the Final Week

Various preparations announce to the public the coming of those paradisiacal hours.

The Corso, one of the few streets in Rome kept clean throughout the year, is now still more carefully swept and cleaned. Workmen are busy repairing the beautiful pavement, which is composed of small, rectangular, fairly uniform pieces of basalt. They dig up these basalt wedges wherever there seems to be even a slight irregularity and reset them properly.

Besides this, there are also living harbingers. As we have already mentioned, every carnival evening concludes with a race. The horses kept for this purpose are mostly small and, because of the foreign origin of the best among them, are called barbs.[193]

A little horse of this kind, with a cover of white linen fitted closely to its head, neck, and body, and trimmed on the seams with colorful ribbons, is brought to the spot in front of the obelisk from which it is subsequently to start running. It is trained to stand still for a while, with its head pointing toward the Corso, then it is gently led along the street and given a small amount of oats up at the Venetian palace, so that it will become interested in running the course that much faster.

This exercise is repeated with most of the horses, often fifteen to twenty at a time, the promenade always being accompanied by a number of merrily shouting boys, and so this already gives a foretaste of the greater noise and jubilation that are soon to follow.

In former times, the leading Roman families maintained this breed in their stables; it was considered an honor for such a horse to win the prize. Bets were placed, and the victory was celebrated with a banquet.

Recently, however, this fancy has abated to a great extent, and the desire to acquire fame with one's horses has descended to the middle and even to the lowest class of people.

It may be a custom going back to those old times that a troop of riders which goes all around Rome, accompanied by trumpeters, to show off the prizes, also rides into the houses of the upper class and, after a little piece has been played on the trumpets, receives a gratuity.

The prize consists of a piece of gold or silver brocade some three and one-half yards long and not quite a yard wide, which, being attached to a colorful pole, floats like a banner; and a picture of some running horses is woven in across the lower end.

This prize is called the *palio,* and, as many days as the carnival lasts, that is how many such quasi-standards are shown through the streets of Rome by the aforementioned procession.

Meanwhile the Corso also begins to change its form; the obelisk now becomes the boundary of the street. A stand with many rows of seats is raised in front of it, looking straight into the Corso. Barriers are set up before the stand, between which the horses are soon to be brought to start off the race.

More large stands are built on both sides, adjoining the first houses on the Corso, and in this way the street is extended into the square. Small elevated and covered arches stand on both sides of the barriers for the persons who are to regulate the starting of the horses.

We also see stands erected before many houses along the Corso. The squares of San Carlo and the Antonine column are closed off from the street by barriers, and everything quite plainly indicates that the whole festivity should and will be limited to the long, narrow Corso.

Finally, the middle of the street is strewn with pozzuolana,[194] so that the competing horses cannot slip so easily on the smooth pavement.

Signal for Complete Carnival Freedom

Thus expectations are fed and stirred every day, until at last, soon after midday, a bell toll from the Capitol gives the sign that permission is granted to act foolish out in the open.

At this moment, the serious Roman, who throughout the year has carefully guarded against any false step, suddenly casts aside his gravity and his caution.

The pavers, who have kept on clattering up to the last moment, pack up their tools and, with a joke, put an end to their work. All the balconies, all the windows, are gradually hung with tapestries, chairs are set out on the raised pavements at either side of the street, the humbler local inhabitants and all the children are in the street, which now ceases to be a street; instead, it looks like a large festival hall, an enormous decorated gallery.

For, just as all the windows are hung with tapestries, so all the stands are covered with old woven wall hangings; the many chairs add to the idea of a room, and the friendly sky seldom reminds one that there is no roof.

So the street gradually seems more and more livable. On stepping out of the house, a person does not think he is in the open air among strangers, but in a salon among acquaintances.

Guards

While the Corso is becoming increasingly crowded, and here and there a Pulcinella appears among the many persons strolling in their ordinary clothes, soldiers have gathered before the Porta del Populo. Led by a general on horseback, they move up the Corso in good array and new uniforms, with a military band, immediately occupy all the entrances to the street, set up a few guardhouses on the main squares, and assume responsibility for maintaining order in the whole affair.

The people who rent out chairs and stands now shout eagerly to the passersby: "Luoghi! Luoghi, padroni! Luoghi!"[195]

Masqueraders

Now the masqueraders begin to multiply. Young men decked out in the festive clothing of women of the lowest class, with bared bosom and impudent smugness, are usually the first to show themselves. They caress any men whom they meet, behave coarsely and familiarly with the women, as if with their own kind, and do whatever else is prompted by their mood, wit, or naughtiness.

Among others, we remember a young fellow who expertly played the role of a passionate, quarrelsome, and totally unmanageable woman and made his way down the whole Corso in that fashion, bickering and finding fault with everyone, while his companions seemed to be trying every means to calm him.

Here a Pulcinella comes running with a big horn rocking at his hips, tied on with colored strings. With a slight movement, while he is chatting with the women, he can brazenly imitate the figure of the ancient god of gardens[196] in holy Rome, and his bawdiness causes more merriment than anger. Here comes another of the kind, who, more modest and content, brings his pretty partner with him.

Since the women take as much delight in appearing in men's clothes as the men do in women's, they have not failed to adopt the popular Pulcinella costume, and it must be admitted that they often succeed in looking extremely charming in this hybrid form.

With quick steps, declaiming as though in court, a lawyer pushes his way through the crowd. He shouts up to the windows, takes hold of costumed and uncostumed strollers, threatens each of them with a lawsuit, reels off to one person a long history of ridiculous crimes that the latter is supposed to have committed, gives another a detailed list of his debts. He scolds the women because of their cicisbei,[197] the girls because of their lovers; he refers to a book he carries with him, produces documents, and all of that with a penetrating voice and fluent tongue. He tries to embarrass and confuse everybody. Just when one thinks he has finished, he really starts in; when one thinks he has gone away, he turns back; he heads straight for one person, and then does not address him, but takes hold of another who has already passed. If a member of his fraternity happens to meet him, then the madness reaches its peak.

But they cannot hold the attention of the public for long; even the maddest impression is soon swallowed up again in the crowd and its variety.

The Quakers, in particular, create just as great a sensation as the lawyers, while making less noise. The Quaker costume seems to have become so general because of the ease with which old-fashioned garments can be found on the second-hand market.

The main requirements of this costume are that the clothes, while old-fashioned, should be in good condition and of expensive materials. These masqueraders are seldom seen dressed in anything but silk or satin, they wear brocaded or embroidered vests, and the Quaker must be corpulent of figure; his mask covers his whole face and has chubby cheeks and little eyes; his wig has odd little pigtails; his hat is small and usually trimmed.

Obviously, this figure is very close to the *buffo caricato* of the comic opera, and, just as this personage usually plays a silly, love-sick, hoodwinked fool, so these also act like tasteless fops. They hop around very lightly on their toes; instead of lorgnettes they carry big black rings without glass, with which they look into all the carriages and up to all the windows. They usually make a deep, stiff bow and demonstrate their joy, especially when they meet each other, by hopping straight up and down several times, with both feet together, and uttering a shrill, penetrating, inarticulate sound that is connected with the consonants *brr*.

Often this sound is a signal they give to each other, and the nearest ones repeat it, so that in a short time the shrill tone runs up and down the whole Corso.

Meanwhile, mischievous boys blow into large spiral shells and offend the ear with unbearable noises.

It soon becomes evident that, considering the narrowness of the space, the similarity of so many masquerade costumes (for there may easily be several hundred Pulcinellas and nearly one hundred Quakers running up and down the Corso), few can have any intention of causing a stir or being noticed. Those who do must appear in the Corso quite early. Rather, each one just goes out to find pleasure, to give vent to his foolishness, and enjoy to the full the freedom of these days.

Especially the girls and women seek amusement in their fashion and know how to do it. Each one just wants to get out of the house and disguise herself in some way or other. While only very few are in a position to spend much money, they are quite resourceful at contriving all sorts of ways not so much of adorning as of concealing themselves.

The costumes of male and female beggars are very easily made; beautiful hair is a prime requisite, then an all-white face mask and a little earthen pot on a colored ribbon, a staff and a hat in their hand. With a gesture of humility they step under the windows and up to everyone and, instead of alms, receive candy, nuts, and whatever other pleasant things people may give them.

Others take even less trouble, wrap up in furs, or appear in a pretty housedress with just a face mask. For the most part they go around without men, carrying as their offensive and defensive weapon a little broom tied together out of the flowering parts of a reed. This they use either to ward off too bothersome admirers or, playfully enough, to wave in the faces of uncostumed people they encounter, whether acquaintances or strangers.

When someone they take aim at finds himself surrounded by four or five such girls, he cannot escape. The throng keeps him from fleeing, and wherever he turns, he feels the brooms under his nose. To defend himself in earnest against this or other forms of teasing would be very dangerous, because the masqueraders are sacrosanct, and every guard has orders to assist them.

The ordinary clothing of all occupations must also serve as costumes. Stable boys come with their big brushes to rub the back of anyone they please. *Vetturini* offer their services in their usual importunate way. More charming costumes are those of the country maids, the women of Frascati, the fishermen, Neapolitan boatmen, Neapolitan *sbirri,* and the Greeks.

Sometimes a theatrical costume is imitated. Some people take very little trouble, wrapping up in tapestries or linen cloths and tying these together over their heads.

The white figure typically steps in the way of other people, and hops on ahead of them, thinking to portray a ghost in this manner. Some distinguish themselves by strange combinations, and the *tabarro* is always considered the noblest disguise, because it is not at all conspicuous.

Witty and satirical masqueraders are very rare, because they do have a purpose, and want to be noticed. But we saw a Pulcinella as a cuckold. The horns were movable, he could pull them in and out like a snail.

He would step under a window where there was a newly married couple, and let one horn be seen just a little, or, in front of another couple, let both horns stretch out quite long, and very lustily ring the bells fastened at their tips; then, for moments, the public would be cheerfully attentive and sometimes laugh loudly.

A magician mingles with the crowd, shows the people a book with numbers, and reminds them of their passion for lotto.

A man with two faces is present in the throng; one cannot tell which is the front, which the back, whether he is coming or going.

The foreign visitor too must submit to being mocked during this time. The long garments of the Northerners, their big buttons, and curious round hats catch the attention of the Romans, and so the foreigner becomes a costume for them.

Because the foreign painters, especially those who study landscapes and buildings, sit out and paint in public everywhere in Rome, they too are enthusiastically portrayed amidst the carnival crowds, and appear with large portfolios and long, closefitting overcoats, working very busily with colossal drawing pens.

German baker's boys in Rome quite often get conspicuously drunk, and they too are portrayed in their actual outfits, or somewhat embellished, staggering around with a wine bottle.

We remember just a single offensive disguise. An obelisk was to be set up before the church of Trinità de' Monti.[198] The public was not very happy about that, partly because the square is narrow, partly because the obelisk was small, and a very tall pedestal had to be built underneath to bring it to a certain height. Someone took this as an incentive for wearing a big white pedestal as a cap, on top of which was fixed a quite small red obelisk. Large letters were written on the pedestal, the meaning of which was perhaps only guessed by a few.

Carriages

While the masqueraders are becoming more numerous, the carriages gradually drive into the Corso, in the same order as we have described above when discussing the Sunday and festival-day promenades, only with the difference that now the vehicles driving down on the left side from the Venetian palace turn where the Via Corso ends and immediately drive back on the other side.

We have already pointed out above that at most places, if one subtracts the elevated sides for pedestrians, the street has the width of little more than three carriages.

The side elevations are all blocked with stands and occupied by chairs, and many spectators have already taken their seats. A line of carriages moves down quite close to the stands and chairs and up the other side. The pedestrians are confined to a space at most eight feet wide between the two rows. Everyone pushes this way and that as well as he can, while another dense crowd looks down on the throng from all the windows and balconies.

In the first days mostly only ordinary equipages are seen, because everybody saves for later anything elegant or magnificent he may want to display. Toward the end of the carnival a greater number of open carriages appear, some of which have room for six: two ladies sit opposite each other on raised seats, so that one can see their whole figure, four gentlemen occupy the four remaining corner seats, coachmen and servants are in costume, the horses adorned with gauze and flowers.

Often a beautiful white poodle, decorated with rose-colored ribbons, stands between the coachman's feet, bells tinkle on the harness, and, for several moments, the attention of the public is fixed on this procession.

As one can easily imagine, only beautiful women dare to be elevated in this manner before the whole populace, and only the most beautiful one lets herself be seen without a face mask. But as the carriage approaches—and usually it must move quite slowly—all eyes are directed to it, and she has the pleasure of hearing from many sides: "O quanto è bella!"

Formerly, these elegant carriages are said to have been much more numerous and costly, as well as more interesting, because of the mythological and allegorical representations. But lately, for whatever reason it may be, the more aristocratic persons seem to want to merge with the whole and, although they still derive pleasure from this festivity, to be partakers rather than stand out from others.

The further the carnival progresses, the gayer the equipages look.

Even serious persons, who sit in the carriages without wearing disguises, allow their coachmen and servants to be costumed. The coachmen generally choose feminine garb, and in the last days it would seem that only women are managing the horses. They are often nicely, even charmingly, dressed; on the other hand, a broad, ugly fellow dressed up in the very latest fashion, with a high coiffure and feathers, becomes a great caricature; and, whereas those beauties could hear themselves being praised, he has to submit to having someone look up at him and shout: "O fratello mio, che brutta puttana sei!"[199]

Usually, the coachman obliges one or two of his girl friends by lifting them up onto the box when he meets them in the crowd. The latter sit beside him, usually in masculine dress, and then their pretty little Pulcinella legs, with little feet and high heels, often rock back and forth around the heads of passersby.

The servants do likewise and take their male and female friends onto the back of the vehicle, and all that is missing is for them even to sit down on its roof, as is done on English stagecoaches.

The masters and mistresses themselves seem to be pleased to see their carriages well laden; during this time, everything is permissible and proper.

Throngs

Let us now cast a glance over the long, narrow street, where crowded spectators look down from all the balconies and out of all the windows, over long, dangling, colorful tapestries, at the stands filled with spectators, and the long rows of occupied chairs, on both sides of the street. Two lines of carriages move slowly in the area between, and the space which could, if need be, accommodate a third carriage is completely filled with people, who do not walk back and forth, but shove their way back and forth. Since the carriages stay a short distance apart as long as that is at all possible, so as not to bump into each other every time the line halts, many pedestrians, just to get a bit of air, venture out of the crush in the middle and walk between the wheels of one carriage and the horses and shaft of the next. The greater the danger and difficulty become for the pedestrians, the bolder their spirit seems to grow.

Since most of the pedestrians moving between the two lines of carriages carefully avoid the wheels and axles, in order to protect their limbs and clothing, they usually leave more room than is necessary between themselves and the vehicles; so whoever can no longer bear to go along with the slow mass and has the courage to slip between the wheels and the pedestrians, between the danger and those who fear it, can go a long way in a short time, until he sees himself stopped by another obstacle.

Even at this point our narrative seems to border on the incredible, and we would hardly dare to continue it if so many persons who have attended the Roman carnival could not testify that we have stayed strictly with the truth, and if it were not a festival repeated annually that will be viewed in future by many an individual with this book in hand.

For what will our readers say when we announce to them that everything related up to now is just, so to speak, the first stage of the crowding, tumult, noise, and boisterousness?

Progress of the Governor and the Senator

While the carriages move cautiously forward and stand quietly whenever there is a stoppage, the pedestrians are harassed in various ways.

The papal guards, individually, ride back and forth through the crowd on their horses, in order to adjust any chance disarray of the carriages and get them moving again; and someone who is dodging the carriage horses may suddenly feel a riding horse's head in his neck. But a greater inconvenience follows.

The governor, in a large state carriage with a retinue of several more coaches, rides down the middle between the two other lines of carriages. The papal guards and the servants walking ahead warn and make room, and, for the moment, this procession takes up the whole space that, shortly before, still remained for the pedestrians. They crowd as best they can in between the other carriages and, in one way or another, to the side. And as water divides only for a moment when a ship sails through and immediately rushes together again behind the rudder, so the mass of masqueraders and other pedestrians also reunites at once behind the procession. Not long afterwards, a new movement disturbs the closely packed group.

The senator approaches with a similar procession; his large state carriage and the carriages of his retinue appear to float on the heads of the crushed throng; and, although every native and foreigner is captivated and bewitched by the charm of the present senator, Prince Rezzonico,[200] this may be the one time when a mass of people are glad to see him depart.

Whereas these processions of the two supreme legal and police authorities of Rome made their way through the Corso only on the first day, to open the carnival ceremoniously, the Duke of Albany greatly inconvenienced the crowd by driving the same route daily and, at a time of general mummery, reminded this city, the old sovereign of kings, of the farcicality of his royal pretensions.

The ambassadors, who have the same right, make use of it sparingly and with humane discretion.

The World of Beauty at the Ruspoli Palace

But it is not these processions alone that interrupt and obstruct circulation in the Corso; at the Ruspoli palace and in its vicinity, where the street does not grow any wider, the raised pavements on both sides are higher. There the world of beauty takes its place, and all the chairs are soon occupied or spoken for. The most beautiful middle-class girls, charmingly costumed, surrounded by their male friends, display themselves there before the gaze of the curious passerby. Everyone who comes into the area lingers to inspect these pleasant ranks; everyone is curious to pick out which are female among the many seemingly masculine figures sitting there, and perhaps to discover the object of his longing in a dainty officer. Here is the spot where movement first comes to a halt, for the carriages linger as long as possible in this area, and if they have to stop sooner or later, surely it is preferable to do so in this agreeable company.

Confetti

If our description up to now has suggested only a cramped, indeed almost alarming situation, then a still odder impression will be made when we go on to relate how these crowded revels start off with a kind of small war, mostly playful, but often all too serious.

Probably it once happened that a pretty girl, trying to make her good friend notice her amidst the crowd in her disguise as he went by, threw sugared kernels at him, since nothing would be more natural than for the victim to turn around and discover his mischievous sweetheart. This has now become a universal custom, and after a volley one often sees a pair of friendly faces greet each other. However, people are in part too thrifty to waste real candy, and in part the misuse of it has made a larger and cheaper supply necessary.

It is now a special occupation to go through the crowd, carrying around for sale big basketsful of little plaster pellets, which are made through a funnel and resemble dragées.

No one is safe from attack; everyone is in a defensive position, and so, out of mischief or necessity, a duel, a skirmish, or a battle ensues, now here, now there. Pedestrians, passengers in carriages, spectators at windows, in the stands, or on chairs alternately attack each other and defend themselves.

The ladies have little gilded and silvered baskets full of these kernels, and the escorts are capable of defending their belles very valiantly. With lowered carriage windows, people await the attack, joking with their friends and stubbornly defending themselves against strangers.

But nowhere does this conflict grow more serious and general than in the vicinity of the Ruspoli palace. All the masqueraders that have sat down there are equipped with little baskets, little sacks, and tied-up handkerchiefs. They attack more often than they are attacked; no carriage passes by with impunity, without at least several masqueraders finding some fault with it. No pedestrian is safe from them; especially when an abbé appears in his black coat, all of them throw at him from all sides, and because plaster and chalk rub off wherever they hit, such a person is soon spotted all over with white and gray. Often the quarrels become very serious and general, and it is astonishing to see how jealousy and personal hatred are given free rein.

Unnoticed, a costumed figure sneaks up and hits one of the most eminent beauties so violently and directly that her face mask resounds, and her lovely throat is hurt. Her escorts on both sides become greatly infuriated, they vehemently rain confetti upon the attacker from their little baskets and sacks; but he is well muffled up, and too heavily padded to feel their repeated volleys. Because he is so secure, he continues his attack the more violently; the defenders shield the girl with their *tabarri,* and since the attacker also wounds the persons nearby in the heat of the fight, and offends everyone in general with his rudeness and vehemence, the people sitting round about join in the fight. They do not spare their plaster kernels and, for such cases, have somewhat larger ammunition in reserve, approximately like sugared almonds. The attacker is eventually so pinned down by their fire, and so assailed from all sides, that he has no alternative but to retreat, especially if he has run out of pellets.

Usually, someone who sets out on such an adventure has an assistant with him who slips ammunition into his hand, while in the meantime the men who sell this plaster confetti are busy with their baskets during the melee, and hurriedly weigh out for each person as many pounds as he desires.

We ourselves had a close view of such a fight, in which the combatants, having no more ammunition, threw the little gilded baskets at each other's heads and could not be restrained by the warnings of the guards, who themselves were also being severely hit.

Surely many such conflicts would end with stabbings if the *corde,*[201] the well-known punitive devices of the Italian police, were not hung up at several corners to remind everyone, in the midst of the revels, that it would be very dangerous at this moment to use dangerous weapons.

There are countless frays like this, and most of them are more comical than serious.

Thus, for example, an open carriage approaches Ruspoli, filled with Pulcinellas. It proposes to drive by the spectators, and hit each one in turn; but, unfortunately, the press is too great, and it stays stuck in the middle. The whole crowd is suddenly of one mind, and confetti hails down on the carriage from all sides. The Pulcinellas use up their ammunition and, for quite a while, remain exposed to the cross fire from all sides, so that, in the end, the carriage is all covered as though with snow and hailstones, and slowly departs amidst general laughter and accompanied by sounds of disapproval.

Dialogue at the Upper End of the Corso

While a large part of the beautiful world is engaged in these rough and lively games at the midpoint of the Corso, another part of the public finds amusement of a different sort at the upper end of the street.

Not far from the French Academy, the so-called *capitano* of the Italian theater, in Spanish dress with a plumed hat, sword, and big gloves, steps out unexpectedly from among the masqueraders watching from a stand, and begins to relate in an emphatic tone his great deeds on land and water. Before long, a Pulcinella confronts him, utters doubts and objections, and, while seeming to agree with everything, makes that hero's boasting ridiculous with his plays on words and interpolated platitudes.

Every passerby stops here too and listens to this lively exchange.

King of Pulcinellas

The crowding is often made worse by new processions. A dozen Pulcinellas convene, elect a king, crown him, put a scepter in his hand, give him musical accompaniment, and amidst loud shouting lead him up the Corso on a little decorated cart. As the procession moves forward, all the Pulcinellas run up and swell the retinue, making way for themselves by shouting and swinging their hats.

Only then do we notice how each one tries to vary this general costume.

One wears a wig, another sets off his black face with a woman's hood, the third, instead of a hat, has a cage on his head, in which a pair of birds, dressed as an abbé and a lady, hop back and forth on the little perches.

Side Streets

The dreadful crowding, which we have tried to describe as vividly as possible for our readers, naturally forces a number of masqueraders out of the Corso and into neighboring streets. Pairs of lovers walk together more quietly and privately there, and merry fellows find room for enacting all sorts of mad plays.

A group of men in the Sunday dress of the common people, with short jackets over gold-embroidered vests, their hair tied up in a long, dangling net, stroll back and forth with youths who have disguised themselves as women. One of the latter looks highly pregnant, and they walk peacefully up and down. Suddenly, the men fall out, the women interfere, vehement words are exchanged, the quarrel intensifies, finally the combatants draw large knives of silvered cardboard, and attack each other. The women scream horribly and keep them apart, one is pulled this way, one that, the bystanders join in, as if it were real, and try to pacify both sides.

Meanwhile, the highly pregnant woman becomes ill with fright; a chair is brought up, the other women assist her, she acts miserable, and in the twinkling of an eye, to the great amusement of the spectators, she gives birth to some grotesque shape or other. The play is over, and the troupe moves on, in order to put on the same play or one similar to it at another place.

Thus the Roman, who always has stories of murder on his mind, likes to play with ideas of *ammazzare*[202] at every opportunity. Even the children have a game they call *chiesa,* which resembles our "prisoner's base," but really depicts a murderer who has taken refuge on the steps of a church; the others represent the *sbirri* and try in every way to catch him, without, however, being permitted to enter the protected zone.

So there is much amusing activity in the side streets, especially in the Strada Babuino and on the Piazza d'Espagna.

The Quakers also come here in groups, so as to have more freedom for exchanging their courtesies.

They have a maneuver that makes everyone laugh. As many as twelve of them come marching up on tiptoe, with quick little steps, forming a very straight front; suddenly, when they come to a square, they make a column with a right or left about-face, and now mince along, one after the other. Suddenly, with a right about-face, the front reforms, and thus they go into a street; then, in the twinkling of an eye, again a left about-face: the column is shoved into the door of a house as though on a spit and the fools disappear.

Evening

Now it is getting towards evening, and everybody crowds more and more into the Corso. The carriages have long since stopped moving, indeed, it sometimes happens as early as two hours before nightfall that not a vehicle can budge from its spot.

The papal guards and the guards on foot are busy now moving all the vehicles as much as possible away from the middle, and into a completely straight line; and on account of the crowd this causes much confusion and vexation. There is backing up, shoving, lifting, and when one driver backs up, all those behind him must also give ground, until one is finally in such a tight corner that he has to turn his horses in toward the middle. Then the papal guards begin to scold, and the other guards curse and threaten.

In vain, the unfortunate coachman points to the obvious impossibility; he is scolded and threatened and either has to get back in line or, if there is a little side street nearby, must leave the row through no fault of his own. Usually the side streets also are occupied by motionless vehicles that came too late and could no longer move in, because the circulation of carriages had already come to a halt.

Preparation for the Race

The moment for the horse race is now swiftly approaching, and this is the moment on which the interest of many thousands of people is concentrated.

The chair hawkers and stand concessioners now multiply their shouted offers: "Luoghi! Luoghi avanti! Luoghi nobili! Luoghi, padroni!"[203] They are determined to have all the seats occupied, at least in these last moments, even if for less money.

And it is fortunate that seats are still to be found here and there, for the general, with part of the guards, now rides his horse down the Corso between the two rows of carriages, crowding the pedestrians out of the only space still left to them. Then everybody still tries to find a chair, a seat on a stand, on a carriage, between the vehicles, or with acquaintances at a window, all of which places swarm to capacity with spectators.

Meanwhile, the space before the obelisk has been entirely cleared of people and affords what is perhaps one of the most beautiful sights to be seen in the modern world.

The fronts of the three stands described above, hung with tapestries, enclose the square. Many thousands of faces look out over each other, giving the impression of an ancient amphitheater or circus. The whole length of the obelisk rises into the air above the middle stand, which just covers its pedestal, and only now, when measured against such a mass of people, is its enormous height noticeable.

The open square is an agreeably restful sight to the eye, and we look expectantly at the empty barriers with a rope stretched in front of them.

Now the general comes down the Corso, as a sign that it is clear, and the guards behind him allow no one to step out from the line of carriages. He takes a seat in one of the loges.

The Race

Now smartly dressed grooms lead the horses, in an order determined by lot, into the barriers, up to the rope. They have no cloth or other covering on their bodies. Spiked balls are tied to them here and there with cords, and the spots where they are to feel these spurs are covered with leather until the moment of starting; large sheets of tinsel are also glued to them.

Most of them are already wild and impatient when they are brought into the barriers, and the grooms need all their strength and skill to restrain them.

Eagerness to begin the race makes them unruly, the presence of so many people makes them shy. They often strike over the neighboring barrier, often over the rope, and this movement and disorder intensify the expectant interest moment by moment.

The grooms are tense and alert in the highest degree because, at the moment of starting, a man's skill in releasing his horse, as well as chance circumstances, can give a decisive advantage to one or the other of them.

At last the rope falls, and the horses begin to run.

On the open square they keep trying to gain the advantage over each other, but once they have entered the narrow space between the two lines of carriages all rivalry is usually in vain.

Ordinarily a few are ahead, straining themselves to the utmost. The pavement throws up sparks despite the strewn pozzuolana, the manes fly, the tinsel rustles, and one scarcely catches sight of them before they are past. The rest of the herd obstruct one another with their crowding and rushing; sometimes one comes galloping along belatedly, and torn pieces of tinsel flutter down singly onto the forsaken track.

Soon the horses have completely disappeared from sight, the populace crowds in, and the racecourse is filled up again.

Other grooms are already waiting at the Venetian palace for the horses' arrival. They are able to catch them skillfully and hold them in an enclosed area. The prize is awarded to the victor.

So this festivity ends with a violent, momentary impression, flashing by like lightning. Many thousands of people were eagerly anticipating it for a long time, but few can explain why they were waiting for this moment and why they enjoyed it so much.

Our description makes it obvious that this game can become dangerous for both humans and animals. We shall cite only a few cases: Considering the narrow spaces between the carriages, a rear wheel need only stand out a little, and by chance a somewhat wider space be left after this particular vehicle. A horse which is hurrying past, closely pressed by the others, tries to use the widened space, leaps ahead, and hits directly against the protruding wheel.

We ourselves saw a case where a horse fell down from such a shock, three of the ones following stumbled over the first and went sprawling, while the last ones successfully jumped over them and continued on their way.

Often such a horse will lie dead on the spot, and spectators more than once have lost their lives under such circumstances. A great catastrophe can also occur if the horses turn around.

It has happened, when a horse was far in the lead, that spiteful, envious persons have hit it in the eye with their cloaks and thereby forced it to turn around and run to the side. It is still worse when the horses are not sucessfully caught on the Venetian square; then it is impossible to keep them from turning back, and, because the racetrack is already full of people again, the horses cause many a mischief that either goes unreported or is disregarded.

Suspended Regulations

Usually the horses do not run until nightfall. As soon as they have arrived up at the Venetian palace, little mortars are fired; this signal is repeated halfway down the Corso, and, for the last time, in the vicinity of the obelisk.

At that moment, the guards leave their posts, the rows of carriages are no longer kept in order, and this is certainly an uneasy and unpleasant period, even for the spectator who is calmly standing at his window. It is worth making a few comments about.

We have already seen above that the moment of nightfall, which decides so many things in Italy, also breaks up the customary Sunday and festival-day promenades. No guards are there, either mounted or on foot, but it is an old tradition, a general convention, for people to drive up and down in proper order. Yet, as soon as the Ave Maria is sounded, no one surrenders his right to turn around when and where he pleases. Since during the carnival the circuit is made in the same street and according to similar rules, no one is willing to yield his right to drive out of line at nightfall, although now the crowd and other circumstances make a great difference.

When we look back now at the tremendous crush in the Corso, and see how the racetrack, cleared only for a moment, has immediately been flooded again with people, reason and fairness would seem to us to suggest the rule that each equipage should simply take its turn to reach the nearest, most convenient side street and hurry home by that route.

But when the signals have gone off, some vehicles immediately turn toward the middle, where they obstruct and confuse the people on foot. Because it occurs to one coachman to drive down the narrow middle space, to another to drive up it, neither can move from the spot, and the more sensible drivers, who have stayed in line, are also prevented from moving.

If, into the bargain, a returning horse meets such an obstacle, the danger, mischief, and vexation increase on all sides.

Night

And yet this confusion does become unraveled, later, of course, but for the most part satisfactorily. Night has fallen, and everybody hopes for some rest.

Theater

From that moment on, all face masks are removed, and a large part of the public hastens to the theater. Perhaps we shall still see some *tabarri* and costumed ladies, but only in the loges; the whole parterre appears again in ordinary clothes.

The Aliberti and Argentina theaters give serious operas, interspersed with ballets; Valle and Capranica give comedies and tragedies, with comic operas as intermezzos; Pace imitates them, although imperfectly, and in addition there are many inferior spectacles, including lowly puppet shows and tightrope walker booths.

The large Tordinone theater, which burned to the ground one day and then, when it was rebuilt, immediately collapsed, unfortunately now no longer entertains the populace with its blood-and-thunder dramas and other extraordinary presentations.

The Romans' passion for the theater is very great and was formerly even more intense at carnival time, because this was the only period when it could be satisfied. Now at least one theater is open also in summer and fall, and the public can satisfy its desire to a certain extent throughout the greater part of the year.

It would lead us too far afield if we were to embark here on a detailed description of the theaters and whatever special features the Roman ones might have. Our readers will remember that this subject was discussed in other places.[204]

Festini

We shall likewise have little to tell about the so-called *festini;* these are large masquerade balls, which are given several times in the beautifully illuminated Aliberti Theater.

Here too, *tabarri* are considered the most appropriate disguise for both ladies and gentlemen, and the whole salon is filled with black figures; a few colorful character costumes mingle with them.

Curiosity, then, is all the livelier when some noble, though rather rare, figures appear who have chosen their disguises from various artistic epochs and in a masterly way imitate various statues which are to be found in Rome.

So Egyptian deities display themselves here, priestesses, Bacchus and Ariadne, the Tragic Muse, the Muse of History, Vestal Virgins, a consul, more or less well executed and authentically costumed.

Dance

The dances at these festivals are usually danced in long rows in the English manner; the only difference is that, in their few figures, usually something characteristic is expressed in pantomime; for example, two lovers quarrel and become reconciled, part and find each other again.

The Romans are accustomed to vividly expressive gesticulation from their pantomimic ballets; in the social dances too, they love attitudes which would seem exaggerated and affected to us. Scarcely anyone will venture to dance unless he has learned to do so correctly; especially the minuet is considered a true work of art, and only a few pairs act it out, so to speak. Such a pair is then encircled by the rest of the company and receives applause at the end.

Morning

While the fashionable world is amusing itself until morning in this manner, already at daybreak there is renewed activity in the Corso, to clean it and put it in order. Special care is taken to strew the pozzuolana evenly and neatly in the middle of the street.

Before long, the racehorse that performed most poorly yesterday is brought to the obelisk by the grooms. They set a little boy on its back, and another rider drives it with a whip, so that it exerts all its strength to run the course as swiftly as possible.

The already described festive cycle begins every day at about two o'clock in the afternoon, after the bell signal has been given. The strollers assemble, the guard marches up, balconies, windows, and stands are hung with tapestries, the masqueraders multiply and carry on their nonsense, the carriages drive up and down, and the street is either more crowded or less so depending on the favorable or unfavorable influence exerted by the weather or by other circumstances. As is natural, the spectators, the masqueraders, the carriages, the finery, and the noise increase toward the end of the carnival. But nothing equals the crowding and excesses of the last day and evening.

Last Day

Mostly the rows of carriages have already been standing still since two hours before nightfall, no vehicle can move anymore, none come in from the side streets. The stands and chairs are taken earlier, although the seats remain expensive; everyone tries to find a place as soon as possible, and the start of the horse race is awaited with greater longing than ever.

Finally this moment also rushes by, the signals are given that the festival is ended, but neither carriages, nor masqueraders, nor spectators budge from the spot.

All is calm, all is quiet, while the twilight gradually darkens into night.

Moccoli[205]

Hardly has it become dark in the narrow, high-walled street when one sees lights appear here and there and move at the windows and on the stands. In a short time the fire has circulated so widely that the whole street is illuminated by burning wax candles.

The balconies are adorned with translucent paper lanterns, each person holds his candle out of the window, all the stands are illuminated, and it is most pleasant to look inside the carriages, where often there are little crystal candelabra at the ceilings that illuminate the passengers; meanwhile in another carriage ladies with colorful candles in their hands seem almost to invite one to contemplate their beauty.

The servants line the edges of the carriage roofs with little candles, open carriages display colorful paper lanterns, some of the pedestrians appear with high pyramids of lights on their heads, others have stuck their candles onto poles made of reeds tied together, which often reach up to the height of two or three stories.

Now it becomes everyone's duty to carry a small lighted candle in his hand, and the favorite Roman curse, "Sia ammazzato," is heard repeatedly here, there, and everywhere.

"Sia ammazzato chi non porta moccolo!" "Death to anyone not carrying a candle!" one calls to the other, while trying to blow out the latter's flame. Lighting, extinguishing, and an unruly shout: "Sia ammazzato!" soon bring life and movement and a mutual interest into the enormous crowd.

Not distinguishing between acquaintances and strangers, everyone just tries to blow out the nearest candle, or relight his own, taking this as an opportunity to extinguish the candle of the rekindler. And the more loudly the roar "Sia ammazzato!" resounds on all sides, the more these words lose their fearful meaning, the more we forget we are in Rome, where this curse can be swiftly carried out, for a trivial reason, on this person or that.

The meaning of the expression is gradually lost entirely. And as in other languages we often hear imprecations and indecent words used to signify admiration and joy, so this evening "Sia ammazzato!" becomes a watchword, a cry of joy, a refrain for all jokes, teasing, and compliments.

So we hear a mocking "Sia ammazzato il Signore Abbate che fa l'amore!"[206] Or someone calling to a good friend passing by: "Sia ammazzato il Signore Filippo!" Or, combined with flattery and compliments, "Sia ammazzata la bella Principessa! Sia ammazzata la Signora Angelica, la prima pittore del secolo!"[207]

All these phrases are shouted quickly and vehemently with a long-drawn-out stress on the penultimate or antepenultimate syllable. Amidst this incessant shouting, the blowing-out and lighting of candles continues unabated. Whether someone is encountered in the house, on the stairs, whether it be a company together in a room, or from one window to the next, everywhere one person is trying to prevail over the other and extinguish his flame.

All classes and ages behave boisterously toward each other, people climb on carriage steps, and no hanging lamps, scarcely even the street lamps, are safe; a boy extinguishes his father's candle and keeps shouting" "Sia ammazzato il Signore Padre!" In vain the father rebukes him for this impropriety; the boy claims the privileges of this evening and only curses his sire the more mischievously. While the tumult soon diminishes at the opposite ends of the Corso, it increases in the middle that much more ungovernably, and the crowding that results is past imagining, indeed cannot be visualized again even by the most retentive memory.

No one is able any longer to stir from the spot where he stands or sits; the heat of so many bodies, so many candles, the smoke of so many blown-out candles, the shouts of so many people, who roar the more furiously, the less they can move a limb, eventually cause the soundest mind to reel. It seems a miracle that no accidents occur, that the carriage horses do not get wild, that some of them are not bruised, squeezed, or otherwise injured.

And yet, because everybody eventually more or less longs to go away, because everybody turns off into some little lane he can reach, or seeks open air and respite on the next square, this mass also dissolves, melting from the ends to the middle, and this festival of universal license and unconstraint, this modern Saturnalia, ends in a universal stupor.

Now the populace hurries to a well-prepared banquet, and, until midnight, will enjoy the meat that is soon to be forbidden, while the elegant world goes to the theater, in order to bid farewell there to the stage performances, which have been very much shortened, for the approaching midnight hour puts an end to these pleasures also.

Ash Wednesday

So, then, an extravagant festival is over, like a dream, like a fairy tale, and perhaps less of it remains in the mind of the participant than of our readers, to whose imagination and understanding we have presented the whole of it in a coherent form.

If, during the course of these follies, the rude Pulcinella indecently reminds us of the joys of love, to which we owe our existence; if a Baubo,[208] on a public square, desecrates the mysteries of a woman in travail; if those many nocturnally lit candles remind us of the last rites, then, in the midst of the nonsense, we are made aware of the most important scenes of our life.

Even more, the long, narrow, full, crowded street reminds us of the paths of earthly life, where every spectator or participant, without a mask or with one, surveys from a balcony or stand just a meager space in front of, or next to, himself, proceeds only step by step in a carriage or on foot, is shoved more than he walks, is obstructed more than he willingly stands still, tries only the more eagerly to arrive at a place where life will be better and happier, then gets into straits again, and at last is crowded out.

If we may continue to speak more seriously than the subject seems to warrant, then we shall make the observation that the most intense and extreme pleasures, like those horses flying past, appear to us only for a moment, stir us, and scarcely leave a mark on our mind; that freedom and equality can be enjoyed only in the frenzy of madness; and that, in order to spur us to the highest pitch of excitement, the greatest delights must come into very close proximity with danger and let us wantonly savor, in their vicinity, feelings of pleasure mixed with fear.

And so, without actually intending to do it, we too have concluded our carnival with an Ash Wednesday meditation, which we trust will not have saddened any of our readers. Rather, since life on the whole, like the Roman carnival, remains incalculable, unenjoyable, and even dubious, we hope that this carefree masquerade may remind every reader, along with us, of the importance of every momentary, often seemingly trivial, enjoyment to be found in it.

February

Correspondence

Rome, February 1.

How happy I shall be when the fools are laid to rest next Tuesday evening! It is a dreadful *seccatura*[209] to see others infected with a madness one does not feel oneself.

As much as possible, I have continued my studies. *Claudina* has also progressed, and, unless all the genii refuse their assistance, the third act will go off to Herder a week from today, and so I would be rid of the fifth volume. Then begins a new misery, in which no one can advise or help me. *Tasso* must be revised; what is written cannot be used for anything. I can neither end it thus nor discard it all. Such is the trouble God has given mankind!

The sixth volume will probably contain *Tasso, Lila, Jerry and Betty,*[210] all of them so revised and perfected as to be unrecognizable.

At the same time, I have looked through my small poems and thought about the eighth volume, which I may publish before the seventh one. It is a strange thing to draw up such a *summa summarum* of one's life. How little trace remains, after all, of a human existence!

Here they plague me with the translations of my *Werther,* showing them to me and asking which is best, and whether everything is really true! That is a nuisance which would pursue me all the way to India.

Rome, February 6.

Here is the third act of *Claudina;* I hope that you get just half the pleasure from it, Herder, that I feel from having finished it. Since I am better acquainted now with the requirements of the lyric theater, I have tried to accommodate the composer and the actors by making some sacrifices. Cloth that is to be embroidered on must have its threads set wide apart, and for a comic opera it must absolutely be woven like marli.[211] But in this work, as in *Erwin,* I have also been concerned about the reader. In a word, I have done what I could.

I am very calm and clear and, as I have already assured all of you, ready to submit to any summons. I am too old for the visual arts, and so it does not matter how much, or how little, I botch things. My thirst is quenched, I am on the right path as far as viewing and study are concerned, my enjoyment is peaceful and modest. Give me your blessing on all of that. I have nothing more pressing now than to finish the last three volumes. Then I shall work on *Wilhelm,* etc.

Rome, February 9.

The fools were still making a real racket on Monday and Tuesday. Especially on Tuesday, when the madness with the *moccoli* was at its height. On Wednesday, we thanked God and the Church for Lent. I did not go to any *festino* (as they call fancy-dress balls), I am diligent and fill my head with whatever it will hold. Since the fifth volume is completed, I only want to finish a few art studies, then go right to the sixth. I have recently read Leonardo da Vinci's book on painting[212] and now understand why I was never able to understand anything in it.

Oh, how happy are those who only look at artworks! They consider themselves so clever, they have such a good opinion of themselves. The connoisseurs and art lovers too! You would not believe, Charlotte, what a self-satisfied lot they are, whereas the poor artist always remains meekly silent. But of late, when I hear someone express opinions who does not work himself, I am filled with an indescribable disgust. Like tobacco smoke, such talk always immediately makes me uncomfortable.

Angelica has indulged herself by buying two paintings. One by Titian, the other by Paris Bordone.[213] Both for a high price. Since she is so rich that she does not use up her investment income and earns an additional amount annually, it is commendable that she is acquiring something that delights her, moreover objects of a kind that increase her artistic zeal. As soon as she had the pictures in her house, she began to paint in a new manner, trying, if possible, to assimilate certain merits of those masters. She is tireless, not only in work but in study. I greatly enjoy viewing artistic objects with her.

Kayser also goes about his work like a true artist. He is making great progress with his music for *Egmont.* I have not yet heard all of it. Each part seems to me to be very well suited to the purpose.

He will also set "Ah, Cupid, naughty little, etc." to music. I shall send it to you at once, so that it can be sung often to remind you of me. It is also my favorite little song. Much writing, doing, and thinking have my head in a muddle. I am not growing any wiser, demand too much of myself, and assume too many burdens.

Rome, February 16.

Some time ago, the Prussian courier delivered a letter to me from our duke, and I doubt that I have ever received one as friendly, nice, kind, and gratifying. Since he could write without reserve, he described the whole political situation to me, as well as his own, and so forth. He expressed himself about me personally in the most affectionate way.

Rome, February 22.

There has been a case this week that grieves our whole group of artists. A Frenchman named Drouais, a young man about 25 years old, the only son of a loving mother, rich and handsome, who was considered the most promising of all the student artists, has died of smallpox. There is universal mourning and dismay. In his forsaken studio, I saw the life-size figure of a Philoctetes[214] cooling the pain of his wound by waving the wing of a slain bird of prey over it. A beautifully conceived painting, of quite meritorious workmanship, but unfinished.

I am industrious and happy, and thus I await the future. It becomes clearer to me daily that I was really born for literature, and that for the next ten years, which is as long as I still expect to work, I should develop this talent, and still produce something good, inasmuch as, thanks to the fire of youth, I once had some success even without great effort. The benefit I shall have from my rather long stay in Rome is that I am giving up the practice of the visual arts.

Angelica pays me the compliment of saying that she knows few people in Rome who *see* better in art than I do. I know very well where and what I do not yet see, and am quite conscious of my steady improvement, and of what must be done to see farther and farther. Suffice it to say, I have already achieved my wish: not to grope around blindly anymore in a matter to which I feel myself passionately drawn.

Charlotte, very soon I shall send you a poem called "Amor as a Landscape Painter," and I wish it good luck. I have attempted to put my small poems in a certain order, and they look strange. The poems on Hans Sachs and on Mieding's death[215] conclude the eighth volume, and so, for the present, my writings. If in the meantime I am laid to rest next to the pyramid,[216] these two poems can serve as my biographical data and funeral oration.

Tomorrow morning is papal chapel, and the famed concerts of old music begin, which later, in Holy Week, become interesting to the highest degree. I intend to go there now every Sunday morning to acquaint myself with the style. Kayser, who really studies these things, will no doubt teach me to appreciate them. In every mail we expect to receive a printed copy of the Maundy Thursday music from Zurich, where Kayser left it. Whereupon it will first be played on the piano and then heard in the chapel.

Report

February

Anyone born to be an artist finds that a great many things appeal to his artistic perception, and the latter served me very well even amidst the tumult of Shrovetide foolishness and absurdities. It was the second time that I had seen the carnival, and inevitably it soon struck me that this popular festival followed a set course, like any other recurrent activity.

On account of this I became reconciled to the turmoil, viewing it as one more significant natural product and national event; in this sense, I became interested in it, and closely observed the progress of the follies, and how everything actually proceeded with a certain form and decorum. In so doing, I noted the individual happenings in turn, which preliminary work I used later for the essay that has just been inserted. I also asked our fellow-lodger Georg Schütz to sketch and color the individual costumes, which, with his usual affability, he did.

These drawings were subsequently etched in quarto format by Melchior Krause of Frankfurt-on-Main, director of the independent drawing institute at Weimar, and were colored on the basis of the originals for the first edition, published by Unger,[217] which has become rare.

For the aforesaid purposes it was necessary to mingle with the masquerading crowd more than before, which, even though viewed artistically, often made a repulsive, weird impression. My spirit was accustomed to the worthy objects that had occupied it all year long in Rome, and always seemed to be well aware that it was out of its proper place.

But something most refreshing to my inner, better sense was now at hand. On the Venetian square, where carriages often stop to look at the passing crowd before rejoining the turbulent lines, I saw Madame Angelica's carriage, and stepped up to its door to greet her. She leaned out in a friendly manner, but immediately drew back to let me see, sitting beside her, the now fully recovered Milanese girl. I found her unchanged, for how could the cure be anything but quick for such healthy youth? Indeed, her eyes seemed to look at me with even more clarity and brilliance, with a joyousness that went right to my heart. Thus we stood for a while, without speaking, whereupon Madame Angelica broke the silence, saying to me, while the girl leaned forward: "I must really act as interpreter, for I see that my young friend will never get around to what she has so long wished and intended to say and has frequently repeated to me, that is, how obliged she is to you for the interest you have shown in her illness, in her fate. Her first consolation, the thing that had a beneficial and restorative effect on her as she reentered life, was the sympathy of her friends, and especially yours. Out from the depths of loneliness she has suddenly found herself in the finest circle, among so many good people."

"That is all true," the girl said, extending her hand to me over her friend, so that I could touch it with mine, but not with my lips.

With quiet satisfaction I went away again into the throng of fools, with the tenderest feeling of gratitude to Angelica, who had been able to take the poor girl under her comforting wing immediately after the calamity and, which is rare in Rome, had accepted a previously unknown young woman into her noble circle. This touched me all the more, since I could flatter myself that my interest in the poor child had been of no small influence.

The Senator of Rome, Count Rezzonico, had already come to visit me when he returned from Germany. He had formed an intimate friendship with Mr. and Mrs. von Diede[218] and brought me cordial greetings from these dear friends and patrons of mine. As usual, I declined a closer relationship, but in the end I was to be drawn inevitably into this circle.

Those aforementioned friends, Mr. and Mrs. von Diede, paid a return visit to their dear bosom comrade, and I could hardly refuse various kinds of invitations when the lady, who was a renowed pianist, agreed to perform in a concert at the senator's Capitoline residence, and when our comrade Kayser, whose skill had become widely known, received a flattering invitation to take part in the program. To be sure, the incomparable view from the senator's windows of the Coliseum at sunset, together with everything adjoining it from the other sides, presented the most magnificent spectacle to us as artists; but we could not show a lack of respect and courtesy to the company by abandoning ourselves to it. First Mrs. von Diede played a significant piece of music, displaying very great abilities, and soon after that our friend was offered her seat, of which he seemed to prove quite worthy, judging from the praise he received. For a while they continued to alternate, and a lady also sang a popular aria; finally, however, when it was Kayser's turn again, he stated a charming theme and varied it in the most manifold way.

Everything had gone well, but during a very pleasant conversation with me the senator could not conceal and, in that soft Venetian manner, half regretfully averred that he really was not partial to such variations, whereas he was always quite enraptured by the expressive adagios of his lady.

Now I by no means wish to say that I have ever found anything distasteful about those typically attenuated, wistful tones in adagio and largo, yet I have always preferred music to have a stimulating quality, since our own feelings, our reflections on loss and failure, threaten only too often to drag us down and overwhelm us.

However, I could not possibly hold it against our senator, in fact had to grant it to him in the friendliest way, that he liked to listen to such sounds, which reassured him that he was entertaining a very much loved and honored friend in the most splendid abode in the world.

For the rest of us listeners, especially us Germans, it was an inestimable pleasure that, at the same moment when we were listening to an old friend, this excellent, respected lady, produce the sweetest sounds on the piano, we were also looking out of the window at the most unique area in the world. By turning our heads slightly, we could survey in the glow of the setting sun the great panorama that extended, on the left, from the arch of Septimius Severus along the Campo Vaccino to the temple of Minerva and Peace, with the Coliseum looking out from behind them; then, by turning our eyes to the right and running them past the arch of Titus, we had the labyrinth of the Palatine ruins, a wilderness adorned with cultivated gardens and wild vegetation, to linger in bemusedly.

(After this, we ask our readers to view a northwest prospect of Rome, drawn and engraved in 1824 by Fries and Thürmer,[219] taken from the tower of the Capitol; it is several stories higher and based on the more recent excavations, but shows the evening light and shadows as we saw them, in addition to which, of course, one must imagine the glowing color, with its shadowy blue contrasts, and all the magic arising from that.)

Next, we considered ourselves fortunate to be able to view unhurriedly at this time the most splendid picture that Mengs ever painted, the portrait of Clement XIII Rezzonico,[220] who had placed our patron, the senator, in this post because he was his nephew. In conclusion, I cite a passage from the diary of our friend[221] concerning its merit:

"Among the portraits painted by Mengs, the one in which his artistry stood the test most impressively is the portrait of Pope Rezzonico. In this work, the artist imitated the palette and method of the Venetians and succeeded very well; the color tone is true and warm, and the

expression of the face is lively and intelligent; the curtain of gold brocade, against which the face and the rest of the figure stand out beautifully, is considered a daring device in painting, but here it has succeeded brilliantly, inasmuch as the picture gains a rich, harmonious
appearance from it, with a pleasing effect on our eye."

March

Correspondence

On Sunday, we went to the Sistine chapel, where the pope was attending mass with the cardinals. Because of Lent, the latter are not dressed in red, but violet, so this was a new spectacle. Several days before, I had seen paintings by Albrecht Dürer, and now was happy to encounter something similar in real life. The whole thing, taken together, was uniquely grand and yet simple, and I am not surprised that foreign visitors who arrive in Holy Week, when everything comes to a climax, can hardly contain themselves. I know the chapel itself quite well, last summer I ate my noon meal there, took an afternoon nap on the pope's throne, and know the paintings almost by heart; and yet, when everything connected with the ritual has been assembled, that is something else again, and it is hard to orient oneself.

An old motet was sung, composed by a Spaniard named Morales,[222] and we had a foretaste of what now will come. Kayser is also of the opinion that this music can, and should, be heard only here, partly because nowhere else could singers be trained to sing without organ and instruments, partly because it is uniquely suited to the antique furnishings of the papal chapel and the total impression made by the Michelangelos, the *Last Judgment*, the prophets, and Biblical history. Kayser will render a precise account of all this at some future time. He is a great admirer of old music and very diligently studies everything pertaining to it.

So we have a noteworthy collection of psalms in the house; they have been put into Italian verse and were set to music by a Venetian *nobile*, Benedetto Marcello,[223] at the beginning of this century. In many of them, he adopted as his motif the intonation of the Jews, partly the Spanish, partly the German ones; in others, he used old Greek melodies as a basis and developed them with great understanding, artistic knowledge, and moderation. They are variously set as solos, duets, and choruses, and are incredibly original, although one must first learn to appreciate them. Kayser has a high opinion of them and will make copies of several. Perhaps, sometime, we can procure the whole work, which was printed in Venice in 1724 and includes the first fifty psalms. I would like Herder to investigate, perhaps he will find this interesting work in some catalog.

I have had the courage to think over my last three volumes all at the same time, and now I know exactly what I want to do; may Heaven give me the disposition and good fortune to do it.

It was a full week, seeming to me in retrospect like a month.

First, I made the plan for *Faust,* and I hope that it has been a successful undertaking. Of course, finishing the play now is different from finishing it fifteen years ago, but I do not think it will suffer on that account, especially since I believe I have found the thread again. I also feel confident about the tone of the whole; I have already written a new scene,[224] and if I were to discolor the paper with smoke, I doubt that anyone would be able to distinguish it from the old ones. My long rest and isolation have brought me back entirely to the level of my own existence, and it is remarkable how much I have remained the same, and how little my inner self has been affected by the years and events. The old manuscript[225] sometimes puts me in a reverie when I see it lying before me. It is still the original one, in fact, just the main scenes, written down spontaneously and without plan; now it is so yellow with age, so worn (the quires were never bound), so brittle, and crumpled at the edges, that it really does look like an old codex. And just as I then, by meditation and surmise, put myself back into an earlier world, I must now put myself back into my own olden times.

The plan for *Tasso* is also in good order, and the miscellaneous poems are mostly in fair copies. "The Artist's Earthly Pilgrimage" is to be reworked and its "Apotheosis"[226] added. Only lately have I applied myself to these youthful fancies, and now all the detail is very alive for me. I am also looking forward to the last three volumes, for which I have the highest hopes, and I can already see them all standing in front of me. I only wish for the leisure and peace of mind to carry out my ideas, step by step.

As a model for the placement of my various small poems, I have used your collections of *Scattered Leaves,* Herder, and hope that I have found good means of combining such disparate items, as well as a way to make these all too individual and evanescent pieces fairly enjoyable.

After these reflections, the new edition of Mengs's writings[227] arrived at my door, a book that is endlessly interesting to me now because I am in possession of the material concepts which must necessarily come first if one is to understand a single line of the work. It is an excellent book in every respect, one cannot read a page without decided benefit. I am also indebted for good insights to his *Fragments concerning Beauty*,[228] which seem so obscure to many a person.

Furthermore, I have been making all manner of speculations about colors, which interest me very much because that is the area I have hitherto understood the least. I see that with some practice and sustained reflection I shall also be able to assimilate this beautiful and pleasant feature of the world's surface.

One morning I was in the Borghese gallery, which I had not seen for a year, and found to my delight that I looked at it with much more comprehending eyes. The prince[229] possesses immense artistic treasures.

Rome, March 7.

Another good, full, and quiet week has now gone by. On Sunday, we omitted the papal chapel, instead I went with Angelica to see a very beautiful painting which is properly considered a Correggio.[230]

I saw the collection of the Academy of San Luca, where Raphael's skull[231] is kept. This relic seems completely authentic to me. A splendid structure of bone, in which a beautiful soul could comfortably roam. The duke wants a cast of it, which I shall probably be able to procure. The picture painted by him[232] that hangs in the same large room is worthy of him.

I have also seen the Capitol again, besides several other things still on my list, particularly Cavaceppi's house,[233] which I had always neglected to see. Among many exquisite things, I was especially delighted with two casts of the heads of the colossal statues on Monte Cavallo. At Cavaceppi's they can be seen close up in their whole grandeur and beauty. It is unfortunate that time and weather have caused the better one to lose almost a straw's thickness of the smooth facial surface, and up close it looks as if it were disfigured by smallpox.

Today was the funeral of Cardinal Visconti,[234] in the church of San Carlo. Since the papal choir was singing for the high mass, we went there to get our ears well washed out for tomorrow. Two sopranos sang a requiem, the most remarkable thing anyone could hear. N.B. There was neither organ nor any other instrumental music.

It struck me yesterday evening in St. Peter's, when the choir was singing the vesper hymn to organ accompaniment, what an odious instrument the organ is. It does not blend with the human voice and is so powerful. On the other hand, how charming the sounds in the Sistine chapel, where the voices are alone.

The weather has been cloudy and mild for several days. The almond trees, for the most part, have already stopped blooming, and are now becoming green; only a few blossoms are still to be seen at their tops. Now the peach trees follow, adorning the gardens with their lovely color. *Viburnum tinus*[235] is blooming on all the ruins, the elderberry bushes in the hedges have all budded, as well as others that I do not know. The walls and roofs are now growing greener, and flowers appear on some of them. In my new little room, into which I have moved because we are expecting Tischbein from Naples, I have a varied view into countless gardens and onto the rear galleries of many houses.

I have begun to model a little in clay. As far as theoretical knowledge is concerned, I feel on sure ground, but I am a little confused when it comes to employing my active power. So it is the same with me as with all my brothers.

Rome, March 14.

Next week there will be no thinking or doing anything here, one must swim with the flood of festivities. After Easter, I shall still see several things I have missed, break off my thread, settle my accounts, pack my bundle, and leave with Kayser. If everything works out as I desire and intend, I shall be in Florence by the end of April. Meantime you will all still hear from me.

Oddly enough, it was a request from outside[236] that obliged me to take various measures which put me into a new situation and made my Roman sojourn increasingly beautiful, profitable, and happy. Yes, I can say that I have enjoyed the greatest satisfaction of my life in these last eight weeks, and now at least I know an extreme point from which in future I can read the thermometer of my existence.

All went well this week in spite of the bad weather. On Sunday, we heard a motet by Palestrina[237] in the Sistine chapel. On Tuesday, it was our good fortune that various parts of the Holy Week music were sung in a salon in honor of a visiting foreign lady. So we heard it in the greatest comfort, and, since we sang it through so often at the piano, we could form a preliminary idea of it. This work of art is incredibly grand and simple, but it could probably not be performed with such regularity anywhere except in this place and under these circumstances. On closer inspection, to be sure, various unsophisticated reports, which describe the thing as strange and unheard of, fall away; nevertheless it remains something extraordinary and an entirely new concept. At some future time Kayser will give an account of it. He will have the privilege of listening to a rehearsal in the chapel, to which otherwise no one is admitted.

Moreover, this week I modeled a foot, after prior studies of bones and muscles, and am praised by my teacher. Anyone who has made a similar study of the whole body would be a great deal wiser—that is to say, in Rome, with all its resources and the manifold advice of experts. I have a skeleton foot, a beautiful anatomical foot cast from nature, a half dozen of the finest ancient feet, and several inferior ones—the former for imitation, the latter as warning; and I can also consult nature, for in every villa that I enter I find an opportunity to look at these body parts, while paintings show me what artists have thought and done. Three or four artists come to my room daily, and I profit from their advice and comments, but, among them, strictly speaking, I have benefited most from Heinrich Meyer's advice and assistance. A ship that does not move in this sea, with this wind, must have no sails or a mad helmsman. Considering that my survey of art has been a general one, it was very necessary for me to proceed attentively and diligently to specific parts. It is pleasant to advance, even in the infinite.

I continue to go around everywhere and see the things I have neglected. So yesterday, for the first time, I was at Raphael's villa,[238] where, at the side of his beloved, he found the enjoyment of life preferable to all art and all fame. It is a sacred monument. Prince Doria has acquired it and apparently intends to treat it as it deserves. Raphael portrayed his beloved on the wall twenty-eight times, in all sorts of clothes and costumes; even in the historical compositions the women resemble her. The location of the house is very beautiful. I shall be able to describe it to you orally better than I can write about it. The entire detail must be noted.

Then I went to the Villa Albani[239] and just looked around in it generally. It was a glorious day. Last night, it rained; now the sun is shining again, and there is a paradise before my window. The almond trees are all green, the peach blossoms are already beginning to fall, and the lemon blossoms are opening on the tops of the trees.

Three persons[240] are deeply grieved by my departure from here. They will never again find what they had in me. It pains me to leave them. In Rome I first found myself, for the first time I achieved inner harmony and became happy and rational, and it is as such an individual that the three of them knew, possessed, and enjoyed me, in various senses and degrees.

Rome, March 22.

Today I am not going to St. Peter's and want to write you a few words. Now Holy Week too is past, with its wonders and inconveniences; tomorrow, we shall still attend a Benediction, and then our hearts and minds will turn completely to another life.

Thanks to the kind efforts of good friends, I have seen and heard everything; the foot washing and the feeding of the pilgrims, in particular, can only be observed at the cost of much pushing and shoving.

The chapel music is unimaginably beautiful. Especially the *Miserere* by Allegri, and the so-called *Improperi*,[241] the reproaches which the crucified God makes to His people. They are sung on Good Friday morning. One of the most beautiful of all the noteworthy ceremonies is the moment when the pope, divested of all his rich apparel, steps down from the throne to worship the cross, and all the others remain in their place, everyone is quiet, and the choir begins: *"Populus meus, quid feci tibi?"*[242] I shall elaborate on all that orally, and Kayser will bring along as much music as is transportable. As was my wish, I enjoyed everything that was enjoyable in the ceremonies, and thought my private thoughts about the rest. Nothing made an effect on me, so to speak, nothing really impressed me, but I admired everything, for it must be said to their credit that they have made a thorough study of the Christian traditions. In the papal ceremonies, especially these in the Sistine chapel, everything that usually appears unpleasant in the Catholic divine service proceeds with great taste and perfect dignity. However, this can only happen in a place where for centuries all the arts have been at the Church's disposal.

Now is not the time to give the details of this. I could leave next week, if, as a result of that request, I had not meanwhile come to a standstill again, expecting to have a rather long stay here. But that too is for the best. I have again studied a great deal during this time, and the period of development I was hoping for has been concluded and rounded off. To be sure, it is always an odd feeling suddenly to leave a path on which one has advanced with bold steps, but one must resign oneself and not make a great fuss. In every great separation there lies a germ of madness; one must take care not to hatch it out and foster it.

Beautiful drawings have come to me from Naples, by Kniep, the painter who accompanied me to Sicily. These are lovely, charming fruits of my journey and will be those that please you most; for something set before one's eyes is what makes the deepest impression. With respect to color tone, some of them have turned out quite exquisitely, and you will hardly believe that the world is so beautiful there.

This much I can say, that I have become ever happier in Rome, and that my pleasure is still increasing daily; and, if it might seem mad that I must depart just when I would most deserve to stay, on the other hand it is a great comfort to me that I have been able to stay long enough to arrive at that point.

Just now the Lord Christ is rising with a fearful noise. The Castel is firing a salvo, all the bells are ringing, and on every side are heard firecrackers, squibs, and exploding trails of gunpowder. At eleven o'clock in the morning.

Report

March

It will be remembered that Filippo Neri frequently made it his duty to visit the seven principal Roman churches, thus giving a clear proof of his ardent devotion. However, it must now be mentioned here that a pilgrimage to the aforesaid churches is absolutely required of every pilgrim who comes to the jubilee; and really, owing to the fact that these stations are separated by great distances which have to be covered in a single day, this amounts to a second strenuous journey.

Those seven churches are: St. Peter's, Santa Maria Maggiore, San Lorenzo outside the Walls, San Sebastiano, St. John Lateran, Santa Croce in Gerusalemme, San Paolo outside the Walls.

Pious local souls also make this circuit in Holy Week, especially on Good Friday. An indulgence is associated with this, so that these souls earn and enjoy a spiritual benefit; but added to it is a material pleasure, in view of which the goal and purpose become still more attractive.

That is to say, whoever finally enters the portals of San Paolo with suitable proofs of having completed the pilgrimage receives a ticket entitling him to participate on specified days in a pious folk festival at the Villa Mattei. There the persons admitted receive a collation of bread, wine, and some cheese or eggs; while eating, they lie about in the garden, mainly in the little amphitheater situated in it. The more distinguished company, cardinals, prelates, princes, and gentlemen, assembles across from them in the pavilion of the villa, in order to enjoy the view and then also to accept their share of the bounty dispensed by the Mattei family.

We saw a procession of boys about ten to twelve years old approaching in pairs, not in ecclesiastical garb, but dressed as might be suitable, say, for apprentices on festival days, in clothes of identical color and identical cut; there may have been forty of them. They sang and said their litanies piously to themselves while walking along quietly and demurely.

An old man of sturdy, artisan-like appearance walked beside them, seeming to lead them and keep them all in order. We were surprised to see, at the end of the well-dressed line passing by, a half-dozen beggarly, barefoot, and ragged children, who nevertheless were walking along in the same proper, demure fashion. Our inquiries about this brought us the following information: This man, a cobbler by profession and childless, had felt moved at some earlier time to adopt a poor boy and teach him the trade; also, with the assistance of other benevolent persons, to clothe him and get him started in life. By giving this example, he had also succeeded in persuading other master artisans to adopt children, whom he then likewise tried to aid. In this way a little troop had been assembled, which he held unremittingly to religious observances, so as to prevent pernicious idleness on Sundays and holidays. Indeed, he even required them to visit the widely separated main churches on a single day. In this way his pious institution had continued to grow; he still made his commendable walking trips and, because there were always more boys pressing to enter this obviously useful institution than could be accepted, he tried to awaken charitable feelings generally by means of adding to the procession the children who still needed to be cared for and clothed. And he succeeded every time in obtaining donations sufficient to provide for one or the other of them.

While we were getting this information, one of the older, clothed boys had approached us also, holding out a plate, and in well-chosen words modestly requested alms for the naked and unshod ones. He not only received gifts in abundance from us foreigners, whose hearts were touched, but also from the usually stingy Romans standing nearby, men and women, who did not fail to attach pious weight to their meager contributions with many words in praise and appreciation of that man's merits.

It was said that this pious foster father always lets his charges partake of that free meal, after being edified by the preceding walk, so that there can never fail to be something worthwhile taken in for his noble purpose.

On the Creative Imitation of Beauty

By Karl Philipp Moritz. Brunswick, 1788.

Under this title was printed a pamphlet of scarcely four sheets, from a manuscript which Moritz had sent to Germany in an effort to pacify his publisher somewhat about the advance payment sent to him in Italy for a travel book. To be sure, the latter could not be written as easily as a book about a quixotic walking tour through England.[243]

But I must not pass over the aforesaid pamphlet in silence: it had resulted from our conversations, which Moritz had used and formed after his fashion. Besides, it possibly has some historical interest, showing what thoughts occurred to us at that time, which, when subsequently developed, tested, applied, and circulated, coincided well with the attitudes of the century.

A few pages from the middle of his presentation can be inserted here, perhaps they will motivate someone to reprint the whole pamphlet.[244]

"In the case of a creative genius, however, the horizon of his active power must be as broad as nature itself: that is, his organic structure must be so finely textured and offer so many points of contact with all-circumfluent nature that, so to speak, the outermost ends of all relations in nature on the grand scale, placed beside each other here on a small scale, have room enough not to crowd each other out.

Now if an organic structure of this finer texture, when fully developed, suddenly, in dim awareness of its active power, grasps a whole entity that came in neither through its eye nor its ear, neither through its imagination nor its thoughts, then a commotion, a tension, will necessarily arise between the swaying forces, until they regain their balance.

If a mind, with dim presentiment, has already grasped the grand, noble entirety of nature solely with its active power, then its clearly discerning power of thought, its still more vividly graphic power of imagination, and its most brightly mirroring external sense can no longer be satisfied with viewing individual things in nature's continuum.

All the relations of that great whole that are only dimly sensed by the active power must necessarily in some way become either visible, audible, or, at any rate, comprehensible to the imagination; and in order for this to happen the active power, in which they slumber, must form them in its own fashion, out of itself.—This power must take all the relations of the great whole and bring the highest beauty in them, as though from the point of its rays, into focus—Out of this focus, within the precise range of the eye, a fragile, yet faithful image of the highest beauty must be rounded out and include in its small compass the most complete relations of the great whole of nature, just as truly and accurately as nature itself does.

Now, however, because this image of the highest beauty must necessarily adhere to something, the creative power, determined by its individuality, chooses some object that is visible, audible, or, at any rate, comprehensible to the imagination, onto which it transfers, on a reduced scale, the reflection of the highest beauty.—And again, because if this object were really what it represents it could not go on existing in the continuum of nature, which tolerates no really independent whole outside itself, this leads us to the point where we were before: namely, that the inner essence must always first be transformed into phenomenon before it can be shaped by art into an independently existing whole and mirror unhindered and in their full scope the relations of the great whole of nature.

Since, however, those great relations, in whose complete compass beauty resides, lie outside the jurisdiction of the power of thought, the living concept of the creative imitation of beauty can only emerge when one is conscious of the active power producing the imitation, in the first moment of origin, when the work, as though already completed, suddenly, in dim presentiment, appears before the mind in all the degrees of its gradual development, and, in this moment of its first conception, is there, so to speak, before it really exists. From this, then, springs that inexpressible charm which impels the creative genius to continue producing art perpetually.

Thanks to our reflections on the creative imitation of beauty, combined with our pure pleasure in the beautiful artworks themselves, something like that living concept can, to be sure, arise in us and enhance our enjoyment of the beautiful artworks.—But nevertheless, since our highest enjoyment of beauty cannot possibly depend on our own power for its genesis, the only supreme enjoyment of it always belongs to the creative genius who produces it; and therefore beauty has already attained its highest goal in its emergence, in its becoming. Our subsequent enjoyment of it is simply a result of its existence—and, consequently, in the great plan of nature the creative genius exists first for his own sake, and only then for ours. For, of course, there are other beings besides him, who themselves do not create and produce art, but nevertheless can grasp the work with their imagination, once it is produced.

The nature of beauty consists in the very fact that its inner essence lies in its emergence and becoming, outside the boundaries of the power of thought. Beauty is beautiful for the very reason that the power of thought cannot inquire of it *why* it is beautiful.—For the power of thought completely lacks a point of comparison by which it could judge and view beauty. What other point of comparison is there for true beauty except the sum of all the harmonious relations of the great whole of nature, which no power of thought can grasp? Every individual beauty strewn here and there in nature is only beautiful insofar as this sum of all the relations of that great whole is more or less revealed in it. Therefore it can never serve as the point of comparison for the beauty of the fine arts, nor as a model for the true imitation of beauty; because the highest beauty in individual things in nature is still not beautiful enough for the proud imitation of the grand and majestic relations of the all-inclusive whole of nature. Consequently, beauty is not discerned, it must be produced—or felt.

Because beauty, with its total lack of a point of comparison, is not a matter for the power of thought, and since we cannot produce it ourselves, we would have to forgo enjoyment of it altogether, for we could never be certain of what was more beautiful, or less so—if the productive power were not replaced in us by something that comes as close to it as is possible without actually being it—this, now, is what we call taste, or the ability to *feel* beauty. When this remains within its bounds, it can replace our lack of the higher pleasure of producing beauty with the undisturbed peace of quiet contemplation.

That is to say, if our organic structure is not textured finely enough to offer the inflowing whole of nature as many points of contact as are needed to mirror completely all its great relations in miniature, and we lack one point for complete closure of the circle, then all we can have, instead of the creative power, is the ability to feel beauty; our every attempt to represent it outside ourselves would fail and make us the more dissatisfied with ourselves, the more closely our ability to feel beauty borders on the creative ability we lack.

That is to say, because the essence of beauty consists in its being complete within itself, the last missing point damages it as much as a thousand, for this shifts all the other points out of the position where they belong.—And if this point of completion is missing, then an artwork is not worth the trouble of beginning it and the time of its formation; it descends below inferiority to uselessness, and its existence is inevitably canceled out again by the oblivion into which it sinks.

The creative capacity implanted in the finer texture of the organic structure is damaged just as much by the last point it lacks in completeness as by a thousand.—The highest value it could have as capacity for feeling is of no more importance to it as creative power than the least would be. At the point where the capacity for feeling oversteps its bounds, it can only sink beneath itself, and cancel and annihilate itself.

The more perfect the capacity for feeling is with respect to a certain species of beauty, the greater risk it runs of being deceived into taking itself for creative power, and so its peace is disturbed by a thousand unsuccessful attempts.

For example, when enjoying beauty in any work of art, the capacity for feeling immediately looks through the formation of that work into the creative power that formed it; and dimly senses the higher degree to which this same beauty can be enjoyed by the individual who feels this power, which is mighty enough to produce the work out of itself.

In order to attain this higher degree of pleasure, which cannot possibly be derived from a work already in existence, the too actively stirred feeling strives in vain to produce something similar out of itself, hates its own work, rejects it, and at the same time spoils its own enjoyment of all beauty that already exists outside of itself and which can no longer delight it because this beauty exists without its help.

Its only wish and aspiration is to partake of the higher pleasure denied it, and which it only dimly senses: to mirror itself, conscious of its own creative power, in a beautiful work which owes its existence to it.

But this wish is never granted, because it arises from self-interest, whereas beauty submits only for its own sake to the artist's hand, and willingly and obediently lets itself be formed by him.

If the creative, formative impulse is simultaneously mixed with an idea of the enjoyment which is to come when the beautiful work is complete; and if this idea becomes the primary and strongest spur to our active power, which does not feel urged in and of itself to do what it is undertaking, then the creative impulse is certainly not pure: the focus, or completion point, of beauty falls outside the work, into its effect; the rays scatter; the work cannot be rounded off in itself.

To imagine oneself so near to the highest enjoyment of something beautiful produced out of oneself, and yet to forgo that enjoyment, surely seems a hard struggle—which nevertheless becomes extremely easy if we expunge from this creative impulse, which we flatter ourselves we have, every trace of self-interest that is still present, thus ennobling its nature; and if we try to banish as much as possible all thought of enjoying the sense of our own power that will be afforded us by the beautiful thing we intend to produce, once it exists. This must go so far that, even if we could only complete it with our last breath, we would still endeavor to complete it.—

If, then, the beautiful thing we dimly foresee still retains enough charm, merely in and of itself, in its production, to stir our active power, we can confidently follow our creative impulse, because it is genuine and pure.—

But if, along with our total dismissal of enjoyment and effect, the charm also disappears, then no further struggle is needed, we are at peace with ourselves, and the capacity for feeling, which has now come into its own again, is rewarded for its modest retreat into its limits by being opened up to the purest enjoyment of beauty consistent with the nature of its being.

To be sure, the point where the creative power and the power of feeling intersect can be missed and overstepped so very easily that it is not at all astonishing if for every genuine reproduction of the highest beauty in artworks there are a thousand false, presumptuous ones, owing to the false creative impulse.

For since the genuine creative power, immediately at the first emergence of its work, already bears the first, highest enjoyment thereof in itself, as a sure reward, and is only differentiated from the false creative impulse by the fact that it receives the very first moment of impetus from itself, and not from any presentiment of its enjoyment of the work; and because in this moment of passion the power of thought itself cannot judge correctly, it is almost impossible to escape this self-deception without first making a number of unsuccessful attempts.

And even these unsuccessful attempts themselves are not always a proof of deficient creative power because, even where this power is genuine, it often takes quite a wrong course, trying to set before its imagination what belongs before its eye, or before the eye what belongs before the ear.

Precisely because nature does not always allow the indwelling creative power to attain full maturity and development or lets it take a wrong path, on which it can never develop, genuine beauty remains rare.

And because nature also lets what is common and inferior be produced without hindrance by the pretended creative impulse, the genuine and beautiful is, for that very reason, distinguished from the inferior and common by its rare value.

So in the capacity for feeling there is always a gap which can only be filled by what the creative impulse produces.—Creative power and the capacity for feeling are in the same relationship to each other as man and woman. For the creative power too, at the original emergence of the work, in the moment of highest enjoyment, is simultaneously the capacity for feeling and, like nature, brings forth the replica of its being from itself.

Capacity for feeling, as well as creative power, are therefore grounded in the finer texture of the organic structure, insofar as the latter is a complete, or at least almost complete, replica, in all its points of contact, of the relations of the great whole of nature.

Capacity for feeling, as well as creative power, encompass more than the power of thought does; and the active power, on which both are based, simultaneously embraces everything that the power of thought embraces, because it bears within itself the first causes of all the concepts we can ever have, continually spinning them out of itself.

Insofar as this active power embraces productively everything that does not fall under the jurisdiction of the power of thought, it is called creative power; and insofar as it includes what lies outside the boundaries of the power of thought, inclining toward production, it is called the power of feeling.

Creative power cannot operate by itself alone, without active power and feeling, but the active power as such can operate on its own without actual creative power and power of feeling, of which it is only the basis.

Now insofar as this active power as such is also grounded in the finer texture of the organic structure, the organ may be in all its points of contact only generally a replica of the relations of the great whole, without the same degree of completeness being required that the creative power and that of feeling presuppose.

That is to say, there are always so many relations of the great whole surrounding us which coincide with all the points of contact of our organ that we feel this great whole dimly in ourselves, without, however, being it. The relations of that whole which are spun into our nature strive to extend themselves again to all sides; the organ wishes to continue itself infinitely in all directions. It not only wants to mirror the surrounding whole in itself, but also, as far as possible, to be *itself* this surrounding whole.

Therefore every higher organic structure, by its nature, seizes the one subordinate to it and absorbs this into its being. The plant absorbs inorganic material by means of mere formation and growth; the animal absorbs the plant through formation, growth, and enjoyment; the human being not only converts animal and plant into his inner substance through formation, growth, and enjoyment, but simultaneously, by means of that mirroring surface of his being which is the most highly polished of them all, takes everything into the sphere of his existence that is subordinate to his organic structure and depicts it outside of himself again, beautified, if his organ is being creatively perfected within him.

If not, he must draw what is around him into the sphere of his real existence by destruction and spread desolation around himself as far as he can, since pure, innocent viewing cannot take the place of his thirst for extended real existence.''

April

Correspondence

I am still in Rome in body, but not in spirit. As soon as I was firmly resolved to leave, I no longer felt any interest and would rather have already been gone for a fortnight. Actually, I am staying for Kayser's sake, and for Bury's sake. The former still has to complete some studies that he can only pursue here and assemble some printed music; the latter still has to finish his sketch for a painting I have suggested, for which he needs my advice.

Nevertheless, I have fixed on April 21 or 22 for my departure.

Rome, April 11.

The days pass, and I can no longer do anything. I scarcely care to see another thing. My honest Meyer is still assisting me, and I am enjoying his instructive company to the last. If I did not have Kayser with me, I would bring Meyer along. If we had only had him for a year, we would have progressed enough. In particular, he would soon have helped us overcome all hesitancy in the drawing of heads.[245]

This morning I was in the French Academy with my good Meyer, where casts of the best ancient statues stand in a group. How can I express what I felt when bidding them farewell? In the presence of these statues we become more than we are; we feel that nothing is as worthy of study as the human figure, which is seen here in all its manifold splendor. But who does not immediately feel at such a sight how inadequate he is? Even though prepared, one stands there as though reduced to nothing. Although I had tried to acquire a fairly clear idea of proportion, anatomy, and regularity of movement, here it struck me only too forcibly that, in the end, *form* includes everything, the suitability of the limbs, their relation, character, and beauty.

Rome, April 14.

I doubt that the confusion can become greater! While I did not stop modeling on that foot, it occurred to me that now I would immediately have to attack *Tasso,* and so I turned my thoughts also to it, as a welcome companion for my impending journey. Meanwhile I am packing, and only at such a moment does one see how much one has accumulated and dragged together.

Report

April

My correspondence from the final weeks offers little of significance; my situation was too caught up between art and friendship, between having and striving, between a present I was accustomed to and a future I would have to become accustomed to all over again. Under these circumstances my letters could not contain much; I expressed my joy quite temperately at the prospect of seeing my tried and true old friends again, whereas I barely concealed the pain I felt at detaching myself. Therefore, in the present supplementary report, I shall sum up some things and record only what has been preserved to me from that time in other papers and mementos, or in my memory.

Tischbein was still lingering in Naples, although he had repeatedly announced that he would return in the spring. He was easy to live with except for one bad habit, which in the long run grew tiresome. That is to say, he was rather vague about all his plans, and so, without actual malicious intent, he brought trouble and annoyance to other people. That happened to me as well in this case. Whenever he returned, I would have to change my living quarters if we were all to be lodged comfortably, and since the upper floor of our house had just been vacated, I quickly rented it and moved in, so that on his arrival he would find everything ready on the lower floor.

The upper rooms were like the lower ones, but to the rear they had the advantage of a most charming view over the back garden and the gardens of the neighborhood, a view extending in all directions, since our house stood on the corner.

Here, now, the most varied gardens were to be seen, regularly separated by walls, laid out and planted with infinite diversity. Nobly simple architecture was in evidence everywhere, enhancing this green and blossoming paradise: garden rooms, balconies, terraces, also an open loggia on the higher rear wing of the house, and in between were all the trees and plants typical of the region.

In our back garden, an old priest tended a number of well-maintained lemon trees of moderate height in decorated terra cotta pots, which enjoyed the open air in summer, but were kept in the garden room in winter. When fully ripe, their fruits were carefully picked, each one wrapped individually in soft paper, packed up like that, and sent off. They are a popular market item because of their special merits. Middle-class families regard an orangery of this kind as a small capital that is certain to yield interest annually.

The same windows out of which, beneath the clearest sky, I peace-fully contemplated so much charm, also provided an excellent light for viewing pictures. Kniep, per arrangement, had just then sent me various watercolor paintings, done from the outlines he had carefully made on our trip through Sicily. Seen now in this most favorable light, they pleased everyone who took an interest in them, and were much admired. Perhaps no one has ever succeeded better in producing clarity and air-iness of this kind than he, whose inclination was to apply himself to this very thing. The sight of these pictures was really enchanting, for I seemed to feel again the dampness of the sea, to see again the blue shadows of the rocks, the yellowish-reddish colors of the mountains, the distances merging with the most brilliant sky. But these were not the only pictures that took on such a favorable appearance; every painting that was placed on the same easel, in the same spot, looked more effective and striking. I remember several times when I entered the room and a picture like that had an almost magical effect on me.

The secret of favorable or unfavorable, direct or indirect atmospheric lighting had not yet been discovered at that time; but the phenomenon itself was certainly felt and marveled at, and considered just accidental and inexplicable.

We had gradually collected a number of plaster casts, and my new lodgings presented an opportunity to set them up in agreeable order and a good light, so that only now did we enjoy our very handsome possessions. If someone is constantly in the presence of ancient statues, as is the case in Rome, he feels himself confronted with something infinite and inscrutable, as one does in the presence of nature. The impression of the sublime, the beautiful, as salutary as it may be, makes us uneasy, and we want to put our feelings, our perceptions, into words: but first, in order to do so, we would have to discern, penetrate, com-prehend; we begin to distinguish, to differentiate, to put in order, and we also find this, if not impossible, nevertheless very difficult, and so, in the end, we go back to viewing, enjoying, and admiring.

In general, however, the most marked effect of all artworks is that they put us back into the situation of the time and the individuals that produced them. Surrounded by ancient statues, we feel ourselves in the midst of a vigorous natural life, we become aware of the diverseness of human forms and are led directly back to the human being in his purest state, with the result that the observer himself becomes alive and purely human. Even the drapery, compatible with nature, to some extent actually emphasizing the figure, is generally pleasing. Being able to enjoy such surroundings every day in Rome, one begins at the same time to covet them; we want to set up such figures next to ourselves, and good plaster casts, as the most genuine facsimiles, provide the best opportunity for this. On opening our eyes in the morning, we feel stirred by the most splendid things; all our thinking and musing is accompanied by such figures, and consequently it becomes impossible to sink back into barbarism.

In our house, the *Juno Ludovisi* claimed first place and was all the more highly esteemed and honored since we could see the original only seldom, only by chance. We considered ourselves very fortunate to have her perpetually in view; for not one of our contemporaries, approaching her for the first time, can claim to be equal to this sight.

Several other, smaller Junos stood next to her for comparison, busts of Jupiter were prominent, and (to pass others by) there was a fine old cast of the *Medusa Rondanini,* a wonderful work expressing the conflict between death and life, grief and sensual pleasure, which, like any other dispute, holds an unutterable fascination for us.

But I shall additionally mention a Hercules Anax, as intelligent and mild as he was big and strong; then a most charming Mercury.[246] The originals of both are now in England.

Works in bas-relief, casts of some beautiful works in terra cotta, also Egyptian casts taken from the apex of the great obelisk, and any number of fragments, among them some marble ones, stood around in neat rows.

I am speaking of these treasures, which stood in rows in the new rooms for only a few weeks, like someone who is thinking about his last will and looks with composure, and yet with emotion, at the possessions surrounding him. The many details involved, the trouble and expense, and a certain awkwardness in such matters restrained me from immediately dispatching the best items to Germany. *Juno Ludovisi* was designated for the noble Angelica, a few other things for the artists closest at hand, some were still part of Tischbein's possessions, others were to remain untouched until used, in his own fashion, by Bury, who would move into these quarters after me.

As I write this, I am carried back in thought to my earliest days, and I recall the occasions that originally acquainted me with such objects, aroused my interest, instilled a boundless enthusiasm in me (though my thinking was totally inadequate), and resulted in an infinite longing for Italy.

In my earliest youth I took no notice of any statuary in my native town. In Leipzig it was the faun coming on stage,[247] as it were, dancing and beating cymbals, that first made an impression on me, so that even now I can imagine that cast in its surroundings, with its individuality. After a long pause I was abruptly plunged into the open sea, that is, when I suddenly saw myself surrounded by the Mannheim collection,[248] in that salon with its excellent lighting from above.

Afterwards, some makers of plaster casts arrived in Frankfurt; they had crossed the Alps with some original casts, which they then sold for a modest price, after having made copies of them. So I obtained a fairly good Laocoon head, Niobe's daughter, a little head that was later declared to be a Sappho, and some more things. These noble forms acted as a kind of antidote when the weak, false, and mannered threatened to overwhelm me. Actually, however, I always suffered inwardly from an unsatisfied desire for the unknown, which, although often suppressed, revived again and again. Therefore my pain was great when, on leaving Rome, I was obliged to relinquish ownership of what I had most ardently wished for and finally attained.

The laws of plant structure, which I had become aware of in Sicily, occupied my mind amidst all of this, as is usual with inclinations which take possession of the inner self and at the same time prove consonant with our abilities. I visited the botanical garden, which, if you will, was not very attractive in its antiquated condition, but nevertheless had a favorable influence on me, since much of what I found there seemed new and unexpected. Consequently I took this opportunity to add some of the rarer plants to my collection, so that I could continue meditating on them, while I also continued observing and tending those I had grown from seeds and fruit pits.

At my departure, several friends wanted to divide especially these latter ones among themselves. I planted the already fairly well-grown stone pine sprout, the little model of a future tree, in Angelica's back garden. There in the course of time it grew to a considerable height, and sympathetic travelers, to my delight and theirs, had much to tell me about it and also about memories of me in that place. Unfortunately, after the death of that highly esteemed friend, the incoming new owner thought it unsuitable to have stone pines growing up, quite out of place, on his flowerbeds. Later, when travelers who thought well of me looked for the spot, they found it empty and the traces of an agreeable existence obliterated, at least here.

Several date palms that I had grown from seeds were more fortunate. From time to time, to be sure, I had sacrificed some specimens, to observe something of their remarkable development; but I entrusted the remaining, newly sprouted ones to a Roman friend, who planted them in a garden in the Via Sistina. There they are still alive and, as a matter of fact, grown to man's height, as an august traveler[249] has graciously assured me. May they not inconvenience the owners, and continue to be green, to grow, and flourish, in memory of me!

Two very disparate things, the Cloaca Maxima and the catacombs next to St. Sebastian, remained on my list of what was still to be seen, if possible. The first proved to be an even more colossal concept than Piranesi had prepared us for;[250] however, the visit to the second locality did not turn out very well. My first steps into these musty chambers made me so uneasy that I immediately climbed back out into the daylight. There in the open air, in a part of the city both distant and unfamiliar, I awaited the return of the rest of the party, who were more composed than I and no doubt viewed the conditions down there calmly.

Long afterwards in the great work by Antonio Bosio Romano, *Roma sotterranea*,[251] I got detailed information about everything I would have seen, or more likely *not* have seen, and felt myself adequately recompensed by this.

However, another pilgrimage was undertaken with more profit and effect: it was to the San Luca Academy, to pay our respects to Raphael's skull, which has been preserved there as a holy relic ever since it was removed from the grave of this extraordinary man (opened in connection with some construction work) and brought to this place.

A truly wonderful sight! A shell, joined together and rounded off as beautifully as can be imagined, without a trace of those elevations, bulges, and bumps which, observed later on other skulls, have acquired such diverse significance in Gall's teachings.[252] I could not tear myself away from the sight and remarked upon leaving how much it would mean to lovers of nature and art to have a cast of it, if that were at all possible. Aulic Councilor Reiffenstein, our influential friend, gave me hope and fulfilled it after some time by really sending such a cast to me in Germany, the sight of which I often still find most manifoldly thought-provoking.

The charming picture by this artist's hand—the Mother of God appearing to St. Luke, so that he can paint her truly and naturally in her full divine majesty—was a most pleasant sight. Raphael himself, still a youth, stands some distance away, watching the Evangelist at work. There could hardly be a more graceful way to express and acknowledge a vocation to which one feels strongly attracted.

Pietro da Cortona[253] formerly owned this work and he bequeathed it to the academy. While damaged and restored in some places, it still remains a painting of significant value.

However, at this time I was exposed to quite a unique temptation, which threatened to prevent my trip and tie me down again in Rome. That is to say, Mr. Antonio Rega,[254] artist and also art dealer, came from Naples to my friend Meyer, confidentially announcing that he had arrived on a ship now docked outside at Ripa grande, and inviting Meyer to go there with him; for he had a significant ancient statue on the ship. It was that dancer, or Muse, which had stood for countless years in a niche in the courtyard of the Caraffa Colombrano palace in Naples along with other statues and without question was considered a good work. He said that he wanted to sell it, but quietly, and therefore was inquiring whether by any chance Mr. Meyer himself, or one of his intimate friends, would be interested in this transaction. He said that he was offering this noble artwork at the indisputably very moderate price of three hundred zechins, a demand which would unquestionably have been higher, if there were not reason to proceed cautiously in consideration of the sellers and the buyer.

I was informed of the matter at once, and the three of us hurried to the landing place, which was at a considerable distance from our lodgings. Rega immediately removed a board from the case, which stood on the deck, and we saw a charming little head, which had never been separated from its trunk,[255] the face looking out from under loose curls; and by degrees a winsomely animated figure was revealed, most gracefully draped, moreover little damaged and with one hand perfectly preserved.

Immediately we remembered quite well having seen it in place, never imagining that someday we would stand so close to it.

Now the following thought occurred to us, and to whom would it not have? "Certainly," we said, "if someone had finally come upon such a treasure after a whole year of expensive digging, he would have considered himself very fortunate." We could hardly take our eyes off it, for surely we had never seen an ancient relic that was so pure, well preserved, and easily restorable. But at last we left, intending and promising to give an answer very soon.

The two of us had a real struggle with ourselves, since in some respects we felt it was inadvisable to make this purchase; therefore we decided to report the matter to our good Madame Angelica, as a person well able financially to make the purchase and sufficiently qualified through her connections to take care of restoration and whatever else might come up. Meyer did the reporting, as he had done before in the case of the picture by Daniele da Volterra, and so we hoped for the best success. But the prudent woman, and more especially her economical husband, refused to buy; for while they spent significant sums on paintings, they could by no means make up their minds to go in for statues.

This negative answer caused us to think the matter over again; fortune seemed to be uniquely favoring us; Meyer inspected the treasure once more and convinced himself that the sculpture should surely be recognized as Greek, since it bore all the earmarks of Greek workmanship. In fact, it could be dated back to long before Augustus, perhaps as far back as Hieron II.[256]

To be sure, I had enough credit to acquire this significant artwork. Rega even seemed willing to accept payment in instalments, and for a moment we believed that we were in possession of the image and already saw it set up, well lighted, in our large salon.

But just as other thoughts are wont to intrude between a passionate attachment and the signing of a marriage contract, so it was here too; and without the advice and consent of our noble art associates, Mr. Zucchi and his kindly wife,[257] we dared not undertake such a relationship, for a relationship it was, in an ideal-Pygmalionic sense, and I do not deny that the thought of possessing this object had become deeply rooted in me. Indeed, let the following confession serve as proof of how greatly I flattered myself in the affair: I regarded this event as a sign that higher daimons intended to keep me in Rome and to strike down very effectively all my reasons for deciding to leave.

Fortunately, we had already reached an age when in such cases reason usually comes to the aid of intellect, and therefore our love of art, desire to possess, and what additionally supported them, namely dialectics and superstition, had to retreat before the wise sentiments our noble friend Angelica was kind enough to express to us sensibly and benevolently. Her objections made us see clearly all the difficulties and risks standing in the way of such a project: If men who had heretofore quietly devoted themselves to the study of art and antiquity were suddenly to meddle in the fine art trade, they would arouse the jealousy of persons who normally have a right to this business. Restoration would present manifold difficulties, and it was uncertain how fairly and honestly we would be served in this. Furthermore, even if everything connected with shipment proceeded in the best possible order, obstacles could still arise at the end in securing permission to export such an artwork, and then all sorts of untoward happenings were to be feared from the sea crossing, the unloading, and the arrival at home. She said that a businessman would look beyond such considerations, because where a large enterprise is concerned the trouble and danger are balanced out, whereas a single undertaking of this kind would be doubtful in every way.

As a result of such remonstrances, my desire, wish, and intent gradually became weaker and more moderate, but were never entirely extinguished, especially since the statue eventually attained to great honor; for at present it stands in the Museo Pio-Clementino, in a little added room, which, however, is connected with the museum, and in whose floor are set very beautiful mosaics of masks and festoons. The other statues grouped in that room are 1) the Venus sitting on her heel, in whose base the name "Bupalos" is carved;[258] 2) a very beautiful little Ganymede;[259] 3) the beautiful statue of a youth, who has been given, I do not know how correctly, the name Adonis;[260] 4) a faun made of *rosso antico* marble;[261] 5) the quietly standing Discobolus.[262]

Visconti,[263] in his third volume, which is dedicated to the aforesaid museum, has described this statue, explained it in his fashion, and had it illustrated in plate 30. And surely every art lover can share our regret that we did not succeed in bringing it to Germany and adding it to some great collection in our fatherland.

It will seem only natural that in making my farewell visits I did not forget that charming Milanese girl. I had lately heard some agreeable things about her: that she had grown ever closer to Angelica and knew very well how to behave in the higher society she had entered as a result. Also, I had reason to suppose and hope that a well-to-do young man,[264] who was on the best terms with the Zucchis, would not be insensitive to her charm and not disinclined to carry out more serious intentions.

Now I found her in a neat morning dress, as I had first seen her in Castel Gandolfo; she received me with unaffected charm, and with natural grace very sweetly repeated many times her gratitude for my interest. "I shall never forget," she said, "that when I recovered from my delirium and heard the beloved and honored names of those who had asked about me, yours was always mentioned; several times I tried to find out whether it was really true. You continued your inquiries for several weeks, until finally my brother visited you and could thank for both of us. I do not know if he did it according to my instructions; I would like to have gone along, if that had been seemly." She inquired about the route I intended to take, and when I told her my travel plans, she replied: "You are fortunate to be so rich that you do not need to deny yourself this; the rest of us must resign ourselves to the place that God and His saints have allotted us. For a long time I have been watching ships come and go, load and unload, in front of my window; that is entertaining, and sometimes I think, where do they all come from, where do they go?" Her windows directly overlooked the steps of the Ripetta, where the activity just then was very lively.

She spoke tenderly of her brother, being happy to manage his household in an orderly fashion and make it possible for him, in spite of his modest salary, to lay something aside for investing in a profitable business; in short, she soon thoroughly acquainted me with her situation. I was glad she was loquacious; for I was really cutting a very strange figure, since I felt an urge quickly to review all the moments, from the first to the last, of our tender relationship. Then her brother entered, and the leave-taking concluded in friendly, temperate prose.

When I went out the door I discovered that my carriage was without its driver, whom an eagerly helpful boy ran to fetch. She looked out at a window in the entresol that they inhabited in a stately building; it was not very high up, so that we could almost have clasped hands.

"He does not want to take me away from you, you see," I cried. "He seems to know that I am loath to leave you."

What she answered to that, what I replied, the rest of our most charming conversation, which, being free of all constraint, revealed the inmost hearts of two people who were only half aware of loving each other, shall not be profaned by me through telling and repeating it. Forced from our lips by an inner impulse, it was a wonderful, inadvertently begun, laconic last confession of the most innocent and tender mutual affection, and therefore it has always stayed in my heart and soul.

However, my departure from Rome was to be initiated with particular ceremony: on the three nights preceding it, a full moon stood in the clearest sky and spread a magic, so often felt but now most vividly palpable, over the enormous city. The great lucent masses, clear as though illuminated by a gentle daylight, with individual details suggested by contrasting deep shadows—which are sometimes brightened by reflections—give us the sensation of being in a different, simpler, grander world.

After some distracting, at times painfully spent days, I made the rounds with a few friends, for once in complete solitude. After I had walked, no doubt for the last time, through the long Corso, I climbed up to the Capitol, which stood there like a fairy palace in the desert. The statue of Marcus Aurelius[265] brought to mind the Commendatore in *Don Giovanni,* and warned this stroller that he was undertaking something unusual. Nevertheless I descended the steps in back. Standing darkly opposite me and casting dark shadows was the triumphal arch of Septimius Severus; in the deserted Via Sacra the otherwise so familiar objects looked strange and ghostly. But when I approached the sublime remains of the Coliseum and looked through the grille into its closed-off interior, I cannot deny that a shudder went through me and hastened my return.

Everything of massive proportions makes the peculiar impression of being both sublime and comprehensible, and so while making these rounds I drew up a vast *summa summarum,* as it were, of my whole sojourn. This, being felt deeply and grandly in my agitated soul, evoked a mood that I may call heroic-elegiac, out of which an elegiac poem began to take form.

And how could I not recall Ovid's elegy[266] at these very moments, for he too was banished and was about to leave Rome on a moonlit night. "Cum repeto noctem!"—his recollection far away at the Black Sea, where he was sad and miserable—kept recurring to me, and I recited the poem, which in part I remembered exactly. But actually it only interfered with and hindered my own production, which, although undertaken again later, never came into existence.

When the mournful image of that night returns to me,
Which was to be my last in the great city,
When I recall the night I left so much that was dear to me,
Even now a tear rolls down from my eye.
Already the voices of men and of dogs had grown silent,
And Luna was driving her nocturnal steeds high above.
I gazed at her, then down at the Capitol's temples,
So near to our Lares and yet all in vain.

Cum subit illius tristissima noctis imago,
Quae mihi supremum tempus in Urbe fuit;
Cum repeto noctem, qua tot mihi cara reliqui;
Labitur ex oculis nunc quoque gutta meis.
Iamque quiescebant voces hominumque canumque:
Lunaque nocturnos alta regebat equos.
Hanc ego suspiciens, et ab hac Capitolia cernens,
Quae nostro frustra iuncta fuere Lari.—

Notes

Part I
Carlsbad to Rome: August 1786–February 1787

[1] Goethe had been vacationing in Carlsbad (today Karlovy Vary) since July 27, 1786. Charlotte von Stein, the Herders, and Duke Carl August had been there at the same time, although Charlotte had left earlier, on August 14.

[2] The Waldsassen monastery dates from 1115.

[3] Here, as elsewhere, "mile" means the German mile, equivalent to approximately four and a half English miles.

[4] Rubens had done sketches for a series of paintings commissioned by Maria de' Medici in 1622 for the new Luxembourg palace in Paris. The sketches are now in the Munich Alte Pinakothek, the finished paintings in the Louvre in Paris.

[5] A copy of the Trajan Column in Rome had been acquired in Italy by the Palatine-Bavarian elector Karl Theodor in 1783.

[6] Begun in 1569, this was one of the oldest museums north of the Alps.

[7] Karl Ludwig von Knebel (1744–1834), an intimate Weimar friend of Goethe. See also the note in Volume 4, p. 517.

[8] Balthasar Hacquet (1739–1815) had traveled in the Alps in 1781 and 1783 before publishing a four-volume work in Leipzig in 1785.

[9] A Benedictine monastery in the Swiss canton of Schwyz, founded in 934. Goethe had visited there on his first Swiss journey in 1775 and wrote about it in Book Eighteen of *Poetry and Truth*.

[10] This was a much-retold anecdote from the life of Emperor Maximilian (1459–1519) and had also been the subject of numerous paintings.

[11] The good-for-nothing son-in-law of the innkeeper in Goethe's early play, *The Accomplices* (1768).

[12] "Blende" or "Plente," Italian "polenta," originally meant either barley or maize.

[13] The *Species Plantarum* published in 1753 by Carl von Linné (1707–1778), which established the classification and nomenclature of flowers and ferns.

[14] The first authorized edition of Goethe's collected works was published in eight volumes by Georg Joachim Göschen (1752–1828) in Leipzig between 1787 and 1790. Work on the last four volumes was completed largely during Goethe's

stay in Italy (including the major plays *Egmont, Iphigenia in Tauris,* and parts of *Torquato Tasso*) and is a recurring theme in the *Italian Journey.* Herder was Goethe's closest advisor during his work on the edition.

[15] Christian Georg Karl Vogel (1760–1819), Goethe's secretary at the time, was later a Weimar councilor.

[16] Goethe had translated and adapted Aristophanes's play, *The Birds,* in which "True Friend" is one of the émigrés.

[17] Goethe's play, written in prose in 1779, had been performed at the Weimar court theater at the time, with Goethe playing the role of Orestes.

[18] Allart van Everdingen (1621–1675), a Dutch landscape painter.

[19] Goethe should rather have written "westwards."

[20] "Just as peaches and melons are reserved for barons, so sticks and switches are kept for madmen, says Solomon."

[21] Johann Heinrich Roos (1631–1685), a landscape painter who settled in Frankfurt. The young Goethe was acquainted with his works and owned some drawings by him.

[22] In reality September 11.

[23] A painting done by Elia Naurizio in 1633 which, however, hung in the church of Santa Maria Maggiore rather than in the Jesuit church, as it would appear from what Goethe writes. The Council of Trent met 1545–1547, 1551/52, and 1562.

[24] The Society of Jesus had been suppressed by Pope Clement XIV in 1773.

[25] Countess Aloysia von Lanthieri (b. 1750), an acquaintance of Goethe's from Carlsbad.

[26] J.J. Volkmann's *Historical and Critical News of Italy,* a three-volume work first published in Leipzig in 1770–1771, was Goethe's principal guidebook.

[27] "O Benacus, resounding to the shore with roaring waves," *Georgica,* 2, 160. In his diary Goethe had quoted the passage correctly, *assurgens* instead of *resonans.*

[28] "You can do it down there." "Where?" "Anywhere, wherever you want."

[29] Mayor.

[30] Goethe had played the role of True Friend on the stage at Ettersburg Castle near Weimar.

[31] Marco Bolongaro (1712–1779) had founded a merchant company in Frankfurt and built a villa in nearby Höchst during the 1770s.

[32] Johann Maria Allesina, a Piedmontese silk merchant in Frankfurt, had married Franziska Clara Brentano (b. 1705). Goethe had known their grandchildren while growing up in Frankfurt.

[33] The Laestrygones, *Odyssey,* X, were cannibalistic giants.

[34] In reality September 14.

[35] Johann Jakob Ferber (1743–1790) published a volume of letters about the curiosities of Italy, Prague, 1773.

[36] Johann Karl Wilhelm Voigt (1752–1823), a geologist and mineralogist, Weimar secretary for mining in Ilmenau, had assembled small mineralogical collections for sale.

[37] An allusion to the controversy over the building of the earth's crust. The Vulcanists considered volcanic action to be the prime factor, whereas the Neptunists considered rock formations to be oceanic deposits. Goethe himself was a Neptunist.

[38] Bullfights had been staged in the amphitheater in honor of Emperor Joseph II in 1771 and Pope Pius VI in 1782.

[39] The name on the monument, which dates from 1569, is actually "Hieronymus Marmoreus."

[40] Built 1542–1551 by the Veronese architect Michele Sanmicheli (1484–1559).

[41] The Teatro Filarmonico was built in 1710 by Francesco Scipione, Marchese di Maffei (1675–1755), a writer and archaeologist. He founded an archaeological museum there in 1719 and was the author of *Verona illustrata,* published in four parts, Verona, 1731, and *Museo Veronese,* 1749.

[42] On the left bank of the river across from the cathedral, the church was built in 1477 on the site of an older edifice.

[43] By Felice Brusasorci the Younger (ca. 1542–1605), dated 1605 and completed by his pupils.

[44] By Paolo Farinato (1524–1606), dated 1602/03.

[45] By Giovanni Francesco Caroto (ca. 1480–1555), dated 1535.

[46] Ca. 1540. This was Goethe's first sight of an original work by Titian.

[47] Alessandro Turchi (1578–1649), called Veronese or l'Orbetto. The painting of Samson and Delilah described here is now in the Louvre.

[48] The Palazzo Canossa, built by Michele Sanmicheli, was begun around 1530. The painting mentioned here has not been identified.

[49] Built by Sanmicheli in the 1530s, it is now a technical institute.

[50] Jacopo Robusti (1518–1594), called Tintoretto, was a pupil of Titian. The work described here is a sketch for a competition in 1579 for the Palace of the Doge in Venice, now in the Louvre. Goethe's praise played a significant role in the history of Tintoretto's reputation.

[51] Paolo Caliari (?1528–1588), called Veronese. One of the portraits seen by Goethe, a young woman holding the hand of a child, is now in the Louvre.

[52] "Marlbrough s'en va-t-en guerre," a popular satirical ballad dating from the Seven Years' War that was being sung everywhere in 1786, half in Italian, half in French.

[53] Cypress branches were usually carried by mourners.

[54] Andrea Palladio (1508–1580), was born and died in Padua, but worked principally in Vicenza. Goethe's architectural taste was greatly influenced by becoming acquainted with Palladio's work and reading Palladio while in Italy. The Teatro Olimpico was finished in 1585 after Palladio's death.

[55] Probably Goethe means Giovanni Montenari's *Discorso del teatro Olimpico,* published in Padua in 1733.

[56] *Les trois sultanes ou Soliman II,* a comedy in verse by Charles-Simon Favart (1710–1792); *The Abduction from the Seraglio* was composed by Mozart in 1782, using a libretto by Gottlob Stephanie.

[57] Goethe is of course alluding again to the Aristophanes play and his own role as True Friend in performances of it.

[58] Antonio Turra, a physician and scientist in Vicenza.

[59] Ottavio Bertotti Scamozzi (1719–1790), an architect, published four volumes of *Fabriche e disegni di Andrea Palladio* between 1776 and 1783. Goethe acquired the volumes later in Venice.

[60] The house, built in 1563 or 1564, was neither built by Palladio nor his residence.

[61] Goethe is referring to the elder Canaletto, Antonio Canale (1697–1768).

[62] A major work of Palladio, begun in 1550. In 1591 it was acquired by the Capra family.

[63] "Marcus Capra, son of Gabriel, who has placed this structure under the strictest primogeniture, together with all rents, fields, valleys, and mountains on this side of the great road, dedicates this to everlasting memory, while he himself endures and abstains."

[64] Founded in 1556 for the encouragement of learned studies.

[65] The palace was actually built in the 15th century.

[66] Driver.

[67] The original edition of Palladio's *I quattro libri dell' Architettura* was published in two volumes, Venice, 1570.

[68] Joseph Smith (1682–1770).

[69] Marcus Vitruvius Pollio, Roman architect and writer in the reign of Augustus.

[70] Pietro Cardinal Bembo (1470–1547) was a famous humanist. The bust was done in 1547 by Danese Cattaneo (ca. 1509–1573).

[71] "Hieronymus Guerinus, son of Ismenus, had the portrait of Pietro Bembo, Cardinal, set up in public, so that also the physical appearance of him whose works of genius are immortal should live on in the memory of posterity."

[72] Founded in 1545, the oldest botanical garden in Europe, it proved of great significance in Goethe's botanical and morphological studies.

[73] A covered marketplace.

[74] Gustav III (1746–1792) became King of Sweden in 1771.

[75] Gustavus II Adolphus (1594–1632) became King of Sweden in 1611.

[76] Archduke Leopold of Tuscany (1747–1792), from 1790 on Emperor Leopold II.

[77] Giovanni Battista Piazzetta (1683–1754), a Venetian painter. The painting is dated 1744.

[78] Andrea Mantegna (1431–1506). Goethe's praise of Mantegna, who was disparaged by Volkmann in the guidebook Goethe used, is evidence of his independent and original thinking.

[79] The Palazzo della Ragione was built in 1218–1219 as a law-court. The audience room was rebuilt after a fire in 1420.

[80] The customs.

[81] Angelo Emo (1731–1792), admiral of the Venetians in their war against Tunis.

[82] Santa Maria della Carità, built 1442–1454 by Bartolomeo Buon (d. 1464). In 1560 Palladio began to build part of the convent next to it.

[83] Begun in 1577, Palladio's last major work.

[84] Paolo Renieri (1710–1789) was doge from 1779 on. His wife, Margareta Dalmaz, who had been a tightrope performer, was not recognized by the government as dogaressa.

[85] Magic spell from the Faust puppet play.

[86] Goethe is referring to the typological characters of traditional Italian comedy. Pantalone is the good-natured old man.

[87] A comedy by Johann Christian Bock (1724–1785), adapted from Calderón.

[88] Built in 1534 by Jacopo Sansovino (1486–1570).

[89] The state shipyard, founded in 1104; the main portal, dating from 1460, is the first early Renaissance structure in Venice.

[90] The state barge. The one Goethe saw was the last one, built in 1728 and destroyed by Napoleon in 1797.

[91] Possibly *La punizione del prezipizio,* by Carlo Gozzi (1720–1806).

[92] Prosper-Jolyot Crébillon the Elder (1674–1762).

[93] The Battle of Lepanto, October 7, 1571. The date is correct in Goethe's diary.

[94] The sixteen ministers of the Republic.

[95] From Rousseau's *Les Consolations des Miséres de ma vie ou Recueil d'Airs, Romances et Duos,* Paris, 1780.

[96] "It is singular how one is moved by this singing, and all the more, the better it is sung."

[97] Veronese's painting, *The Family of Darius before Alexander,* is now in the National Gallery, London.

[98] Built in the 12th and 13th centuries, it is today the city hall.

[99] See for example the end of Book Eleven of *Poetry and Truth* (Volume 4, pp. 371–2).

[100] The sculpture, a Roman copy of a work from the 2nd century B.C., was correctly identified by J.J. Winckelmann as a sleeping Ariadne. It is now in the Vatican.

[101] Jakob Böhme (1575–1624), a shoemaker and influential mystic.

[102] Dedicated by Emperor Antoninus Pius to his deceased wife and consecrated to the imperial couple in 161 A.D.

[103] The lions were brought to Venice in 1687. One of them originally stood on the avenue to the temple of Apollo on Delos and is the oldest work of Greek art Goethe ever saw.

[104] Painted in 1540 for the altar of the church of S. Giovanni e Paulo, destroyed by fire in 1867.

[105] The famous horses are believed originally to have belonged to a monument to the Flavians in Rome. They were brought to Venice from Constantinople in 1204.

[106] Here and elsewhere Goethe means Charlotte von Stein's son Fritz and/or Herder's children.

[107] Long cloaks.

[108] Carlo Goldoni (1707–1793). The comedy dates from 1762.

[109] Antonio Sacchi (b. 1708), famous in the role of Harlequin, was no longer alive at this time. Smeraldina and Brighella are typological characters of Italian comedy.

[110] "It seems that you have not wasted your time."

[111] Bernardo, Marchese Galiani (d. 1771), published a bilingual (Latin/Italian) edition of Vitruvius's *Ten Books on Architecture* in Naples, 1758/59.

[112] The translation of Horace's *Satires* by Christoph Martin Wieland (1733–1813) had appeared recently, in the summer of 1786.

[113] Lodovico Ariosto (1474–1533) lived from 1517 until his death at the court of Alfonso I (1505–1534). Torquato Tasso (1544–1595) lived from 1565 to 1586 at the court of Alfonso II (1559–1597). Tasso was confined to the Hospital Santa Anna from 1579 on. Goethe was carrying the two completed acts of his prose *Tasso* with him when he passed through Ferrara.

[114] At the Wartburg, near Eisenach.

[115] Journeymen are said to have looked for secret marks left by their predecessors in the houses of masters to indicate whether the masters were generous or not.

[116] By the Ferrara painter Carlo Bononi (1569–1632).

[117] Giovanni Francesco Barbieri (1591–1666), called Il Guercino, a Bolognese master.

[118] The painting, dating from the end of the 1620s, is entitled *Noli me tangere.* Today it is in the Pinacoteca Comunale.

[119] Robert Strange (1721–1792), a leading English engraver of the time, praised highly by Winckelmann.

[120] Raphael (Raffaello Santi, 1483–1520) painted the *St. Cecilia* around 1515. It is now in the Pinacoteca Comunale.

[121] Francesco Raibolini (1450–1517), called Il Francia, a Bolognese master. Pietro Vanucci (ca. 1450–1523), called Il Perugino, was an associate of Raphael.

[122] At the time of his journey to Italy Goethe was not well informed about Dürer's biography. The Dürer painting Goethe saw in Venice, a *Feast of the Rosary,* was not commissioned by priests, as he seems to assume, but by German merchants in residence there.

[123] The Torre degli Asinelli, built between 1109 and 1119.

[124] The never-completed Torre dei Garisendi, from the same period as the Torre degli Asinelli (which also leans, though not as much). The tower began to sink during its construction and was partially demolished in the mid-14th century.

[125] Lodovico Carracci (1555–1619); Agostino Carracci (1557–1602); Annibale Carracci (1560–1609); Guido Reni (1575–1642); Domenico Zampieri (1581–1641), called Il Domenichino.

[126] See Genesis 6:2–4.

[127] *Madonna della Pietà,* painted 1614–1616, now in the Pinacoteca Comunale.

[128] *John in the Desert* has been attributed to Simone Cantarini (1612–1648), called Pesarese; it and Guido Reni's *Sebastian* are now in the Pinacoteca Comunale.

[129] The whereabouts of this picture is unknown.

[130] Painted in 1646 as an altar piece, the upper part is in the Bologna gallery and the remainder in the museum of Lyon.

[131] The painting has since been attributed to Guercino.

[132] Goethe never did write the play sketched out here.

[133] The Weimar orphanage had been "opened up" in 1784 and the orphans placed with families.

[134] J.W. von Archenholz (1743–1812) had compared Italy unfavorably with England in his two-volume work, *England and Italy,* published in Leipzig in 1785.

[135] A Gothic double church, built between 1228 and 1253. One sees here and in the following how Goethe downgrades the Gothic in comparison with the temple of Minerva, probably dating from the latter part of the 1st century A.D., which had later been transformed into a church. After the amphitheater in Verona this temple was Goethe's first significant experience of classical architecture.

Part I   455

[136] Goethe is referring to the 1st-century temple of Bel at Palmyra (now in Syria), which he knew from engravings.

[137] Police.

[138] The monastery to which the church of St. Francis of Assisi is attached.

[139] That is, the myth of Arcadia, or the Golden Age.

[140] A huge octagonal castle on the Wilhelmshöhe near Kassel.

[141] Apparently Goethe means the church of San Salvatore, dating from the second half of the 8th century and known as the temple of Clitumnus.

[142] "I come to be crucified again."

[143] This entry is based upon a letter to Duke Carl August of November 3, 1786. Up to this point Goethe had kept the goal of his journey a secret from his friends at home.

[144] The figure in the classical myth is named "Galatea." Goethe had the name "Elisa" from a story by Johann Jakob Bodmer.

[145] Pius VI (1775–1799).

[146] Wilhelm Tischbein (1751–1829). After studies in Germany, Holland, and Italy, Tischbein worked in Zurich in 1781/82 and was acquainted with Johann Caspar Lavater. He was in Rome from 1783 to 1787. Goethe and Tischbein had corresponded since the latter's Zurich years, and their epistolary acquaintance blossomed into friendship in Rome. By the end of the stay in Italy, however, Goethe had cooled towards Tischbein and complained of his egotism in letters to Herder. After ten years as director of the Art Academy in Naples (1789–1799), Tischbein returned to Germany and from 1807 to the end of his life was court painter to the Duke of Oldenburg at Eutin.

[147] The so-called horse tamers or dioscuri, 5.6 meter marble figures dating from late imperial times.

[148] Carlo Maratti (1625–1713), a Roman painter.

[149] *Burial and Adoration of St. Petronilla*, 1621, now in the Vatican art gallery.

[150] *Madonna of San Niccolò de' Frari*, presumably painted in the 1640s, now in the Vatican art gallery.

[151] Guido Reni's frescoes of 1610 illustrating the life of the Virgin Mary are in the Cappella dell'Annunziata in the Quirinal.

[152] At the time the painting was ascribed to Giovanni Antonio de Sacchis (1483–1539), called Pordenone. It is now generally considered to be the work of Paris Bordone (1500–1571), a pupil of Titian, and is in the Vatican gallery.

[153] Johann Heinrich Meyer (1759–1832), a Swiss artist and art historian. Soon a close friend and collaborator, he moved to Weimar in 1791, living in Goethe's house until 1803. Meyer was a professor at the Weimar drawing academy from 1792 on and its director after 1807.

[154] Heinrich Cölla (1757–1789), a painter from Zurich.

[155] Johann Jakob Bodmer (1698–1783), Zurich poet and literary theorist.

[156] The work is entitled *The Strength of Man*, completed as a watercolor in 1790 and done again as a large oil for the castle at Eutin in 1821.

[157] The loggias surrounding the Cortile di San Damaso in the Vatican were begun by Bramante in 1513, continued by Raphael in 1518, and completed by his pupils in 1519. *The School of Athens* is an allegorical fresco in the papal apartments, executed by Raphael between 1509 and 1511.

[158] Goethe was known in Rome as Jean Philippe Möller, merchant, or Filippo Miller, painter.

[159] Johann Friedrich Reiffenstein (1719–1793), a diplomat in the service of Gotha and Russia, had lived in Rome since 1763. A friend of Winckelmann, he was an archaeologist and art connoisseur.

[160] The Palazzo Rondanini, opposite which Goethe and Tischbein lived.

[161] The Pantheon, a monumental circular building with a cupola dating from Hadrian's reign as emperor, restored and renewed an older building from 27 B.C. dedicated to all the deities. It is the only building of Roman antiquity still completely preserved.

[162] The tomb of one C. Cestius, a wealthy citizen, dating from the Augustan period, located at the Porta S. Paolo.

[163] A ruined grotto dedicated to Egeria, reputedly the beloved of King Numa Pompilius.

[164] Now known as the Circus of Maxentius, the anti-emperor of Constantine the Great, built in 309 A.D. It was not known until 1825 that Maxentius had built it.

[165] The tomb of Caecilia Metella, presumed to be the daughter-in-law of the triumvir Marcus Licinius Crassus, dates from the 1st century B.C.

[166] Charlotte von Stein, to whom this letter was directed.

[167] Philipp Hackert (1737–1807), a Prussian-born landscape painter who spent most of his life in Italy. He had until recently lived in Rome, but had become court painter to King Ferdinand IV of Naples, where Goethe met him the following year. In 1811 Goethe wrote a biography based on Hackert's memoirs.

[168] Johann Georg Sulzer (1720–1779), *Allgemeine Theorie der schönen Wissenschaften und Künste (General Theory of the Fine Sciences and Arts)*, Leipzig, 1771–1774. Goethe had reviewed part of this work very negatively in 1772.

[169] Domenichino had decorated the interior of the church between 1624 and 1628.

[170] The decoration of the gallery of the Palazzo Farnese is a major work of Annibale Carracci, executed between ca. 1597 and 1604.

[171] A fresco begun by Raphael and completed by one of his pupils in 1517.

[172] Raphael's last work, now in the Vatican gallery.

[173] Believed to be Blasius Caryophylus, *De antiquis marmoribus,* published in Vienna in 1738.

[174] The Congregatio de propaganda fide, founded by Pope Gregory XV in 1622 to oversee foreign missions.

[175] The Domus Aurea, begun by Nero in 64 A.D. after the great fire.

[176] Chevalier Diel de Marsilly (d. 1761), a retired army officer.

[177] Anton Raphael Mengs (1728–1779), a German painter and theorist who worked in Italy and later in Spain. Many of his paintings are in the Prado in Madrid.

[178] Johann Joachim Winckelmann (1717–1768), *Geschichte der Kunst des Altertums (History of the Art of Antiquity),* 1764, Book VII, Chapter 3. The painting was indeed by Mengs.

[179] Originally from the 3rd century. The contemporary structure dates from the 9th to 12th centuries.

[180] *Tra i due litiganti il terzo gode (When Two Quarrel, the Third is Happy),* an operetta by Giambattista Lorenzi.

[181] Goethe means either Prince Wenzel Joseph von Liechtenstein (1767–1842)

or, more likely, Prince Philipp Joseph von Liechtenstein (1762–1802), both of whom were in Rome.

[182] Marie Josephine Eleonore, Countess von Harrach (1763–1833), whom Goethe knew from Carlsbad.

[183] Vincenzo Monti (1754–1828), an abbé and secretary to the nephew of Pius VI, until 1804 professor of eloquence at Milan.

[184] Charlotte Stuart (1753–1789), the illegitimate daughter of Charles Edward Stuart ("Bonnie Prince Charlie"), Jacobite pretender to the British throne. Declared legitimate and styled Duchess of Albany, she had been in Italy since 1785.

[185] Kaspar Joseph Schwendimann (1741–1786).

[186] Johann Karl Hedlinger (1691–1771), a Swiss medallist.

[187] Winckelmann was murdered in Trieste in 1768.

[188] Karl Philipp Moritz (1756–1793), author, psychologist, antiquarian, and a devoted admirer of Goethe. *Anton Reiser* is a "psychological novel" published in four parts between 1785 and 1790, largely based on Moritz's childhood experiences. His *Travels of a German in England in the Year 1782* appeared in 1783.

[189] Villa Doria Pamphili or Belrespiro, with Rome's largest garden, laid out in 1650.

[190] Today the Astronomical-Meteorological Observatory.

[191] Designed by Raphael and built in the 16th century for Giulio Cardinal de' Medici, unfinished; later the property of Duchess Margaret of Parma.

[192] The Giardino dei Semplici, founded by Pope Alexander VII, no longer in existence.

[193] Carlo Fea (1753–1834), archaeologist. His Italian translation of Winckelmann's history originally appeared in 1783/84, a second edition in 1786.

[194] Death-defying leap.

[195] *Winckelmanns Briefe an seine Freunde (Winckelmann's Letters to his Friends)*, ed. Karl Wilhelm Dassdorf in two volumes, Dresden, 1777–1780.

[196] Johann Michael Franke (1717–1775) was a librarian who had worked with Winckelmann in Dresden.

[197] Friedrich Münter (1761–1830), a theologian and antiquarian.

[198] Roman copy of a Greek original from the 5th century B.C. King Ludwig I of Bavaria acquired it in 1814 for the Munich Glyptothek. Goethe left his cast of it behind in Rome, but obtained another as a gift from Crown Prince Ludwig of Bavaria after it had been taken to Munich.

[199] Presumably the Zeus of Otricoli, a Roman copy of a work by Bryaxis from the 4th century B.C. Goethe also left this cast behind in Rome, but later acquired another one.

[200] The second volume of Herder's *Zerstreute Blätter* (1786), containing essays and translations from the Greek.

[201] Probably the most famous portrait of Goethe, completed in August 1787. It was eventually acquired by the Frankfurt Rothschilds and given by them to the Städel Art Institute there. A copy made by Tischbein and others is in the Goethe Museum in Weimar. The portrait inspired the Andy Warhol design on the dust jackets of this edition.

[202] Actually more like thirty days.

[203] The provenance of the famous colossal head, long thought to be of Juno, is unclear; today it is in the Museo dei Termi in Rome. In the 19th century it was identified as part of a colossal statue erected by Emperor Claudius to portray his mother, Antonia Augusta. Goethe made a present of his cast to Angelica Kauffmann upon leaving Rome, but acquired another as a gift in 1823.

[204] Previously called "of Delphi." Goethe apparently thought Delphi was an island.

[205] In Rome most of the the theaters were open only during the carnival season (in 1787 from January 7 on).

[206] Pasquale Anfossi (1729–1797), composer and conductor.

[207] Moritz's *Versuch einer deutschen Prosodie (Essay on German Prosody)* appeared in 1786, shortly before his own departure for Italy.

[208] Goethe's first play, *Götz von Berlichingen,* was published in 1773.

[209] The Giustiniani *Athena,* the Roman copy of a statue from the school of Phidias around the end of the 5th century B.C. It was acquired by Pope Pius VII for the Vatican collections and is now in the Braccio Nuovo.

[210] A language of southern India.

[211] Albanian.

[212] Romanian.

[213] It is not known what language Goethe means here.

[214] Georgian.

[215] Berber.

[216] Gaelic.

[217] Malayan.

[218] The dialect of an area of Asia Minor, now in Turkey.

[219] Alessandro Cardinal Albani (1692–1779), a famous antiquarian, Vatican librarian, and friend of Winckelmann.

[220] The nephew of Pius VI, Luigi Braschi, Duke of Nemi.

[221] Ferdinand IV (1751–1825).

[222] Replica of a bronze original from the 4th century B.C.

[223] Guglielmo della Porta (ca. 1516–1577), a sculptor. He restored the *Hercules* after a model made by Michelangelo.

[224] Marco Antonio III, Principe di Borghese (1730–1800).

[225] Frederick II, King of Prussia, had died on August 17, 1786, while Goethe was still in Carlsbad, and Goethe had already learned of his death at that time. The odd placement of the remark here is a carryover from the original letter to Charlotte von Stein (January 18, 1787), on which this passage is based, where Goethe had acknowledged information that had become public concerning the king's estate.

[226] Founded in the early 13th century by Pope Innocent III, renovated in the 15th century by Sixtus IV and in the 18th century by Benedict XIV.

[227] Angelica Kauffmann (1741–1807). A Swiss painter, she had been in London from 1766 to 1781. In 1781 she married the painter Antonio Zucchi (1726–1795) and moved with him to Italy. After a short time in Venice they lived in Rome from 1782 on. She was acclaimed as a sentimentalist-classicistic portrait and history painter.

[228] The women of Alba Longa, according to legend destroyed by King Tulius Hostilius in the 8th century B.C.

[229] François Jacquier (1711–1788), a physicist and mathematician.

[230] A replica dating from Roman imperial times; Pius VI had it erected in front of the church of Trinità dei Monti in 1789.

[231] Charles Louis Clérisseau (1722–1820), a painter and architect. His Dalmatian sketches were published in 1764.

[232] A quote from the prologue of one of Goethe's early farces in "knittel verse," the *Carnival at Plundersweilern*.

[233] Moritz began antiquarian studies which eventually led to books on classical mythology and on the antiquities of Rome, both of which were published in 1791.

[234] Claude Gellée, called le Lorrain (1620–1682), a French landscape painter who spent much of his life in Rome.

[235] An illustrated Latin schoolbook by Amos Comenius (1592–1670), published in 1657 and often reprinted, known to Goethe since childhood.

Part II
Naples and Sicily: February–June 1787

[1] Gismondo Maria Giuseppe, Prince of Chigi (1736–1794).

[2] Camillo Borgia, a Knight of Malta, was a brother of Stefano Cardinal Borgia (1731–1804), the director of the Propaganda.

[3] The mysterious young girl in *Wilhelm Meister's Apprenticeship* who, it turns out, was abducted from Italy as a young child. Goethe had worked on the first version of the novel during the 1780s before his trip to Italy. He is referring here to songs she sings in the novel, several of which express longing for Italy and the south.

[4] Maria Carolina (1752–1814), queen of Naples, was a daughter of Empress Maria Theresa and sister of Emperor Joseph II. Maria Carolina was the mother of seventeen children.

[5] Also called the Grotta Vecchia, dating originally from the 3rd century B.C., restored in the 16th, 18th, and 19th centuries.

[6] Christian August von Waldeck (1744–1798), an Austrian general. Goethe had already visited him in January in Rome.

[7] A dramatic poem by the 6th-century Indian poet, Kalidasa, which impressed Goethe greatly. *Sakuntala* was not translated into German, however, until 1791 (by Georg Forster). It is possible, therefore, that Goethe had only written "S." in his diary (for "Spinoza") and later misunderstood the entry, or that the passage is an anachronism dating from the period of editing the *Italian Journey*.

[8] Since Friday was not March 3 this letter is misdated: presumably it was written either on Friday, March 2 or Saturday, March 3.

[9] Summer residence of the Dukes of Weimar.

[10] Luca Giordano (1634–1705) had the reputation of working very fast and was called "Luca Fà Presto." The *Expulsion of Heliodorus* was painted, however, by one of his pupils, Francesco Solimena (1657–1747), in 1725.

[11] "Strand," the road from Naples to Posillipo.

[12] Gaetano Filangieri (1752–1788), a political theorist. His *La Scienza della legislazione* appeared in eight volumes in Naples from 1781 to 1788.

[13] There was some fear that Joseph II, brother of the queen of Naples, had designs on Tuscany and indeed all of Italy.

[14] Cesare Bonesana, Marchese di Beccaria (1738–1794), professor in Milan, was a highly influential criminologist and economist. His book on crimes and punishments, published in 1764, had a broad impact on European legislation during the Enlightenment period.

[15] Giambattista Vico (1668–1744), philosopher and historian, was a professor in Naples. His chief work, *La scienza nuova,* first appeared in 1725. The final and authoritative edition appeared in 1744.

[16] Johann Georg Hamann (1730–1788), the "Magus of the North." See especially *Poetry and Truth,* Book Twelve (Volume 4, pp. 379–82 and notes).

[17] This is what Goethe considered granite to be.

[18] The colossal horse's head is now in the National Museum in Naples. There has been much debate about its origin and provenance. It is believed to be a fragment of a late Hellenistic statue.

[19] The Roman copy of an original from the end of the 5th century B.C. The head does not belong to the statue. Goethe later (see below, the Report for April 1788) had the opportunity to acquire the statue for himself and was sorely tempted. It was finally bought by Pius VI and is now in the Vatican.

[20] An opera by Giambattista Giordani (1753–1794), called Giordaniello.

[21] Filangieri's wife was Caroline, Countess Fremdel, from Pressburg. She had originally been sent by Maria Theresa to the Naples court as a governess.

[22] Filangieri's sister, Teresa, who was married to the then 60-year-old Prince Filippo Fieschi Ravaschieri di Satriano. She became insane soon after Goethe's stay in Naples.

[23] Goethe is referring to the tomb of the priestess Mamia, the temple of Isis, and the so-called villa of Diomedes in front of the Herculaneum Gate.

[24] The beginning of the second part of Wieland's "Winter's Tale" (1776).

[25] Johann Georg Schlosser (1739–1799), Goethe's brother-in-law. See *Poetry and Truth,* Book Seven and elsewhere (especially Volume 4, p. 202 and note).

[26] The tomb of the priestess Mamia, which Goethe had already noted in the letter of March 11 above. The inscription reads: "Mamiae P. f. sacerdoti publicae locus sepulturae datus decurionum decreto" ("this burial place was given to the state priestess Mamia, daughter of Publius, by order of the senators").

[27] Christoph Heinrich Kniep (1748–1825), a German painter, later professor at the Academy in Naples.

[28] A museum for artifacts excavated at Herculaneum was established in the Palazzo Reale in Portici between 1732 and 1752.

[29] Act III, Scene 3. The drawing is now in the Goethe House in Weimar.

[30] The massive palace built by Philipp II outside Madrid during his reign makes an imposing, but cold impression. The new palace at Caserta, north of Naples, had been built by Charles III in 1752.

[31] Friedrich Christian Andres (b. ca. 1735), a pupil of Anton Raphael Mengs. He had been appointed on Hackert's recommendation.

[32] Sir William Hamilton (1730–1803) had been British ambassador to Naples since 1764. He was also an archaeologist and collector.

[33] Emma Lyon (ca. 1761–1815), also called Miss Harte, was from the lower classes. Hamilton married her in 1791. As Lady Hamilton she later became

famous as the mistress of Lord Horatio Nelson (1798) and died in poverty in Calais.

[34] The identity of the "friend" remains unknown.

[35] Gennaro, Bishop of Benevento, was martyred under Diocletian. His dried blood, which is preserved in the cathedral at Naples, supposedly becomes liquid and flows three times a year during special ceremonies. The ceremonies are also instituted when Vesuvius is erupting, and the saint's blood thus protects the city.

[36] Dou (1613–1675), a pupil of Rembrandt, here taken by Goethe as representative of genre painting.

[37] Probably Duke Carl August. Goethe had stopped working on the novel some time before his journey to Italy and was not to revise and complete it until the middle of the 1790s.

[38] Not identified. Correggio's *Vow of St. Catherine,* mentioned below, is now in the National Museum in Naples.

[39] Goethe and Kniep were at Paestum from March 21 to March 23.

[40] Kniep's drawings are now in the Goethe House in Weimar.

[41] The University of Salerno was founded in the 11th century and became the leading medical school of the Middle Ages. It was closed in 1812.

[42] Paestum, the Greek colony of Poseidonia, contains the ruins of three Doric temples, the most recent of them from the 5th century B.C. These are the most ancient structures Goethe was ever to see.

[43] The three-pointed, i.e., Sicily.

[44] Francesco, Marchese di Berio, a Neapolitan aristocrat.

[45] Nothing came of the projected trip and the Prince of Waldeck returned to Rome with Tischbein in May 1787.

[46] This ostensible "letter" has all the earmarks of a later narrative based on notes or even written from memory. Frequent use of the past perfect tense strengthens this conjecture. The first two acts of the prose *Tasso* had been written in 1780/81. The phrase "written ten years ago" is thus, at the least, a misstatement, if applied from the standpoint of the year 1787, and "the present ones" can only refer to the play in its final published form (1790). Goethe's remarks here about working on *Tasso* would seem to sum up the mental activity of several days rather than just reporting for the date March 30, 1787. This is not the only case of such retrospective interpolation—or editorial mistake— to be found in the *Italian Journey*.

[47] The Porta Felice, begun in 1582 and completed in 1644. It is believed, however, that Goethe did not enter Palermo through this gate, but rather through the Porta delle Legne, which no longer exists today.

[48] St. Rosalia, the niece of the Norman king William II, is the patron saint of Palermo. Her feast is celebrated from July 11–15. Her "towering cart," drawn by eight or more mules and also pushed and pulled by the faithful, was several stories high and prone to inflict damage on the houses as it passed by.

[49] The Locanda nobile al Cássaro Morto, in the Via di Porto Salvo, which is no longer standing.

[50] Goethe refers, here as elsewhere, to plans for a *Nausicaa* tragedy which, however, he never seriously undertook to complete.

[51] Caecilius Metellus defeated the Carthaginian general Hasdrubal (not Hannibal!) in a battle at Panormus in 251 B.C.

[52] Goethe is mistaken about the provenance of the fountain on the Piazza Pretoria: it was originally built in 1554/55 by the Florentine sculptors Francesco Camilliani (d. 1586) and Michele Naccherini (1535–1622) for the Florence villa of the Neapolitan viceroy, Don Pedro, and moved to Palermo in 1575.

[53] Patrick Brydone (1736–1818), an English scientist, traveled in Italy in 1767–1771. His 1773 book, *A Tour through Sicily and Malta, in a Series of Letters to William Beckford, Esq.*, was widely praised. German editions appeared in 1774 and 1777.

[54] Abbé Jean-Claude-Richard de Saint-Non, *Voyage pittoresque ou description des Royaumes de Naples et de Sicile*, appeared in five folio volumes in Paris, 1781–1786.

[55] Statue of St. Rosalia by the Florentine sculptor Gregorio Tedeschi (d. 1634), a gift of King Charles III of Naples.

[56] A legendary people visited by Odysseus. See *Odyssey*, V–VIII. According to the diary, Goethe bought (on April 15, not April 7) a Greek-Latin edition of the *Odyssey* by Stephan Bergler published in Padua in 1777. The volume is preserved in Goethe's library in Weimar.

[57] Conte di Statella. Soon afterward he visited Charlotte von Stein in Weimar and conveyed to her Goethe's personal greeting.

[58] The family of Karl Friedrich von Dacheröden, chamber president in Erfurt, whose daughter Caroline married Wilhelm von Humboldt in 1791.

[59] Karl Theodor von Dalberg (1744–1817), governor of Erfurt for the Elector of Mainz since 1772. While in Naples Goethe had learned of Dalberg's election as coadjutor and successor to the Elector of Mainz. Dalberg became Elector in 1802, Prince-Primate of the Rhenish Confederation in 1806, Grand Duke of Frankfurt from 1810 to 1813.

[60] Ferdinando Francesco II. Gravina, Cruylas ed Agliata, Principe di Palagonia (1722–1788). His villa was in La Bagheria, east of Palermo. His somewhat grotesque decorative style used to be regarded, as in Goethe's case, as merely bizarre bad taste, but more recently has come to be seen in the context of late Baroque. Goethe's description is partly based on the book by Patrick Brydone.

[61] The monastery was founded in the 6th century by Pope Gregory I. It is now an agricultural college.

[62] Original works of the early Hellenistic era, probably found in Syracuse. One was melted down during the Revolution of 1848, the other is in the Palermo museum.

[63] Phrixus and Helle were the children of the Boeotian King Athamus and Queen Nephele. Nephele abducted them to save them from the machinations of a rival concubine and sent them away on a golden ram provided by Hermes. Helle became dizzy and fell off into the sea (at the Hellespont), while Phrixus landed safely in the country of the Colchians. He sacrificed the ram and presented the golden fleece to Aeëtes, ruler of the Colchians.

[64] The catacombs at Porta d'Ossuna had been discovered in 1785.

[65] Gabriele Lancelotto Castello, Prince of Torremuzza (1727–1794), a numismatist and writer. Part of his outstanding collection of ancient Sicilian coins is now in the Palermo museum.

[66] Michel-Jean, Comte de Borch (1753–1810), a Polish scientist and traveler. His *Lithologie sicilienne ou Connaissance de la nature des pierres de la Sicile* appeared in Rome, 1778.

[67] Like True Friend, a character in Goethe's adaptation of Aristophanes's *The Birds*.

[68] Giuseppe Balsamo (1743–1795), also called Alessandro, Conte Cagliostro, was the most notorious charlatan and swindler of the 18th century. The following passage on Cagliostro is based on a talk that Goethe gave at the Weimar "Friday Club" and published in 1792. Cagliostro was also the inspiration for the title character of Goethe's play, *The Great Cophta,* published in 1791.

[69] Published in Cagliostro's "Mémoire justicatif," written in the Bastille in Paris.

[70] Baron Antonio Vivona, the French representative in Sicily.

[71] The famous diamond necklace affair of 1785/86. (See the note in Volume 5, p. 789.) Cagliostro was released from prison on May 31, 1786, by the Paris Parlement and banished to England.

[72] Goethe published the family tree in his 1792 essay.

[73] Extracts from the trial records were published in Rome in 1791, translated into German and published in Weimar in the same year by Christian Joseph Jagemann, librarian to Dowager Duchess Anna Amalia. Balsamo-Cagliostro was condemned to death for heresy by order of the Pope in 1790, but the sentence was commuted to life imprisonment in 1791 and he died in prison in 1795.

[74] The *oncia* was a silver coin used in Sicily, equal to three Neapolitan silver ducats. Fourteen *oncie* represented a considerable sum for a family of modest means, perhaps as much as two months' income.

[75] Goethe sent the fourteen *oncie* to the family in Palermo after his return to Weimar and published a German translation of the letter in his 1792 essay.

[76] The Villa La Zisa, begun by the Norman King William I in the 12th century. This was Goethe's first contact with oriental and Byzantine art.

[77] Ruler of the Phaeacians in the *Odyssey*.

[78] An allusion to the marriage at Cana where Jesus' first miracle was performed.

[79] The unfinished Doric temple dates from the 5th century B.C.

[80] Johann Hermann von Riedesel, Freiherr zu Eisenbach und auf Altenberg (1740–1785), a Prussian diplomat. His *Travels through Sicily and Magna Graecia,* dedicated to Winckelmann, were published in 1771. Goethe had known Riedesel's book since his Strassburg student days and it was in his father's library.

[81] The Greek city of Akragas, Roman Agrigentum, was founded in 582 B.C. Destroyed by the Carthaginians in 406 B.C., it was finally conquered by the Romans in 210 B.C. Goethe used the 18th-century name, Girgenti.

[82] Although there is a town, there is no river by this name.

[83] An Attic work of the 3rd century A.D., now in the museum of the Agrigento cathedral. One of the ends of the sarcophagus is pictured in the title vignette of Riedesel's 1771 book (done by the famous Swiss poet and artist Salomon Gessner). Winckelmann had praised the sarcophagus in a 1767 work as perhaps the most beautiful bas-relief preserved from antiquity.

[84] A red-figured krater of Corinthian form, now in the cathedral museum.

[85] A ruin dating from the middle of the 5th century B.C.

[86] Goethe should have written "westward."

[87] Wrongly so-called from a Latin inscription which has nothing to do with the temple. It was built after the middle of the 5th century B.C. and owes its preservation to the fact that it was converted into a Christian church (dedicated to Saints Peter and Paul) in the 6th century A.D.

[88] Begun in 480 B.C. to commemorate the tyrant Theron's victory over the Carthaginians in 486, the temple was never finished. The site was cleared in the early 19th century.

[89] The oldest temple ruin at Agrigento, dating from the end of the 6th century B.C.

[90] The identification with Aesculapius is uncertain. The temple dates from the 5th century B.C.

[91] The so-called tomb of Theron (d. 472 B.C.) actually dates from the Roman period.

[92] The ruins of a small temple of Ceres and Proserpina, in which a small church had been built during the Norman period.

[93] Prince of Eleusis, inventor of the plough and of agriculture, to whom Demeter gave a chariot drawn by winged dragons.

[94] Thirty Sicilian miles are just under twenty-eight English miles.

[95] Goethe never returns to this subject.

[96] Three mountains near Gotha.

[97] Scallops.

[98] An ancient Greek settlement, the town was the center of the cult of Demeter. It was from here that Persephone was kidnapped and taken away to Hades. Goethe generally uses the medieval name Castro Giovanni in his text (the town is again called Enna today) and—perhaps because he was not very warmly received there—completely overlooks its historical and mythological importance.

[99] Goethe probably meant mules. At any rate, in the letter of May 5 (below) he and Kniep are riding mules.

[100] Nicolas Poussin (1594–1665), the most significant French painter of the 17th century, leading representative of classicistic Baroque. Goethe is thinking here of Poussin's landscapes.

[101] The modern name. Goethe used the former name, Ibla Major.

[102] Vincenzo, Prince of Biscari (b. 1742), the wealthiest nobleman in Catania. His house chaplain, Abbé Sestini, was also a scientist and the author of *Descrizione del museo d'Antiquaria e del Gabinetto di Istoria naturale del Signore Principe di Biscari,* published in 1776 (second edition in 1787).

[103] Identified as a Bacchus by Riedesel, who had been the first to call attention to it.

[104] Probably Goethe means the wife of the Prince of Biscari.

[105] Anna, Princess of Biscari, née Morso e Bonnano, Princess of Poggio Reale.

[106] Ignazio Vincenzo Paternò Castello, Prince of Biscari (1719–1786), a collector and antiquarian.

[107] Riedesel had been in Catania in 1767, Münter in 1785 and 1786. Johann Heinrich Bartels (1761–1850), a theologian and jurist who later became mayor

of Hamburg, had been there in 1786 and published a three-volume work, *Letters on Calabria and Sicily*, in Göttingen between 1787 and 1792.

[108] The great organ of the church of San Nicolò, built in the 18th century, has five manuals, seventy-two registers, and 2,916 pipes.

[109] The argument, which divided the "Vulcanists" and the "Neptunists," was important to Goethe's geological theories. He was a "Neptunist" himself, but had tried to mediate in this particular dispute.

[110] Guiseppe Gioeni (1747–1822), a Knight of Malta, was a professor of natural science at the University of Catania.

[111] The seven Scogli de' Ciclopi, said to be the rocks that the blinded Cyclop Polyphemus threw after Odysseus (*Odyssey*, IX). They are north of Catania at Aci Costello.

[112] An ancient basin for naval war games.

[113] The amphitheater was built in the Hellenistic period, around the 2nd century B.C., the stage housing in the Roman imperial period.

[114] In Palermo.

[115] Messina had been almost completely destroyed by earthquakes in February and March of 1783.

[116] Since 1783 an Irishman, Field Marshal Don Michele Odea, had been governor.

[117] The church of S. Gregorio, built in 1542.

[118] Possibly Freemasons? Goethe himself had long been a member.

[119] Joost de Momper the Younger (1564–1635), a Flemish landscape painter, son and pupil of Bartholomäus de Momper.

[120] Kniep's watercolor is in the Goethe House in Weimar.

[121] "Ah! Barlamé! Blessed be Barlamé!" Probably St. Barlaam is meant, who had converted the Indian Prince Josaphat.

[122] A folio Bible illustrated by the engraver Matthias Merian, 1627, known to Goethe since childhood.

[123] The page did not make its way into the *Italian Journey*.

[124] The youngest of the three temples at Paestum, a small so-called temple of Poseidon dating from the mid-5th century B.C., one of the best preserved Greek temples.

[125] At the beginning of May. Tischbein returned to Naples in July.

[126] Presumably Filangieri's wife.

[127] The same that had destroyed Messina in 1783.

[128] St. Filippo Neri (1515–1595). He was ordained in 1550 and canonized in 1622. He founded the order of the Oratorians in 1575. See also Goethe's longer essay below, in the section on the second sojourn in Rome, which repeats much of the same information and the same anecdotes.

[129] "Scorn the world, scorn yourself, scorn being scorned." Later, in his Neri essay (see below), Goethe gives another version ascribed to St. Bernard. It is known in several variants.

[130] Joseph Johann, Count von Fries (1765–1788), an Austrian banker whom Goethe presumably knew from Carlsbad.

[131] It contained a purse from Charlotte von Stein.

[132] Presumably Countess Lanthieri.

[133] Goethe's poem "To Duke Carl August. Farewell in the Name of the En-

gelhaus Peasant Girls,'' was written in Carlsbad at the end of August, 1786. Engelhaus is a town southwest of Carlsbad.

[134] Wilhelm, Duke of Ursel (1750–1816) and Maria Flora, Duchess of Ursel, née Princess of Arenburg (1752–1832), were from Brussels.

[135] The third volume of Herder's *Ideas Toward a Philosophy of the History of Mankind* appeared in Riga in 1787.

[136] Cornelius de Pauw (1739–1799). His *Recherches philosophiques sur les Anciens Grecs* (Goethe has quoted the title incorrectly) appeared in 1787/88.

[137] North of Naples. A type of Roman farce, the "Fabulae Atellanae,'' always used Atella as a setting.

[138] Goethe's account here is based on a letter Tischbein wrote from Naples at a later date (July). He then included the Tischbein letter in its entirety in the account of his second sojourn in Rome.

[139] Aert van der Neer (1603–1677), Dutch landscape painter, famous for his moonlit scenes.

[140] In 1787 Corpus Christi fell on June 7.

[141] Girolamo Lucchesini (1751–1825), Prussian diplomat. He had been sent on a mission to Pius VI by the new Prussian king, Frederick William II, and had stopped in Weimar on the way. Lucchesini's wife, Charlotte, was born a von Tarrach.

[142] Lodovico, Marchese di Venuti (b. 1745), director of the royal porcelain factory from 1781 to 1799. The fate of the Ulysses (which Heinrich Meyer saw in 1789 and wrote about in a letter to Goethe) is unknown.

[143] Giuliana, Duchess of Giovane di Girasole (1766–1805), lady-in-waiting to the queen of Naples. She was originally a von Mudersbach from Würzburg.

[144] Christian Garve (1742–1798), a popular Englightenment writer and philosopher in Breslau.

[145] Ernst II Ludwig, Duke of Saxe-Gotha and Altenburg (1745–1804), known for his wisdom, good government, and patronage of science and learning. Goethe was well acquainted with him.

Part III
The Second Sojourn in Rome: June 1787–April 1788

[1] The conclusion of Romulus's prayer for Rome at its founding, from Ovid's *Fasti*, IV, 831–32: "May she be granted long life and power to rule the world, and may the rising and the setting sun be subject to her.''

[2] Raphael designed the cartoons of ten scenes from the Acts of the Apostles in 1515/16; the tapestries were woven in Brussels and came to Rome in 1519. They adorned the lower walls of the Sistine Chapel, but from 1553 to 1797 they were displayed in public on Corpus Christi. They were heavily damaged in the sack of Rome by Charles V (1527) and carried off to Paris during the Napoleonic period (1798–1808). Today they are in the Vatican gallery. There are several copies in existence and Goethe had already seen one set of them during his student days when Marie Antoinette was received ceremonially in Strassburg (see *Poetry and Truth*, Book Nine, Volume 4, p. 270). Seven of the cartoons are in the Victoria and Albert Museum in London.

[3] Ancient Tibur, northeast of Rome. The ruins include a Corinthian temple of the Sybils and a so-called temple of Tiburtus with Ionian columns.

[4] Daniele Ricciarelli, called da Volterra (?1509–1566), Italian mannerist painter. Both the identity and the whereabouts of the painting are unknown.

[5] The transaction, as Goethe describes it, is somewhat murky. Either Angelica Kauffmann advanced Tischbein all or much of the 500 scudi for his share of the original purchase price, or he only had 500 scudi and she paid the other half. In order to secure sole ownership she then apparently paid Tischbein a premium over his original 500-scudi investment.

[6] Roman adaptation of a marble group by Apollonios and Tauriskos from the 1st century B.C., discovered in 1547. It depicts the death of the evil Dirke, who has been tied to the back of a wild bull by her stepsons, Zethos and Amphion.

[7] Salvatore Rosa (1615–1673), landscape painter.

[8] The portrait was purchased by Goethe's daughter-in-law Ottilie in the 1840s and now hangs in the Goethe House in Weimar.

[9] Corso no. 18, where he had lived before.

[10] Not a castle of Genserich (or Geiserich, ca. 390–477), king of the Vandals, but probably the foundation of a temple of Venus destroyed in the 5th century.

[11] Conradin (1252–1268), Duke of Swabia, last of the Hohenstaufens. He was executed in Naples, an event long remembered with bitterness in German history.

[12] Cicero had a villa near here. Upon hearing that he had been outlawed in 43 B.C. he attempted to flee, but was caught and killed. Marius Gaius (157–86 B.C.), Roman general, hid himself here in flight from Sulla.

[13] The ship that had carried the Farnese *Hercules* to Naples.

[14] The essay on the tapestries was written in 1829, when Goethe was composing the second Roman sojourn.

[15] Goethe is referring especially to the group of early nineteenth-century Romantic religious painters known as the "Nazarenes," whom he and Heinrich Meyer held in low regard.

[16] According to Acts 5:1–6.

[17] Marcantonio Raimondi (ca. 1480–ca. 1534), famous engraver through whose work Raphael became known far and wide. The particular engraving in question, however, was made by Agostini Veneziano.

[18] Nicolas Dorigny (1657–1746), French engraver. In 1711 he was commissioned to engrave the Raphael cartoons in London.

[19] Located before the Porta del Popolo in a spring-house built by Lorenzo Bernini in 1661.

[20] The "compatriots" were Friedrich Bury (1763–1823), a portrait and landscape painter from Hanau who lived in Italy from 1783 to 1799, and Johann Georg Schütz (1755–1815), a landscape painter from Frankfurt. Bury and Schütz lived in the same house as Goethe. The Swiss was Heinrich Meyer.

[21] Of the unfinished dramas Goethe took along to Italy, *Egmont* and *Faust* were the oldest. He had begun work on *Egmont* while still in Frankfurt, in 1775 or earlier. Whereas he turned the prose *Tasso* and *Iphigenia* into verse plays which have come to be regarded as "classical," he left *Egmont* in prose and it retains a close affinity to Goethe's Storm and Stress dramas.

[22] Only in Goethe's thoughts. He did not work on the novel seriously until the mid-1790s, well after his return to Weimar.

[23] James Moore (1740–1793), landscape painter, a Scot by origin.

[24] Goethe is referring to the unrest stirred up by reforms introduced in the Netherlands by Joseph II and the regent, his sister Marie Christine. Crowds had gathered in front of the regent's palace in protest. The unrest eventually grew so serious that civil war threatened and Joseph and his successor, Leopold II, had to rescind many of the attempted reforms. *Egmont* contains several crowd scenes, including some expressing approval of the regent, Margaret of Parma, and popular displeasure with the stricter Spanish rule to be expected under Duke Alba, but no real scenes of vigorous protest.

[25] A round structure on the Field of Mars that served as a mausoleum for the emperors from Augustus to Nerva. In the 16th century it was turned into a park with statues; at the end of the 18th century it was rebuilt into a circus and theater.

[26] Carlo Albacini the Elder, sculptor and restorer.

[27] Now identified as a Dionysos and thought to be a Greek original from the 3rd century B.C.

[28] Abbé Giambattista Casti (1721–1803), court poet to Joseph II in Vienna. *L'Arcivescovo di Praga* appeared in his *Novelle galanti* in 1793. *Il Re Teodoro in Venezia* and *Il Re Teodoro in Corsica* are opera libretti. (*Il Re Teodoro in Venezia* was put to music by Giovanni Paisiello, 1741–1816.) Casti's ottava rima verse in the *Archbishop of Prague* was a model for Goethe and others who experimented with the form (for example Goethe's erotic poem, "The Diary").

[29] Andrea d'Agnolo, called del Sarto (1486–1531). The *Madonna* in question, now in the Rothschild Collection in London, was falsely ascribed to him.

[30] In his essay "Fragment of a Second Replique to Mr. Fabrioni Concerning the Niobe Group."

[31] *Vanity and Modesty,* previously ascribed to Leonardo, now thought to be a work of Bernardo Luini (d. 1532).

[32] The so-called *Fornarina*. The conception is attributed to Raphael with certainty, the painting itself was probably done by Giulio Romano around 1518.

[33] Jean Baptiste Louis Georges Seroux d'Agincourt (1730–1814). Goethe later owned and admired his *Histoire de l'art par les monuments depuis sa décadence au IV. siècle jusqu'à son renouvellement au XVI. siècle,* six volumes, Paris, 1810–1823.

[34] Albert Christoph Dies (1755–1822), German landscape painter and engraver, lived in Rome from 1775 to 1796.

[35] Built in 109 A.D. to celebrate Trajan's victory over the Dacians, with reliefs illustrating scenes from the war. Topped with a statue of St. Peter in the 16th century.

[36] The column celebrates not Antoninus Pius, as was thought in Goethe's time, but Marcus Aurelius's victory over the Danubians in 175 A.D. Like Trajan's column, it has illustrative reliefs. Topped with a statue of St. Paul in the 16th century.

[37] Unidentified.

[38] "Like the sun of England."

[39] *The Anguished Impresario,* an opera by Domenico Cimarosa (1749–1801).

[40] Johann Friedrich Kranz (1754–1807), court musician in Weimar until 1799, then court conductor in Stuttgart.

[41] Thomas Jenkins (1722–1798), English artist, art dealer, and banker, living at that time in Rome. Giovanni Volpato (1733–1803) was an engraver.

[42] Wagon or carriage with bench seats for a large number of passengers.

[43] That is, Miss Harte.

[44] Tischbein's *Orestes and the Furies,* painted for Prince Christian von Waldeck, is now in Arolsen Palace.

[45] Maximilian von Verschaffelt (1754–1818), a painter and architect. He succeeded his father, Peter Anton von Verschaffelt (1710–1793), as director of the Mannheim academy and later moved to Munich.

[46] Dowager Duchess Anna Amalia (1739–1807). She was in Italy from September, 1788 to May, 1790.

[47] These predictions were somewhat optimistic. *Tasso* was not completed until 1789, after Goethe's return to Weimar. Although he worked at *Faust* in Italy and wrote several new scenes, Goethe settled for publishing it in the form of a "Fragment" in the Göschen edition in 1790. The first part of *Faust* was not finally completed and published until 1808.

[48] Herder's birthday was August 25, Goethe and Herder's son were born on August 28, Carl August on September 3, Wieland on September 5.

[49] The works Moritz was planning were *Anthousa or Rome's Antiquities: A Book for Mankind* and *Lore of the Gods, or Mythological Poems of the Ancients,* both published in Berlin in 1791.

[50] Paolo, Prince of Borghese-Aldobrandini (b. 1704). The collection was in the Borghese Palace. The painting in question, *Christ among the Doctors,* is now in the National Gallery in London, the ascription to Leonardo uncertain.

[51] Ignazio Lodovico, Prince of Buoncompagni (1743–1790), Cardinal Secretary of State until 1789.

[52] See Genesis 32:26.

[53] Johann Caspar Lavater (1741–1801), a Pietist theologian and physiognomist from Zurich with whom Goethe had had various and complicated relations since his Storm and Stress days.

[54] Spinoza. Goethe did not write out the name but replaced it with crosses, parodying pious horror of the devil.

[55] Sir Richard Worthley (1751–1805), an archaeologist and collector. Goethe first became acquainted with the Parthenon friezes through Worthley's drawings.

[56] *God. Some Dialogues by J.G. Herder,* Gotha, 1787.

[57] The French Academy in Rome was founded in 1666 by Louis XIV and Colbert and was located in the Mancini Palace on the Corso.

[58] By Jean Baptiste Frédéric Desmarais (1756–1813), a French painter. He lived on a subsidy in Rome from 1786 to 1794.

[59] Alexander Trippel (1744–1793), sculptor, lived permanently in Rome after 1778. The bust was completed in November 1787, and is now in Arolstein Palace. During her stay in Italy Dowager Duchess Anna Amalia met Trippel and ordered a copy of the bust, which was completed in 1790 and is now in the State Library in Weimar.

[60] An allusion to Herder's *God,* where he had criticized the use of the term "fulgurations" by Leibniz to explain the working of God in the universe. Goethe's term "manifestations" is, however, also not in line with Herder's thinking.

[61] Johann Heinrich Lips (1758–1817), a Swiss painter and engraver. Goethe appointed him professor at the Drawing School in Weimar, where he stayed for five years before returning to Zurich in 1794.

[62] Jacques Louis David (1748–1825), the leading history painter of French Classicism. His *Oath of the Horatii,* completed in Rome in 1784, established his fame. The painting is now in the Louvre in Paris.

[63] Tischbein's *Hector* was intended for the Duke of Gotha, but it was never finished and is now lost.

[64] German-Jean Drouais (1763–1788), was living in Rome (Goethe later describes his early death, February 22, 1788); Bénigne Gagneraux (1756–1795); regarding Desmarais, see note 58 above; Louis Gauffier (1761–1801), landscape and history painter supported by the French Academy in Rome; Jean Pierre St.-Ours (1752–1809), a history painter from Geneva; Didier Boquet (1755–1839), landscape painter.

[65] Joachim Heinrich Campe (1746–1818), a leading Brunswick publisher and prominent Enlightenment author in his own right, had financed Moritz's Italian journey in return for a book Moritz had promised to write about it. The only manuscript Moritz sent to Campe, however, was the rather slender tract *On the Creative Imitation of Beauty* (excerpted by Goethe near the end of his treatment of the second sojourn in Rome). Campe and Moritz feuded in public over the rights and expectations of publishers and authors, respectively, and Moritz returned Campe's advance. He did go on to publish a three-volume work, *Travels of a German in Italy in the years 1786–1788,* with another publisher in 1792/93.

[66] Already mentioned above. Now called the *Apollo Pourtalès,* after Jakob Ludwig von Pourtalès (1722–1814), a Neuchâtel merchant who bought it when the Giustiniani collection was auctioned during the Napoleonic period. The head, which inspired Trippel's bust of Goethe, is now in the British Museum.

[67] Philipp Christoph Kayser (1755–1823) lived in Zurich. Goethe had written him on August 14, 1787, requesting that he write the incidental music to *Egmont.* Kayser came to Rome in November.

[68] Actually the obelisk of Psammetich II (594–589 B.C.), from Heliopolis. It was brought to Rome by Augustus and stood on the Field of Mars until into the 9th century. It was rediscovered in 1748 and finally put up again on the Piazza di Montecitorio under Pius VI.

[69] Goethe probably means Moritz's book on classical mythology.

[70] *Hen kai pan,* "one in all." The formulation goes back to Xenophanes of Colophon (6th century B.C.). Goethe had been reminded of it again by reading Herder's *God.*

[71] Palmyra was destroyed in 271 A.D. The architect was Louis François Cassas (1756–1827), a French painter and engraver, whom Goethe met on September 16. Cassas's work, *Voyage pittoresque de la Syrie, de la Phénicie,* etc., including drawings of the ruins of Palmyra, began appearing in Paris in 1799 but was never completed.

[72] Goethe is referring to the tensions that led Prussia to invade Holland in the fall of 1787 to defend the incompetent Stadholder, William V of Orange, and his wife, Wilhelmine (sister of the Prussian king, Frederick William II) against the so-called "patriotic" party. Carl August took part in the diplomacy and the campaign and presumably Goethe, a high Weimar official, was reasonably well informed about events.

[73] That is, back home in Weimar.

[74] Unidentified.

[75] A topic presumably brought up in a no longer extant letter of Herder's, doubtless on the basis of various 17th- and 18th-century reports.

[76] Unidentified.

[77] A musical which Goethe had written in February, 1775, while still in Frankfurt, and revised for the Göschen edition.

[78] Friedrich von der Trenck (1726–1794), a Prussian officer, was a favorite of Frederick II until he was defamed and imprisoned for a number of years. In 1786 he published a three-volume autobiography entitled *The Strange Story of my Life*. He was guillotined in Paris in 1794, just before Thermidor.

[79] Cassas.

[80] A letter of September 17, 1787, describing Cassas's Palmyra drawings, which later became the basis for the passage about them in Goethe's Report for September, below.

[81] A celebration had been organized in Goethe's garden in Weimar by his friend Knebel.

[82] The first four volumes of the Göschen edition, which had just come out.

[83] In a letter to Duke Carl August on August 11 Goethe had called the Weimar-Saxe-Eisenach territories "your provinces."

[84] Great things.

[85] Openly, deliberately.

[86] The Rome art dealer Christian Dehn (ca. 1700–1770) had made impressions of items from the collection of the famous antiquarian Baron Philipp von Stosch (1691–1757). Moritz used engravings based on these impressions to illustrate his book on classical mythology.

[87] Christoph Unterberger (1732–1798), a pupil of Mengs. The copies of Raphael's loggias are now in the Hermitage in Leningrad.

[88] Quiet!

[89] Presentation copies of the four volumes of Goethe's works for Angelica Kauffmann, along with the third part of Herder's *Scattered Leaves* and the third part of the *Ideas,* both of which had just come out.

[90] Stay in the country.

[91] "Conjectures about Persepolis," one of the essays in the newly arrived third part of the *Scattered Leaves.*

[92] Early poems by Herder which he had put together in the third part of the *Scattered Leaves.*

[93] Matthias Claudius (1740–1815), a German popular writer who turned increasingly conservative. The verse "My mother has geese" comes from a Claudius lullaby. The quotation "They are not confused by hay and straw. . ." is unidentified.

[94] See John 1:11: "He came unto his own, and his own received him not."

[95] Friedrich Heinrich Jacobi (1743–1819), a philosopher with whom Goethe had been on good terms in his Storm and Stress days, but from whom he gradually became more and more estranged from the 1780s on. In *Campaign in France 1792* he reports on a somewhat uncomfortable visit to Jacobi in the fall of 1792 (Volume 5 pp. 708–12).

[96] Franz Kaspar Buchholz (1756–1812), a landowner who had mediated Hamann's contact with the Münster circle of pious Catholics around Princess Gallitzin (see *Campaign in France 1792*, Volume 5, pp. 728f. and notes).

[97] Johann Caspar Lavater. Goethe apparently believed, wrongly, that Lavater had put Buchholz up to introducing Hamann to the Gallitzin circle.

[98] *Ageometreton*, someone ignorant of geometry.

[99] Quoted from Lavater's *Nathanael: Or the Divinity of Christianity, as Certain as it is Undemonstrable. For Nathanaels, That is, Persons with an Upright, Healthy, Calm, Ingenuous Sense of Truth,* 1786. The work was dedicated to Goethe as part of Lavater's effort to convert him to proper Christian belief.

[100] See Luke 4:11.

[101] Anton von Maron (1733–1808), painter from Vienna.

[102] Georg Forster (1754–1794) had accompanied Captain James Cook on his second voyage around the world and became a continental celebrity as a result. Forster had been engaged to be the scientific director of a four-year Russian expedition which was supposed to set out in early 1788, and he prepared himself by collecting ideas about things to investigate during the trip. The expedition was called off when Russia went to war with the Turks in the winter of 1787/88.

[103] This is the beginning of a new letter, written from Rome.

[104] Maddalena Riggi (1765–1825). Goethe tells much more about his first acquaintance with her below, in the Report for October. Though he never mentions her name, it is known from a letter of Angelica Kauffmann to Goethe dated November 1, 1788.

[105] L., J., C. = Lavater, Jacobi, Claudius. Claudius was known as the "messenger from Wandsbeck."

[106] Peter Camper (1722–1789), Dutch anatomist. Camper had confirmed Goethe's observations about the intermaxillary bone in higher animals, though not agreeing that the bone was present in human beings. Herder had cited Camper in the *Ideas* for having demonstrated how well the Greek artistic ideal conformed with anatomical principles.

[107] Lavater's *Physiognomic Fragments for the Purpose of Furthering Knowledge and Love of Mankind* were published in four volumes between 1775 and 1778.

[108] Amsterdam capitulated on October 8, 1787.

[109] Firmness, tenacity.

[110] After Scapin and Scapine, commedia dell'arte-type figures in Goethe's operetta *Scherz, List und Rache (Jest, Ruse, and Revenge)*.

[111] The work, to be based on the diamond necklace affair, was to be called *The Dupes*. Goethe later made use of the necklace affair in *The Great Cophta*.

[112] Friedrich Wilhelm Basilius von Ramdohr (1757–1822), Hanoverian official, Prussian diplomat, and aesthetician. His three-volume work on *Painting and Sculpture in Rome for Lovers of the Beautiful in Art* appeared in 1787. Both Goethe and Schiller were extremely critical of Ramdohr.

[113] Wieland had reviewed the first four volumes of Goethe's works in the *German Mercury*.

[114] Pietro Camuccini (1760–1833), a Roman art dealer, brother of the painter Vincenzo Camuccini.

[115] Canon Johann Friedrich Hugo von Dalberg (1752–1812), brother of the Erfurt governor.

[116] The engraving was used in volume five of Goethe's works. It depicts Clare kneeling before Egmont.

[117] *Claudina of Villa Bella,* like *Erwin and Elmira,* an older operetta that was revised for the collected works.

[118] Kniep.

[119] Friedrich Maximilian Klinger was born in 1752. On Klinger see *Poetry and Truth,* Book Fourteen (Volume 4, p. 443f. and note).

[120] Friedrich Christian Daniel Schubart (1739–1791), poet, journalist, and musician. He was a legendary keyboard virtuoso, and after his release from ten years' fortress imprisonment he was appointed director of music at the court of Carl Eugene in Stuttgart.

[121] *Il matrimonio segreto,* opera by Cimarosa, libretto by Giovanni Bertati. It was first performed in Vienna in 1792.

[122] *The Maid as Mistress,* composed by Giovanni Battista Pergolesi (1710–1736) in 1731. It has only two singing roles.

[123] Anton Berger. He had appeared in Weimar as early as 1777.

[124] In *Jest, Ruse, and Revenge* the doctor is tricked into believing he has given Scapine arsenic. As an antidote he brews a theriaca potion, but Scapine is only playing sick.

[125] Mozart's opera, composed in 1782, was performed in Weimar as early as 1785.

[126] Founded in 1698 by Cardinal Casanate, taken over by the government in 1873, still one of the largest and most important libraries in Rome.

[127] By Antonio Lafreri (ca. 1512–1577), published in Rome in 1575.

[128] Giovanni Paolo Lomazzo (1538–1600), *Trattato dell'arte della pittura, scultura ed architettura,* Milan, 1584, the most extensive and detailed Mannerist tract.

[129] Goethe's title is incorrect. *Admiranda Romanarum antiquitatum* was edited by Giovanni Pietro Bellori, Rome, 1693.

[130] A colonnaded building with seven galleries and a waterworks, built by Emperor Septimius, dismantled in the 16th century.

[131] Josephus Johannes Crescentius (Jakob) Seydelmann (1750–1829), well known for his copies of ancient and Renaissance art works in sepia.

[132] The Meyer essay inserted here had originally been written for Goethe's art periodical, *Die Propyläen.*

[133] A late Hellenistic work from the middle of the 1st century B.C. by Hagesandros, Polydoros, and Athanodoros, believed at this time to be considerably older and thus representative of the best period of Greek art. Both Lessing and Goethe wrote influential essays on the group.

[134] Roman copy of a statue of Hermes ascribed to Praxiteles, 4th century B.C.

[135] Colossal statue of a reclining river god, copy of a Hellenistic work.

[136] Roman copy of a Greek work from the middle of the 4th century B.C.

[137] Statue of Hermes with the head of a Greek general not originally belonging to it; copy of a Greek work from the end of the 5th century B.C.

[138] Today thought to represent Apollo; copy of a Hellenistic work.

[139] Roman copy of a Greek work from the 4th century B.C.

[140] Copy of a Greek original from the middle of the 4th century B.C. It was found near Tivoli in 1790 and therefore was not seen by Goethe.

[141] The famous Belvedere *Torso,* an original work of the Athenian sculptor Apollonios, second half of the 1st century B.C. It is unknown where and when it was discovered.

[142] Now identified as Ares, Roman copy of a Hellenistic work.

[143] Roman copy of a Greek work from the end of the 5th century B.C.

[144] The Capitoline *Venus,* an original Greek work from the 3rd or 2nd century B.C.

[145] A draped statue redesigned as Hera, Roman copy of a Greek original from the end of the 5th century B.C.

[146] Now identified as a head of Dionysos, Roman copy of a Hellenistic work.

[147] Aloys Ludwig Hirt (1759–1837), archaeologist and art historian. Hirt later collaborated with Moritz on a journal, *Italien und Deutschland. In Rücksicht auf Sitten, Gebräuche, Litteratur und Kunst (Italy and Germany, with Regard to Mores, Customs, Literature, and Art),* Berlin, 1789–1793. Goethe accepted Hirt's theory deriving Greek architecture from archaic wooden structures.

[148] Imitating one material with another, for example treating wood to look like stone or vice versa.

[149] Goethe prints the letter in French. Its author is unknown.

[150] A Nordic hero who is awakened by his daughter in Herder's collection of folksongs.

[151] Some verses from *Claudina* that Goethe had sent to Charlotte von Stein.

[152] Goethe's "first" Fritz was Charlotte von Stein's son, the "second" was Friedrich Bury.

[153] A colossal head of Antinous, the favorite of Emperor Hadrian who was drowned in the Nile. Today it is in the Louvre. In 1827 Goethe acquired a cast which is in the Goethe House in Weimar.

[154] The Frankfurt merchant Karl Wilhelm Thurneisen.

[155] By the first two Goethe definitely means Moritz and Bury, the third is probably Schütz.

[156] S. Paolo alle Tre Fontane, built in the 5th and restored at the end of the 16th century. The frescoes after Raphael are not, however, in this church, but in the neighboring church of S. Vincenzo e S. Anastasio, founded in the 7th and restored in the 13th century.

[157] The essay on Marcantonio's engravings of Raphael's twelve Apostles actually appeared in the *German Mercury* in December 1789.

[158] S. Paolo fuori le mura is a basilica with a nave and four aisles, begun in 385 over the grave of St. Paul, completed in the 5th century and decorated with frescoes by Pietro Cavallini (ca. 1250–1334). The church was heavily damaged by fire in 1823 and rebuilt in a richer style in the following decades.

[159] See note 164 in Part I.

[160] The pyramid was a landmark especially for German and English visitors because the Protestant cemetery is on the west side of the pyramid.

[161] Begun in 212 A.D.

[162] Giovanni Battista Piranesi (1720–1778), etcher, archaeologist, and architect. Goethe's conception of Rome was greatly influenced by Piranesi's illustrations of Roman buildings and monuments. Goethe owned the first of the four volumes of Piranesi's *Antichità Romane,* which appeared in 1756.

[163] Herman van Swanevelt (ca. 1600–1655), Dutch landscape painter and etcher who lived many years in Rome. Goethe owned copies of a number of his etchings of Roman sights.

[164] Fountain erected in the first quarter of the 17th century under Pope Paul V (Camillo Borghese, 1552–1621). The basin was added under Pope Innocent XII (1691–1700).

[165] Probably completed in 1514, one of the major works of Raphael's Roman period.

[166] Executed by Simone Mosca (1492–1553).

[167] Raffaello Vanni (1587–1673).

[168] Pietro Berettini, called da Cortona (1596–1669).

[169] Giovanni Maria Morandi (1622–1717).

[170] Francesco Albani (1578–1660).

[171] Donato Lazzari, called Bramante (ca. 1444–1514), architect and painter.

[172] The *Mass of Bolsena* and the *Freeing of the Captive St. Peter* were painted for the Stanza d'Eliodoro of the Vatican, 1511–1514, the *Parnassus* for the Stanza della Segnatura, 1509–1511. All three works had to take account of windows set in the walls.

[173] Francis Bacon, in his work *On the Dignity and Advancement of Science,* 1623.

[174] Herder's essay won the prize of the Berlin Academy in 1771.

[175] Goethe had begun the essay in 1810, but only completed it in 1829 while composing the "Second Sojourn in Rome." The passage on Neri published previously (in the section dated ".Naples, Saturday, May 26, 1787") represents an earlier stage of the essay when he may have given up all thought of completing it.

[176] Paolo Fidanza (1731–ca. 1790), *Teste scelte di personaggi illustri.* Goethe owned the five-part work, which appeared between 1756 and 1775.

[177] By German and Spanish troops under Charles V in 1527.

[178] "Scorn the world, scorn no one, scorn yourself, scorn being scorned."

[179] Francisco de Yasu y Xavier, S.J. (1506–1552) undertook missions to Brazil, India, and Japan.

[180] Ippolito Aldobrandini (1536–1605), became pope in 1592.

[181] Giovanni de' Medici (1475–1521), became pope in 1513.

[182] A laxative obtained from the flowering ash in the form of flakes.

[183] A Franciscan nunnery.

[184] Giles Adrian Camper (1759–1820), Dutch anatomist, son of Peter Camper.

[185] The fourth part of Herder's *Ideas* did not appear until 1791!

[186] A reference to his Storm and Stress period before the move to Weimar in 1775.

[187] The poem was inserted into the second act of the revised version of *Claudina of Villa Bella.*

[188] Goethe had actually been inducted into the society on January 4, 1787, before his trip to Naples and Sicily. He had been introduced by the Prince of Liechtenstein. His account of the history of the society is based on Volkmann.

[189] Dante and Petrarch.

[190] Giovanni Maria Crescimbeni (1663–1728), poet and literary historian, custodian of the Arcadian Society from 1690 to the end of his life. He wrote three works on vernacular poetry: *Istoria della volgar poesia* (Rome, 1698); *Trattato della bellezza della volgar poesia* (Rome, 1700); and *Commentario intorno alla volgar poesia* (5 vols., Rome, 1701–1711).

[191] Goethe's description of the Roman carnival was published as a book in 1789 with twenty colored copperplates drawn by Georg Schütz and etched and illuminated by Georg Melchior Kraus, now a great bibliophilic rarity. In 1790 it was published again, without the plates, in the *Journal of Luxury and Fashion*.

[192] Charles Edward Stuart (1720–1788), grandson of James II, who had unsuccessfully tried to invade England and claim the throne in 1745. He retreated to Scotland and was defeated at the battle of Culloden on April 16, 1746.

[193] That is, Barbary horses from North Africa.

[194] Volcanic dust, named after Pozzuoli, where it is found.

[195] "Places! Places, masters! Places!"

[196] Priapus.

[197] Gentlemen escorts.

[198] The project, instituted by Pius VI, was completed in 1789.

[199] "Oh, brother, what an ugly strumpet you are!"

[200] Abbondio Fausto, Prince of Rezzonico (b. 1742), nephew of Pope Clement XIII and Senator of Rome since 1765.

[201] So-called "quick gallows." The culprit was bound and jerked quickly up and down by the body.

[202] To murder.

[203] "Places! Places up front! Fine places! Places, masters!"

[204] In an essay, "Female Roles Played by Men in the Roman Theater," first published as an extract from Goethe's travel journal in the *German Mercury* in 1788.

[205] Candle stumps.

[206] "Death to the abbé who makes love."

[207] "Death to the beautiful princess! Death to Signora Angelica, the greatest woman painter of the century!"

[208] Demeter's nurse, who tried to cheer her up when she lost Persephone by telling her bawdy stories.

[209] A bore.

[210] *Lila* and *Jerry and Betty* are musicals dating from 1780. For *Jerry and Betty* see Volume 7.

[211] A light gauze-like weave.

[212] *Trattato della pittura di Lionardo da Vinci, nuovamente dato in luce con la vita dell'istesso autore scritta da Raff. du Fresnes,* first published in 1651 in Paris, a century after Leonardo's death.

[213] Paris Bordone (1550–1571), a pupil of Titian. Nothing is known about either of these paintings.

[214] German-Jean Drouais's *Philoctetes on Lemnos* is in the Chartres museum.

[215] "Explanation of an old Woodcut Depicting Hans Sachs's Poetic Mission," dating from 1776, was revised in Rome. "On Mieding's Death" dates from 1782 (Mieding was the Weimar theater's carpenter and set-maker).

[216] The pyramid of Cestius, that is, in the Protestant cemetery. In February 1788 Goethe drew a picture of "his" grave. His son, August, died in Rome while traveling in 1830 and is buried there.

[217] Johann Friedrich Unger (1753–1804), Berlin publisher and book dealer who pioneered in the development of attractive new type fonts. Unger also published *Goethe's New Works* in seven volumes from 1792 to 1800.

[218] Wilhelm Christoph von Diede zum Fürstenstein (1732–1807), Danish diplomat, and his wife, Margareta Constantia Luise, née Countess von Callenberg (1752–1803). Goethe had already known the couple in Darmstadt before 1775.

[219] Ernst Fries (1801–1833), landscape painter, and Joseph Thürmer (1789–1833), architect and etcher. The work is entitled *Northwest View of Rome, from the Tower of the Capitol. . . .*

[220] Clement XIII was pope from 1758 to 1769. Mengs did his portrait twice shortly after 1758—one is in the municipal gallery of Bologna, the other in the Ambrosiana in Milan.

[221] Heinrich Meyer.

[222] Cristobal Morales (ca. 1500–1553), a Sevillian, one of the greatest Spanish masters of the motet and the mass.

[223] Benedetto Marcello (1686–1739). His Psalm settings, *Estro poetico-armonico*, were published in Venice in eight volumes, 1724–1727.

[224] The pact scene. The oldest parts of *Faust* date from 1773–1775, before Goethe's move to Weimar.

[225] The earliest *Faust* manuscript is not preserved.

[226] "The Artist's Earthly Pilgrimage" was written in 1773 or 1774. Goethe did not in fact revise it. "The Artist's Apotheosis," written at this time, in 1788, is usually connected with "The Artist's Earthly Pilgrimage" because of this passage.

[227] Presumably not one of the editions of Mengs's collected works, but the *Complete Posthumous Writings of the Chevalier A.R. Mengs*, edited by Christian Friedrich Prange and published in three volumes, Halle, 1786.

[228] *Observations on Beauty and Good Taste in Painting*, in the second volume of the Prange edition.

[229] Paolo, Prince of Borghese-Aldobrandini.

[230] Unidentified.

[231] In 1833 it was discovered that this was definitely not Raphael's skull, as his grave was found in the Pantheon. The cast of the skull is in the Goethe Museum in Weimar.

[232] *St. Luke Paints the Madonna*, believed today to be from Raphael's school rather than by Raphael himself.

[233] Bartolommeo Cavaceppi (ca. 1716–1799), a prominent restorer of ancient sculptures and a friend of Winckelmann.

[234] Antonio Eugenio Cardinal Visconti (1713–1788).

[235] Laurustine, which blooms in the spring and has fragrant white and pink flowers.

[236] Duke Carl August had asked Goethe to remain longer in Rome and make preparations for Anna Amalia's impending visit, which Goethe has already mentioned several times up to this point.

[237] Giovanni Pierluigi da Palestrina (ca. 1525–1594), originator of an influential

new style of church music conforming to the requirements of the Council of Trent.

[238] Raphael neither owned nor lived in the villa in question, and a number of the frescoes considered by Goethe as having been done by Raphael date from the middle of the 16th century. It is not known who built or first owned it. It was acquired by Andrea Doria, Prince of Landi, Pamphili, and Melfi (b. 1744) in 1785. It was largely destroyed during revolutionary disorders in 1849.

[239] Begun by Alessandro Cardinal Albani in 1746.

[240] Moritz, Bury, and probably Schütz (as above). It has, however, also been claimed (for example by Erich Trunz) that Goethe left a mistress behind in Rome, and that she is meant as the third person who will miss him.

[241] The 9-voice *Miserere* by Gregorio Allegri (1584–1652) was reserved for use in the Sistine chapel and was not allowed to be copied. Mozart, however, wrote it out from memory after hearing it. The *Improperi* are a work by Palestrina dating from 1560.

[242] "My people, what have I done to you?"

[243] Moritz had apparently assumed, and assured his publisher, Campe, that it would be as easy to write an Italian travel memoir as it had been to write his *Travels of a German in England in the Year 1782*.

[244] Although Moritz's pamphlet is arguably one of the more important documents of German classical aesthetics, it was not reprinted in full until near the end of the 19th century.

[245] Goethe did get his wish, as Meyer moved to Weimar in 1792.

[246] The Hercules and the Mercury are unidentified.

[247] A Greek bronze from the end of the 3rd century B.C., a cast of which Goethe saw in Leipzig in the company of Adam Oeser in 1765. The original is in the Uffizi in Florence.

[248] Goethe visited it in 1771 on his return from Strassburg to Frankfurt. See *Poetry and Truth,* Book Eleven (Volume 4, pp. 371–2).

[249] King Ludwig I of Bavaria, who acquired the villa in 1827.

[250] Piranesi, *Della Magnificenza ed Architettura dei Romani,* 1761. The Cloaca Maxima was begun under the Tarquinian kings in order to drain the Forum area, then expanded and covered over during the 1st century B.C. The bones of St. Paul and St. Peter had been hidden away in the St. Sebastian catacombs during the persecutions under Valerian in the 3rd century A.D.

[251] Antonio Bosio (1575–1629). His book appeared in 1632. Goethe became acquainted with the work in 1827.

[252] Franz Joseph Gall (1758–1828), physician, anatomist, and phrenologist. Gall traveled to various cities to lecture on his theories in 1805, at which time Goethe heard him in Halle.

[253] Not Pietro de Cortona, but Federigo Zuccaro (1543–1609), the first president of the Academia di S. Luca.

[254] Not further identified.

[255] The claim here, that the head was the original and had never been separated from the statue, contradicts Goethe's earlier statement (Naples, March 7, 1787) that the head had been broken off but repaired well. In fact, the head is that of a Maenad and does not belong to the torso.

[256] Hieron, tyrant of Syracuse (269–215 B.C.). The original statue probably dated from the end of the 5th century B.C.

[257] That is, Angelica Kauffmann and her husband. It is somewhat confusing that here Goethe suddenly reverses his usual way of referring to them.

[258] Roman copy of a work by Doidalsas from the middle of the 3rd century B.C. The signature is a forgery. This entire passage is taken verbatim from a Heinrich Meyer letter of August 20, 1829.

[259] Copy of a work by Leochares from the 4th century B.C.

[260] A statue of Apollo from the 4th century B.C.

[261] A Hellenistic satyr of red marble.

[262] From the school of Polyclitus, 5th century B.C. The statue was not found until 1792, so Goethe did not see it himself.

[263] Ennio Quirino Visconti (1751–1818), archaeologist. His *Il Museo Pio-Clementino* appeared in Rome in seven volumes, 1782–1807.

[264] Giuseppe Volpato (d. 1803), son of the engraver Giovanni Volpato. Maddalena Riggi married again after his death.

[265] A bronze statue, part of a victory monument erected in honor of Marcus Aurelius by the Senate in 164 A.D.

[266] *Tristia: Epistulae ex Ponto,* I, 3, verses 1–4 and 27–30.

Index

Information about a person is usually contained in the first footnote reference to that person. All references to footnotes appear in boldface type.